Higher

MATHEMATICS
GCSE for Edexcel
Student Book

Karen Morrison, Julia Smith, Pauline McLean, Rachael Horsman and Nick Asker

CAMBRIDGE
UNIVERSITY PRESS

University Printing House, Cambridge CB2 8BS, United Kingdom

Cambridge University Press is part of the University of Cambridge.

It furthers the University's mission by disseminating knowledge in the pursuit of education, learning and research at the highest international levels of excellence.

www.cambridge.org
Information on this title:
www.cambridge.org/9781107448001 (Paperback)
www.cambridge.org/9781107449718 (1 year Online Subscription)
www.cambridge.org/9781107449671 (2 year Online Subscription)
www.cambridge.org/9781107447851 (Paperback + Online Subscription)

First published 2015

Printed in the United Kingdom by Latimer Trend

A catalogue record for this publication is available from the British Library

ISBN 978-1-107-44800-1 (Paperback)
ISBN 978-1-107-44971-8 (1 year Online Subscription)
ISBN 978-1-107-44967-1 (2 year Online Subscription)
ISBN 978-1-107-44785-1 (Paperback + Online Subscription)

Additional resources for this publication at www.cambridge.org/ukschools

Cambridge University Press has no responsibility for the persistence or accuracy of URLs for external or third-party internet websites referred to in this publication, and does not guarantee that any content on such websites is, or will remain, accurate or appropriate. Information regarding prices, travel timetables, and other factual information given in this work is correct at the time of first printing but Cambridge University Press does not guarantee the accuracy of such information thereafter.

....

....

In order to ensure that this resource offers high quality support for the associated Edexcel qualification, it has been through a review process by the awarding body to confirm that it fully covers the teaching and learning content of the specification or part of a specification at which it is aimed, and demonstrates an appropriate balance between the development of subject skills, knowledge and understanding, in addition to preparation for assessment.

While the publishers have made every attempt to ensure that advice on the qualification and its assessment is accurate, the official specification and associated assessment guidance materials are the only authoritative source of information and should always be referred to for definitive guidance.

Edexcel examiners have not contributed to any sections in this resource relevant to examination papers for which they have responsibility.

No material from this endorsed GCSE Mathematics Higher Student Book will be used verbatim in any assessment by Edexcel.

Endorsement of this GCSE Mathematics Higher Student Book does not mean that the resource is required to achieve this Edexcel qualification, nor does it mean that it is the only suitable material available to support the qualification, and any resource lists produced by the awarding body shall include this and other appropriate resources.

Contents

Find answers at: cambridge.org/ukschools/gcsemaths-studentbookanswers

Note
The colour of each chapter corresponds to the area of maths that it covers:

- Number
- Algebra
- Ratio, proportion and rates of change
- Geometry and measures
- Probability
- Statistics

 Find answers at: cambridge.org/ukschools/gcsemaths-studentbookanswers

Introduction

This book has been written by experienced teachers to help build your understanding and enjoyment of the maths you will meet at GCSE.

Each chapter opens with a list of skills that are covered in the chapter. The **real-life applications** section describes an example of how the maths is used in real life.

All chapters build on knowledge that you will have learned in previous years. You might need to revise some topics before starting a chapter. To check your knowledge, answer the questions in the **Before you start…** table. You can check your answers using the free answer booklet available at **www.cambridge.org/ukschools/gcsemaths-studentbookanswers**. If you answer any questions incorrectly, you might need to revise the topic from your work in earlier years.

The chapters are divided into sections, each covering a single topic. Some chapters may cover topics that you already know and understand. You can use the **Launchpad** to identify the best section for you to start with. Answer the questions in each step. If you find a question difficult to answer correctly, the step suggests the section that you should look at.

Throughout the book, there are features to help you build knowledge and improve your skills:

 This means you might need a calculator to work through a question.

 This means you should work through a question without using a calculator.

 This shows the question is from a past exam paper.

 Tip

Tip boxes provide helpful hints.

 Calculator tip

Calculator tips help you to use your calculator.

 Learn this formula

Learn this formula boxes contain formulae that you need to know.

 Key vocabulary

Important maths terms are written in green. You can find what they mean in **Key vocabulary** boxes and also in the **Glossary** at the back of the book.

 Did you know?

Did you know? boxes contain interesting maths facts.

WORK IT OUT

Work it out boxes contain a question with several worked solutions. Some of the solutions contain common mistakes. Try to spot the correct solution and check the free answer booklet available at **www.cambridge.org/ukschools/gcsemaths-studentbookanswers** to see if you're right.

WORKED EXAMPLE

Worked examples guide you through model answers to help you understand methods of answering questions.

Some chapters contain a **Problem-solving framework**, which sets a problem and then shows how you can go about answering it.

 Checklist of learning and understanding

At the end of a chapter, use the **Checklist of learning and understanding** to check whether you have covered everything you need to know.

 Chapter review

You can check whether you have understood the topics using the **Chapter review,** which contains questions from the whole chapter.

A booklet containing answers to all exercises is free to download at **www.cambridge.org/ukschools/gcsemaths-studentbookanswers**.

You can find more resources, including interactive widgets, games and quizzes on **GCSE Mathematics Online**.

1 Calculations

In this chapter you will learn how to …

- use non-calculator methods to calculate with positive and negative numbers.
- perform operations in the correct order based on mathematical conventions.
- recognise inverse operations and use them to simplify and check calculations.

 For more resources relating to this chapter, visit GCSE Mathematics Online.

Using mathematics: real-life applications

Everyone uses numbers on a daily basis often without really thinking about them. Shopping, cooking, working out bills, paying for transport and measuring all rely on a good understanding of numbers and calculation skills.

Tip

You probably already know most of the concepts in this chapter. They have been included so that you can revise concepts if you need to and check that you know them well.

"Number puzzles and games are very popular and there are mobile apps and games available for all age groups. I use an app with my GCSE classes where they have to work in the correct order to solve different number puzzles." *(Secondary School Teacher)*

Before you start …

KS3	You should be able to add, subtract, multiply and divide positive and negative numbers.	**1** Copy and complete each statement to make it true. Use only $<$, $=$ or $>$. **a** $2 + 3 \square 4 - 7$ **b** $-3 + 6 \square 4 - 7$ **c** $-1 - 4 \square 20 \div -4$ **d** $-6 \times 2 \square -7 - (-5)$
KS3	You should know the rules for working when more than one operation is involved in a calculation (BODMAS).	**2** Spot the mistake in each calculation and correct the answers. **a** $3 + 8 + 3 \times 4 = 56$ **b** $3 + 8 \times 3 + 4 = 37$ **c** $3 \times (8 + 3) \times 4 = 130$

KS3	You should understand that addition and subtraction, and multiplication and division are inverse operations.	**3** Identify the inverse operation by choosing the correct option.
		
		 a $14 \times 4 = 56$
		    A $56 \times 4 = 14$ **B** $14 \div 4 = 56$ **C** $56 \div 4 = 14$
		
		 b $200 \div 10 = 20$
		    A $200 \div 20 = 10$ **B** $200 = 10 \times 20$ **C** $10 \times 200 = 2000$
		
		 c $27 + 53 = 80$
		    A $80 = 4 \times 20$ **B** $80 - 27 = 53$ **C** $80 + 27 = 107$

Find answers at: cambridge.org/ukschools/gcsemaths-studentbookanswers

Assess your starting point using the Launchpad

STEP 1

❶ Calculate, without using a calculator, and show your working.

a 647 + 786

b 1406 − 289

c 45 × 19

d 414 ÷ 23

?

GO TO
Section 1:
Basic calculations

STEP 2

❷ Choose the correct answer.

a 9 ÷ (2 + 1) − 2

A 9   **B** $3\frac{1}{2}$ **C** 1   **D** 0

b (3 × 8) ÷ 4 + 8

A 2   **B** 30   **C** 16   **D** 14

c 12 − 6 × 2 + 11

A 78   **B** 23   **C** 1   **D** 11

d [5 × (9 + 1)] − 3

A 53   **B** 47   **C** 40   **D** 43

e (6 + 5) × 2 + (15 − 2 × 3) − 6

A 40   **B** 20   **C** 32   **D** 25

?

GO TO
Section 2:
Order of operations

STEP 3

❸ The perimeter of a square is equal to four times the length of a side. If the perimeter is 128 cm, what is the length of a side?

❹ What should you add to 342 to get 550?

❺ If a number divided by 45 is 30, what is the number?

?

GO TO
Section 3:
Inverse operations

GO TO
Chapter review

Assess your starting point using the Launchpad

Section 1: Basic calculations

You will not always have a calculator so it is useful to know how to do calculations using mental and written strategies.

It is best to use a method that you are confident with and always **show your working**.

Remember that when a question asks you to find the:

- **sum** you need to add
- **difference** you need to subtract the smaller number from the larger number
- **product** you need to multiply
- **quotient** you need to divide.

Tip

Some examination papers will not allow you to use your calculator.

WORK IT OUT 1.1

Look at these calculations carefully.

Discuss with a partner what methods these students have used to find the answer.

Which method would you use to do each of these calculations? Why?

① $489 + 274$

$$400 + 200 \rightarrow 600$$
$$80 + 70 \rightarrow 150$$
$$9 + 4 \rightarrow \underline{13}$$
$$ 763$$

② $284 - 176$

$$\begin{array}{r} {}^{7}\;{}^{1} \\ 28\!\!\!/4 \\ -\;176 \\ \hline 108 \end{array}$$

③ 29×17

$$\rightarrow 30 \times 17 - 17$$
$$\rightarrow 3 \times 170 - 17$$
$$\rightarrow 510 - 17$$
$$\rightarrow \;493$$

④ 15×62

$$= 30 \times 31 \qquad 310$$
$$= 930 \qquad\qquad 310$$
$$\qquad\qquad\quad \underline{310}$$
$$\qquad\qquad\quad 930$$

⑤ 207×47

×	200	0	7
40	8000	0	280
7	1400	0	49

$$9400 + 0 + 329$$
$$= 9729$$

⑥ $2394 \div 42$

$$\begin{array}{r} 2394 \\ -\;1680 \\ \hline 714 \\ -\;420 \\ \hline 294 \\ -\;210 \\ \hline 84 \\ -\;84 \\ \hline = 57 \end{array}$$

(40) (10) (5) (2)

$$42 \times 10 = 420$$
$$42 \times 20 = 840$$
$$42 \times 40 = 1680$$
$$42 \times 5 = 210$$
$$42 \times 2 = 84$$

 Find answers at: cambridge.org/ukschools/gcsemaths-studentbookanswers

Problem-solving strategies

There are some useful strategies and techniques that you can use to break down complex problems to help you solve them more easily.

If you follow these steps each time you are faced with a problem, you will become more confident at problem solving and more able to check that your answers are sensible.

These are important skills both for your GCSE courses and for everyday life.

Problem-solving framework

Sally buys, repairs and sells used furniture at a market.

Last week she bought a table for £32 and a bench for £18.

She spent £12 on wood, nails, varnish and glue to fix them up.

She then sold the two items on her stall for £69.

How much profit did she make on the two items?

Steps for solving problems	What you would do for this example
Step 1: Work out what you have to do. Start by reading the question carefully.	Find the profit on the two items.
Step 2: What information do you need? Have you got it all?	Cost of items = £32 + £18 Cost of repairs = £12 Selling price = £69
Step 3: Is there any information that you don't need?	In this problem you don't need to know what she spent the money on, you just need to know how much she spent. Many problems contain extra information that you don't need so as to test your understanding.
Step 4: Decide what maths you can do.	Profit = selling price − cost You can add the costs and subtract them from the selling price.
Step 5: Set out your solution clearly. Check your working and make sure your answer is reasonable.	Cost = £32 + £18 + £12 = £62 Profit = £69 − £62 = £7 Sally made £7 profit.
Step 6: Check that you have answered the question.	Yes. You needed to find the profit and you have found it.

EXERCISE 1A

Solve these problems using written methods.

Set out your solutions clearly to show the methods you chose.

1 Nola checked the prices of pens at three different supermarkets. She found that the cheapest pack of pens was £3.90 for three. She bought 15 pens.

How much did she pay in total and how much did she pay for each pen?

a What two things are you asked to find here?

b How many packs of pens did she buy? Why do you need to know this?

c What operation would you do to find the total cost? Why?

d How would you work out the cost of each pen?

e Does a price of £1.30 for a pen seem reasonable to you?

Tip

You don't always need to write something for the first few steps in the problem-solving framework, but you should still consider these steps mentally when approaching a problem in order to help you decide what to do. You should **always** show your working fully.

2 Sandra bought a pair of jeans for £34, a scarf for £9.50 and a top for £20.

If she had saved £100 to buy these items, how much money would she have left?

3 How many 16-page brochures can you make from 1030 pages?

4 Jason can type 48 words per minute.

a How many words can he type in an hour and a half?

b Approximately how long would it take him to type an article of 2000 words?

5 At the start of a year the population of Greenside Village was 56 309.

During the year 617 people died, 1835 babies were born, 4087 people left the village and 3099 people moved into the village.

What was the population at the end of the year?

6 The Amazon River is 6448 km long, the Nile River is 6670 km and the Severn is 354 km long.

a How much longer is the Nile than the Amazon?

b How much shorter is the Severn than the Amazon?

Did you know?

The Severn is the longest river in the UK.

7 What is the combined sum of 132 and 99 plus the product of 36 and 127?

8 What is the result when the difference between 8765 and 3087 is added to the result of 1206 divided by 18?

Find answers at: cambridge.org/ukschools/gcsemaths-studentbookanswers

Key vocabulary

integers: whole numbers belonging to the set {... −3, −2, −1, 0, 1, 2, 3, ...}; they are sometimes called directed numbers because they have a negative or positive sign.

Tip

You will be expected to work with negative and positive values in algebra, so it is important to make sure you can do this early on in your GCSE course.

Working with negative and positive integers

When doing calculations involving positive and negative **integers**, you need to remember the following:

- Adding a negative number is the same as subtracting the number:
  $4 + -3 = 1$
- Subtracting a negative number is the same as adding a positive number:
  $5 - -3 = 8$
- Multiplying or dividing the same signs gives a positive answer:

  $-4 \times -2 = 8$ and $\dfrac{-4}{-2} = 2$

- Multiplying or dividing different signs gives a negative answer:

  $4 \times -2 = -8$ and $\dfrac{-4}{2} = -2$

EXERCISE 1B

1 What would you add to each number to get a result of 5?

   a 7   **b** 3   **c** −1   **d** −4   **e** −24

2 What would you subtract from each number to get a result of −8?

   a 7   **b** 3   **c** −1   **d** −4   **e** −24

3 −4 is multiplied by another number to get each of the following results.

   Work out what the other number is in each case.

   a 12   **b** −100   **c** −36   **d** 504   **e** 0

4 By what would you divide −64 to get the following results?

   a 8   **b** −8   **c** 2   **d** $-\dfrac{1}{2}$ **e** −256

5 Here is a set of integers:

   {−8, −6, −3, 1, 3, 7}

   From the numbers in this set:

   a Find two numbers with a difference of 9.

   b Find three numbers with a sum of 1.

   c Find two numbers whose product is −3.

   d Find two numbers which, when divided, will give an answer of −6.

6 One more than −6 is added to the product of 7 and 6 less than 3.

   What is the result?

7 Saleem has a container of wooden dowels.

Some are 5 cm long and some are 7 cm long.

If the dowels are joined end to end, investigate what lengths between 5 cm and 150 cm **cannot** be made.

Section 2: Order of operations

Jose posted this calculation on his wall on social media.

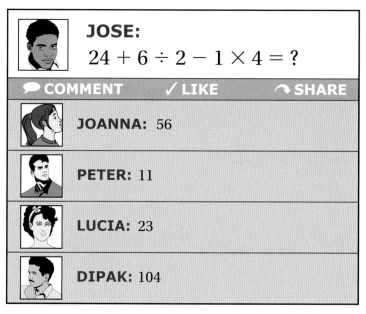

JOSE:
$24 + 6 \div 2 - 1 \times 4 = ?$

💬 COMMENT ✓ LIKE ↱ SHARE

JOANNA: 56

PETER: 11

LUCIA: 23

DIPAK: 104

Within minutes, his friends had posted four different answers.

Which one (if any) do you think is correct? Why?

There is a set of rules that tell you the order in which you need to work when there is more than one operation.

The order of operations is:

1 Do any operations in brackets first.

2 If there are any '**powers of**' or '**fractions of**' in the calculation, do them next.

3 Do division and multiplication next, working from left to right.

4 Do addition and subtraction last, working from left to right.

Brackets and other grouping symbols

Brackets are used to group operations. For example:

$(3 + 7) \times (30 \div 2)$

When there is more than one set of brackets, you work from the **innermost set** to the **outermost set**.

 Tip

Many people remember these rules using the letters **BODMAS**. (or sometimes BIDMAS).
Brackets
Of ('powers **o**f' or 'fractions **o**f'; in BIDMAS, I stands for Indices)
Divide and/or **M**ultiply
Add and/or **S**ubtract.

Find answers at: cambridge.org/ukschools/gcsemaths-studentbookanswers

WORKED EXAMPLE 1

Calculate $2((4 + 2) \times 2 - 3(1 - 3) - 10)$

$2((4 + 2) \times 2 - 3(1 - 3) - 10)$

> Highlight the different pairs of brackets to help if you need to.

$2((4 + 2) \times 2 - 3(1 - 3) - 10)$
$= 2(6 \times 2 - 3(-2) - 10)$
$= 2(6 \times 2 - 3 \times -2 - 10)$

> The red brackets are the innermost, so do the calculations inside these ones first. There are two lots of red brackets, so work from left to right. **Note** that you can leave -2 inside brackets if you prefer because $3(-2)$ is the same as 3×-2.

$2(6 \times 2 - 3 \times -2 - 10)$
$= 2(12 - -6 - 10)$
$= 2(8)$
$= 2 \times 8$
$= 16$

> Blue brackets are next. Do the multiplications first from left to right, then the subtractions from left to right.

Often a different style of bracket will be used to make it easier to identify each pair.

For example, the following different types of brackets have been used below: $(\,), [\,], \{\,\}$.

$\{2 - [4(2 - 7) - 4(3 + 8)] - 2\} \times 8$

Other symbols can also be used to group operations.

For example:

fraction bars: $\dfrac{5 - 12}{3 - 8}$

roots: $\sqrt{16 + 9}$

These symbols are treated like brackets when you do a calculation.

Tip

$\dfrac{5 - 12}{3 - 8}$ is the same calculation as $(5 - 12) \div (3 - 8)$

WORK IT OUT 1.2

Which of the solutions is correct in each case?

Find the mistakes in the incorrect option.

	Option A	Option B
1	$7 \times 3 + 4$ $= 21 + 4$ $= 25$	$7 \times 3 + 4$ $= 7 \times 7$ $= 49$
2	$(10 - 4) \times (4 + 9)^2$ $= 6 \times 16 + 81$ $= 96 + 81$ $= 177$	$(10 - 4) \times (4 + 9)^2$ $= 6 \times (13)^2$ $= 6 \times 169$ $= 1014$
3	$45 - [20 \times (4 - 3)]$ $= 45 - [20 \times 1]$ $= 45 - 21$ $= 24$	$45 - [20 \times (4 - 3)]$ $= 45 - 20 \times 1$ $= 45 - 20$ $= 25$
4	$30 - 4 \div 2 + 2$ $= 26 \div 2 + 2$ $= 13 + 2$ $= 15$	$30 - 4 \div 2 + 2$ $= 30 - 2 + 2$ $= 30$
5	$\dfrac{18 - 4}{4 - 2}$ $= \dfrac{18}{2}$ $= 9$	$\dfrac{18 - 4}{4 - 2}$ $= \dfrac{14}{2}$ $= 7$
6	$\sqrt{36 \div 4} + 40 \div 4 + 1$ $= \sqrt{9} + 10 + 1$ $= 3 + 11$ $= 14$	$\sqrt{36 \div 4} + 40 \div 4 + 1$ $= \sqrt{9} + 40 \div 5$ $= 3 + 8$ $= 11$

Calculator tip

Most modern calculators are programmed to use the correct order of operations. Check your calculator by entering $2 + 3 \times 4$. You should get 14.

If the calculation has brackets, you need to enter the brackets into the calculator to make sure it does these first.

EXERCISE 1C

1 Check whether these answers are correct.

If the answer is wrong, work out the correct answer.

a $12 \times 4 + 76 = 124$

b $8 + 75 \times 8 = 698$

c $12 \times 18 - 4 \times 23 = 124$

d $(16 \div 4) \times (7 + 3 \times 4) = 76$

e $(82 - 36) \times (2 + 6) = 16$

f $(3 \times 7 - 4) - (4 + 6 \div 2) = 12$

 Find answers at: cambridge.org/ukschools/gcsemaths-studentbookanswers

2 Use the numbers listed to make each number sentence true.

a $\square - \square \div \square = \square$ 9, 11, 13, 18

b $\square \div (\square - \square) - \square = \square$ 1, 3, 8, 14, 16

c $(\square + \square) - (\square - \square) = \square$ 4, 5, 6, 9, 12

3 Insert brackets into each calculation to make it true.

a $3 \times 4 + 6 = 30$ **b** $25 - 15 \times 9 = 90$ **c** $40 - 10 \times 3 = 90$

d $14 - 9 \times 2 = 10$ **e** $12 + 3 \div 5 = 3$ **f** $19 - 9 \times 15 = 150$

g $10 + 10 \div 6 - 2 = 5$ **h** $3 + 8 \times 15 - 9 = 66$ **i** $9 - 4 \times 7 + 2 = 45$

j $10 - 4 \times 5 = 30$ **k** $6 \div 3 + 3 \times 5 = 5$ **l** $15 - 6 \div 2 = 12$

m $1 + 4 \times 20 \div 5 = 20$ **n** $8 + 5 - 3 \times 2 = 20$ **o** $36 \div 3 \times 3 - 3 = 6$

p $3 \times 4 - 2 \div 6 = 1$ **q** $40 \div 4 + 1 = 11$ **r** $6 + 2 \times 8 + 2 = 24$

4 Each $\bigcirc$ represents an operation.

Fill in the missing operations to make these statements true.

a $12 \bigcirc (28 \bigcirc 24) = 3$ **b** $88 \bigcirc 10 \bigcirc 8 = 8$

c $40 \bigcirc 5 \bigcirc (7 \bigcirc 5) = 4$ **d** $9 \bigcirc 15 \bigcirc (3 \bigcirc 2) = 12$

5 Calculate:

a $\dfrac{7 \times \sqrt{16}}{2^3 + 7^2 - 1}$ **b** $\dfrac{5^2 \times \sqrt{4}}{1 + 6^2 - 12}$ **c** $\dfrac{2 + 3^2}{5^2 + 4 \times 10 - \sqrt{25}}$

d $\dfrac{6^2 - 11}{2(17 + 2 \times 4)}$ **e** $\dfrac{3^2 - 3}{2 \times \sqrt{81}}$ **f** $\dfrac{3^2 - 5 + 6}{\sqrt{4} \times 5}$

g $\dfrac{36 - 3 \times \sqrt{16}}{15 - 3^2 \div 3}$ **h** $\dfrac{-30 + [18 \div (3 - 12) + 24]}{5 - 8 - 3^2}$

6 Work with a partner.

a Find a quick method for adding a set of consecutive whole numbers.

b Explain why your method works.

c Test your method on a set of consecutive negative integers.

d Does it work? Explain why or why not.

Section 3: Inverse operations

The four operations (add, subtract, multiply and divide) are related to each other. Operations are inverses of each other if one undoes (cancels out) the effect of the other.

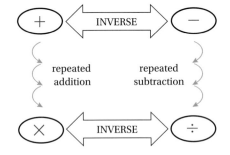

- Adding is the inverse of subtracting, e.g. add 5 is undone by subtract 5.

- Multiplying is the inverse of dividing, e.g. multiply by 2 is undone by divide by 2.

- Taking a square root is the inverse of squaring a number, e.g. 4^2 is undone by $\sqrt{16}$.

- Taking the cube root is the inverse of cubing a number, e.g. 2^3 is undone by $\sqrt[3]{8}$.

Additive inverse

The additive inverse of 1 is −1 (add 1 is undone by subtract 1).

The additive inverse of −5 is 5 (subtract 5 is undone by add 5).

When you add a number to its inverse the answer is always 1.

Multiplicative inverse

The multiplicative inverse of 2 is $\frac{1}{2}$ (multiply by 2 is undone by divide by 2).

The multiplicative inverse of $\frac{1}{4}$ is 4 (divide by 4 is undone by multiply by 4).

When you multiply a number by its inverse, the answer is always 1.

Tip

The multiplicative inverse of a number is also called its **reciprocal**. For example, $\frac{1}{3}$ is the reciprocal of 3.

Inverse operations are useful for checking the results of your calculations because carrying out the inverse operation gets you back to the number you started with.

For example,

is $4320 - 500 = 3820$ correct?

Check by adding 500 back to the result (i.e. doing the inverse operation) to see whether it gives you 4320.

$3820 + 500 = 4320$

Tip

You will use inverse operations to solve equations and when you deal with functions, so it is important that you understand how they work.

When there is more than one operation involved, you have to reverse the order of the inverse operations to return to the starting number.

For example, is $(50 + 62) \div 8 = 14$?

Check by working backwards and applying inverse operations:

$14 \times 8 - 62 = 50$

EXERCISE 1D

1 Use inverse operations to find the missing values in each of these calculations.

    a $\square + 217 = 529$ **b** $\square + 388 = 490$ **c** $\square - 218 = 182$

    d $121 \times \square = -605$ **e** $-6 \times \square = 870$ **f** $\square \div 40 = 5400$

2 Use inverse operations to check these calculations.

    a $45 \times 5 - 8 = 217$ **b** $14 + 5 \times 9 - 9 = 50$

    c $(23 + 48) \times 4 = 284$ **d** $(412 - 128) \div 4 = 71$

3 The formula for finding the area of a triangle is $A = \dfrac{bh}{2}$ (where b = base length and h = height).

    a Find the height of a triangle with an area of 54 cm^2 and a base length of 9 cm.

    b A triangle has an area of 64 cm^2.

        Find the height and the base length if the base is twice the height.

4 Three boys each have 15 pence in their left pockets.

They also have the same amount as each other in their right pockets.

The total of all their money is 120 pence.

a Using R to represent the money in the right-hand pocket, write a sum to show how you can work out the total.

b Use your sum to find out how much each boy has in their right pocket.

5 Here is an expression which includes different operations:

$$1 - \left(\frac{2}{3}(4 + 5) + 6\right) \times 7$$

a Calculate the value of the expression.

b Keep the numbers in order (from 1 to 7) but change the operations as necessary to:

i find the highest possible answer

ii find the lowest possible answer.

c Comment on how changing the operations affected your results.

Checklist of learning and understanding

Basic calculations

- Written methods are important for when you do not have a calculator.

- You can use any method as long as you show your working.

- Negative and positive numbers can be added, subtracted, multiplied and divided as long as you apply the rules to get the correct sign in the answer.

Order of operations

- In maths there is a conventional order for working when there is more than one operation.

- Always work out brackets (or other grouping symbols) first, then powers. Multiply and/or divide next, then add and/or subtract.

- A useful memory aid for the order of operations is BODMAS.

Inverse operations

- An inverse operation undoes the previous operation.

- Addition is the inverse of subtraction.

- Multiplication is the inverse of division.

- Squaring is the inverse of taking the square root.

Chapter review

For additional questions on the topics in this chapter, visit GCSE Mathematics Online.

1 These are the solutions to a cross-number puzzle.

The clues are all calculations that involve using the correct order of operations.

Write a set of clues that would give these results.

	¹2	²7					³3		
⁴1	4	8	⁵6		⁶1	9	7	⁷4	
⁸3	0		7					5	
	⁹4	¹⁰9		¹¹3	2	7		¹²2	¹³4
		2		1					8
		0		¹⁴4	¹⁵2	5		¹⁶2	6
	¹⁷4	1	¹⁸7		1			0	
¹⁹2	3		²⁰3	²¹2	0	4		²²9	0
²³7	9	4		1			²⁴7	9	

2 Use integers and operations to write ten different calculations that give an answer of −17.

3 **a** Work out $2 \times (8 - 3)$ *(1 mark)*

    b Work out $32 + 4 \times 5$ *(2 marks)*

©Pearson Education Ltd 2013

4 On a page of a magazine there are three columns of text.

Each column contains 42 rows.

If there is an average of 32 letters per column row, approximately how many letters are there on a page?

5 A stadium has seats for 32 000 people. How many rows of 125 is this?

6 Two numbers have a sum of −15 and a product of −100.

What are the numbers?

7 The sum of two numbers is 1, but their product is −20.

What are the numbers?

8 Josie's bank account was overdrawn.

She deposited £1000 and this brought her balance to £432.

By how much was her account overdrawn to start with?

9 You can use the formula $F = 2C + 30$ to convert approximately temperatures from Celsius to Fahrenheit.

Find the temperature in degrees Celsius when it is:

a 68 °F   **b** 100 °F

Find answers at: cambridge.org/ukschools/gcsemaths-studentbookanswers

2 Shapes and solids

In this chapter you will learn how to ...

- use the correct geometrical terms to talk about lines, angles and shapes.
- recognise and name common 2D shapes and 3D objects.
- describe the symmetrical properties of various polygons.
- classify triangles and quadrilaterals and use their properties to identify them.
- use properties of shapes to find missing angles and sides.

 For more resources relating to this chapter, visit GCSE Mathematics Online.

Using mathematics: real-life applications

Artists, craftspeople, builders, designers, architects and engineers use shape and space in their jobs, but almost everyone uses lines, angles, patterns and shapes in different ways every day.

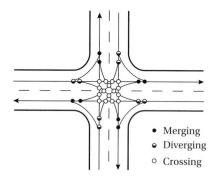

- Merging
- Diverging
- Crossing

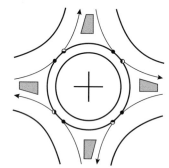

"I use a CAD package to plot lines and angles and show the direction of traffic flow when I design new road junctions." *(Civil engineer)*

Before you start ...

KS3	You need to use geometrical terms correctly.	**1** Choose the correct label for each letter on the diagram.
		base vertex acute angle point edge right angle height face
KS3	You should be able to recognise and name different types of shapes.	**2** Identify three different shapes in this diagram and use letters to name them correctly. **3** *ABCE* is one face of a solid with eight faces. What type of solid could it be?

Assess your starting point using the Launchpad

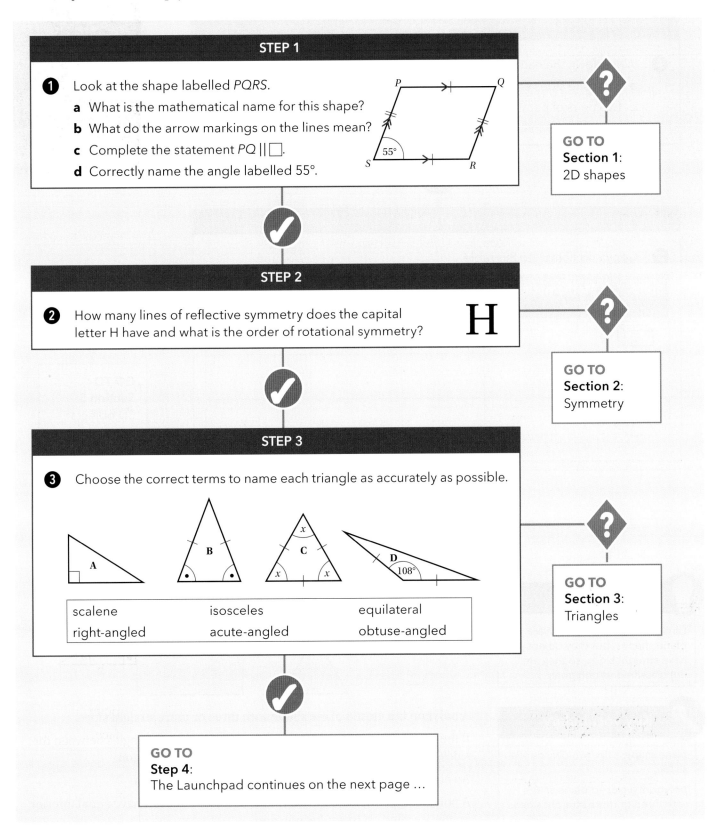

STEP 1

❶ Look at the shape labelled *PQRS*.

   a What is the mathematical name for this shape?

   b What do the arrow markings on the lines mean?

   c Complete the statement *PQ* || ☐.

   d Correctly name the angle labelled 55°.

GO TO
Section 1:
2D shapes

STEP 2

❷ How many lines of reflective symmetry does the capital letter H have and what is the order of rotational symmetry?

H

GO TO
Section 2:
Symmetry

STEP 3

❸ Choose the correct terms to name each triangle as accurately as possible.

scalene	isosceles	equilateral
right-angled	acute-angled	obtuse-angled

GO TO
Section 3:
Triangles

GO TO
Step 4:
The Launchpad continues on the next page …

Find answers at: cambridge.org/ukschools/gcsemaths-studentbookanswers

Launchpad continued …

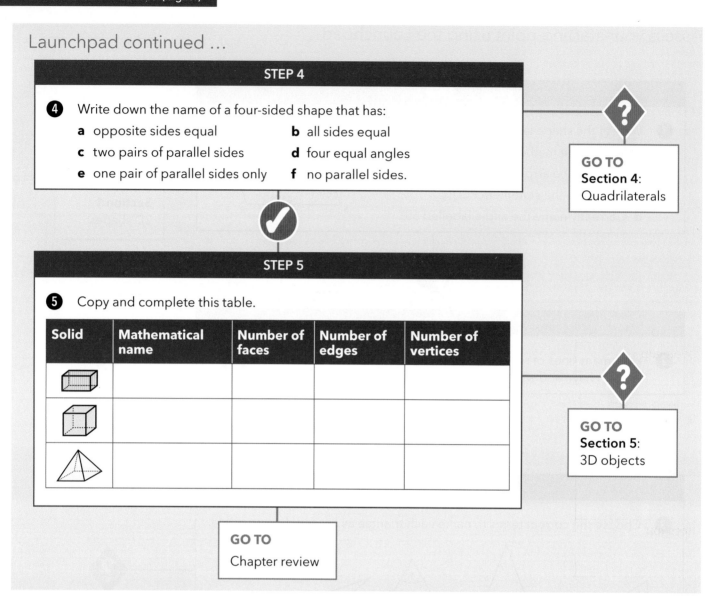

STEP 4

4 Write down the name of a four-sided shape that has:

a opposite sides equal   **b** all sides equal

c two pairs of parallel sides   **d** four equal angles

e one pair of parallel sides only   **f** no parallel sides.

GO TO
Section 4:
Quadrilaterals

STEP 5

5 Copy and complete this table.

Solid	Mathematical name	Number of faces	Number of edges	Number of vertices

GO TO
Section 5:
3D objects

GO TO
Chapter review

Tip

Circles and ellipses (ovals) are plane shapes, but they do not have straight sides, so they are not classified as polygons.

Key vocabulary

plane shape: a flat, two-dimensional shape.

polygon: a closed plane shape with three or more straight sides.

regular polygon: a polygon with equal straight sides and equal angles.

irregular polygon: a polygon that does not have equal sides or equal angles.

Section 1: 2D shapes

Flat shapes are called **plane shapes** or two-dimensional (2D) shapes.

A **polygon** is a closed plane shape with three or more straight sides.

If the sides of a polygon are all the same length and the angles between the sides (interior angles) are equal, then it is a **regular polygon**.

An equilateral triangle is an example of a regular polygon.

A polygon that does not have all sides equal or does not have equal interior angles is called an **irregular polygon**.

A rectangle is an irregular polygon because its sides are not all equal in length.

The fact that the angles of a rectangle are all equal to 90° does not make it a regular polygon.

Naming polygons

Polygons can be named according to the number of sides they have.

Name of polygon	Number of sides	Regular polygon	Irregular polygon
triangle	3	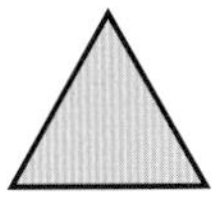	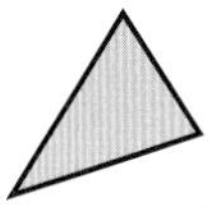
quadrilateral	4		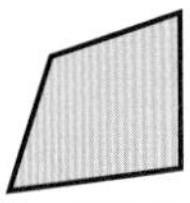
pentagon	5	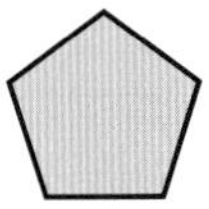	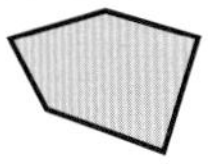
hexagon	6	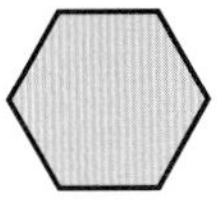	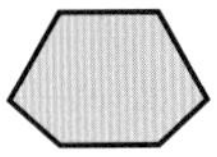
heptagon	7	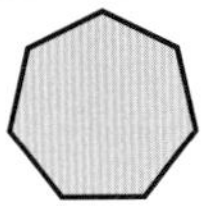	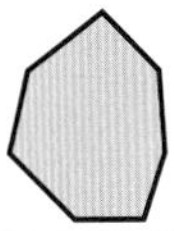
octagon	8	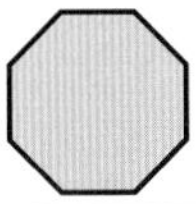	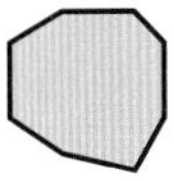
nonagon	9	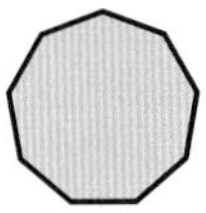	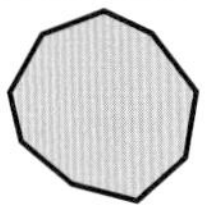
decagon	10	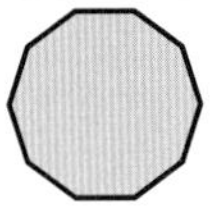	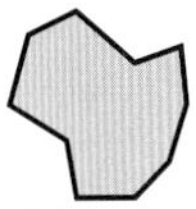

EXERCISE 2A

1 What is the correct mathematical name for each of the following shapes?

a A plane shape with three equal sides.

b A polygon with five equal sides.

c A polygon with six vertices and six equal angles.

d A plane shape with eight equal sides and eight equal internal angles.

2 Which of the following is not a polygon?

A square   **B** sector   **C** parallelogram   **D** triangle

3 Where might you find the following in real life?

a a regular octagon

b a circle

c a regular quadrilateral

d an irregular pentagon

Find answers at: cambridge.org/ukschools/gcsemaths-studentbookanswers

Perpendicular and parallel lines

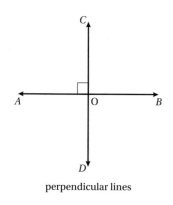

perpendicular lines

Perpendicular lines meet at right angles (90°).

The symbol $\perp$ means 'perpendicular to'.

In the diagram (left) $AB \perp CD$.

The shortest distance from a point to a line is the perpendicular distance between them.

The sides of shapes are perpendicular if they form a 90° angle.

Lines are parallel if they are the same perpendicular distance apart at any point along their length.

You can say that parallel lines are equidistant along their length, i.e. always an equal distance apart and never meeting.

The symbol $\parallel$ means 'parallel to'.
In the diagram $AB \parallel CD$ and $MN \parallel PQ$.

Small arrow symbols are drawn on lines to indicate that they are parallel to each other

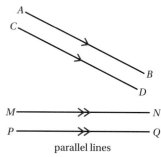

parallel lines

When there is more than one pair of parallel lines in a diagram, each pair is usually given a different set of arrow markings.

In the diagram below, $AB \parallel DC$, $AD \parallel EG$ and $EF \parallel BC$.

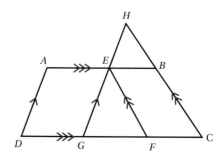

Drawing and labelling diagrams

Mathematical diagrams are drawn and labelled in standard ways so that their meaning is clear to anyone who uses them.

Sides and angles

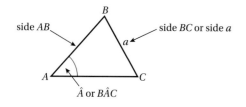

side AB

side BC or side a

$\hat{A}$ or $B\hat{A}C$

Shapes are labelled using capital letters on each vertex, which are usually written in alphabetical order as you move round the shape.

The shape on the left would be called $\triangle ABC$.

Each side of this triangle can be named using the capital letters on the vertices: AB, BC and CA.

Sometimes single letters are used to name the sides.

In this example, side *BC* can also be called side a because it is opposite angle *A*.

This convention is often used when you work with Pythagoras' theorem and in trigonometry, which explore angles and lengths of sides in triangles.

The angles can be named in different ways.

The angle at vertex *A* can be named *A*, *BAC* or *CAB*.

Symbols can be used to label angles. For example, ∠*BAC* or *BÂC*.

Tip

Greek letters are sometimes used to label angles. Don't be surprised to see α (alpha), β (beta), γ (gamma), δ (delta), and θ (theta) used to label angles, particularly in trigonometry.

Marking equal sides and angles

Small lines can be drawn on the sides of a shape to show whether the sides are equal or not.

Curved lines and symbols such as dots or letters can be used to show whether angles are equal or not.

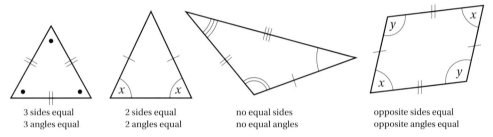

| 3 sides equal
3 angles equal | 2 sides equal
2 angles equal | no equal sides
no equal angles | opposite sides equal
opposite angles equal |

EXERCISE 2B

1 Read each clue in Column A. Match it to a term in Column B.

	Column A	Column B
a	a shape that has two fewer sides than an octagon	decagon
b	a shape that has two sides more than a triangle	hexagon
c	a shape with four sides	equilateral triangle
d	a traffic stop sign is an example of this shape	two-dimensional
e	a figure that has length and height	pentagon
f	a closed plane shape with all sides x cm long and all angles the same size	quadrilateral
g	a ten-sided figure	square
h	another name for a regular four-sided polygon	regular polygon
i	the more common name for a regular three-sided polygon	octagon

2 Look at this diagram.

Say whether each of the following statements is true or false.

a $AF \parallel EC$.

b $\triangle BFD$ is isosceles.

c $CE \perp BC$.

d $AE \parallel BD$.

e $ABCE$ is a regular polygon.

f $GB \parallel BC$.

g In $\triangle DHJ$, angle H = angle J = angle D.

h $\triangle GHJ$ is a regular polygon.

3 Draw and correctly label a sketch of each of the following shapes.

a A triangle, ABC with angle B = angle C and side $AB \perp AC$.

b A regular four-sided polygon $DEFG$.

c Quadrilateral $PQRS$ such that $PQ \parallel SR$ but $PQ \neq SR$ and $\angle PSR = \angle QRS$.

4 a In the diagram, why can you not use just the single letter A to represent the angle labelled x?

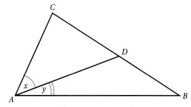

b How should it be labelled?

5 A quadrilateral has both pairs of opposite sides parallel.

Explain mathematically why the opposite sides of the shape must also be equal.

Section 2: Symmetry

Some shapes and objects are symmetrical.

Symmetry is a property that can be used to help identify shapes, find missing lengths and angles, and solve problems.

You need to recognise two types of symmetry in plane shapes: line symmetry and rotational symmetry.

Line symmetry

Tip

The line of symmetry is sometimes called the mirror line. If you place a small mirror on the line of symmetry you will see the whole shape reflected in the mirror.

If you can fold a shape in half to create a mirror image (**reflection**) on either side of the fold the shape has line symmetry.

The fold is known as the **line of symmetry**.

Each half of the shape is a reflection of the other half so this type of symmetry is also called reflection symmetry.

Triangle A has line symmetry. The dotted line is the line of symmetry.

If you fold the shape along this line the two parts will fit onto each other exactly.

Triangle B is not symmetrical. You cannot draw a line to divide it into two identical parts.

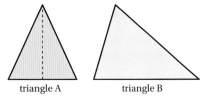

triangle A   triangle B

A shape can have more than one line of symmetry.

A regular pentagon has five lines of symmetry.

Lines of symmetry can be horizontal, vertical or diagonal.

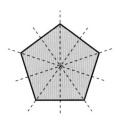

Key vocabulary

reflection: an exact image of a shape about a line of symmetry.

line of symmetry: a line that divides a plane shape into two identical halves, each the reflection of the other.

Rotational symmetry

A shape has **rotational symmetry** if you rotate it around a fixed point and it looks identical in different positions.

The **order** of rotational symmetry tells you how many times the shape will look identical before it returns to the starting point.

If you can only rotate the shape a full 360° before it appears identical again then it does **not** have rotational symmetry.

Key vocabulary

rotational symmetry: symmetry by turning a shape around a fixed point so that it looks the same from different positions.

Tip

You will deal with reflections in mirror lines and rotations about a fixed point again in Chapter 40 when you deal with transformations using coordinates.

The order of rotational symmetry of a regular polygon depends on the number of sides it has.

A square has an order of rotational symmetry of 4 around its centre.

The star is just to show the position of one vertex of the square as it rotates.

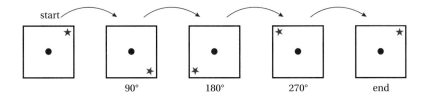

start   90°   180°   270°   end

This is the national symbol for the Isle of Man.

It has an order of rotational symmetry of 3 about its centre.

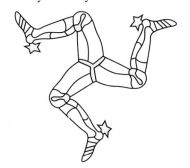

Find answers at: cambridge.org/ukschools/gcsemaths-studentbookanswers

EXERCISE 2C

1 Which of the dotted lines in each figure are lines of symmetry?

a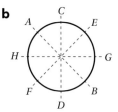

b

c

d

2 By sketching, investigate and work out the number of lines of symmetry and the order of rotational symmetry of each shape.

Copy and complete the table to summarise your results.

Shape	Number of lines of symmetry	Order of rotational symmetry
square		
rectangle		
isosceles triangle		
equilateral triangle		
parallelogram		
regular hexagon		
regular octagon		

3 Give an example of a shape that has rotational symmetry of order 3 but is not a triangle.

4 Which of the following letters have rotational symmetry?

C   H   A   R

5 Describe the symmetrical features of this design in as much detail as possible.

Use sketches if you need to.

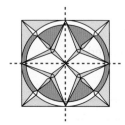

6 Metal alloy rims for tyres are very popular on modern cars.

Find and draw five alloy rim designs that you like.

For each one, state its order of rotational symmetry.

7 Sketch five different symmetrical designs or logos that you can find in your environment.

Label your sketches to indicate how the design is symmetrical.

Section 3: Triangles

Triangles are three-sided polygons which are given special names according to their properties.

Type of triangle	Properties
scalene	No equal sides. No equal angles. No line of symmetry. No rotational symmetry.
isosceles	Two equal sides. Angles at the base of the equal sides are equal. One line of symmetry. Line of symmetry is the perpendicular height. No rotational symmetry.
equilateral	All sides equal. Three equal angles, each is 60°. Three lines of symmetry. Rotational symmetry of order 3.
acute-angled	All angles are less than 90° (acute).
right-angled	One angle is a right angle (90°).
obtuse-angled	One angle is greater than 90° (obtuse).

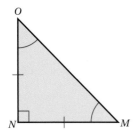

Triangles can be a combination of types.

For example, an isosceles triangle could be a right-angled isosceles triangle, an acute-angled isosceles triangle or an obtuse-angled isosceles triangle depending on the size of the angles.

Triangle *MNO* (left) is a right-angled isosceles triangle.

You will need to know and apply the basic properties of triangles when you work with theorems and proofs.

For example, you will use triangle properties extensively when you deal with circle theorems in Chapter 27.

Angle properties

The angles inside a triangle are called interior angles.

The three interior angles of any triangle always add up to 180°.

If you extend the length of one side of a triangle you form another angle outside the triangle, called an exterior angle.

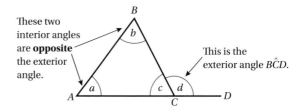

If you tear off the angles of any triangle and place them against a straight edge (180°) you can see that the interior angles add up to 180°.

You can also see that the exterior angle is equal to the sum of the two interior angles that are opposite it.

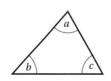  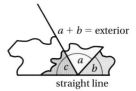

Tip

Rearranging pieces of a triangle demonstrates the angle properties. You will learn how to prove these properties using mathematical principles in Chapter 26.

Using the properties of triangles to solve problems

You can use the properties of triangles to solve problems involving unknown angles and lengths of sides.

Problem-solving framework

Triangle *ABC* is isosceles with perimeter 85 mm.

AB = *BC* and *AC* = 25 mm. Angle *ABC* = 48°.

Calculate:

a the length of each equal side

b the size of each equal angle.

Continues on next page …

Steps for solving problems	What you would do for this example
Step 1: Work out what you have to do. Start by reading the question carefully.	You need to use the properties of isosceles triangles and the given information to find the length of two sides and the size of two angles.
Step 2: What information do you need? Have you got it all?	You should draw a labelled sketch to see whether you have the information you need. *B* 48° *x* *x* *A* 25 mm *C*
Step 3: Decide what maths you can do.	You can use the values you already have to make equations to find the missing values.
Step 4: Set out your solution clearly. Check your working and that your answer is reasonable.	**a** Perimeter = $AC + AB + BC = 85$ mm So, $85 = 25 + AB + BC$ $85 - 25 = AB + BC$ $60 = AB + BC$ But $AB = BC$, so $AB = BC = 60 \div 2 = 30$ mm Check: $30 + 30 + 25 = 85$. **b** Let each equal angle be $x°$. $48 + 2x = 180$ (angle sum of triangle) $2x = 180 - 48$ $2x = 132$ $x = 66$ Check: $66 + 66 + 48 = 180$
Step 5: Check that you've answered the question.	Each equal side is 30 mm long. Each equal angle is 66°.

Tip

You will use these properties often when you deal with trigonometry in Chapter 33.

In many problems you will have to find the size of unknown angles before you can move on and solve the problem.

 Find answers at: cambridge.org/ukschools/gcsemaths-studentbookanswers

EXERCISE 2D

1 What type of triangle is this? Explain how you decided without measuring.

2 What type of triangle is shown on the left?

Choose the correct answer.

A obtuse-angled scalene   **B** right-angled isosceles

C acute-angled isosceles   **D** obtuse-angled isosceles

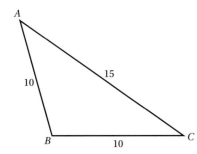

3 Which of the following triangles are not possible?

Explain why.

a An isosceles triangle with a right angle.

b A scalene triangle with two angles $> 90°$.

c A scalene triangle with three angles $34°$, $64°$ and $92°$.

d An obtuse equilateral triangle.

e An isosceles triangle with side lengths 6.5 cm, 7 cm and 7.5 cm.

4 Two angles in a triangle are $38°$ and $104°$.

a What is the size of the third angle?

b What type of triangle is this?

5 Find the size of the unknown angles a to i in the following diagrams.

Show your working and give mathematical reasons for any deductions you make.

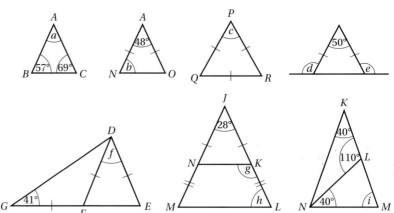

6 Isosceles triangle DEF with $DE = EF$ has a perimeter of 50 mm.

Find the length of EF if:

a $DF = 15$ mm   **b** $DE = \sqrt{130}$ mm   **c** $DE = (3x + 2)$ and $DF = (x + 4)$

Section 4: Quadrilaterals

A quadrilateral is a four-sided plane figure.

In the photographs to the right you can find rectangles, squares and more than one trapezium.

Quadrilaterals are classified and named according to their properties.

- A trapezium has one pair of opposite sides parallel.
- A kite has two pairs of adjacent sides equal.
- A parallelogram has both pairs of opposite sides parallel.
- A rhombus is a parallelogram with all sides equal.
- A rectangle is a parallelogram with angles of 90°.
- A square is a rectangle with all sides equal.

Some properties overlap, for example, a rectangle is actually a special type of parallelogram.

The rectangle meets the definition of a parallelogram (it has both pairs of opposite sides parallel and equal in length), so all rectangles are parallelograms.

In this case the reverse of the statement is not true. All parallelograms are not rectangles.

Quadrilateral		Properties
trapezium		• One pair of opposite sides are parallel.
kite		• Two pairs of **adjacent** sides are equal. • Diagonals are perpendicular. • One diagonal **bisects** the other at right angles (and this is a line of symmetry). • One diagonal bisects the angles.
parallelogram		• Both pairs of opposite sides are parallel. • Both pairs of opposite sides are equal. • Both pairs of opposite angles are equal. • Diagonals bisect each other. Continues on next page …

Key vocabulary

adjacent: next to each other; in shapes, sides that meet at a common vertex.

bisect: to divide exactly into two halves.

Quadrilateral		Properties
rhombus		As for parallelogram, plus: • All sides are equal. • Diagonals bisect at right angles. • Diagonals bisect the angles.
rectangle		As for parallelogram, plus: • All angles are 90°. • Diagonals are equal in length.
square		As for a rectangle, plus: • All sides are equal. • Diagonals bisect at right angles. • Diagonals bisect the angles.

Using the properties of quadrilaterals to solve problems

You can use the given or marked properties of a quadrilateral to identify and name it.

You should always state what properties you are using to justify your answer.

WORKED EXAMPLE 1

A plane shape has two diagonals.

The diagonals are perpendicular.

a What shape(s) could this be?

b The diagonals are not the same length.
Which shape(s) could it not be?

a Two diagonals means that the shape is a quadrilateral.

Only the square, rhombus and kite have diagonals that intersect at 90°.

The shape could be a square, rhombus or kite.

b Of the three shapes, only the square has diagonals that are equal in length.

Therefore, it could not be a square.

The angle sum of quadrilaterals

All quadrilaterals have two (and only two) diagonals. If you draw in one diagonal you divide the quadrilateral into two triangles.

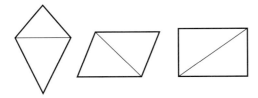

You already know that the interior angles of a triangle add up to 180°.

Therefore, the interior angles of a quadrilateral are equal to $2 \times 180° = 360°$.

WORK IT OUT 2.1

Find the sizes of the missing angles, x, y and z.

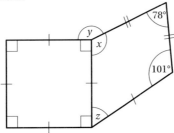

Identify the correct solution. Find the error in the other two.

Option A	Option B	Option C
$x = 180° - 78° = 102°$ (angles on a straight line $= 180°$)	$x = 101°$ as the shape is a kite and opposite angles are equal	The shape is a square and a rhombus
$x + 90° + y = 360°$ $192° + y = 360°$	If $x = 101°$ then the angles in any quadrilateral $= 360°$	Angle $x = 101°$
$y = 360° - 192° = 168°$ (angles in a quadrilateral add to 360°)	$z = 360° - 78° - 101° - 101° = 80°$	Angle $z = 78°$
$x + 78° + 101° + z = 360°$ $102° + 78° + 101° + z = 360°$	Angles round a point add to 360° $x + y + 90° = 360°$	Angle $y = 360° - 101° - 90°$ $y = 360° - 192°$
$281° + z = 360°$	$360° - 90° - 101° = y$	$y = 168°$
$z = 360° - 281° = 79°$	$y = 169°$	

EXERCISE 2E

1 Identify the quadrilateral from the description.

There may be more than one correct answer.

a All angles are equal.

b Diagonals are equal in length.

c Two pairs of sides are equal and parallel.

d No sides are parallel.

e The only regular quadrilateral.

f Diagonals bisect each other.

2 You can identify a quadrilateral by considering its diagonals.

Copy and complete this table.

Shape	Diagonals are equal in length	Diagonals bisect each other	Diagonals are perpendicular
rhombus			
parallelogram			
square			
kite			
rectangle			

3 What is the most obvious difference between a square and a rhombus?

4 Millie says that a quadrilateral has all four sides the same length.

Elizabeth says it must be a square.

Is Elizabeth correct? Give an explanation for your answer.

5 A kite has one angle of 47° and one of 133°. What sizes are the other two angles?

6 State whether each statement is always true, sometimes true or never true.

Give a reason for your answer.

a A square is a rectangle.　　　　　**b** A rectangle is a square.

c A rectangle is a rhombus.　　　　**d** A rhombus is a parallelogram.

e A parallelogram is a rhombus.

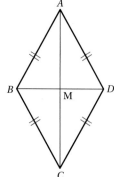

7 *ABCD* (left) is a rhombus.

Which of the following statements are true? Justify your answers.

a $\angle AMB = 90°$　　　　　**b** $DB = AC$

c $\angle BDC + \angle ACD = 180°$　　**d** $\angle ABC = \angle ADC$

8 Calculate the value of *x* in rhombus *ABCD*.

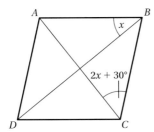

9 In the figure on the right *ABCD* and *ADEF* are parallelograms.

Show mathematically that *FECB* is a parallelogram.

10 Jason says that if two opposite sides of a quadrilateral are equal in length then the quadrilateral must be a parallelogram.

Is he correct?

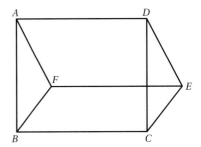

Section 5: 3D objects

Solids

Solids are three-dimensional (3D) objects.

The parts of a solid are given specific names.

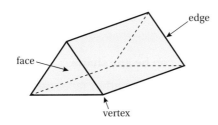

A solid, such as a triangular prism, that has only flat (plane) surfaces can also be called a **polyhedron**.

Cylinders, spheres and cones are not polyhedra. They are solids with a curved surface.

Two faces of a solid meet at an edge.

Three or more faces meet at a point called a vertex. (The plural of vertex is vertices.)

Each type of polyhedron has some properties that are not shared by the others.

Cubes and cuboids

Cubes and cuboids are box-shaped polyhedra.

They have six faces, twelve edges and eight vertices.

A cuboid has six rectangular faces.

Tip

3D means an object has three dimensions or measurements: length, width and height.

Key vocabulary

polyhedron (plural: polyhedra): a solid shape with flat faces that are polygons.

Tip

You need to know the properties of the basic polyhedra and other 3D solids.

You will use these properties to draw plans, elevation and nets of solids in Chapter 3 and you will apply them when you solve problems relating to volume and surface area in Chapter 18.

Key vocabulary

congruent: identical in shape and size.

A cube also has six faces, but to be classified as a cube, the faces must all be **congruent** squares.

All cubes are cuboids, but not all cuboids are cubes.

Prisms

A prism is a 3D object with two congruent, parallel faces.

If the prism is sliced parallel to one of these faces the cross-section will always be the same shape.

The diagram below shows a prism with two triangular end faces.

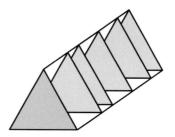

You can see that slicing it anywhere along its length gives a triangular cross-section.

The parallel faces of a prism can be any shape.

If the prism is a polyhedron all of the other faces are rectangular.

Prisms are named according to the shape of their parallel faces.

pentagonal prism	**hexagonal prism**	**octagonal prism**
2 pentagonal faces	2 hexagonal faces	2 octagonal faces
5 rectangular faces	6 rectangular faces	8 rectangular faces

Although you do not normally refer to them as prisms, a cube is a square prism and a cuboid is a rectangular prism.

Pyramids

A pyramid is a polyhedron with a base and triangular faces which meet at a vertex (sometimes called the apex of the pyramid).

Pyramids are named according to the shape of their base.

triangular pyramid   square pyramid   pentagonal pyramid   hexagonal pyramid

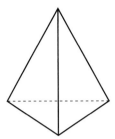 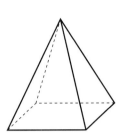 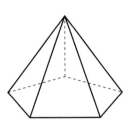 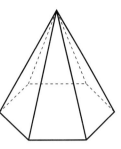

The number of sides of the base can be used to work out how many triangular faces the pyramid has.

A square has four sides, so a square pyramid has four triangular faces.

The Louvre Museum in Paris is famous for the massive glass square pyramid at its entrance.

There is another smaller, inverted square pyramid in the underground shopping mall behind the museum.

A regular polyhedron is a solid whose faces are all congruent regular polygons.

There are only five regular polyhedra.

Other solids

Cylinders, cones and spheres are also 3D objects.

They do not have straight edges or flat faces that are polygons so they are not polyhedral.

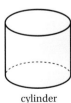 

cylinder   cone   sphere

A cylinder has two circular end faces and a curved surface along its length.

A cone has a circular base and a curved surface that forms a point.

A sphere is shaped like a ball. It has only one continuous curved surface.

EXERCISE 2F

1 Sketch a possible solid you could make by combining the given solids.

For each one, state whether it is a polyhedron and how many faces, vertices and edges it would have.

a A large and a small cylinder.

b A cube and a square-based pyramid.

c Two identical pentagonal-based pyramids.

d A triangular prism and a cuboid.

2 Copy and complete this table.

3D Shape	Faces (F)	Vertices (V)	Edges (E)
cube			
cuboid			
triangular-based pyramid			
square-based pyramid			
triangular-based prism			
hexagonal-based prism			

a Write an expression to show the relationship between F, V and E in these solids.

b Use your expression to find the number of faces in a polyhedron with 12 vertices and 30 edges.

c Show whether your expression works for each of these solids.

If it doesn't work, suggest a reason for this.

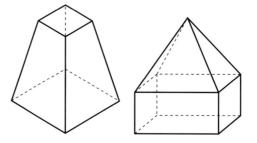

d Is it possible to have a polyhedron with 25 faces, 45 edges and 30 vertices?

Justify your answer.

3 Janice is building wire models of 3D objects for a school project.

How much wire would she need to build each of these shapes?

Assume there is no overlap at the vertices or joins.

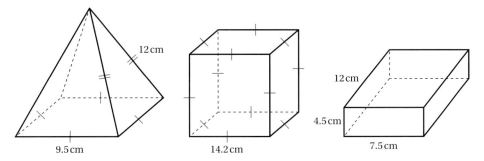

 Checklist of learning and understanding

Types of shapes

- Polygons are closed plane shapes with straight sides.
- Triangles, quadrilaterals, pentagons and hexagons are all polygons.
- Circles and ovals are plane shapes, but they are not polygons.

Symmetry

- Shapes have line symmetry if they can be folded along a line of symmetry to produce two identical mirror images.
- Shapes have rotational symmetry if they fit onto themselves more than once during a 360° rotation.

Triangles

- Triangles are three-sided polygons.
- Triangles can be classified and named using their side and angle properties.
- The sum of the interior angles of a triangle is 180°.

Quadrilaterals

- Quadrilaterals are four-sided polygons.
- Quadrilaterals can be classified and named using their side, angle and diagonal properties.
- The sum of the interior angles of a quadrilateral is 360°.

Properties of 3D objects

- 3D objects are solids with length, breadth and height.
- Polyhedra are solids with flat faces and straight edges.
- Prisms and pyramids are polyhedral.
- Cylinders, cones and spheres are 3D objects but they are not polyhedral.

 Find answers at: cambridge.org/ukschools/gcsemaths-studentbookanswers

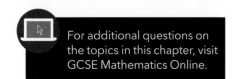
For additional questions on the topics in this chapter, visit GCSE Mathematics Online.

 Chapter review

1 True or false?

   a A slice of pizza can be accurately described as a triangle.

   b A triangular pyramid has 4 vertices, 4 faces and 6 edges.

   c A pair of lines that are equidistant and never meet are described as being perpendicular.

   d A pyramid with a polygon base of n sides will have $n + 1$ vertices.

   e A cylinder has a uniform circular cross-section.

2 Describe the symmetrical features of a regular hexagon as fully as possible.

3 Find the values of the missing angles in this trapezium.

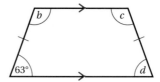

4 Is the missing angle a right angle? Explain.

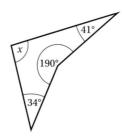

5 Find the value of the angle marked x.

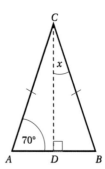

6 A quadrilateral has two pairs of equal sides. Opposite sides are not equal. What shape is it?

7 What is the difference between a polygon and a polyhedron?

8 A solid has two surfaces and no straight edges. What is the name of the solid?

9 Find the unknown angles denoted by variables.

a

b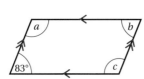

10 Is this quadrilateral a parallelogram?

Justify your answer.

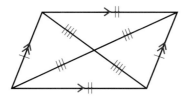

11 Niresh states that if the diagonals of a quadrilateral intersect at right angles, the quadrilateral must be a square.

Is he correct?

Justify your answer.

12 Here is a list of the names of five types of quadrilateral:

   trapezium   parallelogram   square   rhombus   rectangle

a From the list, write down the names of two quadrilaterals which must have all four sides the same length.   *(1 mark)*

   trapezium   parallelogram   square   rhombus   rectangle

b From the list, write down the name of the quadrilateral that has only one pair of parallel sides.   *(1 mark)*

   trapezium   parallelogram   square   rhombus   rectangle

For one of these quadrilaterals,

   the corners are not right angles,
   the quadrilateral has rotational symmetry of order 2
and   the diagonals cross at right angles.

c Write down the name of this quadrilateral.   *(1 mark)*

Find answers at: cambridge.org/ukschools/gcsemaths-studentbookanswers

3 2D representations of 3D shapes

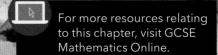

In this chapter you will learn how to ...

- apply what you already know about the properties of 3D objects.
- work with 2D representations of 3D objects.
- construct and interpret plans and elevations of 3D objects.

For more resources relating to this chapter, visit GCSE Mathematics Online.

Using mathematics: real-life applications

Buildings, engine parts, vehicles and packaging are all carefully planned and designed before they are built or made. Most design work starts on paper or screen using two-dimensional images to represent the final three-dimensional objects.

"No one will buy an apartment that isn't built yet if they don't know what it is going to look like. When we sell a development we show people floor plans as well as elevations from all four sides. Sometimes we also have a 3D scale model of the development."

(Estate agent)

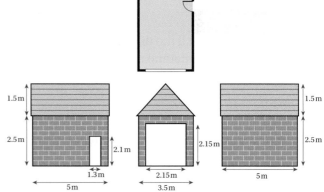

Before you start ...

Ch 2	You must be able to identify and name some common 3D objects.	**1** Name each of these 3D objects. **a** **b** **c** **d**
Ch 2	You should know the basic properties of polygons and other 3D objects.	**2** True or false? Correct the false statements. **a** A cube has 4 faces. **b** A cube has 12 edges. **c** A cuboid has 8 vertices. **d** For any polyhedral, $F + V + E = 2$.
KS3	You must be able to accurately use a ruler, protractor and compasses to draw shapes.	**3** Draw a triangle with a base of 8 cm and angles at the ends of 45° and 60°. What are the lengths of the other two sides? **4** Use a pair of compasses to draw a circle of radius 5 cm. Construct a hexagon inside the circle.

Assess your starting point using the Launchpad

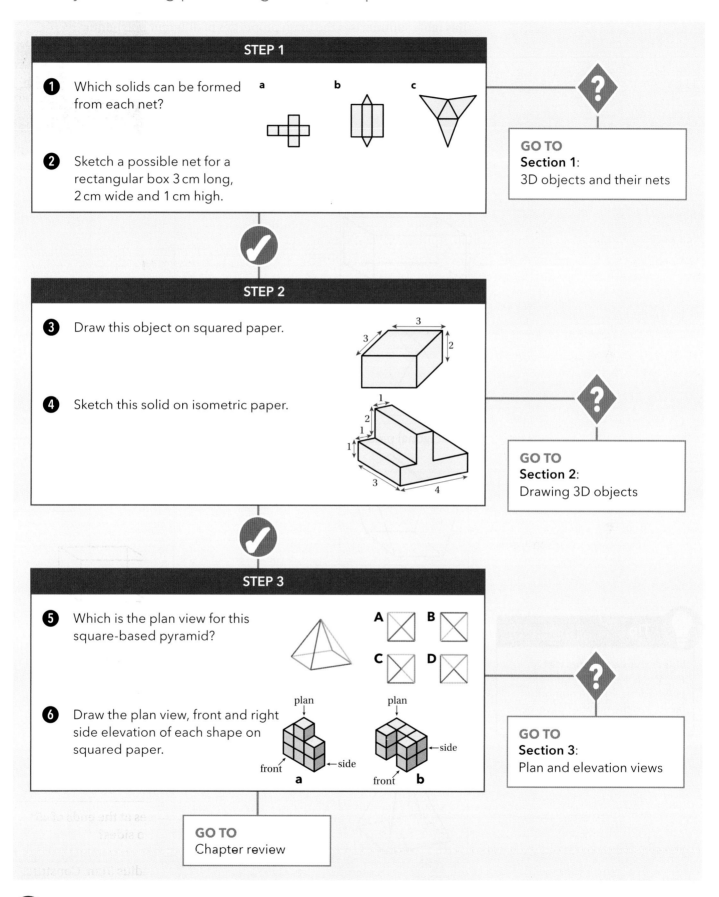

STEP 1

1 Which solids can be formed from each net?

a   b   c

2 Sketch a possible net for a rectangular box 3 cm long, 2 cm wide and 1 cm high.

GO TO
Section 1:
3D objects and their nets

STEP 2

3 Draw this object on squared paper.

4 Sketch this solid on isometric paper.

GO TO
Section 2:
Drawing 3D objects

STEP 3

5 Which is the plan view for this square-based pyramid?

A   B   C   D

6 Draw the plan view, front and right side elevation of each shape on squared paper.

plan   plan

front   side   side   front

a   b

GO TO
Section 3:
Plan and elevation views

GO TO
Chapter review

Find answers at: cambridge.org/ukschools/gcsemaths-studentbookanswers

Section 1: 3D objects and their nets

This table summarises the main properties of different polyhedra.

Polyhedron	Faces	Vertices	Edges
cube (square prism)	6 square faces	8	12
cuboid (rectangular prism)	3 pairs of congruent rectangular faces	8	12
triangular prism	2 congruent triangular end faces 3 rectangular faces	6	9
pentagonal prism	2 congruent pentagonal end faces 5 rectangular faces	10	15
triangular pyramid	1 triangular base 3 triangular faces that meet at an apex	4	6
square-based pyramid	1 square base 4 triangular faces that meet at an apex	5	8

Tip

Euler's theorem states that $F + V = E + 2$ for any convex polyhedron. F is the number of faces, V is the number of vertices and E is the number of edges.

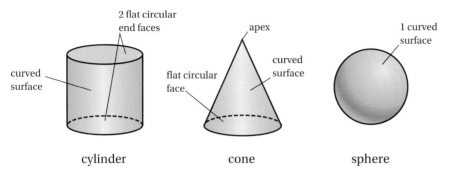

cylinder · cone · sphere

Nets of 3D objects

A **net** is a 2D representation of a 3D shape. You can fold up a net to make the 3D shape.

For printed packaging the design is printed onto the net, and then the net is folded up to make the box itself.

A cube has six square faces. There are 11 possible ways of arranging the faces to make the net of a cube. These are the two nets most commonly used.

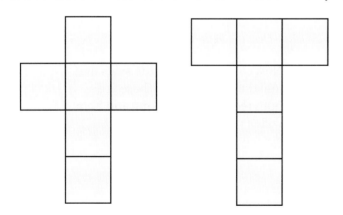

You can see from the net on the right that the object has one square face and four triangular faces. When this net is folded up, the triangular faces will meet at a common point.

You know that a square-based pyramid has a square base and four triangular faces that meet at an apex. So this must be the net of a square-based pyramid.

You can use the properties of a 3D shape to help you recognise nets and identify the shapes they will make. You can also use the properties to sketch or construct the net of a shape.

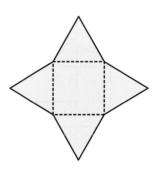

WORKED EXAMPLE 1

Construct an accurate net of this rectangular prism.

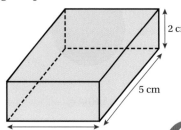

You know that a cuboid has six rectangular faces, so your net will have six faces.

Draw a rough sketch.

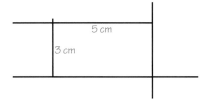

> **Tip**
>
> When you draw a net, always start in the middle of the page to give yourself space to construct all the faces.

To construct an accurate net you need to use the measurements given on the diagram.

Use a ruler and pencil to draw the net.

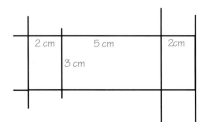

Draw the bottom face first. This is a rectangle 3 cm wide and 5 cm long.

Next construct two of the sides that join onto the bottom. These are both rectangles 3 cm long and 2 cm wide.

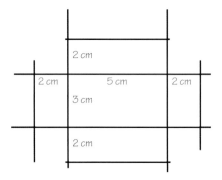

Construct the other two sides that join onto the bottom. These are both rectangles 5 cm long and 2 cm wide.

Continues on next page ...

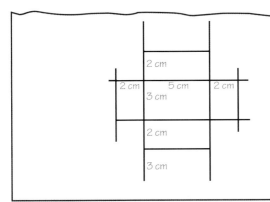

Lastly, draw the top face. This can be joined onto either the back or the front face or either of the sides. It is a rectangle 3 cm wide and 5 cm long.

EXERCISE 3A

1 You have seen the two most commonly used nets of a cube. Draw the other nine.

2 Which of the 3D shapes shown below can be created from this net?

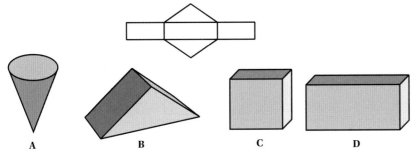

A   B   C   D

3 Which of these nets could be used to make a cylinder?

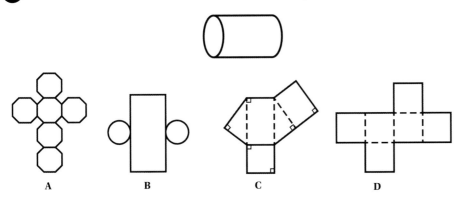

A   B   C   D

4 Which dice is represented by this net?

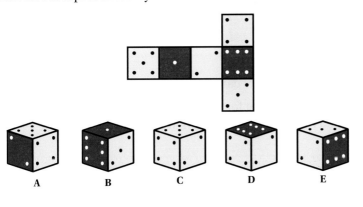

A   B   C   D   E

Tip

The numbers on the opposite faces of a dice add up to 7.

Find answers at: cambridge.org/ukschools/gcsemaths-studentbookanswers

5 Which 3D shapes can be formed from these nets?

a **b**

6 The six faces of a cube are shown here.

Here are three different views of the cube.

Here is the net of the cube. Only one of the faces has been recorded.

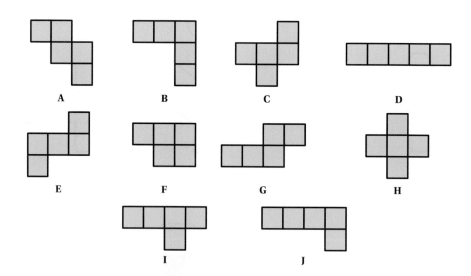

Copy and complete the net.

7 Here are some possible arrangements of five square faces.

A   B   C   D

E   F   G   H

I   J

a Which of these nets cannot be folded up to form an open box?

b Draw one more net for an open box. Make sure your net is not just a turned or flipped over version of the ones shown here.

8 A Year 10 class plan to sell popcorn to raise funds. They will charge £1.50 per litre box of popcorn. They have two box designs, a 'chunky' cube, and the 'tall boy' cuboid.

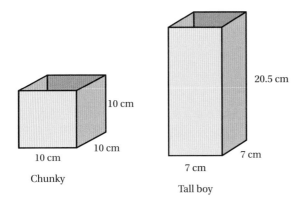

Chunky

Tall boy

The price of popcorn boxes is based on how much material is used to make them. The more expensive the box, the less profit the class will make.

a Sketch the net of each box and label its dimensions.

b Use the nets to work out the area of cardboard needed to make each box. (Ignore the tabs needed to fold up the box.)

c If it costs 5p for every $100\,\text{cm}^2$ of card used, what is the cost, to the nearest penny, of each type of box.

Section 2: Drawing 3D objects

You need to be able to make drawings of 3D objects and to interpret and make sense of drawings of 3D objects from different perspectives.

It can be challenging to draw a 3D object because you are trying to show three dimensions on a two-dimensional plane (your paper).

There are a number of ways of drawing 3D objects to show their features in 2D. As you read through each method, try it out on rough paper.

Prisms and cylinders using end faces

For prisms and cylinders, visualise the position of their end faces and draw these first.

A cuboid (rectangular prism):

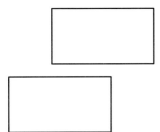

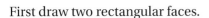

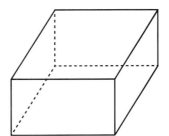

First draw two rectangular faces.

Then draw lines to join the vertices.

 Tip

Once you've drawn the end faces, you can join them by drawing lines to represent the edges. For prisms make sure you match up the corresponding vertices.

A cylinder:

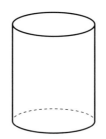 

First draw the two circular end faces by drawing ovals.

Then draw in two lines to join the end faces.

Shading can make the cylinder look more realistic.

A triangular prism:

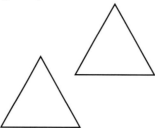 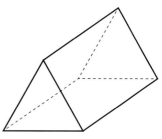

First draw the two triangular end faces.

Then draw in lines to join the vertices.

Any shaped prism:

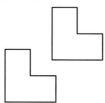 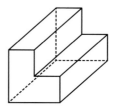 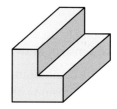

First draw the end faces.

Then draw lines to join the vertices.

Prisms and pyramids from parallel lines

You can draw square and rectangular prisms and square-based pyramids using two pairs of parallel lines as a starting point.

To draw a prism:

 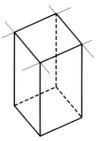

Begin by drawing two pairs of parallel lines that intersect.

Then draw four lines of equal length down (or up) from the intersections. Complete the shape by joining the ends to make a prism.

To draw a square-based pyramid:

 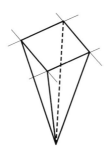 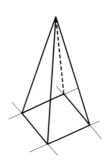

Start by drawing two pairs of parallel lines.

Mark a point and draw lines from three intersections of the parallel lines to the point.

Drawing shapes on squared or isometric grids

3D objects can be drawn on squared or isometric grids. The grid may be made from dots or from faintly printed lines.

This diagram shows a cube and a cuboid drawn on a square grid.

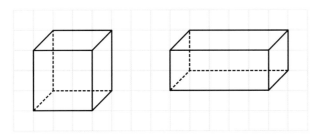

This diagram shows the same objects drawn on an **isometric grid**.

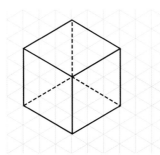 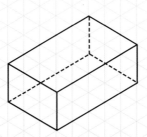

 Key vocabulary

isometric grid: special drawing paper based on an arrangement of equilateral triangles.

The vertical lines on the grid are used to represent the vertical edges of the 3D object. You draw along the lines at an angle on the paper to represent the horizontal edges of the 3D object.

When you draw shapes on both square and isometric grids you use broken lines to show the edges that would not be seen if you viewed the shape from that angle.

Isometric drawings

Isometric drawings are used to visually represent three-dimensional objects in two dimensions in technical and engineering drawings.

 Find answers at: cambridge.org/ukschools/gcsemaths-studentbookanswers

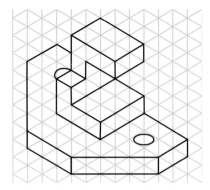

The diagram on the left shows the design of an engineering component on isometric paper.

Isometric paper is very useful for drawing solids built from cubes.

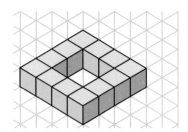 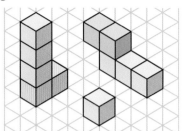

WORKED EXAMPLE 2

Draw this shape on the grid provided.

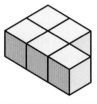

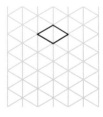

Start by drawing the horizontal face of one of the cubes. Here, one of the top yellow faces has been drawn.

Use that face to draw in the other horizontal faces.

Use the vertical lines on the grid to draw in the vertical edges.

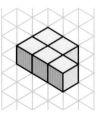

Use the angled lines to draw in the bottom horizontal edges.

WORK IT OUT 3.1

Students were asked to draw this view of a shape on an isometric grid.

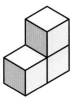

This is how they started their sketches.

Student A	Student B	Student C
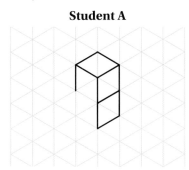	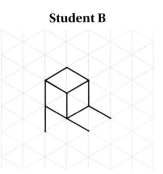	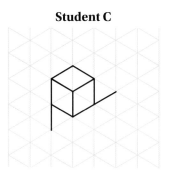

Which student is likely to end up with the correct view of the shape?

What are the others doing incorrectly?

EXERCISE 3B

1 Draw the following objects without using a grid.

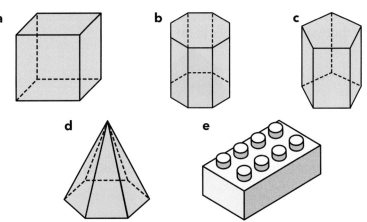

2 One of the parallel end faces of each of three different prisms is shown here.

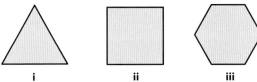

| i | ii | iii |

a Sketch each prism on squared paper.

b Use isometric paper to draw each prism.

c Compare the two drawings of each prism. How does the grid affect what your drawing looks like?

Draw the following shapes on an isometric grid.

a 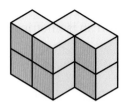 **b** 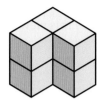 **c**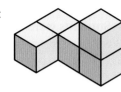

4 The diagrams show different shapes made from cubes. If there are no cubes missing from the layers you cannot see, how many cubes would you need to build each shape?

a 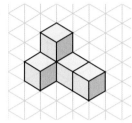 **b**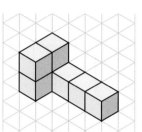

c 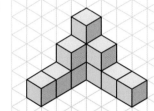 **d**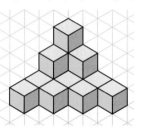

5 Shading 3D drawings can create optical illusions like these.

a Are there six or seven cubes in this diagram?

b Is this a large cube with a black cube cut out of it or a small black cube in the corner of a large white cube?

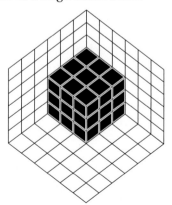

c Use an isometric grid to reconstruct these diagrams accurately. Shade your diagrams to form the illusion.

Section 3: Plan and elevation views

A **plan view** shows a 3D object from above. That is the top view of the object that you would see if you looked at it from directly above.

You can also view objects from the front, sides or back.

The **front elevation** is the view from the front of the object.

The **side elevation** is the view from the side of the object.

This diagram shows the plan view, front elevation and the left side elevation of a shape built out of cubes.

Key vocabulary

plan view: the view of an object from directly above.

elevation view: a view of an object from the front, side or back (front elevation, side elevation or back elevation).

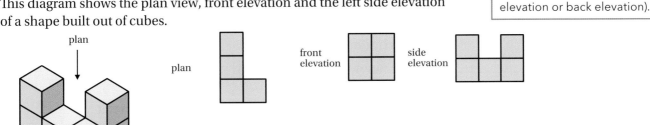

The shape below is a prism with trapezium-shaped ends. The front is higher than the back.

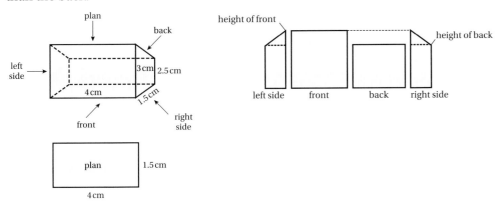

The plan view is a rectangle. Even though the top of the object slopes down to the back, if you look at it from above, it will look like a rectangle. The plan view is normally drawn above the front view because the two views will be the same width.

The left and right elevations are reflections of each other. They are drawn on the left and right side of the front elevation.

The front elevation is a rectangle. So is the back, but it is not at tall as the front, so it looks different when you draw it accurately.

You get different information from different views because each one shows two of the three dimensions of the solid.

- The plan view shows the length and width of the solid.
- The front view shows the length and height of the solid.
- The side views show the width and height of the solid.

When you draw plans or elevations you show any immediate changes in height as solid lines. Use dotted lines to indicate any hidden edges.

 Find answers at: cambridge.org/ukschools/gcsemaths-studentbookanswers

WORKED EXAMPLE 3

Draw the plan, front and side elevations of this solid.

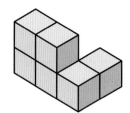

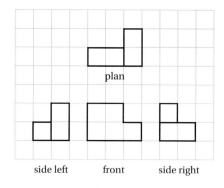

plan

side left   front   side right

Start by drawing the plan view.

Next, draw the front view below it. It will be the same width as the plan view.

Work out what the right side will look like if you view it face on.

Draw it next to the front view. It will be the same height.

You can't see the left view, so you have to visualise it.

Draw it in the correct place.

When you draw views of a shape, you have to think quite carefully about what the parts you cannot see clearly will look like.

For example, the shape on the right is built from **four** cubes.

You can only see three cubes. You have to work out that the fourth one is supporting the 'top' cube.

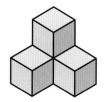

EXERCISE 3C

1 Select the correct plan view of each object.

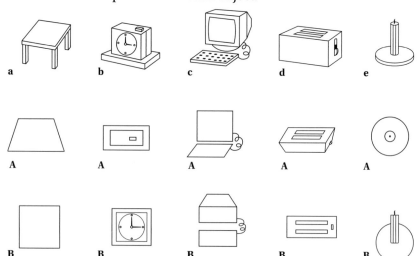

2 **a** Match each shape to its plan and elevation image.

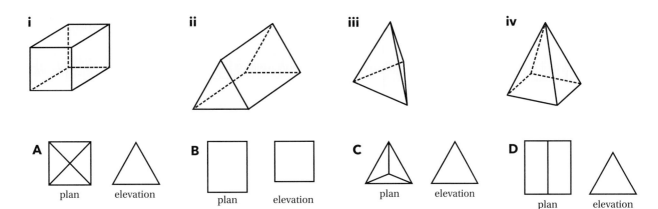

b Sketch and label the elevations that are not shown for each shape.

3 For each set of cubes, draw plan, front and side elevations:

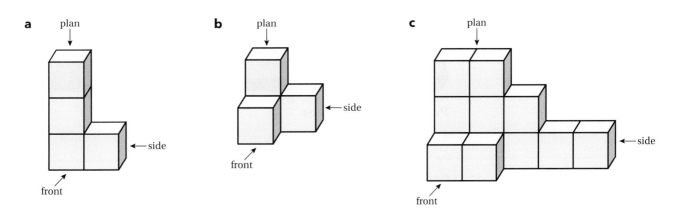

4 Draw the plan, the front elevation and the side elevation of the shape below.

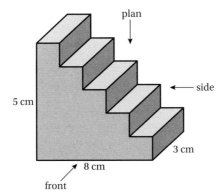

5 The plan view and elevations of different solids are shown below. Use these to work out what each solid looks like and draw it on an isometric grid.

a

plan   front   side

b

plan

front   right side

c

plan

left side   front   right side

d

front   right   plan

Checklist of learning and understanding

Properties of 3D shapes

- Prisms are shapes with congruent polygonal faces and a regular cross-section.
- Pyramids have a base and triangular sides that meet at an apex.
- Cylinders, cones and spheres are 3D shapes, but they are not polyhedra.
- The number and shape of the faces and the number of edges and vertices can be used to identify and name shapes.

2D representations of 3D shapes

- 3D shapes can be drawn on squared or isometric grids.
- Hidden edges are shown as dotted lines.

Plans and elevations

- A plan is a view from above a shape.
- An elevation is a view from the front, sides or back of a shape.

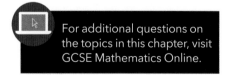
For additional questions on the topics in this chapter, visit GCSE Mathematics Online.

Chapter review

1 Which 3D objects can be formed from these nets?

a   **b**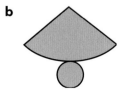

2 **a** Match each block of cubes to the correct plan and elevation.

b Identify any missing elevations and draw them for each shape.

i   ii   iii   iv

A   **B**   **C**    **D**

3 The plan and elevation of a solid built from cubes is shown below. Work out what the solid looks like and sketch it accurately on an isometric grid.

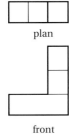

plan

front   side

4 The front elevation and the side elevation of a cuboid are drawn on the grid. On a copy of the grid, draw the plan of the cuboid.   *(1 mark)*

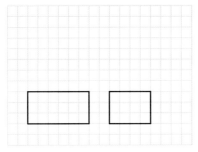

5 **a** Draw the plan, front and side elevation for the solid on the left.

b How many cubes are in the solid?

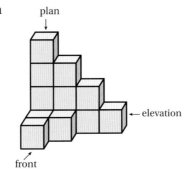

6 This is a solid built from cubes.

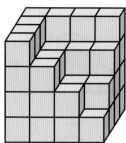

    a Draw one possible plan view of this shape.

    b Draw a plan view that is not possible for this shape.

    c What is the least and greatest number of cubes that the shape could be built from to have these elevations?

7 This is the plan view and front elevation of a computer-generated solid built using 32 cubes.

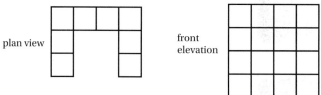

Work out what the shape might look like and draw an accurate diagram of the 3D shape on an isometric grid.

4 Properties of whole numbers

In this chapter you will learn how to ...

- identify the properties of different types of number and use the correct words to talk about them.
- identify prime numbers and write any whole number as a product of its prime factors.
- find the HCF and LCM of two numbers by listing and by prime factorisation.

 For more resources relating to this chapter, visit GCSE Mathematics Online.

Using mathematics: real-life applications

People use numbers and basic calculations on a daily basis. A market stall holder has to quickly calculate the cost of a customer's order; a logistics manager has to order stock and divide the supplies so that they are never over or under stocked. There are many applications of basic calculation.

 Tip

You probably already know most of the concepts in this chapter. They have been included so you can revise the concepts if you need to and check that you know them well.

> "Counting in multiples saves quite a bit of time. If I know that each shelf has 15 boxes and each box contains 5 reams of paper, then I know straight away that I have 75 reams on each shelf without having to count each ream." *(Logistics manager)*

Before you start ...

KS3	You should be able to recognise and find the factors of a number and to list multiples of a number.	**1** If these are the factors, what is the number? **a** 1, 5, 25 **b** 1, 2, 3, 6 **c** 1, 11 **2** If these are all multiples of a number (that isn't 1), what is the number? **a** 8, 10, 12, 14 **b** 18, 21, 27, 33 **c** 5, 20, 35, 60
KS3	You should know the first few prime numbers, square numbers and cube numbers.	**3** Which of the numbers below are: **a** prime numbers **b** square numbers **c** cube numbers? 0, 1, 2, 3, 4, 5, 6, 7, 8, 9, 10, 11, 12, 13, 14, 15, 16, 17, 18, 19, 20
KS3	You will need to be able to write a number as a product of its prime factors.	**4** Match each number to the product of its prime factors: **a** 450 **b** 180 **c** 120 **d** 72 **A** $2^3 \times 3^2$ **B** $2^2 \times 3^2 \times 5$ **C** $2^3 \times 3 \times 5$ **D** $2 \times 3^2 \times 5^2$

Find answers at: cambridge.org/ukschools/gcsemaths-studentbookanswers

Assess your starting point using the Launchpad

STEP 1

1 Say whether each statement is true or false.

  a 1 is the smallest prime number.

  b If you square 7 you get 14.

  c 8 is the cube of 2.

  d Any whole number that ends in 1 is an odd number.

  e 33, 43 and 53 are prime numbers.

  f 7, 14 and 21 are factors of 7.

2 There is one incorrect number in each of the following sets.
Work out what the set is and find the incorrect number.

  a 20, 22, 24, 26, 28, 29, 30   **b** 11, 22, 33, 44, 56, 66

  c 1, 2, 3, 4, 8, 12   **d** 27, 30, 33, 36, 39, 41

  e 1, 2, 3, 4, 6, 9, 12, 18, 24, 36   **f** 12, 24, 48, 60, 72, 86

  g 2, 3, 5, 7, 9, 11, 13, 17, 19

GO TO
Section 1:
Reviewing number properties

STEP 2

3 Choose the correct way of writing each number using prime factors.

  a 48

   A $2^3 \times 3^2$ **B** $2^4 \times 3$

  b 100

   A $2^2 \times 5^2$ **B** 2×5^2

GO TO
Section 2:
Prime factors

STEP 3

4 Given that $72 = 2^3 \times 3^2$ and $120 = 2^3 \times 3 \times 5$, choose the correct answers.

  a The HCF of 72 and 120 is:

   A 360   **B** 12   **C** 24   **D** 5

  b The LCM of 72 and 120 is:

   A 30   **B** 2   **C** 120   **D** 360

GO TO
Section 3:
Multiples and factors

GO TO
Chapter review

Section 1: Reviewing number properties

Mathematical terms and their meanings

You need to remember the correct mathematical terms for the different types of numbers shown in the table.

Mathematical term	Definition	Example
Odd number	A whole number that cannot be divided exactly by 2; it has a remainder of 1.	1, 3, 5, 7, …
Even number	A whole number that can be divided exactly by 2 (no remainder).	0, 2, 4, 6, 8, …
Prime number	A whole number greater than 1 that can only be divided exactly by itself and by 1. (It only has two factors.)	2, 3, 5, 7, 11, 13, 17, 19, …
Square number	The product when an integer is multiplied by itself. For example $2 \times 2 = 4$, so 4 is a square number.	1, 4, 9, 16, … 3×3 can be written using powers as 3^2.
Cube number	The product when an integer is multiplied by itself twice. For example $2 \times 2 \times 2 = 8$, so 8 is a cube number.	1, 8, 27, 64, … $5 \times 5 \times 5$ can be written using powers as 5^3.
Root $\left(\sqrt{\ }\right)$	The number that produces a square number when it is multiplied by itself is a square root. The number that produces a cubed number when it is multiplied by itself and then by itself again is a cube root.	The square root of 25 is 5. $\sqrt{25} = 5$ $(5 \times 5 = 25)$ The cube root of 8 is 2. $\sqrt[3]{8} = 2$ $(2 \times 2 \times 2 = 8)$
Factor (also called divisor)	A number that divides exactly into another number, without a remainder.	Factors of 6 are 1, 2, 3 and 6. Factors of 7 are 1 and 7. Factors of 25 are 1, 5 and 25.
Multiple	A multiple of a number is found when you multiply that number by a whole number. Your times tables are really just lists of multiples.	Multiples of 3 are 3, 6, 9, 12, … Multiples of 7 are 7, 14, 21, …
Common factor	A common factor is a factor shared by two or more numbers. 1 is a common factor of all numbers.	Factors of 6 are 1, 2, 3, and 6. Factors of 12 are 1, 2, 3, 4, 6 and 12. 1, 2, 3 and 6 are common factors of 6 and 12.
Common multiple	A common multiple is a multiple shared by two or more numbers. It is in both of their times tables.	Multiples of 2 are 2, 4, 6, 8, 10, 12, … Multiples of 3 are 3, 6, 9, 12, … 6 and 12 are common multiples of 2 and 3.

ℹ Did you know?

Mathematicians use the following arguments to define zero as an even number:
- When divided by two, it results in zero; and there is no remainder.
- In a list of consecutive numbers, an even number has an odd number before and after it; −1 and 1 are either side of zero.
- When an even number is added to another even number it will give an even result, but when added to an odd number it will give an odd result; when zero is added to any number, the result is the number you started with.
- Numbers that end in 0 are even.
- It is the next number in a pattern of even numbers: 8, 6, 4, 2, …

 Find answers at: cambridge.org/ukschools/gcsemaths-studentbookanswers

EXERCISE 4A

1 Here is a set of numbers.

1	2	3	4	5	6	7	8	9	10
11	12	13	14	15	16	17	18	19	20
21	22	23	24	25	26	27	28	29	30

Choose and list the numbers from the box that are:

a odd　　　　**b** even　　　　**c** prime

d square　　　　　　　　　**e** cube

f factors of 24　　　　　　**g** multiples of 3

h common factors of 8 and 12　　**i** common multiples of 3 and 4.

2 Write down:

a the next four odd numbers after 207

b four **consecutive** even numbers between 500 and 540

c the square numbers between 20 and 70

d the factors of 23

e the next four prime numbers greater than 13

f the first ten cube numbers

g the first five multiples of 8

h the factors of 36.

Key vocabulary

consecutive: following each other in order. For example 1, 2, 3 or 35, 36, 37.

3 Say whether the results of the following calculations will be odd or even.

a The sum of two odd numbers.

b The sum of two even numbers.

c The difference between two even numbers.

d The square of an odd number.

e The product of an odd and an even number.

f The cube of an odd number.

4 **a** Write down all the factors of:　　**i** 4　　**ii** 9　　**iii** 16.

b Write down all the factors of:　　**i** 6　　**ii** 12　　**iii** 20.

c What do you notice about the number of factors and the properties of the numbers from your answers to **a** and **b**?

5 From your answer to question **2h** above (write down all the factors of 36), which factors are:

a even　　**b** prime　　**c** square?

Place value

Consider the number 22<u>2</u>222.

Each of the 2s in the number has a different place value.

The place value tells you the value of the digit; the underlined 2 in the number has a value of 2 thousands or 2000.

Hundred thousands 100 000	Ten thousands 10 000	Thousands 1000	Hundreds 100	Tens 10	Ones/units 1
2	2	2	2	2	2

Each column in the place-value table is 10 times the value of the place to the right of it.

EXERCISE 4B

1 Write these sets of numbers in order from smallest to biggest.

   a 432   456   348   843   654

   b 606   660   607   670   706

   c 123   1231   312   1321   231

   d 12 700   71 200   21 700   21 007

2 The prices of some second hand cars are given. Write the list in order, starting with the most expensive.

   £5490   £3645   £5250   £3700   £4190

3 The table shows the population of five small towns. Write the list in order starting with the most populous.

Town	Population
Besbrough	467 542
Attleton	793 963
Witten	340 415
Thetham	351 000
Pullinge	627 250

4 What is the value of the 5 in each of these numbers?

   a 35   **b** 534   **c** 256   **d** 25 876

   e 50 346 987   **f** 1 532 980   **g** 5 678 432   **h** 356 432

5 What is the biggest and smallest number you can make with each set of digits?

Use each digit only once in each number.

   a 4, 0 and 6   **b** 5, 7, 3 and 1   **c** 1, 0, 3, 4, 6 and 2

Section 2: Prime factors

The number 1 is not a prime number because it only has one factor.

2 is the only even prime number.

If a factor of a number is a prime number it is called a **prime factor**.

Tip

It will help you work faster if you can learn to recognise all the prime numbers up to 100.

Key vocabulary

prime factor: a factor that is also a prime number.

Tip

Remember that 1 is **not** a prime number because it only has one factor, and 2 is the only even prime number.

Every whole number greater than 1 can be written as a product of its prime factors.

Finding the prime numbers that multiply together to make a given number is known as **prime factorisation**.

You can find the prime factors of a number by **repeatedly dividing by prime numbers**, or by using **factor trees**.

WORKED EXAMPLE 1

Express 48 as a product of its prime factors by:

a division   **b** using a factor tree.

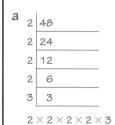

Divide by prime numbers.

Start with the lowest divisor that is prime (always try 2 first).

Continue dividing, moving to higher prime numbers as necessary.

Write the prime numbers you have used for dividing as a product.

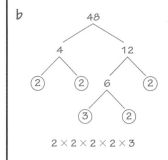

Write the number as a product of any two of its factors (but **not** 1 and the number itself).

Keep doing this for the factors until you cannot divide a factor any more (i.e. until you get to a prime factor).

Write the prime numbers you have used for dividing as a product.

Tip

The **unique factorisation theorem** in mathematics states that each number can be written as a product of prime factors in one way only.

It means that different numbers cannot have the same product of prime factors.

Both methods give the same result because a whole number can only be expressed in terms of its prime factors in one way. This is called the **unique factorisation theorem**.

Even if you do the division in a different order and split the factors differently in the factor tree, you will always get the same result for a given number.

Here are three ways of finding the prime factors of 280.

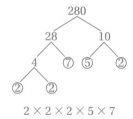

$2 \times 2 \times 2 \times 5 \times 7$

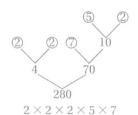

$2 \times 2 \times 2 \times 5 \times 7$

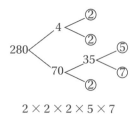

$2 \times 2 \times 2 \times 5 \times 7$

The examples show the product of factors in expanded form, but you can write them in a more efficient way using powers.

$2 \times 2 \times 2 \times 5 \times 7 = 2^3 \times 5 \times 7$

expanded form   index form using powers

EXERCISE 4C

1 Identify the prime numbers in each set.

  a 1, 2, 3, 4, 5, 6, 7, 8, 9, 10

  b 50, 51, 52, 53, 54, 55, 56, 57, 58, 59, 60

  c 95, 96, 97, 98, 99, 100, 101, 102, 103, 104, 105

2 Write each of the following numbers as a product of their prime factors. Use the method you prefer. Write your final answers using powers.

  a 36   **b** 65   **c** 64   **d** 84

  e 80   **f** 1000   **g** 1270   **h** 1963

3 A number is expressed as $2^3 \times 3^3 \times 5$.

  a What is the number?

  b Could it be any other number? Explain why.

4 Find out about the 'sieve of Eratosthenes' and show how it can be used to identify prime numbers up to 100.

5 Mathematicians have tried to find ways of identifying larger and larger prime numbers.

  It is very time consuming, testing them by dividing by all integers up to the square root of the number!

  Computers have made this task easier and larger prime numbers have been found by sharing computer power.

  In January 2013, a mathematician called Dr Curtis Cooper found that the number $2^{(57\,885\,161)} - 1$ was a prime number with 17 425 170 digits!

  This is the 48th known 'Mersenne prime'. It has been verified.

  a Find out about Marin Mersenne and why prime numbers in the form of $2^p - 1$ are known as Mersenne primes.

  b The Great Internet Mersenne Prime Search is a project that anyone can join.
  Find out what it aims to do and whether or not any new primes have been discovered since 2013.

6 There are four prime numbers between 10 and 20.

  a Can you find any other sets of four prime numbers between two consecutive multiples of 10?

  b Explain why you cannot expect to find four prime numbers between most other consecutive multiples of 10.

Section 3: Multiples and factors

The lowest common multiple (LCM)

The lowest common multiple (LCM) of two or more numbers is the smallest number that is a multiple of all the given numbers.

To find the LCM, list the multiples of the given numbers until you find the first multiple that appears in all the lists.

WORKED EXAMPLE 2

Find the LCM of 4 and 7.

$M_4 = 4, 8, 12, 16, 20, 24,$
$\quad\quad 28, 32, \ldots$

Begin to list the multiples of 4.

$M_7 = 7, 14, 21, 28, \ldots$

Begin to list the multiples of 7.

LCM of 4 and 7 = 28

Stop listing at 28 as it appears in both lists.

The highest common factor (HCF)

The highest common factor (HCF) of two or more numbers is the largest number that is a factor of all the given numbers.

To find the HCF, list all the factors of each number then pick out the highest number that appears in all the lists.

WORKED EXAMPLE 3

Find the HCF of 8 and 24.

$F_8 = \underline{1}, \underline{2}, \underline{4}, \underline{8}$

Write out all the factors of 8 and 24.

$F_{24} = \underline{1}, \underline{2}, 3, \underline{4}, 6, \underline{8}, 12, 24$

Underline the common factors.

HCF of 8 and 24 = 8

The highest underlined number is the HCF.

Tip

The LCM is used to find the lowest common denominator when you add or subtract fractions.

The HCF is useful for cancelling fractions. You will also use them in Chapter 5 to factorise algebraic expressions.

With word problems you need to work out whether to use the LCM or HCF to find the answers.

- Problems involving the LCM usually include repeating events. You might be asked how many items you need to 'have enough' or when something will happen again at the same time.

- Problems involving the HCF usually involve splitting things into smaller pieces or arranging things in equal groups or rows.

Using prime factors to find the HCF and LCM

When you work with larger numbers you can find the HCF and LCM by writing the numbers as products of prime factors (i.e. by prime factorisation).

Once you've done that you can use the factors to quickly find the HCF and LCM.

WORKED EXAMPLE 4

Find **a** the HCF and **b** the LCM, of 72 and 120.

a $72 = \underline{2} \times \underline{2} \times \underline{2} \times \underline{3} \times 3$
   $120 = \underline{2} \times \underline{2} \times \underline{2} \times \underline{3} \times 5$

First express each number as a product of prime factors.

Underline the common factors.

$2 \times 2 \times 2 \times 3 = 24$
HCF of 72 and 120 = 24

Write down the common factors and multiply them out.

b $72 = \underline{2} \times \underline{2} \times \underline{2} \times \underline{3} \times \underline{3}$
   $120 = 2 \times 2 \times 2 \times 3 \times \underline{5}$

First express each number as a product of prime factors.

Underline the largest set of multiples of each factor across **both** lists.

Here, 2 appears three times in each list, so underline the 2s in one of the lists. 3 appears twice in the first list, but only once in the second, so underline the top two 3s. 5 only appears in the bottom list, so underline that one.

Tip

Use the letters to help you remember what to do. LCM requires the **L**argest set of **M**ultiples.

$2 \times 2 \times 2 \times 3 \times 3 \times 5 = 360$
LCM of 72 and 120 is 360

Write down each set of multiples and multiply them out.

EXERCISE 4D

1 Find the LCM of the given numbers.

a 9 and 18	**b** 12 and 18	**c** 15 and 18	**d** 24 and 12
e 36 and 9	**f** 4, 12, and 8	**g** 3, 9 and 24	**h** 12, 16 and 32

2 Find the HCF of the given numbers.

a 12 and 18	**b** 18 and 36	**c** 27 and 90	**d** 12 and 15
e 20 and 30	**f** 19 and 45	**g** 60 and 72	**h** 250 and 900

3 Sian has two rolls of cotton fabric.

One roll has 72 metres on it, the other has 90 metres on it.

She wants to cut the rolls to make pieces of equal length without wasting any of it.

What is the longest possible length the pieces can be?

4 In a shopping centre promotion every 30th shopper gets a £10 voucher and every 120th shopper gets a free meal.

How many shoppers must enter the mall before one receives both a voucher and a free meal?

5 Amanda has 40 pieces of fruit and 100 sweets to share among the students in her class.

She is able to give each student an equal number of pieces of fruit and an equal number of sweets.

What is the largest possible number of students in her class?

6 Samir and Li start to walk in opposite directions around a walking track.

They start at the same point at the same time.

It takes Samir 5 minutes to walk round the track and it takes Li 4 minutes.

If they walk at this pace, how long will it be before they meet again at the starting point?

7 In a group of four cyclists, Lana cycles every 2nd day, Pete cycles every 3rd day, Karen cycles every 4th day and Anna cycles every 5th day.

They all cycle on 1 January this year.

  a How many days will pass before they all cycle on the same day again?

  b How many times a year will they all cycle on the same day?

8 Mr Abbot has three pieces of ribbon with lengths 2.4 m, 3.18 m and 4.26 m.

He wants to cut the ribbons into pieces that are all the same length.

He doesn't want any of the ribbon left over.

What is the greatest possible length for the pieces?

9 Two warning lights in a tunnel flash every 20 seconds and 30 seconds, respectively.

They flashed together at 4.30 pm.

When will they next flash at the same time?

10 Francesca, Ayuba and Claire are Olympic and Paralympic contenders.

They all train on the same track.

Francesca cycles round the track and completes a lap in 20 seconds.

Ayuba runs and completes a lap in 84 seconds and Claire goes round the track in her wheelchair, taking 105 seconds.

They start at the same place at the same time.

How long will it take for all three women to be at the same point again?

How many laps will they each have completed?

11 Mr Smith wants to tile a rectangular veranda with dimensions 4.2 m × 8.1 m with a whole number of identical square tiles.

Mrs Smith wants the tiles to be as large as possible.

a Find the area of the largest possible tiles in cm².

b How many tiles will Mr Smith need to tile the veranda?

12 In an earthquake relief operation, supplies are handed out equally to all affected people at a relief centre.

On one day, 284 items of clothing, 426 food packets and 710 bottles of water are handed out.

How many people were in the relief centre on that day?

 ### Checklist of learning and understanding

Properties of whole numbers

- Even numbers are multiples of 2, odd numbers are not.
- Factors are numbers that divide exactly into a number.
- Prime numbers have only two factors, 1 and the number itself.
- Square numbers are the product of a number and itself ($n \times n = n^2$).
- Cube numbers are the product of a number multiplied by itself twice ($n \times n \times n = n^3$).
- The value of a digit depends on its place in the number.

Prime factors

- If a factor is a prime number it is called a prime factor.
- Whole numbers can be written as the product of their prime factors.

  You find the prime factors by:

  ○ repeated division by prime numbers (starting from 2 and working upwards)

  ○ using a factor tree and breaking down factors until they are prime numbers.

Factors and multiples

- The lowest common multiple (LCM) of two numbers can be found by:

  ○ listing the multiples of both numbers and selecting the lowest multiple that appears in both lists

  ○ finding the largest set of multiples of each of the prime factors and multiplying them together.

- The highest common factor (HCF) of two numbers can be found by:

  ○ listing the factors of both numbers and selecting the highest factor that appears in both lists

  ○ finding the common prime factors and multiplying them together.

For additional questions on the topics in this chapter, visit GCSE Mathematics Online.

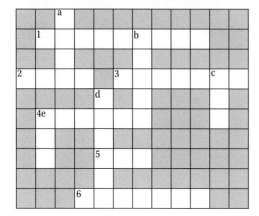

Chapter review

1 Complete the crossword puzzle provided by your teacher.

Across

1 The times tables are examples of these.

2 Whole numbers divisible by 2.

3 Another word used for factor.

4 Numbers in the sequence 1, 4, 9, 16, ...

5 An even prime number.

6 The result of a multiplication.

Down

a $n \times n \times n$ is the __ of n.

b Numbers with only two factors.

c Whole numbers that are not exactly divisible by 2.

d Number that divides into another with no remainder.

e HCF of 12 and 18.

2 Is 149 a prime number? Explain how you decided.

3 Find the HCF and the LCM of 20 and 35 by listing the factors and multiples.

4 Express 800 as a product of prime factors, giving your final answer using powers.

5 Determine the HCF and LCM of the following by prime factorisation.

a 72 and 108   **b** 84 and 60

6 **a** Express 54 as a product of its prime factors.   *(2 marks)*

b Find the Lowest Common Multiple (LCM) of 45 and 54   *(2 marks)*

©Pearson Education Ltd 2012

7 Jo, Mo and Jenny were jumping up a flight of stairs.

Jo jumped 2 steps at a time, Mo jumped 3 steps at time while Jenny managed 4 steps at a time.

They started together on the first step. What is the next step they will all jump on together?

8 Nick starts an exercise programme on 3 March.

After doing two activities on his first day, he decides to swim every third day and to cycle every fourth day.

On which other dates in March will he swim and cycle on the same day?

9 A Year 10 class consists of 32 boys and 52 girls.

The teachers want to divide the students into the greatest possible number of groups, splitting the boys and girls equally among the groups.

How many boys and girls would be in each group?

5 Introduction to algebra

In this chapter you will learn how to ...

- use algebraic notation and write algebraic expressions.
- simplify and manipulate algebraic expressions.
- multiply out (expand) algebraic expressions with brackets.
- use common factors to factorise expressions.
- use algebra to solve problems in different contexts and prove statements.

For more resources relating to this chapter, visit GCSE Mathematics Online.

Using mathematics: real-life applications

Algebra lets you describe and represent patterns using concise mathematical language.

This is useful in many different careers including accounting, navigation, building, plumbing, health, medicine, science and computing.

> **Tip**
>
> You will do more work with the rules of indices in Chapter 8.

"You are unlikely to think about algebra when you watch cartoons or play video games, but animators use complex algebra to program the characters and make objects move." *(Games designer)*

Before you start ...

KS3	You need to understand the basic conventions of algebra.	**1**	Choose the correct way to write each of these.
			a $n \times n$
			  A $2n$ **B** n^2 **C** 2^n **D** $2(n)$
			b c multiplied by 3 and then added to 5
			  A $3c + 5$ **B** $3(c + 5)$ **C** $c + 15$
			c n squared and then multiplied by 2
			  A $2n^2$ **B** $(2n)^2$ **C** $4n^2$

KS3	You should be able to substitute numbers for letters and evaluate expressions.	**2**	**a** Evaluate the following expressions for $n = 5$ and $n = -5$. **i** $3n + 4$ **ii** $3(n + 4)$ **b** What is the value of $\dfrac{(2 + 4)^2}{6}$?
Ch 4	You should be able to find the highest common factor in a group of terms.	**3**	Write down the HCF of: **a** $12xy$ and $18y^2$ **b** $45x$ and $50xy$.
KS3	You need to know how to apply the rules of indices to simplify expressions.	**4**	Match the simplified expressions (**i–iv**) to the mathematical statements **a–d**: **a** $a^m \times a^n$ **b** $a^m \div a^n$ **c** $(a^m)^n$ **d** a^0 **i** 1 **ii** a^{m-n} **iii** a^{m+n} **iv** $a^{m \times n}$

Assess your starting point using the Launchpad

STEP 1

1 Use the correct notation and conventions to write each statement as an algebraic expression.

a Multiply n by 3 and add 4 to the result.

b Subtract 4 from n and multiply the result by 3.

c Multiply n squared by 4, add 3 and divide the result by 2.

GO TO
Section 1:
Using algebraic notation

STEP 2

2 Simplify these expressions by collecting like terms.

a $3a + 2b + 2a - b$ **b** $4x + 7 + 3x - 3 - x$

c $4a^2 + 8ab - 10a^2 - 5ab$

GO TO
Section 2:
Simplifying expressions

STEP 3

3 Multiply out the brackets and simplify.

a $m(n - p)$ **b** $3(x + 5) + 4(x + 2)$

c $2z(z + 4) - z(z + 5)$

GO TO
Section 3:
Multiplying out brackets

STEP 4

4 Complete the following.

a $3x + 12 = \square(x + 4)$ **b** $5x + 10y = \square(x + 2y)$

c $x^2 - 3x = \square(x - 3)$ **d** $ab - ac = a(\square - \square)$

e $-x + 7x^2 = -x(\square\,\square\,\square)$

5 Factorise each expression and write it as a product of its factors.

a $2x + 4y$ **b** $-3x - 9$

c $5x + 5y$

GO TO
Section 4:
Factorising expressions

Section 5:
Solving problems and algebraic proof

GO TO
Chapter review

Section 1: Using algebraic notation

In algebra letters are used to represent unknown numbers.

For example, $x + y = 20$.

The letters can represent many different values so they are called **variables**.

Letters and numbers can be combined with operation signs to form an **expression**, such as $5a^3 - 2xy + 3$.

This expression has three **terms**.

Terms are separated by + or − signs; the sign belongs to the term that follows it.

Terms should always be written in the shortest, simplest way:

$2 \times h$ is written as $2h$ and $x \times x \times y$ is written as x^2y.

$4x \div 3$ is written as $\dfrac{4x}{3}$ and $(x + 4) \div 2$ is written as $\dfrac{x + 4}{2}$.

To find a **product**, you multiply the factors.

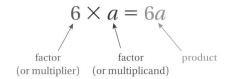

$$6 \times a = 6a$$

factor
(or multiplier)
factor
(or multiplicand)
product

In algebraic notation, multiplication is shown by writing the factors next to each other.

You write $a \times b$ as ab and $5 \times z$ as $5z$.

$a \times b \equiv ab$ and $5 \times z \equiv 5z$ are called **identities**.

The symbol $\equiv$ means exactly the same as, or identical to.

For division, you write $a \div b$ as $\dfrac{a}{b}$ and $5 \div z$ as $\dfrac{5}{z}$.

Key vocabulary

variable: a letter representing an unknown number.

expression: a group of numbers and letters linked by operation signs.

term: a combination of letters and/or numbers.

product: the result of multiplying numbers and/or terms together.

identity: an equation that is true no matter what values are chosen for the variables.

Tip

When you have numbers and letters in a term, the number is written first and letters are usually written in alphabetical order. So, you write $5x$ not $x5$ and $3xy$ not $3yx$.

EXERCISE 5A

1 Match the statements (**a**–**i**) to their correct algebraic expression from (**A**–**I**).

a Take a number and multiply it by 3 then add 2 to it.   **A** $\dfrac{6x + 2}{3}$

b Take a number and add 3 to it, then double it.   **B** $3x + 2$

c Take a number and multiply it by itself then add 3 to it.   **C** $5(x - 4)$

d Add 6 to a number then divide it by 2.   **D** $(3x)^2$

e Take 4 away from a number and multiply the result by 5.   **E** x^5

f Square a number then multiply by 9.   **F** $2x^2 - 3x^3$

g Square a number and multiply by 2 and subtract the number cubed multiplied by 3.   **G** $2(x + 3)$

h Twice the sum of one-third and a number.   **H** $\dfrac{6 + x}{2}$

i The cube of a number multiplied by the square of a number.   **I** $x^2 + 3$

 Find answers at: cambridge.org/ukschools/gcsemaths-studentbookanswers

2 Write the algebraic expression for:

   a x multiplied by 3 and added to y multiplied by 7.

   b 4 subtracted from x squared and the result multiplied by 5.

   c x cubed added to y squared and the result divided by 4.

   d 6 added to x and the result multiplied by 4 minus y.

   e x multiplied by itself and then divided by 2.

   f Five less than three-fifths of a number.

3 Use algebra to write these in as short a form as possible.

   a $2 \times 3a$ **b** $4b \times 5$ **c** $d \times (-9)$

   d $4a \times 3b$ **e** $5c \times 2d$ **f** $-3m \times 4n$

   g $-2p \times (-3q)$ **h** $a \times a$ **i** $m \times m$

   j $2a \times 4a$ **k** $-3a \times 5a$ **l** $-2m \times (-4m)$

   m $7a \times 8ab$ **n** $-6cd \times (-2de)$ **o** $2a \times 2a \times 2a$

4 Rewrite each division using algebraic conventions. Simplify them if possible.

   a $15x \div 5$ **b** $27y \div 3$ **c** $24a^2 \div 8$

   d $7 \times 15p \div 21$ **e** $24x \div (8 \times 3)$ **f** $18y \div (6 \times 2)$

   g $-18x^2 \div 9$ **h** $-16a^2 \div (-4)$ **i** $15 \div (3 \times n \times n)$

5 Simplify:

   a $x^6 \times x^7$ **b** $y^4 \times y^9$ **c** $3a^4 \times 5a^5$

   d $2x^3 \times 5x^6$ **e** $a^2 \div a^4$ **f** $\dfrac{12b^7}{6b^2}$

   g $\dfrac{18p^{10}}{9p^{11}}$ **h** $(x^4)^3$ **i** $(2a^7)^3$

   j $4x^2y^3 \times 5xy^4 \div 2x^5y^3$ **k** $5x^0$

Tip

Use the laws of indices for this question:
$a^m \times a^n = a^{m+n}$
$a^m \div a^n = a^{m-n}$
$(a^m)^n = a^{m \times n}$
$a^0 = 1$

6 Write expressions to represent the perimeter and area of each shape:

a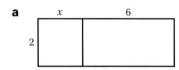

b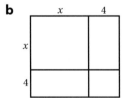

c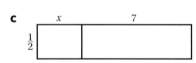

d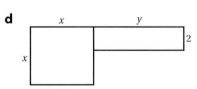

7 A man is x years old.

   a How old will he be 10 years from now?

   b How old was he 10 years ago?

   c His daughter is a third of his age. How old is his daughter?

8 A CD and a DVD together cost C pounds.

    a If the CD cost £5, what did the DVD cost?

    b If the DVD cost twice as much as the CD, what did the CD cost?

    c If the CD cost £$(C - 15)$, what did the DVD cost?

Substitution

You can evaluate expressions if you are told what values the letters represent.

If $x = -2$, then:

$2x + 1 = 2 \times -2 + 1 = -4 + 1 = -3$.

Tip

When you substitute values into a term such as $2y$ you need to remember that $2y$ means $2 \times y$. So, if $y = 6$, you need to write $2y$ as 2×6 and not as 26.

WORKED EXAMPLE 1

Given that $a = -2$ and $b = 8$, evaluate:

a ab **b** $3b - 2a$ **c** $2a^3$ **d** $2(a + b)$

a $ab = a \times b$
    $= -2 \times 8$
    $= -16$

b $3b - 2a = 3 \times b - 2 \times a$
    $= 3 \times 8 - 2 \times -2$
    $= 24 - (-4) = 28$

c $2a^3 = 2 \times a^3 = 2 \times (-2)^3$
    $= 2 \times -8 = -16$

d $2(a + b) = 2 \times (a + b)$
    $= 2 \times (-2 + 8)$
    $= 2 \times 6$
    $= 12$

Remember to do the calculation in brackets first.

Tip

Substitution is an important skill. You will need to substitute values for letters when you work with formulae for perimeter, area and volume of shapes and when you solve problems involving Pythagoras' theorem.

EXERCISE 5B

1 Given that $x = 3$ and $y = 6$, evaluate these expressions.

    a $2x + 3y$ **b** $3x + 2y$ **c** $10y - 2x$ **d** $x + 2y$

2 Given that $x = 2$ and $y = 7$, evaluate these expressions.

    a $6x + y$ **b** $5x - 5y$ **c** $2xy$ **d** $\dfrac{1}{2}xy$

    e $-3x^2$ **f** $4 - 3(xy)^2$ **g** $\dfrac{3x^2y^4}{2y^3}$ **h** $-12x^2y \div -2xy^2$

3 Find the value of each expression when $a = -2$ and $b = 5$.

    a $-5ab + 10$ **b** $-3ab - 6$ **c** $\dfrac{10}{b}$ **d** $\dfrac{400}{a}$

4 Find the value of each expression when $a = 2$ and $b = -3$.

    a $\dfrac{6}{a} - \dfrac{15}{b}$ **b** $\dfrac{15}{b} - \dfrac{24}{2a}$ **c** $8 - 2a + 2b$ **d** $7a - 4 + 2b$

5 Evaluate each expression when $a = 3$ and $b = 7$.

    a $2(a + b)$ **b** $3a(15 - 2b)$ **c** $\dfrac{2}{3}(2b - a + 1)$ **d** $2(b - a) + b(a - 1)$

Find answers at: cambridge.org/ukschools/gcsemaths-studentbookanswers

Section 2: Simplifying expressions

Adding and subtracting like terms

Like terms have exactly the same letters or combination of letters and powers.

You can simplify expressions by adding or subtracting like terms.

$3a$ and $4a$ are **like** terms: $3a + 4a = 7a$

$7xy$ and $2xy$ are **like** terms: $7xy - 2xy = 5xy$

$5x^2$ and $3x^2$ are **like** terms: $5x^2 - 3x^2 = 2x^2$

$5ab^2$ and $2a^2b$ are **not like** terms so $5ab^2 - 2a^2b$ **cannot** be simplified further.

WORK IT OUT 5.1

Here are two terms: $3x^2y$ and $2xy^2$.

Student A said that these two terms are like terms and can be added together to be written as:

$5x^2y^2$

Student B said that these two terms are not like terms and can only be written added together as:

$3x^2y + 2xy^2$

Which student is correct? Why?

When an expression contains many different terms you might be able to simplify it by collecting and then combining like terms.

WORKED EXAMPLE 2

Simplify $2x - 4y + 3x + y$

$2x - 4y + 3x + y$

$= 2x + 3x - 4y + y$ Rearrange the terms so like terms are together. Keep the signs with the terms they belong to.

$= 5x - 3y$ Combine the like terms. Remember $y \equiv 1y$.

Multiplication and division

WORKED EXAMPLE 3

Simplify:

a $5 \times 4a$ **b** $2x \times 6y$ **c** $2a^2 \times 7ab$ **d** $12a \div -4$

e $\dfrac{6x^2}{2}$ **f** $\dfrac{-8xy}{-16}$ **g** $\dfrac{12ab^2}{36ab}$

Continues on next page …

---

a $5 \times 4a = 20a$

b $2x \times 6y = 12xy$

> Multiply numbers by numbers and write letters in alphabetical order.

c $2a^2 \times 7ab = 14a^3b$

> $a^2 = a \times a$, so $a^2 \times a = a \times a \times a = a^3$

d $12a \div -4$

$= \dfrac{12a}{-4} = -3a$

> Write the division as a fraction.
> Cancel the fraction to its lowest terms.

e $\dfrac{6x^2}{2} = 3x^2$

> Cancel by 2 to lowest terms.

f $\dfrac{-8xy}{-16} = \dfrac{xy}{2}$

> Cancel by -8 to lowest terms.

g $\dfrac{12ab^2}{36ab} = \dfrac{b}{3}$

> Write the numerator as b not $1b$ by convention.

EXERCISE 5C

1 Say whether each of these pairs are like or unlike terms.

a $4a$ and $3b$ b $5b$ and $-3b$ c $3b$ and $9b$

d $4p$ and $6p$ e $8p$ and $-4q$ f $5a$ and $6b$

g $7mn$ and $3mn$ h $4ab$ and $-2ab$ i $-6xy$ and $-7x$

j $9ab$ and $3a$ k $9x^2$ and $6x^2$ l $6a^2$ and $-7a^2$

2 Simplify.

a $9x + 4y - 4y - 3x + 5y$ b $3c + 6d - 6c - 4d$

c $2xy + 3y^2 - 5xy - 4y^2$ d $2a^2 - ab^2 + 3ab^2 + 2ab$

e $5f - 7g - 6f + 9g$ f $7a^2b + 3a^2b - 4a^2b$

g $6mn^3 - 2mn^3 + 8mn^3$ h $3st^2 - 4s^2t + 5s^2t + 6st^2$

3 Find the value of the missing term to complete the following.

a $2a + \square = 7a$ b $5b - \square = 2b$

c $8mn + \square = 12mn$ d $11pq - \square = 6pq$

e $4x^2 + \square = 7x^2$ f $6m^2 - \square = m^2$

g $8ab - \square = -2ab$ h $-3st + \square = 5st$

4 Find the value of the missing term to complete the following.

a $8a \times \square = 16a$ b $9b \times \square = 18b$

c $8a \times \square = 16ab$ d $5m \times \square = 15mn$

e $3a \times \square = 12a^2$ f $6p \times \square = 30p^2$

g $-5b \times \square = 10b^2$ h $4m \times \square = 12m^2n$

Find answers at: cambridge.org/ukschools/gcsemaths-studentbookanswers

5 Rewrite each expression in the simplest possible form.

a $7 \times 2x \times -2$ **b** $4x \times 2y \times 2z$ **c** $2a \times 5 \times a$

d $ab \times bc \times cd$ **e** $-4x \times 2x \times -3y$ **f** $\dfrac{1}{4x} \times 4y \times -y$

g $-9x \div 3$ **h** $-24y \div 2x$ **i** $18x^2 \div 6$

6 Simplify.

a $\dfrac{4x}{6}$ **b** $\dfrac{3}{15}a$ **c** $\dfrac{-12}{54}m$ **d** $\dfrac{35}{49}p$

e $\dfrac{22}{132}x^2$ **f** $\dfrac{15xy}{20}$ **g** $\dfrac{12ab}{a}$ **h** $\dfrac{2xy}{6xy}$

Section 3: Multiplying out brackets

Removing (multiplying out) brackets is called **expanding** the expression.

To expand an expression such as $2(a + b)$ you multiply each term inside the bracket by the value outside the bracket.

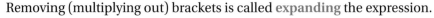

$$2(a + b) = 2 \times a + 2 \times b$$
$$= 2a + 2b$$

$$-2(a + b) = -2 \times a + (-2 \times b)$$
$$= -2a - 2b$$

WORKED EXAMPLE 4

Expand:

a $3x(y + 2z)$ **b** $-2x(4 + y)$ **c** $-(3x - 2)$

a $3x(y + 2z) = 3x \times y + 3x \times 2z$
$= 3xy + 6xz$

b $-2x(4 + y) = -2x \times 4 + (-2x \times y)$
$= -8x - 2xy$

c $-(3x - 2) = -1 \times 3x - (-1 \times 2)$
$= -3x - -2$
$= -3x + 2$

Expanding and simplifying

After expanding a bracket, an expression might contain like terms, so it can be simplified.

WORKED EXAMPLE 5

Expand and simplify:

a $6x - 3(2x + 1)$ **b** $2x(x + y) - x(3x - 4y)$

a $6x - 3(2x + 1)$
$= 6x - 6x - 3$
$= -3$

Combine the x terms.

b $2x(x + y) - x(3x - 4y)$
$= 2x^2 + 2xy - 3x^2 + 4xy$
$= -x^2 + 6xy$

Combine the x^2 terms and the xy terms.

EXERCISE 5D

1 Some of these expansions are incorrect.

Check each one and correct those that are wrong.

a $4(a + b) = 4a + b$ **b** $5(a + 1) = 5a + 6$

c $8(p - 7) = 8p - 56$ **d** $-3(p - 5) = -3p - 15$

e $a(a + b) = 2a + ab$ **f** $2m(3m + 5) = 6m^2 + 10m$

g $-6(x - 5) = 6x + 30$ **h** $3a(4a - 7) = 12a^2 - 7$

i $4a(3a + 5) = 12a^2 + 20a$ **j** $3x(2x - 7y) = 6x^2 - 21y$

2 Expand and simplify.

a $2(c + 7) - 9$ **b** $(a + 2) + 7$ **c** $5(b + 3) + 10$

d $2(e - 5) + 15$ **e** $3(f - 4) - 6$ **f** $2a(4a + 3) + 7a$

g $5b(2b - 3) + 6b$ **h** $2a(4a + 3) + 7a^2$ **i** $3b(3b - 5) - 7b^2$

3 Expand and simplify.

a $2(y + 1) + 3(y + 4)$ **b** $2(3b - 2) + 5(2b - 1)$

c $3(a + 5) - 2(a + 7)$ **d** $5(b - 2) - 4(b + 3)$

e $x(x - 2) + 3(x - 2)$ **f** $2p(p + 1) - 5(p + 1)$

g $3z(z + 4) - z(3z + 2)$ **h** $3y(y - 4) + y(y - 4)$

4 The expression in each box is obtained by adding the expressions in the two boxes directly below it.

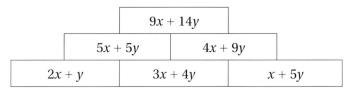

Copy and complete these two pyramids.

a

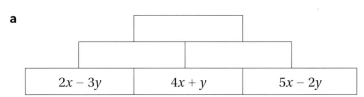

b

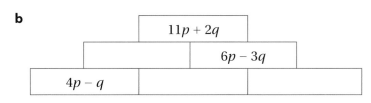

5 Use substitution to show that the following expressions are **not** identities.

a $a + a$ and a^2 **b** $3x + 4 - x + 2$ and $2x + 2$

c $(m + 2)^2$ and $m^2 + 4$ **d** $\dfrac{x+3}{3}$ and $x + 1$

Find answers at: cambridge.org/ukschools/gcsemaths-studentbookanswers

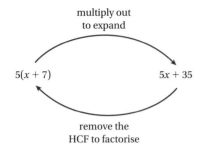

multiply out
to expand

$5(x + 7)$ $5x + 35$

remove the
HCF to factorise

Section 4: Factorising expressions

Factorising is the reverse of expanding.

When you factorise an expression you use brackets to write it as a product of its factors.

If you expand $5(x + 7)$ you get $5x + 35$.

To factorise $5x + 35$ you find the highest common factor of the terms.

5 is the HCF of $5x$ and 35, so 5 is written outside the bracket and the remaining factors are written in brackets.

> **Tip**
>
> The highest common factor can be a number or a variable. It can also be a negative quantity.

WORKED EXAMPLE 6

Factorise each expression.

a $10a + 15b$ **b** $-2x - 8$ **c** $3x^2 - 6xy$ **d** $3(m + 2) - n(m + 2)$

a $10a + 15b$
$10a + 15b = 5(2a + 3b)$

> HCF of 10 and 15 is 5. There are no common variables.

b $-2x - 8$
$-2x - 8 = -2(x + 4)$

> HCF of -2 and -8 is -2.

c $3x^2 - 6xy$
$3x^2 - 6xy = 3x(x - 2y)$

> HCF is $3x$.

d $3(m + 2) - n(m + 2)$
$3(m + 2) - n(m + 2) =$
$(m + 2)(3 - n)$

> This looks like an expansion, but you are asked to factorise!
>
> $(m + 2)$ is common to both terms, so **it** is the HCF.

EXERCISE 5E

1 Factorise each expression and write it as the product of its factors.

a $2x + 4$	**b** $12m - 18n$	**c** $3a - 3b - 6$
d $xy - xz$	**e** $5xy - 15xyz$	**f** $14ab - 21bc$
g $pq - pr$	**h** $x^2 - x$	**i** $18abc - 12ac$
j $2x^2 - 4xy$	**k** $2x^2y - 4xy^2$	**l** $-6a - 12$
m $-3a - 9$	**n** $-xy - 5x$	**o** $-x^2 + 6x$

> **Tip**
>
> You will learn other methods of factorising expressions in Chapter 13.

2 Factorise.

a $7x - xy + x^2$	**b** $2xy + 4xz + 10x$	**c** $10x - 5y + 15z$
d $x(x - 2) + 5(x - 2)$	**e** $a(a - 7) - (a - 7)$	**f** $(x - 3) - 3(x - 3)$
g $3x^2y + 6xy^2$	**h** $36x^3 - \frac{1}{4}x^4$	**i** $-ax^2 - ay^2$

Section 5: Solving problems and algebraic proof

You can use algebra to solve problems, particularly if they involve unknown amounts.

You can also use algebra to prove statements.

WORKED EXAMPLE 7

Prove that the sum of any three consecutive numbers is a multiple of three.

Let the first number be n.

State your variable.

The next number must be 1 more than n, so let it be $n + 1$.
The third number is 1 more than $n + 1$, so let it be $n + 1 + 1 = n + 2$.

Use your variable to express the other numbers.

The sum of the three numbers is $n + n + 1 + n + 2 = 3n + 3$.

Use your expressions to form the sum in the question.

This factorises to give $3(n + 1)$.

Show that 3 is a factor.

Since 3 is a factor, the sum of any three consecutive numbers must be a multiple of three.

State your conclusion.

WORKED EXAMPLE 8

Prove that the sum of any odd number and any even number is odd.

Let the odd number be $2n + 1$.
Let the even number be $2m$.

$2n + 1 + 2m$
$= 2(n + m) + 1$

This has a remainder of 1, so the sum will always be odd.

Use a different letter for the even number so that you are not proving for just consecutive numbers.

 Tip

n could be odd or even but $2n$ must be even as it is a multiple of two. Since $2n$ must be even, $2n + 1$ and $2n - 1$ must be odd numbers.

EXERCISE 5F

1 Are the following statements true or false?

a The expression $3z^2 + 5yx - z^2 - 6yx$ simplified is $2z^2 - 11xy$.

b If you expand the brackets $2p(3p + q)$ you get the expression $6p^2 + 2pq$.

c This is a correct use of the identity symbol: $4(a + 1) \equiv 4a + 4$.

d $\dfrac{4}{x}$ always has the same value as $\dfrac{x}{4}$.

e x squared and added to 7 with the result divided by 3 is $\dfrac{x^2 + 7}{3}$.

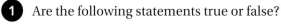 Find answers at: cambridge.org/ukschools/gcsemaths-studentbookanswers

79

2 In a magic square the sum of each row, column and diagonal is the same.

Is the square on the right a magic square?

$m - p$	$m + p - q$	$m + q$
$m + p + q$	m	$m - p - q$
$m - q$	$m - p + q$	$m + p$

3 **a** Write an expression for each missing length in this rectangle.

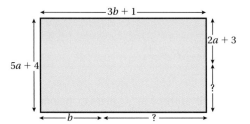

b Write an expression for P, the perimeter of the rectangle.

c Given that $a = 2.1$ and $b = 4.5$, calculate the area of the rectangle. (Area = length × width)

4 **a** The area of a rectangle is $2x^2 + 4x$. Suggest possible lengths for its sides.

b If the perimeter of a rectangle is $2x^2 + 4$, what could the lengths of the sides be?

5 Draw two diagrams representing areas to prove that $(3x)^2$ and $3x^2$ are different?

6 The diagram represents a room with an area of floor covered by carpet (shaded).

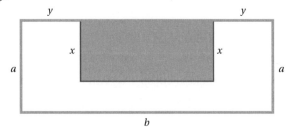

Divide the room into rectangles in different ways to find different, but equivalent, expressions for the floor area that is not covered by carpet.

Multiply out the expressions to confirm that they are equivalent.

7 Copy and fill in the missing cells. The entry for each cell is formed from the two cells beneath it by addition or subtraction and collecting like terms from the two cells beneath it. Write each expression as simply as possible. The first missing entry for diagram **a** has been completed in red for you.

a

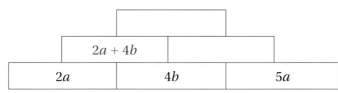

b

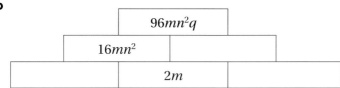

c

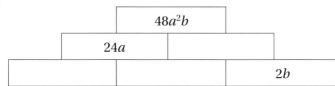

8 **a** Paul plays a 'think of a number game' with his friends and predicts what their answer will be.

The steps he tells his friends to follow the steps in the box.

Think of a number.

Double it.

Add 6.

Halve it.

Take away the number you first thought of.

Paul then guesses that the answer is 3.

Use algebra to show why Paul will guess correctly, no matter what number his friends choose as a starting number.

b Make up a 'think of a number' problem of your own.

Use algebra to check that it will work and to see which number you end up with.

Try it out with another student to check that it works.

9 The expression $7(x + 4) - 3(x - 2)$ simplifies to $a(2x + b)$.

Work out the values of a and b.

10 Check whether each expression has been fully simplified.

If not, simplify it further.

a $5(g + 2) + 8g = 5g + 10 + 8g$ **b** $4z(4z - 2) - z(z + 2) = 15z^2 - 10z$

c $-5ab \times (-3bc) = 15ab^2c$ **d** $\dfrac{18x^3}{3x} = \dfrac{6x^3}{x}$

e $\dfrac{(x^5 \times x^7)}{x^4} = \dfrac{x^{12}}{x^4}$

11 Simplify:

a $\dfrac{2x}{y^3} + \dfrac{7x}{3y^3}$ **b** $\dfrac{3a}{b} + \dfrac{5}{2b}$

c $-\dfrac{4}{5}(25x - 100)$ **d** $-\dfrac{3}{5}\left(\dfrac{a}{3} - \dfrac{2}{3}\right)$

12 Simplify:

a $\dfrac{6x^3y^3}{xy} + \dfrac{2x^3y^2}{y^2} - \dfrac{14x^5y}{2x^2y} + \dfrac{12x^4y^2}{3x^2}$

b $\dfrac{4p^2q^3}{2pq} + 3p^2 - \dfrac{6p^5q^2}{3pq^2} + 5pq^2$

13 Prove that the sum of two odd numbers is even.

Checklist of learning and understanding

Algebraic notation

- You can use letters (called variables) in place of unknown quantities in algebra.
- An expression is a collection of numbers, operation signs and at least one variable.
- Each part of an expression is called a term.
- To evaluate an expression you substitute numbers in place of the variables.
- If two expressions are identical, this is called an identity.

Simplifying expressions

- Like terms have exactly the same variables.
- Expressions can be simplified by adding or subtracting like terms.
- You can multiply and divide unlike terms.

Multiplying out brackets

- If an expression contains brackets you multiply them out and then add or subtract like terms to simplify it further.

Factorising

- Factorising involves putting brackets back into an expression.
- If terms have a common factor, write it in front of the bracket and write the remaining terms in the bracket as a factor. (You can check by multiplying out.)

Solving problems

- Algebra allows you to make general rules that apply to any number. This is useful in problem solving.

Chapter review

For additional questions on the topics in this chapter, visit GCSE Mathematics Online.

1 Expand and simplify:

   a $3b(3b - 5) - 7b^2$ **b** $2x(5x + 4) - 6x(3x - 7)$

   c $\dfrac{3}{4}(p + 2) + \dfrac{1}{2}(p - 1)$ **d** $\dfrac{2y}{3}(y + 5) + \dfrac{y}{3}(y - 4)$

2 **a** Expand and simplify $5(x + 7) + 3(x - 2)$ *(2 marks)*

   b Factorise completely $3a^2b + 6ab^2$ *(2 marks)*

                                             ©Pearson Education Ltd 2012

3 Two of these expressions have been incorrectly simplified.

Find them and correct them.

$2x \times 6y = 12xy$

$2a^2 \times 7ab = 14a^3b$

$\dfrac{12a}{4} = 3a$

$\dfrac{6x^2}{2} = 3x^2$

$\dfrac{8xy}{16} = \dfrac{xy}{4}$

$\dfrac{12ab^2}{36ab} = \dfrac{b}{3}$

$\dfrac{15}{2x} \times \dfrac{2}{3x} = \dfrac{10}{x^2}$

$\dfrac{6a}{7b} \div \dfrac{2ab}{3} = \dfrac{9}{7b^2}$

4 Determine by substitution whether the following pairs of expressions are identities or not.

   a $5(x + 3)$ and $5x + 3$

   b $-3(m - 2)$ and $-3m - 6$

   c $4(y - 3) + 2(y + 4)$ and $6y - 4$

5 The generalised rule for adding or subtracting fractions states that:

$$\dfrac{a}{b} \pm \dfrac{c}{d} = \dfrac{(ad \pm bc)}{bd}$$

A student wrote the following:

$$\dfrac{1}{t} + \dfrac{1}{w} = \dfrac{2}{(t + w)}$$

Show algebraically that this is incorrect.

6 Prove, using algebra, that the sum of two consecutive whole numbers is always an odd number.

7 Prove algebraically that the difference between the squares of any two consecutive integers is equal to the sum of these two integers.

 Find answers at: cambridge.org/ukschools/gcsemaths-studentbookanswers

6 Fractions

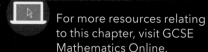
Using mathematics: real-life applications

Nurses and other medical support staff work with fractions, decimals, percentages, rates and ratios every day. They calculate medicine doses, convert between different systems of measurement and set the patients' drips to supply the correct amount of fluid per hour.

"I have to work out a treatment plan for patients who are going to have radiation treatment for various cancers. The patient has to receive a certain fraction of the total dose of radiation at each treatment session."   *(Oncologist)*

Before you start …

Ch 4	Check that you can find common factors of sets of numbers.	**1** From the set above, choose numbers that have:

18	24	27	28	30	32	36

1 From the set above, choose numbers that have:

    a a common factor of 9   **b** common factors 2 and 3

    c common factors 3, 4 and 12   **d** common factors 3 and 6.

Ch 4 — Find the lowest common multiple of sets of numbers.

2 Choose the lowest common multiple of each set of numbers.

    a 5 and 10

        A 15   **B** 50   **C** 10   **D** 20

    b 8 and 12

        A 12   **B** 96   **C** 36   **D** 24

    c 2, 3 and 5

        A 1   **B** 30   **C** 10   **D** 6

Ch 1 — Know the correct order for performing operations (BODMAS).

3 Which calculation is correct in each pair? Why?

	Student A	Student B
a	$-3 - 2 \times -6 - 4 = 5$	$-3 - 2 \times -6 - 4 = 50$
b	$-60 \div 5 + 3 \times -4 - 8 = 28$	$-60 \div 5 + 3 \times -4 - 8 = -32$
c	$13 - 2 \times -6 - 5 \times 4 = 80$	$13 - 2 \times -6 - 5 \times 4 = 5$

Assess your starting point using the Launchpad

STEP 1

 1 Which fraction does not belong in each set?

a $\dfrac{3}{15}, \dfrac{1}{5}, \dfrac{6}{30}, \dfrac{5}{35}, \dfrac{4}{20}$

b $\dfrac{4}{7}, \dfrac{8}{14}, \dfrac{12}{21}, \dfrac{9}{16}, \dfrac{52}{91}$

c $\dfrac{22}{10}, \dfrac{11}{4}, 2\dfrac{3}{4}, \dfrac{33}{12}, 2\dfrac{18}{24}$

**GO TO
Section 1:**
Equivalent fractions

STEP 2

 2 Each calculation contains a mistake. Find the mistake and write the correct answer.

a $\dfrac{2}{3} + \dfrac{3}{4} = \dfrac{5}{7}$

b $\dfrac{4}{5} - \dfrac{9}{10} = \dfrac{1}{10}$

c $\dfrac{2}{7} \times \dfrac{4}{5} = \dfrac{6}{35}$

d $30 \div \dfrac{1}{2} = 15$

**GO TO
Section 2:**
Operations with fractions

STEP 3

3 Which is greater in each pair?

a $\dfrac{5}{8}$ of 40 or $\dfrac{3}{5}$ of 60

b $\dfrac{3}{4}$ of 240 or $\dfrac{7}{10}$ of 300

c $\dfrac{1}{4}$ of $\dfrac{1}{2}$ or $\dfrac{1}{2}$ of $\dfrac{3}{4}$

4 If you have read 45 pages of a 240 page book, what fraction of the book remains unread?

5 What fraction of 30 minutes is 45 seconds?

**GO TO
Section 3:**
Finding fractions of a quantity

GO TO

Chapter review

 **Find answers at: cambridge.org/ukschools/gcsemaths-studentbookanswers**

Section 1: Equivalent fractions

Equivalent fractions represent the same value.

For example, $\frac{1}{4}, \frac{2}{8}$ and $\frac{16}{64}$ are equivalent.

You can find equivalent fractions by multiplying the numerator and denominator by the same number.

You can also find equivalent fractions by dividing the numerator and denominator by the same number (cancelling).

This is known as simplifying, or reducing the fraction to simplest terms.

When you give an answer in the form of a fraction, you usually give it in simplest form.

$$\frac{6}{18} = \frac{1}{3} \qquad \frac{12}{27} = \frac{4}{9} \qquad 3\frac{5}{30} = 3\frac{1}{6}$$

When you are asked to compare fractions that look different, you can write them both with the same denominator so that you can compare them by size, or you can cross multiply to find out whether they are equivalent or not.

Tip

You can use the LCM of the denominators to find a common denominator, but any common denominator works (not just the lowest).

WORKED EXAMPLE 1

Are the following pairs of fractions equivalent or not?

a $\frac{5}{6}$ and $\frac{7}{8}$ **b** $3\frac{3}{4}$ and $\frac{45}{12}$

Method 1: Using common denominators

$\frac{5}{6} = \frac{20}{24}$ and $\frac{7}{8} = \frac{21}{24}$ — Write both fractions with the same denominator.

$\frac{5}{6} \ne \frac{7}{8}$ — When the fractions have the same denominator it is easy to see whether they are equivalent or not.

It is also easy to compare them by size.

$3\frac{3}{4} = \frac{15}{4}$ — Write the mixed number as an improper fraction.

$\frac{15}{4} = \frac{45}{12}$ — Write $\frac{15}{4}$ with a denominator of 12, or write $\frac{45}{12}$ with a denominator of 4.

Method 2: By cross multiplying

$\frac{5}{6} \diagdown \frac{7}{8}$ — $5 \times 8 = 40$
$6 \times 7 = 42$

$40 \ne 42$

∴ the fractions are not equivalent.

40 is also smaller than 42, so $\frac{5}{6} < \frac{7}{8}$

This is a useful strategy for comparing the size of fractions.

$3\frac{3}{4} = \frac{15}{4}$ — Write the mixed number as an improper fraction.

$\frac{15}{4} \diagdown \frac{45}{12}$ — $15 \times 12 = 180$
$4 \times 45 = 180$

$180 = 180$ — ∴ the fractions are equivalent.

EXERCISE 6A

1 Determine whether the following pairs of fractions are equivalent ($=$) or not ($\neq$).

a $\dfrac{2}{5}$ and $\dfrac{3}{4}$ **b** $\dfrac{2}{3}$ and $\dfrac{3}{4}$ **c** $\dfrac{3}{8}$ and $\dfrac{5}{12}$ **d** $\dfrac{2}{11}$ and $\dfrac{1}{10}$

e $\dfrac{3}{5}$ and $\dfrac{9}{15}$ **f** $\dfrac{10}{25}$ and $\dfrac{4}{10}$ **g** $\dfrac{6}{24}$ and $\dfrac{5}{20}$ **h** $\dfrac{11}{9}$ and $\dfrac{121}{99}$

2 Find the equivalent fractions of $\dfrac{1}{4}$ with:

a denominator 32   **b** numerator 48

c numerator 27   **d** denominator 52

3 How could you use cross multiplication to find the missing values in examples like these?

a $\dfrac{3}{5} = \dfrac{18}{x}$ **b** $\dfrac{x}{51} = \dfrac{2}{17}$

4 Reduce the following fractions to their simplest form.

a $\dfrac{3}{15}$ **b** $\dfrac{4}{6}$ **c** $\dfrac{25}{100}$ **d** $\dfrac{5}{10}$ **e** $\dfrac{4}{12}$ **f** $\dfrac{-7}{21}$

g $\dfrac{36}{-24}$ **h** $\dfrac{60}{100}$ **i** $\dfrac{-14}{-21}$ **j** $\dfrac{18}{27}$ **k** $\dfrac{15}{21}$ **l** $\dfrac{-18}{-42}$

Tip

You can use the LCM of the denominators to find a common denominator, but any common denominator works (not just the lowest).

5 Write each set of fractions in ascending order.

a $\dfrac{3}{5}, \dfrac{1}{4}, \dfrac{9}{4}, 1\dfrac{3}{4}, \dfrac{4}{7}$ **b** $\dfrac{5}{6}, \dfrac{3}{4}, \dfrac{11}{3}, \dfrac{19}{24}, 2\dfrac{2}{3}$ **c** $2\dfrac{3}{7}, \dfrac{1}{7}, \dfrac{7}{7}, \dfrac{8}{14}, \dfrac{10}{21}, \dfrac{13}{7}$

EXERCISE 6B

A mediant fraction is a fraction that lies between two other fractions.

They follow the general rule:

If $\dfrac{a}{b}$ and $\dfrac{c}{d}$ are two fractions and $\dfrac{a}{b} < \dfrac{c}{d}$, then the fraction $\dfrac{a+c}{b+d}$ lies between them such that

$$\frac{a}{b} < \frac{a+c}{b+d} < \frac{c}{d}$$

1 Use this general rule to find a fraction between:

a $\dfrac{1}{4}$ and $\dfrac{3}{5}$ **b** $\dfrac{4}{5}$ and $\dfrac{9}{11}$

Find answers at: cambridge.org/ukschools/gcsemaths-studentbookanswers

2 Show how you could apply the rule to find three fractions between $\frac{1}{3}$ and $\frac{3}{4}$.

3 Test your results to show that the answers are correct.

4 How does this work?

Find out what you can and try to explain the general rule in simple terms.

Section 2: Operations with fractions

Multiplying fractions

Tip

Mediant fractions should not be confused with the median value in a set of data. These concepts are not related.

To multiply fractions multiply the numerators and then multiply the denominators.

WORKED EXAMPLE 2

a $\frac{3}{4} \times \frac{2}{7} = \frac{3 \times 2}{4 \times 7}$

Multiply numerators by numerators and denominators by denominators.

$= \frac{6}{28}$

$= \frac{3}{14}$

Give the answer in its simplest form.

b $\frac{5}{7} \times 3 = \frac{5 \times 3}{7 \times 1}$

Think of a whole number as a fraction with a denominator of 1.

$= \frac{15}{7}$

$\frac{15}{7}$ cannot be simplified further but it can be written as a mixed number.

$= 2\frac{1}{7}$

c $\frac{3}{8} \times 4\frac{1}{2} = \frac{3}{8} \times \frac{9}{2}$

Rewrite the mixed number as an improper fraction.

$= \frac{27}{16}$

$\frac{27}{16}$ cannot be simplified but it can be written as a mixed number.

$= 1\frac{11}{16}$

Tip

You can cancel before you multiply to make it easier to simplify the answers.

Adding and subtracting fractions

To add or subtract fractions they must have the same denominator.

Find a common denominator and then find the equivalent fractions before you add or subtract the numerators.

WORKED EXAMPLE 3

a $\dfrac{1}{2} + \dfrac{1}{4} = \dfrac{2}{4} + \dfrac{1}{4}$

Use 4 as a common denominator.
Write $\dfrac{1}{2}$ as its equivalent, $\dfrac{2}{4}$

$= \dfrac{3}{4}$

Add the numerators.

b $2\dfrac{1}{2} + \dfrac{5}{6} = \dfrac{5}{2} + \dfrac{5}{6}$

Rewrite mixed numbers as improper fractions.

$= \dfrac{15}{6} + \dfrac{5}{6}$

Find a common denominator.

$= \dfrac{20}{6}$

Add the numerators.

$= \dfrac{10}{3}$ or $3\dfrac{1}{3}$

Simplify the answer.

c $2\dfrac{3}{4} - 1\dfrac{5}{7} = \dfrac{11}{4} - \dfrac{12}{7}$

Rewrite mixed numbers as improper fractions.

$= \dfrac{77}{28} - \dfrac{48}{28}$

Find a common denominator.

$= \dfrac{29}{28}$ or $1\dfrac{1}{28}$

Subtract the numverators.
Simplify the answer.

Tip

Think of $\dfrac{3}{7}$ and $\dfrac{2}{7}$ as 3 lots of 7ths and 2 lots of 7ths. If you combine them, you have 5 lots of 7ths, or $\dfrac{5}{7}$.

You **never add the denominators**.

Dividing fractions

To divide one fraction by another fraction you multiply the first fraction by the reciprocal of the second fraction.

To find the reciprocal of a fraction you invert it.

The reciprocal of $\dfrac{3}{4}$ is $\dfrac{4}{3}$

The reciprocal of a whole number is a unit fraction.

The reciprocal of 3 is $\dfrac{1}{3}$

To divide one fraction by another fraction you multiply the first fraction by the **reciprocal** of the second fraction.

Key vocabulary

reciprocal: the value obtained by inverting a fraction. Any number multiplied by its reciprocal is 1.

unit fraction: a fraction with numerator 1 and denominator a positive integer.

Tip

The reciprocal of $\frac{3}{4}$ is $\frac{4}{3}$. The reciprocal of a whole number is a **unit fraction**. For example, the reciprocal of 3 is $\frac{1}{3}$.

WORKED EXAMPLE 4

a $\quad \frac{3}{4} \div \frac{1}{2} = \frac{3}{4} \times \frac{2}{1}$

Multiply by the reciprocal of $\frac{1}{2}$.

$\qquad = \frac{6}{4}$

$\qquad = \frac{3}{2}$ or $1\frac{1}{2}$

b $\quad 1\frac{3}{4} \div 2\frac{1}{3} = \frac{7}{4} \div \frac{7}{3}$

Convert mixed numbers to improper fractions.

$\qquad = \frac{\cancel{7}}{4} \times \frac{3}{\cancel{7}}$

Multiply by the reciprocal of $\frac{7}{3}$. Cancel the 7s.

$\qquad = \frac{3}{4}$

c $\quad \frac{6}{7} \div 3 = \frac{6}{7} \times \frac{1}{3}$

Multiply by the reciprocal of 3.

$\qquad = \frac{6}{21}$

$\qquad = \frac{2}{7}$

The rules for order of operations and negative and positive signs also apply to calculations with fractions.

EXERCISE 6C

1 Simplify:

a $\quad \frac{3}{4} \times \frac{2}{5}$ b $\quad \frac{1}{5} \times \frac{1}{9}$ c $\quad \frac{5}{7} \times \frac{1}{5}$ d $\quad \frac{7}{10} \times \frac{2}{3}$

e $\quad \frac{1}{5} \times \frac{3}{8} \times \frac{-5}{9}$ f $\quad \frac{2}{3} \times \frac{-3}{4} \times \frac{-4}{5}$ g $\quad \frac{1}{2} \times \frac{2}{3} \times \frac{4}{11}$ h $\quad \frac{5}{8} \times \frac{3}{7} \times \frac{2}{3}$

i $\quad \frac{4}{25} \times \frac{-3}{5} \times \frac{-7}{8}$ j $\quad \frac{9}{20} \times \frac{10}{11} \times \frac{1}{12}$ k $\quad 1\frac{2}{9} \times 1\frac{5}{22} \times 1\frac{1}{6}$ l $\quad 1\frac{3}{4} \times 2\frac{1}{3} \times \frac{-3}{5}$

2 Simplify:

a $\quad \frac{2}{7} + \frac{1}{2}$ b $\quad \frac{1}{2} + \frac{1}{4}$ c $\quad \frac{5}{8} - \frac{1}{4}$ d $\quad \frac{7}{9} - \frac{1}{3}$

e $\quad 4\frac{3}{4} + \frac{15}{6}$ f $\quad 8\frac{2}{5} - 3\frac{1}{2}$ g $\quad 7\frac{1}{4} - 2\frac{9}{10}$ h $\quad 9\frac{3}{7} - 2\frac{4}{5}$

3 Simplify:

a $\dfrac{1}{8} \div \dfrac{7}{9}$ **b** $\dfrac{2}{11} \div \dfrac{-3}{5}$ **c** $3\dfrac{1}{5} \div 2\dfrac{1}{2}$ **d** $1\dfrac{7}{8} \div 2\dfrac{3}{4}$

4 What should be added to $4\dfrac{3}{5}$ to get $9\dfrac{7}{20}$?

5 What should be subtracted from $13\dfrac{3}{4}$ to get $5\dfrac{1}{3}$?

6 Subtract the product of $\dfrac{1}{6}$ and $20\dfrac{4}{7}$ from the sum of $4\dfrac{7}{9}$ and $5\dfrac{5}{18}$.

7 Simplify:

a $4 + \dfrac{2}{3} \times \dfrac{1}{3}$ **b** $2\dfrac{1}{8} - \left(2\dfrac{1}{5} - \dfrac{7}{8}\right)$ **c** $\dfrac{3}{7} \times \left(\dfrac{2}{3} + 6 \div \dfrac{2}{3}\right) + 5 \times \dfrac{2}{7}$

d $2\dfrac{7}{8} + \left(8\dfrac{1}{4} - 6\dfrac{3}{8}\right)$ **e** $\dfrac{5}{6} \times \dfrac{1}{4} + \dfrac{5}{8} \times \dfrac{1}{3}$ **f** $\left(5 \div \dfrac{3}{11} - \dfrac{5}{12}\right) \times \dfrac{1}{6}$

g $\left(\dfrac{5}{8} \div \dfrac{15}{4}\right) - \left(\dfrac{5}{6} \times \dfrac{1}{5}\right)$ **h** $\left(2\dfrac{2}{3} \div 4 - \dfrac{3}{10}\right) \times \dfrac{3}{17}$ **i** $\left(7 \div \dfrac{2}{9} - \dfrac{1}{3}\right) \times \dfrac{2}{3}$

j $\left(\dfrac{5}{9} \times \dfrac{27}{35}\right) \div \dfrac{6}{9} + \dfrac{2}{3}$ **k** $1\dfrac{2}{3} \div \dfrac{5}{6} \times \dfrac{24}{35} \times \dfrac{1}{3}$

l $2\dfrac{1}{9} + \left[3\dfrac{20}{27} + \left\{\dfrac{5}{14} - \left(\dfrac{3}{35} - \dfrac{3}{7}\right) - \dfrac{1}{5}\right\} \times \dfrac{7}{9}\right]$

EXERCISE 6D

1 Kevin is a professional deep-sea diver.

He needs to keep track of how much time he spends underwater to make sure he has enough air left in his tank.

If he spends $9\dfrac{3}{4}$ minutes diving to a wreck, $12\dfrac{5}{6}$ minutes exploring the wreck and $3\dfrac{5}{6}$ minutes examining corals, how much time has he spent underwater in total?

2 In a public park, $\dfrac{2}{3}$ of the area is grassed, $\dfrac{1}{5}$ is taken up by flower beds and the rest is paved.

How much of the park area is paved?

3 The perimeter of a quadrilateral is $18\dfrac{23}{60}$ m.

If the lengths of three sides are $6\dfrac{1}{6}$ m, $7\dfrac{2}{3}$ m and $1\dfrac{2}{15}$ m, find the length of the other side.

4 A tank contains $\dfrac{7}{30}$ of a litre of water.

The water has to be removed by a piece of equipment that draws out the water at a rate of $\dfrac{3}{5}$ of a litre per minute.

How long will it take to remove all the water?

Tip

Remember that addition and subtraction are inverse operations.

Tip

Remember the rules for order of operations apply to fractions as well. Simplify brackets first, then powers, then multiplication and/or division, then addition and/or subtraction. When there is more than one set of brackets, work from the inner ones to the outer ones.

Find answers at: cambridge.org/ukschools/gcsemaths-studentbookanswers

5 There are $1\frac{3}{4}$ cakes left over after a party.

These are shared out equally among six people.
What fraction does each person get?

6 If I have $5\frac{2}{3}$ litres of juice, how many cups containing $\frac{2}{15}$ of a litre can I pour?

7 Nico buys six trays of chicken pieces for his restaurant.
Each tray contains $2\frac{1}{2}$ kg of chicken.

Each chicken meal served uses $\frac{3}{8}$ kg of chicken.
How many meals can he serve?

8 A mountaineer inserts a bolt into the rock face every $5\frac{3}{4}$ metres she climbs.

If she uses 32 bolts, what is the maximum height she has climbed?

9 Ted has marked out three lengths of wood.
Length C is $\frac{2}{3}$ of the length of B, and length B is $1\frac{1}{3}$ times as long as A.

What is the length of piece C if A is $\frac{97}{3}$ m long?

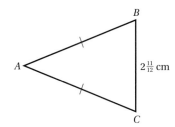

10 Triangle *ABC* to the left is isosceles with a perimeter of $12\frac{3}{4}$ cm.

Find the length of sides *AB* and *AC* given that *BC* is $2\frac{11}{12}$ cm.

11 What is the length of the side of a square of perimeter $9\frac{3}{7}$ m?

12 On a holiday weekend Salma read $\frac{2}{9}$ of her book on Saturday, $\frac{1}{6}$ on Sunday and $\frac{5}{12}$ on Monday.

a What fraction of the book does she still have to read?

b If there are still 49 pages left for her to read, how many pages were in the book?

Section 3: Finding fractions of a quantity

Expressing one quantity as a fraction of another

It is easy to express one quantity as a fraction of another if you remember that the numerator in a fraction tells you how many parts of the whole quantity you are dealing with and the denominator represents the whole quantity.

So, a fraction of $\frac{3}{5}$ means you are dealing with 3 of the 5 parts that make up the whole.

WORKED EXAMPLE 5

a What fraction is 20 minutes of 1 hour?

b Express 35 centimetres as a fraction of a metre.

a 20 minutes is the part of the whole, so it is the numerator.

The hour is the whole, so it is the denominator.

20 minutes is part of 60 minutes:

$$\frac{20}{60} = \frac{2}{6} = \frac{1}{3} \text{ of an hour.}$$

You cannot form a fraction using one unit for the numerator and another for the denominator, so you need to convert the hour to minutes. There are 60 minutes in one hour.

b 35 cm is the part of the whole, so it is the numerator.

The metre is the whole, so it is the denominator.

35 cm is part of 100 cm:

$$\frac{35}{100} = \frac{7}{20} \text{ of a metre.}$$

Again, you cannot use centimetres and metres in the same fraction, so you convert 1 m to 100 cm.

 Tip

To write a quantity as a fraction of another quantity make sure the two quantities are in the same units and then write them as a fraction and simplify.

EXERCISE 6E

1 Calculate.

a $\frac{3}{4}$ of 12   **b** $\frac{1}{3}$ of 45   **c** $\frac{2}{9}$ of 36   **d** $\frac{3}{8}$ of 144

e $\frac{4}{5}$ of 180   **f** $\frac{1}{3}$ of 96   **g** $\frac{1}{2}$ of $\frac{3}{4}$ **h** $\frac{1}{3}$ of $\frac{3}{10}$

i $\frac{4}{9}$ of $\frac{3}{14}$ **j** $\frac{1}{4}$ of $2\frac{1}{2}$ **k** $\frac{3}{4}$ of $2\frac{1}{3}$ **l** $\frac{5}{6}$ of $3\frac{1}{2}$

2 Calculate the following quantities.

a $\frac{3}{4}$ of £28   **b** $\frac{3}{5}$ of £210   **c** $\frac{2}{5}$ of £30   **d** $\frac{2}{3}$ of £18

e $\frac{1}{2}$ of 3 cups of sugar   **f** $\frac{1}{2}$ of 5 cups of flour

3 Calculate the following quantities.

a $\frac{3}{4}$ of $2\frac{1}{3}$ cups of flour   **b** $\frac{2}{3}$ of $1\frac{1}{2}$ cups of sugar

c $\frac{2}{3}$ of 4 hours   **d** $\frac{1}{3}$ of $2\frac{1}{2}$ hours   **e** $\frac{3}{4}$ of 5 hours

f $\frac{1}{3}$ of $\frac{3}{4}$ of an hour   **g** $\frac{2}{3}$ of $3\frac{1}{2}$ minutes   **h** $\frac{3}{15}$ of a minute

4 Express the first quantity as a fraction of the second.

a 35 cm of a 2 m length   **b** 12 mm of 30 cm

c 45 minutes per 8-hour shift   **d** 5 minutes per hour

e 150 m of a kilometre   **f** 45 seconds of 30 minutes

g 575 ml of 4 litres   **h** 12 000 g of 40 kg

5 Nick earns £18 000 per year. His friend Samir earns £24 000 per year.

What fraction of Samir's salary does Nick earn?

6 The floor area of a room is 12 m². Pete buys a rug that is 110 cm wide and 160 cm long.

What fraction of the floor area will be covered by this rug?

7 A technical college has 8400 books in their library.

Of these, $\frac{1}{7}$ are general reference books, $\frac{3}{7}$ are technology related, $\frac{4}{35}$ are engineering related and the rest are computer related.

Find the total number of books in each subject category.

8 A section of road $1\frac{1}{2}$ km long is to be tarred.

$\frac{1}{6}$ is tarred in week 1, $\frac{3}{5}$ in week 2 and the rest is to be completed in week 3.

Calculate the length of road tarred each week.

9 Of 60 000 people passing through a major airport in one week, $\frac{1}{6}$ are travelling first class, $\frac{1}{4}$ are travelling business class, $\frac{3}{8}$ are travelling in economy class and the rest are using no-frills, low-cost tickets.

Work out the number of people travelling in each class.

EXERCISE 6F

The Ancient Egyptians believed that anything other than a unit fraction was unacceptable (a unit fraction has a numerator of 1).

So they wrote all fractions as the sum or difference of unit fractions.

The sum or difference always started with the largest possible unit fraction and they did not allow repetition.

So, for example, $\frac{2}{3}$ would be written as $\frac{1}{2}+\frac{1}{6}$ and not as $\frac{1}{3}+\frac{1}{3}$

1 Try to write each of the following as the sum or difference of unit fractions:

a $\frac{5}{8}$　　**b** $\frac{3}{5}$　　**c** $\frac{2}{7}$　　**d** $\frac{2}{9}$　　**e** $\frac{3}{10}$

2 Find three unit fractions that have a sum of $\frac{2}{5}$ when added together.

3 Find a unit fraction greater than $\frac{1}{9}$ with a denominator that is a multiple of 4 and which has three additional factors.

4 Can all fractions be written as the sum or difference of unit fractions? Justify your answer.

 Checklist of learning and understanding

Equivalent fractions

- Fractions that represent the same amount are called equivalent fractions.
- You can change fractions to their equivalents by multiplying the numerator and denominator by the same value or by dividing the numerator and denominator by the same value (simplifying).

Operations on fractions

- To add or subtract fractions, find equivalent fractions with the same denominator.
- Add or subtract the numerators once the denominators are the same. Do not add or subtract denominators.
- To multiply fractions, multiply numerators by numerators and denominators by denominators.
- To divide fractions, multiply by the reciprocal of the divisor.

Fractions of a quantity

- The word 'of' means multiply.
- A quantity can be written as a fraction of another as long as they are in the same units. Write one quantity as the numerator and the other as the denominator and simplify.

Find answers at: cambridge.org/ukschools/gcsemaths-studentbookanswers

For additional questions on the topics in this chapter, visit GCSE Mathematics Online.

Chapter review

1 Simplify.

a $\dfrac{15}{90}$ **b** $\dfrac{195}{230}$ **c** $4\dfrac{18}{48}$

2 Write each set of fractions in ascending order.

a $\dfrac{8}{9}, \dfrac{4}{5}, \dfrac{5}{6}, \dfrac{3}{7}$ **b** $2\dfrac{2}{5}, \dfrac{23}{7}, 1\dfrac{3}{5}, \dfrac{16}{9}$

3 Evaluate:

a $\dfrac{7}{5} + \dfrac{3}{8} - \dfrac{1}{2}$ **b** $\dfrac{7}{5} \times \dfrac{3}{8} + \dfrac{1}{2}$ **c** $\dfrac{7}{5} \div \dfrac{3}{8} \times 3$

d $3\dfrac{1}{7} + 2\dfrac{2}{5}$ **e** $3\dfrac{1}{15} - 1\dfrac{3}{5}$ **f** $\dfrac{1}{7}$ of $3\dfrac{3}{11} + \dfrac{3}{4}$

g $\dfrac{2}{7} \times \dfrac{8}{18} \div 3$ **h** $28 \div \dfrac{3}{4} - \dfrac{5}{7}$ **i** $\dfrac{2}{9}$ of $\dfrac{3}{4} - \dfrac{1}{8}$

4 Simplify.

a $\left(\dfrac{3}{8} \div \dfrac{13}{4}\right) + \left(\dfrac{5}{9} \times \dfrac{3}{5}\right)$ **b** $2\dfrac{2}{3} \times \left(8 \div \dfrac{4}{7} + \dfrac{7}{8}\right)$

c $4\dfrac{2}{5} + 3\dfrac{1}{2} + 5\dfrac{5}{6} - 4\dfrac{11}{12} + 2\dfrac{7}{9}$ **d** $\left(7 \div \dfrac{2}{9} - \dfrac{1}{3}\right) \times \dfrac{2}{3}$

  5 Work out $3\dfrac{1}{3} \div 4\dfrac{3}{4}$

(2 marks)

©Pearson Education Ltd 2012

6 Express $425\,g$ as a fraction of $2\dfrac{1}{2}\,kg$.

7 Sandy has $12\dfrac{1}{2}$ litres of water. How many bottles containing $\dfrac{3}{4}$ litre can she fill?

8 A surveyor has to divide a $15\,km^2$ area of land into equal plots each measuring $\dfrac{1}{2}\,km^2$.

How many plots can she make?

9 A ladder $7\dfrac{1}{5}$ m long is lowered into a manhole.

If $\dfrac{15}{32}$ parts of the ladder are outside the manhole when the bottom of the ladder touches the ground, how deep is the manhole?

7 Decimals

In this chapter you will learn how to ...

- convert decimals to fractions and fractions to decimals.
- order fractions and decimals.
- carry out the four basic operations on decimals without using a calculator.
- solve problems involving decimal quantities.
- convert recurring decimals to proper fractions.

For more resources relating to this chapter, visit GCSE Mathematics Online.

Using mathematics: real-life applications

Food technologists analyse the contents of different raw and prepared foods to work out what they contain and how much there is of each ingredient. For example, how much water, protein and fat there is in a cut of meat. They use decimal fractions to give the quantities correct to tenths, hundredths or even smaller parts of a gram.

"Think about a product like a vitamin pill. We may have to list the mass of 30 different ingredients in fractions of milligrams. A milligram is 0.001 grams, a microgram (µg) is 0.001 mg and a nanogram (ng) is 0.000 001 mg, so decimal fractions (and negative indices) are very important in my work."

(Food technologist)

Before you start ...

KS3	You need to be able to work confidently with place value.	31.098 0.0398 300.098 0.98308 19.308
		
		1 Choose the number from the set that has a 3 in the:
		  a hundreds position **b** hundredths position
		  c tenths position **d** thousandths position
		  e tens position.

KS3	Check that you can compare decimal fractions and order them by size.	**2** Fill in <, = or > between each pair of decimal fractions.
		  a 0.65 ☐ 0.7 **b** 0.08 ☐ 0.01 **c** 0.8 ☐ 0.85
		  d 2.87 ☐ 0.99 **e** 4.230 ☐ 4.23

KS3	You need to know the fractional equivalents of some common decimals.	**3** Make equivalent pairs by matching the decimal in the upper box with the fraction in the lower box.
		
		  a 0.25 **b** 0.375 **c** 0.4 **d** 0.75 **e** 0.5 **f** 0.025
		
		  $\dfrac{2}{5}$ $\dfrac{3}{4}$ $\dfrac{45}{90}$ $\dfrac{1}{40}$ $\dfrac{4}{16}$ $\dfrac{3}{8}$

Find answers at: cambridge.org/ukschools/gcsemaths-studentbookanswers

Assess your starting point using the Launchpad

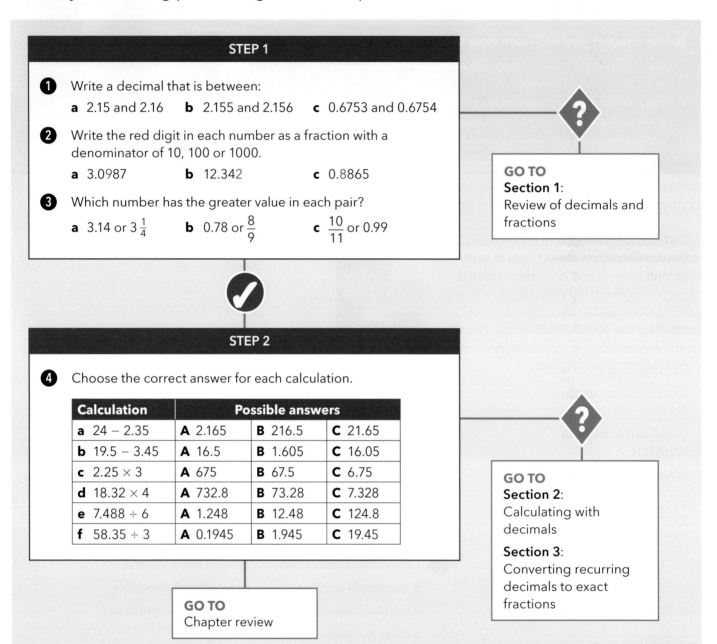

STEP 1

1 Write a decimal that is between:

  a 2.15 and 2.16   **b** 2.155 and 2.156   **c** 0.6753 and 0.6754

2 Write the red digit in each number as a fraction with a denominator of 10, 100 or 1000.

  a 3.0987   **b** 12.342   **c** 0.8865

3 Which number has the greater value in each pair?

  a 3.14 or $3\frac{1}{4}$ **b** 0.78 or $\frac{8}{9}$ **c** $\frac{10}{11}$ or 0.99

GO TO
Section 1:
Review of decimals and fractions

STEP 2

4 Choose the correct answer for each calculation.

Calculation	Possible answers		
a 24 − 2.35	**A** 2.165	**B** 216.5	**C** 21.65
b 19.5 − 3.45	**A** 16.5	**B** 1.605	**C** 16.05
c 2.25 × 3	**A** 675	**B** 67.5	**C** 6.75
d 18.32 × 4	**A** 732.8	**B** 73.28	**C** 7.328
e 7.488 ÷ 6	**A** 1.248	**B** 12.48	**C** 124.8
f 58.35 ÷ 3	**A** 0.1945	**B** 1.945	**C** 19.45

GO TO
Section 2:
Calculating with decimals

Section 3:
Converting recurring decimals to exact fractions

GO TO
Chapter review

Section 1: Review of decimals and fractions

Team	Time (seconds)
Australia	39.14
Bahamas	39.27
England	38.74
India	38.89
Jamaica	38.79

Five teams completed the men's 4 × 100 m relay final at the 2010 Commonwealth Games in New Delhi.

The times are given as decimals.

The numbers that follow the decimal point indicate parts (decimal fractions) of a second.

There are two digits after the decimal place so the times are given correct to a hundredth of a second.

Comparing decimals

To write the times in order from fastest to slowest, compare the whole number parts of each first. If those are the same, compare the decimal parts.

England, India and Jamaica ran the relay in 38 seconds and a fraction of a second.

This is less time than Australia and the Bahamas who ran the race in 39 seconds and a fraction of a second.

To decide first, second and third place, you need to look at the decimal parts.

Here are the times written in a place value table.

Team	Tens	Ones/units	.	tenths	hundredths
England	3	8	.	7	4
India	3	8	.	8	9
Jamaica	3	8	.	7	9

Start by looking at the tenths.

India has 8 in the tenths place. This is greater than the others, so India came third.

England and Jamaica both have 7 in the tenths place, so compare the hundredths.

England has 4 in the hundredths and Jamaica has 9, this means that England was faster.

The places were: England (1st), Jamaica (2nd) and India (3rd), followed by Australia then the Bahamas.

 Tip

Remember you are comparing winning times, so you are looking for the smallest time as this is the fastest time. The greater the time, the slower the team ran.

Converting decimals to fractions

The decimal times can be written as fractions using place value.

Tens	Ones/units	.	tenths	hundredths
3	8	.	7	4

The England team ran the relay in 38 seconds and $\dfrac{74}{100}$ of a second.

The fraction part can be simplified further: $\frac{74}{100} = \frac{37}{50}$. So, $38.74 = 38\frac{37}{50}$

Any decimal can be converted to a fraction in this way. For example:

$$0.6 = \frac{6}{10} = \frac{3}{5} \qquad 0.25 = \frac{25}{100} = \frac{1}{4} \qquad 0.075 = \frac{75}{1000} = \frac{3}{40}$$

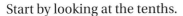 **Find answers at: cambridge.org/ukschools/gcsemaths-studentbookanswers**

Converting fractions to decimals

There are different methods for converting fractions to decimals. You should choose the method that is easiest for the fraction involved.

Method 1: Equivalent fractions with denominators of 10, 100, 1000 and so on.	**Method 2:** Pen and paper division.	**Method 3:** Calculator division.
Express $\dfrac{61}{125}$ as a decimal. $\dfrac{61}{125} = \dfrac{122}{250} = \dfrac{244}{500}$ $= \dfrac{488}{1000}$ $\dfrac{61}{125} = 0.488$ This method works well if the denominator is a factor of 10, 100 or 1000.	Express $\dfrac{5}{8}$ as a decimal. Work out $5 \div 8$ using division. insert decimal point when you cross the decimal point in the number you are dividing $\begin{array}{r} 0 \cdot 6\,2\,5 \\ \hline 8\,)\,5\,.\,0 \\ 4\,.\,8 \qquad 0.6 \times 8 \\ \hline 0\,.\,2\,0 \\ 0\,.\,1\,6 \quad 0.02 \times 8 \\ \hline 0\,.\,0\,4\,0 \\ 0\,.\,0\,4\,0 \; 0.005 \times 8 \\ \hline 0\,.\,0\,0 \end{array}$	Express $\dfrac{2}{3}$ as a decimal. Input $2 \div 3$ on your calculator. 0.666666666 The 6s continue forever (they recur). Show this by writing the answer as $0.\dot{6}$ **Tip** Remember that you write a dot above the first and last digit of the recurring numbers if more than one digit recurs.

Tip

When you have to compare and order ordinary fractions you can convert them all to decimals and compare them easily using place value. This is often quicker than changing them all into equivalent fractions with a common denominator.

EXERCISE 7A

1 Write each of the following decimals as a fraction in its simplest form.

   a 0.6   **b** 0.84   **c** 1.64   **d** 0.385   **e** 0.125

   f 1.08   **g** 0.875   **h** 0.008   **i** 3.064   **j** 0.333

2 Convert the following fractions to decimals without using a calculator.

   a $\dfrac{3}{5}$ **b** $\dfrac{3}{4}$ **c** $\dfrac{18}{25}$ **d** $\dfrac{19}{20}$ **e** $\dfrac{34}{50}$

   f $\dfrac{110}{250}$ **g** $\dfrac{89}{200}$ **h** $\dfrac{76}{500}$ **i** $\dfrac{185}{20}$ **j** $\dfrac{145}{50}$

   k $\dfrac{11}{6}$ **l** $\dfrac{3}{8}$ **m** $\dfrac{9}{4}$ **n** $\dfrac{8}{9}$ **o** $\dfrac{19}{8}$

3 Use a calculator to convert the fractions from $\frac{1}{9}$ to $\frac{8}{9}$ into decimals.

    a What pattern do you notice?

    b What do you call decimals of this nature?

    c Repeat this for the fractions from $\frac{1}{6}$ to $\frac{5}{6}$.

    d Convert $\frac{1}{11}$ and $\frac{2}{11}$ to decimals.

    e Predict what $\frac{3}{11}$ and $\frac{4}{11}$ will be if you convert them to decimals.

       Check your prediction using a calculator.

4 Arrange the following in descending order.

    a 5.2, 5.29, 8.62, 4.92, 4.09   **b** 7.42, 0.76, 0.742, 0.421, 3.219

    c 14.3, 14.72, 14.07, 14.89, 14.009   **d** 0.23, 0.26, 0.273, 0.287, 0.206

    e 0.403, $\frac{1}{2}$, $\frac{2}{3}$, 0.68, 0.45, $\frac{5}{11}$ **f** $\frac{7}{9}$, $\frac{3}{8}$, 0.625, 0.88, 0.718

5 Fill in the boxes using $<$, $=$ or $>$ to make each statement true.

    a 13.098 $\square$ 13.099   **b** 0.312 $\square$ 0.322   **c** $\frac{5}{6}$ $\square$ 0.84

    d 0.375 $\square$ $\frac{3}{8}$ **e** 2.05 $\square$ $\frac{205}{1000}$ **f** $\frac{3}{5}$ $\square$ 0.7

    g $\frac{2}{5}$ $\square$ 0.35   **h** $\frac{18}{25}$ $\square$ 0.67   **i** $\frac{1}{3}$ $\square$ 0.37

6 Write a decimal fraction that is between each pair of decimals.

    a 3.135 and 3.136   **b** 0.6645 and 06646   **c** 4.998 and 4.999

7 The lengths of some of the world's longest roller coaster rides are given in the table.

Roller coaster	Length of ride (km)
The Beast (USA)	2.243
California Screaming (USA)	1.851
Formula Rossa (United Arab Emirates)	2.0
Fujiyama (Japan)	2.045
Steel Dragon (Japan)	2.479
The Ultimate (UK)	2.268

    a Which is the longest roller coaster?

    b Which is the shortest?

    c Is the Steel Dragon longer or shorter than $2\frac{1}{2}$ km?

    d Which roller coasters are longer than $2\frac{1}{4}$ km?

    e Write the lengths in order from longest to shortest.

Find answers at: cambridge.org/ukschools/gcsemaths-studentbookanswers

Section 2: Calculating with decimals

You need to be able to add, subtract, multiply and divide decimals without using a calculator.

When you calculate with decimals it is useful to estimate the answer so that you can tell whether your solution is reasonable and whether you have the decimal point in the correct place. There's a big difference between £10 and £0.10.

Adding and subtracting decimals

Add or subtract decimals in columns by lining up the places and the decimal points.

WORKED EXAMPLE 1

Calculate.

a 12.7 + 18.34 + 3.087   **b** 399.65 − 245.175

a   12.7
        18.34
     + 3.087
      34.127

b   399.650   Write a 0 as a place
   − 245.175   holder here.
    154.475

Multiplying and dividing decimals

Andy made the following notes about multiplying and dividing decimals when he was studying for exams at the end of last year.

- When multiplying or dividing by a power of 10 (10, 100, 1000, and so on):

  Move the digits as many places to the left as the number of zeros when multiplying.

  Move the digits as many places to the right as the number of zeros when dividing.

- When multiplying decimal fractions by decimal fractions:

  Ignore the decimal points and multiply the numbers.

  Place the decimal point in the answer so it has the same number of digits after the decimal point as there were altogether in the multiplication problem.

- When dividing by a decimal:

  Make the divisor a whole number by multiplying the divisor and the dividend by the same power of 10.

  Then divide as normal, keeping the decimal point in the answer directly above the decimal point in the number you are dividing.

Tip

The dividend is the amount you are dividing up; the divisor is the quantity you are dividing it by. If you are asked to divide 18 by 9, then 18 is the dividend and 9 is the divisor.

EXERCISE 7B

Work with a partner.

1 **a** Read through Andy's summary notes.

   b Provide one or two examples for each summary point using actual numbers to show what he means.

   c Write your own summary point for dividing a decimal by a whole number.

   Include two numerical examples to illustrate your point.

2 Use a place value chart and provide some examples to show why you can multiply and divide decimals in the way Andy summarised.

EXERCISE 7C

1 Estimate first then calculate.

   a $0.8 + 0.78$ **b** $12.8 - 11.13$ **c** $0.8 + 0.9$

   d $15.31 - 1.96$ **e** 2.77×8.2 **f** 9.81×3.5

2 Evaluate without a calculator.

   a $12.7 + 18.34 + 35.01$ **b** $12.35 + 8.5 + 2.91$ **c** $6.89 - 3.28$

   d $34.45 - 12.02$ **e** $345.297 - 12.39$ **f** $56 + 8.345 - 34.65$

3 Without using a calculator, work out the value of the following.

   a 0.786×100 **b** 54.76×2000 **c** 1.234×0.65

   d 87.87×2.34 **e** $1.83 \div 61$ **f** $0.358 \div 4$

   g $5.053 \div 0.62$ **h** $31.72 \div 0.04$ **i** $86 \div 0.02$

4 The world record for the women's 4×100 m relay is 40.82 seconds (USA, 2012) and the Commonwealth Games record is 41.83 seconds (Jamaica, 2014).

   a What is the time difference between the World Record and the Commonwealth Games Record?

   b In the 2010 Commonwealth Games, the winning time for this relay was 44.19 seconds.

   How much slower is this than the 2014 record?

   c Each of the four runners in a relay runs 100 m.

   Calculate the average time taken for 100 m during the world record winning race.

   d Do you think each runner takes the same amount of time? Explain your reasoning.

5 Nadia wants to make a dish that requires 1.5 litres of cream.

   She has four 0.385 litre cartons of cream. Does she have enough?

Find answers at: cambridge.org/ukschools/gcsemaths-studentbookanswers

Tip

In Question 6, mg stands for milligrams; 'milli' means one thousandth. There are one thousand millimetres (mm) in one metre.
In 'kilowatt', 'kilo' means 'one thousand'; 1 kilowatt is 1000 watts.

6 Josh takes a multivitamin tablet every morning.

He calculates that if he takes one tablet every day for a week he will take in 1166.69 mg of vitamin C, 54.6 mg of boron and 257.95 mg of calcium.

Work out how much of each ingredient there is in a tablet.

7 The Chetty household uses about 25.75 kilowatt hours of electricity per day. Calculate how much they will use in:

a one week   **b** one (non-leap) year.

Decimals in context

In daily life you use decimals when you deal with money, distances and other measurements.

When you solve problems involving decimals you need to make sure that your answer is both reasonable and sensible in the context.

For example, if you work out the price of an item and you get an answer of £15.987, it makes sense to round it to £15.99 because we don't have coins smaller than 1p (a hundredth of a pound).

EXERCISE 7D

Use a calculator if you need one to solve these problems.

1 Sandra has £87.50 in her purse. She buys two sweaters that cost £32.99 each.

How much money does she have left?

2 George travels from York to Oxford by car.

His odometer reads 123 456.8 km when he leaves York and 123 642.7 km when he arrives in Oxford.

How far did he travel?

3 If I have 5.67 litres of juice, how many cups containing $\frac{2}{15}$ of a litre can I pour?

4 Find 0.75 of 2400

5 Sheldon places fence posts 0.84 m apart all along his boundary fence.

If the total fence is 59.64 metres long, how many posts will there be?

6 June bought 6.65 litres of petrol at £1.29 per litre. How much did she pay?

7 Toni earns £28 650 per year.

a How much is this per day? Remember there are 365.25 days in a year.

b How much is this per five-day week? Give your answer correct to 2 decimal places.

c If Toni is paid the amount in part **b** every week for 52 weeks of a year, will she earn more or less than the original total? Why?

Section 3: Converting recurring decimals to exact fractions

There are three types of decimal fractions:

- exact or terminating decimals such as 0.25 and 0.375
- non-terminating and recurring decimals in which a set of digits repeats to infinity
- other decimals which are non-terminating and non-recurring (irrational numbers) such as π (3.141592654...) and $\sqrt{2}$ (1.414213562...).

EXERCISE 7E

How do you know whether a fraction will give you a terminating or recurring decimal?

1 Nazeem says you can work this out by writing the denominator of the fraction as the product of its prime factors.

Any denominator that has only 2s and/or 5s as prime factors will produce a terminating decimal.

All the others will produce recurring decimals.

Do you agree?

Test Nazeem's hypothesis and state whether it is correct or not.

2 Andy says Nazeem is wrong and he uses sixths to show this:

$6 = 2 \times 3$, so it should produce recurring decimals according to Nazeem.

But $\dfrac{3}{6}$ gives an exact decimal of 0.5, so Nazeem is wrong.

Consider Andy's argument and use it to adapt Nazeem's hypothesis so that it holds for fractions such as $\dfrac{3}{6}$ as well.

Writing decimals as fractions in the form of $\dfrac{a}{b}$

Exact and recurring decimals can be written as fractions in the form of $\dfrac{a}{b}$, so that they are rational numbers.

To convert a recurring decimal to an exact fraction you can set up a pair of equations using the decimal and then use algebra to solve for x.

The answer should always be given in its simplest form.

 Calculator tip

It is important to understand how your calculator deals with recurring decimals. Some calculators will round them off and other calculators will just cut them off (truncate them) at the end of the display area.

To find out what your calculator does, enter 2 ÷ 3 on your calculator.

If you get 0.666 666 666 then your calculator truncates the recurring decimal.

If you get 0.666 666 667 then your calculator rounds the last available decimal place.

WORKED EXAMPLE 2

Convert each of the following recurring decimals to fractions:

a $0.\dot{4}$ b $0.\dot{2}\dot{4}$ c $0.2\dot{3}$

a $0.\dot{4}$

Let $x = 0.444\ldots$ (1)   ◁ Equation 1.

Then $10x = 4.444\ldots$ (2)   ◁ There is **one** digit recurring so multiply equation 1 by 10 to get equation 2.

$10x - x = 4.444 - 0.444$ ◁ Subtract (1) from (2). This gets rid of the recurring digits.

$9x = 4$

So, $x = \dfrac{4}{9}$ ◁ Divide both sides by 9 to get x.

b $0.\dot{2}\dot{4}$

Let $x = 0.\dot{2}\dot{4}$ (1)   ◁ Equation 1.

Then $100x = 24.\dot{2}\dot{4}$ (2)   ◁ There are **two** digits recurring so multiply equation 1 by 100 to get equation 2.

$99x = 24.\dot{2}\dot{4} - 0.\dot{2}\dot{4}$ ◁ Subtract (1) from (2).

$99x = 24$

So, $x = \dfrac{24}{99} = \dfrac{8}{33}$ ◁ Divide both sides by 99 (and simplify if possible).

c $0.2\dot{3}$

Let $x = 0.2\dot{3}$ (1)   ◁ Equation 1.

Then $10x = 2.\dot{3}$ (2)   ◁ The recurring digit does not start immediately to the right of the decimal point, so multiply x by the appropriate power of ten until it does to get equation 2.

and $100x = 23.\dot{3}$ (3)   ◁ There is now **one** digit recurring so multiply equation 2 by 10 to get equation 3.

$100x - 10x = 23.\dot{3} - 2.\dot{3}$ ◁ Subtract (2) from (3).

$90x = 21$

So, $x = \dfrac{21}{90} = \dfrac{7}{30}$

EXERCISE 7F

1 Express each rational number as a decimal:

a $\dfrac{3}{8}$ b $\dfrac{5}{16}$ c $\dfrac{5}{11}$ d $\dfrac{4}{9}$

e $\dfrac{18}{7}$ f $\dfrac{7}{15}$ g $\dfrac{23}{7}$ h $\dfrac{8}{7}$

2 Express each decimal as a rational number:

a 0.888...   **b** 2.777...   **c** 0.812 812...   **d** 3.454 545...

e 1.999...   **f** 0.6565...   **g** 0.277 777...   **h** 2.499 999...

3 Write the following as exact fractions in simplest form:

a 0.$\dot{4}$ **b** 0.$\dot{7}\dot{4}$ **c** 0.8$\dot{7}$ **d** 0.11$\dot{4}$

e 0.$\dot{9}4\dot{3}$ **f** 0.1$\dot{8}5\dot{7}$ **g** 4.5$\dot{6}\dot{7}$ **h** 0.11$\dot{3}$

> **Calculator tip**
>
> Most calculators cannot deal with recurring fractions such as 0.$\dot{1}$ (although they can easily deal with 0.1), so you have to know how to convert these to exact fractions using algebra.

4 What is the exact length of line *AC* in this diagram?

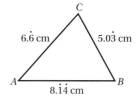

EXERCISE 7G

1 Write the following pairs of decimals as pairs of fractions in the form of $\dfrac{a}{b}$.

a 0.3 and 0.$\dot{3}$ **b** 0.17 and 0.$\dot{1}\dot{7}$ **c** 0.173 and 0.$\dot{1}7\dot{3}$

2 Use your results to make a conjecture about writing recurring decimals as fractions.

3 Test your conjecture using a few examples of your own.

Comment on what you find out.

 Checklist of learning and understanding

Decimals and fractions

- You can express decimals as fractions by writing them with a denominator that is a power of ten and then simplifying them. $0.4 = \dfrac{4}{10} = \dfrac{2}{5}$

- You can change fractions to decimals by dividing the numerator by the denominator. $\dfrac{3}{4} = 3 \div 4 = 0.75$

- Changing ordinary fractions to decimals makes it easier to compare their sizes using place value.

Calculations with decimals

- Pen and paper methods are important in the non-calculator exam paper.

- You can use any method as long as you show your working.

- Decimals can be added and subtracted by lining up the places and the decimal points.

Find answers at: cambridge.org/ukschools/gcsemaths-studentbookanswers

- Decimals can be multiplied like whole numbers as long as you insert the decimal point so there are the same number of decimal places in the answer as there were altogether in the numbers being multiplied.
- Decimals can be divided by making the divisor a whole number (multiply both numbers by a power of ten to do this). Then divide normally and insert the decimal point in the answer when you cross the decimal point in the number being divided.

Recurring decimals

- Recurring decimals can be written as fractions in the form of $\dfrac{a}{b}$. To do this, set up a pair of equations and subtract to get rid of the recurring digits, then simplify to get an answer.

 For additional questions on the topics in this chapter, visit GCSE Mathematics Online.

 Chapter review

1 Arrange each set of numbers in ascending order.

  a 4.2, 4.8, 4.22, 4.97, 4.08

  b 2.96, 2.955, $2\frac{46}{50}$, $2\frac{9}{25}$, 2.12

  c $\dfrac{3}{4}$, 0.86, $\dfrac{4}{5}$, 0.78, $\dfrac{5}{6}$, 0.91

2 Convert to decimals and insert $<$, $=$ or $>$ to compare the fractions.

  a $\dfrac{3}{5}\,\square\,\dfrac{12}{20}$ **b** $\dfrac{5}{6}\,\square\,\dfrac{7}{11}$ **c** $\dfrac{2}{9}\,\square\,\dfrac{1}{7}$

3 Write each as a fraction in its simplest terms.

  a 0.88   **b** 2.75   **c** 0.008

4 **a** Increase $\dfrac{2}{5}$ by 2.75   **b** Reduce 91.07 by $\dfrac{1}{2}$ of 42.8

  c Divide 4 by 0.125   **d** Multiply 0.4 by 0.8

5 **a** Add 4.726 and 3.09   **b** Subtract 2.916 from 4.008

  c Multiply 8.76 by 100   **d** Divide 18.07 by 1000

  e Multiply 4.12 by 0.7   **f** Simplify $\dfrac{32.64}{2.4}$

6 Jarryd and Kate have £16 each. Jarryd spends 0.415 of his money and Kate spends $\dfrac{7}{20}$ of hers.

Who has more money left? How much more?

7 Convert each recurring decimal to a fraction in its simplest form:

  a $0.\dot{2}$ **b** $0.\dot{5}\dot{4}$ **c** $0.8\dot{5}$ **d** $2.4\dot{3}\dot{8}$

  8 Express $0.2\dot{5}$ as a fraction in its simplest form.   *(3 marks)*

8 Powers and roots

In this chapter you will learn how to ...

- use integers and fractions to represent numbers in index notation.
- calculate with powers and roots.
- apply the rules for multiplying and dividing indices.

 For more resources relating to this chapter, visit GCSE Mathematics Online.

Using mathematics: real-life applications

Financial advisors and investors have to perform calculations involving powers and roots to work out the value of investments. They may use computer technology (apps) to work out different options to help their clients invest their money wisely.

 Calculator tip

Make sure you know which buttons to use to evaluate different powers and find different roots of numbers.

"I have to be able to understand, manipulate and evaluate different formulae to find the best investment. Many of these formulae involve fractional powers and different roots."

(Personal financial adviser)

Before you start ...

Ch 1	You should be able to quickly add and subtract pairs of integers mentally.	**1** Choose the correct sign: $<$, $=$ or $>$. **a** $-3 + -3 \;\square\; 4 + 2$ **b** $6 - 7 \;\square\; 3 - 4$ **c** $4 - (-5) \;\square\; -3 + -6$ **d** $-2 + 6 \;\square\; 9 - 5$

Ch 4	You need to be able to find the squares, cubes, square roots and cube roots of numbers.	**2** Choose the correct answer.
		a The area of a square with sides of 3 cm.
		    A $6\,\text{cm}^2$ **B** $9\,\text{cm}^2$ **C** $12\,\text{cm}^2$
		b $\sqrt[3]{27}$
		    A 9 **B** 5.2 **C** 3
		c $\sqrt{810000}$
		    A 9 **B** 90 **C** 900

Ch 6	You need to be able to find the reciprocal of a number or fraction.	**3** Find the reciprocal of each number. Choose from the values in the box. **a** $\frac{3}{4}$ **b** 12 **c** $1\frac{2}{5}$ $\boxed{\dfrac{12}{1} \quad \dfrac{4}{3} \quad \dfrac{1}{12} \quad \dfrac{7}{5} \quad \dfrac{5}{7}}$

Find answers at: cambridge.org/ukschools/gcsemaths-studentbookanswers

Assess your starting point using the Launchpad

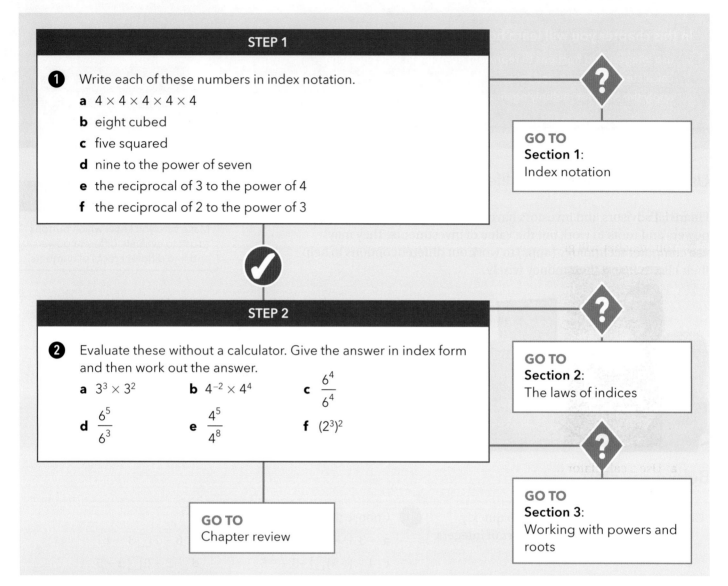

STEP 1

① Write each of these numbers in index notation.

a $4 \times 4 \times 4 \times 4 \times 4$

b eight cubed

c five squared

d nine to the power of seven

e the reciprocal of 3 to the power of 4

f the reciprocal of 2 to the power of 3

GO TO
Section 1:
Index notation

STEP 2

② Evaluate these without a calculator. Give the answer in index form and then work out the answer.

a $3^3 \times 3^2$ **b** $4^{-2} \times 4^4$ **c** $\dfrac{6^4}{6^4}$

d $\dfrac{6^5}{6^3}$ **e** $\dfrac{4^5}{4^8}$ **f** $(2^3)^2$

GO TO
Section 2:
The laws of indices

GO TO
Chapter review

GO TO
Section 3:
Working with powers and roots

Key vocabulary

index: a power or exponent indicating how many times a base number is used in a multiplication: index 2 means the number is squared (5×5); index 3 means it is cubed ($5 \times 5 \times 5$).

index notation: writing a number as a base and index, for example 2^3.

Tip

Any number to the power of 1 stays the same number so you don't usually write powers of 1.

Section 1: Index notation

You can use powers to write repeated multiplications in a shorter form.

For example: $6 \times 6 = 6^2$ and $5 \times 5 \times 5 = 5^3$

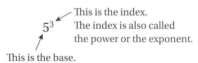

This is the index.
The index is also called the power or the exponent.

5^3

This is the base.

The **index** tells you how many times the base number is used in a multiplication.

When you write a number using an index you are using **index notation**.

7^4 is in index notation.

When you write the multiplication out in full you are using expanded form.

$7 \times 7 \times 7 \times 7$ is in expanded form.

The plural of index is indices.

Roots

You know that $5^2 = 25$ and so $\sqrt{25} = 5$.

Also, $2^3 = 8$ and so $\sqrt[3]{8} = 2$.

Mathematically, finding the root of a number is the inverse of working out the power of the number.

Powers of 2, 3, 4 and 5

It is useful to recognise the first few powers of 2, 3, 4 and 5. This can help you to work out their roots as well.

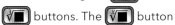

Calculator tip

You can find the square root or cube root of a number with your calculator using the $\boxed{\sqrt{\blacksquare}}$ and $\boxed{\sqrt[3]{\blacksquare}}$ buttons. The $\boxed{\sqrt[x]{\blacksquare}}$ button allows you find any root (fourth root, fifth root, and so on).

EXERCISE 8A

1 Your teacher will give you a copy of this table to complete.

Base \ Index	−3	−2	−1	0	1	2	3	4	5
2	$2^{-3} = \dfrac{1}{8}$	$2^{-2} =$	$2^{-1} = \dfrac{1}{2}$	$2^0 = 1$	$2^1 = 2$	$2^2 = 4$	$2^3 =$	$2^4 = 16$	$2^5 =$
3									
4									
5									

    a Use a calculator to work out the missing values in the table.

    b Compare the positive and negative values for the same index. What do you notice?

    c Compare the powers of 2 with the powers of 4. What do you notice?

    d How can you decide quickly that a whole number is *not* a power of 5?

2 Use the table that you completed in question 1 to decide whether each statement is true or false.

    a $2^4 = 4^2$ **b** $2^5 > 3^5$ **c** $2^0 = 5^0$

    d $2^1 = 2^{-1}$ **e** $3^4 > 4^3$ **f** $4^4 < 3^4$

    g $5^2 = 2^5$ **h** $3^5 > 5^3$ **i** $2^{-3} > 3^{-2}$

    j $3^{-3} = \dfrac{1}{27}$ **k** $5^{-1} = 4^{-1}$ **l** $2(2^{-1}) = 1$

3 Use your table to work these out without using a calculator.

    a $\sqrt{25}$ **b** $\sqrt[3]{8}$ **c** $\sqrt[4]{256}$

    d $\sqrt[3]{125}$ **e** $\sqrt[5]{243}$ **f** $\sqrt[3]{64}$

    g $\sqrt[3]{8} + \sqrt[4]{625}$ **h** $\sqrt{2500}$ **i** $\sqrt[5]{32} + \sqrt[4]{81}$

    j $\sqrt[3]{27\,000}$ **k** $\sqrt[4]{160\,000}$ **l** $\sqrt[5]{3125} \times \sqrt[4]{625}$

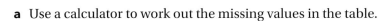

Find answers at: cambridge.org/ukschools/gcsemaths-studentbookanswers

Index notation on your calculator

Most calculators have one key to square a number:

Your calculator is also likely to have a key that allows you to enter any other powers quickly and easily. It may be y^x or x^y or a^b.

To enter 13^4, you press: 1 3 y^x 4 =

You will get a result of $28\,561$.

EXERCISE 8B

 1 Evaluate each expression without using a calculator.

a 2^3	**b** 6^2	**c** 1^8
d 8^3	**e** 10^4	**f** 10^6
g $2^3 - 1^5$	**h** $1^6 + 7^2$	**i** $2^4 \times 2^2$
j $2^4 + 4^2$	**k** $2^3 \times 2^4$	**l** $3^3 \times 3^3$
m $2^4 \div 2^3$	**n** $4^5 \div 4^3$	**o** $7^2 \times 10^3$
p 7×10^6	**q** $2 \times 10^2 + 3 \times 10^3$	**r** $6^2 \times 10^6$

2 Use your calculator to evaluate the following.

a 4^6	**b** 12^3	**c** 8^5	**d** 7^4
e 15^3	**f** 10^4	**g** 28^2	**h** 25^3

3 Use a calculator to find the value of each expression.

a $12^3 - 2^8$	**b** $20^4 - 15^2$	**c** $15^3 \times 15^2$
d $3^{12} + 3^4$	**e** $3^6 + 2^8$	**f** $35^3 \div 5^3$

4 Fill in $<$ or $>$ to make each statement true.

a $4^6 \;\square\; 6^4$	**b** $10^3 \;\square\; 3^{10}$	**c** $4^9 \;\square\; 9^4$
d $15^2 \;\square\; 2^{15}$	**e** $9^8 \;\square\; 8^9$	**f** $2^{10} \;\square\; 10^2$

Zero and negative indices

Look at this table of powers of 10.

Index notation	Expanded form	Value
10^6	$10 \times 10 \times 10 \times 10 \times 10 \times 10$	$1\,000\,000$
10^5	$10 \times 10 \times 10 \times 10 \times 10$	$100\,000$
10^4	$10 \times 10 \times 10 \times 10$	$10\,000$
10^3	$10 \times 10 \times 10$	$1\,000$
10^2	10×10	100
10^1	10	10

In the table each value is $\frac{1}{10}$ of the value above it. (In other words $10^6 \div 10 = 10^5$).
If you continue dividing by 10 you get this pattern for smaller and smaller indices:

Index notation	Expanded form	Value
10^0	$10 \div 10 = 1$	1
10^{-1}	$1 \div 10$	$\frac{1}{10}$
10^{-2}	$\frac{1}{10} \div 10$	$\frac{1}{100}$
10^{-3}	$\frac{1}{100} \div 10$	$\frac{1}{1000}$
10^{-4}	$\frac{1}{1000} \div 10$	$\frac{1}{10000}$

Tip

Remember that we use the reciprocals to change fraction divisions into multiplications.

$\frac{1}{10} \div 10 = \frac{1}{10} \times \frac{1}{10} = \frac{1}{100}$

The pattern in the table shows two very useful features of indices.

> Any number with an index of 0 is equal to 1
> $a^0 = 1$ (except for 0^0 which is undefined).
>
> So, for example, $5^0 = 1$ and $7^0 = 1$

Tip

An index can also be a fraction. You will deal with fractional index notation in *Section 2* because it is easier to understand how it works when you know the laws of indices.

> Any number with a negative index is equal to its reciprocal with a positive index $a^{-m} = \frac{1}{a^m}$
>
> So, for example, $4^{-2} = \frac{1}{4^2}$ and $5^{-3} = \frac{1}{5^3}$

EXERCISE 8C

1 Write each of the following using positive indices only.

a 2^{-1} **b** 3^{-1} **c** 4^{-1} **d** 3^{-2}

e 4^{-3} **f** 3^{-5} **g** 3^{-4} **h** 6^{-6}

i 34^{-5} **j** x^{-3} **k** m^{-2} **l** $3x^{-4}$

2 Express the following with negative indices.

a $\frac{1}{3}$ **b** $\frac{1}{5}$ **c** $\frac{1}{7}$ **d** $\frac{1}{3^2}$

e $\frac{1}{4^5}$ **f** $\frac{1}{2^6}$ **g** $\frac{1}{7^2}$ **h** $\frac{1}{10^5}$

i $\frac{1}{2^2}$ **j** $\frac{1}{12^3}$ **k** $\frac{1}{10^4}$ **l** $\frac{1}{3(2)^2}$

m $\frac{1}{x^2}$ **n** $\frac{1}{x^3}$ **o** $\frac{4}{y^2}$

Find answers at: cambridge.org/ukschools/gcsemaths-studentbookanswers

3 Fill in = or ≠ in each of these statements.

a $10^{-1} \square \dfrac{1}{10}$ **b** $6^0 \square 1$ **c** $6^{-1} \square \dfrac{1}{6}$

d $10^{-2} \square \dfrac{2}{10}$ **e** $6^{-3} \square \dfrac{1}{6^3}$ **f** $10^0 \square 1$

g $6^{-4} \square \dfrac{1}{6^4}$ **h** $\dfrac{1}{10^4} \square 10^{-4}$ **i** $\dfrac{1}{6^3} \square \dfrac{3}{6}$

j $\dfrac{1}{4}(x^{-1}) \square 4x$ **k** $\dfrac{10}{m^5} \square -10m^5$ **l** $0.5x^{-3} \square \dfrac{1}{2x^3}$

4 Write each of the following in the form of 2^x.

a 2   **b** 16   **c** 64

d $\dfrac{1}{8}$ **e** 0.25   **f** 1

g $\dfrac{1}{32}$ **h** $\sqrt{16}$ **i** $-\sqrt{64}$

Section 2: The laws of indices

The laws of indices are a set of rules that allow you to multiply and divide powers without writing them out in expanded form.

Law of indices for multiplication

Consider: $3^4 \times 3^2 = (3 \times 3 \times 3 \times 3) \times (3 \times 3) = 3^6$

Can you see a short-cut?

$3^4 \times 3^2 = 3^{4+2} = 3^6$

You get the same result by adding the indices.

To multiply two numbers in index notation you add the indices.

$a^m \times a^n = a^{m+n}$

This law works for all indices, including negative indices.

For example $2^3 \times 2^{-2} = 2^{3+(-2)} = 2^1 = 2$

Tip

Note that this only works if it is the **same base number**.
So, $2^3 \times 2^5 = 2^8$
but $4^3 \times 5^6$ cannot be simplified by this rule.

Law of indices for division

Consider: $2^5 \div 2^2 = \dfrac{2 \times 2 \times 2 \times 2 \times 2}{2 \times 2} = 2^3$

You should notice that:

$2^5 \div 2^2 = 2^{5-2} = 2^3$

You get the same result by subtracting the indices.

To divide two numbers in index notation you subtract the indices.

$a^m \div a^n = a^{m-n}$

This law works for all indices, including negative indices.

$2^2 \div 2^4 = 2^{2-4} = 2^{-2}$

Tip

$a^m \div a^n$ can be written as $\dfrac{a^m}{a^n}$

You can understand how this works by looking at the expanded notation:

$2^2 \div 2^4 = \dfrac{2 \times 2}{2 \times 2 \times 2 \times 2}$

If you cancel you get $\dfrac{1}{2 \times 2}$

$\dfrac{1}{2^2}$ is equal to 2^{-2}

Law of indices for powers of indices

$(3^2)^3$ means 3^2 all to the power of 3 which is $3^2 \times 3^2 \times 3^2$

$3^2 \times 3^2 \times 3^2 = 3^6$ (applying the law of indices for multiplication).

You should notice that:

$(3^2)^3 = 3^{(2 \times 3)} = 3^6$

To find the power of a power you multiply the indices.

$(a^m)^n = a^{mn}$

This law works for all indices, including negative indices.

$(4^3)^{-4} = 4^{(3) \times (-4)} = 4^{-12}$

> **Tip**
>
> The laws of indices also help to show that $a^0 = 1$
>
> $4^3 \div 4^3 = 4^{3-3} = 4^0$
>
> You already know that any number divided by itself is 1, so $4^3 \div 4^3 = 1$
>
> But this is also equal to 4^0, so 4^0 must equal 1.

EXERCISE 8D

1 Simplify. Leave the answers in index notation.

a $2^4 \times 2^3$
b $10^2 \times 10^5$
c $4^3 \times 4^3$

d 5×5^6
e $2^4 \times 2^7$
f $3^2 \times 3^{-4}$

g $2^{-2} \times 2^5$
h $3^0 \times 3^2$
i $2 \times 2^3 \times 2^{-5}$

j $3^2 \times 3^2 \times 3$
k $10^2 \times 10^{-3} \times 10^2$
l $10^0 \times 10^{-2} \times 10^2$

2 Simplify. Leave the answers in index notation.

a $6^4 \div 6^2$
b $10^5 \div 10^2$
c $6^5 \div 6^3$

d $6^3 \div 6^5$
e $10^3 \div 10^5$
f $3^{10} \div 3^0$

g $3^8 \div 3$
h $10^4 \div 10^4$
i $\dfrac{5^4}{5^{-2}}$

j $\dfrac{10^6}{10^{-4}}$
k $\dfrac{3^{-2}}{3^{-3}}$
l $\dfrac{2^0}{2^3}$

3 Simplify each expression. Give the answers in index notation.

a $(2^2)^3$
b $(2^3)^3$
c $(2^4)^2$

d $(10^2)^2$
e $(10^2)^3$
f $(10^4)^2$

g $(2^4)^{-3}$
h $(10^{-2})^2$
i $(10^2)^{-3}$

j $(3^4)^{-2}$
k $(2^3)^0$
l $(2^2 \times 2^3)^2$

4 Say whether each statement is true or false. If it is false, write the correct answer.

a $3^3 \times 3^5 = 3^8$
b $3^8 \div 3^2 = 3^4$
c $10^8 \div 10^2 = 10^6$

d $(3^3)^2 = 3^6$
e $121^0 = 1$
f $4^5 \times 4^2 = 4^7$

g $3^{10} \div 3^2 = 3^5$
h $(4^2)^4 = 4^8$
i $(3^2)^0 = 1$

Find answers at: cambridge.org/ukschools/gcsemaths-studentbookanswers

Fractional indices

The law of indices for multiplication can be used to explain the meaning of fractional indices.

$$3^{\frac{1}{2}} \times 3^{\frac{1}{2}} = 3^{\frac{1}{2}+\frac{1}{2}} = 3^1 = 3$$

Add the indices using the law above.

But you also know that $\sqrt{3} \times \sqrt{3} = 3$

So, $3^{\frac{1}{2}}$ must equal $\sqrt{3}$ for this to be the case.

Similarly:

$$8^{\frac{1}{3}} \times 8^{\frac{1}{3}} \times 8^{\frac{1}{3}} = 8^{\left(\frac{1}{3}+\frac{1}{3}+\frac{1}{3}\right)} = 8^1 = 8$$

Add the indices using the law above.

But you also know that $\sqrt[3]{8} \times \sqrt[3]{8} \times \sqrt[3]{8} = 8$

$8^{\frac{1}{3}}$ must equal $\sqrt[3]{8}$ for this to be the case.

From this you can see that $x^{\frac{1}{2}}$ is the square root of x and $y^{\frac{1}{3}}$ is the cube root of y. This gives us a general rule:

$$\sqrt{x} = x^{\frac{1}{2}} \qquad \text{and} \qquad \sqrt[3]{x} = x^{\frac{1}{3}}$$

So, $\sqrt[n]{x} = x^{\frac{1}{n}}$ (the nth root of x is the same as x to the power of $\frac{1}{n}$).

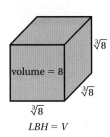

area = 3

$S^2 = A$

volume = 8

$LBH = V$

WORKED EXAMPLE 1

Rewrite as roots.

a $5^{\frac{1}{2}}$ **b** $4^{\frac{1}{5}}$

a $5^{\frac{1}{2}} = \sqrt{5}$ **b** $4^{\frac{1}{5}} = \sqrt[5]{4}$

> The denominator tells you what root you are dealing with.

WORKED EXAMPLE 2

Express each value in index notation.

a $\sqrt{90}$ **b** $\sqrt[4]{2-x}$

a $\sqrt{90} = 90^{\frac{1}{2}}$ **b** $\sqrt[4]{2-x} = (2-x)^{\frac{1}{4}}$

> The root tells you the denominator of the fraction.

Other fractional indices

The general law above applies to fractions where the numerator is 1. You may also get indices where the fraction does not have a numerator of 1.

The index law for raising a power of a power can be used to make a general rule for these fractions.

$$4^{\frac{2}{3}} = \left(4^{\frac{1}{3}}\right)^2 \qquad \frac{1}{3} \times 2 = \frac{2}{3}$$

$$2^{\frac{3}{4}} = \left(2^{\frac{1}{4}}\right)^3 \qquad \frac{1}{4} \times 3 = \frac{3}{4}$$

You already know that a unit fraction gives a root. So you can rewrite these expressions by writing the part inside the bracket as a root like this:

$$\left(4^{\frac{1}{3}}\right)^2 = \left(\sqrt[3]{4}\right)^2 \qquad \text{and} \qquad \left(2^{\frac{1}{4}}\right)^3 = \left(\sqrt[4]{2}\right)^3$$

So, $4^{\frac{2}{3}} = \left(\sqrt[3]{4}\right)^2$ and $2^{\frac{3}{4}} = \left(\sqrt[4]{2}\right)^3$

In general terms:

$$x^{\frac{m}{n}} = \left(x^{\frac{1}{n}}\right)^m = \left(\sqrt[n]{x}\right)^m \qquad \text{(the nth root of x to the power of m).}$$

Tip

When you work with fractional indices, it is important to remember that $\sqrt{(x)^n}$ is equivalent to $\left(\sqrt{x}\right)^n$ and that the operations can be done in any order.

For example, $(16)^{\frac{5}{2}} = \sqrt{(16)^5} = \sqrt{1048576} = 1024$

But you can also work this out as $\left(\sqrt{16}\right)^5 = 4^5 = 1024$, which can be done without using a calculator to find the root.

WORKED EXAMPLE 3

Write using root notation and then work out the value of each expression.

a $27^{\frac{2}{3}}$ **b** $5^{\frac{3}{4}}$

a $27^{\frac{2}{3}} = \left(\sqrt[3]{27}\right)^2$

Remember, the denominator gives the root.

$= (3)^2$
$= 9$

You should know that the cube root of 27 is 3, but you can work it out if you need to.

b $5^{\frac{3}{4}} = \left(\sqrt[4]{5}\right)^3$

$= 3.344$ (correct to 3 decimal places)

Tip

The index laws apply to all indices, including negative and fractional indices.

$2^3 \times 2^{-2} = 2^{3 + (-2)} = 2^1 = 2$ and $3^{\frac{1}{2}} \times 3^{\frac{1}{4}} = 3^{\left(\frac{1}{2} + \frac{1}{4}\right)} = 3^{\frac{3}{4}}$

$2^2 \div 2^4 = 2^{2-4} = 2^{-2}$ and $3^{\frac{3}{4}} \div 3^{\frac{1}{2}} = 3^{\left(\frac{3}{4} - \frac{1}{2}\right)} = 3^{\frac{1}{4}}$

$(4^3)^{-4} = 4^{(3) \times (-4)} = 4^{-12}$ and $\left(2^{\frac{1}{4}}\right)^{\frac{1}{2}} = 2^{\left(\frac{1}{4} \times \frac{1}{2}\right)} = 2^{\frac{1}{8}}$

Find answers at: cambridge.org/ukschools/gcsemaths-studentbookanswers

EXERCISE 8E

1 Rewrite each expression using root signs.

a $3^{\frac{1}{2}}$　　b $4^{\frac{1}{3}}$　　c $5^{\frac{1}{4}}$　　d $6^{\frac{1}{2}}$

e $4^{\frac{1}{9}}$　　f $5^{\frac{2}{3}}$　　g $4^{\frac{3}{8}}$　　h $6^{\frac{2}{9}}$

2 Write in index notation.

a $\sqrt{6}$　　b $\sqrt[3]{4}$　　c $\sqrt[3]{11}$　　d $\sqrt[4]{9}$

e $\left(\sqrt[3]{3}\right)^4$　　f $\sqrt[5]{7}$　　g $\left(\sqrt[3]{7}\right)^2$　　h $2\left(\sqrt[3]{3}\right)^5$

3 Evaluate.

a $8^{\frac{1}{3}}$　　　　　b $32^{\frac{1}{5}}$　　　　　c $8^{\frac{4}{3}}$

d $216^{\frac{2}{3}}$　　　　e $256^{\frac{3}{4}}$　　　　f $256^{-\frac{1}{4}}$

g $125^{-\frac{4}{3}}$　　　h $\left(\dfrac{8}{27}\right)^{-\frac{1}{3}}$　　i $\left(\dfrac{8}{18}\right)^{-\frac{1}{2}}$

Section 3: Working with powers and roots

Estimating powers and roots

You can use what you already know about square and cube numbers and their roots to estimate the approximate value of other powers and roots. For example, you can estimate the square root of a number that is not a perfect square by working out where it lies on a number line in relation to the square number below it and above it.

WORKED EXAMPLE 4

Estimate $\sqrt{98}$.

$\sqrt{81} < \sqrt{98} < \sqrt{100}$

> First find the perfect squares closest to 98. These are 81 and 100.

$9 < \sqrt{98} < 10$

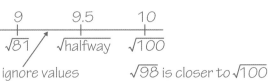

> Now use trial and improvement to estimate more accurately.

ignore values <9.5　　　$\sqrt{98}$ is closer to $\sqrt{100}$ so try 9.9

Check: $9.9 \times 9.9 = 98.01$
As $98.01 \approx 98$, we can state $\sqrt{98} \approx 9.9$

Tip

Remember your estimate may not be an exact value, but it should be close. Usually a value correct to two decimal places is good enough. If you use a calculator you will see that $\sqrt{98}$ is 9.899..., so 9.9 is a fairly accurate estimate.

You can use a similar method using your calculator to find the approximate value of a power by trial and error.

WORKED EXAMPLE 5

If $2^x = 18$, estimate the value of x.

$2^4 = 16$
$2^5 = 32$
So $4 < x < 5$

Use what you know.

Close to 16, so x must be closer to 4 than to 5.

Try
   $2^{4.1} = 17.14...$ Too small
   $2^{4.2} = 18.37...$ Too big
x must be between 4.1 and 4.2

Now use trial and improvement.

Try
   $2^{4.15} = 17.75...$ Too small
   $2^{4.16} = 17.87...$ Too small
   $2^{4.17} = 18.00$ Correct (to 2 decimal places)

So $x \approx 4.17$

EXERCISE 8F

1 Estimate the following roots. Show your working.

   a $\sqrt{72}$ **b** $\sqrt{33}$ **c** $\sqrt{6}$ **d** $\sqrt[3]{29}$ **e** $\sqrt[3]{-200}$ **f** $\sqrt[4]{37}$

2 Use a calculator to find the roots in question 1 correct to 2 decimal places. How good were your estimates?

3 Find the value of x in each of the following by trial and improvement. Show your working.

   a $2^x = 25$ **b** $3^x = 36$ **c** $2^x = 280$

   d $x^4 = 1296$ **e** $x^3 = 12$ **f** $x^3 = 7000$

4 Find four different pairs of values for a and m which will satisfy the equation $a^m = 81$

5 Use trial and improvement methods to find the length of sides of a square piece of plastic with an area of $90\,mm^2$.

6 A cube of sodium has a volume of $800\,mm^3$. Find the lengths of the side of the cube correct to 2 decimal places using trial and improvement methods.

Find answers at: cambridge.org/ukschools/gcsemaths-studentbookanswers

Solving problems involving powers and roots

Some problems seem difficult and confusing because they are so long and wordy. A good strategy for these problems is to rewrite the problem using only the most important words and numbers.

Problem-solving framework

Naresh wants to have £5000 saved in three years' time to buy a car.

He finds an account that offers an interest rate of 2.9% compounded annually.

His sister tells him that you can work out how much you need to put away now to have an amount in the future using the formula:

Principal amount (P) = Future value $(F) \times (1.029)^{-3}$

Use the formula to calculate how much Naresh should put into the account to have £5000 in 3 years' time.

Steps for solving problems	What you would do for this example
Step 1: Read the problem carefully and highlight the important words and numbers.	Naresh wants to have **£5000 saved in three years' time** to buy a car. He finds an account that offers an **interest rate of 2.9% compounded annually**. His sister tells him that you can work out how much you need to put away now to have an amount in the future using the formula: **Principal amount (P) = Future value $(F) \times (1.029)^{-3}$** **Use the formula** to calculate how much Naresh should put into the account to have £5000 in 3 years' time.
Step 2: Jot down the important words and numbers only.	Future value: £5000 Formula: $P = F(1.029)^{-3}$ We need to find P.
Step 3: Rewrite the problem again in mathematical terms to show what you need to do.	$P = £5000 \times (1.029)^{-3}$ Now you can see that the complicated word problem is really quite a simple substitution problem that you can work out in one step with your calculator.
Step 4: Do the necessary calculation.	4589.061... Naresh needs to put £4589.06 into the account now. **Calculator tip** On some calculators you might have to enter Work out how to enter a negative index number on your calculator.

EXERCISE 8G

 1 Shamila received an inheritance of £2500. She wants to invest it for 10 years in an account that offers 5% growth but she wants to know how much money she will have after the 10-year period. Her auntie works in a bank and she tells Shamila how to work this out quickly using the formula:

Value of future investment = Original amount $\times (1.05)^{10}$

a Work out how much money Shamila will have in 10 years.

b How much will she have if she decides to spend £500 and put the rest of the money into this investment?

c How could you change this formula to work out the future value of an investment if the interest rate is 3% and the period of the investment is 18 months?

d Use your formula to find the future value of £3200 invested under these conditions.

 2 Many hot and cold drinks contain caffeine. A 350 ml energy drink contains 120 mg of caffeine.

Caffeine is a stimulant and it takes time for your body to break it down.

You can use the formula $100\left(\dfrac{1}{2}\right)^{\frac{n}{5}}$ to find the percentage of caffeine still in your system a number of hours (n) after drinking something containing caffeine.

Marie and Suki apply the formula to find out how many milligrams of caffeine will remain in their system 3 hours after drinking a 350 ml energy drink. This is how each student worked:

Marie's working	Suki's working
% caffeine $= 100(\frac{1}{2})^{\frac{n}{5}}$ $= 100(0.5)^{\frac{3}{5}}$ $= 2.5\%$ 2.5% of 120 mg = 3 mg	% C $= 100(0.5)^{\frac{3}{5}}$ $= 65.98...\%$ $65.98...\%$ of 120 mg = 79.17 mg (to 2 d.p.)

a Which answer is correct? What did the other student do wrong?

b What percentage of caffeine is left in your body $\dfrac{1}{2}$ hour after drinking any caffeinated drink?

 3 The time (t seconds) a ball takes to hit the ground after being dropped

from a height (h metres) can be found using the formula $t = \sqrt{\dfrac{h}{4.9}}$

a Work out how long it will take a ball dropped from a height of 3.6 m to hit the ground.

b Matt drops a ball from a height of 2.5 m and Nina drops a ball from a height of 3.6 m.

I Whose ball will hit the ground first?

ii How many seconds later will the second ball hit the ground?

 Find answers at: cambridge.org/ukschools/gcsemaths-studentbookanswers

4 Biologists have discovered that many measurements in humans and other mammals are in proportion to the mass of the body. This has allowed them to develop a number of formulae for estimating a number of different measurements. Here are four different formulae which use mass (m) in kilograms to determine other measurements.

Tip

These formulae are all based on a constant of proportionality (k). You will learn more about this in Chapter 35 when you deal with direct and inverse proportion.

Mass of the brain (B) in kilograms	Surface area of the skin (S) in square metres	Resting metabolic rate (C) (calories consumed at rest)	Time (T) it takes for the blood to circulate in seconds
$B = 0.01\,m^{\frac{2}{3}}$	$S = 0.0096\,m^{\frac{7}{10}}$	$C = 70\left(\sqrt[4]{m}\right)^{3}$	$T = 17.4\left(\sqrt[4]{m}\right)$

a Work out all of these values based on your own mass in kilograms.

b Compare the circulation time for an elephant (average mass 5000 kg) and a human male (average mass 70 kg).

c What is the brain of a 4.5 kg cat likely to weigh?

d Find the surface area of the skin of a mouse of mass 0.3 kg and a cat of mass 4.5 kg.

e How many calories does a 145 kg lion consume while lying in the sun sleeping?

f Why are all the values found using these formulae only approximates?

5 Kepler's law can be used to work out the time (T) in Earth days that it takes for a planet to complete an orbit around the sun. The formula for this is $T = 0.2\,R^{\frac{3}{2}}$, where R is the mean distance from the planet to the Sun in millions of kilometres.

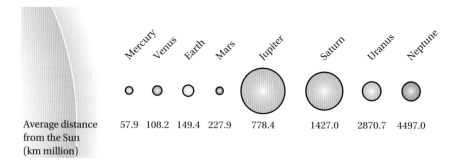

	Mercury	Venus	Earth	Mars	Jupiter	Saturn	Uranus	Neptune
Average distance from the Sun (km million)	57.9	108.2	149.4	227.9	778.4	1427.0	2870.7	4497.0

a Use the formula to find to the nearest day the time it takes the Earth to orbit the Sun. (If you don't get 365 days as an answer you know you are doing something wrong!)

b Which takes longer to orbit the Sun: Jupiter or Uranus? How much longer does it take?

c Which planet orbits the Sun in the shortest time? Explain how you know this and then work out how long it takes.

Checklist of learning and understanding

Index notation

- Numbers can be expressed as powers of their factors using index notation.
  - $2 \times 2 \times 2 \times 2$ can be written in index notation as 2^4.
  - The 4 is the index (also called the power or the exponent) and it tells us how many times the base (2) must be multiplied by itself.
- Any number to the power of 0 is equal to 1: $a^0 = 1$
- A negative index is the reciprocal of a positive index: $a^{-m} = \dfrac{1}{a^m}$

Laws of indices

- Multiplication: $a^m \times a^n = a^{m+n}$
- Division: $\dfrac{a^m}{a^n} = a^{m-n}$
- Raising to a power: $(a^m)^n = a^{mn}$

Working with powers and roots

- Finding the root of a number is the inverse of raising the number to a power.

  For example, $4^2 = 16$ and $\sqrt{16} = 4$

- Powers and roots can be estimated using a number line to locate them in relation to known powers and roots and then finding an accurate estimate by trial and improvement.

- Many real-life calculations rely on formulae containing integer and fractional indices and roots.

Chapter review

For additional questions on the topics in this chapter, visit GCSE Mathematics Online.

1 Write each number in index form.

   a $8 \times 8 \times 8 \times 8 \times 8$ **b** three cubed   **c** $\dfrac{1}{64}$ **d** $\left(\sqrt{5}\right)^3$

2 **a** Find the value of 5^0 *(1 mark)*

     b Find the value of $27^{\frac{1}{3}}$ *(1 mark)*

     c Find the value of 2^{-3} *(1 mark)*

©*Pearson Education Ltd 2012*

3 Put each set of expressions in order from smallest to greatest.

   a $3^4, \sqrt{81}, 10^2, 4^3, 2 \times \sqrt{121}$ **b** $4^5, 5^4, 10^3, 96^0, 3^2, 20^2$

   c $\sqrt[3]{4}, 4^{\frac{3}{2}}, 4^2, \left(\dfrac{1}{4}\right)^{\frac{3}{2}}$

4 Write these numbers with positive indices.

   a 3^{-3} **b** 2^{-10} **c** 5^{-2}

 Find answers at: cambridge.org/ukschools/gcsemaths-studentbookanswers

5 Use the laws of indices to simplify each expression and write it as a single power of 4.

a $4^2 \times 4^2$ **b** $4^6 \times 4^{-3}$ **c** $4^7 \div 4^3$

d $4^3 \div 4^5$ **e** $(4^3)^2$ **f** $(4^{-2})^2$

6 Evaluate. Check your answers with a calculator.

a $\sqrt{121}$ **b** $\sqrt{0.25}$ **c** $\sqrt[3]{125}$

d $\sqrt[5]{32}$ **e** $\sqrt[4]{81}$ **f** $\sqrt{\dfrac{1}{4}}$

g $9^{\frac{3}{2}}$ **h** $(-27)^{\frac{2}{3}}$ **i** $8^{\frac{4}{3}}$

7 Estimate the length of each side of a cube of volume $35\,\text{cm}^3$. Show your working.

8 Electricians use the formula $V = \sqrt{PR}$ to work out voltage (V) when P is the power in watts and R is the resistance in ohms. Calculate the voltage when $P = 2000$ and $R = 24.2$.

9 The length of time (T seconds) it takes for a pendulum of length (L) in metres to swing through one complete movement can be calculated using the formula $T = 2\pi\left(\dfrac{L}{9.8}\right)^{\frac{1}{2}}$

a Work out how long it will take for a pendulum of length $0.25\,\text{m}$ to complete one swing.

b How does the length of the pendulum affect how long it takes to complete one swing? Justify your answer.

10 The radius of a cylindrical container can be found using the formula $r = \sqrt{\dfrac{V}{\pi h}}$, where V is the volume and h is the height of the container.

Pete has a $12\,\text{cm}$ tall cylindrical tin with a volume of $500\,\text{cm}^3$. He wants to use it to store round biscuits of diameter $7\,\text{cm}$. Will they fit?

9 Rounding, estimation and accuracy

In this chapter you will learn how to …

- approximate values by rounding them to different degrees of accuracy.
- recognise the difference between rounding and truncating.
- use approximations to estimate and check the results of calculations.
- understand and apply limits of accuracy in numbers and measurements.
- calculate the upper and lower bounds of a calculation (for discrete and continuous quantities).

 For more resources relating to this chapter, visit GCSE Mathematics Online.

Using mathematics: real-life applications

When you read that 34 000 people attended a festival, the actual number is likely to be slightly less or slightly more than that. When you roughly estimate what you spent over the weekend, look at an object and guess it is about $2\frac{1}{2}$ m long or say things like, "I live about 15 kilometres from school," you are estimating and using approximate values.

"I round off the prices to the nearest pound and keep a mental running total of the costs of things I put in my trolley so I know that I am not over-spending."

(Consumer)

Before you start …

Chs 1, 4	You should be able to use rounding to quickly estimate the answers to calculations.	**1** Use rounded values to estimate and decide whether each answer is correct without doing the calculation. **a** $312 - 56 = 256$ **b** $479 \times 17 = 3142$ **c** $350 + 351 - 96 = 798$
Ch 7	You should be able to calculate with decimals and estimate to decide whether an answer is reasonable.	**2** Say whether each statement is true or false. **a** $5.8 \times 6.72 \approx 42$ **b** $3.789 + 234.6 \approx 4 + 230$ **c** $0.00432 + 3.55 \approx 4$ **d** $4 \times \pi \approx 12$
Ch 7	You need to be able to work confidently with decimals and place value.	**3** Write the number halfway between: **a** 3.0 and 5.0 **b** 3.5 and 3.6 **c** 0.02 and 0.07

Find answers at: cambridge.org/ukschools/gcsemaths-studentbookanswers

Assess your starting point using the Launchpad

STEP 1

1 Round each value to the degree of accuracy specified.

   a 86 to the nearest 10.

   b 1565 to the nearest 1000.

   c 134.1234 to 2 decimal places.

   d 19.999 to 1 decimal place.

   e 1235.26 to 1 significant figure.

   f 234 650 034 to 3 significant figures.

2 The length of a metal component is found to be 0.937 cm. What is its length to the nearest millimetre?

3 The cost of an international call on an itemised phone bill is given as £5.159 32.

   a What is this amount truncated to the nearest penny?

   b What is this amount rounded to 2 decimal places?

GO TO
Section 1:
Approximate values

STEP 2

4 Estimate the cost of 12 packets of seeds at £1.36 each.

5 Approximately how many litres of petrol can you get for £20 if each litre costs £1.89?

6 Use rounding to find an approximate answer to each calculation.

   a $\dfrac{784 + 572}{109}$ **b** $(2.099)^2$ **c** $\dfrac{3.803 + 7.52}{3.29}$

7 A piece of wire is 10 m long, correct to the nearest metre. Complete the following statement to show the longest and shortest possible lengths that this wire could be.

$$\square \leqslant 10 \text{ m} < \square$$

8 If $a = 3.6$ (correct to 1 decimal place) and $b = 14$ (correct to the nearest whole number), find the upper and lower bounds of:

   a $a + b$ **b** ab **c** $\dfrac{a+b}{a}$

GO TO
Section 2:
Approximation and estimation

GO TO
Section 3:
Limits of accuracy

GO TO
Chapter review

Section 1: Approximate values

If someone asks you what you spend on mobile phone calls each week you are more likely to answer "about £10" than to say "exactly £10 and 24 pence". In the same way, the weather service will report that temperatures reached a record high of 37° rather than saying 36.895 79°.

Approximation allows you to give numbers in a more convenient form by writing them in a simpler, but less accurate way.

Rounded values

Rounding is used in calculations where a precise answer is not required because of the size of the numbers involved or the purpose for which you need the answer.

Numbers can be rounded to:

- the nearest whole number or place value (tens, hundreds or thousands)
- a particular number of decimal places
- a particular number of significant figures.

To round, or approximate, a number correct to a given place value, find the specified place value and look at the next digit to the right. If this is 5 or greater, you round up. If it is less than 5, you round down.

This rule applies to whole numbers and decimals whether you are rounding to given place values or to a given number of significant figures.

Rounding whole numbers

Consider the number 456 789. It can be rounded to different degrees of accuracy.

456 789 rounded to the nearest ten	456 790
456 789 rounded to the nearest hundred	456 800
456 789 rounded to the nearest thousand	457 000

In a test or exam you may be told to round numbers to a given **degree of accuracy**.

EXERCISE 9A

1 Choose the correct approximation of each animal's weight.

Weight of an animal		Rounded to	Identify the correct one	
a cow	635 kg	nearest 10 kg	**A** 630 kg	**B** 640 kg
b horse	526 kg	nearest 100 kg	**A** 500 kg	**B** 600 kg
c sheep	96 kg	nearest 10 kg	**A** 90 kg	**B** 100 kg
d dog	32 kg	nearest 10 kg	**A** 30 kg	**B** 40 kg
e cat	5.2 kg	nearest 10 kg	**A** 0 kg	**B** 10 kg

Key vocabulary

rounding: writing a number with zeros in the place of some digits.

Tip

You may need to write in some zeros so that the digits of your answer have the correct place value.

Key vocabulary

degree of accuracy: the number of places to which you round a number.

2 **a** Round each value to the nearest whole number.

    i 54.8   **ii** 10.6   **iii** 9.4   **iv** 12.3

    b Round each value to the nearest 10.

    i 26   **ii** 57.5   **iii** 111.1   **iv** 35 814

    c Round each value to the nearest 100.

    i 458   **ii** 5732   **iii** 2389   **iv** 35 814

    d Round each value to the nearest 1000.

    i 2590   **ii** 176   **iii** 35 814   **iv** 66 876

    e Round the following to the nearest hundred thousand.

    i 123 456   **ii** 1 234 567   **iii** 12 354 642   **iv** 123 456 789

    f Round the following to the nearest million.

    i 545 000   **ii** 555 000   **iii** 14 354 642   **iv** 546 267 789

3 **a** A food bill is £27.60. How much is this to the nearest pound?

    b There are 27 students in a class. What is this to the nearest 10 students?

    c I have £175 saved up. What is this to the nearest £100?

    d You need 167 cm of material to make a kite. Approximately how many metres do you need?

    e Sue says that the population of the United Kingdom is 63 793 234 which is 63.7 million to the nearest hundred thousand people. Is she correct?

4 What is $\sqrt{21}$ rounded to the nearest whole number?

Rounding decimals

In calculations you will often get answers with many more decimal places than you need. You will usually be told to give your answers to a specific number of decimal places.

Tip

The same rules for rounding whole numbers apply to decimals, but you also leave off any digits after the required number of decimal places.

WORKED EXAMPLE 1

Round:

a 54.149 to 1 decimal place   **b** 0.8751 to 2 decimal places

c 0.100 24 to 3 decimal places.

a 54.149
   54.1

> There is a 1 in the first decimal place. The next digit is 4, so round down.
>
> Leave the 1 unchanged and take off the digits to the right of it.

b 0.8751
   0.88

> There is a 7 in the second decimal place. The next digit is 5.
>
> Round 7 up to 8 and take off the digits to the right of it.

Continues on next page …

c 0.100 24
0.100

There is a 0 in the third decimal place. The next digit is 2.

Leave the 0 unchanged and take off the digits to the right of it.

In part **c**, the answer 0.100 is the same as 0.1, but you write the two zeros to show that the number is rounded to 3 decimal places.

Suitable levels of accuracy

Some questions will ask you to round answers to a suitable degree of accuracy. You will have to decide what to round to. This will depend on the degree of accuracy required by the situation or problem.

If the question involves quantities that can only be whole numbers, you round to the nearest whole number. It does not make sense to talk about 5.45 bricks or 9.15 tins of paint.

If the question involves money, you always round to 2 decimal places. An answer of £4.568 96 would be rounded to £4.57.

In mathematical or scientific calculations you usually work to a higher degree of accuracy than when you describe quantities in real life. If you are working with small values you might round them to tenths; if you are working with large numbers you might round to the nearest ten thousand or million.

When you calculate with decimals or significant figures, you generally round answers to no more than the number of places in the original values.

Tip

If you need 9.15 tins of paint, you can't round down to 9 tins. You need 10 tins. With only 9 tins, you might not have enough paint to finish the job.

EXERCISE 9B

1 Round each number to:

   i 1 decimal place **ii** 2 decimal places **iii** 3 decimal places.

a 4.526 38   **b** 25.256 37   **c** 125.617 38

d 0.537 921   **e** 32.3972

2 Write each value correct to 2 decimal places.

a 19.869 03   **b** 302.0428   **c** 0.292

d 0.205 28   **e** 21 245.8449   **f** 0.0039

g 0.0972   **h** 0.999 999 9   **i** 99.997

3 Round each value to a suitable level of accuracy. Explain your decisions.

a A large dog weighs 24.4872 kg.

b To calculate a circumference I use the value
π = 3.141 592 653 589 793 238 46...

c Dan's car can travel 13.7895 km per 1.000 098 7 litres of petrol.

d My share of a phone bill is £14.098 76

4 Bricks cost 83p each.

    a Ian wants 45 bricks, how much should this cost?

    b Ian pays £40 and tells the merchant to keep the change. How much has he paid per brick? (Give your answer to a suitable accuracy.)

5 A motorist travels 379 miles on 43 litres of petrol. How many miles per litre is this? (Give your answer to a suitable accuracy.)

6 What is $\sqrt{21}$ to 1 decimal place?

7 The department of the environment stated that, "The overall total extent of land and sea protected in England through national and international protected areas increased from 1 million to 2 million hectares between 2000 and 2013."

    a What level of accuracy do you think was used in each of these figures?

    b What is the smallest and greatest possible areas that the statement could refer to? Why?

Significant figures

In measurement and scientific calculations values are normally given to a level of accuracy that is certain to be correct. For example, a measure of 10.0 ml means the person measuring is certain that the measurement is 10 point something and not 9 point something or 11 point something. This measurement is given to three significant figures.

When you need to work with values with many digits or decimal places it is useful to **round to significant figures (s.f.)**.

The first **significant figure** in a number is the first non-zero digit when you read the number from left to right. All digits that follow are significant.

For example:

120 000 000	208.130	1.000 87	0.000 560 3

1st s.f.   1st s.f.   1st s.f.   1st s.f.

①20 000 000   ②08.130   ①.000 87   0.000⑤60 3

significant figures   significant figures   significant figures   significant figures

Tip

One significant figure does not mean that you will have only one digit in the answer. 12 756 is 10 000 correct to 1 significant figure, not '1' on its own.

Key vocabulary

significant figure (s.f.): a position in a number used to decide the level of accuracy. The first significant figure is the first non-zero digit when reading a number from the left.

round to significant figures: round to a specified level of accuracy from the first significant figure.

WORKED EXAMPLE 2

Write each figure correct to the given number of significant figures (s.f.).

a 308 000 000 (2 s.f.)   **b** 476.372 (4 s.f.)   **c** 2531.8 (2 s.f.)   **d** 0.004 36 (1 s.f.)

a

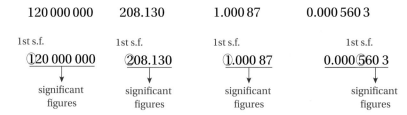

30|8 000 000

1st significant figure   digit to the right of the specified place
2nd significant figure

Read the number from left to right. Mark the first non-zero digit.

30|8 000 000 ≈ 310 000 000 (2 s.f.)

1st s.f.   >5

round to 2 s.f.   round up   state the level of accuracy

Include the zeros. 31 is not the same as 310 000 000

Continues on next page …

b
$$476.3|72 \approx 476.4 \ (4 \ \text{s.f.})$$
>5

1st s.f. round to 4 s.f. round up state the level of accuracy

Ignore digits after the rounding point if they are decimals

Count the required number of significant figures from there to find the rounding place.

c
$$25|31.8 \approx 2500 \ (2 \ \text{s.f.})$$
<5

1st s.f. round to 2 s.f. Leave as it is (round down) state the level of accuracy

Replace digits before the decimal point with zeros. Ignore digits after the decimal point.

Look at the digit to the right of this. If it is 5 or more round up; if it is less than 5 leave the digit unchanged.

d
$$0.004|36 \approx 0.004 \ (1 \ \text{s.f.})$$
<5

1st s.f. round to 1 s.f. Leave unchanged state the level of accuracy

Ignore digits to the right.

Use 0 as a place holder to fill any gaps between the rounding place and the decimal point (if there is one). Leave off any digits past your rounding place if they are after the decimal point.

EXERCISE 9C

1 **a** Round each value to 1 significant figure.

   i 789 **ii** 3874 **iii** 69 356 **iv** 0.0456

b Write correct to 2 significant figures.

   i 789 **ii** 3145 **iii** 0.003 325 **iv** 0.000 749 9

c Express each number correct to 3 significant figures.

   i 789 **ii** 46 712 **iii** 0.004 214 **iv** 753 413

d Round each value to 2 significant figures.

   i 37.673 **ii** −4127 **iii** 3.0392 **iv** 1 999 000

e Write correct to 3 significant figures.

   i 37.673 **ii** −4127 **iii** 3.0392 **iv** 1 999 000

2 Explain why it is more useful to round a value such as 0.000 134 567 to 2 significant figures than to 2 decimal places when you need to work with it.

3 **a** $\pi \approx 3.141\,592\,6$. What is this to 3 significant figures?

b The density of a gas is $1.234\,\text{kg/m}^3$. What is this to 2 significant figures?

c The speed of light is 299 792 458 m/s. What is this to 2 significant figures?

d The strength of gravity at the Earth's surface is $9.806\,65\,\text{m/s}^2$. What is this to 3 significant figures?

4 **a** What is $\sqrt{21}$ to 2 significant figures?

b How might it affect the accuracy of your results if you rounded $\sqrt{21}$ to 2 decimal places in one part of the calculation and to 2 significant figures in another?

Tip

Rounding numbers to a given number of decimal places means that you start the rounding at the decimal point.

Rounding numbers to significant figures means you start at the first significant figure, which can be before or after the decimal point.

Key vocabulary

truncation: cutting off all digits after a certain point without rounding.

Tip

When you calculate with rounded or truncated values your results will not be completely accurate. You will learn more about this in Section 3.

Did you know?

Truncation is used in statistics. A truncated mean is an average worked out by discarding (cutting off) very high or very low values in the data.

Truncation

Truncated means 'cut off'.

A decimal can be truncated by cutting off all the digits past a given point without rounding.

You will not generally use **truncation** to approximate values for calculation. However, you need to be aware that some calculator displays give a truncated rather than rounded value.

You can see this if you enter 2 ÷ 3. The display may show 0.66666666666

You know that $\frac{2}{3}$ can be expressed as the recurring decimal $0.\dot{6}$. So the calculator is showing a truncated value.

If you enter $\frac{20}{3}$ your screen will either show 6.6666666666 or 6.6666666667.

The first value is truncated, the second is rounded to 10 decimal places.

EXERCISE 9D

1 Truncate each number after the second decimal place.

    a 37.673   **b** −4.1275   **c** 3.0392   **d** 0.997

2 Truncate each number after the third significant figure.

    a 4.52638   **b** 25.25637   **c** 125.61738

    d 0.537921   **e** 32.397   **f** 200.6127

3 Consider splitting a bill of £20 equally between three people. What would each person pay? What method of approximation is most useful for deciding?

4 The interest on four accounts is accurately recorded as: £17.525, £8.327, £14.986 and £2.139.

Two accountants use different spreadsheets to add up the amounts. A's spreadsheet rounds the value to the nearest penny before adding. B's truncates to 2 decimal places before adding.

    a What difference does this make to the total?

    b Will this always be the case?

Section 2: Approximation and estimation

Approximate values are useful for estimating or checking the results of calculations without using a calculator.

An **estimate** is a very useful tool for checking whether your answer is sensible. If your estimate and your actual answer are not similar, then you may have made a mistake in your calculation.

Key vocabulary

estimate: an approximate answer or rough calculation.

"I estimate measurements and prices to give customers a fairly accurate quote telling them what a building job will cost." *(Builder)*

For estimating an approximate answer you generally round the original figures to 1 significant figure.

WORKED EXAMPLE 3

Estimate the value of $\dfrac{8.3 \times 536}{2.254 \times 9.612}$.

$$\frac{8.3 \times 536}{2.254 \times 9.612} \approx \frac{8 \times 500}{2 \times 10}$$

Start by rounding each number to 1 significant figure.

$$= \frac{4000}{20}$$

$$= 200$$

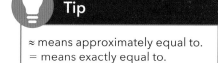

Tip

≈ means approximately equal to.
= means exactly equal to.

If you work out this problem using a calculator, the answer is actually 205.34 (to 2 decimal places).

Comparing this with your estimate tells you that your calculated answer is reasonable.

WORK IT OUT 9.1

A group of four friends are travelling to a festival. They intend to split the cost of everything between them.

The costs are: tent hire, £86.50; travel, 140 mile round trip with petrol costing roughly 20p per mile and camping entry tickets at £44 per night for three nights.

They decide to estimate how much they will each have to pay.

Which is the best estimate? Why is it better than the others?

Estimate A	Estimate B	Estimate C
The cost of tent hire is roughly £88, which is £22 per person split between four.	The tent hire is roughly £100 which is £25 per person.	The tent hire is roughly £80, which is £20 each.
Petrol costs roughly £28 (140 × 0.2) which is £7 per person.	The petrol is roughly £150 × 0.2, which is £30, so split four ways is £7.50.	Petrol is about £100 × 0.2 = £20 so £5 per person.
The camping ticket costs are £44 × 3 nights, which is roughly £120 which is £30 per person.	The camping costs about £50 × 3 = £150, which is about £40 each.	Camping cost is about £40 × 3 = £120 for three nights, so about £30 each.
So total cost per person is £22 + £7 + £30 = £59	Total cost is approximately £25 + £7.50 + £40 = £72.50	Total cost is approximately £20 + £5 + £30 = £55

Find answers at: cambridge.org/ukschools/gcsemaths-studentbookanswers

Tip

Always re-write the calculation with your rounded values before working out your estimate.

EXERCISE 9E

1 Estimate the following by rounding each number to 1 significant figure.

a 111.11×3.6 **b** 378×1.07 **c** 0.99×16.7 **d** -13.6×0.48

e $\pi \times (5.3)^2$ **f** 4.8×12.5 **g** $\dfrac{192}{17.2}$ **h** $\dfrac{58.38}{0.5185}$

2 Which calculation would provide the best estimate (A, B or C)?

a 186×9.832 **A** 200×10 **B** 190×9 **C** 190×10

b $15.76 \div 7.6$ **A** $15 \div 7$ **B** $16 \div 8$ **C** $16 \div 7$

3 Estimate the following by rounding each number to 1 significant figure.

a $\dfrac{82.65 \times 0.4654}{42.4 \times 2.53}$ **b** $\dfrac{16.96 + 3.123}{16.96 - 6.432}$ **c** $\dfrac{879 \div 43.6}{2.36 \times 0.23}$ **d** $\dfrac{976.9 \div 492.9}{21.6 \div 43.87}$

4 Estimate the following.

a $\sqrt{\dfrac{3.2 \times 4.05}{0.39 \times 0.29}}$ **b** $\sqrt{\dfrac{4.1 \times 11.9}{7.9 \times 0.25}}$

5 Shafiek runs a cross country race at an average speed of $6.25\,\text{m/s}$.

a Estimate how far he will have run after 6 minutes.

b Estimate how long it takes him to cover $1467\,\text{m}$. Assume he runs at a steady speed.

6 Look at the calculator display answers for each calculation. Use your estimation skills to say whether the answer is sensible or not without actually doing the calculation.

a $3 \times \pi \times 5^2$ `125.6637061`   **b** 5×8.9 `445`

c 50×8.9 `445`   **d** 3×192.5 `57.75`

e $\dfrac{\sqrt{86}}{2.8 \times 16.18}$ `0.204697565`   **f** $0.0253 \div 0.45$ `56.222222222`

7 A rectangle has an area of $54.67\,\text{cm}^2$. The base of the rectangle is $7.9\,\text{cm}$ long.

a When a student tries to find the height on his calculator, he gets a result of $69\,202\,531$. This is clearly wrong. Give the height correct to 2 significant figures.

b Estimate the perimeter of the rectangle to the nearest cm.

8 Estimate the square root of 50 if the square root of 49 is 7 and the square root of 64 is 8.

9 Given that $\dfrac{0.514 \times 76.3}{2.4^2} = 6.8087$ to 4 decimal places, work out $\dfrac{51.4 \times 7.63}{24^2}$.

10 Find an approximate value of $\dfrac{2876}{31 \times 33}$.

Section 3: Limits of accuracy

All recorded measurements are given to a certain level of accuracy. Even with very accurate measuring instruments, quantities such as mass, length and capacity cannot be measured exactly.

When you are given a measurement you assume it is accurate except for the last digit. However, the rules of rounding mean the measurement has to fall within certain limits.

A piece of wood that is 47 cm to the nearest centimetre, could be anything from 46.5 cm up to, but not including, 47.5 cm long.

You can see this on the number line.

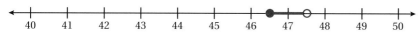

If the length was less than 46.5, it would have been rounded down to 46.

If it was 47.5, it would have been rounded up to 48.

If we let l represent the length of the piece of wood, the possible measurements can be expressed as $46.5 \leqslant l < 47.5$

This is called inequality notation and it means the length is greater than or equal to 46.5 and smaller than 47.5.

The smallest value a measurement can take is called the **lower bound** of the measurement.

The largest value it can take is called the **upper bound**.

WORKED EXAMPLE 4

Use inequality notation to write down an **error interval** for each value.

a 10 cm correct to the nearest cm.

b 22.5 kg to 1 decimal place.

c 128 000 correct to 3 significant figures.

a Let the length be x.
$9.5 \leqslant x < 10.5$

b Let the mass be m.
$22.45 \leqslant m < 22.55$

c Let the value be x.
$127\,500 \leqslant x < 128\,500$

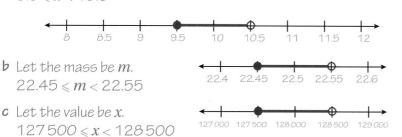

> **Tip**
>
> It is helpful to draw a number line to work out the upper and lower bounds of a value.

> **Key vocabulary**
>
> **lower bound**: the smallest value that a number (given to a specified accuracy) can be.
>
> **upper bound**: the largest value that a number (given to a specified accuracy) can be.
>
> **error interval**: the difference between the upper and lower bounds.

> **Tip**
>
> | $\leqslant$ | means | less than or equal to. |
> | $\geqslant$ | means | greater than or equal to. |
> | $<$ | means | less than. |
> | $>$ | means | greater than. |

Find answers at: cambridge.org/ukschools/gcsemaths-studentbookanswers

For any measurement correct to a given level of accuracy, the exact values lie in a range half a unit below and half a unit above the measurement.

Look at the following examples and note the rules that apply for decimals and significant figures:

Example	Lower and upper bounds	Let the value be x
0.5 rounded to 1 d.p.	0.45 and 0.55	$0.45 \leqslant x < 0.55$
0.65 rounded to 2 d.p.	0.645 and 0.655	$0.645 \leqslant x < 0.655$
0.7663 rounded to 3 d.p.	0.76625 and 0.76635	$0.76625 \leqslant x < 0.76635$
15 rounded to 2 s.f.	14.5 and 15.5	$14.5 \leqslant x < 15.5$
320 rounded to 2 s.f.	315 and 325	$315 \leqslant x < 325$

EXERCISE 9F

1 Find the lower and upper bound of each value.

    a 96 rounded to 2 s.f.   **b** 96.0 rounded to 3 s.f.

    c 96.00 rounded to 4 s.f.   **d** 0.6 rounded to 1 d.p.

    e 0.06 rounded to 1 d.p.   **f** 0.60 rounded to 2 d.p.

    g 3.142 rounded to 3 d.p.   **h** 9.9 rounded to 2 s.f.

    i 3.07 rounded to 3 s.f.

2 The following lengths were measured to the nearest millimetre. Write down the possible values for each one using inequality notation. Let the length be L in each case.

    a 4.9 cm   **b** 12.520 m   **c** 43.0 cm   **d** 29 mm

3 **a** There are 36 litres of petrol in a car's tank, to the nearest litre. What is the least and greatest possible volume of petrol in the tank?

    b A length of wood is 1.40 m to the nearest cm. Is it possible for the wood to be 137 cm long?

    c The weight of a stone is 43.4 kg to the nearest tenth of a kg. What is the least and greatest weight it could be?

4 Verna is a jeweller. She buys 9 carat gold for £10.66 per gram and platinum for £33.46 per gram.

    a Use this information to complete the table.

Mass of a piece of jewellery	Maximum value of gold (to nearest pence)	Maximum value of platinum (to nearest pence)
18 grams to nearest gram		
18 grams to nearest 0.1 gram		
18 grams to nearest 0.01 gram		

b Use your data to explain why jewellers tend to use scales that are accurate to a hundredth of a gram or more to weigh the metal they use to make jewellery.

5 Hilal ran 100 m in 15.3 seconds. The distance is correct to the nearest metre and the time is correct to 1 decimal place. Write down the upper and lower bounds of:

a the distance he ran

b the actual time taken.

6 The length of a rope is 4.5 metres to the nearest 10 cm. The actual length of the rope is L metres. Find the range of possible values for L, giving the answer as an inequality.

The upper and lower bounds of a calculation

When you do calculations with approximate values your answers are only as accurate as the specified accuracy of the values you use. In most cases, approximation errors are compounded and this produces an even larger interval of error in the results.

Tip

In real terms this means that your area calculation could be out by 16 cm². If you were coating the area with platinum this could make quite a difference to the amount you needed and the cost.

WORKED EXAMPLE 5

A rectangle has sides of 10 cm and 6 cm given to the nearest centimetre. Calculate the limits of accuracy of the area of the rectangle.

Possible lengths
$9.5 \leqslant l < 10.5$

10 cm

6 cm — Possible widths
$5.5 \leqslant b < 6.5$

Draw a sketch and find the error interval of each measurement.

The smallest possible area is:
$5.5 \times 9.5 = 52.25\,\text{cm}^2$

The lower bound of the length is 9.5 cm and the lower bound of the width is 5.5 cm.

The greatest possible area is:
$10.5 \times 6.5 = 68.25\,\text{cm}^2$

The upper bound of the length is 10.5 cm and the upper bound of the width is 6.5 cm.

The limits of accuracy for the area are
$52.25\,\text{cm}^2 \leqslant \text{Area} < 68.25\,\text{cm}^2$

Discrete and continuous quantities

When working with upper and lower bounds, it is important to understand the difference between **discrete** and **continuous** quantities.

Measurements are continuous quantities. Length, mass, capacity and other measures can take any value between the given points (in the range).

Key vocabulary

discrete quantities: countable values using whole numbers.

continuous quantities: measurements that can take any value in a range.

Quantities that can be counted, such as the number of people, number of cars or number of buildings in a given area are discrete values. When you count people there are no in-between values – there are either 5 or 6 people, never $5\frac{1}{2}$.

The limits of accuracy for discrete values can be expressed in different ways. Suppose you know the population of a village is 500 to the nearest 100. The number of people that live in the village (n) can be expressed as

$450 \leqslant n \leqslant 549$　as well as　$450 \leqslant n < 550$

If more than 549 people live in the village, this means that at least 550 people are residents because n is a discrete variable (there must be a whole number of people), and 550 would be round to 600 to the nearest 100.

EXERCISE 9G

1 12 kg of sugar are removed from a sack containing 50 kg. Each measurement is correct to the nearest kilogram. Find the upper and lower bounds of the mass of the sugar left in the container.

2 The dimensions of a rectangle are 3.61 cm and 2.57 cm, each correct to 3 significant figures.

　a Write down the upper and lower bounds of each measurement.

　b Find the upper and lower bounds of the area of the rectangle.

　c Write the upper and lower bounds of the area correct to 3 significant figures.

3 In the diagram, the measurements of a piece of land are given correct to 1 decimal place.

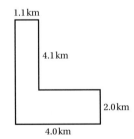

　a Calculate the limits of accuracy of the area of the land.

　b A surveyor calculates the area to be 12.51 km². What is the greatest possible error in taking that value? Give your answer as a percentage of the surveyor's value.

　c Comment on whether that is a significant error or not, giving reasons for your answer.

4 Henry has £100 to the nearest £1 and he spends £30 to the nearest £1. What is the least amount of money he can have left?

5 A rectangle measures 5 cm by 6 cm to the nearest cm. What is:

　a the greatest perimeter

　b the maximum area

　c the smallest diagonal length?

6 In order to try to calculate pi (π) John measures a circle. The circumference (C) is 40 cm to the nearest cm and the diameter (d) is 12 cm to the nearest cm.

Given that $\pi = \dfrac{C}{d}$, what are the highest and lowest values for John's calculation of π?

7 An athlete runs 100 m in 12.32 seconds, correct to 2 decimal places. Find the range of values for her average speed.

8 A chocolate manufacturer recently reduced the weight of its standard chocolate bar from 49 g to 45 g, to the nearest gram. What is the maximum weight of chocolate that could have been removed?

9 In an experiment, the velocity of a model race car is worked out by timing how long it takes to cover a marked length on a track. The velocity is found using the formula $v = \dfrac{d}{t_2 - t_1}$, where d is the distance covered in metres, t_1 is the starting time and t_2 is the finishing time on a stopwatch, measured in seconds.

In a particular trial, the car travels 1.000 m (to the nearest mm), starting at 0.2 s and ending at 1.4 s (both correct to the nearest 0.1 second).

Write an inequality to express the values between which v falls in this trial.

Checklist of learning and understanding

Approximate values

- When you round to a specified place, if the number following is 5 or above, then the original number goes up to the next number. If it is not 5 or greater, then the number stays the same.

- Rounding to a given number of significant figures specifies the number of digits, starting from the first non-zero digit, that are used to express a number.

- Truncating a decimal number, means removing all digits after a specified number of decimal places and expressing the number that remains without rounding.

Estimation

- Complex calculations can be estimated without using a calculator by using approximations of each term in the calculation to make a simple calculation.

- Visual estimation techniques can also be used to approximate sizes and measurements.

Level of accuracy

- Measurement is really approximation within a range of values. A measurement can be expressed using inequality notation ($\leqslant$, $<$).

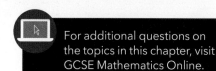

For additional questions on the topics in this chapter, visit GCSE Mathematics Online.

Chapter review

1 Estimate the value of $\dfrac{6.68^2}{4.76 \times 21.2}$

2 A market trader sells 470 apples for £73. Roughly how much does an apple cost?

3 If $521 \times 32 = 16\,672$, what is $16\,672 \div 3.2$?

4 Estimate the value of $\dfrac{39.9 + \sqrt{0.0934}}{(15.4 - 4.3)^2}$

5 Chocolate bars are supposed to weigh 50 g with a tolerance of 5%. If they are weighed to the nearest 10 grams, will they be within this tolerance?

6 The voltage V of an electronic circuit is given by Ohm's law, which is the formula:

$V = IR$

where I is the current in amps and R is the resistance in ohms.

Given that $V = 316$ correct to 3 significant figures and $R = 19.2$ correct to 3 significant figures, calculate the lower bound of I.

7 Quantity x is 45 to the nearest integer. Quantity y is 98 to the nearest integer. Calculate upper and lower bounds for x as a percentage of y to 1 decimal place.

  8 $m = \dfrac{\sqrt{s}}{t}$

$s = 3.47$ correct to 2 decimal places
$t = 8.132$ correct to 3 decimal places

By considering bounds, work out the value of m to a suitable degree of accuracy.

You must show all your working and give a reason for your final answer.

(5 marks)

©Pearson Education Ltd 2013

10 Mensuration

In this chapter you will learn how to …

- work with and convert standard units of measurement.
- use and convert compound units of measurement.
- work with map scales and bearings.
- construct and use scale diagrams to solve problems.

 For more resources relating to this chapter, visit GCSE Mathematics Online.

Using mathematics: real-life applications

Measurement has practical applications in many jobs, and also in everyday activities. Being able to read and work with measurements is important when you make or alter clothes, work out what materials you need to build things, and weigh ingredients to make a recipe.

"I use accurate measurements to work out the scale when I draw maps. The people who use maps need to understand the scale so that they can make sense of map distances." *(Cartographer)*

Before you start …

Ch 7	You must be able to multiply and divide using multiples of 10.	**1** Work out. **a** 1000×10 **b** $340 \div 100$ **c** $16 \div 1000$	
Ch 5	You should be able to substitute numbers into a simple formula.	**2** Use the formula to work out the pay of each person: pay = hours worked × rate of pay **a** Amelia: 20 hours worked at £7 per hour. **b** Billy: 15 hours worked at £6 per hour. **c** Catrin: 40 hours worked at £5.50 per hour.	
KS3	You should be able to solve problems involving direct proportion.	**3** Six pencils cost 90p. Work out the cost of: **a** 12 pencils **b** 1 pencil **c** 4 pencils.	

Find answers at: cambridge.org/ukschools/gcsemaths-studentbookanswers

Assess your starting point using the Launchpad

STEP 1

1 Convert.

a 11 569 grams into kilograms

b $4\frac{1}{2}$ hours into seconds

c 123 456 pence into pounds (£)

d 5 cm² into m²

GO TO
Section 1:
Standard units of measurement

STEP 2

2 A car travels 16 kilometres in 20 minutes.

a What is the average speed of the car in kilometres per hour (km/h)?

b Express this speed in metres per second (m/s).

3 Annie is stuck in traffic.

She works out that her taxi is travelling at an average speed of $6\frac{2}{3}$ m/s.

a Express that speed in km/h.

b How long will it take her to cover a distance of 600 m at this speed?

c The traffic clears slightly and the average speed increases to 30 km/h. How far will she travel in 20 seconds at this speed?

GO TO
Section 2:
Compound units of measurement

STEP 3

4 A helicopter is drawn using a scale of 1 : 100.

On the scale drawing the length of the helicopter blade is 8 cm.

How long is the actual blade?

5 A helicopter takes off from a point X and flies due north for 30 km to reach point Y.

It then flies on a bearing of 150° for 15 km to reach point Z.

a Use a scale of 1 cm to represent 10 km to make a scale drawing showing this journey.

b Use your diagram to find the bearing from X to Z.

c By measuring your diagram, find the actual distance directly between X and Z.

GO TO
Section 3:
Maps, scale drawings and bearings

GO TO
Chapter review

Section 1: Standard units of measurement

In the metric system, units of measurement are divided into sub-units with prefixes such as milli-, centi-, deci-, deca-, hecto- and kilo-.

The same prefixes are used for length, mass and capacity.

Each sub-unit is 10 times bigger than the one before it. Centimetres are 10 times bigger than millimetres, decimetres are 10 times bigger than centimetres and so on.

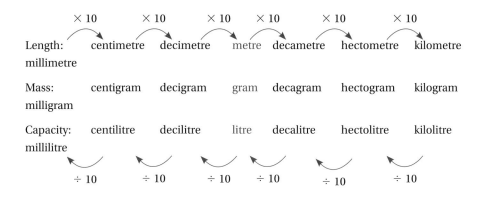

Tip

When you convert from a smaller to a larger unit there will be fewer of the larger units, so you divide by a power of 10.

When you convert from a larger to a smaller unit there will be more of the smaller units, so you multiply by a power of 10.

Converting between units

To convert between units in the metric system you need to multiply or divide by powers of 10.

This diagram shows how to convert between centimetres and metres.

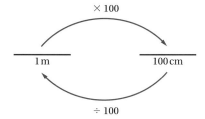

Tip

Not all the prefixes are in common use.

For example, length is usually only measured using mm, cm, m and km.

Key vocabulary

conversion factor: the number that you multiply or divide by to convert one measure into another smaller or larger unit.

The **conversion factor** is 100 because you are changing across two sub-units.

Each sub-unit is 10 times greater or smaller than the one next to it, so here you have to multiply or divide by $10^2 = 100$.

You will use the following conversions often, so it is useful to try and remember them.

1 centimetre (cm) = 10 millimetres (mm)

1 metre (m) = 100 centimetres (cm)

1 kilometre (km) = 1000 metres (m)

1 kilogram (kg) = 1000 grams (g)

1 tonne (t) = 1000 kilograms (kg)

1 litre (l) = 1000 millilitres (ml)

1 litre (l) = 1000 cubic centimetres (cm^3)

1 cubic centimetre (cm^3) = 1 millilitre (ml)

Tip

In the UK, the imperial unit the mile is used for measuring long distances.
1 mile ≈ 1.6 km.

WORK IT OUT 10.1

In a sponsored swim the total number of lengths swum is 94. Each length is 25 metres.

How many kilometres were swum in total?

Which of the answers below is correct?

Option A	Option B	Option C
Total number of metres $= 25 \times 94 = 2350$ metres Conversion: 100 metres $= 1$ km $2350 \div 100 = 23.5$ km swum in total.	Total number of metres $= 25 \times 94 = 2350$ metres Conversion: 100 metres $= 1$ km $2350 \times 100 = 235\,000$ km swum in total.	Total number of metres $= 25 \times 94 = 2350$ metres Conversion: 1000 metres $= 1$ km $2350 \div 1000 = 2.35$ km swum in total.

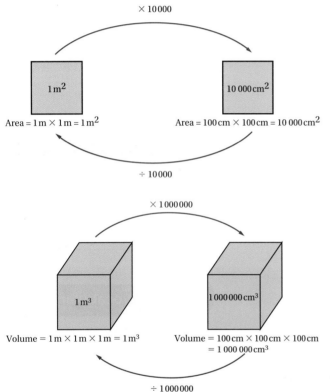

Converting areas and volumes

Area is measured in square units such as mm² (square millimetres), cm², m² or km² so any conversion factor also has to be squared.

For example, to convert cm to mm you would multiply by 10, but to convert cm² to mm² you would need to multiply by 10^2 which is 100.

The two squares on the left have the same area.

The conversion factor from m² to cm², and vice versa, is 10 000.

Volume is measured in cubic units such as mm³ (cubic millimetres), cm³ or m³ so any conversion factor also has to be cubed.

Again, to convert cm to mm you would multiply by 10, but to convert cm³ to mm³ you would need to multiply by 10^3 which is 1000.

The two cubes on the left have the same volume.

The conversion factor from m³ to cm³, and vice versa, is 1 000 000.

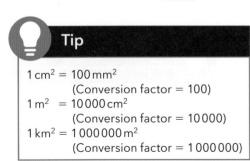

Tip

1 cm² = 100 mm²
    (Conversion factor = 100)
1 m² = 10 000 cm²
    (Conversion factor = 10 000)
1 km² = 1 000 000 m²
    (Conversion factor = 1 000 000)

WORKED EXAMPLE 1

Convert each measure to the units given.

a 10 m² to cm²   **b** 8.6 km² to m²   **c** 3500 mm² to cm²

a 10 m² to cm²
  = 10 × 10 000 = 100 000 cm²
                    Conversion factor = 10 000

b 8.6 km² to m²
  = 8.6 × 1 000 000
  = 8 600 000 m²
                    Conversion factor = 1 000 000

c 3500 mm² to cm²
  = 3500 ÷ 100 = 35 cm²
                    Conversion factor = 100

WORKED EXAMPLE 2

Convert each measurement to the unit given.

a $6.3\,m^3$ to cm^3 **b** $96\,500\,000\,cm^3$ to m^3 **c** $750\,cm^3$ to mm^3

a $6.3\,m^3$ *to* cm^3
$= 6.3 \times 1\,000\,000 = 6\,300\,000\,cm^3$

Conversion factor $= 1\,000\,000$

b $96\,500\,000\,cm^3$ *to* m^3
$= 96\,500\,000 \div 1\,000\,000 = 96.5\,m^3$

Conversion factor $= 1\,000\,000$

c $750\,cm^3$ *to* mm^3
$= 750 \times 1000 = 750\,000\,mm^3$

Conversion factor $= 1000$

This is the plan of a room.

The real length of each section of wall is given but the units of measurement are different.

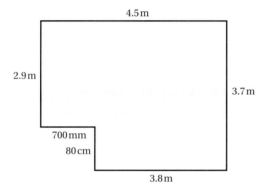

Tip

$1\,cm^3 = 1000\,mm^3$
(Conversion factor $= 1000$)
$1\,m^3 = 1\,000\,000\,cm^3$
(Conversion factor $= 1000000$)
1 litre $= 1000\,cm^3$
(Conversion factor $= 1000$)

Tip

You will use measurement conversions when you deal with scale drawings and maps in Section 3 and when you deal with perimeter, area and volume in Chapters 11, 12 and 18.

You can make mistakes if you try to calculate with measurements in different units.

Convert the measurements to the same unit before doing any calculations.

WORKED EXAMPLE 3

A builder is to put a wallpaper border around the ceiling of the room drawn above.

How many metres of wallpaper border does the builder need?

$80\,cm \div 100 = 0.8\,m$
$700\,mm \div 1000 = 0.7\,m$

The answer needs to be given in metres so it makes sense to work in metres.

$2.9 + 4.5 + 3.7 + 3.8 + 0.8 + 0.7 = 16.4\,m$

Add the given lengths.

The builder needs $16.4\,m$ of wallpaper border.

EXERCISE 10A

1 Match each measurement with one from the box.

    a 10 000 mm   **b** 10 000 ml   **c** 10 kg

    d 0.01 kg   **e** 0.1 cm

10 l	10 g	10 m	1 mm	10 000 g

2 Convert the following lengths and masses into the given units to complete the following.

    a 2.5 km = ☐ m   **b** 85 cm = ☐ mm   **c** 34 m = ☐ mm

    d 1.55 m = ☐ mm   **e** 0.07 m = ☐ cm   **f** 5.4 kg = ☐ g

    g 0.9 kg = ☐ g   **h** 102 g = ☐ kg   **i** 14.5 g = ☐ kg

3 Add the following capacities. Give your answers in the units indicated in brackets.

    a 3.5 l + 5 l (ml)   **b** 2.3 l + 450 ml (l)   **c** 20 l + 4.5 l + 652 ml (l)

4 Mandy wants to use concrete slabs to form a border round a rectangular garden. The garden is 480 cm wide and 7.2 metres long.

    a Draw a diagram to represent the garden.

    b Calculate the perimeter of the garden in metres.

    c If the concrete slabs are square with sides of 120 cm, how many will Mandy need to form the border?

    d The slabs cost £4.55 each. Work out how much it will cost Mandy to buy the slabs she needs.

    e What is the cost per metre for the concrete border?

5 Convert each of the following into the required units.

    a Total weight in kg of three bags of flour, each of mass 1200 g.

    b The length in cm of a 7.763 m long whale.

    c 3567 kg of lead into tonnes.

    d Area of 5 m^2 into mm^2.

    e 96.35 m^3 of sand into cm^3.

    f 345 cm^3 of water into litres.

Tip

Think units!

It is important to consider the units in which you are working. Always look back to the original question to determine the units. With a formula, whatever units you put in must match the units that come out.

6 An area of 250 000 cm^2 needs to be painted. A pot of paint can cover an area of 10 m^2. How many pots of paint are needed?

7 Fill in < , = or > between the two measurements.

Then calculate the difference between the greater and smaller measurement.

Give your answer in the most appropriate units.

a 55.9 cm ☐ 560 mm

b 8 kg ☐ 7900 g

c 590 l ☐ 59 015 cl

d 19.3 cm ☐ 189 mm

e 101 cl ☐ 0.99 l

f 198 cm ☐ 0.001 99 km

g 145 g ☐ 1.45 kg

h 1987 t ☐ 10 987 kg

i 2 m³ ☐ 2 000 000 cm³

8 The actual dimensions of a new kitchen sink are given on the diagram in millimetres.

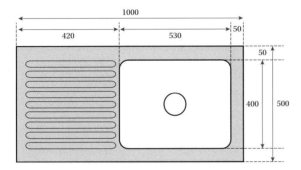

a Calculate the total perimeter of the unit in centimetres.

b What is the area of the draining board section in square millimetres?

c Convert the area of the draining board to square metres.

d The sink is 170 mm deep.

What is the approximate capacity of the sink in:

  i cubic millimetres **ii** litres?

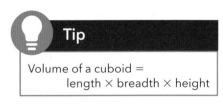

Tip

Volume of a cuboid =
    length × breadth × height

Time

The units of time we use on a daily basis are not decimal units.

To convert from weeks to days, you would need to multiply by 7 as there are 7 days in a week.

To convert from seconds to hours, you would need to divide by 60 to get minutes and then by 60 again to get hours. (You can also do this in one step by dividing by 3600.)

Time is sometimes given in decimal form, for example, 4.8 hours.

You can convert these times back to ordinary units in different ways.

There are 60 minutes in an hour, so

4.8 × 60 minutes = 288 minutes = 4 hours 48 minutes.

Or, you can think of this as 4 hours and 0.8 hours.

0.8 × 60 = 48, so the time is 4 hours and 48 minutes.

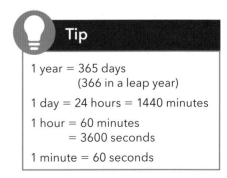

Tip

1 year = 365 days
        (366 in a leap year)
1 day = 24 hours = 1440 minutes
1 hour = 60 minutes
       = 3600 seconds
1 minute = 60 seconds

In athletics, and other timed sporting events, the times are often given using decimal fractions of a second.

For example, in August 2009, Usain Bolt ran the 100 m in the World Record time of 9.580 seconds.

In the metric system, 1 second = 1000 milliseconds.

9.580 is time recorded exact to $\frac{1}{1000}$ of a second.

This is 9 seconds and 580 milliseconds. You cannot convert it in any other way.

12-hour and 24-hour times

The 12-hour time system uses am to show times from midnight to noon and pm for time from noon till midnight.

The 24-hour time system shows the times 00:00–23:59. Midnight is 00:00.

Calculator tip

Modern scientific calculators have a mode that you can use to do sexagesimal calculation (hours, minutes and seconds). Different models work in different ways, so read the manual or check online to see how your calculator works.

Tip

Add 12 to write a pm time using the 24-hour clock, for example
10.35 pm + 12 = 22:35

Subtract 12 to write a time between 13:00 and 23:59 using the 12-hour clock, for example 15:40 − 12 = 3.40 pm

Problem-solving framework

DEPARTURES

ЕНИЕ ATION	ЧЕРЕЗ VIA	ВРЕМЯ/TIME ПО РАСПИСАНИЮ SCHEDULED	ОЖИДАЕМОЕ EXPECTED	СТОЙКА РЕГИСТРАЦИИ CHECK-IN	ПРИМЕЧАНИЕ REMARKS
AMSTERDAM		17:25		41-›	
ROME		17:35		31-33-›	
WARSAW		18:35		‹-16-20	CHECK IN NOW
ISTANBUL		18:40		25-29-›	CHECK IN NOW
PRAHA		18:45		‹-16-20	CHECK IN NOW
HANOI		18:50		37-38-›	CHECK IN NOW
LONDON		18:55		‹-16-20	CHECK IN NOW
BEIJING		18:55		‹-1-5	CHECK IN NOW
BELGRADE		19:00		34-36-›	CHECK IN NOW
MALAGA		19:20		‹-16-20	CHECK IN NOW
PARIS		19:30		45-48-›	
BANGKOK		19:40		‹-7-10	
TOKYO		19:40		40-42-›	
PARIS		19:45		‹-16-20	CHECK IN NOW

Mr Smith is in Moscow.

He needs to return to London for an urgent meeting in the morning.

The flight from Moscow to London takes 3.6 hours. The local time in Moscow is 3 hours ahead of the UK.

The flight is scheduled for take-off at 18:55 local time, and on arrival it will take 45 minutes to pass through customs and exit the airport.

Mr Smith will stop to buy a coffee, sandwich and newspaper for the train.

Trains for central London leave at 5, 27 and 46 minutes past the hour, and the journey will take 29 minutes.

There is a 7-minute walk from the train station to the meeting location.

What is the earliest time that Mr Smith can expect to arrive at his meeting? Give your answer using the 12-hour system of time.

Tip

When you work with time, treat hours and minutes separately. If you carry over from hours to minutes, remember you are carrying 60 minutes.

Continues on next page …

Steps for solving problems	What you would do for this example
Step 1: What have you got to do?	First work out the time of arrival in London and then work out how long it takes from there to the meeting location.
Step 2: What information do you need?	Flight departure time: 18:55 (local time) Time difference between London and Moscow: 3 hours Flight time: 3.6 hours Time to pass through customs: 45 minutes Train departure times: 5 past, 27 minutes past, 46 minutes past the hour Length of train journey: 29 minutes Walk time: 7 minutes
Step 3: What information don't you need?	Assume time to buy a coffee, sandwich and newspaper is negligible (as no time for this is provided).
Step 4: What maths can you do?	18:55 minus 3 hours = 15:55 (London time) Convert 3.6 from a decimal to time in hours and minutes: 3 hours and 0.6×60 = 3 hours 36 minutes Arrival time in London: 15:55 + 3 hours 36 minutes = 19:31 Add on time in customs: 19:31 + 45 minutes = 20:16 Next possible train is 20:27 Time at end of train journey: 20:27 + 29 minutes = 20:56 Arrival time at venue following walk: 20:56 + 7 minutes = 21:03 21:03 − 12 = 9.03 pm or three minutes past nine in the evening
Step 5: Have you used all the information? At this point you should check to make sure you have calculated what was asked of you.	Flight departure time ✓ Train departure times ✓ Time difference ✓ Length of train journey ✓ Flight time ✓ Walk time ✓ Time through customs ✓
Step 6: Is it correct?	Estimate to check $3\frac{1}{2}$ hours flying + 45 min at airport + 10 min wait + 30 min train + 7 min walk = about 5 hours Take off the time difference leaves 2 hours Leave 7 pm + 2 hours = 9 pm

Key vocabulary

exchange rate: the value of one currency used to convert that currency to an equivalent value in another currency.

Tip

Exchange rates can change over short periods of time due to economic and political factors. So, unlike conversions for distance, time and so on, you shouldn't memorise a particular exchange rate.

Money

$£1 = 100p$ so $£x = 100x$ pence and x pence $= £\dfrac{x}{100}$

The rate at which one currency is converted to another is called an **exchange rate**. For example, $£1 = €1.26$ and $€1 = £0.794$ or 79.4p (at 2014 rates).

WORKED EXAMPLE 4

If the exchange rate for the pound to the euro is $£1 = €1.26$, convert:

a £400 to euros   **b** €400 to pounds.

a $£400 = 400 \times 1.26 = €504$

> When the exchange rate is given as 1 unit of A = x units of B, you can convert A to B by multiplying by x.

b $€400 = \dfrac{400}{1.26} = £317.46$

> Currency B can be converted to currency A by dividing by x.

EXERCISE 10B

1 The starting pistol for a road race is fired at 12:15:30.

The first runner crosses the finishing line at 14:07:22.

What was the winning time for the race?

2 Sandra is exactly 16 years old. Calculate her age in:

a weeks   **b** days   **c** hours   **d** seconds.

3 A boat leaves port at 14:35 and arrives at its destination $6\frac{1}{2}$ hours later. At what time does the boat arrive?

4 Ashwin and Luke plan to meet up in London. Ashwin's journey will take 2 hours and 27 minutes. Luke's journey will take 1.3 hours.

What time must each set off if they are to meet at 11:15?

5 The table (left) gives the value of the pound against four other currencies in July 2014.

a Calculate the value of each of the other currencies in pounds at this rate.

b Convert £125 to US dollars.

c How many Indian rupees would you get if you converted £45 at this rate?

d Dilshaad has 8000 Indian rupees. What is this worth in pounds at this rate?

e Explain why tourists from the UK may find India a cheap place to visit.

f How can a weaker exchange rate affect the economy of a country?

Consider the cost of imports and the value of exports in your answer.

British pound (£)	1
Euro (€)	1.26
US dollar ($)	1.70
Australian dollar (AS$)	1.80
Indian rupee (INR)	102.28

Section 2: Compound units of measurement

Compound measures involve more than one unit of measurement.

- Rates of pay (such as pounds per hour) involve units of money and time.
- Unit pricing (such as pence per gram) involves units of money and mass (or capacity or volume).

Compound measures usually express how many of the first unit correspond with 1 of the second unit. A rate of pay of £8.30/hour shows how many pounds you earn for 1 hour of work.

You can simplify compound measures by multiplying or dividing both units by the same factor.

WORKED EXAMPLE 5

40 litres of petrol cost £52.

a What is the cost in £/litre?

b Convert the cost in £/litre to pence per millilitre.

a $\dfrac{52}{40}$ = £1.30/litre

The compound measure £/litre tells you that pounds are the first unit.

b Convert pounds to pence:
£1.30 = 130p
Convert litres to millilitres:
1 l = 1000 ml

You want a compound measure comparing pence and millilitres.

130 p per 1000 ml

Compare the two quantities

130 ÷ 1000 = 0.13
1000 ÷ 1000 = 1

You want a rate per **one** millilitre, so divide both quantities by 1000.

So 130 p per 1000 ml = 0.13 p/millilitre

Tip

A forward slash symbol / is often used instead of the word "per". So £8.30/hour means the same as £8.30 per hour.

Speed

Speed compares the distance travelled to the time taken. The units of speed depend on the situation.

A car or train's speed is often given in km/h or mph (kilometres or miles per hour).

An athlete's running speed may be given in m/s (metres per second).

You need to know the formula for calculating speed:

$$\text{Average speed} = \frac{\text{distance travelled}}{\text{time taken}}$$

Did you know?

Speed isn't just a measure of how fast something is travelling. Run rates per over in cricket and the number of words you can type per minute are both examples of speed.

Learn this formula

$$\text{Average speed} = \frac{\text{distance travelled}}{\text{time taken}}$$

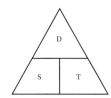

The speed is an average speed because a journey may involve faster and slower speeds over the given period. You can see the different speeds at different points in a car journey by looking at the speedometer. The speed shown on the speedometer is the speed at that particular time.

The triangle on the left shows the relationship between speed, distance and time.

Using the triangle:

- To find distance: cover D with your finger.
  The position of S next to T tells you to multiply speed by time.
  Distance = Speed × Time

- To find time: cover T with your finger. The position of D over S tells you to divide distance by speed. Time = Distance ÷ Speed

- To find speed: cover S with your finger. The position of D over T tells you to divide distance by time. Speed = Distance ÷ Time

The units of speed given in a problem usually let you know what units to use.

For example, if the problem talks about km/h, then express distances in kilometres and time in hours to calculate the speed.

Tip

Unless the unit is specified in the question, you can use any suitable unit you like. If you change the unit from the one in which the question is written, you must state the units you are using.

WORK IT OUT 10.2

A car travels 330 miles in $5\frac{1}{2}$ hours.

What is the average speed of the car in miles per hour (mph)?

Which of the answers below is correct?

Option A	Option B	Option C
Speed = Distance ÷ Time	Speed = Distance × Time	Speed = Distance – Time
D = 330 miles	D = 330 miles	D = 330 miles
T = $5\frac{1}{2}$ hours = 5.5 hours	T = $5\frac{1}{2}$ hours = 5.5 hours	T = $5\frac{1}{2}$ hours = 5.5 hours
S = 330 ÷ 5.5 = 60 mph	S = 330 × 5.5 = 1815 mph	S = 330 – 5.5 = 324.5 mph

To convert speeds from one set of units to another, you need to work systematically and take care with the units.

WORKED EXAMPLE 6

An athlete runs at an average speed of 10.16 m/s. Is this faster or slower than an average speed of 40 km/h?

Convert 10.16 m/s so that both speeds are in km/h.

× 60 to get metres per minute
    10.16 × 60 = 609.6 m/min   Convert seconds to hours.
× 60 to get metres per hour
    609.6 × 60 = 36 576 m/hour

÷ 1000 to get kilometres per hour   Convert metres to kilometres.
$\dfrac{36576}{1000} = 36.576$ km/h

So the athlete's speed is slower than 40 km/h.

EXERCISE 10C

1 Joe is 18 years old and works for a minimum wage of £5.03 per hour.

If he works for 14 hours, how much will he earn?

2 Henry earns £8.75 per hour. Sian earned £220.44 for working 22 hours.

How much more does Sian earn per hour than Henry?

3 A bricklayer lays 680 bricks in 4 hours.

How many does she lay per minute, to the nearest brick?

4 Bernie cycles 168 km in 8 hours. What is his average speed?

5 A car travels 528 km at an average speed of 88 km/h. Work out the time taken.

6 Usain Bolt set an Olympic record over 100 m at the London Olympics in 2012 with a time of 9.63 seconds.

  a Express this speed in m/s.   **b** How fast is this in km/h?

  c Usain Bolt is also the world record holder for the 100 m event.

    He set a world record of 9.58 s in August 2009.

    How much faster is the world record speed than the Olympic record speed?

7 How long would it take a zebra running at 42 km/h to cover a distance of 6.3 km?

8 A train leaves Liverpool Street at 9:37 am and arrives at Norwich at 11:43 am, a distance of 189.9 km.

What is the average speed of the train?

9 A marathon runner starts a 42 km race at 05:54:10 and finishes at 08:12.37.

What was her average speed for the race? Give the answer in km/h and m/s.

10 A car travelled for 20 minutes at 85 km/h and then for another 25 minutes at 100 km/h.

What was its average speed over the journey?

Density and pressure

Density is the ratio between the mass and the volume of an object.

The triangle on the right helps you see the relationship between density, mass and volume.

    Mass = Density × Volume

    Volume = Mass ÷ Density

The units of density are grams per cubic centimetre (g/cm³) or kilograms per cubic metre (kg/m³).

Express the mass and the volume in the units given when you solve problems involving density.

Learn this formula

Density = Mass ÷ Volume

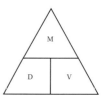

WORKED EXAMPLE 7

A gold bar has a volume of 725 cm^3 and a mass of 14.5 kg. What is the density of the gold bar in g/cm^3?

$M = 14.5\,kg = 14.5 \times 1000 = 14\,500\,g$

> Units of density are g/cm^3 so mass must be in g.

Density = Mass ÷ Volume

> Write the formula you are using.

Density = 14 500 ÷ 725
= 20 g/cm^3

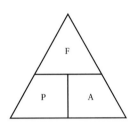

Pressure is defined by the formula:

Pressure = Force ÷ Area

The units given for force and area give you compound units for the pressure.

For example, if force is measured in newtons and area in mm^2, the compound unit of pressure would be N/mm^2 (newtons per mm^2).

WORKED EXAMPLE 8

A brick exerts a force of 5 N.

a Calculate the pressure exerted on the ground when the brick is in each of the following positions.

b Which brick exerts the strongest pressure? Why?

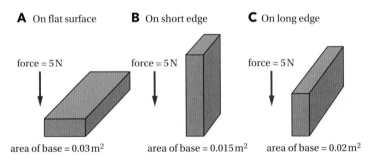

A On flat surface   **B** On short edge   **C** On long edge

force = 5 N   force = 5 N   force = 5 N

area of base = 0.03 m^2 area of base = 0.015 m^2 area of base = 0.02 m^2

A Pressure = $\dfrac{5\,N}{0.03\,m^2}$ = 167 N/m^2 (to the nearest unit)

B Pressure = $\dfrac{5\,N}{0.015\,m^2}$ = 333 N/m^2 (to the nearest unit)

C Pressure = $\dfrac{5\,N}{0.02\,m^2}$ = 250 N/m^2

b The middle brick (B) exerts the strongest pressure.

The force of 5 N is pushing down on a smaller area, so the pressure is greater.

EXERCISE 10D

1 The mass of 1 cm³ of different substances is shown in the diagram.

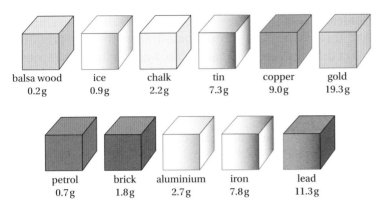

balsa wood	ice	chalk	tin	copper	gold
0.2 g	0.9 g	2.2 g	7.3 g	9.0 g	19.3 g

petrol	brick	aluminium	iron	lead
0.7 g	1.8 g	2.7 g	7.8 g	11.3 g

a Express the density of each substance in g/cm³.

b Calculate each density in g/m³ and then convert each to kg/m³.

2 A cube of material with side length 30 mm has a mass of 0.0642 kg.

Calculate the density of the material in g/cm³.

3 Calculate the volume of a piece of wood with a mass of 0.1 kg and a density of 0.8 g/cm³.

4 Two metal blocks both exert a force of 18 N.

Block A is a cube with sides 100 cm long. Block B is a cuboid with a base of area 6 m² in contact with the floor.

Calculate the pressure exerted by each block in N/m².

5 A car exerts a force of 6000 N on the road.

Each of the four wheels has an area of 0.025 m² in contact with the road.

What pressure does the car exert on the road?

Section 3: Maps, scale drawings and bearings

A **scale drawing** is a diagram in which measurements are either reduced or enlarged by a scale factor.

The scale tells you how much the dimensions are reduced or enlarged.

Maps are scaled representations of areas of the real world.

The scale of a map describes the relationship between lengths in real life and lengths on the map.

The scale allows you to convert distances that you measure on the map to real-life distances.

Map scales are shown in different ways.

Key vocabulary

scale factor: a number that scales a quantity up or down.

- **Bar or line scales.** The divided line or bar shows you distances on the map but the number on the bar tells you what the real distances are (usually in km).

- **Ratio scales.** You will often see scale given as a ratio, for example: 1 : 25 000. This means that one unit measured on the map is equivalent to 25 000 of the same units in real life. So, 1 cm on the map represents 25 000 cm = 0.25 km in real life.

Bar or line scales are useful for finding small distances. You measure the distance and then compare it with the line scale.

On the line scale below, each block is 1 cm long, and 1 cm on the map represents 1 km in real life.

To find a distance in real life:

- Measure the map distance using a piece of paper.

- Make pencil marks on the paper to record the distance.

- Compare your marked distance with the line scale.

- Read off the real distance.

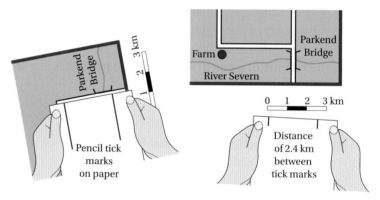

For bigger distances it is more efficient to use the ratio scale. You can convert any distance on a map to a real distance using the following formula.

Distance on the map × Scale = Distance on the ground

WORKED EXAMPLE 9

A scale drawing has a scale of 1 : 10.

a Calculate the real-life length when a length on the drawing is 5 cm.

b Calculate the length on the drawing when the real-life length is 30 cm.

a 5 cm on the drawing = 5 × 10 = 50 cm in real life

b 30 cm in real life = 30 ÷ 10 = 3 cm on the drawing.

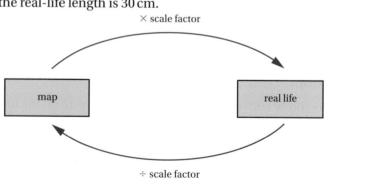

Take care with the units. When you multiply by the scale your answer will be in the same units that you used to measure on the map.

If the question asks for different units, you will need to convert the measurement to get the units you need.

WORK IT OUT 10.3

The distance between two towns on a 1 : 25 000 map is 3.4 cm.

How many kilometres apart are these towns in reality?

Which student has worked out the correct answer?

What have the other two done incorrectly?

Student A	Student B	Student C
$\dfrac{1}{25\,000} \times \dfrac{3.4}{1}$ $= 0.000\,136\,\text{cm}$ $= 1.36\,\text{km}$	Map distance = 34 mm Scale = 1 : 25 000 Real distance 34 × 25 000 = 850 000 mm = 8.5 km	3.4 × 25 000 = 85 000 The distance is 85 000 cm ÷ 100 = 850 m ÷ 1000 = 0.85 km

EXERCISE 10E

1 Here are three line scales. Work out what distance is represented by 1 cm in each case.

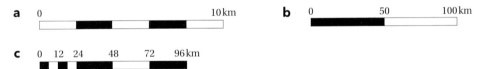

a 0   10 km   **b** 0   50   100 km

c 0   12   24   48   72   96 km

2 Work out the real distance (in kilometres) that a map distance of 45 mm would represent at each scale.

    a 1 : 120   **b** 1 : 1200   **c** 1 : 12 000   **d** : 120 000

    e 1 : 1 200 000   **f** 1 : 12 000 000   **g** 1 : 120 000 000

3 Andrew says that a map drawn to a scale of 1 : 15 000 is a larger scale map than one drawn to 1 : 150 000.

Is he correct? How do you know?

4 The map to the right shows three towns: Coltown, Bracwich and Nostley.

The map has a scale of 1 : 75 000.

Work out the actual distance directly from Coltown to Bracwich.

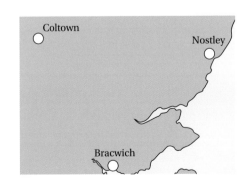

Find answers at: cambridge.org/ukschools/gcsemaths-studentbookanswers

1 : 10 000 000

Tip

You will use scale factors again in Chapter 30 when you deal with similar triangles and with enlargements of shapes.

5 The red line on the map (left) shows the flight path of a plane flying from Edinburgh to London. The flight took 55 minutes.

  a Calculate the distance flown in kilometres.

  b What was the plane's average speed on this flight?

6 A set of toy furniture is manufactured using a scale of 1 : 50.
Work out:

  a the height of a cupboard if the model is 5 cm high

  b the width of the model bed if the actual bed is 1.5 m wide

  c the length of a table if the model is 2.7 cm long.

7 A model of an F15 fighter jet has a scale of 1 : 32.

The real aircraft is 12.5 m long.

What is the length of the model?

8 A map of Scotland on an A4 sheet of paper has a scale of 1 : 2 000 000.

  a The map distance from Inverness to Glasgow is 90 mm.

  What is the real distance between these places?

  b The actual distance by road from Aberdeen to Dundee is 96.5 km.

  How long would this road be on the map?

9 The distance between places is often printed on road maps.

Pete has a road map that shows the driving distance from Birmingham to London as 192 km.

He estimates that $2\frac{1}{2}$ cm on the map represents a distance of 50 km.

  a Work out the scale of the map.

  b How long would the roads shown on the map be for Pete's journey at this scale?

Constructing scale drawings

To make a scaled drawing or simple map you need to:

● Find out or measure the real lengths involved.

● Decide what size your drawing is going to be so you can work out a scale.

● Choose an appropriate scale (if you are not given one to use). Use ratio to work this out.

  scale = length on drawing : length in real life.

● Use the scale to convert the real lengths to ones you need for the scaled drawing.

WORKED EXAMPLE 10

Draw a scale plan of a rectangular park that is 115 m long and 85 m wide.

Your plan must fit into a space 7.5 cm long and 5 cm wide.

A scale drawing 6 cm long will fit into the given space.

> Don't try to draw to the edge of the paper. Choose a convenient length.

Scale = length on drawing : length in real life
$= 6\,cm : 115\,m$

> Work out the scale.

$= 6\,cm : 11\,500\,cm$

> Convert the metres to centimetres.

$= 1 : 1917$

> Divide both sides of the ratio by 6 to get 1 on the left.

$\approx 1 : 2000$

> 1 : 1917 is a clumsy scale. Most scales are rounded.

Scaled length = 115 m ÷ 2000 = 0.0575 m = 5.75 cm
Scaled width = 85 m ÷ 2000 = 0.0425 m = 4.25 cm

> Use the scale to convert the real distances.
>
> 4.25 cm is less than the width of the paper, so your choice of about 6 cm for the length was a good choice.

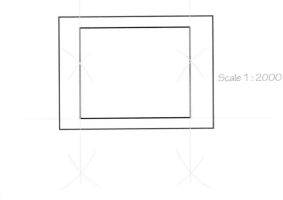

Scale 1 : 2000

> Draw a 5 cm by 7.5 cm frame.
>
> Draw an accurate rectangle 4.25 cm by 5.75 cm within the frame.
>
> Remember to write the scale you used on the diagram.

EXERCISE 10F

1 The floor of a school hall is 40 m long and 20 m wide.

Draw scaled diagrams to show what it would look like at each of these scales.

a 1 : 500 **b** 1 : 1000

2 Measure the dimensions of your desk in centimetres.

Work out a suitable scale and draw a scaled diagram of your desk, including anything on it.

3 Jules drew this rough plan of a classroom block at her school.

She wrote the actual measurements on the plan.

Use the dimensions on the plan to draw a scaled diagram of this classroom block that fits into the width of your exercise book.

Indicate windows and doors as shown on the plan.

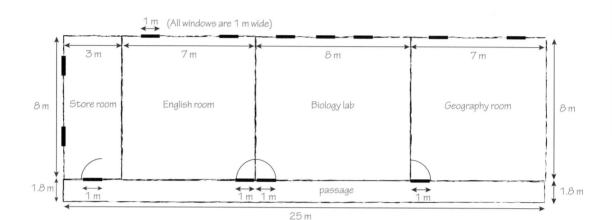

4 A plan of a house is to be drawn at a scale of 1 : 80.

a What should the scaled dimensions of the kitchen be if the real dimensions are 4900 mm by 3800 mm?

b Calculate the scaled length of the sink unit if it is 1.2 metres long in reality.

Bearings

> **Tip**
>
> You may need to create your own north line if it is not on the diagram.

Compass directions can be given using cardinal points as shown on the compass rose.

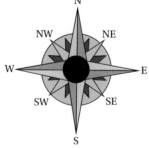

More accurate directions can be given using degrees or bearings.

Bearings are measured in degrees from 0° (north) around in a clockwise direction to 360° (which is back at north).

Bearings are written as three-figure numbers. East is 90° clockwise from north and, as a bearing, is written as 090°.

WORKED EXAMPLE 11

Find the bearings from:

a A to B   **b** B to A.

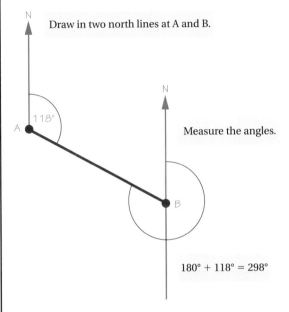

Draw in two north lines at A and B.

Measure the angles.

There are no north lines on the diagram so you have to draw them on before you can measure the bearings.

$180° + 118° = 298°$

a Bearing from A to B is 118°

To measure bearings, you must place the baseline of your protractor in line with the compass direction north. Then you measure the angle clockwise from there to the given point.

b Bearing from B to A is 298°

With your protractor, measure the angle anti-clockwise from B and subtract this from 360°.

EXERCISE 10G

1 Write the three-figure bearing that corresponds with these directions:

   a due south   **b** north-east   **c** west.

 Find answers at: cambridge.org/ukschools/gcsemaths-studentbookanswers

2 Use a protractor to measure each of the following bearings on the diagram. Give your answer to the nearest 5°.

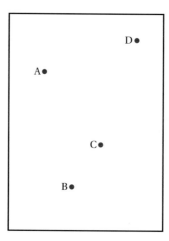

a A to B	**b** B to A	**c** A to C
d B to D	**e** D to A	**f** D to B

3 Beville is 140 km west and 45 km north of Lake Salina.

Draw a scale drawing with a scale of 1 cm to 20 km and use it to find:

a the bearing from Lake Salina to Beville

b the bearing from Beville to Lake Salina

c the shortest distance between the two places in kilometres.

4 Find the bearing from B to A, if the bearing from A to B is:

a 120°   **b** 045°   **c** 210°

5 Village Q is 7 km from Village P on a bearing of 060°.

Village R is 5 km from Village P on bearing of 315°.

Using a scale of 1 : 100 000, draw a diagram and use it to find:

a the direct distance from Village Q to Village R.

b the bearing of Village Q from Village R.

 Checklist of learning and understanding

Standard units of measurement

- You can convert between metric units of length, mass and capacity by multiplying or dividing by powers of ten.

- To convert squared units, you need to square the conversion factors.

- To convert cubed units, you need to cube the conversion factors.

- Units of time are not metric, so you need to use the number of parts in the sub-units when you convert units of time.

Compound units of measurement

- Compound units of measurement involve more than one unit.
- Rates such as £/hour or cost per kilogram are compound units.

- Speed $= \dfrac{\text{distance}}{\text{time}}$

- Density $= \dfrac{\text{mass}}{\text{volume}}$

- Pressure $= \dfrac{\text{force}}{\text{area}}$

Maps, scales and bearings

- The scale of a map or diagram describes how much smaller (or bigger) the lengths on the diagram are compared to the original lengths.
- Real length = map length × scale.
- The scale can be written as, length on diagram : real length.
- Bearings are accurate directions given in degrees from 0° to 360°. 0° corresponds with north.
- Bearings are measured clockwise from 0° and written using three figures.

 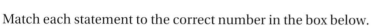

Chapter review

 For additional questions on the topics in this chapter, visit GCSE Mathematics Online.

1 Match each statement to the correct number in the box below.

5	475	182.5	259 200

   a The number of seconds in 3 days.

   b The number of kilometres travelled in $2\frac{1}{2}$ hours by a car travelling at 73 km/h.

   c The distance in km in real life of a length of 5 cm on a map with a scale of 1 : 100 000.

   d The number of litres in 475 000 millilitres.

2 True or false?

   a Tony's fish tank contains 72 litres of water.

      He says this is 72 000 millilitres.

   b The school is 15 km from the bus stop. The bus travels at 40 km/h.

      Molly says it will take her half an hour to get to school.

   c The distance from Liverpool to Manchester is about 55 km.

      The scale of a map is 1 : 250 000.

      The distance on the map would be 5.2 cm.

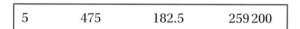

3 Convert $60\,000\,\text{cm}^2$ into m^2.

4 How many mm^2 are there in $2\,\text{m}^2$?

5 Margaret is in Switzerland.

The local supermarket sells boxes of Reblochon cheese.

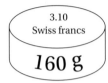

3.10
Swiss francs

160 g

Each box of Reblochon cheese costs 3.10 Swiss francs.

It weighs 160 g.

In England, a box of Reblochon cheese costs £13.55 per kg.

The exchange rate is £1 = 1.65 Swiss francs.

Work out whether Reblochon cheese is better value
for money in Switzerland or in England. *(4 marks)*

©Pearson Education Ltd 2010

6 A car is travelling at an average speed of $80\,\text{km/h}$ for one hour on a
bearing of $120°$.

a Use a scale of 1 cm to 20 km to show this journey.

b After 45 km, the driver stopped for petrol. Mark this spot on the
diagram. If this was after 40 minutes, calculate his speed for that part
of the journey.

7 The density of an object is $8\,\text{kg/m}^3$.

Work out the mass of $25\,\text{m}^3$ of the object.

8 A cyclist travels due east from point A for 10 km to reach point B.

She then travels 6 km on a bearing of $125°$ from B to reach point C.

a Use a scale of 1 cm to 2 km to represent her journey on a scale
diagram.

b Find the bearing from C to A.

c Find the direct distance from C to A in kilometres.

d If it takes the cyclist $1\frac{1}{2}$ hours to cycle back using the direct route

from C to A, find her average speed:

i in km/h **ii** in m/s.

9 Two motorcyclists set off from point A at the same time.

One travels at $60\,\text{km/h}$ on a bearing of $045°$.

The other travels at $55\,\text{km/h}$ on a bearing of $072°$.

Using a scale of 1 cm to 10 km, make a scaled diagram to show their
journey and work out how far apart they are after $1\frac{1}{2}$ hours.

11 Perimeter

In this chapter you will learn how to ...

- calculate the perimeter of simple shapes such as rectangles and triangles.
- find the perimeter of composite shapes.
- calculate the circumference of a circle.
- calculate the perimeter of composite shapes including circles or parts of circles.

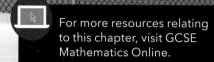
For more resources relating to this chapter, visit GCSE Mathematics Online.

Using mathematics: real-life applications

Working out the amount of fencing needed for a field, or the number of tiles needed to edge a swimming pool, or the number of perimeter security cameras needed to secure an area all require the calculation of a perimeter.

"Security cameras in a car park are only effective if they can see all round the perimeter of the car park."

(Security camera technician)

Before you start ...

Ch 2	You must be able to recognise and name some common polygons.	**1** Match each name to the correct shape. octagon pentagon hexagon **a** **b** **c**
Ch 10	You must be able to convert between basic metric units.	**2** Convert these units. **a** 5 km into m **b** 12 km into cm **c** 8500 mm into m **d** 4.8 m to mm
KS3	You need to know and use the correct names of circle parts.	**3** True or false? **a** The diameter is twice the length of the radius. **b** The diameter is always shorter than the radius. **c** The angles at the centre of a circle add up to 180°.
Ch 5	You should be able to expand brackets and factorise expressions.	**4** Which is the correct expansion of $3(x + 2)$? **A** $3x + 2$ **B** $3x + 5$ **C** $3x + 6$ **5** Factorise $3\pi + 6$.
KS3	You should be able to change the subject of a simple formula.	**6** Make l the subject of the formula $P = 2(l + w)$. **7** Make r the subject of the formula $P = \pi r + 2r$.

Find answers at: cambridge.org/ukschools/gcsemaths-studentbookanswers

Assess your starting point using the Launchpad

STEP 1

1 A football pitch is 90 m long and 55 m wide.

What is the distance around the pitch?

2 Calculate the perimeter of each shape.

a

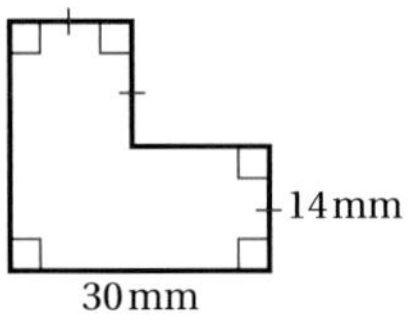

b

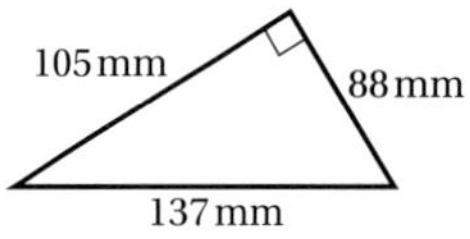

105 mm   88 mm

14 mm

30 mm   137 mm

3 A square has a perimeter of 168 mm. What is the length of a side?

4 A rectangle with a length of 4 cm, has a perimeter of 150 mm. Calculate the width of the rectangle. (Pay attention to the units.)

GO TO
Section 1:
Perimeter of simple and composite shapes

STEP 2

5 Determine the circumference of each circle. Use the π button on your calculator and give your answers correct to two decimal places.

a

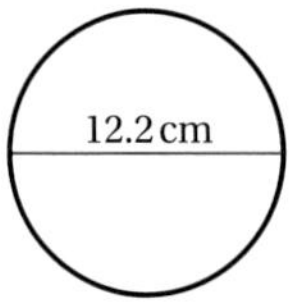

12.2 cm

b

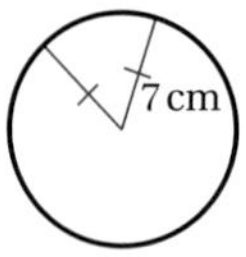

7 cm

6 Determine the diameter of a circle to the nearest centimetre given that its circumference is 37.7 cm (correct to one decimal place).

7 What is the perimeter of a semi-circular rug of radius 1.6 m to two decimal places?

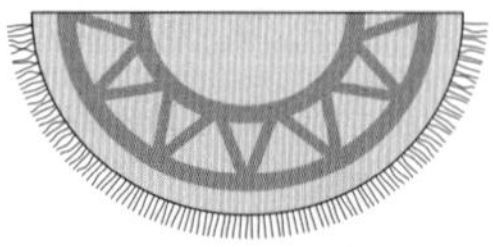

Give your answer to 2 decimal places.

GO TO
Section 2:
Circumference of a circle

GO TO
Section 3:
Problems involving perimeter and circumference

GO TO
Chapter review

Section 1: Perimeter of simple and composite shapes

The **perimeter** of a shape is the total distance around the boundaries of the shape. To calculate the perimeter of a shape:

- determine the lengths of all the sides, making sure they are in the same units
- add the lengths together.

Tip

The perimeter must include **all** the lengths. You can use what you know about the properties of shapes to deduce missing lengths.

WORKED EXAMPLE 1

Find the perimeter (P) of this T-shaped piece of cardboard.

All angles are right angles and all dimensions are in centimetres.

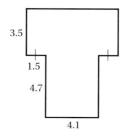

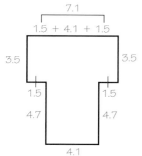

Start by working out the lengths of the missing sides.

$P = 7.1 + 3.5 + 1.5 + 4.7 + 4.1 + 4.7 + 1.5 + 3.5$
$ = 30.6$

Add up the side lengths.

Using formulae to find perimeter

The properties of different polygons can be used to derive formulae for calculating the perimeter without adding up all the sides.

Tip

You might remember some of these formulae from KS3. You do not need to memorise them, but you must be able to apply and manipulate them.

Find answers at: cambridge.org/ukschools/gcsemaths-studentbookanswers

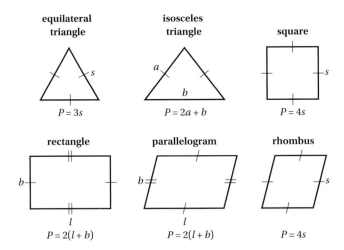

Tip

Writing a general expression is a way of showing the quantity of something when the actual numbers are not known. Numbers can be substituted into the expression to find the quantity required.

For **regular polygons** you only need the length of one side to find the perimeter.

Multiply the side length by the number of sides.

Each side length of this regular hexagon is 6 cm so the perimeter is: $6 \times 6 = 36$ cm.

If each side length was a cm, the expression for the perimeter would be $6 \times a$ or $6a$.

WORKED EXAMPLE 2

Write an expression for the the perimeter of this shape in terms of x.

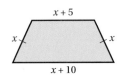

Perimeter $= x + (x + 5) + x + (x + 10)$

> Start at one side and move systematically round the shape.

Tip

Simplifying expressions by collecting like terms was covered in Chapter 5.

$= x + x + 5 + x + x + 10$
$= 4x + 15$

> Remove the brackets and gather like terms.

EXERCISE 11A

1 What is the perimeter of an equilateral triangle of side length 10 cm?

2 A yard is fully enclosed by a fence of lengths 12 m, 4.7 m, 354 cm, 972 cm. What is the perimeter of the yard?

3 Write expressions for the perimeter of these shapes.

a An equilateral triangle, side length *a*.

b A rectangle, width *x* and length *y*.

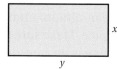

c A regular octagon, side length *z*.

4 Work out the perimeter of this shape.

Each side length is 10 cm.

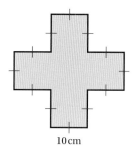

10 cm

5 A tessellated hexagon, where each hexagon fits exactly with the next, creates a pattern for a patchwork quilt.

If the side length of each hexagon is 8 cm, what is the perimeter of this shape?

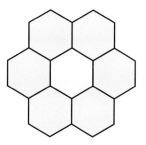

6 Each side length of this tiling pattern is 15 cm.

Work out its perimeter.

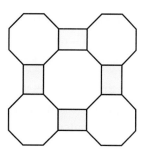

7 A field with dimensions shown on the diagram is to be fenced to protect the vegetation growing there. The fence consists of upright posts and four strands of wire (as shown).

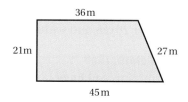

36 m

21 m   27 m

45 m

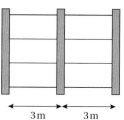

3 m   3 m

maximum distance apart
(from middle of posts)

a Find the total length of wire needed for the fencing (the wire runs through the fence posts).

b The fence posts are placed a maximum distance of 3 m apart (measured from the middle of the post to the middle of the next post). Work out the minimum number of fence posts needed for the whole perimeter fence. Make sure to include one fence post at each corner. (Assume there is no gate, only a stile to get over the fence.)

c Calculate the cost of fencing if each post costs £2.39 and the wire costs £1.78 per metre.

8 An international football field is 64 m by 75 m. (The minimum allowed size). Three teams are training on the field.

Team A warms up by running 10 times around the field.

Team B runs round half the field 15 times cutting across the half-way line.

Team C also runs round half the field 15 times but they cut through the penalty spots and kickoff spot.

The routes followed by each team are shown on the diagram.

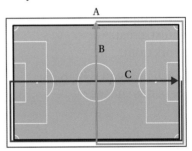

a Calculate the total distance run by each team.

b If it takes Team C a quarter of an hour to complete their warm-up laps, work out their average running speed in km/h.

Finding lengths when the perimeter is known

You can calculate missing side lengths of shapes if you know the perimeter and have enough information about the shape. For example, if you know a regular hexagon has a perimeter of 72 cm, you can deduce that each of the six equal sides are 12 cm long because 72 cm ÷ 6 = 12 cm.

WORKED EXAMPLE 3

What is the length of a rectangle of perimeter 20 cm and width 5.5 cm?

$P = 2(L + W)$
$P = 20, W = 5.5$

> Think about the information you have.

$20 = 2L + 2(5.5)$
$20 = 2L + 11$
$20 - 11 = 2L$
$9 = 2L$
$L = 4.5$ cm

> Substitute the values into the formula and solve for L.

WORKED EXAMPLE 4

Calculate the length of each side of a rhombus of perimeter 1.8 m.

$P = 4s$ Write down the formula.

$s = \dfrac{P}{4}$

$s = \dfrac{1.8}{4}$ Change the subject of the formula and substitute the values you know to find s.

$s = 0.45\,m$

> **Tip**
>
> You will do more work with changing the subject in Chapter 17.

Perimeter of composite shapes

Composite shapes are formed by combining shapes or by removing parts of a shape.

This shape (right) is made up of a rectangle and a triangle.

You add up the side lengths around the outside boundary of the shape to find the perimeter. The perimeter is:
$4 + 3 + 3 + 4 + 3 = 17\,cm$

The rectangle below a parallelogram cut out of it. The perimeter of the shape must include all of the boundaries, so, in examples like these, you must include the outer and inner boundaries of the shape.

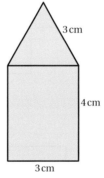

$P = 2(20 + 10) + 2(10 + 5)$

$\quad = 2(30) + 2(15)$

$\quad = 60 + 30$

$\quad = 90\,cm$

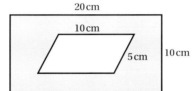

WORK IT OUT 11.1

This shape was made by combining five identical squares with sides of 6.5 cm with four identical equilateral triangles.

Which calculation will result in the correct perimeter? Why?

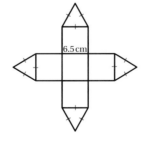

Option A	Option B	Option C
$P = 16 \times 6.5$	$P = 20 \times 6.5$	$P = 24 \times 6.5$
$- 104\,cm$	$= 130\,cm$	$= 156\,cm$

EXERCISE 11B

1 Work out the lengths of the sides in each shape.

a A rectangle has a perimeter of 242 mm and a longer side length of 77 mm.

b A parallelogram has a perimeter of 200 mm. One side length is 55 mm.

c A rhombus has a perimeter of 14 cm.

d A square has a perimeter 47.2 cm.

2 Calculate the perimeter of each shape.

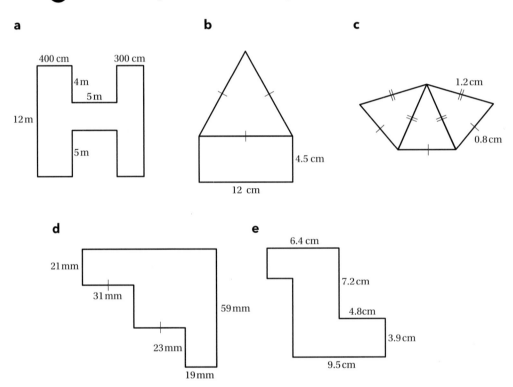

3 Petra is a mosaic artist. She has the following mosaic tiles:

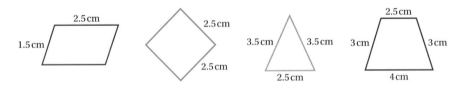

She arranges the tiles to make the following shapes.

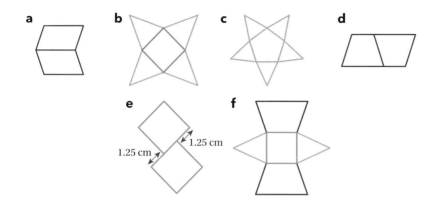

Use the dimensions above to find the perimeter of each shape.

4 The end of a maze consists of a regular pentagon with side length 5 m.

If a child runs round this three times, how far will they run in total?

5 A rectangular allotment has a perimeter of 25 metres.

If the length of one side is 6.8 metres, how wide is the allotment?

Section 2: Circumference of a circle

Make sure you remember these names for different parts of a circle.

The perimeter of a circle is called its **circumference (C)**.

The radius (r) is the distance from the centre to the circumference.

The diameter (d) is a line through the centre of a circle. The diameter is twice the radius ($2r$).

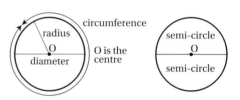

The Ancient Greeks discovered that when you measured the circumference of a circle and divided it by its diameter you got a constant ratio of approximately 3.142.

This ratio is called pi and the symbol π is used to represent it.

$$\pi = \frac{C}{d}$$

This ratio can be rearranged to give two formulae for finding the circumference of any circle.

Pi has no exact decimal or fractional value (it is an irrational number). When you do calculations involving pi you might need to give rounded or approximate answers.

Your calculator can work with more precise values of π but you might be given an approximate value of π to use in a problem context.

Learn this formula

$C = \pi d$ and $C = 2\pi r$

WORKED EXAMPLE 5

a Calculate the circumference of a circle with diameter 7 cm.

Give your answer to the nearest cm.

b Calculate the circumference of a circle with radius 4.5 m.

Leave your answer as a multiple of π.

a $C = \pi d$

> Use the version of the formula with d, as you are given the diameter.

$$= \pi \times 7$$
$$= 21.991\,149 \approx 22\,\text{cm}$$

> Substitute $d = 7$ and use the $\boxed{\pi}$ button on your calculator.

b $C = 2\pi r$

> Use the version of the formula with r, as you are given the radius.

$$= 2 \times \pi \times 4.5$$
$$= 9\pi\,\text{m}$$

> Substitute $r = 4.5$. **Do not** put in a value for π.

Problem solving

Problem-solving framework

Racing wheelchairs can travel at speeds of up to 45 mph and can cost up to £20 000.

The rear wheels of a chair have a diameter of 70 cm.

The hand wheels have a radius of 20 cm.

a Find the difference in circumference between the two wheels.

b Find the number of revolutions that the rear wheels will make over a 100 m race.

Steps for solving problems	What you would do for this example
Step 1: What have you got to do?	Find the difference in circumference between the two wheels, and find the number of revolutions (turns) that the rear wheels will make over 100 m.
Step 2: What information do you need?	Diameter (d) of rear wheel = 70 cm Radius (r) of hand wheel = 20 cm Length of race = 100 m Circumference formula: $C = \pi d$ or $2\pi r$
Step 3: What information don't you need?	The speed of the wheelchair and its cost are irrelevant.

Continues on next page …

Step 4: What maths can you do?	Circumference of rear wheel $- \pi d = \pi \times 70 = 219.9$ cm (to 1 decimal place)
	Circumference of hand wheel $= 2\pi r = 2 \times \pi \times 20 = 125.7$ cm (to 1 decimal place)
	Difference in circumference $= 219.9 - 125.7 = 94.2$ cm
	Change the units so that they are the same:
	100 m $= 100 \times 100$ cm $= 10\,000$ cm
	Number of revolutions made by rear wheel $= 10\,000 \div 219.9 = 45.5$ (to 1 decimal place)
Step 5: Have you used all the information? At this point you should check to make sure you have calculated what was asked of you.	All information used ✓ Calculated part **a** ✓ Calculated part **b** ✓
Step 6: Is it correct?	Used diameter for rear wheel ✓ Used radius for hand wheel ✓ Converted cm into m correctly ✓

Knowing the circumference of a circle means that you can calculate the diameter and/or radius.

WORKED EXAMPLE 6

A circle has a circumference of 200 cm.

Calculate the diameter of the circle to 1 decimal place.

$C = \pi d$
Use the version of the formula with d.
You *could* re-arrange the formula here to give $d = \dfrac{C}{\pi}$

$200 = \pi \times d$
Substitute $C = 200$.
$200 \div \pi = d$

$d = 63.7$ cm

Tip

If you are asked to find r and use $C = \pi d$, remember to divide d by 2 to get r.

EXERCISE 11C

1 Use the π key on your calculator to calculate the circumference of each circle.

Give your answer correct to 2 decimal places if necessary.

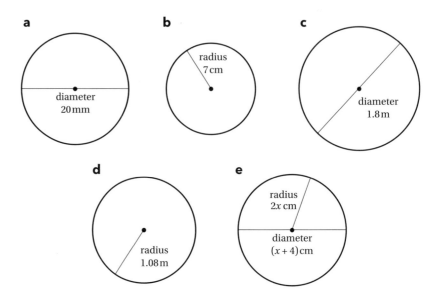

a

diameter 20 mm

b

radius 7 cm

c

diameter 1.8 m

d

radius 1.08 m

e

radius 2x cm

diameter (x + 4) cm

2 A car rim has a diameter of 42 cm. Calculate the circumference of the rim.

3 A plastic toy (left), called a slinky spring, consists of 36 coils of plastic.

If the diameter of one coil is 55 mm, what length of plastic is needed to make the spring?

4 Nate has a square piece of metal with sides of 8.5 cm. He wants to cut out a round disc with a radius of at least 4 cm from the square.

a Draw a rough sketch to show this shape.

b Calculate the circumference of the disc if the radius is 4 cm.

c When he cuts the disc out, Nate finds the diameter is actually 8.3 cm.

What is the circumference of this disc?

d What is the perimeter of the piece of metal left after cutting out a disc of:

   i radius 4 cm   **ii** diameter 8.3 cm?

5 Find the diameter, correct to 2 decimal places, of a circle of circumference:

a 20 mm   **b** 15.2 cm.

6 Find the radius of a round CD to the nearest mm, if its circumference is 36.33 cm.

7 What is the smallest possible square plate that you can use for a round cake of circumference 77 cm?

8 The minute hand of a clock is 75 mm long.

How far will the tip of the hand travel in one hour? Give your answer correct to the nearest centimetre.

9 A circular boating lake has a diameter of 8 m. What is its circumference? Give your answer in terms of π.

10 The radius of a circular stained glass window is 60 cm. In terms of π, what is its circumference?

Sectors of a circle

A sector is a 'slice' of a circle. The perimeter of a sector is formed by two radii and a section of the circumference called an arc.

Perimeter of a sector = radius + radius + arc length.

To find the perimeter of a sector you have to work out the length of the arc.

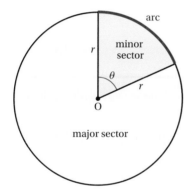

The angle at the centre of a circle is a fraction of 360°. You can express this as $\dfrac{x}{360}$.

The arc length is a fraction of the circumference. To find the length of the arc, use the size of the angle and the circumference of the circle.

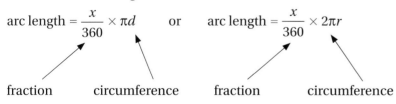

$$\text{arc length} = \frac{x}{360} \times \pi d \qquad \text{or} \qquad \text{arc length} = \frac{x}{360} \times 2\pi r$$

fraction   circumference   fraction   circumference

The angle θ is said to be **subtended** at the centre. A subtended angle is one whose sides pass through the ends of an arc (or other curved line).

> **Tip**
>
> The term circumference is only used to describe the distance around a whole circle. For the distance around the boundary of a shape that is part of a circle, you use the term perimeter.

Find answers at: cambridge.org/ukschools/gcsemaths-studentbookanswers

WORKED EXAMPLE 7

Find the length of the arc in each of these circle sectors.

a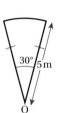

b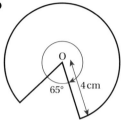

a Arc length $= \dfrac{30}{360} \times 2\pi r$

Use $2\pi r$ here as you have been given the radius.

$= \dfrac{1}{12} \times 2 \times \pi \times 5$

$= 2.62$ m

Correct to 2 decimal places.

b $360° - 65° = 295°$

The angle inside the sector is not given.

Work it out using angles round a point.

Arc length $= \dfrac{295}{360} \times 2 \times \pi \times 4$

Correct to 2 decimal places.

$= 20.59$ cm

The semi-circle and quarter-circle (quadrant) are special cases.

- In a semi-circle, the angle at the centre is 180° and the arc length is half the circumference.
- In a quarter-circle, the angle at the centre is 90° and the arc length is a quarter of the circumference.

EXERCISE 11D

1 Find l in each of the following circles.

a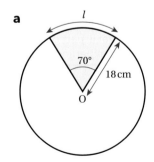

b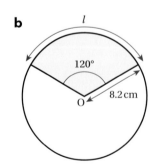

c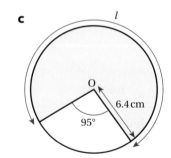

d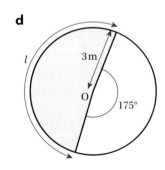

2 Find the perimeter of each shape.

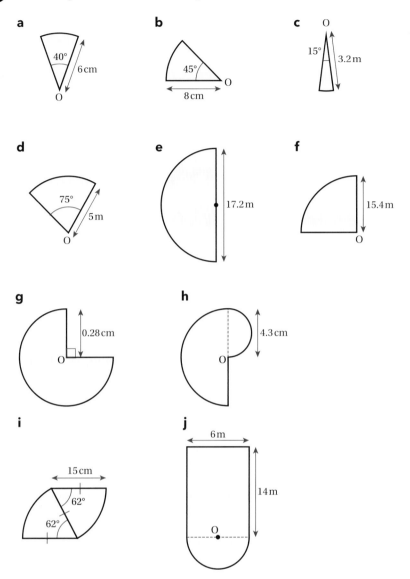

a 40° 6cm O

b 45° 8cm O

c O 15° 3.2m

d 75° 5m O

e 17.2m

f 15.4m O

g 0.28cm O

h 4.3cm O

i 15cm 62° 62°

j 6m 14m O

Section 3: Problems involving perimeter and circumference

In this section you are going to combine what you have learned about perimeter and circumference to solve problems involving composite shapes.

To work with irregular and composite shapes you divide them up into known shapes to make it easier to do the calculations.

An athletics track can be divided up into a rectangle and two semi-circles, one at either end. By splitting the shape into known shapes, you can find the perimeter of the track.

Two semi-circles make one circle, so

perimeter = circumference of circle + the lengths of the two straight sides.

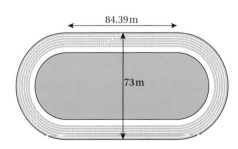

84.39 m

73 m

WORKED EXAMPLE 8

The diagram shows a baseball field which is $\frac{1}{4}$ of a circle.

Calculate the perimeter of the field correct to the nearest metre.

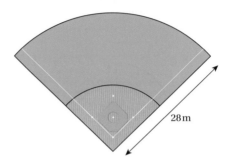

Circumference of whole circle
$= 2\pi r = 2 \times \pi \times 28$

Arc length of $\frac{1}{4}$ circle $= \frac{C}{4}$

> Remember, a quarter-circle is a special case, with the angle at the centre being 90°.

$$= \frac{2 \times \pi \times 28}{4}$$

$$= 43.98\,m$$

Perimeter $= 2r + arc\ length$
$$= 2 \times 28 + 43.98$$
$$= 56 + 43.98$$
$$= 99.98\,m$$

$P = 100\,m$ correct to the nearest metre.

WORK IT OUT 11.2

This is a plan of a children's play area.

Scale 1 : 25

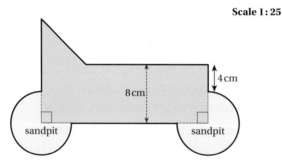

Edging is to be placed around the curved edges of the yellow sandpits.

Using $\pi = 3.14$, what is the total length of edging required?

Which of the answers below is the correct answer?

What mistakes have been made in the other workings?

Continues on next page …

Option A	Option B	Option C
Circumference $= \pi d = 2\pi r$ of a circle $r = 4\,\text{cm}$	Circumference $= \pi d = 2\pi r$ of a circle $r = 4\,\text{cm}$	Circumference $= 2\pi d = \pi r$ of a circle $r = 4\,\text{cm}$
$C = 2 \times 3.14 \times 4$ $\quad = 3.14 \times 8$ $\quad = 25.12\,\text{cm}$	$C = 2 \times 3.14 \times 4$ $\quad = 3.14 \times 8$ $\quad = 25.12\,\text{cm}$	$C = 2 \times 3.14 \times 8$ $\quad = 3.14 \times 16 = 50.24\,\text{cm}$
Scale $1 : 25$ So, actual circumference of the circle $= 25.12 \times 25$ $\quad = 628\,\text{cm} = 6.28\,\text{m}$	Only $\dfrac{3}{4}$ of the sandpit needs edging: $\dfrac{3}{4} \times 25.12\,\text{cm} = 18.84\,\text{cm}$	Only $\dfrac{3}{4}$ of the sandpit needs edging: $\dfrac{3}{4} \times 50.24\,\text{cm} = 37.68\,\text{cm}$
Two sandpits so total edging required $= 6.28 \times 2 = 12.56\,\text{m}$	Two sandpits: $18.84\,\text{cm} \times 2 = 37.68\,\text{cm}$ of edging Scale $= 1 : 25$ So actual amount of edging required: $37.68\,\text{cm} \times 25 = 942\,\text{cm}$ $\quad\quad\quad\quad\quad\quad\quad = 9.42\,\text{m}$	Two sandpits: $37.68\,\text{cm} \times 2 = 75.36\,\text{cm}$ of edging Scale $= 1 : 25$ So actual amount of edging required: $75.36\,\text{cm} \times 25 = 1884\,\text{cm}$ $\quad\quad\quad\quad\quad\quad\quad = 18.84\,\text{m}$

Tip

Perimeter can be worked out by measuring lengths, or by using lengths from a scale diagram.

EXERCISE 11E

The diagram shows the shape and dimensions of different throwing event field areas in international competitions. Use the information on the diagram to answer questions 1 to 5.

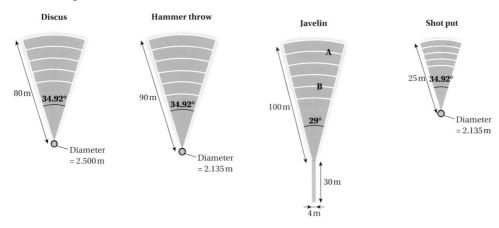

1 Calculate the length of the white line painted around the outside of:

   a the discus area   **b** the hammer throw area.

2 Competitors in the discus, shot put and hammer throw have to remain inside a marked circle while the equipment is in their hands (before they throw it).

   a Which sport has the largest marked circle?

   b What is the circumference of the circle in the discus throwing cage?

   c In shot put and hammer throw, a raised edge is built around the circumference of the starting circle. If this edge is 10 cm wide, calculate its inner and outer circumference.

3 Calculate the perimeter of the event space for javelin.

4 The curved measurement lines on each event space are 10 m apart.

   Using the javelin field, calculate the length of the lines marked A and B.

5 The position of a winning discus throw is shown on the field by a red dot. The angle between its path and the edge of the marked area closest to it is 10°.

   a How far is the discus from the throwing area?

   b Work out the shortest curved distance along the white line to the edge of the throwing area.

6 The average radius of the Earth is 6378.1 km at the Equator.

   Calculate the circumference of the Earth, assuming the Earth is a sphere. Give your answer correct to 2 decimal places.

7 A large pizza has a circumference of 94 cm.

   What is the side length of the smallest cardboard box it will fit into?

8 Find the perimeter of the symmetrical logo (left).

   Use a ruler and protractor to measure and find the dimensions you need.

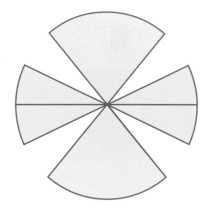

9 The diagram (right) shows the design of a small stained glass window consisting of a composite shape - a rectangle with a semi-circle on top. Take π as 3.14. Give your answer to the nearest whole number.

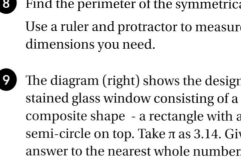

420 mm

340 mm

10 The London Eye is a good example of a structure involving angles and sectors of circles.

   a The London Eye has a diameter of 122 m. What is its circumference?

   b There are 32 equally spaced pods on the outside of the wheel. Calculate the curved distance between them.

   c The curved boarding platform at the base of the eye is 58 m long. How far does a capsule travel from where it leaves this platform to where it meets it again after a revolution?

   d One capsule takes 30 minutes to make a complete revolution. What is its speed in metres per second?

   e The London Eye rotates 7668 times per year. How many kilometres does one capsule travel in a year?

 Checklist of learning and understanding

Perimeter

- Perimeter is the total distance around the boundaries of a shape.
- You can calculate perimeter by adding the lengths of the sides or by applying a formula based on the properties of the shape.

Circumference

- The perimeter of a circle is called its circumference.
- $C = \pi d$ or $C = 2\pi r$
- A sector is a part of a circle between two radii. You can find the arc length of a sector by working out what fraction of a circle the sector represents.

 Chapter review

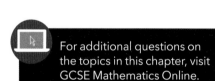

For additional questions on the topics in this chapter, visit GCSE Mathematics Online.

1 The perimeters of the two shapes on the right are equal.

   What is the side length of the square?

8 cm

6 cm

2 The perimeter of a regular pentagon is 90 cm.

   Work out the length of each side.

3 A rectangular vegetable plot has a perimeter of 50 metres.

   If the width is 6.5 m, what is the length of the plot?

4 An irrigator in a field can water a circular area of radius 14.5 m.

   What is the circumference of the area that can be irrigated?
   Use $\pi = 3.14$.

 Find answers at: cambridge.org/ukschools/gcsemaths-studentbookanswers

5 Susan has a round cake.

The cake has a diameter of 20 cm.

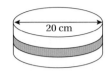

20 cm

Diagram **NOT** accurately drawn

Susan wants to put a ribbon round the cake.

What is the least length of ribbon she can use? *(3 marks)*

©Pearson Education Ltd 2012

6 A pizza has a diameter of 28 cm. It is placed in a cardboard box.

Calculate the perimeter of the smallest box that it will fit into.

7 Calculate the perimeter of the shape shown.

Give your answer correct to 1 decimal place.

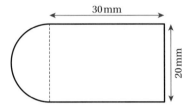

30 mm

20 mm

8 The diagram shows some staging for a concert.

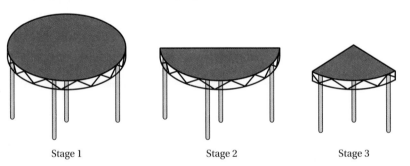

Stage 1   Stage 2   Stage 3

The main stage is a circle of diameter 6 m. The smaller stages can be made by splitting up a main stage into smaller pieces, with stage 2 being half the size of stage 1, and stage 3 being half the size of stage 2. The curved edges of the staging pieces have a patterned edge.

a Work out the total length of the patterned edging on the stage sections shown in the diagram.

b A rubber safety strip is to be applied along all the edges of the staging.

Work out the length of strip required for the three stages sections shown in the diagram.

12 Area

In this chapter you will learn how to ...

- apply formulae to find the area of different shapes, including circles and parts of circles.
- use appropriate formulae to calculate the area of composite shapes.

 For more resources relating to this chapter, visit GCSE Mathematics Online.

Using mathematics: real-life applications

Ordering the right quantity of turf for a sports field, preparing detailed floor plans, and determining how much fertiliser is needed to treat a field crop all require knowledge and calculation of areas.

 Did you know?

The area of farmland is sometimes given in acres. An acre was traditionally the area of farmland that could be ploughed in one day by oxen. In the metric system, the acre was replaced by the hectare.
1 hectare = $10000\,m^2$
1 hectare = 2.471 054 acres

"Fertiliser application rates are normally given in kilograms per hectare. One hectare is an area of $100\,m \times 100\,m$ or $10000\,m^2$. Applying too much or too little fertiliser to an area can have disastrous results for the crops."

(Farmer)

Before you start ...

Ch 2	You should remember the properties of quadrilaterals.	**1** Use the marked properties to name the quadrilaterals correctly. 
Ch 4	You should be familiar with square numbers and square roots.	**2** Calculate. **a** 5^2 **b** 2×10^2 **c** $3^2 + 4^2$ **3** Find the number which is squared to give each of these. **a** 144 **b** 10000 **c** 0.25
Ch 10	You need to be able to convert between square units of measurement.	**4** Complete these. **a** $5\,m^2 = \square\,cm^2$ **b** $\square\,cm^2 = 87000\,mm^2$ **c** $4\,km^2 = \square\,m^2$

Assess your starting point using the Launchpad

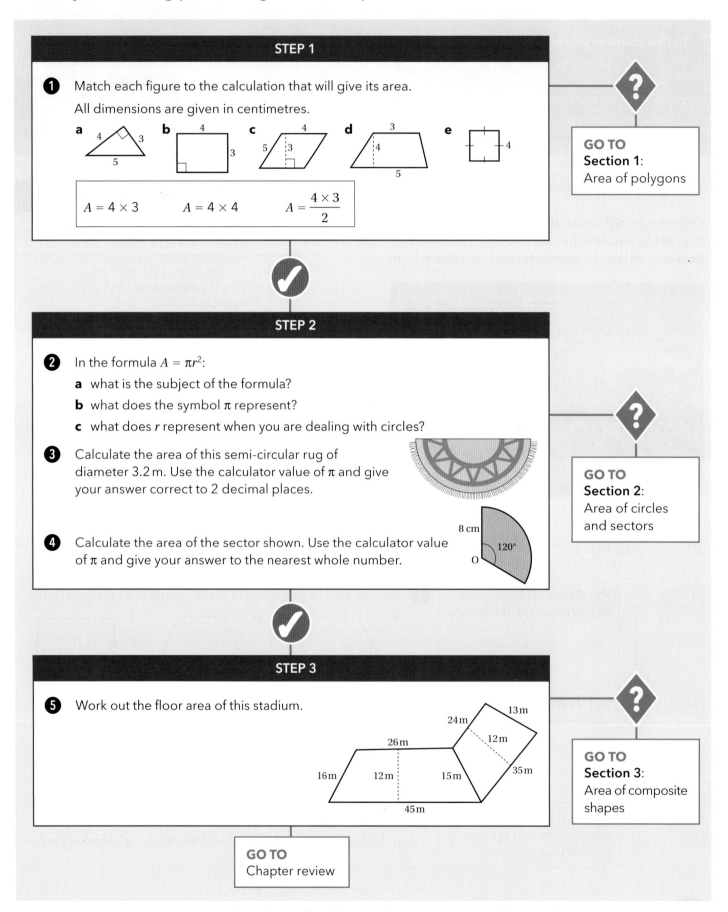

STEP 1

1 Match each figure to the calculation that will give its area.

All dimensions are given in centimetres.

a   **b**   **c**   **d**   **e**

$$A = 4 \times 3 \qquad A = 4 \times 4 \qquad A = \frac{4 \times 3}{2}$$

**GO TO
Section 1:**
Area of polygons

STEP 2

2 In the formula $A = \pi r^2$:

a what is the subject of the formula?

b what does the symbol π represent?

c what does r represent when you are dealing with circles?

3 Calculate the area of this semi-circular rug of diameter 3.2 m. Use the calculator value of π and give your answer correct to 2 decimal places.

4 Calculate the area of the sector shown. Use the calculator value of π and give your answer to the nearest whole number.

8 cm

120°

O

**GO TO
Section 2:**
Area of circles and sectors

STEP 3

5 Work out the floor area of this stadium.

13 m
24 m
26 m
12 m
16 m   12 m   15 m   35 m
45 m

**GO TO
Section 3:**
Area of composite shapes

GO TO
Chapter review

Section 1: Area of polygons

The **area** of a plane shape is the amount of space it takes up. You can think of area of a plane, or flat, shape as the number of squares (square units) that will fit inside the boundary of the shape.

Area is always given in square units. Common units are mm² (square millimetres), cm² (square centimetres), m² and km².

Area of rectangles and squares

The formula for finding the area of a rectangle is:

area = length × width

$A = lw$

A square is a special case of a rectangle, the length and width are equal, so the formula is:

area of the square $= l \times l = l^2$

$A = l^2$

Area of a triangle

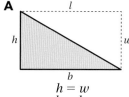
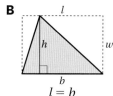

Figure A shows a right-angled triangle. Figure B shows a scalene triangle. In both diagrams the area of the shaded and unshaded parts are equal.

Area of the rectangle $= l \times w$

So, the area of the triangle $= \frac{1}{2} \times l \times w$

But, l is equal to the base of the triangle and w is equal to the height of the triangle, so the area of the triangle $= \frac{1}{2} \times$ length of its base $\times$ its height.

This gives a formula for the area of any triangle.

Continues on next page …

Tip

Base (b) and height (h) may be used instead of length and width, so you may see this area formula written as $A = bh$.

Tip

Sometimes the side length is written as s (for side) instead of l. In this case the formula for the area of a square is written as $A = s^2$.

Learn this formula

Area of a triangle
$= \frac{1}{2} \times$ base $\times$ perpendicular height
$= \frac{1}{2} \times b \times h$

WORKED EXAMPLE 1

Calculate the area of each triangle.

a

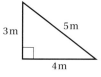

b

c

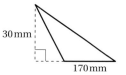

Tip

The order of the multiplication is not important:

$\frac{1}{2} \times 4 \times 3 = \frac{1}{2} \times 12 = 6$

$\frac{1}{2} \times 4 \times 3 = 2 \times 3 = 6$

$0.5 \times 3 \times 4 = 1.5 \times 4 = 6$

Did you know?

Two triangles that look completely different might still have the same area.

These two triangles are equal in area.

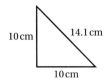

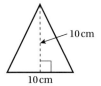

a $\text{Area} = \frac{1}{2} \times b \times h$

        $= \frac{1}{2} \times 4 \times 3$

        $= \frac{1}{2} \times 12$

        $= 6\,\text{m}^2$

Write down the formula you are going to use.

In a right-angled triangle the two shorter (perpendicular) sides can be used as the base and height.

Remember to include the units in your answer.

b $\text{Area} = \frac{1}{2} \times b \times h$

        $= \frac{1}{2} \times 1.9 \times 0.9$

        $= \frac{1}{2} \times 1.71$

        $= 0.855\,\text{m}^2$

Use the side marked 1.9 as the base because the height is perpendicular to it.

c $\text{Area} = \dfrac{bh}{2}$

        $= \dfrac{(170 \times 30)}{2}$

        $= \dfrac{5100}{2}$

        $= 2550\,\text{mm}^2$

This is the same formula expressed differently. Multiplying by $\frac{1}{2}$ is the same as dividing by 2.

When you extend a base line so that you can find a perpendicular height outside the triangle, it does not change the base length you use in your calculations.

EXERCISE 12A

1 Calculate the area of each triangle.

a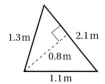

b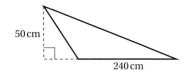

2 The area of a triangle is $36\,\text{m}^2$ and its perpendicular height is $6\,\text{m}$.

Work out the length of its base.

3 Work out the total area of this kite.

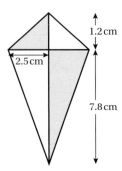

4 A triangle has a base of 3.6 m and a height of 50 cm. What is its area in metres squared?

5 A triangle of area 0.125 m² has a base 25 cm long. What is its height in centimetres?

6 Calculate the total area of the sails on this small boat (right). The larger sail is 2.7 m tall. The smaller sail extends $\frac{2}{3}$ of the way up the larger sail.

7 These flags were seen at an international convention centre.

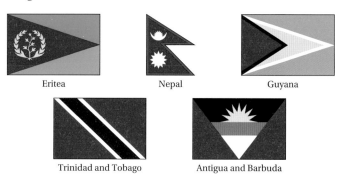

a The flag of Nepal is the world's only non-quadrilateral flag. It consists of two triangles, one above the other. The bottom triangle overlaps the top triangle by $\frac{1}{4}$ of its area. The dimensions of the top triangle to the bottom one are in the ratio 3 : 4.

If the top flag is 84 cm high and 63 cm wide at its base, what is the area of the whole flag?

b The flag of Eritrea contains three triangles. The tip of the red triangle is at the midpoint of the edge of the flag. If the flag dimensions are 1.2 m by 60 cm, calculate the area of each triangle on the flag.

c If the flag of Trinidad and Tobago is 1.3 m by 87 cm and the width of the black and white flash is 32.5 cm along the edges of the flag, calculate the area of each red triangle.

d A small decorative flag of Antigua and Barbuda is 210 mm × 297 mm.

  i The red triangles meet at the centre of the long edge of the flag. What is the area of each red triangle?

  ii Estimate the area of the white triangle based on these dimensions. Show how you made your estimate.

e On the flag of Guyana, the triangles are isosceles, so the tips of the triangles lie along the centre line of the flag. The point of the black line around the red triangle extends $\frac{4}{9}$ of the length of the flag.

Assuming a flag is 270 mm by 450 mm, calculate:

  i the area covered by the red and black triangle

  ii the area of each green triangle

  iii the area of the 'golden arrow' made by the yellow and white colour on the flag.

f Investigate the dimensions of the Union Jack. What percentage of the flag area is each colour?

Tip

If you need more information about ratios, refer to Chapter 20.

Find answers at: cambridge.org/ukschools/gcsemaths-studentbookanswers

Area of a parallelogram

The base of this parallelogram is b and the **perpendicular height** is h.

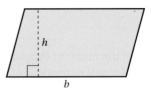

By removing a triangle from one end and joining it to the other end, you can form a rectangle.

The parallelogram and rectangle have the same area.

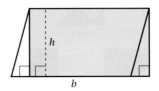

Learn this formula

Area of a parallelogram
= base × perpendicular height
= $b \times h$

Tip

You must use the perpendicular height and not the slant height.

WORKED EXAMPLE 2

Calculate the area of the parallelogram.

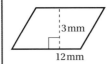

Area = $b \times h$

$= 12 \times 3 = 36\,\text{mm}^2$

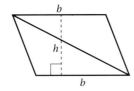

You can use the formula for the area of a triangle to derive the formula for the area of a parallelogram.

A parallelogram can be divided into two triangles.

So, area of parallelogram = $(\frac{1}{2} \times b \times h) + (\frac{1}{2} \times b \times h) = b \times h$

WORK IT OUT 12.1

A parallelogram is made by combining a rectangle and two right-angled triangles like this.

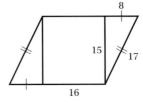

Which of these options will give the correct area?

Which dimensions are incorrect in the other two? Why?

Option A	Option B	Option C
$A = bh$	$A = bh$	$A = bh$
$= 16 \times 17$	$= 24 \times 17$	$= 24 \times 15$

Area of a trapezium

A **trapezium** has parallel sides a and b, and perpendicular height h.

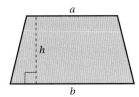

If you join two identical trapezia, you can form a parallelogram.

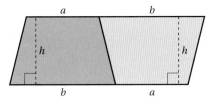

The parallelogram has a base of length $a + b$, and perpendicular height h.

The area of a parallelogram = base × perpendicular height.

So area $= (a + b) \times h$

But, each trapezium is half the area of the parallelogram.

So, area of a trapezium $= \dfrac{1}{2} \times (a + b) \times h$, where a and b are the lengths of the parallel sides.

WORKED EXAMPLE 3

Calculate the area of the trapezium.

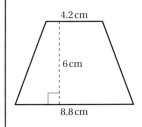

$$\text{Area} = \frac{1}{2} \times (a + b) \times h$$

$$= \frac{1}{2} \times (4.2 + 8.8) \times 6$$

$$= \frac{1}{2} \times 13 \times 6$$

$$= 39 \, \text{cm}^2$$

Tip

You might see the trapezium area formula written as $\dfrac{(a + b)h}{2}$.

WORK IT OUT 12.2

A solar farm is being built in a field.

Each solar panel measures 98 cm by 150 cm.

If 500 panels can fit onto the field, what is the area of panels being used, in m²?

Continues on next page …

Find answers at: cambridge.org/ukschools/gcsemaths-studentbookanswers

Which of the answers below is correct?

What errors were made in each of the others?

Answer A	Answer B	Answer C
Area of one panel:	Area of one panel:	Area of one panel:
$98 \times 150 = 14\,700\,\text{cm}^2$	$\frac{1}{2} \times (98 \times 150) = 7350\,\text{cm}^2$	$98 \times 150 = 14\,700\,\text{cm}^2$
$1\,\text{m}^2 = 10\,000\,\text{cm}^2$	$1\,\text{m}^2 = 10\,000\,\text{cm}^2$	$1\,\text{m}^2 = 100\,\text{cm}^2$
1 panel $= 14\,700 \div 10\,000 = 1.47\,\text{m}^2$ 500 panels $= 1.47\,\text{m}^2 \times 500$ $\qquad = 735\,\text{m}^2$	1 panel $= 7350 \div 10\,000 = 0.735\,\text{m}^2$ 500 panels $= 0.735\,\text{m}^2 \times 500$ $\qquad = 367.5\,\text{m}^2$	1 panel $= 14\,700 \div 100 = 147\,\text{m}^2$ 500 panels $= 147\,\text{m}^2 \times 500$ $\qquad = 73\,500\,\text{m}^2$

EXERCISE 12B

1 Calculate the area of each parallelogram.

a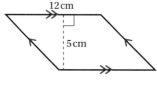

b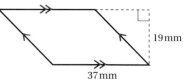

c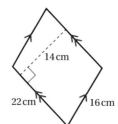

d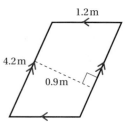

2 Calculate the area of each trapezium.

a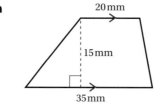

b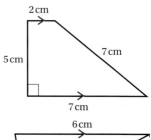

c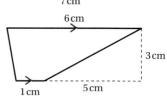

d

3 The area of this rectangle is $96\,\text{cm}^2$.

What is its length?

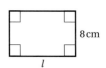

4 The area of a parallelogram is $40\,\text{m}^2$.

If the perpendicular height is $10\,\text{cm}$, what is the length of the base?

5 The area and one other measurement are given for each shape. Use the given information to find the unknown length in each figure.

a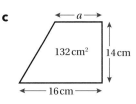

24 cm² with base 8 cm and height h

b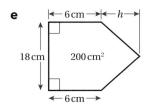

289 cm², b, 17 cm

c 132 cm², a, 14 cm, 16 cm

d 15 cm, 75 cm², b

e 6 cm, h, 18 cm, 200 cm², 6 cm

6 Amira works in a community development programme that helps people to grow organic vegetables. The area of land available in one community is shown on the plan (right).

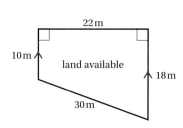

a Calculate the area of the available land.

b To prepare the soil, the community has to lay down 25 kg of soil and 10 kg of compost per square metre of land. Work out how much soil and compost they will need.

c There is a gate 2 m wide along the 22 m boundary. The rest of the land needs to be fenced. Work out the total amount of fencing needed.

d Once the first crop is planted an organic fertiliser is mixed with water and applied to the area. The instructions for mixing the powdered fertiliser with water are:

Mix 43 g/litre and the application rate is 125 litres per hectare.

  i Work out how many litres are needed for this area. Remember one hectare is 10 000 m².

  ii The powder comes in $\frac{1}{2}$ kg tubs. How many applications can the community get from one tub?

7 Write an expression in simplest terms for the area of each shape.

a  x + 7, 2x

b 4x + 6, 2x − 1

c 3x, x + 4, 3x

d $\frac{7x}{y}$, $\frac{4y}{x}$

e  3x + 1, 4x, 3(x + 4)

f 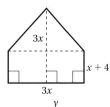 $\frac{y}{6x}$, $\frac{3x^2}{y}$

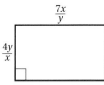
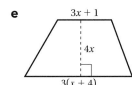
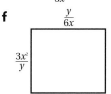

Find answers at: cambridge.org/ukschools/gcsemaths-studentbookanswers

Learn this formula

Area of a circle, $A = \pi r^2$
where r = radius

Tip

Use the π key of your calculator to find the area and circumference of circles unless you are given an approximate value to use.

Leave the value you get on the display for the next step and only round off to the required number of places when you have a final value.

Remember always to calculate r^2 before you multiply by π. The rules of BODMAS apply.

Tip

If you are asked to find the diameter (d) remember it is twice the radius ($2 \times r$).

Tip

A semi-circle is half a circle, so its area is half the area of a circle $\left(\dfrac{\pi r^2}{2}\right)$.

A quarter-circle is one quarter of a circle, so its area is one quarter of the area of a circle $\left(\dfrac{\pi r^2}{4}\right)$.

Section 2: Area of circles and sectors

In Chapter 11 you worked with the diameter, radius and circumference of circles and sectors of circles. You also used approximate and calculator values of π in circle calculations. You will meet these terms again in this section.

The area of a circle is calculated using the formula:

area, $A = \pi r^2$

where r = radius.

If you are given the diameter, d, you can still use this formula by remembering that:

$$r = \frac{1}{2}d$$

WORKED EXAMPLE 4

Calculate the area of this circle correct to 2 decimal places.

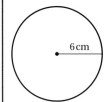

$A = \pi r^2$

$\quad = \pi \times 6 \times 6 = 113.0973355\,cm^2$

$\quad = 113.10\,cm^2$ (to 2 decimal places)

When you know the area of a circle you can find the length of a radius (or the diameter).

WORKED EXAMPLE 5

Calculate the radius of a circle with area $50\,cm^2$.

$A = \pi r^2$

$50 = \pi \times r^2$

$r^2 = \dfrac{50}{\pi}$

$r = \sqrt{\dfrac{50}{\pi}} = 3.989422804$

$\quad = 3.99\,cm$ (to 2 decimal places)

Area of a sector

A sector is a fraction of the area of the whole circle. To find the area of a sector you need to know what fraction the sector is of the circle.

You find this by dividing the sector angle by 360 in the same way that you did to find the arc length in Chapter 11.

WORKED EXAMPLE 6

Calculate the area of the sector shown.

$$\text{Area of the sector} = \frac{\theta}{360} \times \pi r^2$$

$$= \frac{135}{360} \times \pi \times r^2$$

$$= 0.375 \times \pi \times 14^2$$

$$= 230.90706$$

$$= 230.91 \text{ m}^2 \text{ (to 2 decimal places)}$$

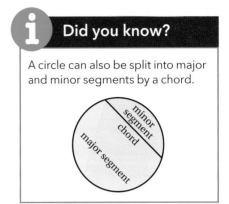

135°

14 m

Did you know?

A circle can also be split into major and minor segments by a chord.

minor segment

chord

major segment

EXERCISE 12C

Use the calculator value of π and give your final answers correct to 2 decimal places.

1 Find the area of each circle.

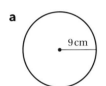 **a** 9 cm

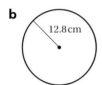 **b** 12.8 cm

 c 14 cm

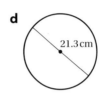 **d** 21.3 cm

2 Calculate the area of each sector.

 a 18 mm 53°

 **b** 105° 2 cm

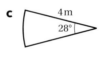 **c** 4 m 28°

 d 122° 19 mm

3 What is the difference in area between these two sectors?

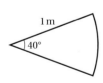 1 m 40°

 50 cm 80°

4 A pizza has a diameter of 14 cm.

a Calculate the area of the pizza.

b Estimate the area of a round plate that the pizza can fit onto with about 1 cm space around the edge.

5 A pair of sunglasses has circular lenses each 5.4 cm in diameter.

a What is the total area of the tinted surface of the lenses?

Find answers at: cambridge.org/ukschools/gcsemaths-studentbookanswers

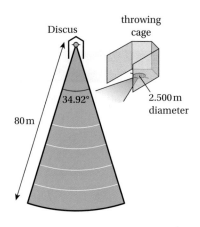

6 The area for discus at an international event has the dimensions shown in the diagram (left).

   a Calculate the area of the grass in the landing zone.

   b What is the area of the starting circle in the throwing cage?

7 A circular disc has a circumference of 75.398 mm. Show clearly how you could use this information to find the area of the disc.

8 A jeweller is making a tapered tube to set a diamond. She works out the dimension of the curved piece of metal she needs based on the diameter and depth of the stone and draws a rough sketch like this.

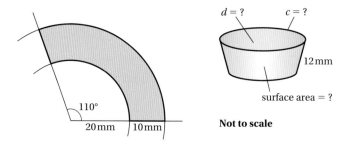

Apply what you know about the area and circumference of circles to work out:

   a the area of the flat curved section shown on the diagram

   b the diameter and circumference of the top of the finished tube

   c the diameter and circumference of the bottom of the finished tube.

Section 3: Area of composite shapes

Addition of parts

- Divide the figure into smaller known shapes whose area can be found directly.
- Calculate the area of each part separately.
- Add the areas of all the parts to find the total area.

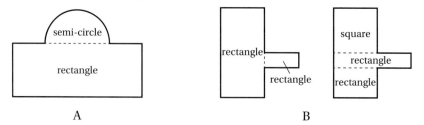

Figure A can be divided into a rectangle and a semi-circle.

Figure B can be divided in different ways. The first way requires fewer calculations.

Subtraction of parts

When one figure is 'cut out' of another you have to find the area of the larger figure and subtract the area of the cut-out figure.

The shaded area = area of square – area of circle.

In some cases, you can find the area by viewing the figure as part of a larger known shape and subtracting the parts that have been 'removed'.

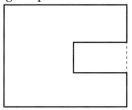

In this shape you can work out the area of the large rectangle (made by drawing the dotted line) and subtract the smaller cut-out rectangle from it.

(You could also find this area by addition, but you would need to do more calculations.)

> **Tip**
>
> Some problems can be solved either way. Think carefully about which method will be more efficient before you decide which one to use.

> **Tip**
>
> Copy diagrams into your exercise book so you can draw on them and mark dimensions. This helps you keep track of your working.

WORKED EXAMPLE 7

Calculate the area of this shape.

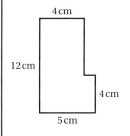

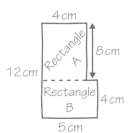

Split the shape into:

Rectangle A: 4 cm × 8 cm

Rectangle B: 4 cm × 5 cm

Area of rectangle A
$= bh = 4 \times 8 = 32\,cm^2$
Area of rectangle B
$= bh = 4 \times 5 = 20\,cm^2$

Calculate the area of each smaller rectangle.

Make sure you label the working so that someone else knows which calculation goes with each part.

Area of shape = 32 + 20 = 52 cm²

> **Tip**
>
> This shape can also be split into:
> Rectangle A: 12 cm × 4 cm
> Rectangle B: 4 cm × 1 cm

EXERCISE 12D

1 Find the total area of each of these shapes. Show all your working.

a

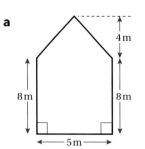

b

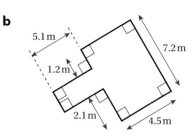

c

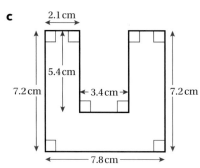

d

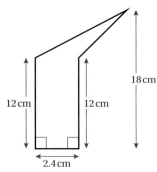

e

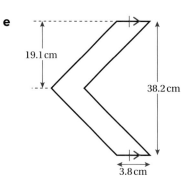

f

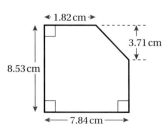

g

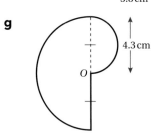

h

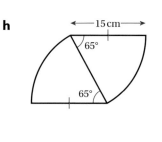

2 Find the area of the shaded part of each figure.

a

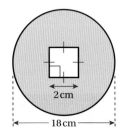

b

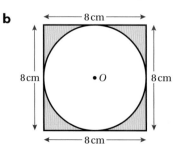

c

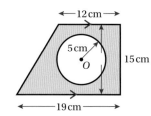

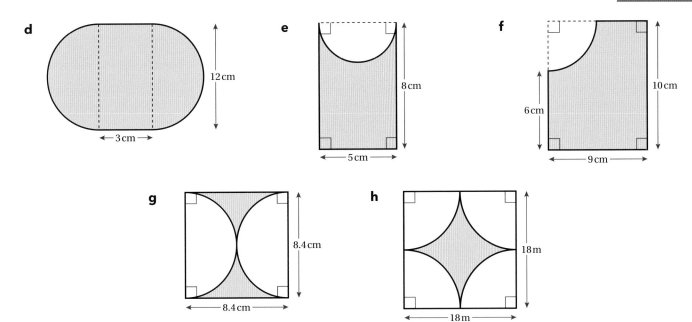

d 12 cm 3 cm

e 8 cm 5 cm

f 6 cm 10 cm 9 cm

g 8.4 cm 8.4 cm

h 18 m 18 m

3 Calculate the perimeter and area of the shaded region in each figure.

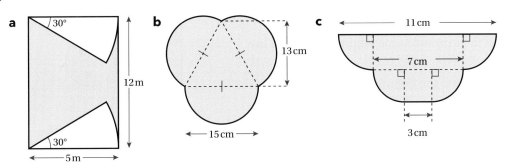

a 30° 12 m 30° 5 m

b 13 cm 15 cm

c 11 cm 7 cm 3 cm

side length of triangle = diameter of semi-circle

Problem solving

Perimeter, circumference and area are often combined with other calculations in problem-solving situations.

WORKED EXAMPLE 8

This face of a house is to be painted.

If each pot of paint can cover an area of $12 \, \text{m}^2$, how many pots of paint will be needed?

15 m h 7.5 m 12 m

Continues on next page ...

Find answers at: cambridge.org/ukschools/gcsemaths-studentbookanswers

Area of rectangle = $l \times w$
$$= 12 \times 7.5 = 90\,m^2$$

Area of triangle = $\frac{1}{2} \times b \times h$

Height, h, of triangle = $15 - 7.5 = 7.5\,m$

Area = $\frac{1}{2} \times 12 \times 7.5$
$$= 45\,m^2$$

Area to be painted = $90 + 45 = 135\,m^2$

Number of pots of paint
$$= 135 \div 12 = 11.25$$

So 12 pots of paint are needed.

> Split the shape into a rectangle and a triangle.
>
> Work out the area of each smaller shape.

> Calculate the number of pots needed.

WORKED EXAMPLE 9

A garden pond has a radius of 5 m.

The pond needs netting across the top, and some edging all around the water's edge.

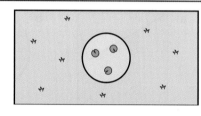

Using 3.14 as the value for π, calculate the quantities of:

a netting and **b** edging required.

The pond lies in a rectangular area, of width 15 m and length 20 m, which is to be made into a lawn.

Grass seed is required for the lawn. Packets of grass seed cover 25 m² and cost £3.75 each.

c What is the cost of seeding the lawn area?

a Area of pond = $\pi r^2 = 3.14 \times 5 \times 5 = 78.5\,m^2$
A minimum of 78.5 m² of netting is required.

> You are told to use the approximate value of 3.14 for π here.

b Circumference of pond = $2\pi r = 2 \times 3.14 \times 5 = 31.4\,m$
31.4 m of edging is required for the pond.

c Rectangular lawn area = $l \times w = 20 \times 15 = 300\,m^2$
Area for seeding = 300 – 78.5 (area of pond)
$$= 221.5\,m^2$$

> Use the 'subtraction of parts' to find the area of lawn.
>
> You already have the circular area from part **a**.

$221.5 \div 25 = 8.86$
So, 9 packets of grass seed will be needed.

> Remember, you have to buy whole numbers of packets.

Cost of seed = $9 \times 3.75 = £33.75$

EXERCISE 12E

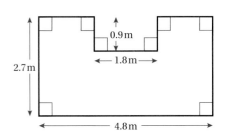

1 How many rectangular tiles 20 cm wide by 30 cm tall would you need to tile the area of wall shown (right)?

2 The net of a cylinder is shown.

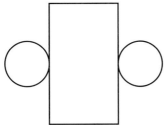

The rectangle has dimensions 10 cm × 16 cm, and each circle has radius 2.55 cm. Using 3.14 as an approximate value of π, calculate the total surface area of the cylinder.

3 The diagram (right) shows a circular mirror that has a decorative metal surround.

The mirror has an edge which is 12 cm wide. The width of the edge is $\frac{4}{5}$ of the radius of the whole mirror.

Calculate the area that the mirror and its surround would cover on a wall. Use 3.14 as an approximate value of π.

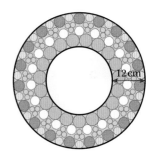

4 A piece of fondant icing is rolled out into the shape of a square. A circle with radius 11 cm is cut out from the square.

Given that the largest circle possible is cut out, find the difference between the area of the circular icing and the area of the square.

5 A semi-circular sandpit sits at the end of a lawn (right). A cover is to be placed over the sandpit.

What is the area that needs to be covered?

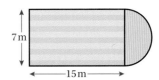

6 A circular photo frame has a plastic surround. The width of the plastic surround is 8 cm. The diameter of the complete photo frame is 28 cm.

Calculate the area available for the photo.

7 The shapes below have the same area. What is the side length of the square?

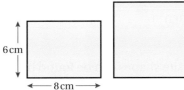

8 Guy is paid £0.15 for every square metre of grass he cuts.

How much would he be paid for cutting the grass in this garden (right)?

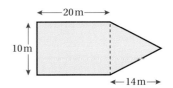

9 A stained glass window is a semi-circle with radius 30 cm. Calculate:

    a the perimeter of the window

    b the area of glass.

10 Car parking bays are either based on rectangles or parallelograms, as shown on this model.

    a The Department of the Environment's Planning Service specifies the following minimum standing space dimensions for cars and light vans:

        Cars 2.4×4.8 m

        Vans 2.4×5.5 m

    These dimensions do not take into account space between vehicles and space for access and/or unloading.

    Based on this, suggest some suitable dimensions for both rectangular and parallel parking bays.

    b Is it feasible for both shapes to have the same area? Give a reason for your answer.

    c What are the advantages and disadvantages of using each type of parking bay?

    d Given a rectangular area 120 m by 200 m, with access possible from all sides, sketch the parking arrangement you would recommend and justify your choices.

Checklist of learning and understanding

Area of polygons

- Area is the amount of space occupied by a plane shape. Area is always given in square units as it describes 2D shapes. You find the area by multiplying the two dimensions.

- Area can be calculated using formulae.

Rectangle	Square	Triangle	Parallelogram	Trapezium
$A = lw$	$A = l^2$	$A = \dfrac{1}{2}bh$	$A = bh$	$A = \dfrac{1}{2}(a + b)h$

Area of circles

- Area of a circle $= \pi r^2$.

- Area of a circle sector is a fraction of the area of the whole circle.

- Area of a sector $= \dfrac{\theta}{360} \times \pi r^2$.

Composite shapes

- The area of composite shapes can be found by splitting them into known shapes.

- Areas of smaller shapes can be calculated separately and added to find the total area.

- The area of a given shape can be subtracted from a known shape to find the total area.

Chapter review

For additional questions on the topics in this chapter, visit GCSE Mathematics Online.

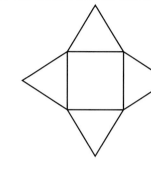

1 A rectangular vegetable plot has an area of $100\,\text{m}^2$.

If the width is $6.5\,\text{m}$, what is the length of the plot?

2 The net of a square-based pyramid is shown (right). The square base has side length $5\,\text{cm}$. The triangles have a perpendicular height of $4.3\,\text{cm}$.

Calculate the total surface area of the square-based pyramid.

3 A square flower bed, with side length $3\,\text{m}$, sits exactly in the middle of a rectangular lawn of side length $5\,\text{m}$ and width $450\,\text{cm}$.

Calculate the area of grass.

4 Mr Weaver's garden is in the shape of a rectangle.

In the garden there is a patio in the shape of a rectangle and two ponds in the shape of circles with diameter $3.8\,\text{m}$.

The rest of the garden is grass.

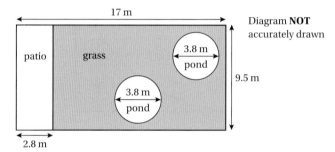

Diagram **NOT** accurately drawn

Mr Weaver is going to spread fertiliser over all the grass.

One box of fertiliser will cover $25\,\text{m}^2$ of grass.

How many boxes of fertiliser does Mr Weaver need?

You must show your working. *(5 marks)*

©Pearson Education Ltd 2012

5 An irrigator in a field can water a circular area of crops within a radius of $14.5\,\text{m}$.

What is the total area of field that can be irrigated?

6 The diagram (below) shows a shape made from a square and a semi-circle. Calculate the area of the shape. Give your answer in cm^2.

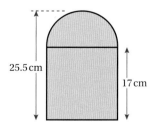

Find answers at: cambridge.org/ukschools/gcsemaths-studentbookanswers

7 Calculate the area of this shape.

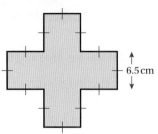

6.5 cm

8 A jeweller charges by the centimetre for gold rings. If the charge is £28.50 per cm for a 9 carat ring, what is the cost of a ring to fit a finger that is 2.5 cm wide?

9 *PQRS* is a square of side *x* cm. The shaded area is formed by drawing arcs from corners *P* and *R* with a radius equal to the length of the side of the square.

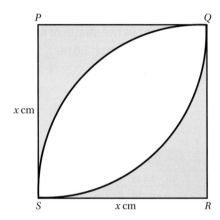

Prove that the total shaded area is $\dfrac{x^2(4 - \pi)}{2}$

10 A running track has semi-circular ends. The internal radius of each end is 30 m. If the distance round the inside of the track is to be 400 m, what is the length of the straight section of the track *XY*?

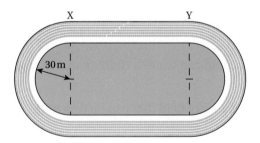

13 Further algebra

In this chapter you will learn how to ...

- expand the product of two or more binomial expressions and use the difference of two squares identity.
- factorise quadratic expressions of the form $ax^2 + bx + c$.
- complete the square on a quadratic expression.
- simplify and manipulate algebraic fractions.

For more resources relating to this chapter, visit GCSE Mathematics Online.

Using mathematics: real-life applications

Situations that involve motion, including acceleration, stopping distance, velocity and distance travelled (displacement) can be modelled using quadratic expressions and formulae.

"At the site of a crash, I measure the length of the tyre skid marks and apply an equation to work out the speed at which vehicles were moving before the accident."

(Police road accident investigator)

Before you start ...

Ch 5	Check that you can simplify expressions.	**1**	**a** Simplify: $5x^2y^2 + 6xy - 11x^2y^2 - 7xy$ **b** Why are terms that are multiples of x^2y^2 and terms that are multiples of xy not 'like' terms?
Ch 5	Make sure you can multiply out brackets.	**2**	Expand and simplify: $3(2x + 3y) + 2(3x - 2y)$
Ch 5	You should be able to recognise an identity.	**3**	Is the identity symbol used correctly in this example? Explain why or why not. $3b(3b - 5) - 7b^2 \equiv 2b^2 - 15b$
Ch 5	You should be able to express situations using algebra.	**4**	The square root of a number (x) is cubed and this is added to 36 divided by a number (y) squared. Write an expression to represent this.
Chs 1, 5	Make sure you remember the rules for multiplying and dividing in algebra.	**5**	Simplify: **a** $6a \times -5a$ **b** $-3y \times -7y^2$ **c** $-2ab \div b$ **d** $-6y \div -5y$ **e** $-2x \times -5x \div -4x$
KS3	Check that you remember how to apply the four operations to fractions.	**6**	Match each calculation to the correct answer: **a** $\frac{1}{3} + \frac{1}{4} = ?$ **b** $\frac{2}{3} - \frac{1}{8} = ?$ **c** $\frac{5}{6} \times \frac{3}{8} = ?$ **d** $\frac{2}{7} \div \frac{1}{14} = ?$ **A** 4 **B** $\frac{7}{12}$ **C** $\frac{13}{24}$ **D** $\frac{5}{16}$

Find answers at: cambridge.org/ukschools/gcsemaths-studentbookanswers

Assess your starting point using the Launchpad

STEP 1

1 Multiply out these expressions.

  a $(x + 3)(x + 5)$ **b** $(x - 3)(x + 5)$ **c** $(x - 3)(x - 5)$

GO TO
Section 1:
Multiplying two binomials

STEP 2

2 Write each expression as the product of two binomials.

  a $a^2 + 5a + 6$ **b** $x^2 - 3x + 2$
  c $p^2 - 4p - 45$ **d** $y^2 - 16$

GO TO
Section 2:
Factorising quadratic expressions

STEP 3

3 Complete these identities by filling in the missing values:

  a $x^2 + 12x - 11 \equiv (x + \square)^2 - \square$ **b** $x^2 + 8x + 20 \equiv (x + \square)^2 + \square$
  c $x^2 - 5x - 9 \equiv (x - \dfrac{5}{2})^2 - \square$

GO TO
Section 3:
Completing the square

STEP 4

4 Express as a single fraction:

  a $\dfrac{3x}{10} + \dfrac{x}{10}$ **b** $\dfrac{3}{x + 1} + \dfrac{1}{x + 3}$

GO TO
Section 4:
Algebraic fractions

Section 5:
Apply your skills

GO TO
Chapter review

Key vocabulary

binomial: an expression consisting of two terms.

binomial product: the product of two binomial expressions; for example, $(x + 2)(x + 3)$.

Section 1: Multiplying two binomials

A **binomial** is an expression that contains two terms.

For example, $x + 2$ or $2x^2 - 5y^3$

A **binomial product** is the product of two binomials.

For example, $(x + 2)(3x^2 + 4)$

The area of a rectangle is useful for showing how to multiply two binomials.

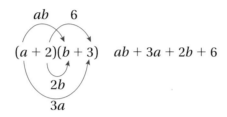

Consider a large rectangle of length $(a + 2)$ metres and breadth $(b + 3)$ metres.

The area of the whole rectangle is its length × breadth. This is the binomial product $(a + 2)(b + 3)$.

The area of the whole rectangle must also be equal to the sum of the four smaller rectangles.

This means $(a + 2)(b + 3) = ab + 3a + 2b + 6$

To multiply two brackets together each term in the first bracket must be multiplied by each term in the second bracket.

You can use arrows to keep track of your multiplication.

You can also use a grid to make sure you have multiplied all the terms.

> **Tip**
>
> Breadth is another word for width.

WORKED EXAMPLE 1

Expand and simplify, if possible.

$(x + 3)(x + 5)$.

×	x	3
x	x^2	$3x$
5	$5x$	15

Put the terms of the first binomial on the top row and of the second in the first column.

$(x + 3)(x + 5) = x^2 + 3x + 5x + 15$

Write out the terms in the smaller boxes to show your expansion.

$= x^2 + 8x + 15$

$5x$ and $3x$ are like terms, so add them.

> **Tip**
>
> When the product contains like terms you add these to simplify the expression.

The expression $x^2 + 8x + 15$ is an example of a quadratic expression. The highest power of x in the expression is x squared (x^2).

The general form of a quadratic equation is

$ax^2 + bx + c$

where a, b and c are real numbers and $a \neq 0$.

> **Key vocabulary**
>
> **real numbers**: all the numbers that can be placed on a number line. They include the set of rational and irrational numbers. Numbers that are not real are called imaginary. You will meet these numbers in the next stage of mathematics.

Find answers at: cambridge.org/ukschools/gcsemaths-studentbookanswers

Tip

Finding a binomial product is the same process we could apply to a long multiplication calculation. For example 14×27 can be rewritten as the product of two binomials:

$(10 + 4) \times (20 \times 7)$

We can illustrate this in a grid (the same method we used in Worked example 1)

×	10	4
20	200	80
7	70	28

Total represented in the grid = 200 + 80 + 70 + 28
= 378

Key vocabulary

quadratic expression: an expression in which the highest power of x is x^2.

WORKED EXAMPLE 2

Use substitution to determine whether $(a + b)^2 = a^2 + b^2$.

Let $a = 1$ and $b = 2$

Choose small values to make your calculations as simple as possible.

$(a + b)^2 = (1 + 2)^2 = (3)^2 = 9$
$a^2 + b^2 = 1^2 + 2^2 = 1 + 4 = 5$

Calculate the value for each side.

$9 \neq 5$ so the expressions are not identical.

Check to see if the values are the same.

WORKED EXAMPLE 3

Expand and simplify.

a $(x - 2)(x + 9)$ **b** $(x - 4)(x - 7)$

a $(x - 2)(x + 9) = x^2 + 9x - 2x - 18$
$= x^2 + 7x - 18$

Notice that you get a positive and a negative 'like' term here.

b $(x - 4)(x - 7) = x^2 - 7x - 4x + 28$
$= x^2 - 11x + 28$

Notice that the 'like' terms are both negative here.

Tip

Pay careful attention to the signs when you multiply binomials.

A negative quantity multiplied by a positive quantity gives a negative product.

A negative quantity multiplied by another negative quantity gives a positive product.

Squaring a binomial

You know that a^2 is short for writing $a \times a$.

So, for a binomial, $(x + 8)^2 = (x + 8)(x + 8)$

WORKED EXAMPLE 4

Expand $(x + 8)^2$

$(x + 8)^2 = (x + 8)(x + 8)$

Write as a product of two brackets.

$= x^2 + 8x + 8x + 64$

Write down the result of multiplying out.

$= x^2 + 16x + 64$

Simplify by gathering any like terms.

EXERCISE 13A

1 Expand and simplify.

a $(x + 2)(x + 5)$ **b** $(x - 2)(x - 5)$ **c** $(x + 2)(x - 5)$

d $(x - 2)(x + 5)$ **e** $(x + 3)(x - 4)$ **f** $(x + y)(x + y)$

2 Expand and simplify.

a $(2x + 4)(3x + 3)$ **b** $(3x + 4)(5x + 2)$ **c** $(2x - 5)(3x + 1)$

d $(4y - 3)(5y + 1)$ **e** $(3a - 5)(2a - 1)$ **f** $(2b - 5)(b - 3)$

g $(2y - 3)(3y - 5)$ **h** $(2x + 4)(2x - 6)$ **i** $(5x - 3)(4x - 1)$

3 If $A = 3x + 2$ and $B = 2x - 1$ determine:

a AB **b** $A^2 + B^2$ **c** $(A - B)(A + B)$

4 Determine each product.

a $\left(\dfrac{2}{x} + \dfrac{x}{2}\right)^2$ **b** $[2x - (4x + 3y)]^2$ **c** $[2x - (y + z)]^2$

5 What is the value of a if $(2x - 3)$ is a factor of $(6x^2 + ax - 12)$?

The difference of two squares identity

Squaring a binomial produces a pattern that can be used to expand them without doing any working.

Work through the investigation in Exercise 13B to find a shortcut for expanding binomials in the form

$(a + b)(a - b)$

EXERCISE 13B

1 Expand each of the following binomials:

a $(x + 1)(x - 1)$ **b** $(a + 2)(a - 2)$

c $(2x - 1)(2x + 1)$ **d** $(x - 2y)(x + 2y)$

2 Write down a rule that you can use to quickly find the answer to any similar expansion.

3 In general,

$(x + y)(x - y) \equiv x^2 - y^2$

This is called the **difference of two squares identity**.

a How can you recognise when a binomial expansion is a difference of two squares?

b Are each of these expressions a difference of squares?

Explain why or why not.

i $(3x + 2y)(2x - 3y)$ **ii** $25a^2 - 81b^2$ **iii** $16 - \left(\sqrt{11}\right)^2$

Find answers at: cambridge.org/ukschools/gcsemaths-studentbookanswers

Expanding more than two factors

Consider the multiplication $3 \times 4 \times 5$.

To do this you have to multiply two numbers at a time.

For example:

$$3 \times 4 \times 5 = 12 \times 5 = 60$$

or:

$$3 \times 4 \times 5 = 3 \times 20 = 60$$

or:

$$3 \times 5 \times 4 = 15 \times 4 = 60$$

The order in which you multiply does not change the answer.

Tip

It is worth doing the multiplication of three or more binomials one step at a time. You are less likely to make sign errors and more likely to get the answer correct.

Tip

To work most efficiently, always check whether some factors form the square of a binomial or the difference of two squares and expand these first using the rules that you know.

WORKED EXAMPLE 5

Expand $(3x + 2)(2x + 1)(x - 1)$.

$(3x + 2)(2x + 1)(x - 1)$

$= (6x^2 + 3x + 4x + 2)(x - 1)$ Expand the first two factors.

$= (6x^2 + 7x + 2)(x - 1)$ Add the like terms.

$= 6x^3 + 7x^2 + 2x - 6x^2 - 7x - 2$ Expand the remaining two factors.

$= 6x^3 + x^2 - 5x - 2$ Collect like terms to simplify.

EXERCISE 13C

1 Expand and simplify.

    a $(x + 1)(x + 2)(x + 3)$ **b** $(2x - 3)(x - 2)(2x - 1)$

    c $(x + 1)(x + 2)(x - 2)$ **d** $(x - 3)(2x + 1)(3x - 2)$

2 Expand and simplify.

    a $(3x - 4)^3$ **b** $(x + 3)(x^2 - 3x + 9)$

    c $\left(\dfrac{1}{5x} + \dfrac{1}{3y}\right)\left(\dfrac{1}{25x^2} - \dfrac{1}{15xy} + \dfrac{1}{9y^2}\right)$ **d** $(x^2y^2 + x^2)(xy + x)(xy - x)$

3 The volume of a cuboid can be found using the formula LBH, where L is the length, B is the breadth and H is the height.

    Given a cuboid of length $(2x + \dfrac{1}{2})$ cm, breadth $(x - 2)$ cm and height $(x - 2)$ cm:

    a Write an expression for the volume of the cuboid in factor form.

    b Expand the expression.

    c Why is it sensible to expand the factors $(x - 2)(x - 2)$ first?

Section 2: Factorising quadratic expressions

Expanding a binomial such as $(x + 3)(x + 4)$ gives you a quadratic expression.

Factorising the quadratic expression involves writing it as the product of its factors.

expanding

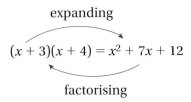

$$(x + 3)(x + 4) = x^2 + 7x + 12$$

factorising

Key vocabulary

coefficient: the number in front of a variable in a mathematical expression. In the term $5x^2$, 5 is the coefficient and x^2 is the variable.

In this section you will learn how to factorise quadratic expressions.

You need to be able to factorise quadratic expressions in the form of $x^2 + bx + c$ as well as those where the x^2 term has a **coefficient** that is not 0 or 1.

These quadratic expressions are in the form $ax^2 + bx + c$.

In general:

$$(x + a)(x + b) = x^2 + (a + b)x + ab$$

So, the middle term is the sum of a and b in the original binomials or $(a + b)$.

The third term is the product of a and b or (ab).

This pattern can be used to develop a strategy for factorising quadratic expressions.

Problem-solving framework

Factorise $x^2 + 7x + 12$.

Steps for factorising a quadratic expression	What you would do for this example
Step 1: Write down the expression you have been asked to factorise.	$x^2 + 7x + 12$
Step 2: Write two pairs of brackets, writing x in each bracket. You can put x in each bracket because to get x^2 you need to multiply x by x.	$x^2 + 7x + 12$ $= (x + \Box)\,(x + \Box)$
Step 3: Now look at the value of the constant. What are the factor pairs of this constant?	Factor pairs are: 1×12 2×6 3×4

Continues on next page …

Step 4: Which factor pair, when added, will give the coefficient of the middle term?	$3 + 4 = 7$ $3 \times 4 = 12$ So, $x^2 + 7x + 12 = (x + 3)(x + 4)$
Step 5: Check your answer.	Expand the brackets to check your answer: $(x + 3)(x + 4) = x^2 + 3x + 4x + 12$ $\qquad\qquad\qquad\;\; = x^2 + 7x + 12$ Yes, this is the expression you started with.

Quadratic expressions that have negative terms need a bit more care.

WORKED EXAMPLE 6

Factorise $x^2 - 7x + 12$.

$x^2 - 7x + 12 = (x - \Box)(x - \Box)$

Start by writing two pairs of brackets with x to the left of each.

Put negative signs in **both** brackets because the constant is $+12$ but the coefficient of x this time is a negative number, -7.

-1×-12
-2×-6
-3×-4

Write the factor pairs of the constant term.

The product of two negative numbers is positive so the factor pairs must be negative.

$-3 + (-4) = -7$

Determine which factor pair, when added, will give the coefficient of the middle term.

$x^2 - 7x + 12 = (x - 3)(x - 4)$

Complete your solution. (You can expand the brackets to check that it is correct.)

The example below shows you how to work systematically to factorise a quadratic expression which has two negative terms.

WORKED EXAMPLE 7

Factorise $x^2 - 4x - 12$

$x^2 - 4x - 12 = (x + \Box)(x - \Box)$

Start by writing two pairs of brackets with x to the left of each.

The constant is negative.

To get a negative product you have to multiply a negative number by a positive number. This means one bracket will have a negative sign and the other will have a positive sign.

1×12
2×6
3×4

Write the factor pairs of the constant term.

Which of these pairs has a difference of 4 (the value of the number in front of the x term)?

Continues on next page …

$-2 + 6 = 4$
$-6 + 2 = -4$

There is a difference of 4 between 2 and 6.

So this is the pair you need.

Notice that the middle term is negative, so the larger number of the factor pair needs to be negative.

$x^2 - 4x - 12 = (x + 2)(x - 6)$

Complete your solution. (Expand the brackets to check that it is correct.)

Work out the signs before you factorise by looking at the signs in the expression.

If the **constant is positive**, the brackets will have the same sign.

- If the middle term (the x term) is positive, both brackets will have positive signs.
- If the middle term is negative, both brackets will have negative signs.

If the **constant is negative**, the brackets will have different signs.

- When the signs are different, the middle term is the difference between the two factors.
- The largest number in the factor pair will have the same sign as the middle term in the expression.

When you factorise any expression, the first step should be to check for, and remove, common factors.

Key vocabulary

constant: in algebra, a constant is a value that does not change. It is usually a number. It could be a letter with a fixed value, like π.

WORKED EXAMPLE 8

Factorise $4x^2 - 12x - 40$

$4x^2 - 12x - 40$
$= 4(x^2 - 3x - 10)$

Take out the common factor of 4.

$= 4(x - 5)(x + 2)$

Factorise the quadratic.

EXERCISE 13D

1 Factorise:

  a $x^2 + 5x + 6$ **b** $x^2 + 11x + 18$ **c** $x^2 + 7x + 10$

  d $x^2 + 11x + 30$ **e** $x^2 + 9x + 14$ **f** $x^2 + 19x + 90$

2 Factorise:

  a $x^2 - 5x + 6$ **b** $x^2 - 14x + 33$ **c** $x^2 - 17x + 30$

  d $x^2 - 13x + 42$ **e** $x^2 - 15x + 44$ **f** $x^2 - 25x + 100$

3 Factorise fully:

  a $2x^2 + 6x + 4$ **b** $6x^2 - 24x + 18$ **c** $5x^2 - 5x - 10$

  d $2x^2 + 14x + 20$ **e** $2x^2 + 4x - 6$ **f** $3x^2 - 30x - 33$

Find answers at: cambridge.org/ukschools/gcsemaths-studentbookanswers

Factorising the difference of two squares

In Exercise 13B, you saw that multiplying out binomials in the form $(a + b)(a - b)$ gives a product that is the difference of two squares.

$$(a - b)(a + b) = a^2 + ab - ab - b^2$$
$$= a^2 - b^2 \text{ (simplifying)}$$

The reverse of this expansion is factorising the difference of two squares.

WORKED EXAMPLE 9

Factorise:

a $x^2 - 4$ **b** $x^2 - 36$ **c** $4a^2 - 9$

d $5x^2 - 45$ **e** $2(x - 1)^2 - 50$ **f** $x^2 - 2$

a $x^2 - 4 = x^2 - (2)^2$ Express both terms as squares.

$= (x + 2)(x - 2)$ Apply the identity: $a^2 - b^2 \equiv (a + b)(a - b)$.

b $x^2 - 36 = x^2 - (6)^2$
$= (x + 6)(x - 6)$

c $4a^2 - 9 = (2a)^2 - (3)^2$
$= (2a + 3)(2a - 3)$

d $5x^2 - 45 = 5(x^2 - 9) = 5(x + 3)(x - 3)$ Take out a common factor of 5.

e $2(x - 1)^2 - 50 = 2((x - 1)^2 - 25))$ Take out a common factor of 2.

$= 2(x - 1 + 5)(x - 1 - 5)$

$= 2(x + 4)(x - 6)$ Add like terms.

f $x^2 - 2 = (x + \sqrt{2})(x - \sqrt{2})$ The square root of an imperfect square is a surd (see Chapter 14).

Tip

Some expressions are not a difference of squares until you have removed the common factor. Checking for a common factor should always be the first step when you are factorising.

Tip

You can also think of factorising a difference of squares as taking the square root of each term and writing these in brackets, one with a negative sign and one with a positive sign. The order in which you write down the brackets doesn't matter.
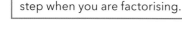
$(a - b)(a + b) = (a + b)(a - b)$

Mathematically, a difference of squares such as $x^2 - 4$ is a special case of the quadratic expression $x^2 + bx + c$.

In a difference of squares, the coefficient of x is 0, so there is no x term $(x \times 0 = 0)$ and the constant (c) is a negative number.

Using the difference of two squares in number problems

You can use the difference of squares to subtract square numbers such as $86^2 - 14^2$ without working out the square values, which can be very large numbers.

WORKED EXAMPLE 10

Find the value of $86^2 - 14^2$

$86^2 - 14^2 = (86 + 14)(86 - 14)$ Write the subtraction as the product of its factors.

$= 100 \times 72$ Add and subtract the values in each bracket.

$= 7200$ Find the product.

EXERCISE 13E

1 Factorise each of the following.

  a $x^2 - 36$ **b** $p^2 - 81$ **c** $w^2 - 16$

  d $p^2 - 36q^2$ **e** $144s^2 - c^2$ **f** $64h^2 - 49g^2$

2 Factorise:

  a $8x^2 - 2y^2$ **b** $3x^2y^2 - 12z^2$ **c** $1 - (2x - 3)^2$

  d $3(x + 4)^2 - 12$ **e** $7(x - 5)^2 - 7y^2$ **f** $(x + 5)^2 - (y + 3)^2$

3 Using $(a - b)(a + b) = a^2 - b^2$, evaluate the following:

  a $100^2 - 97^2$ **b** $50^2 - 48^2$ **c** $639^2 - 629^2$

  d $98^2 - 45^2$ **e** $83^2 - 77^2$ **f** $1234^2 - 999^2$

Further quadratic expressions

The quadratic expressions you have factorised so far have had an x^2 term with a coefficient of 1, or you have been able to take out a common factor so that the x^2 term has a coefficient of 1.

To factorise quadratic expressions in the form $ax^2 + bx + c$ (where $a \neq 1$) you still need two particular numbers which have a sum equal to b (the coefficient of the x term).

However, the two numbers must now have a product which is equal to ac (rather than just c as before).

WORKED EXAMPLE 11

Factorise: $2x^2 + 9x + 4$

$a = 2, b = 9$ and $c = 4$.   There are no common factors.

$ac = 2 \times 4 = 8$ Work out ac.

$8 \times 1 = 8$
$8 + 1 = 9$ Find factors of 8 that add up to 9.

$2x^2 + 8x + x + 4$ Re-write the x term, using the factors in the previous step (make sure you use the correct signs).

$(2x^2 + 8x) + (x + 4)$ Group the terms in pairs.

$2x(x + 4) + 1(x + 4)$ Take out any common factors (write the 1 here as a reminder).

$(x + 4)(2x + 1)$ Combine the two common factors to make the second bracket.

EXERCISE 13F

1 Factorise each quadratic expression fully:

    a $2x^2 + 7x + 5$ **b** $3x^2 + 10x + 8$ **c** $2x^2 + 8x - 90$

    d $4x^2 + 16x + 15$ **e** $4x^2 - 24x + 27$ **f** $3x^2 - 6x - 105$

    g $12x^2 + 9x - 30$ **h** $3x^2 + x - 10$ **i** $2x^2 - 6x - 260$

    j $3x^2 - 13x - 10$

2 A rectangle has an area of $(5x^2 - 13x + 6)$ cm.

    Find the length in terms of x if the breadth is $(x - 2)$ cm.

3 A triangle of base $(2x + 8)$ cm has an area of $(2x^2 + 11x + 12)$ cm.

    Use this information to determine an expression for the perpendicular height of the triangle.

4   **a** Use the substitution $a = x + y$ to factorise the expression

       $3(x + y)^2 + 13(x + y) + 12$

       and show that it factorises to $(3x + 3y + 4)(x + y + 3)$.

    b Apply your method to factorise these expressions:

       i $3(x - 3)^2 - (x - 3) - 24$ **ii** $8(5x + 2)^2 - 14(5x + 2) + 3$

Section 3: Completing the square

You previously used the squaring of a binomial and difference of squares identities:

$$(a + b)^2 \equiv a^2 + 2ab + b^2$$
$$(a - b)^2 \equiv a^2 - 2ab + b^2$$
$$a^2 - b^2 \equiv (a + b)(a - b)$$

Completing the square uses a combination of these two identities so that any quadratic expression can be written so that one term is a perfect square (i.e. the square of a binomial).

Tip

Completing the square is a very useful technique that can be used to:
- factorise quadratic expressions
- solve quadratic equations that do not factorise
- find the turning point of a quadratic graph.

EXERCISE 13G

1 Expand these perfect squares:

    a $(x + 3)^2$ **b** $(y - 5)^2$ **c** $(2x + 7)^2$

    d $(3a - 4b)^2$ **e** $(x - \frac{1}{2})^2$ **f** $\left(2x - \dfrac{5}{9}\right)^2$

2 Factorise using the difference of two squares rule:

    a $x^2 - 1$ **b** $25x^2 - 1$ **c** $(x + 2)^2 - 4$

    d $9x^2 - \dfrac{1}{4}$ **e** $2x^2 - 32$ **f** $4x^2 - 16$

3 Write each expression as a product of linear factors:

    a $x^2 - 3$ **b** $x^2 - 7$ **c** $x^2 - 18$

    d $15 - 10x^2$ **e** $(x - 3)^2 - 15$ **f** $(x + \dfrac{1}{2})^2 - \dfrac{1}{5}$

    g Explain how you could treat these expressions like a difference between two squares even though one of the terms is not a perfect square.

4 Find the missing terms in these quadratic expressions to make them equivalent to the perfect square:

    a $x^2 + 6x + \square = (x + 3)^2$ **b** $x^2 + 12x + \square = (x + 6)^2$

    c $x^2 + 5x + \square = \left(x + \dfrac{5}{2}\right)^2$ **d** $x^2 + 7x + \square = \left(x + \dfrac{7}{2}\right)^2$

    e $x^2 - 12x + \square = (x - 6)^2$ **f** $x^2 - 10x + \square = (x - 5)^2$

In question **4** you found the constant term in each expression to make it a perfect square.

If you look at your answers, you will see that the constant term can be found by halving the coefficient of the x term and then squaring it.

WORKED EXAMPLE 12

Find the constant term that will make $x^2 - 8x$ a perfect square and hence write the expression in completed square form.

$x^2 - 8x$	Half the coefficient of x is -4.
$x^2 - 8x + 4^2$	Add the square of half the coefficient of x.
$= (x - 4)^2$	Re-write as the square of a binomial.
so $x^2 - 8x = (x - 4)^2 - 16$	Expanding the perfect square would give an answer that is larger than the original expression, so the extra part must be subtracted.

WORKED EXAMPLE 13

Complete the square on $x^2 + 9x$.

$$x^2 + 9x$$

$$x^2 + 9x + \left(\frac{9}{2}\right)^2 = \left(x + \frac{9}{2}\right)^2$$

Half the coefficient of x is $\frac{9}{2}$. Leave this as a fraction.

$$\text{so } x^2 + 9x = \left(x + \frac{9}{2}\right)^2 - \left(\frac{9}{2}\right)^2$$

$$= \left(x + \frac{9}{2}\right)^2 - \frac{81}{4}$$

WORKED EXAMPLE 14

By completing the square for the first two terms, re-write $x^2 + 8x + 2$ in completed square form.

$x^2 + 8x$	
$x^2 + 8x + 4^2 = (x + 4)^2$	Find the perfect square for the first two terms.
$x^2 + 8x + 2$ $= [(x + 4)^2 - 4^2] + 2$	Re-write the first two terms using the square of a binomial but remember to subtract the extra constant.
$= (x + 4)^2 - 14$	Simplify the constant.

EXERCISE 13H

1 Find the missing value that would make each expression the square of a binomial.

a $x^2 - 2x + \square$ **b** $x^2 + 2x + \square$ **c** $x^2 + 4x + \square$

d $x^2 + 6x + \square$ **e** $x^2 - \square x + \dfrac{1}{9}$ **f** $x^2 - \square x + 5$

g $x^2 - \square x + 25$ **h** $x^2 - \square x + 11$ **i** $x^2 + \square x + 7$

j $x^2 - 12x + \square$

2 Use the method of completing the square to re-write the following with a perfect square term:

a $x^2 + 2x - 5$ **b** $x^2 + 2x + 7$ **c** $x^2 + 4x + 1$

d $x^2 + 6x - 3$ **e** $x^2 - 6x + 6$ **f** $x^2 - 8x - 5$

g $x^2 + 8x + 25$ **h** $x^2 + 12x - 11$ **i** $x^2 + 11x + 7$

j $x^2 - 10x - 3$

Tip

Completing the square can be used to solve quadratic equations when the quadratic expression does not factorise.

This is covered in Chapter 15.

Section 4: Algebraic fractions

You can simplify algebraic fractions using the same rules that apply to arithmetic fractions.

The rules for the four operations are:

Tip

Remember that letters represent unknown numbers.

- Multiplication $\dfrac{a}{b} \times \dfrac{c}{d} = \dfrac{ac}{bd}$

- Division $\dfrac{a}{b} \div \dfrac{c}{d} = \dfrac{ad}{bc}.$ Remember $\dfrac{a}{b} \div \dfrac{c}{d} = \dfrac{a}{b} \times \dfrac{d}{c}$

- Addition $\dfrac{a}{b} + \dfrac{c}{d} = \dfrac{ad + bc}{bd}$ bd is the lowest common denominator of the two fractions

- Subtraction $\dfrac{a}{b} - \dfrac{c}{d} = \dfrac{ad - bc}{bd}$

Tip

You learned how to simplify algebraic terms in the form of fractions by dividing (cancelling) in Chapter 5.

Multiplying and dividing

You can simplify algebraic fractions by cancelling terms (using a common factor).

You may need to factorise the numerator and/or the denominator before you can cancel terms.

Tip

Remember you cannot cancel out only part of a bracket.

$\dfrac{(x-2)}{(x-2)}$ can be simplified to give 1.

$\dfrac{(x-2)}{2}$ cannot be simplified any further.

WORKED EXAMPLE 15

Simplify:

a $\dfrac{8xy^2}{4z} \times \dfrac{yz}{-2x}$ b $\dfrac{x^2 + 2x - 3}{x - 1}$ c $\dfrac{4x^2 - 9}{x + 1} \div \dfrac{2x + 3}{x^2 - 1}$

a $\dfrac{\overset{2}{\cancel{8}} \, x y^2}{\cancel{4} \, \cancel{z}} \times \dfrac{y\cancel{z}}{-2\cancel{x}} = \dfrac{2y^3}{-2} = -y^3$

b $\dfrac{x^2 + 2x - 3}{x - 1} = \dfrac{(x - 1)(x + 3)}{x - 1}$

$= x + 3$

> Factorise the quadratic expressions in the numerator and then cancel the factors $(x - 1)$.

c $\dfrac{4x^2 - 9}{x + 1} \div \dfrac{2x + 3}{x^2 - 1} = \dfrac{4x^2 - 9}{x + 1} \times \dfrac{x^2 - 1}{2x + 3}$

> Rewrite the division as the equivalent multiplication by the reciprocal.

$= \dfrac{(2x + 3)(2x - 3)}{x + 1} \times \dfrac{(x + 1)(x - 1)}{2x + 3}$

> Factorise the difference of squares.

$= \dfrac{\cancel{(2x + 3)}(2x - 3)}{\cancel{x + 1}} \times \dfrac{\cancel{(x + 1)}(x - 1)}{\cancel{2x + 3}}$

> Cancel common brackets.

$= (2x - 3)(x - 1)$

WORK IT OUT 13.1

Zoey got these three homework questions wrong.

Find her mistakes.

Simplify each fraction correctly.

1	$\dfrac{3\cancel{x} + 2}{2\cancel{x} + 3} = \dfrac{5}{5} = 1$
2	$\dfrac{\cancel{x^2} - \cancel{x} - 6}{\cancel{x^2} + 3\cancel{x} + 2} = \dfrac{6}{5}$
3	$\dfrac{\overset{x}{\cancel{x^2}} - 1}{\underset{1}{\cancel{2x}} + \underset{1}{\cancel{4}}} \times \dfrac{\overset{2x}{\cancel{4x^2}} - \overset{4}{\cancel{16}}}{\underset{1}{\cancel{x}} + 1} = \dfrac{(x - 1)(2x - 4)}{4}$

Adding and subtracting

To add or subtract fractions you find a common denominator.

WORKED EXAMPLE 16

Type 1: Denominators are numbers

a $\dfrac{2x}{5} + \dfrac{x}{3}$ **b** $\dfrac{(x+2)}{5} + \dfrac{(x-1)}{4}$

a $\dfrac{2x}{5} + \dfrac{x}{3}$ $\quad$ LCD $= 15$

$\quad = \dfrac{6x}{15} + \dfrac{5x}{15}$

$\quad = \dfrac{11x}{15}$

b $\dfrac{(x+2)}{5} + \dfrac{(x-1)}{4}$ $\quad$ LCD $= 20$

$\quad = \dfrac{4(x+2)}{20} + \dfrac{5(x-1)}{20}$

$\quad = \dfrac{4x+8+5x-5}{20}$ $\quad$ Expand the brackets.

$\quad = \dfrac{9x+3}{20}$ $\quad$ Collect like terms.

$\quad = \dfrac{3(3x+1)}{20}$ $\quad$ Take out a common factor to simplify.

WORKED EXAMPLE 17

Type 2: Denominator is an algebraic expression

a $\dfrac{4}{x} + \dfrac{3}{2x}$ **b** $\dfrac{5}{2x^2} + \dfrac{11}{2x}$ **c** $\dfrac{x}{x-2} - \dfrac{3}{x+2}$

a $\dfrac{4}{x} + \dfrac{3}{2x} = \dfrac{8}{2x} + \dfrac{3}{2x}$ $\quad$ LCD $= 2x$

$\quad = \dfrac{11}{2x}$

b $\dfrac{5}{2x^2} + \dfrac{11}{2x} = \dfrac{5}{2x^2} + \dfrac{11x}{2x^2}$ $\quad$ LCD $= 2x^2$

$\quad = \dfrac{(5+11x)}{2x^2}$

Continues on next page …

c $\dfrac{x}{x-2} - \dfrac{3}{x+2}$

$= \dfrac{x(x+2) - 3(x-2)}{(x-2)(x+2)}$ ◁ LCD $= (x-2)(x+2)$

$= \dfrac{x^2 + 2x - 3x + 6}{(x-2)(x+2)}$ ◁ Expand the brackets.

$= \dfrac{x^2 - x + 6}{(x-2)(x+2)}$ ◁ Collect like terms.

EXERCISE 13I

1 Simplify:

a $\dfrac{8x}{10}$　　　　　**b** $\dfrac{9x+3}{3x+1}$　　　　　**c** $\dfrac{x^2-9}{x+3}$

d $\dfrac{4x^2-81}{2x-9}$　　　**e** $\dfrac{(x-3)(x+2)}{(x+4)(x+2)}$　　**f** $\dfrac{(2x-5)(x+4)}{(x-4)(5-2x)}$

g $\dfrac{2x^2-5x+3}{2x^2-x-3}$

2 Express as single fractions:

a $\dfrac{4x}{5} - \dfrac{2x}{5}$　　**b** $\dfrac{2x}{3} + \dfrac{x}{2} - \dfrac{3x}{4}$　　**c** $\dfrac{7}{2x} - \dfrac{4}{3x}$

d $\dfrac{2}{x+1} + \dfrac{1}{x+2}$　**e** $\dfrac{7}{x-2} - \dfrac{4}{x-1}$　**f** $\dfrac{1}{(x-7)^2} - \dfrac{2}{x-7}$

3 Express as single fractions:

a $\dfrac{2}{x+1} + \dfrac{3}{x}$　　**b** $\dfrac{x}{x-2} - \dfrac{3}{x+2}$　　**c** $\dfrac{x+3}{x+2} - \dfrac{x+2}{x+3}$

d $\dfrac{1}{2x-3} + \dfrac{1}{2x+3}$　**e** $\dfrac{5}{2p+1} + \dfrac{1}{p}$　　**f** $\dfrac{p+2}{p-1} + \dfrac{p-1}{p+2}$

g $\dfrac{1}{x-2} - \dfrac{2}{x-1} + \dfrac{1}{x-3}$

Section 5: Apply your skills

Algebraic manipulation skills can be used to solve problems in many different contexts.

For example, you will use factorising to simplify expressions, solve equations and to sketch curves, and you will complete the square to solve some quadratic equations and find the turning points of curved graphs.

EXERCISE 13J

1 Read each statement and apply what you have learned to decide whether it is true.

If not, state why not.

a $2(3b - 2) + 5(2b - 1) = 11b + 9$

b $(3x - 2)(4x + 7) = 12x^2 + 13x - 14$

c $3x^2 + 11x + 6 = (3x + 2)(3x + 3)$

d $9x^2 - 2 = (3x + \sqrt{2})(3x - \sqrt{2})$

e $x^2 + 2x - 6 = (x + 1)^2 - 7$

f $\dfrac{5}{x - 1} + \dfrac{3}{x + 2} = \dfrac{9x + 7}{(x - 1)(x + 2)}$

2 The area of a quadrilateral is expressed as $x^2 - 25$.

a Explain why this quadrilateral cannot be a square.

b Another quadrilateral has an area of $x^2 + 10x + 25$.

Is it a square?

How do you know that?

3 Use the difference between two squares to simplify the expression $(x + 8)^2 - (x - 8)^2$.

4 Show algebraically that $(x - 1)$ is not a factor of $(-2x^2 - 13x - 15)$.

5 A rectangular slot $(x - y)$ cm wide and $(x + y)$ cm long is cut out of a square metal plate with sides of $(2x - y)$ cm.

Calculate the area of metal remaining.

6 Given that $A = 5x + 3$ and $B = 4x - 1$, write each of the following expressions in terms of x in their simplest form:

a AB **b** $A^2 + B^2$ **c** $(A - B)(A + B)$

7 Evaluate the following using $(a + b)^2 \equiv a^2 + 2ab + b^2$ and $(a - b)^2 \equiv a^2 - 2ab + b^2$:

a $(1.01)^2$ **b** $(0.99)^2$ **c** $(4.02)^2$ **d** $(0.98)^2$

8 Use the method of completing the square to show that:

a $x^2 + 4x + 15 \geqslant 11$ **b** $x^2 + 2x + 15 \geqslant 14$

Find answers at: cambridge.org/ukschools/gcsemaths-studentbookanswers

Tip

The converse of Pythagoras' theorem states that if the square of the longest side of a triangle is equal to the sum of the squares of the other two sides, then the triangle must be right-angled. You will deal with this in more detail in Chapter 32.

9 The three sides of a triangle are $(x + 8)$ cm, $(x + 6)$ cm and $(x - 1)$ cm. If the square of the longest side is equal to the sum of the squares of the other two sides, the triangle is right-angled.

Show algebraically that the triangle is right-angled when $x = 9$.

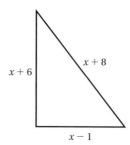

10 **a** Show that the area, A cm^2, of a rectangle of perimeter 20 cm is given by the formula $A = w(10 - w)$, where w cm is the width.

b Complete the square for the quadratic expression $10w - w^2$ and hence show that $A \leqslant 25$.

11 By considering $\left(\sqrt{x} - \dfrac{1}{\sqrt{x}} \right)^2$, prove that 'the sum of a positive number and its reciprocal is greater than or equal to 2'.

12 Simplify:

a $\dfrac{x^2 - x - 6}{x^2 - 8x + 15}$ **b** $\dfrac{9x^2 - 4}{12x - 8}$ **c** $\dfrac{a^2 + ab}{a^2 - ab} \times \dfrac{ab^2 + b^2}{a^3 + a^2 b}$

 Checklist of learning and understanding

Expanding expressions

- Expand binomials by multiplying each term in the first bracket by each term in the second bracket.

- The squaring of a binomial (perfect square) identity is $(a \pm b)^2 \equiv a^2 \pm 2ab \pm b^2$

- The difference of two squares identity is $(a + b)(a - b) \equiv a^2 - b^2$

Factorising

- Factorising is the inverse of expanding.

- Check for common factors first, then write expressions as a product of their factors.

- Apply the perfect square and difference of square identities where possible.

- When the terms in a bracket no longer have a factor, number or letter in common, the expression is factorised fully.

Completing the square

- Completing the square is a technique that turns a quadratic into an equivalent expression containing a perfect square.

Algebraic fractions

- Algebraic fractions can be simplified using the same rules that apply to arithmetic fractions.

 Chapter review

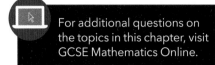For additional questions on the topics in this chapter, visit GCSE Mathematics Online.

1 Expand and simplify:

a $(y + 1)^2 + (y + 2)^2 + (y + 3)^2$

b $(x + 1)(x + 2)(x - 3)$

2 Factorise:

a $2x^2 - 11x - 21$

b $-6x^2 - 14x - 8$

3 Use the difference of two squares identity to calculate $1999^2 - 1998^2$.

4 The diagram shows a trapezium.

The lengths of three of the sides of the trapezium are $x - 5$, $x + 2$ and $x + 6$.

All dimensions are in centimetres.

The area of the trapezium is $36\,\text{cm}^2$.

Show that $x^2 - x - 56 = 0$.

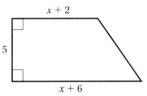

5 Write as single fractions in simplest form:

a $\dfrac{x + 3}{4} + \dfrac{x - 5}{3}$

b $\dfrac{1}{x + 4} + \dfrac{2}{x - 4}$

c $\dfrac{2x}{3x - 3} \div \dfrac{4y}{x^2 - x}$

d $\dfrac{3}{4p + q} + \dfrac{3}{p - 2q}$

e $\dfrac{1}{x - 2} + \dfrac{5}{x - 2} + \dfrac{1}{1 - 3x}$

f $\dfrac{2}{x + 5} + \dfrac{1}{x - 5} + \dfrac{5}{x^2 - 25}$

6 **a** Simplify $\dfrac{2y - 12}{y^2 - 8y + 12}$ *(3 marks)*

b Write as a single fraction $\dfrac{3}{x - 4} - \dfrac{1}{x + 5}$ *(2 marks)*

©*Pearson Education Ltd 2011*

 Find answers at: cambridge.org/ukschools/gcsemaths-studentbookanswers

14 Surds

In this chapter you will learn how to ...

- calculate exactly with surds.
- simplify expressions containing surds.
- manipulate surds.

For more resources relating to this chapter, visit GCSE Mathematics Online.

Using mathematics: real-life applications

Surds are only really used when you are doing mathematical calculations that require exact answers. For all practical purposes surds are approximated. You cannot tell a builder to cut a length of steel that is $\sqrt{2}$ metres long, because $\sqrt{2}$ is an irrational number; so you would be more likely to specify an approximate length of 1.41 metres.

"The widths and lengths of A-series rectangular paper were developed using the ratio $1 : \sqrt{2}$ to mathematically construct a rectangle of area $1m^2$ (A0 size). In real life paper is cut to exact millimetre sizes, so A0 is 841 mm × 1189 mm rather than $841(\sqrt{2})$ which is 1189.353606 ... mm."

Before you start ...

Ch 4	You need to be able to write numbers as a product of their factors.	**1** Match the equivalent pairs. **a** $3^2 \times 5$ **b** $3 \times 2 \times 5$ **c** $2^3 \times 3$ **A** 24 **B** 30 **C** 45
KS3	You should be familiar with Pythagoras' theorem.	**2** For each triangle, state Pythagoras' theorem. **a** (triangle with sides a, b, c) **b** (triangle with sides x, y, z)
Ch 8	You need to be able to simplify expressions with powers.	**3** Decide whether each statement is true or false. **a** $\dfrac{18x^3}{6x^3} = 3$ **b** $\dfrac{\left(2y^3\right)^4}{\left(4y^6\right)^2} = y$

Assess your starting point using the Launchpad

STEP 1

1. A square has an area of 13 cm².

   a What is the length of each side correct to 2 decimal places?

   b What is the exact length of each side?

   c Square the values you gave in **a** and **b** and explain your results.

2. How could you construct a line segment of each of these lengths?

   a $\sqrt{25}$ cm   **b** $\sqrt{10}$ cm

GO TO
Section 1:
Approximate and exact values

STEP 2

3. Simplify the following without using a calculator.

   a $\sqrt{3} \times \sqrt{3}$ **b** $\sqrt{\dfrac{32}{2}}$ **c** $\sqrt{4} \times \sqrt{3}$

   d $\sqrt{3} + 2\sqrt{3}$ **e** $\sqrt{12} - \sqrt{3}$

4. Write each expression with a whole number denominator.

   a $\dfrac{2}{\sqrt{5}}$ **b** $\dfrac{3}{1-\sqrt{2}}$

5. Expand and simplify the following.

   a $(x - 2)(x + 4)$ **b** $(4 + \sqrt{3})(\sqrt{3} - 3)$

GO TO
Section 2:
Manipulating surds

GO TO
Section 3:
Working with surds

GO TO
Chapter review

Section 1: Approximate and exact values

Non-square numbers, such as 2 and 11, have roots that are **irrational** numbers. Irrational roots are commonly called **surds**.

The value $\sqrt{2}$ is the number which produces 2 when it is squared ($\sqrt{2} \times \sqrt{2} = 2$). A surd can only be expressed as an exact value using the root sign ($\sqrt{}$).

The expressions $\sqrt{12}$, $\sqrt{3}$ and $\sqrt[3]{7}$ are all surds. Expressions such as $\sqrt{81}$, $\sqrt[3]{125}$ and $\sqrt[4]{1296}$ are not surds because they have **rational** solutions: $\sqrt{81} = 9$, $\sqrt[3]{125} = 5$ and $\sqrt[4]{1296} = 6$.

Key vocabulary

irrational number: a number that cannot be written in the form of $\dfrac{a}{b}$ or as a terminating or repeating decimal.

surd: if $\sqrt[n]{a}$ is an irrational number, then $\sqrt[n]{a}$ is called a surd.

rational number: a number that can be expressed in the form of $\dfrac{a}{b}$ (or as its equivalent as a terminating or repeating decimal).

Find answers at: cambridge.org/ukschools/gcsemaths-studentbookanswers

Approximate values

Approximate values of surds are useful in many situations. For example, if you want to know the length of a diagonal path across a rectangular 12 m by 7 m field, you can use Pythagoras' theorem and rounding to work out that the path is approximately 13.89 m in length.

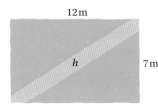

$$h^2 = 12^2 + 7^2$$
$$h^2 = 193$$
$$h = \sqrt{193} \approx 13.89$$

EXERCISE 14A

1 Use a calculator to find the approximate value of each of the following surds. Give your answers correct to 3 decimal places.

  a $\sqrt{7}$ **b** $\sqrt{12}$ **c** $\sqrt{51}$

  d $\sqrt{75}$ **e** $-\sqrt{3}$ **f** $-\sqrt{47}$

2 Use a calculator to find the approximate value of each expression correct to 3 decimal places.

  a $2\sqrt{2}$ **b** $3\sqrt{5}$ **c** $-3\sqrt{12}$

  d $10\sqrt{2}$ **e** $4(2\sqrt{3})$ **f** $-3(2\sqrt{18})$

3 Find the approximate value of each expression. Give your answers correct to 3 decimal places.

  a $\sqrt{2} + \sqrt{3}$ **b** $\sqrt{8} - \sqrt{2}$ **c** $\sqrt{2} + 3$

  d $\sqrt{8 - 2}$ **e** $2\sqrt{3} + 3\sqrt{5}$ **f** $-2\sqrt{3} + 3\sqrt{5}$

Exact values

Values are left as surds when you need to express an answer **exactly**.

> **WORKED EXAMPLE 1**
>
> Use Pythagoras' theorem to calculate the following exactly.
>
> **a** Length AC **b** Height EG
>
> 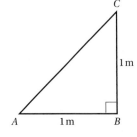   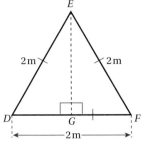
>
> Continues on next page …

a $(AC)^2 = 1^2 + 1^2$

You are finding the longer side so you use the addition form of Pythagoras.

$(AC)^2 = 1 + 1 = 2$
$AC = \sqrt{2}$

2 is not a perfect square, so using your calculator will give a rounded answer. The question states 'exact', so leave your answer in surd form.

b $(EG)^2 = 2^2 - 1^2$

You are finding a shorter side so rearrange the theorem to use subtraction.

$(EG)^2 = 4 - 1 = 3$
$EG = \sqrt{3}$

EXERCISE 14B

1 Find the exact length of a side of a square with area:

   a $14\,\text{cm}^2$ **b** $20\,\text{m}^2$ **c** $17\,\text{cm}^2$

2 What is the exact circumference of a coin with a radius of $\sqrt{3}\,\text{cm}$?

3 What is the exact value of $\left(\dfrac{9}{\sqrt{3}}\right)^2$?

4 Two identical square mosaic tiles have a combined area of $14\,\text{cm}^2$. What is the exact length of a side of each square?

5 The area of a square plot of land is $50\,\text{m}^2$.

   a What is the exact length of each side of the plot?

   b What is the exact diagonal distance across the plot?

Tip

For Question **5b** use Pythagoras' theorem (see Chapter 32).

6 Nico is a jeweller who makes square plates of platinum to use in various pieces of jewellery. Each square has a diagonal of $4\,\text{cm}$.

   a What is the exact length of each side of such a square?

   b Use the exact length to calculate the exact area of a square.

   c Give the length of the sides correct to:

      i 2 decimal places   **ii** 3 decimal places   **iii** 4 decimal places.

   d Calculate the area of each square using the approximate values.

   e Nico works out the cost of the metal used by finding the area of 100 squares and then multiplying this amount by £1245. Use the exact area from part **b** and the three approximate areas from part **d** to show how Nico's calculated costs vary, depending on which area value he uses.

   f Which value would you suggest he uses to work out the cost of each piece of jewellery? Why?

Section 2: Manipulating surds

Tip

Remember that taking a square root and squaring are inverse operations.

You already know some general rules for working with square roots. These rules apply to surds as well and they are useful for simplifying and manipulating surds.

If x and y represent *positive* integers, then by definition:

$\left(\sqrt{x}\right)^2 = x$ For example, $\left(\sqrt{25}\right)^2 = \sqrt{25} \times \sqrt{25} = 5 \times 5 = 25$

$\sqrt{x^2} = x$ For example, $\sqrt{5^2} = \sqrt{25} = 5$

$\sqrt{x} \times \sqrt{y} = \sqrt{xy}$ For example, $\sqrt{9} \times \sqrt{4} = 3 \times 2 = 6$ and $\sqrt{9 \times 4} = \sqrt{36} = 6$

$\sqrt{x} \div \sqrt{y} = \sqrt{\dfrac{x}{y}}$ For example, $\sqrt{36} \div \sqrt{9} = 6 \div 3 = 2$ and $\sqrt{\dfrac{36}{9}} = \sqrt{4} = 2$

WORK IT OUT 14.1

Is each statement true or false?

a $\sqrt{35} = \sqrt{5} \times \sqrt{7}$ **b** $\left(\sqrt{49}\right)^2 = 49$ **c** $\sqrt{30} \div \sqrt{6} = 5$ **d** $3\sqrt{3} = \sqrt{9} \times \sqrt{3}$

Simplifying surds

Tip

The term 'surd' is commonly used for any expression containing a surd. This includes expressions such as $2\sqrt{5}$, which is a product of a whole number and a surd, and $\sqrt{3} + \sqrt{5}$, which is the sum of two surds.

A surd is in its simplest form when the number under the root sign is as small as possible. This means that it has no factors greater than 1 that are perfect squares.

WORKED EXAMPLE 2

Write $\sqrt{18}$ in its simplest form

$18 = 9 \times 2$
so $\sqrt{18} = \sqrt{9} \times \sqrt{2}$

> Look for a factor that is a perfect square.

But $\sqrt{9 \times 2}$ can be written as $\sqrt{9} \times \sqrt{2}$ and $\sqrt{9}$ can be written as 3

> Use the fact that $\sqrt{xy} = \sqrt{x} \times \sqrt{y}$

$\therefore \sqrt{18} = 3\sqrt{2}$

> Remember, $3\sqrt{2}$ is the simpler form of $3 \times \sqrt{2}$

WORKED EXAMPLE 3

Simplify the following surds.

a $3\sqrt{32}$ **b** $-2\sqrt{320}$ **c** $2\sqrt{12} \times 4\sqrt{3}$

a $3\sqrt{32} = 3 \times \sqrt{16} \times \sqrt{2}$

> $32 = 16 \times 2$

$= 3 \times 4 \times \sqrt{2}$

$= 12 \times \sqrt{2}$

> Multiply the integers.

$= 12\sqrt{2}$

Continues on next page ...

b $-2\sqrt{320} = -2 \times \sqrt{16} \times \sqrt{20}$

Look for a factor that is a perfect square.

$= -2 \times 4 \times \sqrt{4} \times \sqrt{5}$
$= -2 \times 4 \times 2 \times \sqrt{5}$
$= -16\sqrt{5}$

Check to see if the second factor can also be written as the product of a perfect square.

c $2\sqrt{12} \times 4\sqrt{3}$

$= 2 \times \sqrt{4} \times \sqrt{3} \times 4\sqrt{3}$

Only the $\sqrt{12}$ can be simplified here.

$= 2 \times 2 \times \sqrt{3} \times 4\sqrt{3}$

$= 16 \times \sqrt{3} \times \sqrt{3}$

Remember, $\sqrt{x} \times \sqrt{x} = x$

$= 16 \times 3$

$= 48$

Tip

Check whether the number in the root sign can be divided by a perfect square (4, 16, 25, 36, 49, 64, 81, 100, …) If it can, then use the largest possible square number as one of the factors to make simplification easier.

EXERCISE 14C

1 What is the simplest form of each surd? Choose the correct answer.

a $\sqrt{28}$	**A** $4\sqrt{7}$	**B** $\sqrt{4} \times \sqrt{7}$	**C** $2\sqrt{7}$	**D** $2\sqrt{14}$	**E** $28\sqrt{1}$
b $\sqrt{12}$	**A** $12\sqrt{1}$	**B** $2\sqrt{3}$	**C** $3\sqrt{4}$	**D** $4\sqrt{3}$	**E** $\sqrt{3} \times \sqrt{4}$
c $\sqrt{72}$	**A** $2\sqrt{36}$	**B** $6\sqrt{2}$	**C** $\sqrt{36} \times \sqrt{2}$	**D** $\sqrt{8} \times \sqrt{9}$	**E** $3\sqrt{8}$
d $5\sqrt{12}$	**A** $5\sqrt{4} \times \sqrt{3}$	**B** $15\sqrt{4}$	**C** $10\sqrt{3}$	**D** $3\sqrt{10}$	**E** $7\sqrt{3}$
e $\sqrt{320}$	**A** $\sqrt{16} \times \sqrt{20}$	**B** $\sqrt{16} \times 4 \times 5$	**C** $4\sqrt{20}$	**D** $32\sqrt{10}$	**E** $8\sqrt{5}$

2 Simplify.

a $\sqrt{8}$ **b** $\sqrt{24}$ **c** $\sqrt{28}$ **d** $\sqrt{45}$

e $\sqrt{54}$ **f** $\sqrt{68}$ **g** $\sqrt{60}$ **h** $\sqrt{126}$

i $\sqrt{90}$ **j** $\sqrt{200}$ **k** $\sqrt{117}$ **l** $\sqrt{243}$

3 These surds are already in their simplest form. Explain how you can tell just by looking.

$\sqrt{2}$ $\sqrt{11}$ $\sqrt{13}$ $\sqrt{53}$ $\sqrt{83}$ $\sqrt{101}$

4 Write each surd in its simplest form.

a $3\sqrt{8}$ **b** $-4\sqrt{24}$ **c** $5\sqrt{20}$

d $-5\sqrt{60}$ **e** $3\sqrt{56}$ **f** $-2\sqrt{128}$

g $-4\sqrt{45}$ **h** $-3\sqrt{68}$ **i** $7\sqrt{108}$

5 **a** Complete the following.

i $2\sqrt{7} = 2 \times \sqrt{7}$

$= \sqrt{\Box} \times \sqrt{7}$

$= \sqrt{\Box \times 7}$

$= \sqrt{\Box}$

ii $-3\sqrt{6} = -3 \times \sqrt{6}$

$= -\sqrt{\Box} \times \sqrt{6}$

$= -\sqrt{\Box \times 6}$

$= -\sqrt{\Box}$

b Why do you leave the minus sign outside the root in part **ii**?

6 Rewrite each of the following in the form of $\sqrt{n}$

a $3\sqrt{2}$ **b** $4\sqrt{3}$ **c** $3\sqrt{6}$

d $4\sqrt{11}$ **e** $-2\sqrt{7}$ **f** $-3\sqrt{3}$

g $-4\sqrt{17}$ **h** $-2\sqrt{11}$ **i** $12\sqrt{3}$

7 **a** What would you need to do to be able to arrange the sets of surds, given below, in order from smallest to largest (without using your calculator)?

i $4\sqrt{2}$ $2\sqrt{3}$ $3\sqrt{3}$ **ii** $8\sqrt{3}$ $6\sqrt{7}$ $5\sqrt{7}$

iii $3\sqrt{7}$ $2\sqrt{10}$ $4\sqrt{3}$ **iv** $5\sqrt{6}$ $8\sqrt{2}$ $6\sqrt{3}$

b Apply your method and arrange the surds in order.

c Compare your answers and your method with a partner. Could you work more efficiently? If so, how?

Adding and subtracting surds

You can use algebra to simplify expressions containing surds. For example, $3\sqrt{5} + 4\sqrt{5}$ can be added because $\sqrt{5}$ is common to both terms. Using factorising you can take out a common factor of $\sqrt{5}$ to get

$$\sqrt{5}(3 + 4) = \sqrt{5}(7) = 7\sqrt{5}$$

An expression such as $2\sqrt{5} + 4\sqrt{3}$ cannot be added because it has no surds that are common factors. (You can also think about $\sqrt{5}$ and $\sqrt{3}$ as unlike surds.) As with like terms in algebra, you can only add or subtract terms which have the same surds in them.

Before you add or subtract you may need to express surds in their simplest terms.

> **Tip**
>
> If a number and a surd are multiplied together, the number is usually written first. So, write $7\sqrt{5}$ rather than $\sqrt{5}(7)$.

WORKED EXAMPLE 4

Simplify $5\sqrt{2} - 2\sqrt{8}$

$5\sqrt{2} - 2\sqrt{8}$

$= 5\sqrt{2} - 2 \times \sqrt{4} \times \sqrt{2}$ $\sqrt{2}$ is in its simplest form. See if you can simplify $\sqrt{8}$

$= 5\sqrt{2} - 2 \times 2 \times \sqrt{2}$

$= 5\sqrt{2} - 4\sqrt{2}$ Now the surds are the same, you can simplify further.

$= \sqrt{2}$

WORK IT OUT 14.2

A teacher gave her class some multiple choice questions for homework. One student's answers are given below. Three of the answers are correct and two are incorrect. What errors do you think this student made to get the incorrect answers? What are the correct answers for these questions?

Circle the correct answers.

1 $8\sqrt{6} - \sqrt{6} =$ ✓

  A $8\sqrt{6}$ (B) $7\sqrt{6}$ C 8   D 0   E 7

2 $7\sqrt{3} + 3\sqrt{2} + 5\sqrt{3} =$ ✗

  A $15\sqrt{5}$ B $15\sqrt{8}$ C $12\sqrt{3} + 3\sqrt{2}$ (D) $12\sqrt{6} + 3\sqrt{2}$ E $15\sqrt{3}$

3 $5\sqrt{2} - 2\sqrt{8} =$

  A 1   B 0   C $-3\sqrt{2}$ (D) $\sqrt{2}$ ✓   E $3\sqrt{-6}$

4 $4\sqrt{5} - \sqrt{2} + 6\sqrt{5} - 3\sqrt{2} =$ ✓

  A $10\sqrt{5} - 3$ B $6\sqrt{3}$ (C) $10\sqrt{5} - 4\sqrt{2}$ D $10\sqrt{10} - 4\sqrt{2}$ E $2\sqrt{5} - 2\sqrt{2}$

5 $\sqrt{27} + 2\sqrt{5} + \sqrt{20} - 2\sqrt{3} =$ ✗

  (A) $2\sqrt{8} + \sqrt{47}$ B $\sqrt{3} + 4\sqrt{5}$ C $4\sqrt{3} + \sqrt{5}$ D $5\sqrt{3} - 4\sqrt{5}$ E $-\sqrt{3} + 4\sqrt{5}$

EXERCISE 14D

1 Provide examples using square numbers to show that when x and y are positive integers:

  a $\sqrt{x} + \sqrt{y} \neq \sqrt{x+y}$ **b** $\sqrt{x} - \sqrt{y} \neq \sqrt{x-y}$

2 Simplify by adding or subtracting.

  a $2\sqrt{6} + 3\sqrt{7} + 4\sqrt{6}$ **b** $\sqrt{2} + 3\sqrt{2} + 2\sqrt{5}$

  c $2\sqrt{5} + 3\sqrt{3} + 2\sqrt{5} + 5\sqrt{3}$ **d** $9\sqrt{2} + 2\sqrt{3} - 7\sqrt{2} + 3\sqrt{3}$

  e $4\sqrt{5} - 2\sqrt{2} + 2\sqrt{5} + 5\sqrt{2}$ **f** $4\sqrt{2} + 4\sqrt{3} - 3\sqrt{2} - 6\sqrt{3}$

3 Simplify.

  a $\sqrt{2} + \sqrt{8}$ **b** $\sqrt{28} - \sqrt{7}$ **c** $3\sqrt{6} + \sqrt{24}$

  d $3\sqrt{5} - \sqrt{20}$ **e** $5\sqrt{63} - 7\sqrt{28}$ **f** $4\sqrt{45} - 2\sqrt{20}$

4 Simplify.

  a $\sqrt{75} + \sqrt{27} - 2\sqrt{3}$ **b** $-4\sqrt{11} + 8\sqrt{10} - 2\sqrt{11} - 2\sqrt{10}$

  c $2\sqrt{75} - \sqrt{45} + 2\sqrt{20}$ **d** $2\sqrt{12} - \sqrt{20} - \sqrt{27} + 2\sqrt{45}$

  e $3\sqrt{54} + 4\sqrt{24} - 2\sqrt{96}$ **f** $6\sqrt{50} - 2\sqrt{24} + 4\sqrt{32} + \sqrt{54}$

5 A rectangular component has side dimensions $(3 - \sqrt{3})$ cm by $(3 + \sqrt{48})$ cm. Calculate the exact perimeter of the component.

Find answers at: cambridge.org/ukschools/gcsemaths-studentbookanswers

Multiplying surds

Some expressions will contain both surds and brackets. To simplify these, you apply the basic rules you know from algebra.

WORKED EXAMPLE 5

Simplify.

a $\sqrt{5} \times \sqrt{7}$ **b** $2\sqrt{7} \times 3\sqrt{3}$ **c** $\sqrt{2}(4 - 3\sqrt{2})$ **d** $(3 + \sqrt{2})(3 - \sqrt{2})$ **e** $(\sqrt{2} + \sqrt{3})^2$

a $\sqrt{5} \times \sqrt{7} = \sqrt{35}$

> Use the rule $\sqrt{x} \times \sqrt{y} = \sqrt{xy}$

b $2\sqrt{7} \times 3\sqrt{3} = 2 \times 3 \times \sqrt{7} \times \sqrt{3}$

$= 6\sqrt{21}$

> Multiplication can be done in any order.

c $\sqrt{2}(4 - 3\sqrt{2}) = \sqrt{2} \times 4 - \sqrt{2} \times 3\sqrt{2}$

$= 4\sqrt{2} - 3 \times 2$

$= 4\sqrt{2} - 6$

> Multiply both terms in the brackets by $\sqrt{2}$ paying attention to the negative sign.

> There is now no surd in the second term because $\sqrt{x} \times \sqrt{x} = x$

d $(3 + \sqrt{2})(3 - \sqrt{2})$

$= 3 \times 3 - 3 \times \sqrt{2} + \sqrt{2} \times 3 - \sqrt{2} \times \sqrt{2}$

$= 9 - 3\sqrt{2} + 3\sqrt{2} - 2$

$= 9 - 2$

$= 7$

> Use the rules for binomial products (see Chapter 13).

e $(\sqrt{2} + \sqrt{3})^2 = (\sqrt{2} + \sqrt{3})(\sqrt{2} + \sqrt{3})$

$= \sqrt{2} \times \sqrt{2} + \sqrt{2} \times \sqrt{3} + \sqrt{3} \times \sqrt{2} + \sqrt{3} \times \sqrt{3}$

$= 2 + \sqrt{6} + \sqrt{6} + 3$

$= 5 + 2\sqrt{6}$

Dividing surds

You may need to simplify surds so that you can find common factors and cancel them.

WORKED EXAMPLE 6

Simplify.

a $\sqrt{104} \div \sqrt{13}$ **b** $\dfrac{3\sqrt{21}}{\sqrt{3}}$ **c** $\dfrac{6 + 2\sqrt{20}}{2}$

a $\sqrt{104} \div \sqrt{13} = \sqrt{\dfrac{104}{13}}$ Apply the rule $\sqrt{x} \div \sqrt{y} = \sqrt{\dfrac{x}{y}}$

$= \sqrt{8}$

$= 2\sqrt{2}$ Give your answer in simplest form.

b $\dfrac{3\sqrt{21}}{\sqrt{3}} = 3\sqrt{\dfrac{21}{3}}$ Apply the rule $\sqrt{x} \div \sqrt{y} = \sqrt{\dfrac{x}{y}}$

$= 3\sqrt{7}$ Simplify $\sqrt{\dfrac{21}{3}}$

c $\dfrac{6 + 2\sqrt{20}}{2} = \dfrac{6}{2} + \dfrac{2\sqrt{20}}{2}$ Remember the rules for dividing fractions.

$= 3 + \sqrt{20}$ Divide both terms by 2

$= 3 + 2\sqrt{5}$ Write the surd in simplest form.

Rationalising the denominator

Many calculations in algebra can be made easier if any surds in a fraction are only in the numerator and the denominators are integers.

Removing surds from the denominator of a fraction is called **rationalising the denominator**.

$\dfrac{x}{\sqrt{y}}$ is equivalent to $\dfrac{x}{\sqrt{y}} \times \dfrac{\sqrt{y}}{\sqrt{y}}$ (because $\dfrac{\sqrt{y}}{\sqrt{y}} = 1$).

Multiplying will give you $\dfrac{x\sqrt{y}}{y}$ (because $\sqrt{y} \times \sqrt{y} = y$).

WORKED EXAMPLE 7

Rationalise the denominators.

a $\dfrac{5}{\sqrt{7}}$ **b** $\dfrac{2\sqrt{5}}{\sqrt{6}}$

a $\dfrac{5}{\sqrt{7}} = \dfrac{5}{\sqrt{7}} \times \dfrac{\sqrt{7}}{\sqrt{7}} = \dfrac{5\sqrt{7}}{7}$

> Multiply by $\dfrac{\sqrt{7}}{\sqrt{7}}$

b $\dfrac{2\sqrt{5}}{\sqrt{6}} = \dfrac{2\sqrt{5}}{\sqrt{6}} \times \dfrac{\sqrt{6}}{\sqrt{6}}$

> Multiply by $\dfrac{\sqrt{6}}{\sqrt{6}}$

$= \dfrac{2\sqrt{30}}{6}$

> Multiply.
> Write $\sqrt{5} \times \sqrt{6}$ as a single surd.

$= \dfrac{\sqrt{30}}{3}$

> Cancel $\dfrac{2}{6} = \dfrac{1}{3}$

Binomial denominators

Tip

This uses the principle of the difference of squares rule that you have met in Chapter 13.

In Worked example 5d, you should have noticed that $(3 + \sqrt{2})(3 - \sqrt{2})$ gave a result that had no surd component.

This is always the case when the terms are the same but the sign between them is different.

We can use this principle to rationalise the denominator when it is a binomial.

WORKED EXAMPLE 8

Write $\dfrac{3}{2 - \sqrt{3}}$ with a rational denominator.

$\dfrac{3}{2 - \sqrt{3}}$

$\dfrac{3}{2 - \sqrt{3}} = \dfrac{3}{2 - \sqrt{3}} \times \dfrac{2 + \sqrt{3}}{2 + \sqrt{3}}$

> Use the same two terms as in the denominator but with the sign between them changed.

Continues on next page …

$$= \frac{3(2+\sqrt{3})}{4-3}$$

$$= 6 + 3\sqrt{3}$$

$(2 + \sqrt{3})(2 - \sqrt{3}) = 4 - 3$
Expansions of this type will always give the square of the first term minus the square of the second term.

Multiply to remove the brackets.

Tip

Rationalising the denominator is useful for simplifying in exact calculations. If you only need an approximate value, use your calculator and you won't need to rationalise the denominator.

EXERCISE 14E

1 Simplify.

a $\sqrt{7} \times \sqrt{3}$ **b** $\sqrt{3} \times \sqrt{5}$ **c** $\sqrt{3} \times \sqrt{12}$

d $2\sqrt{7} \times 3\sqrt{5}$ **e** $-3\sqrt{11} \times 4\sqrt{3}$ **f** $2\sqrt{15} \times 3\sqrt{3}$

g $2\sqrt{13} \times 3\sqrt{13}$ **h** $2\sqrt{6} \times 5\sqrt{3}$ **i** $4\sqrt{2} \times 5\sqrt{3}$

j $\sqrt{27} \times \sqrt{72}$ **k** $\sqrt{48} \times \sqrt{45}$ **l** $2\sqrt{20} \times 3\sqrt{24}$

2 Simplify.

a $\sqrt{14} \div \sqrt{2}$ **b** $\sqrt{26} \div \sqrt{13}$ **c** $\dfrac{\sqrt{5}}{\sqrt{10}}$ **d** $\dfrac{\sqrt{2}}{\sqrt{20}}$

e $\dfrac{\sqrt{45}}{\sqrt{5}}$ **f** $\dfrac{3\sqrt{7}}{3}$ **g** $\dfrac{5\sqrt{6}}{10}$ **h** $4\sqrt{\dfrac{60}{5}}$

i $6\sqrt{\dfrac{22}{2}}$ **j** $\dfrac{12\sqrt{12}}{4\sqrt{3}}$ **k** $\dfrac{-3\sqrt{24}}{\sqrt{6}}$ **l** $\dfrac{-2\sqrt{27}}{\sqrt{12}}$

3 Simplify fully.

a $\dfrac{3\sqrt{6} \times 4\sqrt{3}}{4}$ **b** $\dfrac{2\sqrt{5} \times 4\sqrt{6}}{\sqrt{10}}$ **c** $\dfrac{3\sqrt{5} \times 2\sqrt{8}}{6\sqrt{20}}$

d $\dfrac{\sqrt{3} \times \sqrt{15}}{3\sqrt{5}}$ **e** $\dfrac{5\sqrt{6} \times -2\sqrt{5}}{2\sqrt{15}}$ **f** $\dfrac{-\sqrt{12} \times \sqrt{27}}{2\sqrt{6} \times 2\sqrt{2}}$

Tip

Simplify the surds first so that you work with smaller numbers.

4 Expand and simplify.

a $\sqrt{5}(\sqrt{3} + 2)$ **b** $2\sqrt{3}(5 - \sqrt{3})$ **c** $(\sqrt{2} + 1)(\sqrt{6} - 2\sqrt{3})$

d $(2\sqrt{5} + \sqrt{7})^2$ **e** $(\sqrt{2} + 3)(\sqrt{3} + 5)$ **f** $(2 - \sqrt{5})(\sqrt{5} - 1)$

g $(4\sqrt{3} - \sqrt{2})(4\sqrt{3} + \sqrt{2})$ **h** $(\sqrt{7} + \sqrt{2})^2$ **i** $(\sqrt{3} - \sqrt{5})^2$

5 Express each of the following in simplest form with a rational denominator.

a $\dfrac{5}{\sqrt{3}}$ **b** $\dfrac{1}{\sqrt{5}}$ **c** $\dfrac{-2}{\sqrt{3}}$

d $\dfrac{\sqrt{2}}{\sqrt{3}}$ **e** $4\sqrt{\dfrac{3}{2}}$ **f** $\dfrac{-3}{4\sqrt{7}}$

g $\dfrac{2 + \sqrt{3}}{2\sqrt{3}}$ **h** $\dfrac{2 + \sqrt{5}}{\sqrt{5}}$ **i** $\dfrac{\sqrt{10} - \sqrt{5}}{5\sqrt{10}}$

 Find answers at: cambridge.org/ukschools/gcsemaths-studentbookanswers

6 Rationalise each denominator and simplify.

a $\dfrac{3}{3 - \sqrt{2}}$ **b** $\dfrac{\sqrt{2}}{\sqrt{11} + 3}$ **c** $\dfrac{\sqrt{3}}{\sqrt{5} - \sqrt{2}}$

d $\dfrac{3}{3\sqrt{2} + 4}$ **e** $\dfrac{8}{\sqrt{5} + 1}$ **f** $\dfrac{1 - \sqrt{3}}{2 - \sqrt{5}}$

g $\dfrac{\sqrt{5} + 1}{7 - 3\sqrt{5}}$ **h** $\dfrac{2 + \sqrt{3}}{5 - \sqrt{3}}$ **i** $\dfrac{\sqrt{2} - 3}{\sqrt{6} + 2\sqrt{3}}$

Section 3: Working with surds

In this section, you are going to apply the skills you've just learned to solve problems where some or all of the values are expressed as surds. Unless you are asked to give an approximate value, leave your answers in exact form.

Problem-solving framework

Find length *DE* in this figure. Give the answer in the simplest possible exact form.

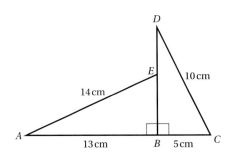

Steps for solving problems	What you would do for this example
Step 1: Read the question carefully to work out what you have to do.	Find length *DE*. Give the answer in the simplest possible exact form.
Step 2 Write down any information that might be useful.	$DE = BD - BE$ *BD* and *BE* are sides of right-angled triangles.
Step 3: Decide what method you'll use.	The triangles are right-angled, so use Pythagoras. Find *BE* and *BD* and then subtract them.

Step 4: Set out your working clearly.	$BE = \sqrt{14^2 - 13^2}$ $BD = \sqrt{10^2 - 5^2}$
	   $= \sqrt{196 - 169}$ $= \sqrt{100 - 25}$
	   $= \sqrt{27}$ $= \sqrt{75}$
	   $= 3\sqrt{3}$ $= 5\sqrt{3}$
	$BD - BE = 5\sqrt{3} - 3\sqrt{3} = 2\sqrt{3}$ cm

Step 5: Write an answer and check that it makes sense.	$DE = 2\sqrt{3}$ cm

EXERCISE 14F

1 Find the exact area and perimeter of each shape.

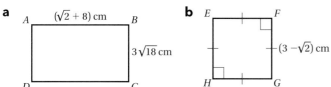

a
A $(\sqrt{2} + 8)$ cm *B*

$3\sqrt{18}$ cm

D *C*

b
E *F*

$(3 - \sqrt{2})$ cm

H *G*

c
J

$(\sqrt{2} + \sqrt{3})$ cm

L *K*

d

O

Diameter = $2(\sqrt{10} - 3)$ cm

e
M

$(\sqrt{11} + \sqrt{3})$ cm

P $(\sqrt{11} - \sqrt{3})$ cm *N*

2 Calculate the exact area of a rectangle *ABCD* with sides of $(6 + \sqrt{5})$ cm and $(6 - \sqrt{5})$ cm.

3 The area of a circle can be found using the formula $A = \pi r^2$. If a circle is found to have an area of 12π cm^2, what is the exact radius of the circle?

4 The chart shows the relationship of paper sizes in the A-series papers. The ratio of sides of each sheet is $1:\sqrt{2}$.

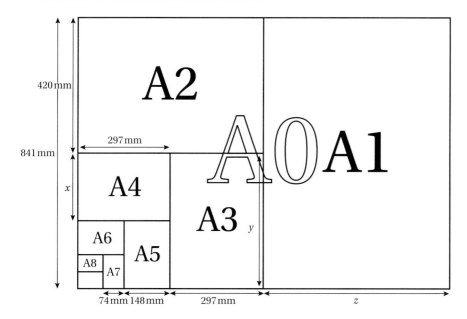

a Calculate the length of the sides marked *x*, *y* and *z*, giving your answers to the nearest whole millimetre.

b Size A0 paper is a rectangle of area 1 m^2.

  i Express the area in cm^2.

  ii Use the ratio of sides $1:\sqrt{2}$ to determine the length of the diagonal of a sheet of A0 paper given the width is 841 mm.

c For any sheet of A-series paper with shorter side *x* wide, express the length of the diagonal (*z*) in terms of *x*.

5 A metal cube $(2\sqrt{3} + 4\sqrt{5})$ cm high is to be coated with a rust inhibitor. Calculate the exact area of the surface to be painted.

6 In a right-angled triangle, the sine (sin) of each acute angle, is found by dividing the short side opposite to it by the hypotenuse of the triangle.

Given that ABC is a right-angled isosceles triangle with $AB = BC$, determine sin A, leaving your answer in surd form.

7 If x is a positive integer, find $\sqrt{x^3 + 2x^2 + x}$

8 A square has sides of length $3\sqrt{8}$. Find:

    a the area of the square   **b** the length of a diagonal.

9 Find the exact perimeter of a square of area 150 cm².

10 In the diagram (left), $AB = 5\sqrt{3}$, $XB = 2\sqrt{3}$, $CB = \dfrac{5\sqrt{5}}{3}$ and $YX = \sqrt{5}$. Find:

    a AX **b** AY **c** CZ **d** YC

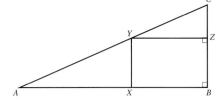

Checklist of learning and understanding

Surds are exact values

- Surds can only be expressed exactly using the root sign. Using a calculator to get a decimal value for a surd gives an approximate value.

Surds can be simplified

- Surds can sometimes be simplified by writing them as factors and taking the roots of any factors that are perfect squares.

Adding and subtracting surds

- Expressions containing surds can be simplified by adding or subtracting common factors.

Multiplying and dividing surds

- Surds can be multiplied and divided using the rules:
  - $\left(\sqrt{x}\right)^2 = x$
  - $\sqrt{x^2} = x$
  - $\sqrt{x} \times \sqrt{y} = \sqrt{xy}$
  - $\sqrt{x} \div \sqrt{y} = \sqrt{\dfrac{x}{y}}$

- When expanding expressions with brackets, apply the rules of algebra.

Rationalising the denominator

- Fractions with a surd in the denominator can be rewritten as equivalent fractions with an integer denominator.

- When the denominator is a binomial, for example $\left(\sqrt{x} + \sqrt{y}\right)$, you can use a binomial with the same terms but different sign between them, i.e. $\left(\sqrt{x} - \sqrt{y}\right)$, to rationalise the denominator.

Chapter review

For additional questions on the topics in this chapter, visit GCSE Mathematics Online.

Two sets of answers to an exercise involving simplifying surds are given below. For each of Questions 1 to 10:

a Decide whether either of the answers is correct. List the answers that you think are correct.

b If neither answer is correct, find the correct answer, showing your working.

	Question	Answer A	Answer B
1	$\sqrt{18}$	$\sqrt{6} \times \sqrt{3}$	$3\sqrt{2}$
2	$\sqrt{45}$	$3\sqrt{5}$	$5\sqrt{3}$
3	$3\sqrt{5} + \sqrt{3} + \sqrt{5} - 2\sqrt{3}$	$3\sqrt{5} - \sqrt{3}$	7.2122
4	$\sqrt{14} + \sqrt{8}$	$\sqrt{22}$	$\sqrt{112}$
5	$\sqrt{5} \times \sqrt{5} \times \sqrt{5} \times \sqrt{5}$	25	$4\sqrt{5}$
6	$\sqrt{3} \times \sqrt{3} \times \sqrt{3} + \sqrt{3}$	$4\sqrt{3}$	$3\sqrt{3}$
7	$\dfrac{6\sqrt{35}}{2\sqrt{5}}$	$3\sqrt{30}$	$3\sqrt{7}$
8	$\dfrac{1 + \sqrt{5}}{\sqrt{5}}$	2	$\dfrac{2}{\sqrt{5}} + 1$
9	$\dfrac{10 + 5\sqrt{7}}{5}$	$\sqrt{7} + 2$	$2 + 5\sqrt{7}$
10	$\dfrac{2}{2\sqrt{7} + 5}$	$\dfrac{2\left(\sqrt{7} - 5\right)}{2}$	$\dfrac{4\sqrt{7} - 10}{3}$

11 **a** Rationalise the denominator of $\dfrac{5}{\sqrt{2}}$ *(2 marks)*

   b Expand and simplify $(2 + \sqrt{3})^2 - (2 - \sqrt{3})^2$ *(2 marks)*

©Pearson Education Ltd 2012

15 Equations

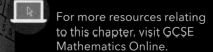

In this chapter you will learn how to …

- solve linear equations and apply them in context.
- solve quadratic equations.
- set up and solve simultaneous equations.
- use graphs and iteration methods to find approximate solutions to equations.

For more resources relating to this chapter, visit GCSE Mathematics Online.

Using mathematics: real-life applications

Accounting involves a great deal of mathematics. Accountants set up computer spreadsheets to calculate and analyse data. Programs such as Microsoft Excel® work by applying different equations to values in columns or cells, so you need to know what equations or formulae to use to get the results you need.

"Although the computer does the actual calculations, I have to insert different equations to tell it what operations to perform and in which order to perform them." *(Accountant)*

Before you start …

Chs 5, 13	Apply your skills in using the conventions of algebraic notation to form equations.	**1** Match each statement to the correct equation: **a** y is one half the size of x **b** y is 2 more than x **c** y is the same as x multiplied by x **d** x is the square root of y **A** $y = x^2$ **B** $y = x + 2$ **C** $x = \pm\sqrt{y}$ **D** $y = \frac{1}{2}x$
Ch 5	Check you can write an equation to represent a problem mathematically.	**2** Which of the equations below correctly represents this problem? "I think of a number, multiply it by 6 and add 1. The answer is 37. What is my number?" **A** $6x + 1 = 37$ **B** $y \times 6 = 37 + 1$ **C** $6a = 37$ **D** $6(x + 1) - 37 = 0$
Ch 1	You should be able to recognise and apply inverse operations.	**3** Complete the following statements. **a** $7 + \Box = 0$ **b** $\Box - 8 = 0$ **c** $-4a + \Box = 0$ **d** $5 \times \Box = 1$ **e** $\frac{1}{6} \times \Box = 1$ **f** $\Box \times 12x = x$
Ch 13	You need to know how to factorise quadratic expressions.	**4** Match each expression to its factors. **a** $x^2 - 5x + 6$ **A** $x(x + 3)$ **b** $x^2 + 3x$ **B** $(x + 5)(x - 5)$ **c** $x^2 - 25$ **C** $(x - 2)(x - 3)$ **d** $x^2 - 5$ **D** $(x + \sqrt{5})(x - \sqrt{5})$
Ch 13	You should be able to complete the square on a quadratic expression.	**5** Complete the square on each expression: **a** $x^2 + 4x + 10 = (x + \Box)^2 + \Box$ **b** $x^2 - 8x - 5 = (x - \Box)^2 - \Box$

Assess your starting point using the Launchpad

STEP 1

1 Match each equation to its solution.

Equations

a $x + 7 = 19$ **b** $x - 6 = 11$ **c** $2x + 5 = 7$

d $8x = -24$ **e** $2 - 3x = 8$

Solutions

A $x = 1$ **B** $x = 17$ **C** $x = -2$

D $x = 12$ **E** $x = -3$

f How can you check whether a solution is correct?

2 Solve.

a $9a - 7 = 7a + 3$ **b** $3(x + 5) = 2(x + 6)$

c $\dfrac{3a}{2} - 4 = \dfrac{1}{2}$ **d** $6(5 - 3x) = 5(x^2 - 5)$

3 Is $5x + 3 = 18$ equivalent to $6x + 3 = x + 18$?

How do you know?

4 When 16 is added to twice Jack's age, the answer is 44.

Write an equation and solve it to find Jack's age.

GO TO
Section 1:
Linear equations

STEP 2

5 If $x^2 - 2x - 3 = 0$, which pair of values is the solution?

A $x = 3$ or $x = -1$ **B** $x = -3$ or $x = 1$

6 What are the possible values of x given that $x^2 - 16 = 0$

7 Complete the square for this expression $(x - 3)^2 \underline{\hspace{2cm}} \equiv x^2 - 6x - 2$

8 Given $x^2 - 6x - 2 = 0$, identify the values of a, b and c in the

equation $x = \dfrac{-b \pm \sqrt{b^2 - 4ac}}{2a}$

Then substitute these and solve for x.

GO TO
Section 2:
Quadratic equations

GO TO
Step 3:
The Launchpad continues on the next page …

 Find answers at: cambridge.org/ukschools/gcsemaths-studentbookanswers

Launchpad continued ...

STEP 3

9 **a** How many positive whole number solutions can you find for $x + y = 6$?

b Which of those solutions are correct if $x + y = 6$ and $x - y = 4$?

GO TO
Section 3:
Simultaneous equations

STEP 4

10 A company hires out meeting rooms.

The total cost (y) can be worked out using the equation $y = 15x + 40$, where x represents the number of hours the room is hired for.

The graph of this equation is the straight line shown here.

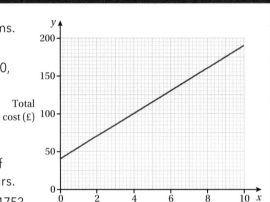

a Use the graph to find the cost of hiring a meeting room for 4 hours.

b What is the value of x when y is 175?

c What is the value of y when x is 5?

GO TO
Section 4:
Using graphs to solve equations

STEP 5

11 What is the maximum number of solutions a quadratic equation can have?

Can you find an approximate solution to $x^2 - 5x + 2 = 0$ using the iteration

$$x_{n+1} = 5 - \frac{2}{x_n} \text{ with } x_1 = 4?$$

GO TO
Chapter review

GO TO
Section 5:
Finding approximate solutions by iteration

Section 6:
Using equations and graphs to solve problems

Section 1: Linear equations

Solving an equation involves working out the value of the **unknown** letter.

When the highest power of the unknown is 1 the equation is a **linear equation**.

WORKED EXAMPLE 1

Solve for x.

a $5x - 5 = 3x + 1$ **b** $2y + 17 = 5 - 6y$ **c** $2(3x - 1) = 2(x + 1)$

a $5x - 5 = 3x + 1$

$5x - 5 - 3x = 3x + 1 - 3x$ | Subtract $3x$ from each side.

$2x - 5 = 1$ | Add like terms.

$2x - 5 + 5 = 1 + 5$ | Add 5 to each side.

$2x = 6$ | Simplify.

$x = 3$ | Divide both sides by 2.

b $2y + 17 = 5 - 6y$

$2y + 17 + 6y = 5 - 6y + 6y$ | Add $6y$ to both sides (this helps you get rid of negative signs).

$8y + 17 = 5$ | Add like terms.

$8y + 17 - 17 = 5 - 17$ | Subtract 17 from each side.

$8y = -12$ | Simplify.

$\dfrac{8y}{8} = \dfrac{-12}{8}$ | Divide both sides by 8.

$y = \dfrac{-3}{2}$ | Reduce the fraction to its simplest terms.

c $2(3x - 1) = 2(x + 1)$

$6x - 2 = 2x + 2$ | Expand the brackets paying attention to the signs.

$6x - 2 - 2x = 2x + 2 - 2x$ | Subtract $2x$ from each side.

$4x - 2 = 2$ | Add like terms.

$4x - 2 + 2 = 2 + 2$ | Add 2 to each side.

$4x = 4$ | Divide both sides by 4.

$x = 1$

Find answers at: cambridge.org/ukschools/gcsemaths-studentbookanswers

EXERCISE 15A

1 Solve the following equations. Check each answer by substitution.

a $3y + 10 = 5y + 3$ **b** $12x + 1 = 7x + 11$

c $5x - 2 = 3x + 6$ **d** $5x + 12 = 20 - 11x$

e $8 - 8a = 9 - 9a$ **f** $5x + 3 = 2(x + 2)$

2 Solve these equations by expanding the brackets first.

a $5(t + 3) = 3(2t + 1)$ **b** $7(x + 2) = 4(x + 5)$

c $4(x - 2) + 2(x + 5) = 14$ **d** $3(x + 1) = 2(x + 1) + 2x$

e $-2(x + 2) = 4x + 9$ **f** $4 + 2(2 - x) = 3 - 2(5 - x)$

3 **a** Try to solve these two equations.

     i $2(x + 8) - 3x = x + 16$ **ii** $4(3 + x) + 4x = 4(2x + 3)$

b If an equation is true for any value of x, it is an identity.

Which of these two equations is an identity? How do you know this?

c Do you think there is a solution for the other equation? Give a reason for your answer.

Equations containing fractions

When an equation contains fractions, your first steps should be to find a common denominator and multiply each side by it to get rid of the denominators.

WORKED EXAMPLE 2

Solve for x:

$$\frac{x - 1}{5} = \frac{2x + 1}{4}$$

$$\frac{(x - 1)}{5} = \frac{(2x + 1)}{4}$$

As a first step, insert brackets.

$$4(x - 1) = 5(2x + 1)$$

Cross multiply by 4 and 5. This is the same as multiplying both sides by the LCD of 20 and cancelling.

$$4x - 4 = 10x + 5$$

Expand the brackets.

$$-4 = 6x + 5$$

Subtract $4x$ from both sides.

$$-9 = 6x$$

Subtract 5 from both sides.

Continues on next page …

$$-\frac{9}{6} = x$$

Divide both sides by 6.

$$x = -\frac{3}{2}$$

Cancel by 3 to lowest terms.

LHS: $\dfrac{\left(-1\frac{1}{2}-1\right)}{5} = \dfrac{-2\frac{1}{2}}{5} = -\dfrac{1}{2}$

Check the answer by substitution.
LHS = RHS, so the solution is correct.

RHS: $\dfrac{\left(2\left(-1\frac{1}{2}\right)+1\right)}{4} = \dfrac{-2}{4} = -\dfrac{1}{2}$

Tip

You can combine steps in your own working. This example shows all the steps in detail.

WORKED EXAMPLE 3

Solve $\dfrac{x}{2} + \dfrac{x-1}{3} = \dfrac{x+1}{4}$

$$\frac{x}{2} + \frac{x-1}{3} = \frac{x+1}{4}$$

$$12 \times \frac{x}{2} + 12 \times \frac{(x-1)}{3} = 12 \times \frac{(x+1)}{4}$$

$$6x + 4(x-1) = 3(x+1)$$

The LCD of 2, 3 and 4 is 12, so multiply both sides by 12 and cancel to eliminate the fractions.

$$6x + 4x - 4 = 3x + 3$$

Expand the brackets.

$$10x - 4 = 3x + 3$$

Subtract $3x$ from both sides and add 4 to both sides.

$$7x = 7$$
$$x = 1$$

Divide both sides by 7

$$\frac{1}{2} + \frac{1-1}{3} = \frac{1+1}{4}$$

Check the solution.

$$\frac{1}{2} + 0 = \frac{2}{4}$$

$$\frac{1}{2} = \frac{1}{2}$$

The solution is correct.

EXERCISE 15B

1 Solve for x:

a $\dfrac{2x}{3} + \dfrac{1}{4} = 1$

b $2x - 3x = 4x + 3$

c $3(x - 5) = 2(4 - x)$

d $\dfrac{x}{3} + \dfrac{x}{2} = 10$

e $\dfrac{2x - 3}{4} = \dfrac{x + 1}{3}$

2 Solve for x:

a $\dfrac{x + 20}{9} + \dfrac{3x}{7} = 6$

b $\dfrac{2}{x - 1} = \dfrac{3}{x - 4}$

c $\dfrac{7x + 3}{2} = \dfrac{18x - 16}{8}$

d $\dfrac{-3(4 + x)}{2} = -9$

e $\dfrac{3x - 11}{5} - \dfrac{3x}{4} = 7 + 4x$

Forming and solving linear equations

When you set up an equation you must say what the letters stand for. Identify the value the letter represents.

WORKED EXAMPLE 4

The sum of two numbers is 54. If one number is 14 more than the other number, find the two numbers.

Let one of the numbers be x.

> Start by giving a letter to one of the unknown values.

So the other number is $(x + 14)$.

> You are told that the other number is 14 more than this.

$x + (x + 14) = 54$

> Use the information that the two numbers add up to 54 to form an equation.

$2x + 14 = 54$
$2x = 54 - 14$
$2x = 40$
$x = 20$

> Solve the equation to find one of the numbers.

$x = 20, \therefore x + 14 = 34$

> Use the value of x to find the value of the other number.

The two numbers are 20 and 34.

> Check that this works:
> $20 + 34 = 54$
>
> Yes, the solution is correct.

When the problem involves a shape it is useful to draw a sketch and label it to help you set up the equation.

WORKED EXAMPLE 5

In a triangle, the largest angle is four times the size of the smallest angle.

The third angle is 24° bigger than the smallest angle.

a Write an equation and solve it to find the size of each angle in this triangle.

b What type of triangle is this?

a

total of 3 angles = 180°

Draw a sketch and mark the angles using the information given.

Let the smallest angle be x.

The greatest angle is therefore $4x$.

The other angle is $(x + 24)$

$x + 4x + x + 24 = 180$
$6x = 180 - 24$
$6x = 156$
$x = 26$

You know that the sum of angles in a triangle is 180°.

So $4x = 4 \times 26 = 104$
And $x + 24 = 26 + 24 = 50$

Use $x = 26$ to find the size of the other angles.

The angles are 26°, 50° and 104°.

b The triangle is obtuse-angled and scalene.

EXERCISE 15C

1 For each of the following, write an equation and solve it to find the unknown number.

    a Three times a certain number is 348, what is the number?

    b 7 less than a number is −2, what is the number?

    c 6 greater than a number is −4, what is the number?

    d Two less than four times a number is 66, what is the number?

    e Two consecutive numbers have a sum of 63, what are the numbers?

    f Three less than twice a number is −2. What is the number?

    g When $1\frac{1}{2}$ is added to twice a certain number, the result is $4\frac{3}{4}$. What is the number?

---

2 Form an equation and solve it to answer each question.

a When 16 is added to twice Lucy's age, the answer is 44.

How old is Lucy?

b Stephen buys eight pens and receives 80p change from £20.00.

How much does a pen cost, assuming each pen costs the same amount?

c Multiplying a number by 2 and then adding 5 gives the same answer as subtracting the number from 23.

What is the number?

d Nick is 20 years older than his daughter.

His daughter has worked out that in five years' time, she will be half her father's age.

How old is she now?

e Gina is 4 years older than her sister.

When their ages are added together the result is 22.

How old is Gina?

f A woman is three times as old as her daughter.

In four years' time she will be only two and a half times as old as her daughter.

What is the woman's present age?

3 A square has sides of $3x$ cm. A parallelogram has sides of $2x$ cm and $(x + 9)$ cm.

a Write an expression for the perimeter of the square.

b Write an expression for the perimeter of the parallelogram.

c Given that the two quadrilaterals have the same perimeter, form an equation and solve it to find the length of one side of the square.

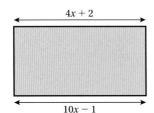

4x + 2

10x − 1

4 The area of this rectangle (left) is 10 cm^2.

Calculate the value of x and use it to find the length and width of the rectangle.

5 In a triangle ABC, angle B is three-quarters of angle A and angle C is one-half of angle A.

Find the size of each angle.

6 In a game of netball, the winning team won by nine goals.

In total, 83 goals were scored in the game.

How many goals did each team score?

7 A cellar contains only bottles of orange, apple, blackcurrant and mango juice.

Of these, $\frac{1}{5}$ of the bottles are orange juice and $\frac{1}{5}$ are apple juice.

The cellar also contains 15 dozen bottles of blackcurrant and 30 bottles of mango juice.

How many bottles of orange and apple juice does it contain?

8 A stallholder at a local market sells articles at either £2 or £5 each.

On a particular market day, he sold 101 articles and took £331 in revenue.

How many articles were sold at each price?

9 Ten thousand tickets were sold for a concert.

Some tickets sold for £80 each and the remainder sold for £60 each.

If the total receipts were £640 000, how many tickets at each price were sold?

Section 2: Quadratic equations

To solve the simple **quadratic equation** $x^2 = 9$, you have to find the square root of 9.

You know that $\sqrt{9} = 3$.

But, 3 is not a complete solution because $\sqrt{9}$ can also be -3. $(-3 \times -3 = 9)$

So, $\sqrt{9} = 3$ **or** -3, written as $\sqrt{9} = \pm 3$.

Because you are dealing with a squared variable, quadratic equations have two solutions, known as **roots**.

When you are asked to solve a quadratic equation you need to give a **solution** that contains both roots.

The solution to the equation $x^2 = 9$ is $x = \pm 3$

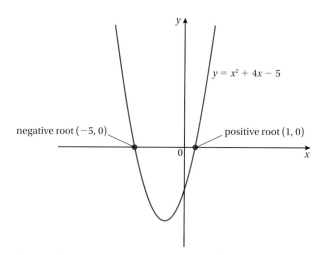

This diagram shows the quadratic function $y = x^2 + 4x - 5$. It cuts the x-axis in two places marked as the positive root and the negative root.

These are the points at which $y = 0$ so you can solve for x by writing the equation as $0 = x^2 + 4x - 5$.

Key vocabulary

quadratic equation: an equation that contains a variable squared term, like x^2, but no variable term with a power greater than 2. $x^2 = 4$ and $x^2 + 2x - 6 = 0$ are quadratic equations. $x^3 - 1 = 0$ and $6x + 7 = 35$ are not quadratic equations.

Tip

Some equations have only one root. For example
$x^2 - 2x + 1 = 0$ and
$x^2 + 4x + 4 = 0$
$(x - 1)(x - 1) = 0$
$(x + 2)(x + 2) = 0$
$x = 1$
$x = -2$

The root is said to repeat. Here the graphs of the equations will just touch the x-axis at the root.

Others equations are said to have no real roots. This means that the graphs of these equations do not cut the y-axis.

In solving some problems using quadratic equations, only one of the roots will be valid.

Key vocabulary

roots: the individual values of x in a quadratic equation.

solution: both possible values of x in a quadratic equation.

Tip

You will deal with graphs of quadratic equations in more detail in Chapter 25.

Solving quadratic equations by factorising them

The general form of a quadratic equation is $x^2 + bx + c = 0$ (when the coefficient of x^2 is 1).

Before you learn how to solve quadratic equations by factorising them, you need to consider what it means if the product of two factors equals 0.

For example, if $7 \times a = 0$, then you know that $a = 0$.

Similarly, if $a \times b = 0$ then either $a = 0$ or $b = 0$ or both $a = 0$ and $b = 0$.

This means that if $(x - 1)(x - 2) = 0$ then either $(x - 1) = 0$ or $(x - 2) = 0$.

If $x - 1 = 0$, then $x = 1$.

If $x - 2 = 0$, then $x = 2$.

This zero factor principle allows you to factorise the left-hand side of a quadratic equation and use the fact that one of the factors must be zero to solve it and find the roots of the equation.

Tip

Make sure you remember these three methods of factorising quadratic expressions:

$x^2 - 6x \equiv x(x - 6)$	taking out a common factor
$x^2 + 5x + 4 \equiv (x + 1)(x + 4)$	writing a quadratic expression as a product of binomials
$x^2 - 100 \equiv (x + 10)(x - 10)$	applying the difference of two squares identity

Read through Chapter 13 again if you have forgotten anything.

WORKED EXAMPLE 6

Solve

a $x^2 - 3x + 2 = 0$ **b** $9x^2 - 4 = 0$ **c** $x^2 - 6x = 0$

d $3x^2 - 5x = 2$ **e** $x + 5 = \dfrac{14}{x}$ **f** $\dfrac{1}{x - 1} - \dfrac{1}{x + 3} = \dfrac{1}{35}$

a $(x - 1)(x - 2) = 0$ Factorise the left-hand side.

Either $(x - 1) = 0$ or $(x - 2) = 0$ Apply the zero factor principle.

$x - 1 = 0$
$\therefore \quad x = 1$ Solve both equations:

Add 1 to each side.

$x - 2 = 0$
$\therefore \quad x = 2$ Add 2 to each side.

$x = 1$ or $x = 2$ State the solution.

Continues on next page …

b $(3x + 2)(3x - 2) = 0$

Factorise using the difference of squares identity.

Either $3x + 2 = 0$ or $3x - 2 = 0$

Apply the zero factor principle.

$3x + 2 = 0$
$\therefore \quad x = -\dfrac{2}{3}$
$3x - 2 = 0$
$\therefore \quad x = \dfrac{2}{3}$

Solve the equations.

$x = -\dfrac{2}{3}$ or $x = \dfrac{2}{3}$

State the solution.

c $x(x - 6) = 0$

Factorise by taking out a common factor of x.

Either $x = 0$ or $(x - 6) = 0$

Apply the zero factor principle.

$x - 6 = 0$
$\therefore \quad x = 6$

In this case you already have one value for x so you need only solve one equation.

$x = 0$ or $x = 6$

State the solution.

d $3x^2 - 5x - 2 = 0$

Subtract 2 from each side to get the equation in general form.

$3x(x - 2) + 1(x - 2) = 0$

Factorise the quadratic.

$(x - 2)(3x + 1) = 0$

$x - 2 = 0$ or $3x + 1 = 0$

Apply the zero factor principle.

$x - 2 = 0$
$\therefore \quad x = 2$

Solve the equations.

$3x + 1 = 0$
$\therefore \quad x = -\dfrac{1}{3}$

$x = 2$ or $x = -\dfrac{1}{3}$

State the solution.

e $x + 5 = \dfrac{14}{x}$

This equation doesn't look like a quadratic until you rearrange it.

$x(x + 5) = 14$

Multiply by x to get rid of the fraction.

$x^2 + 5x = 14$

Expand the brackets – now you can see the squared variable.

Continues on next page ...

$x^2 + 5x - 14 = 0$

Subtract 14 to get the equation into general form.

$(x + 7)(x - 2) = 0$

Factorise.

Either $x + 7 = 0$ or $x - 2 = 0$

$\therefore x = -7$ or $x = 2$

f $35(x + 3) - 35(x - 1) = (x - 1)(x + 3)$

Multiply by the LCD $35(x - 1)(x + 3)$ and cancel to get rid of the denominators.

$35x + 105 - 35x + 35 = x^2 + 2x - 3$

Expand the brackets.

$140 = x^2 + 2x - 3$

Collect like terms.

$x^2 + 2x - 143 = 0$

Rewrite in standard form.

$(x + 13)(x - 11) = 0$

Factorise.

Either $x = -13$ or $x = 11$

After working through these examples you should be able to see a clear set of steps for solving a quadratic equation in the form of $x^2 + bx + c = 0$.

Step 1

Take all the terms to the left-hand side so the right-hand side is 0. This might involve expanding brackets. Make sure the x^2 term is positive. You might need to change signs.

Step 2

Factorise the left-hand side:

- check for common factors.
- check for difference of squares.
- write quadratic expressions as a product of two terms.

Step 3

Write each factor equal to 0.

Solve the equations to find the roots.

Tip

When you are dealing with a difference of two squares you can solve in the following way as well:

$4x^2 - 9 = 0 \quad \rightarrow \quad 4x^2 = 9 \quad \rightarrow \quad x^2 = \frac{9}{4} \quad \rightarrow \quad x = \pm\sqrt{\frac{9}{4}} \quad \rightarrow \quad x = \pm\frac{3}{2}$

EXERCISE 15D

1 Find the roots of each equation.

a $x^2 + 9x + 18 = 0$ **b** $x^2 - 10x + 9 = 0$ **c** $x^2 + 2x - 8 = 0$

d $x^2 - 9x + 20 = 0$ **e** $x^2 - 4x - 12 = 0$ **f** $x^2 + 4x - 21 = 0$

g $x^2 - 6x + 9 = 0$ **h** $x^2 + 10x + 25 = 0$ **i** $x^2 - 14x + 49 = 0$

2 Solve the following equations by factorising.

a $x^2 + 12x^2 + 27 = 0$ **b** $x^2 - x - 30 = 0$ **c** $6x^2 - 7x - 10 = 0$

d $9x^2 + 4x - 5 = 0$ **e** $x^2 + 3x = 0$ **f** $5x^2 - 4x = 0$

g $x^2 - 100 = 0$

3 Find the exact solutions to the following (that is, leave your answer in square root (surd) form).

a $x^2 - 5 = 0$ **b** $x^2 - 6 = 0$

4 Can you solve the quadratic equation $x^2 + 4 = 0$ by factorising it?

Explain.

5 Solve for x:

a $x^2 = 4(x + 8)$ **b** $(x - 1)(3x + 2) = 2$

c $3x - 8 = \dfrac{x^2}{4}$ **d** $2(x + 1)^2 = (x + 1)^2 + 9$

6 Solve for x:

a $\dfrac{x + 1}{3} = \dfrac{10}{x}$ **b** $\dfrac{2}{x - 3} = \dfrac{x}{3x - 4}$

c $\dfrac{4}{x - 1} - \dfrac{5}{x + 2} = \dfrac{3}{x}$ **d** $6(4x + 5) + \dfrac{7}{x}(4x + 5) = 0$

7 **a** Is it possible to factorise this quadratic equation applying one of the methods above?

$x^2 - 2x + 2 = 0$

Explain your answer.

b What can you say about the roots of this equation?

Tip

Quadratic equations are very useful for modelling situations in which a parabolic curve would be produced, or a curve very close to a parabola. The parabola occurs widely in the real world. You can see it in the jets from water fountains and in the path followed by the ball in various sports, as well as in the design of modern buildings.

Solving quadratic equations by completing the square

In Chapter 13 you learned how to factorise quadratic expressions by completing the square.

This method is used to solve quadratic equations if the left-hand side doesn't have integral factors.

Tip

Remember:
$(a + b)^2 = a^2 + 2ab + b^2$
$(a - b)^2 = a^2 - 2ab + b^2$

Find answers at: cambridge.org/ukschools/gcsemaths-studentbookanswers

WORKED EXAMPLE 7

Solve: $x^2 - 6x + 1 = 0$

$x^2 - 6x + 1 = 0$

> The LHS cannot be factorised.

$x^2 - 6x + 9 - 9 + 1 = 0$

> Add and subtract the square of half the coefficient of x.

$x^2 - 6x + 9 = 8$

> Keep the perfect square on the left-hand side.

$(x - 3)^2 = 8$

> Factorise the perfect square.

$x - 3 = \pm\sqrt{8}$

> Take the square root of both sides. Remember a square root has two possible answers.

So, $x = 3 + \sqrt{8}$ or $x = 3 - \sqrt{8}$

> These are **exact** solutions.

$x = 5.83$ or $x = 0.17$

> These solutions are rounded to 2 decimal places.

The quadratic formula

Completing the square results in a formula that can be used to solve quadratic equations.

Consider the general quadratic equation $ax^2 + bx + c = 0$.

$ax^2 + bx + c = 0$

$x^2 + \dfrac{b}{a}x + \dfrac{c}{a} = 0$

> Divide all terms by a.

$x^2 + \dfrac{b}{a}x = -\dfrac{c}{a}$

> Rearrange to get the terms in x and x^2 on one side of the equation.

$x^2 + \dfrac{b}{a}x + \dfrac{b^2}{4a^2} = -\dfrac{c}{a} + \dfrac{b^2}{4a^2}$

> Complete the square by adding $\dfrac{b^2}{4a^2}$ to both sides.

$\left(x + \dfrac{b}{2a}\right)^2 = \dfrac{b^2 - 4ac}{4a^2}$

> Factorise the LHS and write the RHS as a single fraction.

$x + \dfrac{b}{2a} = \dfrac{\pm\sqrt{b^2 - 4ac}}{2a}$

> Take the square root of each side.

$x = -\dfrac{b}{2a} \pm \dfrac{\sqrt{b^2 - 4ac}}{2a}$

> Isolate x by subtracting $\dfrac{b}{2a}$.

$x = \dfrac{-b \pm \sqrt{b^2 - 4ac}}{2a}$

This shows that for an equation in the general form $ax^2 + bx + c = 0$, the two roots are:

$$x = \frac{-b + \sqrt{b^2 - 4ac}}{2a} \quad \text{and} \quad x = \frac{-b - \sqrt{b^2 - 4ac}}{2a}$$

Learn this formula

$$x = \frac{-b \pm \sqrt{b^2 - 4ac}}{2a}$$

WORKED EXAMPLE 8

Solve $3x^2 + 7x - 13 = 0$, using the quadratic formula and giving your answer correct to 2 decimal places.

$a = 3, b = 7, c = -13$

$$x = \frac{-b \pm \sqrt{b^2 - 4ac}}{2a}$$

Start by identifying the values of a, b and c.

$$x = \frac{-7 \pm \sqrt{7^2 - 4 \times 3 \times (-13)}}{2 \times 3}$$

Substitute the values into the formula.

$$x = \frac{-7 \pm \sqrt{49 + 156}}{6}$$

$$x = \frac{-7 \pm \sqrt{205}}{6} = \frac{-7 \pm 14.317}{6}$$

Either $x = \dfrac{-7 + 14.317}{6}$ or $x = \dfrac{-7 - 14.317}{6}$

$x = 1.22$ or $x = -3.55$

Correct to 2 decimal places.

Tip

If you are asked to solve a quadratic equation to a given number of decimal places, it usually means the roots are irrational and you should apply the quadratic formula to find the solution.

Tip

When you use the quadratic formula, it is best to work systematically using a step-by-step approach and paying careful attention to negative values to make sure you get an accurate solution.

EXERCISE 15E

1 Solve each equation by completing the square.

a $x^2 - x - 10 = 0$ **b** $x^2 + 3x - 6 = 0$ **c** $x(6 + x) = 1$

d $2x^2 + x = 98$ **e** $5x = 10 - \dfrac{1}{x}$ **f** $x - 5 = \dfrac{2}{x}$

g $(x - 1)(x + 2) - 1 = 0$ **h** $(x - 4)(x - 2) = 5$ **i** $x^2 = x + 1$

2 Solve each of the following equations using the quadratic formula. Round the answers to three significant figures where necessary.

a $2x^2 - x + 6 = 4x + 5$ **b** $7x^2 - 3x - 6 = 3x - 7$ **c** $x(6x - 3) - 2 = 0$

d $0.5x^2 + 0.8x - 2 = 0$ **e** $(x + 7)(x + 5) = 9$ **f** $\dfrac{1}{x} + x = 7$

3 Use the quadratic formula to solve each quadratic equation.

Give your answers in simplest surd form.

a $x^2 + 5x + 5 = 0$ **b** $x^2 + 2x - 4 = 0$ **c** $x^2 + 12x + 3 = 0$

d $3x^2 + 2x - 7 = 0$ **e** $5x^2 + 3x - 1 = 0$ **f** $4x^2 - 6x + 1 = 0$

Find answers at: cambridge.org/ukschools/gcsemaths-studentbookanswers

Tip

It is possible to solve all quadratic equations by completing the square or using the formula. In many cases the graphical method will give sufficient accuracy for answers. However, if a quadratic factorises that is usually the most efficient method to apply.

Forming and solving quadratic equations

As with linear equations, you can set up and solve quadratic equations.

Always define the letters you are using in your equation.

WORKED EXAMPLE 9

A number is added to its square and the result is 12. What could the number be?

Let the number be x.
∴ its square is x^2.

Define the unknown values.

$x + x^2 = 12$

Set up an equation using the information in the problem.

∴ $x^2 + x - 12 = 0$

Rearrange the equation so that it is in the general form $ax^2 + bx + c = 0$ and the right-hand side is equal to 0.

∴ $(x + 4)(x - 3) = 0$

Factorise the quadratic.

Either $x + 4 = 0$ or $x - 3 = 0$

$x + 4 = 0$	$x - 3 = 0$
∴ $x = -4$	∴ $x = 3$

Solve the equations.

The number could be 3 or -4.

State the solution **in the context of the problem**.

Tip

If the problem involves square units then you can probably use a quadratic equation to solve it.

When you use quadratic equations to model real-life situations you might find that one of the solutions is not possible.

For example, if x is the length of the side of a box in metres, and you get the roots $x = 2.5$ or $x = -1.75$, you can ignore the value of -1.75 as this cannot be the length of an object.

You use 2.5 as the length of the side.

WORKED EXAMPLE 10

A rectangle with an area of $28\,\text{cm}^2$ has one side 3 cm longer than the other. How long are each of the shorter sides?

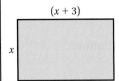

Draw a diagram and label the sides.

Let the shorter side be x.

∴ the longer side is $x + 3$.

Continues on next page ...

$A = x(x + 3)$

Next form your equation.

The area of a rectangle is length × breadth.

$28 = x(x + 3)$

But you are told the area is 28.

$x(x + 3) = 28$
$x^2 + 3x = 28$
$x^2 + 3x - 28 = 0$

Rearrange the equation so that it is in the general form $ax^2 + bx + c = 0$ and the right-hand side is equal to 0.

$(x + 7)(x - 4) = 0$

Factorise.

Either $(x + 7) = 0$ or $(x - 4) = 0$

Apply the zero factor principle.

$x + 7 = 0 \qquad x - 4 = 0$
$\therefore \quad x = -7 \quad \therefore \quad x = 4$

Solve the equations.

The shorter sides are 4 cm long.

State the answer.

In this problem you can ignore the $x = -7$ solution because -7 cm is not a possible length for the side of a rectangle.

EXERCISE 15F

1 Form an equation and solve it to find the unknown numbers.

a The product of a certain whole number and four more than that number is 140.

What could the number be?

b The product of a certain whole number and three less than that number is 108.

What could the number be?

c When three times a number is subtracted from the square of the number the answer is 10.

What are possible values of the number?

d The product of two consecutive positive even numbers is 48.

What are the numbers?

2 The base and height of a triangle in cm are $(x + 3)$ and $(2x - 1)$. The area of the triangle is 36 cm². Form a quadratic equation and find the value of x. Give the values of the base and height of the triangle.

Find answers at: cambridge.org/ukschools/gcsemaths-studentbookanswers

Tip

If you need more information, refer to Chapter 32.

3 Use Pythagoras' theorem to find the value of x in the diagram below and state the length of the three sides.

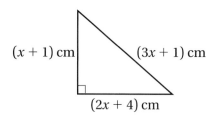

4 A piece of card measures 50 cm by 60 cm. Squares are cut out of the corners so it can be folded to form a box with a base area of 1200 cm². Find the length of the side of the squares to be cut out of the corners.

5 A rectangular lawn is 18 m long and 12 m wide.

The lawn is surrounded by a path of width x m.

The area of the path is equal to the area of the lawn.

Find x.

6 The rectangles shown are equal in area.

Find the value of x and hence the dimensions of each rectangle.

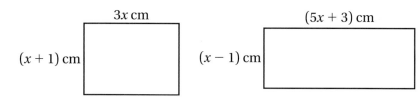

7 The perimeter of a rectangular field is 500 m and its area is 14 400 m².

Find the lengths of the sides.

Section 3: Simultaneous equations

The equations in Sections 1 and 2 all had only one unknown (for example, x).

Some equations contain two unknowns. For example, $x + y = 4$.

You can't work out a single solution to this equation. You can find many values for x and y, for example, $1 + 3 = 4$ or $2 + 2 = 4$.

The equation $3x - y = 2$ also has many solutions.

But if you are told that $x + y = 4$ and $3x - y = 2$, you have a pair of equations in two unknowns that are true at the same time for a particular value of x and y.

These are called **simultaneous equations**.

You can use the fact that both these equations are true to solve them at the same time (simultaneously).

You can draw graphs to solve simultaneous solutions but this method takes a

Key vocabulary

simultaneous equations: a pair of equations with two unknowns that can be solved at the same time.

WORKED EXAMPLE 11

There are 30 rose bushes in a nursery. Some are red and others are white.

There are twice as many red rose bushes as white.

How many rose bushes of each colour are there?

Let w = the number of white rose bushes, r = the number of red rose bushes.

State the letters you will use for your variables.

$r + w = 30$
$w = 2r$

To solve this you need to set up two equations.

There are 30 rose bushes altogether.

The number of red bushes is twice the number of white bushes.

$r + w = 30$

r	0	10	20	30
w	30	20	10	0

You can draw up a table for each equation to show some values of r and w.

$w = 2r$

r	0	5	10	15
w	0	10	20	30

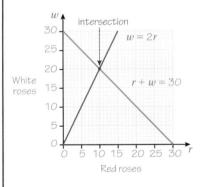

If you draw the graph of each set of values you get two lines that intersect in one place only.

Where the graphs intersect, the values on the axes must be the same.

The coordinates (r, w) of the point of intersection are $(10, 20)$, so $r = 10$ and $w = 20$.

This is the simultaneous solution of the two equations.

$r + w = 30$
$10 + 20 = 30$

Check by substitution in both equations.

$w = 2r$
$20 = 2(10) = 20$

Tip

This method is suitable when one of the equations already has x or y on its own on one side or when you can easily rearrange one of the equations to have x or y on its own.

long time and it might not be very accurate, especially if the solution values are fractions.

There are two methods of solving simultaneous equations using algebra: substitution and elimination.

The method you choose depends on how the equations are written.

Solving simultaneous equations by substitution

Problem-solving framework

Solve these simultaneous equations.

$x - 2y + 1 = 0$ and $y + 4 = 2x$

Steps for solving simultaneous equations by substitution	What you do in this example
Step 1: Number the equations (1) and (2).	$x - 2y + 1 = 0$ (1) $y + 4 = 2x$ (2)
Step 2: Rearrange one of the equations.	Equation (2) is simpler to rearrange. You get: $y = 2x - 4$ (2)
Step 3: Substitute the right-hand side of the rearranged equation into the other equation.	Substitute $(2x - 4)$ in place of y in (1). $x - 2(2x - 4) + 1 = 0$
Step 4: Solve the new equation (which now only has one unknown).	$x - 2(2x - 4) + 1 = 0$ $x - 4x + 8 + 1 = 0$ $-3x + 9 = 0$ $-3x = -9$ $x = 3$
Step 5: Substitute the solution into either of the original equations to find the other unknown.	Substitute $x = 3$ into (2) and solve. $y + 4 = 2(3)$ $y + 4 = 6$ $y = 6 - 4$ $y = 2$
Step 6: Check your solutions to both equations.	Substitute the values $x = 3$ and $y = 2$ in (1): $3 - 2(2) + 1 = 0$ ✓

EXERCISE 15G

1   Solve the following pairs of simultaneous equations by substitution.

Check that your solutions satisfy **both** equations.

a $y = x - 2$
     $y = 3x + 4$

b $y = 2x + 6$
     $y = 4 - 2x$

c $y = x + 1$
     $x + y = 3$

d $y = x - 2$
     $3x + y = 14$

e $y = 2x + 1$
     $x + 2y = 12$

f $y = 1 - 2x$
     $x + y = 2$

2   Solve these simultaneous equations.

a $x + 2y = 11$
     $2x + y = 10$

b $x - y = -1$
     $2x + y = 4$

c $5x - 4y = -1$
     $2x + y = 10$

d $3x - 2y = 29$
     $4x + y = 24$

e $3x + y = 2$
     $9x + 2y = 10$

f $3x - 2 = -2y$
     $2x - y = -8$

Solving simultaneous equations by elimination

In this method you add or subtract the equations to get rid of one of the unknown variables.

You might need to multiply or divide one equation by a factor before you do this.

Problem-solving framework

Solve the simultaneous equations $2x + y = 8$ and $x - y = 1$.

Steps for solving simultaneous equations by elimination	What you do in this example
Step 1: Number the equations (1) and (2).	$2x + y = 8$ (1) $x - y = 1$ (2)
Step 2: Decide whether you can add or subtract to get rid of a variable.	(1) has a variable of y and (2) has a variable of $-y$. If you add the equations, these terms will cancel out. (1) + (2) $(2x + y) + (x - y) = 8 + 1$ $2x + y + x - y = 9$ $3x = 9$
Step 3: Solve the combined equation (which now only has one unknown.	$3x = 9$ $x = 3$
Step 4: Substitute the solution into either of the original equations to find the other unknown.	Substitute $x = 3$ into (2). $3 - y = 1$ $-y = 1 - 3$ $-y = -2$ $y = 2$
Step 5: Check your solutions to both equations.	Substitute the values $x = 3$ and $y = 2$ in (1): $2(3) + 2 = 8$ ✓

In some examples, you will need to form new equations before you can add or subtract to eliminate one variable. Sometimes one new equation will be sufficient.

In the following example, you could rewrite one of the equations to make either x or y the subject and use substitution, but this involves introducing fractions into the equations.

The best strategy is to create multiples of these equations, to get one pair of identical coefficients for either x or y.

 Find answers at: cambridge.org/ukschools/gcsemaths-studentbookanswers

WORKED EXAMPLE 12

Solve this pair of simultaneous equations:

$3x - 2y = 5$ (1) $4x + 3y = 18$ (2)

$9x - 6y = 15$ (3)
$8x + 6y = 36$ (4)

> Multiply (1) by 3 and (2) by 2 to get equations (3) and (4).
>
> This creates a pair of coefficients for y which we can eliminate.

$17x = 51$
$x = 3$

> Add (3) and (4).

$4 \times 3 + 3y = 18$
$3y = 6$
$y = 2$

> Substitute in (2).

So $x = 3$ and $y = 2$

> Check you solution in both equations.

EXERCISE 15H

1   Solve the following pairs of simultaneous equations by elimination.

Check your solutions satisfy **both** equations.

   a $x - y = 2$ **b** $2x - 3y = 3$ **c** $3x + y = 4$

        $3x + y = 14$ $x + 3y = 6$ $2y - 3x = -10$

   d $x + 2y = 7$ **e** $2x - y = 14$ **f** $-x - y = 3$

        $3x - 2y = 13$ $5x + y = 14$ $x + 5y = -11$

   g $x + y = 5$ **h** $3x + 4y = 15$ **i** $2x - y = 7$

        $3x + y = 9$ $x + 4y = 13$ $4x - y = 15$

2   Solve each pair of simultaneous equations. Choose the most suitable method for doing this.

   a $2x + y = 7$ **b** $x + 2y = 7$ **c** $4x + 2y = 50$

        $3x + 2y = 12$ $3x - 2y = 5$ $x + 2y = 20$

   d $x + y = -7$ **e** $y = 1 - 2x$ **f** $y = 2x - 5$

        $x - y = -3$ $5x + 2y = 0$ $y = 3 - 2x$

3   Solve simultaneously:

   a $2x + 5y = 10$ **b** $x - 3y = 0$ **c** $-3x - 2y = 4$

        $x - 3y = 5$ $2x - 4y = 2$ $x + 7y = 5$

   d $2x + 3y = 12$ **e** $5x - 2y = 17$ **f** $2x + 3y = 1$

        $3x - 4y = -1$ $4x + 3y = 9$ $5x + 4y = -1$

Tip

If a problem asks for two different pieces of information then it means there are two unknowns and you will need two equations to solve it.

Forming and solving simultaneous equations

Some problems can be described using a pair of simultaneous equations.

Once you have defined the variables and set up the equations you can use algebra to solve them.

Problem-solving framework

A field contains a number of goats and chickens.

Altogether there are 60 heads and 200 legs.

How many are there of each type of animal?

Steps for solving problems	What you would do for this example
Step 1: Work out what you have to do. Start by reading the question carefully.	You have to find the number of goats (g) and the number of chickens (c).
Step 2: What information do you need? Have you got it all?	You need to know how many there are altogether. You're not told this, but you can work it out because each goat and each chicken must have one head. $g + c = 60$ Now you need another equation to link the goat and chickens. You've already used the number of heads, so it must be something to do with the legs. Goats have 4 legs each, so the number of goat legs is $4 \times g$. Chickens have 2 legs each, so the number of chicken legs is $2 \times c$. There are 200 legs in total so: $4g + 2c = 200$.
Step 3: Decide what maths you can do.	There are two unknowns so you should use simultaneous equations.
Step 4: Set out your solution clearly. Check your working and that your answer is reasonable.	Let the number of goats = g and the number of chickens = c. $g + c = 60$ (1) $4g + 2c = 200$ (2) Make g the subject of equation (1). $g = 60 - c$
	Substitute $(60 - c)$ for g in (2) and solve. $4(60 - c) + 2c = 200$ $240 - 4c + 2c = 200$ $240 - 2c = 200$ $240 - 200 = 2c$ $40 = 2c$ $20 = c$ Substitute $c = 20$ into equation (1) to find g. $g + 20 = 60$ so $g = 40$ Check your result by substituting c and g into original equation (2). $4(40) + 2(20) = 200$ $160 + 40 = 200$ Yes, this works.
Step 5: Check that you've answered the question.	There are 20 chickens and 40 goats.

Find answers at: cambridge.org/ukschools/gcsemaths-studentbookanswers

EXERCISE 15I

1 Sam got eighteen 5p and 10p coins totalling £1.65 as change when he went to the shop.

How many of each coin did he get?

2 Two children have a total of 264 stickers between them.

One child has 6 fewer stickers than 5 times the other child's stickers.

How many do they each have?

3 The sum of two numbers, a and b, is 120.

When b is subtracted from $3a$, the result is 160.

Find the value of a and b.

4 Two numbers have a sum of 76 and a difference of 48.

What are the numbers?

5 A taxi company charges a flat fee plus an amount per mile.

A journey of 10 miles costs £7 and a journey of 15 miles costs £9.

What would you pay for a journey of 8 miles?

6 Josh and Sanjita both spent £2.20 on sweets.

Josh bought five fizzers and four toffees.

Sanjita bought two fizzers and six toffees.

Work out the cost of each type of sweet.

7 A computer store sold 4 hard drives and 10 flash drives for £200 and 6 hard drives and 14 flash drives for £290. Find the cost of a hard drive and the cost of a flash drive.

8 A large stadium has 21 000 seats. The seats are organised in blocks of either 400 or 450 seats. There are three times more blocks of 450 seats than blocks of 400 seats. How many blocks of seats are there?

Simultaneous linear and quadratic equations

When the graphs of a linear equation and a quadratic equation are plotted on the same set of axes there are three possible arrangements.

Either the graphs don't intersect at all, or they intersect at one point, or they intersect at two points.

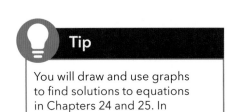

Tip

You will draw and use graphs to find solutions to equations in Chapters 24 and 25. In this chapter you will focus on algebraic solutions.

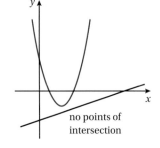

no points of intersection

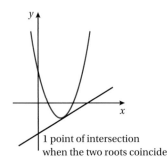

1 point of intersection when the two roots coincide

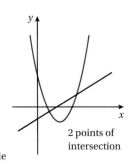

2 points of intersection

If the graphs intersect their equations can be solved simultaneously by substitution or elimination to find the point(s) of intersection.

WORKED EXAMPLE 13

Determine the point(s) of intersection for the following pairs of equations algebraically:

$y = x^2 - 1$ ___(1)

$y = -x + 5$ ___(2)

$x^2 - 1 = -x + 5$

Substitute $(x^2 - 1)$ for y in (2).

$x^2 + x - 6 = 0$

Arrange the equation into the general form.

$(x + 3)(x - 2) = 0$

Factorise.

Either $x = -3$ or $x = 2$

You are asked to find the points of intersection.

These are given as the ordered pair (x,y) so you cannot simply give values of x and y, you need to give the ordered pairs.

Substituting $x = -3$ in (2):
$y = -(-3) + 5$
$y = 8$

Substituting $x = 2$ in (2):
$y = -2 + 5$
$y = 3$

∴ the two points of intersection are $(-3, 8)$ and $(2, 3)$.

Make sure you match the correct value of x with the correct value of y.

Using $(-3, 8)$:
In (1),   LHS $= 8$
          RHS $= (-3)^2 - 1 = 9 - 1 = 8$
In (2),   LHS $= 8$
          RHS $= -(-3) + 5 = 8$
Using $(2, 3)$:
In (1),   LHS $= 3$
          RHS $= (2)^2 - 1 = 3$
In (2),   LHS $= 3$
          RHS $= -(2) + 5 = 3$

Substitute to check that the values for x and y satisfy both equations.

Continues on next page …

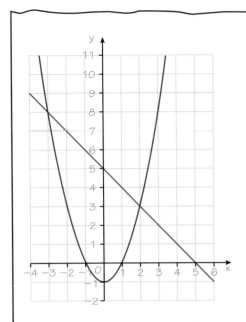

If you draw the graphs of these equations on the same set of axes, you can see that this solution works.

WORKED EXAMPLE 14

$y = x^2 - 3x$ (1)

$y = x - 4$ (2)

$x - 4 = x^2 - 3x$ Substitute (2) in (1).

$x^2 - 4x + 4 = 0$ General form.

$(x - 2)^2 = 0$

$x = 2$

$y = 2 - 4$ Substitute x in (2).

$y = -2$

The point of intersection is $(2, -2)$

In this example there is only one solution, so the graphs will intersect at one point only.

You can always verify this graphically.

EXERCISE 15J

 Solve each pair of simultaneous equations by substitution:

a $y = x^2$

   $y = 2x - 1$

b $y = x^2$

   $y = x + 2$

c $y = x^2$

   $y = x - 1$

d Given that the graph of $y = x^2$ is a U-shaped parabola that goes through the origin, explain why there was no possible solution in part **c** above.

2 Find the coordinates of the point(s) of intersection of the following graphs:

a $y = x^2 + 3x + 3$ and $y = x + 2$ **b** $y = x^2 + 5x + 2$ and $y = x + 7$

c $y = x^2 + 2x + 4$ and $y = x + 6$ **d** $y = 2x^2 + 3x + 1$ and $y = 2x + 1$

e $y = 3x^2 + x + 2$ and $y = 3x + 3$ **f** $y = 6x^2 + 9x + 5$ and $y = 2x + 3$

3 The diagram (right) shows the circular graph plotted from the equation $x^2 + y^2 = 17$ and the graph $x + y = 5$ which cuts the circle in two places.

Find the coordinates of the points of intersection of the graphs.

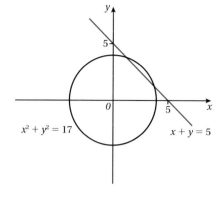

Section 4: Using graphs to solve equations

If you have a graph you can use it to solve an equation or to answer questions based on the equations. Graphs are an excellent means to visualise the algebra.

 Tip

You will work with graphs and equations again in Chapters 24 and 25.

WORKED EXAMPLE 15

This is the graph of the equation $4x + y = 2$.

a Use the graph to estimate the value of y when:

    i $x = 0$

    ii $x = 1$

    iii $x = 2$

b What is the value of x when $y = -4$?

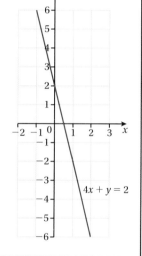

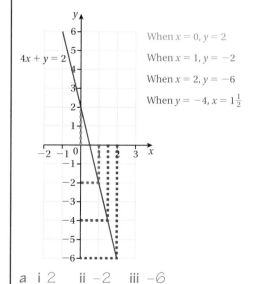

When $x = 0$, $y = 2$

When $x = 1$, $y = -2$

When $x = 2$, $y = -6$

When $y = -4$, $x = 1\frac{1}{2}$

Each point on the graph represents a value of x and y that work in this equation.

To find the solutions for different values of x or y, you need to use the value you have been given as one of the coordinates of a point. If you take a line from this point to the graph you can estimate the value of the other coordinate.

The solutions are shown on this graph in different colours.

a **i** 2   **ii** −2   **iii** −6

b 1.5

Find answers at: cambridge.org/ukschools/gcsemaths-studentbookanswers

EXERCISE 15K

1 Use this graph of the equation $y = 3x - 2$ to estimate the value of y for the following values.

a $x = 0$ **b** $x = 1$ **c** $x = 2$

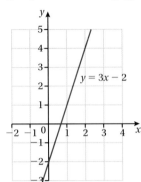

2 This graph (left) shows the distance covered over time by a motorist in a car.

a Estimate how long it took the driver to travel 70 km.

b How far did the driver travel in the first 20 minutes?

c By using two points on the graph, estimate the speed at which the driver was travelling.

3 This graph (right) represents the distance travelled by a cyclist over time.

a Use the graph to estimate how far the cyclist has travelled after 30 minutes.

b How long did it take the cyclist to cover a distance of 8 miles?

c The equation $s = \dfrac{d}{t}$ can be used to work out the speed (s) of the cyclist.

Use values for d and t from the graph to estimate the speed at which this cyclist was travelling.

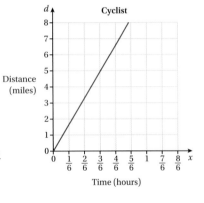

4 This graph (below) shows how water drains from a tank at a constant rate.

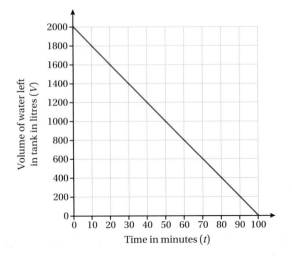

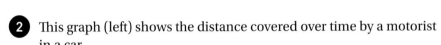

a How much water was in the tank to start with?

b How long did it take for the tank to empty?

c Zena says the equation for this graph is $y = 2000 - 20x$ and Leane says it is $y + 20x = 2000$.

Show using different points from the graph that they are both correct.

5 This graph shows the cost of producing goods and how much money is earned from sales (revenue).

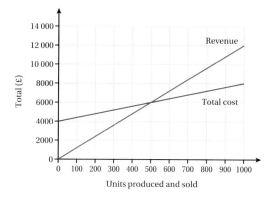

a Use the graph to estimate the point at which the costs and revenue are equal.

b The point at which costs and revenue are equal is called the break even point.

How does this information help a business owner?

6 This diagram shows the graphs of two linear equations $y = 2x$ and $y = -2x + 8$.

Use the graph below to find the simultaneous solution to the two equations.

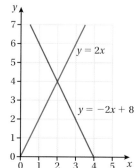

7 This graph (right) of a quadratic equation models a stunt rider's path in the air as he does a jump.

a What do you think the axes represent in this case?

b What values on the horizontal axis represent the rider taking off and landing again?

c Why are these two values useful in terms of the equation?

d Use the graph to estimate the coordinates of the maximum height reached during this jump.

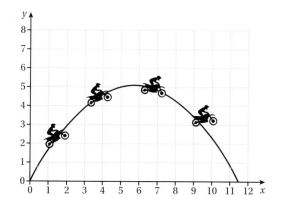

Find answers at: cambridge.org/ukschools/gcsemaths-studentbookanswers

8 This is the graph of the quadratic equation $y = -x^2 + 8x - 12$

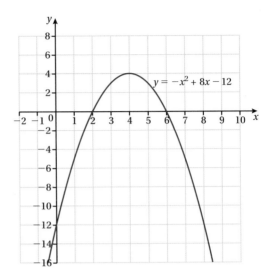

a Explain how you can use the graph to find the roots of the equation.

b What are the solutions of the quadratic equation this graph represents?

c We know the equation of the graph is $y = -x^2 + 8x - 12$. Substitute the solutions for x you have found in part b to show $y = 0$ for each value.

d Where would the line $y = -2x + 3$ cut the graph?

Find the solution algebraically and give your answers correct to 2 decimal places.

9 Two linear graphs are shown here.

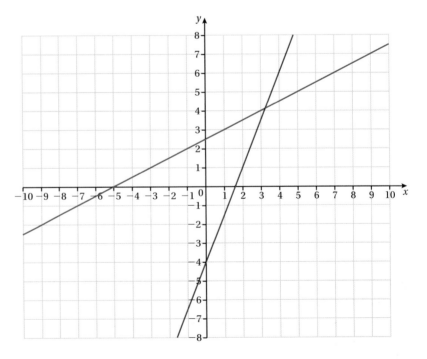

a Use the graph to estimate the values of *x* and *y* that are true for both equations.

b Find the simultaneous solution algebraically.

c What are the limitations of solving a pair of linear simultaneous equations from drawing a graph and finding the point of intersection?

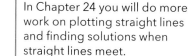

Tip

In Chapter 24 you will do more work on plotting straight lines and finding solutions when straight lines meet.

10 The graph shows the bounce height of a ball dropped from different heights.

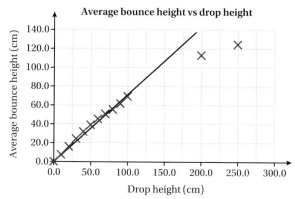

a Using the line of best fit, estimate the average bounce height for a drop of 150 cm.

b Give an alternative estimate given the results for 200 cm and 300 cm.

c Estimate the average bounce height from a drop of 300 cm.

Tip

In Chapter 38 you will do further work on lines of best fit.

11 The graph shows the final height of the swing of a pendulum against its mass.

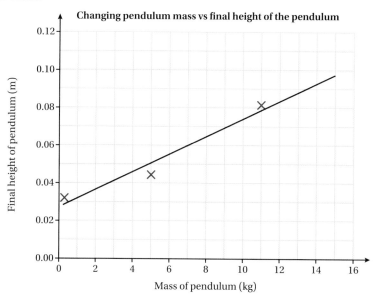

a If the height of the swing of the pendulum is 0.07 m, estimate the mass of the pendulum.

b Estimate the height of the swing for a pendulum of mass approximately 6.5 kg.

c Estimate the height of the swing achieved for a pendulum of mass 16 kg.

Section 5: Finding approximate solutions by iteration

The process of iteration is a numerical method of solving equations.

It is useful for finding solutions to equations that cannot be solved in any other way.

Iteration finds successively better approximations to the roots of the equation.

These three methods:

- iteration formula
- the decimal method
- the bisection method

should only be used when factorising methods cannot be applied or when working with higher-order equations.

In each case you can use your calculator carefully or set up a table of values in a spreadsheet to help you calculate values and take the next steps to get closer to approximate solutions.

Using an iterative formula

Iterate means 'repeat' or 'perform again'.

Mathematically, iteration means repeating a series of steps using the 'answer' from the previous step to get an improved 'answer' on the next step.

The starting value of x, x_1, is used to calculate x_2, which in turn is used to calculate x_3, and so on.

Did you know?

An iterative formula is created by rearranging the original equation you want to solve, to make x the subject. Subscript notation is used to indicate that you use the previous approximation of x to generate the next approximation of x.

Tip

In mathematics, **convergence** is when the terms within a sequence get increasingly close to a value L, which is called the limit of the sequence.

WORKED EXAMPLE 16

Find the positive root of the quadratic equation $x^2 - 7x - 3 = 0$ to 3 decimal places given the iterative formula

$x_{n+1} = 7 + \dfrac{3}{x_n}$, where $x_1 = 7$.

By inspection:

$x = 7$: $49 - 49 - 3 = -3$

$x = 8$: $64 - 56 - 3 = 5$

0 lies between -3 and 5, so one of the roots of the equation lies between 7 and 8.

First, use inspection to estimate the range in which the solution of the quadratic equation will lie. This gives a value for x when $y = 0$. This is the point at which the graph of the function crosses the x-axis.

$x_1 = 7$

$x_2 = 7 + \dfrac{3}{7}$

$x_3 = 7 + \dfrac{3}{x_2}$

Substitute the starting value of $x_1 = 7$ into the iterative formula provided.

Store the answer on your calculator (or spreadsheet) and substitute it (x_2) back into the iterative formula to get x_3.

Continues on next page …

The values for each step:

$x_1 = 7$ (first estimate)

$x_2 = 7.428571429\ldots$

$x_3 = 7.403846154\ldots$

$x_4 = 7.405194805\ldots$

$x_5 = 7.40512101\ldots$

$x_6 = 7.405125047\ldots$

$x_7 = 7.405124826\ldots$

$x = 7.405$ (3 decimal places)

$(7.405)^2 - 7 \times 7.405 - 3 \approx 0$

Repeat the process until the values can be estimated with confidence to the required number of decimal places.

You can see the value of x converging, and after 5 calculated values you can see what the value of x is to 3 decimal places.

Check solution by substitution.

EXERCISE 15L

1. Find an approximate solution to $x^2 - 5x + 2 = 0$, using the iteration $x_{n+1} = 5 - \dfrac{2}{x_n}$ with $x_1 = 4$, correct to 3 decimal places.

2. Find an approximate solution to the square root of 18, using the iteration $x_{n+1} = \dfrac{1}{2}\left(x_n + \dfrac{18}{x_n} \right)$ with $x_1 = 4$, correct to 4 significant figures.

3. Find an answer correct to 2 decimal places for x, using the iteration $x_{n+1} = \dfrac{4}{x_n} + 1$ with $x_1 = 2$.

4. $x^3 - 3x + 1 = 0$

   Use the iteration $x_{n+1} = \dfrac{-1}{x_n - 3}$ with $x_1 = 0.5$ to approximate a solution for x correct to 4 significant figures.

5. Use the iteration formula $x_{n+1} = \dfrac{2x_n}{3} + \dfrac{4}{x_n^2}$, starting with $x_1 = 2$, to find one of the roots of the cubic equation $x^3 - 12 = 0$.

   Give your answer correct to 2 decimal places.

Looking for the change of sign

In terms of the graph of an equation, the change of sign indicates that the y-value has gone from positive to negative, or negative to positive.

This tells you that the graph has crossed the x-axis, i.e. this is a root of the equation.

Decimal search

You can use your calculator or a spreadsheet to help you calculate the values.

Here is the graph for the cubic equation $y = x^3 - 3x + 1$.

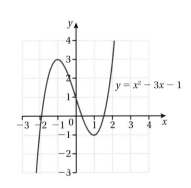

$y = x^2 - 3x - 1$

From the graph you can see there are three roots, and that the equation does not have integral solutions.

WORKED EXAMPLE 17

Find the third root of the function $y = x^3 - 3x + 1$ to 2 decimal places, using the decimal method.

$$y = x^3 - 3x + 1$$

From the graph, the third root lies between $(1, 0)$ and $(2, 0)$.

Take increments of 0.1 from $x = 1$ until you get a change of sign.

Record your results in a table, or an ordered list.

x	$f(x)$
1	−1
1.1	−0.969
1.2	−0.872
1.3	−0.703
1.4	−0.456
1.5	−0.125
1.6	0.96

Tip

You can plot the graph using IT and trace the curve to see how the values change from negative to positive when you cross the x-axis.

y has gone from a negative value to a positive value.

This indicates that the graph has crossed the x-axis.

So, the root lies between $x = 1.5$ and $x = 1.6$

x	$f(x)$
1.5	−0.125
1.51	−0.087
1.52	−0.0482
1.53	−0.0084
1.54	0.03226

Calculate a second table of values with increments of 0.01, starting from $x = 1.5$

y has gone from a negative value to a positive value.

So, the root lies between $x = 1.53$ and $x = 1.54$

x	$f(x)$
1.53	−0.0084
1.531	−0.0044
1.532	−0.0004
1.533	0.00369

Calculate a third table of values with increments of 0.001

The solution is between 1.532 and 1.533 (the sign changes so the curve crosses the x-axis at the value at which $y = 0$).

$x = 1.53$ (2 decimal places)

If more decimal places are required then more tables of values could be calculated.

Tip

This method is sometimes called trial and improvement.

Bisection method

This method looks at the values calculated at half-interval sections.

From the graph of $y = x^3 - 3x + 1$, you can see there is a solution between $(-1, 0)$ and $(-2, 0)$.

WORKED EXAMPLE 18

Find the root between $x = -1$ and $x = -2$ to 1 decimal place for the cubic function $y = x^3 - 3x + 1$

For $y = x^3 - 3x + 1$, when
$x = -1, y = 3$
$x = -2, y = -1$

x	$f(x)$
-1.5	2.125

Take the half interval between $x = -1$ and $x = -2$ as the value of x: -1.5. Substitute this value of x into the cubic function.

-1.75	0.8063

Substitute in the value of x that is the half interval between $x = -1.5$ and $x = -2$: -1.75

-1.875	0.332

Substitute in the value of x that is the half interval between $x = -1.75$ and $x = -2$: -1.875

-1.9375	-0.4607

Substitute in the value of x that is the half interval between $x = -1.875$ and $x = -2$

$x = -1.9$ (1 decimal place)

y has gone from a positive value to a negative value.

This indicates that the graph has crossed the x-axis.

So, the root lies between $x = -1.875$ and $x = -1.9375$.

The method could continue to produce better accuracy.

The advantage of these methods is that the solution bounds indicate the interval in which the root lies.

The disadvantage is that an initial search may miss one or more of the roots; for example, when the x-axis is a tangent to the curve or when several roots are very close together.

Tip

You will learn about tangents to the curve in Chapter 27.

EXERCISE 15M

1 Find an approximate solution to $x^3 + 2x - 1 = 0$ using the iteration

$$x_{n+1} = \frac{1}{x_n^2 + 2} \text{ with } x_1 = 0.5$$

Give the final answer correct to 3 decimal places and check by substitution in the original equation.

2 $y = x^3 - 6x - 4$

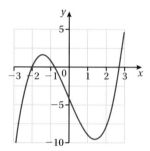

a Use the decimal search method to find the root of the cubic function $f(x) = x^3 - 6x - 4$ which lies between $(2, 0)$ and $(3, 0)$ correct to 2 decimal places.

b Use the interval bisection method to find the root of the cubic function $f(x) = x^3 - 6x - 4$ which lies between $(0, 0)$ and $(-1, 0)$ correct to 1 decimal place.

Section 6: Using equations and graphs to solve problems

Work through this mixed exercise to practise and apply your skills.

EXERCISE 15N

1 Read each statement and decide whether it is true or false.

If it is false, explain why.

a $\frac{1}{2}(x - 3) = \frac{1}{3}(2x + 1)$

$x = -11$ is the solution to this equation.

b $10x^2 - 25x + 10 = 0$

$(10x - 5)(x - 2) = 0 \rightarrow x = \frac{1}{2}$ and $x = -2$.

c $30\frac{1}{4}$ must be added to $x^2 - 11x$ to make a perfect square.

d $x = 3 - 4y$ (1)

$7y - 3x = 21$ (2)

Substituting equation (1) in equation (2) $\rightarrow 19y - 9 = 29 \rightarrow y = 2, x = -5$.

e The diagram shows a pair of simultaneous equations, one linear and one quadratic.

The simultaneous solutions for x are both positive.

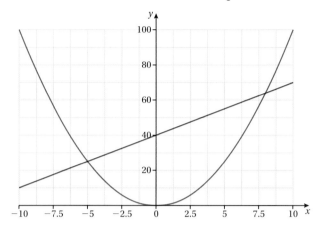

2 Solve:

a $4(x - 3) = 3x + 4$

b $3(2x - 5) = 2\left(4x + \dfrac{3}{2}\right)$

3 A gardener has 60 m of garden edging, which she uses to set out a rectangular garden with its width 5 m less than its length.

If the length of the garden is x metres:

a Find the width of the garden in terms of x.

b Hence, form an equation and solve it to find the length and width of the garden.

4 A father is 28 years older than his daughter.

In six years' time, he will be three times her age.

Find their present ages.

5 Find a number such that if 5, 15 and 35 are added separately to it, the product of the first and third results is equal to the square of the second.

6 This diagram consists of two rectangles with dimensions in centimetres.

The total area is 95 cm².

a Show that $2y^2 + 6y - 95 = 0$.

b Solve the equation $2y^2 + 6y - 95 = 0$ correct to 3 significant figures.

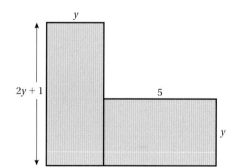

7 Solve the following equations by completing the square:

a $x^2 - 4x - 2 = 0$ **b** $n^2 = 5n + 4$

8 **a** Show that the equation $\dfrac{5}{x + 2} = \dfrac{4 - 3x}{(x - 1)}$

simplifies to give $3x^2 + 7x - 13 = 0$.

b Solve the equation $3x^2 + 7x - 13 = 0$ correct to 2 decimal places.

9 The base and height of a triangle are $x + 3$ and $2x - 5$.

If the area of the triangle is 20, find x.

Find answers at: cambridge.org/ukschools/gcsemaths-studentbookanswers

Tip

Consider what happens to the value of the square root in the quadratic formula.

10 For the quadratic equation $ax^2 - 4x + 3 = 0$, find the values of a for which the equation has:

a one solution   **b** two solutions   **c** no solutions.

11 The sum of two numbers is 112 and their difference is 22.

Write a pair of simultaneous equations and solve to find the two numbers.

12 A manufacturer of lawn fertiliser produces bags of fertiliser in two sizes, Standard and Jumbo.

To transport the bags to retail outlets, he uses a van with a carrying capacity of one tonne.

He discovers that he can transport either 110 Standard bags and 60 Jumbo bags or 50 Standard bags and 100 Jumbo bags at any one time.

Find the weight of each type of bag in kg.

13 Estimate from the graph the simultaneous solutions of $y - 2x = 1$ and $x + y = 10$.

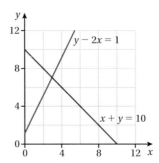

14 **a** Use the graph to estimate the solutions to the two equations.

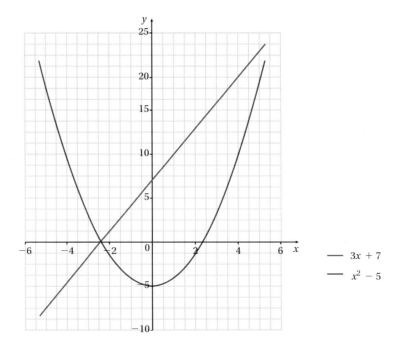

$\qquad$ $3x + 7$

$\qquad$ $x^2 - 5$

b Solve the simultaneous equations $y = x^2 - 5$ and $y = 3x + 7$ algebraically.

15 The equation $x^3 - 7x + 3 = 0$ has three solutions.

   a Find an approximate solution to $x^3 - 7x + 3 = 0$ in the interval between $(0, 0)$ and $(1, 1)$ using the iteration $x_{n+1} = \dfrac{-3}{x_n - 7}$ with $x_1 = 1$

      Answer correct to 2 decimal places.

   b Find a second root that lies between the interval $(2, 0)$ and $(3, 0)$ using the decimal search method.

      Answer correct to 2 decimal places.

   c Find the third root that lies between the interval $(-3, 0)$ and $(-2, 0)$ using the interval bisection search method.

Checklist of learning and understanding

Linear and quadratic equations

- A linear equation has one unknown and will have one unique value as a solution.

- A quadratic equation has a square as the highest power for the variable.

- Quadratic equations can be solved by factorising, completing the square or using the formula $x = \dfrac{-b \pm \sqrt{b^2 - 4ac}}{2a}$

- Quadratic equations have a maximum of two roots. Sometimes there is only one because the values are the same, and sometimes there is only one because one value doesn't work in a particular context. Some quadratic equations have no solutions.

Simultaneous equations

- Simultaneous equations are a pair of equations that have solutions that satisfy both equations.

- Simultaneous equations can be solved algebraically by substitution or by elimination.

Iteration

- A method used to solve higher-order equations by finding successively better approximations to the real values for the roots of an equation. The three methods discussed were:

   – iteration formulae

   – decimal search

   – bisection.

Graphs and problems

- Equations are useful for setting up problems mathematically.

- You can find or estimate the solutions of equations using graphs.

- You need two graphs to solve simultaneous equations. The solution is the point of intersection of the graphs.

For additional questions on the topics in this chapter, visit GCSE Mathematics Online.

 Chapter review

1 Solve by the most efficient method.

Leave your answers in square root form when necessary.

a $x^2 - 4x = 21$ **b** $x^2 + 10x = 2x - 12$

c $9 + x^2 + 11x = 2x - 11$ **d** $x^2 + 10x = 5$

e $2x^2 - 4x - 1 = 0$ **f** $3x^2 + 2x = 3$

2 An object is thrown upwards so that its height (h) in metres after a certain time (t) in seconds can be described using the formula $h = 20t - 4t^2$

a How long does it take the object to first reach a height of 24 m?

b At what time does it come down to reach this height again?

3

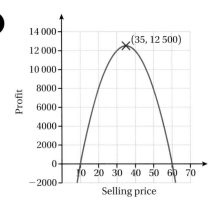

a What are the roots of the quadratic equation modelled by this parabola?

b Write the equation represented by the graph (think carefully about the shape of the parabola).

c What does the graph tell you about the selling price?

4 Are these two equations a pair of simultaneous equations?

$y = x + 2, 5y = 5x + 10$

5 Solve the simultaneous equations $x^2 + y^2 = 25$ and $y = 3x + 1$.

  6 Solve the simultaneous equations

$x^2 + y^2 = 25$

$y = 2x + 5$

(6 marks)

7 Prove algebraically that the difference between the squares of any two consecutive integers is equal to the sum of these two integers.

8 The product of a number and four less than the number is equal to 16 more than twice the number.

Find the number.

9 **a** Show, by completing the square, that $y = 3x^2 + 6x - 7$ can be written in the form $y = 3(x + 1)^2 - 10$.

b Solve the equation $3(x + 1)^2 - 10 = 0$, giving your answer correct to three significant figures.

10 **a** Find an answer correct to 3 decimal places for x using the iteration

$$x_{n+1} = \frac{1}{x_n} + 2 \text{ with a starting value of } x_1 = 2.$$

b Verify that this value of x is the positive solution to the quadratic equation $x^2 - 2x - 1 = 0$.

16 Functions and sequences

In this chapter you will learn how to ...

- generate sequences and find unknown terms in a sequence.
- interpret expressions as functions with inputs and outputs.
- work with inverse and composite functions.
- use correct notation to write rules or functions to find any term in a sequence.
- recognise and use a variety of special sequences.

For more resources relating to this chapter, visit GCSE Mathematics Online.

Using mathematics: real-life applications

Finding a pattern and working out how the parts of the pattern fit together is important in scientific discovery. Scientists use sequences to model and solve real-life problems, such as estimating how quickly diseases spread.

Tip

When you work with sequences you can draw diagrams, flow charts or tables to organise the patterns and make sense of them.

"When a new outbreak of a disease occurs I need to work out how quickly it is spreading. To do this I look at the sequence in which the numbers of victims are increasing. I use the sequence to predict how many people will become infected in a certain length of time."
(Medical researcher)

Before you start ...

Ch 4	You need to know your multiplication tables and recognise multiples of numbers.	**1**	**a** What are the first five multiples of 7? **b** Which of these are multiples of 6? 56, 66, 86, 18, 54, 36
Ch 4	You need to recognise square numbers and cube numbers.	**2**	**a** Which of these are square numbers? 1, 16, 66, 50, 25, 4, 6, 9, 49 **b** Which of these are **not** cube numbers? 9, 15, 27, 64, 1, 8, 125
KS3	You need to be able to spot and describe patterns.	**3**	**a** Describe this pattern in words. Shape 1 Shape 2 Shape 3 **b** How many matchsticks would you need to build the sixth shape in the pattern?

Assess your starting point using the Launchpad

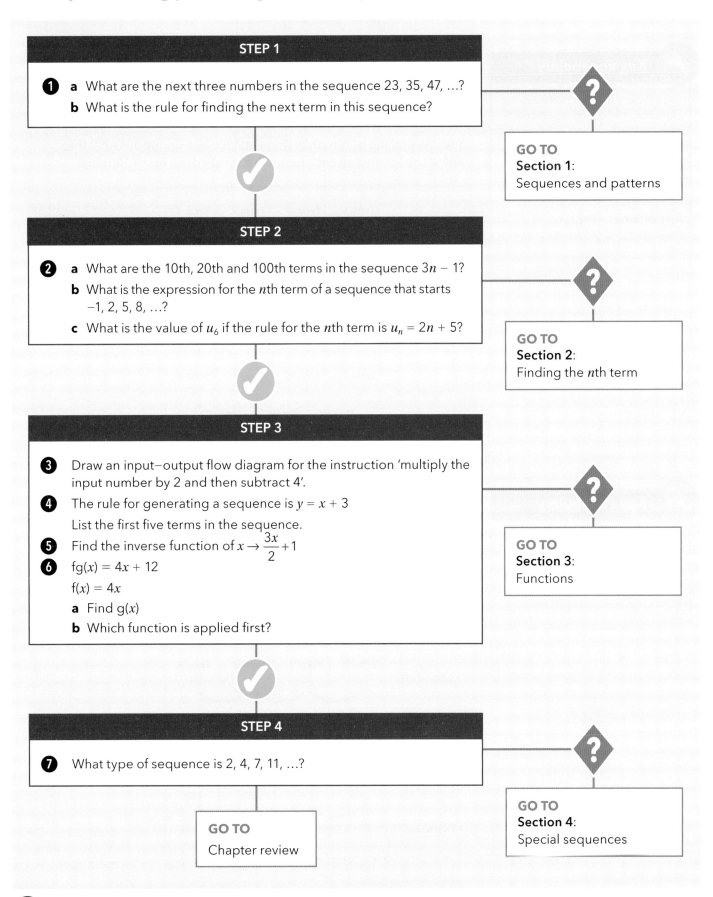

STEP 1

1   **a**   What are the next three numbers in the sequence 23, 35, 47, …?

    b   What is the rule for finding the next term in this sequence?

GO TO
Section 1:
Sequences and patterns

STEP 2

2   **a**   What are the 10th, 20th and 100th terms in the sequence $3n - 1$?

    b   What is the expression for the nth term of a sequence that starts $-1, 2, 5, 8, …$?

    c   What is the value of u_6 if the rule for the nth term is $u_n = 2n + 5$?

GO TO
Section 2:
Finding the nth term

STEP 3

3   Draw an input–output flow diagram for the instruction 'multiply the input number by 2 and then subtract 4'.

4   The rule for generating a sequence is $y = x + 3$

    List the first five terms in the sequence.

5   Find the inverse function of $x \rightarrow \dfrac{3x}{2} + 1$

6 $fg(x) = 4x + 12$

    $f(x) = 4x$

    a   Find $g(x)$

    b   Which function is applied first?

GO TO
Section 3:
Functions

STEP 4

7   What type of sequence is 2, 4, 7, 11, …?

GO TO
Chapter review

GO TO
Section 4:
Special sequences

Find answers at: cambridge.org/ukschools/gcsemaths-studentbookanswers

Section 1: Sequences and patterns

The term-to-term rule

A **sequence** is an ordered list or pattern.

Terms that follow each other in a sequence are called **consecutive terms**.

The first term in a sequence is called T(1), the second T(2) and so on.

You can find the next term in the sequence by working out what the difference is between each term. This is called the **first difference**.

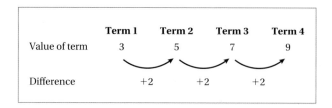

The **term-to-term rule** for this sequence is 'add two'.
9 + 2 = 11, so the next term in the sequence is 11.

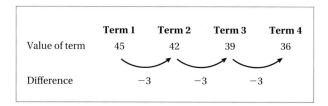

The term-to-term rule for this sequence is 'subtract three'.

3, 5, 7, 9, ... and 45, 42, 39, 36, ... are both **arithmetic sequences**.
In an arithmetic sequence the terms are generated by adding or subtracting a constant difference.

In a **geometric sequence**, the terms are generated by multiplying or dividing by a constant ratio. This ratio isn't always a whole number, and could for example be a surd.
3, 6, 12, 24, ... and 1000, 500, 250, 125, ... are both geometric sequences.

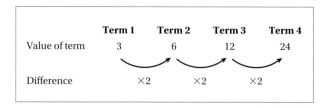

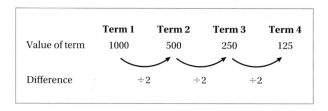

WORKED EXAMPLE 1

"I use term-to-term rules in my job. I know that each row of bricks will have three fewer bricks than the row below it, so I can work out how many bricks I need in each row."

(Bricklayer)

The first row of the wall has 57 bricks.

Use a term-to-term rule to find the number of bricks in the next three rows.

The term-to-term rule is 'subtract three'.	The number of bricks decreases by 3 for each new row.
57 in the first row 57 − 3 = 54 in the second row	Subtract 3 from 57 to get the next term.
54 − 3 = 51 in the third row 51 − 3 = 48 in the fourth row	Continue to do this for the next two terms.

EXERCISE 16A

1 Find the next three terms in each of these sequences.
Explain how you found them.

a 4, 7, 10, 13, …   **b** 38, 43, 48, 53, …

c 27, 23, 19, …   **d** 63, 57, 51, …

e 1, 2, 4, 8, …   **f** 64, 32, 16, …

g 4, 12, 36, …   **h** 729, 243, 81, …

2 Give the term-to-term rule for each of these sequences.

a 7, 14, 21, 28, …   **b** 19, 15, 11, 7, …

c 2, 8, 32, 128, …   **d** 84, 42, 21, …

3 Find the term-to-term rule for each of these sequences.

Use it to generate the next three terms in each sequence.

a 3.5, 5.5, 7.5, …   **b** 1.2, 2.4, 4.8, …

c $1\frac{1}{2}$, 3, $4\frac{1}{2}$, …   **d** 8, 5, 2, …

e 72, 36, 18, …   **f** −10, −7, −4, …

> **Tip**
>
> It can help to write out the sequence and label the difference between each term.

 Find answers at: cambridge.org/ukschools/gcsemaths-studentbookanswers

Tip

Look for the term-to-term rule to answer this question.

4 When a ball is dropped it bounces back to half its original height.

With each new bounce it bounces back to half the height of the previous bounce.

a If a ball is dropped from 96 cm, how high will it bounce on its fourth bounce?

b How many times will it bounce before it bounces to below 1 cm?

5 T(1) of a sequence is 4 and the term-to-term rule for the sequence is 'add x'.

Find a value for x so that:

a every second term is an integer

b every third term is a multiple of 4

c T(2) is smaller than T(1).

Section 2: Finding the nth term

The position-to-term rule

Key vocabulary

position-to-term rule: operations applied to the position number of a term in a sequence in order to generate that term.

Term-to-term rules are useful for generating the first few terms of a sequence and for finding the next term in a given sequence. They are less useful when you want to find the 50th or 100th term.

A **position-to-term** rule allows you to work out the value of any term in a sequence if you know its position in the sequence.

The sequence 1, 3, 5, 7, ... can be generated using the position-to-term rule 'position number $\times 2$, subtract 1'.

To find a sequence using a position-to-term rule, you substitute the position number into the rule.

For example, the tenth term of this sequence is $(10 \times 2) - 1 = 19$.

The nth term

The notation T(n) refers to 'any term' in the sequence, where n is the position of the term. T(n) is known as the 'nth term'.

Sometimes you will be given a sequence and you will need to find a rule to find any term, T(n), in that sequence. You can usually find a rule for a sequence by looking at the difference between consecutive terms.

Remember that this is called the **first difference**.

Once you have found the first difference you can compare it with number patterns you already know to find the rule for the sequence.

Problem-solving framework

Find an expression for the nth term of the sequence: 5, 8, 11, 14, 17, ...

Steps for approaching a problem-solving question	What you would do for this example
Step 1: Identify what you have to do.	You are trying to find an expression to work out the value of any term in the sequence.
Step 2: If it is useful to have a table draw one.	Draw a table showing the position and the term:
Step 3: Start working on the problem using what you know.	Label the table with the difference between each term:
Step 4: Connect to other sequences and compare.	Another sequence that has the same term-to-term rule of 'add 3' is the multiples of 3.
Step 5: Check your working and that your answer is reasonable.	Test for $n = 5$:
Step 6: Have you answered the question?	Yes. The expression for the nth term is $3n + 2$

Step 2:

n	1	2	3	4	5
$T(n)$	5	8	11	14	17

Step 3:

n	1	2	3	4	5
$T(n)$	5	8	11	14	17

$+ 3 \quad + 3 \quad + 3 \quad + 3$

The difference in this sequence is '$+ 3$'.

Step 4:

(If the difference was '$+2$' you would compare to $2n$; if it was '-4' you would compare it to $-4n$.)

Add this sequence to your table:

n	1	2	3	4	5
$T(n)$	5	8	11	14	17
Multiples of 3n	3	6	9	12	15

$+2$

Compare the multiples of 3 to the terms of the original sequence.

Each term is the corresponding multiple of 3 with 2 added.

So the expression for the nth term of this sequence could be $3n + 2$.

Step 5:

$(3 \times 5) + 2 = 15 + 2$

$15 + 2 = 17$

The fifth term is 17 so the expression is correct.

Tip

If you are struggling to find the rule for an arithmetic sequence, you can use the following formula: $(a + d(n - 1))$ where a = first term, and d = common difference. The **common difference** is the constant difference between terms.

 Find answers at: cambridge.org/ukschools/gcsemaths-studentbookanswers

WORK IT OUT 16.1

A sequence is defined by the rule $T(n) = 3n - 2$

What are the first five terms of the sequence?

Only one answer below is correct. Explain why the other two are wrong.

Option A	Option B	Option C
$-2, 1, 4, 7, 10$	$1, 4, 7, 10, 13$	$-1, 1, 3, 5, 7$

Subscript notation

The nth term, where u is a sequence, can be written as u_n.

This is read as 'u sub n' and is known as **subscript notation**.

u_1 is used to denote the first term, u_2 is used to denote the second term and so on.

You can use this notation to write term-to-term and position-to-term rules.

For example, the **position-to-term rule** of $3n - 4$ for the sequence u, would be written as: $u_n = 3n - 4$.

If you want to find the value of the sixth term, substitute 6 into the equation in place of n:

$u_6 = (3 \times 6) - 4$

$u_6 = 14$

The **term-to-term rule** '$+2$' would be written as: $u_{n+1} = u_n + 2$

The '$n + 1$' indicates that it is the term one more than the current term (u_n).

So, if $u_3 = 7$ then,

$u_4 = u_3 + 2$

$\quad = 7 + 2$

$\quad = 9$

EXERCISE 16B

1 A sequence is created using the position-to-term rule 'position $\times$ 3, subtract 1.'

   a What are the first six terms of the sequence?

   b What is the 20th term of the sequence?

   c Would the 40th term of the sequence be double the value of the 20th term? Explain your answer.

2 Find the value of the following terms for each position-to-term rule.

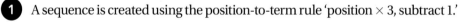

   i 1st term   **ii** 2nd term   **iii** 3rd term   **iv** 4th term

   v 10th term   **vi** 20th term   **vii** 100th term

   a $4n + 1$ **b** $4n - 5$ **c** $8n + 2$

   d $5n - \dfrac{1}{2}$ **e** $\dfrac{n}{2} + 1$ **f** $-2n + 1$

3 Find the expression for the nth term in the sequence that begins
5, 9, 13, 17, ...

4 Find the rules for the nth term of the following sequences.

Write the rule using u_n notation.

a 3, 5, 7, 9, ... **b** 3, 7, 11, 15, ... **c** −1, 4, 9, 14, ...

d 7, 12, 17, 22, ... **e** −3, 0, 3, 6, ... **f** −1, 6, 13, 20, ...

5 Majid conducts an experiment in science and gets the following pattern of results:

67, 73, 79, 85

Write an expression for the nth term of Majid's results.

6 Sam has planted a sunflower and notices that it measures 4.5 cm at the end of the first week, 6.7 cm at the end of the second week and 8.9 cm at the end of the third week.

a Find an expression for the nth term of this sequence, assuming the sunflower continues to grow at the same rate.

b How big will the sunflower be at the end of the 100th week?

c Explain why this is unlikely to be true.

7 Tammy has £100 saved.

She deposits £4 per week. At the end of the first week she has £104.

a If she continues to save at this rate, how much will she have after 52 weeks?

b How long will it take her to save £400?

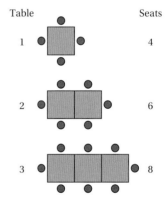

Table	Seats
1	4
2	6
3	8

8 A restaurant uses square tables that can seat four people.

Tables can be pushed together to create different seating arrangements.

a How many people can fit around six tables pushed together in this way?

b How many people can fit around 10 tables pushed together this way?

c Is it possible to seat 31 people around tables pushed together like this with no empty seats?

Section 3: Functions

A **function** is a rule for changing one number into another.

'Multiply by two', 'add three' and 'divide by 2 and then add 1' are examples of functions.

You can use algebra to write functions, for example 'multiply by 2' can be written as the expression '$2n$'.

Functions can be expressed in different ways:

$y = x + 3$ $\qquad x \rightarrow x + 3 \qquad$ f$(x) = x + 3$

> ### Key vocabulary
>
> function: a set of instructions for changing one number (the input) into another number (the output).

 Find answers at: cambridge.org/ukschools/gcsemaths-studentbookanswers

Tip

You can think of a function as 'the answer you will get' if you apply this rule to a number.

These mean the same thing: take any value of x and add 3 to it to get a result.

$f(x)$ is called **function notation**.

input into the function

identifies the expression as a function; it can be any letter but the most commonly used are f, g, and h

---

WORKED EXAMPLE 2

$f(x) = 3x - 2$

a Find the value of

    i $f(0)$ **ii** $f(2)$ **iii** $f(-2)$

b Find the value of x for which $f(x) = 16$

a **i** $f(x) = 3x - 2$
$$= (3 \times 0) - 2$$
$$= 0 - 2$$
$$= -2$$
$$x = -2$$

Substitute the value of 0 in place of x.
Solve the equation.

  ii $f(x) = 3x - 2$
$$= 6 - 2$$
$$x = 4$$

Substitute the value of 2 in place of x.
Solve the equation.

  iii $f(x) = 3x - 2$
$$= -6 - 2$$
$$= -8$$

Substitute the value of -2 in place of x.
Solve the equation.

b $f(x) = 3x - 2$
$$16 = 3x - 2$$
$$18 = 3x$$
$$x = 6$$

Substitute the value of 16 in place of $f(x)$.
Solve the equation.

The steps you take to work out the value of a function can be shown as a simple flow diagram or function machine.

A function machine shows the input, operation and output for a given rule.

Input $\longrightarrow$ | rule $\rangle$ $\longrightarrow$ Output

In a function there is only **one** possible output for each input.

Generating a sequence using a function

You can generate a sequence using a function.

The table shows the outputs when you input the values 1 to 10 into the function $y = 2n + 4$

$n \longrightarrow$ | $\times 2$ $\rangle \longrightarrow$ | $+4$ $\rangle \longrightarrow 2n + 4$

Input	Function	Output
1	× 2 + 4	6
2	× 2 + 4	8
3	× 2 + 4	10
4	× 2 + 4	12
5	× 2 + 4	14
6	× 2 + 4	16
7	× 2 + 4	18
8	× 2 + 4	20
9	× 2 + 4	22
10	× 2 + 4	24

So the function $y = 2n + 4$ generates the sequence
6, 8, 10, 12, 14, 16, 18 , 20, 22, 24, ...

If you know the values of a sequence, you can find the function that generates the sequence by finding the position-to-term rule.

Composite functions

Composite functions are formed by combining two or more functions.

If you have two functions, the composite function is the result of entering the output of the first function as the input of the second function.

Using a function machine, this would look like:

Input → | Function 1 ⟩ → Output of function 1 → | Function 2 ⟩ → Output

Or more simply:

Input → | Function 1 ⟩ → | Function 2 ⟩ → Output

For example, if the first function is $x + 1$, and the second function is $2x$, you would have:

x → | +1 ⟩ → $(x + 1)$ → | ×2 ⟩ → $2(x + 1)$

You can also combine two functions **before** entering the input, and still get the same output as applying the functions separately.

To do this, substitute the value of x that would be the output of the first function $(x + 1)$ into the value of x in the second function: $2(x + 1)$

Then multiply out the brackets to write the rule in its simplest form

$y = 2x + 2$

Function notation can be used to identify different functions within a composite function without needing to draw a function machine.

Suppose $f(x)$ is used to denote one function, and $g(x)$ to denote another function. Then, you can write a composite function as $fg(x)$ or $gf(x)$.

Key vocabulary

composite function: a function created by combining two or more functions.

Find answers at: cambridge.org/ukschools/gcsemaths-studentbookanswers

In fg(x), the output of g(x) is the input of f(x); g(x) is done first.

In gf(x), the output of f(x) is the input of g(x); f(x) is done first.

You can combine the two functions to create a third function.

If f(x) = 2x, and g(x) = x + 1, then the composite function fg(x) can be written as h(x) = 2(x + 1).

Multiplying out, h(x) = 2x + 2

Inverse functions

Most functions have an inverse. Applying this **inverse function** will 'undo' the original function.

For example, the operation 'times two' can be reversed by 'dividing by two', so the function $x \rightarrow 2x$ has the inverse function $x \rightarrow \dfrac{x}{2}$

Using function notation, the inversion of the function f(x) is denoted as f^{-1}(x).

Key vocabulary

inverse function: a function that reverses another function.

WORKED EXAMPLE 3

Find f^{-1}(x) if f(x) = 3n − 1.

$$n \rightarrow \boxed{\times 3} \rightarrow \boxed{-1} \rightarrow 3n - 1$$

First write out the given function using function machines.

$$\frac{(n+1)}{3} \leftarrow \boxed{\div 3} \leftarrow \boxed{+1} \leftarrow n$$

To find the inverse, work in the opposite direction, applying the inverse operations.
The inverse operation of 'subtract 1' is 'add 1'.
The inverse operation of 'multiply by 3' is 'divide by 3'.

$$f^{-1}(x) = \frac{(n+1)}{3}$$

Write out the steps as a function.

Did you know?

$x \rightarrow x$ is called the identity function.

In this function the inverse is the same as the original function.

EXERCISE 16C

1 The numbers 1 to 10 are the input for the function $x \rightarrow x + 3$.
What sequence does this create?

2 The numbers 1 to 10 are input into the function f(x)= x + 7 to make a sequence.
What are the last three numbers of the sequence?

   A 8, 9, 10   **B** 15, 16, 17   **C** 7, 14, 21   **D** 56, 63, 70

3 Input the numbers 1 to 10 into each function to generate a sequence.

   a $x \rightarrow x - 5$ **b** $x \rightarrow 3x$ **c** $n \rightarrow n + 7$ **d** $n \rightarrow \dfrac{n}{2}$

4 Input the numbers 21 to 30 into each function to generate a sequence.

   a $y = 2x$ **b** $y = x - 8$ **c** $y = \dfrac{x}{3}$ **d** $y = x + \dfrac{1}{2}$

5 Input the numbers 11 to 20 into each function to generate a sequence.

  a $n \rightarrow 3n + 5$ **b** $n \rightarrow 2n - 7$ **c** $n \rightarrow \dfrac{n}{2} + 4$

  d $n \rightarrow 4n + \dfrac{1}{2}$ **e** $n \rightarrow \dfrac{4}{n} + 4$

6 Three consecutive numbers have been inputted into the function $f(x) = 3x - 1$
The sequence created was $-4, -1, 2$
Which three numbers were inputted into the function?

  A $-1, 0, 1$ **B** $1, 2, 3$ **C** $0, 1, 2$ **D** $2, 3, 4$

7 Write down the inverse of each of the following functions.

  a $x \rightarrow x - 7$ **b** $x \rightarrow 4x$ **c** $x \rightarrow x + 5$

  d $x \rightarrow \dfrac{x}{3}$ **e** $x \rightarrow 2x + 4$ **f** $x \rightarrow 4x - 5$

  g $x \rightarrow \dfrac{x}{5} + 3$ **h** $x \rightarrow \dfrac{4}{x} - 2$

8 Write down the composite function $fg(x)$ formed by each of these pairs of functions:

  a $f(x) = 4x, g(x) = x - 7$ **b** $f(x) = 2x, g(x) = x + 4$

  c $f(x) = 3x, g(x) = x - 2$ **d** $f(x) = x^2, g(x) = x + 1$

9 **a** Write down the inverse function of $f(x) = 2x$

  b What is the composite function of $f(x)$ and its inverse function?

Section 4: Special sequences

Some patterns and sequences of numbers are well known.
You need to be able to recognise and use the following patterns.

Special sequence	Description
Simple arithmetic progression (or linear sequences)	The **difference** between each term is constant, for example, 3, 5, 7, ... or 14, 11, 8, ...
Geometric sequences	The **ratio** between each term is constant, for example, 3, 6, 12, 24, ...
Square numbers	A square number is the product of multiplying a whole number by itself. For example, $3^2 = 3 \times 3 = 9$ Square numbers form the sequence: 1, 4, 9, 16, 25, 36, ...
Triangular numbers	These are made by arranging dots to form equilateral triangles. 1 dot 3 dots 6 dots 10 dots 15 dots Continues on next page ...

Find answers at: cambridge.org/ukschools/gcsemaths-studentbookanswers

Special sequence	Description
Quadratic sequences	These sequences are linked to square numbers. A quadratic sequence has a position-to-term rule that involves squaring one of the variables. For example, the sequence formed by the rule $n^2 + 3$ is: 4, 7, 12, 19, 28, ... The terms in a quadratic sequence do **not** increase or decrease by a constant amount. The first difference is **not** constant but the **second difference** is constant. The second difference is the difference between each term in the first difference.
Cube numbers	A cube number is the product of multiplying a whole number by itself and then by itself again. 64 is a cube number because $4^3 = (4 \times 4 \times 4) = 64$. Cube numbers form the sequence: 1, 8, 27, 64, 125, ...
Fibonacci sequences	Leonardo Fibonacci was an Italian mathematician who developed the number pattern 1, 1, 2, 3, 5, 8, 13, 21, ... while he was trying to work out how many offspring a pair of rabbits would produce over different generations. These numbers are now called Fibonacci numbers. If you start the sequence with the numbers 1 and 1, the term-to-term rule is 'add the previous two terms together'.

 Did you know?

The Fibonacci pattern is found in many natural situations.

In the Fibonacci series, the sequence of numbers is created by adding the 1st and 2nd term together to make the 3rd term; adding the 2nd and 3rd terms together to make the 4th term, and so on.

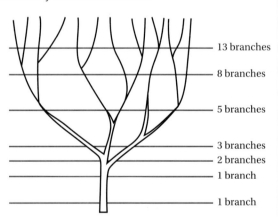

13 branches
8 branches
5 branches
3 branches
2 branches
1 branch
1 branch

EXERCISE 16D

 a Write down the sequence of the first 10 square numbers.

b Find the difference between consecutive terms in the sequence.

c How could you use this new sequence to find the next two square numbers?

2 **a** What type of number is shown on the right? Explain how you know this.

b The picture represents the fifth term in the sequence.
Write down the first 10 numbers in the same sequence.

c Find the first and second differences between the terms of the sequence.

d What type of sequence is this?

3 Honeybees live in colonies known as hives.

There is one queen bee, a female, who is the only one able to lay eggs.

All the other female bees are called workers. They are made when a male fertilises the queen's eggs. This means that a worker bee has a mother and a father.

The male bees are called drones. Drones are made when the queen's eggs hatch without being fertilised by a male. This means that a drone has a mother but not a father.

This is a family tree of a drone; a family tree shows each generation of bee in terms of their parents.

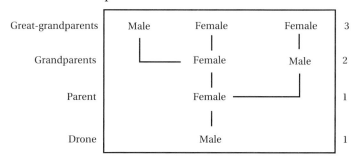

Great-grandparents	Male	Female	Female	3
Grandparents		Female	Male	2
Parent		Female		1
Drone		Male		1

a How many great-great-grandparents does the male bee have?

b The family tree shows four generations of bee.

i Copy and complete the tree so that it shows six generations.

ii Use the family tree to write a sequence for the number of bees there are in each generation.

iii Continue the sequence to find how many bees there are in the ninth generation.

iv What is the relationship between the number of bees in each generation? Do you recognise the sequence?

4 **a** Find the first 10 terms of a sequence that follows the same rules as the Fibonacci sequence that starts with the numbers 3, 4, …

b Start a Fibonacci sequence with the numbers −2 and 3.
Write down the first 10 terms of the sequence.

c Compare your sequence in part **b** with a Fibonacci sequence starting with 2, −3. What do you notice?

5 The sixth and seventh terms of a sequence that follows the same rules as the Fibonacci sequence are 31 and 50. What are the first two terms?

> **Tip**
>
> You know the term-to-term rule of the Fibonacci sequence. How can you use this to help you?

6 Copy and complete the table below.

Position-to-term rule	1st term	2nd term	3rd term	5th term	10th term	20th term	50th term
$n^2 + 5$							
$n^2 - 3$							
$2n^2 + 1$							
$2n^2 - 7$							

7 Write down the first six terms of the sequence formed by the rule $n^3 + 1$.

8 Write down the first 10 terms of the sequence formed by using the rule $n^2 + n$.

9 Compare your answer to Question **8** with your answer from Question **2**.

    a What is the position-to-term rule for triangular numbers?

    b Use your rule to find the 10th and 25th triangular numbers.

The nth term of a quadratic sequence

You can find the rule for the nth term of a quadratic sequence in a similar way to how you find the nth term of an arithmetic sequence.

WORKED EXAMPLE 4

Find the expression for the nth term in the following sequence: 4, 7, 12, 19, 28

n	1	2	3	4	5
$T(n)$	4	7	12	19	28

Draw a table showing the position and the term.

n	1	2	3	4	5
$T(n)$	4	7	12	19	28

$+3 \quad +5 \quad +7 \quad +9$

$+2 \quad +2 \quad +2$

Label the table with the difference between each term.
The first difference is not constant, it is increasing.

Find the second difference by calculating the difference between the first differences.
The second difference is constant, which means this is a quadratic sequence and it will involve n^2.

n	1	2	3	4	5
$T(n)$	4	7	12	19	28
n^2	1	4	9	16	25

$\big)+3$

Square each position number and compare the resulting sequence to the original.

The square numbers are 3 fewer than the corresponding term. The expression could be $n^2 + 3$

$T(n) = n^2 + 3$
$n = 4: (4 \times 4) + 3 = 16 + 3 = 19\checkmark$
$n = 5: (5 \times 5) + 3 = 25 + 3 = 28\checkmark$

Test the rule works.

The general formula for finding the nth term of a quadratic sequence is

$u_n = an^2 + bn + c$

where the value of a is half the second difference; the value of b depends on the first term and c is the imaginary term before the first term, T(0).

The value of a helps you determine if the sequence involves square numbers or multiples of square numbers.

WORKED EXAMPLE 5

What is the nth term in the sequence 4, 13, 28, 49, ... ?

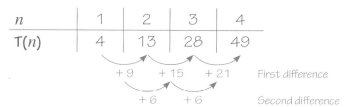

Draw a table showing the position, term and first difference. The first difference isn't constant, so find the second differences.

$u_n = an^2 + bn + c$

$a = \dfrac{6}{2} = 3$

Using the general formula, a is half of the second difference.

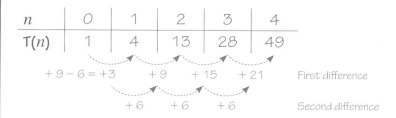

The value of c can be found by working out the value of the imaginary term before the first term T(0).

Apply inverse operations to count back and find T(0).

$u_n = 3n^2 + bn + 1$

Substitute $a = 3$ and $c = 1$ into the general formula.

$T_1 = 4$, so
$u_1 = 3(1)^2 + b(1) + 1 = 4$
$\quad\quad 3 + b + 1 = 4$
$\quad\quad\quad b = 4 - 3 - 1$
$\quad\quad\quad b = 0$

To work out the value of b you need to substitute the value of T(1) into the formula to solve for b.

If $b = 0$, then $bn = 0$

The formula for the nth term of the sequence 4, 13, 28, 49, ... is therefore $u_n = 3n^2 + 1$

Substitute b into the general formula to give you the rule for the nth term.

EXERCISE 16E

1 Find a formula for the nth term for each of these sequences:

   a 3, 8, 15, 24, 35   **b** 3, 10, 21, 36, 55

   c 7, 22, 45, 76, 115   **d** 6, 17, 32, 51, 74

   e 1, 8, 21, 40, 65   **f** 3, 6, 23, 40, 81

   g −2, −8, −18, −32, −50   **h** 0, −4, −12, −24, −40

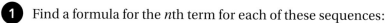

Find answers at: cambridge.org/ukschools/gcsemaths-studentbookanswers

2 Find the next three terms in this sequence:

$1, \sqrt{2}, 2, 2\sqrt{2}, \square, \square, \square$

3 A sequence is defined as

$$x_n = \frac{n}{n+1}$$

a List the first five terms of this sequence.

b Determine the value of the 10th term.

4 A sequence is defined as

$$u_n = n^2 + 2n - 3$$

a List the first five terms of this sequence.

b Determine the value of the 15th term.

5 Look at this pattern.

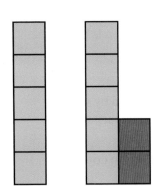 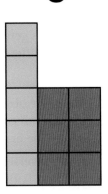 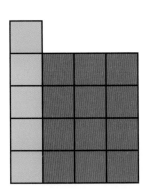 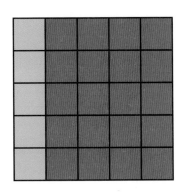

a How many tiles are there in each shape?

b How many tiles will there be in the sixth shape?

c How many tiles will there be in the nth shape?

📎 **Checklist of learning and understanding**

Sequences

- Sequences can be formed using a term-to-term rule. Each term is generated by applying the same rule to the previous term.

- The position-to-term rule is used to find the value of any term in a sequence using its position in the sequence.

- Subscript notation can be used to describe position-to-term and term-to-term rules.

Functions

- A function is an expression or rule for changing one number (the input) into another number (the output).

- A sequence can be generated by inputting an ordered set of numbers into a function.

- When two or more function are applied one after the other, they make a composite function.

- An example of function notation is $f(x) = x + 3$. A composite function might be written as $fg(x)$ where the output of the function $g(x)$ is the input of the function $f(x)$.

- A function that reverses the result of another function is called the inverse function. In function notation, the inverse of the function $f(x)$ is denoted by $f^{-1}(x)$.

Special sequences

- It is important to recognise familiar sequences such as square numbers, cube numbers, triangular numbers and Fibonacci numbers.

- In a quadratic sequence the first difference between the terms is not constant but the second difference is, and the pattern is linked to square numbers.

- It is possible to find an expression for the nth term quadratic sequences by looking at first differences and second differences.

 Chapter review

For additional questions on the topics in this chapter, visit GCSE Mathematics Online.

1 This array of numbers is called Pascal's triangle.

```
          1
        1   1
      1   2   1
    1   3   3   1
  1   4   6   4   1
1   5  10  10   5   1
```

Each number is the sum of the two numbers above it, except for the edges which are all 1.

The first row (containing the number 1) is the 0th row.

a Copy and complete Pascal's triangle to the 8th row.

b Find the total for each row.

Describe the sequence that is created by these totals.

c What sequence is represented by the diagonal series of numbers that begins in the second row 1, 3, 6, 10, …?

d Write an expression for the nth term of the sequence 1, 3, 6, 10, …

2 A virus is infecting the population of a village.

Day	1	2	3	4
Number of infections	8	13	18	23

a If the virus continues to infect people at the same rate, how many people will be infected on day 5?

b Assume the infection rate is constant.

Find an expression to calculate how many people will be affected on any day.

c There are 126 people in the village. How long will it be before everyone is infected?

Find answers at: cambridge.org/ukschools/gcsemaths-studentbookanswers

3 The number of rabbits on an island is recorded each month.

After 1 month there are 9 rabbits.

After 2 months there are 19 rabbits.

After 3 months there are 33 rabbits.

a If the population keeps growing at the same rate, and no rabbits die, how many rabbits will there be at the end of the year?

b Explain why this sequence is not likely to reflect the real number of rabbits.

4 The number of hits on a website increases daily.
On day 1 there were 13 hits.
On day 2 there were 27 hits.
On day 3 there were 65 hits.

Assuming the number of hits continues to grow at the same rate, how many hits will there be on day 20?

5 Look at this pattern.

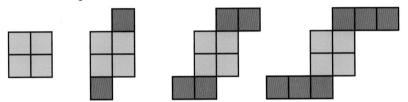

a Complete this function machine for calculating the number of tiles used to make any shape in the pattern:

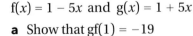

input $(n) \rightarrow$ ⬡ $\rightarrow$ ⬡ $\rightarrow$ output

b Use your function to work out the number of tiles you'd need to build the 20th, 25th and nth pattern.

6 Tamsyn is an ecologist.

She gets 28 days holiday every year plus $\frac{1}{2}$ a day holiday for each overnight bat survey she completes.

a Write a function for calculating how much holiday she will get if she does 10, 15 and b overnight bat surveys in a year.

b Tamsyn's boss knows how much holiday each of her staff have. She wants to work out how many overnight bat surveys they did. What function can she use to calculate this?

c Tamsyn's colleague Sofia has 30 days of holiday this year. How many surveys must she have done?

7 The functions f and g are such that

$f(x) = 1 - 5x$ and $g(x) = 1 + 5x$

a Show that $gf(1) = -19$ *(2 marks)*

b Prove that $f^{-1}(x) + g^{-1}(x) = 0$ for all values of x. *(3 marks)*

©*Pearson Education Ltd 2012*

17 Formulae

In this chapter you will learn how to ...

- use formulae to express and solve problems.
- substitute numbers into formulae to find the value of the subject.
- change the subject of a formula.
- understand and use a range of formulae, including kinematics formulae.

 For more resources relating to this chapter, visit GCSE Mathematics Online.

Using mathematics: real-life applications

Vets use formulae to make sure they are giving animals the correct dosage of medicines for their age and weight. A poodle weighing 6 kg needs a far smaller dose of medicine than a 35 kg retriever.

"I need to make sure I give my animal patients the correct amount of medicine. I do this by using formulae that take into account their age, weight and the ratio between any prescribed medicines."

(Veterinarian)

 Did you know?

Einstein's famous formula $E = mc^2$ looks deceptively simple. It describes the relationship between energy, mass and the speed of light (c). Find out more about this formula and why it is linked to the theory of relativity.

 Tip

Formulae often use letters for the variables that relate to the value they represent. For example, in formulae for area, A is often used to represent the value for **a**rea and h to represent the value for **h**eight.

Before you start ...

Chs 1 and 5	You need to be able to substitute values into expressions.	**1** Evaluate $\dfrac{x + 2y}{z}$ when: **a** $x = 7, y = 4$ and $z = 2$ **b** $x = 7, y = -2$ and $z = 2$ **c** $x = -7, y = 4$ and $z = 4$ **d** $x = -7, y = -2$ and $z = 2$
Ch 15	You should be able to solve simple equations.	**2** Solve. **a** $6x = x + 35$ **b** $5x = 64 - 3x$ **c** $2(2x + 3) = x + 7$ **d** $5x - 8 = 3x + 12$
Chs 2, 5, 10, 13, 15	You should be familiar with some formulae already, and be able to identify the subject, variable(s) and any constants.	**3** Look at these two formulae for finding the area of shapes. $A = \dfrac{1}{2}bh \quad A = \pi r^2$ **a** What do the variables represent? **b** What is the constant in each formula? **c** What is the subject of each formula? **d** What tells you that the second formula applies to circles?

Find answers at: cambridge.org/ukschools/gcsemaths-studentbookanswers

Assess your starting point using the Launchpad

STEP 1

1 Match each formula **A–F** with the correct statement **a–f**.

A $y = x - 3$ **a** y is eight times the square root of one-fifth of x.

B $y = x^2 + 4$ **b** y is four more than the square of x.

C $y = 8\sqrt{\dfrac{x}{5}}$ **c** A car travelled 80 km in x hours at an average speed of y km/h.

D $y = 180 - x$ **d** x and y are supplementary angles.

E $y = \dfrac{80}{x}$ **e** A car used x litres of petrol on a trip of 80 km and the fuel consumption was y litres/100 km.

F $y = \dfrac{5x}{4}$ **f** x is three more than y.

2 The cooking instructions to cook a leg of lamb are as follows:

Preheat oven to 220°C and cook for 45 min per kg, plus an additional 20 min.

Write a formula relating the cooking time T minutes and weight w kg.

GO TO
Section 1:
Writing formulae

STEP 2

3 Given the expression $\dfrac{x + 2y}{3z}$

if $x = -7$, $y = -2$ and $z = 2$, what is the value of the expression?

4 One of the kinematic equations that describes motion is

$s = \dfrac{t(u + v)}{2}$

a How many variables does this equation contain?

b How many do you need to know to use the formula to evaluate?

c If $u = 3.5$, $v = 6.1$ and $t = 9$, what is the value of s?

GO TO
Section 2:
Substituting values into formulae

STEP 3

5 The formula for the area of a circle is

$A = \pi r^2$

a What do each of the letters represent?

b Rewrite the formula and make r the subject.

c Can the value of r ever be a negative value?

GO TO
Section 3:
Changing the subject of a formula

Section 4:
Working with formulae

GO TO
Chapter review

Section 1: Writing formulae

A **formula** is a rule that shows you how to work out one quantity by combining other quantities.

For example, the rule for working out cooking time for a roast chicken might be 'cook for 40 minutes per kilogram plus an extra 20 minutes'.

The rule for finding the area of a triangle is to multiply half the length of the base by the height.

In mathematical language, the formula for the area of a triangle is $A = \frac{1}{2}bh$.

To make sense of a formula you need to know what the variables represent. In this example:

- A is the area in square units.
- b is the length of the base of the triangle.
- h is the perpendicular height of the triangle.

A, b and h are variables. The letters can be replaced by many different values. $\frac{1}{2}$ is a constant. No matter what value you use for b, you have to multiply it by $\frac{1}{2}$ in the formula.

A single variable on one side of the formula is called the **subject** of a formula.

The subject is the variable (or quantity) that is being **expressed in terms of** the other variables in the formula.

In $A = \frac{1}{2}bh$, A is the subject of the formula.
In $y = 3x$, y is the subject of the formula.

Writing formulae to represent real-life contexts

In Chapter 15 you formed equations to represent information given in problems and then solved them to get the answer to a question. You use the same procedures to set up formulae.

Key vocabulary

formula: a general rule or equation showing the relationship between unknown quantities; the plural is formulae.

Tip

For a reminder about variables, see Chapter 5.

Key vocabulary

subject: the variable which is expressed in terms of other variables; it is the variable on its own on one side of the equals sign. In the formula $s = \frac{d}{t}$, s is the subject.

WORKED EXAMPLE 1

Mary and Peter are sharing half a circular pizza.

Peter cuts himself a slice that makes an angle of a with the straight edge of the pizza half.

He tells Mary that he will cut another slice the same size, and then she can have what is left.

Write a formula for the size of Mary's share of the pizza.

Subject = Size of Mary's share
Variable = Peter's share
Constant = Size of starting slice

List the quantities involved.

Work out whether they represent the subject, a variable, a constant or a coefficient.

Continues on next page …

Peter's share = $2a$

Angles on a straight line equal $180°$

$180° - 2a$ = size of Mary's share

Let the size of Mary's share = M

$M = 180° - 2a$

> Establish the relationship between each quantity. What is the subject being expressed in terms of?
>
> Peter takes two slices, each with an angle of a, so you can write an expression for the total size of Peter's share.
>
> You know that angles on a straight line add up to $180°$.
>
> The size of Mary's share is expressed in terms of the size of the pizza half and the size of Peter's slice.

> Write the formula as concisely as possible using the language of algebra.

Problem-solving framework

A group of sixth form students are planning to run a day conference.

The local university offers conference rooms for hire at a daily rate.

The students think they will have a maximum of 60 delegates and want to offer refreshments costing £4 per delegate.

The largest room they can hire costs £160 for the day.

They want to charge each delegate enough to cover the costs of running the conference.

Write a formula for calculating how much they should charge each delegate.

Steps for approaching a problem-solving question	What you would do for this example
Step 1: If it is useful, draw a diagram.	A diagram is not particularly useful for this question.
Step 2: Identify what you have to do.	Calculate how much to charge each delegate at the conference by writing a formula using the information given.
Step 3: Test the problem with what you already know.	You know a formula is a general rule showing the relationship between quantities.
Step 4: What maths can you do?	**1** List the quantities involved, and establish if they are the subject, a variable, a constant or a coefficient: Number of delegates (d) = 60 (variable, as this can change). Cost of refreshments = £4 per delegate (coefficient, as this value is multiplied by how many delegates there are). Cost of the room = £160 (constant, this is fixed by the university). Cost to charge each delegate = C (subject, this is what we want to find out).

Continues on next page …

2 Establish what the relationship is between each quantity.

The cost to charge each delegate is the same as the cost of having each delegate at the conference, which is the total cost divided by the number of delegates.

The total cost is equal to the cost of refreshments for each delegate and the cost of the room hire.

Now put this together using algebra:

Cost of conference = $4d + 160$

Cost of one delegate is this value divided by the number of delegates (d).

3 Write the formula as concisely as possible using the language of algebra.

$$C = \frac{4d + 160}{d}$$

EXERCISE 17A

1 Two friends Simon and Lucy are going to Europe on holiday. Simon has x euros and Lucy has y euros. Write an equation for each of these statements:

a Simon and Lucy have a total of 2000 euros.

b Lucy has four times as many euros as Simon.

c If Lucy spent 400 euros she would then have three times as many euros as Simon.

d If Lucy gave 600 euros to Simon they would both have the same number of euros.

e Half of Simon's euros are equivalent to two-fifths of Lucy's.

> **Tip**
>
> You can look up any standard formulae that you are not sure of in the relevant chapters.

2 When y is the subject and x is an unknown value, write a formula to determine y, when y is:

a three more than x

b six less than x

c ten times x

d the sum of -8 and x

e the sum of x and the square of x

f twice x more than x plus 1

g double x divided by the sum of x and -2

h half the product of π and the cube root of x divided by 3.

3 In general, temperature decreases with height above sea level. This formula shows how temperature and height above sea level are related.

$$T = \frac{h}{200}$$

where T is the temperature decrease in degrees Celsius and h is the height increase in metres.

 Find answers at: cambridge.org/ukschools/gcsemaths-studentbookanswers

a If the temperature at a height of 500 m is 23 °C, what will it be when you climb to 1300 m?

b What increase in height would result in a 5 °C decrease in temperature?

 4 a The population of a town decreases by 2% each year. The population was initially P, and is Q after n years.

What is the formula relating Q, P and n?

b The population of a town decreases by 5% each year. The percentage decrease over a period of n years is a%.

What is the formula relating a and n?

Section 2: Substituting values into formulae

To find the value of the subject (or any variable) in a formula you need to know the value of all the other variables. The values are substituted into the formula to work out the missing value.

Substitute means replace the letters with the numbers you have been given.

Evaluate means work out the numerical value of a given calculation.

Key vocabulary

substitute: to replace letters with numbers.
evaluate: to calculate the numerical value of something.

WORKED EXAMPLE 2

The perimeter of a square can be found using the formula $P = 4s$, where s is the length of a side.

What is the perimeter of a square with sides of:

a 10 cm   **b** 2.5 mm?

a $P = 4 \times 10$
$P = 40$ cm   Substitute (replace) s with 10

b $P = 4 \times 2.5$
$P = 10$ mm   Substitute (replace) s with 2.5

Tip

It is good practice to show you can correctly substitute values into a formula before calculating the answer. Write down what you need to work out and then calculate the value.

WORKED EXAMPLE 3

The volume of an object can be found using the formula $V = \dfrac{1}{3}Ah$

Find the volume of an object when $A = 30\,\text{cm}^2$ and $h = 6\,\text{cm}$.

$V = \dfrac{1}{3} \times 30 \times 6$ Substitute $A = 30$, and $h = 6$.

$= \dfrac{1}{3} \times 180$ Remember volume is given in cubic units.

$= 60\,\text{cm}^3$

WORK IT OUT 17.1

The surface area of a sphere given by the formula

$A = 4\pi r^2$

where r is the radius of the sphere.

Calculate the surface area of a sphere of radius 8 cm in exact form.

Which is the correct answer?

What mistakes have been made in the incorrect answers?

Option A	Option B	Option C
$A = 4 \times \pi \times 8^2$	$A = 256\pi \text{ cm}^2$	60 cm^3

Tip

Make sure you include units in an answer when appropriate.

EXERCISE 17B

1 Evaluate these expressions:

a $2a(a - 3b)$ when:

   i $a = 2$ and $b = -5$ **ii** $a = -3$ and $b = -2$ **iii** $a = \dfrac{1}{3}$ and $b = \dfrac{1}{2}$

b $x^2 - 2y$ when:

   i $x = -7, y = 2$ **ii** $x = -\dfrac{1}{3}, y = \dfrac{5}{6}$

2 For $x = -\dfrac{a}{2} - \dfrac{b}{c}$, find the exact value of x if:

   a $a = 2, b = -2, c = -1$ **b** $a = 7, b = 3, c = -4$

   c $a = -10, b = \sqrt{3}, c = \sqrt{3}$ **d** $a = \sqrt{2}, b = \sqrt{2}, c = 4$

   e $a = 0, b = 0, c = 5$ **f** $a = \pi, b = \pi, c = 7$

3 For the formula $v = u + at$, find v if $u = 6$, $a = 3$ and $t = 5$.

4 Given $v^2 = u^2 + 2ax$ and $v > 0$, find the value of v (correct to 1 decimal place) when:

   a $u = 0, a = 5$ and $x = 10$ **b** $u = 6, a = 4$ and $x = 15$

   c $u = 2, a = 9.8$ and $x = 22$ **d** $u = 2.3, a = 4.9$ and $x = 10.6$

5 Given $\dfrac{1}{f} = \dfrac{1}{u} + \dfrac{1}{v}$, find the value of f when:

   a $u = 2$ and $v = 4$ **b** $u = 2$ and $v = 15$

6 When a stone is thrown upward at 25 m/s, the height h metres it reaches after t seconds is given by the formula

$h = 25t - 4.9t^2$

Find the height of the stone after:

   a 1 second   **b** 2 seconds.

Find answers at: cambridge.org/ukschools/gcsemaths-studentbookanswers

7 $V = \pi l(r^2 - (r - t)^2)$ is the volume of metal in a tube where l is the length of the tube, r is the radius of the outside surface and t is the thickness of the material.

Find V when $l = 40$, $r = 5$ and $t = 0.5$ (Leave π in your answer).

8 Find the value of h, correct to 1 decimal place, if

$$h = \frac{9gRs}{2v}$$

when $g = 9.8$, $R = 2.5$, $s = 3$ and $v = 7.4$

9 The length of the hypotenuse c cm in a right-angled triangle is given by

$$c^2 = a^2 + b^2$$

where a cm and b cm are the lengths of the perpendicular sides, as in the diagram.

Calculate, correct to the nearest 0.1 cm, the length of the hypotenuse in the right-angled triangle whose perpendicular sides have lengths 14 cm and 25 cm.

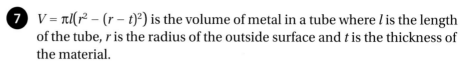

10 The time T (in seconds) taken for one complete swing of a pendulum is given to the nearest centimetre by

$$T = 2\pi \sqrt{\frac{L}{g}}$$

where $g = 9.8 \, \text{m/s}^2$ and L is length of the pendulum.

Find, correct to the nearest centimetre, the length of the pendulum that takes 2 seconds to complete one swing.

Section 3: Changing the subject of a formula

There are times when you might want to find the value of a variable that is not the subject of a formula.

To do this, rearrange the formula to make the letter you are trying to find the subject of the formula.

Since a formula is a type of equation you can use inverse operations to 'solve' the formula for the letter you want.

WORKED EXAMPLE 4

Given the kinematic formula $v^2 = u^2 + 2as$

a make s the subject of the formula

b make u the subject of the formula.

a $u^2 + 2as = v^2$ Swap the sides to get $2as$ on the left.

   $2as = v^2 - u^2$ Subtract u^2 from each side.

   $\dfrac{2as}{2a} = \dfrac{(v^2 - u^2)}{2a}$ Divide both sides by $2a$.

   $s = \dfrac{v^2 - u^2}{2a}$ You can leave out the brackets because the fraction line acts as a bracket.

Continues on next page …

---

b $u^2 + 2as = v^2$ — Swap the sides to get u^2 on the left.

$u^2 = v^2 - 2as$ — Subtract $2as$ from each side.

$\sqrt{u^2} = \sqrt{(v^2 - 2as)}$ — Take the square root of each side to get u on its own.

$u = \sqrt{v^2 - 2as}$ — Note that we are not considering the negative square root in this situation as we are working with positive values of u.

Tip

When u has a positive value, the square root is positive. However, when u can be positive or negative, the correct notation is $u = \pm\sqrt{v^2 - 2as}$.

WORKED EXAMPLE 5

Given the formula
$P = \pi r + 2r + 2a$
make r the subject.

$P - 2a = \pi r + 2r$ — Move the term that does not contain r to the LHS. Take $2a$ from both sides.

$P - 2a = r(\pi + 2)$ — r is now a common factor of the two terms on the RHS. Factorise so that r is only written down once.

$\dfrac{(P - 2a)}{(\pi + 2)} = r$ — Divide both sides by $\pi + 2$

$r = \dfrac{P - 2a}{\pi + 2}$ — Write the subject on the LHS.

WORKED EXAMPLE 6

Given the formula
$y = \dfrac{2pt}{p - t}$
make t the subject.

$y(p - t) = 2pt$ — Cross multiply by $(p - t)$.

$yp - yt = 2pt$ — Expand the brackets and add yt to both sides.

$yp = 2pt + yt$

$yp = t(2p + y)$ — Factorise the RHS by t.

$\dfrac{yp}{(2p + y)} = t$ — Divide both sides by $(2p + y)$ and write t on the LHS.

$t = \dfrac{yp}{2p + y}$

Find answers at: cambridge.org/ukschools/gcsemaths-studentbookanswers

You can calculate the value of **any** variable in a formula provided all the other variables are known.

WORKED EXAMPLE 7

Given the formula $v^2 = u^2 + 2as$ find the value of s when $u = 8$, $v = 10$ and $a = 3$.

$$v^2 = u^2 + 2as$$
$$v^2 - u^2 = 2as$$
$$\frac{(v^2 - u^2)}{2a} = s$$

Rearrange the formula to make s the subject:

Subtracting u^2 from both sides.

Dividing by 2as.

$$s = \frac{v^2 - u^2}{2a}$$

The subject is normally written on the left.

$u = 8$, $v = 10$ and $a = 3$

$$s = \frac{10^2 - 8^2}{2 \times 3}$$

Substitute in the values you know.

$$s = \frac{100 - 64}{6}$$
$$s = \frac{36}{6}$$
$$s = 6$$

$$10^2 = 8^2 + 2 \times 3s$$
$$100 = 64 + 6s$$
$$100 - 64 = 6s$$
$$36 = 6s$$
$$\frac{36}{6} = s$$
$$6 = s$$
$$s = 6$$

Alternatively, you can substitute the numbers first and then solve for s.

EXERCISE 17C

1 Rearrange each of these formulae to make the letter in the bracket the subject.

a $a(q - c) = d$ (q) **b** $4(p - 2q) = 3p + 2$ (p)

c $5(x - 3) = y(4 - 3x)$ (x) **d** $d = \sqrt{\dfrac{3h}{2}}$ (h)

e $y = \dfrac{2pt}{p - t}$ (t) **f** $a = \dfrac{2 - 7b}{b - 5}$ (b)

g $\dfrac{x}{x + c} = \dfrac{p}{q}$ (x)

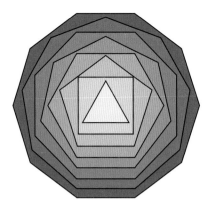

2 The formula for the sum S of the interior angles in a convex n-sided polygon is

$S = 180(n - 2)$

Rearrange the formula to make n the subject and use this to find the number of sides in the polygon if the sum of the interior angles is:

a 1080°   **b** 1800°   **c** 3240°

3 The kinetic energy E joules of a moving object is given by

$E = \dfrac{1}{2}mv^2$

where m kg is the mass of the object and v m/s is its speed.

Rearrange the formula to make m the subject and use this to find the mass of the object when its energy and speed are, respectively:

a 400 joules, 10 m/s   **b** 28 joules, 4 m/s   **c** 57.6 joules, 2.4 m/s

4 The formula for finding the number of degrees Fahrenheit (F) for a temperature given in degrees Celsius (C) is

$F = \dfrac{9}{5}C + 32$

Rearrange the formula to make C the subject. Use this formula to convert these Fahrenheit temperatures to Celsius temperatures:

a 68 °F   **b** 23 °F   **c** 212 °F

5 The formula for the perimeter P of a rectangle l by w is

$P = 2(l + w)$

If $P = 20$ cm and $l = 7$ cm, what is the length of w?

6 The area A cm² enclosed by an ellipse is given by

$A = \pi ab$

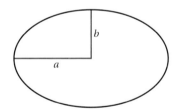

> **Tip**
>
> These are questions where you may decide to rearrange first and then substitute the values given to solve, or substitute the values first and then evaluate.

Calculate to 2 decimal places the length a cm if $b = 3.2$ and $A = 25$.

7 When an object is shot up into the air at a speed of u metres per second, its height above the ground h metres and time of flight t seconds are related (ignoring air resistance) by

$h = ut - 4.9t^2$

Find the speed at which an object was fired if it reached a height of 30 metres after 5 seconds.

8 For the formula

$I = \left(\dfrac{180n - 360}{n} \right)$

find n when $I = 108$.

Find answers at: cambridge.org/ukschools/gcsemaths-studentbookanswers

9 Given the formula

$$t = 2\pi\sqrt{\dfrac{L}{g}}$$

find L given $t = \pi$ and $g = 9.8$.

Section 4: Working with formulae

You will now apply your skills with formulae to a set of general problems.

Things to remember:

- Substitute in the correct values.
- Include appropriate units in your answer.
- When constructing a formula try some values to make sure it works.
- It can be useful to rearrange a formula to change the subject, but it is not always necessary when using a formula to evaluate.

EXERCISE 17D

1 Decide whether each of the following statements is true or false. Correct any false statements to make them true.

a Using the formula

$$s = ut + \dfrac{1}{2}at^2$$

to find the value of s when $u = 4.6$, $a = 9.8$ and $t = 4$, the answer is $s = 96.8$

b The formula

$$A = \pi r(r + l)$$

rewritten to make l the subject becomes $l = \dfrac{A - \pi r}{r}$

c A formula to calculate the number n half way between two numbers x and y can be written as

$$n = \dfrac{x + y}{2}$$

d In the formula to calculate the area of a circle

$$A = \pi r^2$$

π is a constant and A and r are the variables.

e $V = \pi r^2 h$

This formula calculates the volume of a triangular prism.

2 The Greek mathematician Hero showed that the area of a triangle with sides a, b and c is given by the formula:

$$A = \sqrt{s(s - a)(s - b)(s - c)}$$

where $s = \dfrac{1}{2}(a + b + c)$.

Use Hero's formula to find the area of the triangle on the left.

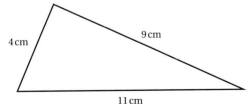

4 cm   9 cm   11 cm

3 Compound interest is calculated by the interest being added to a principal amount at the end of each year.

If P is the principal amount, r is the interest rate over a given period and n is number of years that the interest is compounded:

Total accrued $= P\left(1 + \dfrac{r}{100}\right)^n$

Find to the nearest whole £ the total accrued when £6000 is borrowed for three years at a rate of 4%. How much interest was paid?

4 What does this formula calculate?

$x = \dfrac{-b \pm \sqrt{b^2 - 4ac}}{2a}$

Why is the sign $\pm$ included in this formula?

5 Given that the general form of a quadratic equation is

$ax^2 + bx + c = 0$

use the method of completing the square to prove the formula in question **4**.

6 $n,\ n^2,\ \sqrt{n},\ 8n,\ \dfrac{36}{n},\ \dfrac{n}{2} + 1$

a If $n = 4$ arrange in ascending numerical order.

b Arrange in ascending numerical order if $n = \dfrac{1}{4}$.

Learn this formula

You are expected to know the formula $x = \dfrac{-b \pm \sqrt{b^2 - 4ac}}{2a}$ from memory. See Chapter 15 if you need a reminder.

7 Conversion of a given temperature from the Fahrenheit scale to the Centigrade scale is done by means of the formula

$C = \dfrac{5(F - 32)}{9}$

a Gallium is a soft, silvery metal that melts at temperatures above 85.57 °F. Given that your normal body temperature is about 37 °C, would gallium be likely to melt if you held it in your hand? Explain your answer.

b Cast iron becomes molten at 1204 °C. Determine the Fahrenheit equivalent.

8 A formula used in life insurance is

$Q = \dfrac{2m}{2 + m}$

a Calculate Q if $m = -0.7$ (correct to 4 significant figures).

b Calculate m if $Q = 3$.

9 For a rectangle of length l cm and width w cm, the perimeter P cm is given by

$P = 2(l + w)$

Use this formula to calculate the length of a rectangle which has width 15 cm and perimeter 57 cm.

10 The distance d metres Jim's car takes to stop once the brakes are applied is given by the formula

$$d = 0.2v + 0.005v^2$$

where v km/h is the speed of the car when the brakes are applied.

Find the distance the car takes to stop if the brakes are applied when it is travelling at each of the speeds given below.

a 60 km/h   **b** 65 km/h   **c** 70 km/h

d Comment on how stopping distances vary with increasing speed and what this means for road safety.

11 A rocket scientist is trying to calculate how long a Lunar Explorer Vehicle will take to descend towards the surface of the moon. He knows that if u = initial speed and v = speed at time t seconds, then:

$$v = u + at$$

where a is the acceleration and t is the time that has passed.
Rearrange the formula to make t the subject.

12 A statistician has been asked to write a report on some data he has been investigating. He needs to know if the mean of the data is representative of his data set. The formula given here calculates the maximum value of the mean:

$$b = a + 3\frac{s}{\sqrt{n}}$$

where s = sample spread about the mean, n = the sample size, a = the school mean and b = the mean maximum value.
Rewrite the formula making s the subject, to provide the statistician with a formula for calculating the spread of the data about the mean.

13 When an object is thrown up into the air at a speed of u metres per second, its height above the ground h metres and time of flight t seconds are related (ignoring air resistance) by

$$h = ut - 4.9t^2$$

Find the speed at which a javelin was thrown if it reached a height of 12.5 metres after 5 seconds.

14 The general form of a quadratic equation is

$$ax^2 + bx + c = 0$$

Solve this equation with the formula

$$x = \frac{-b \pm \sqrt{b^2 - 4ac}}{2a}$$

given $a = 1$, $b = 9$ and $c = 20$.

Checklist of learning and understanding

Writing formulae

- A formula is a general rule showing the relationship between quantities.
- You can use formulae to represent real-life problems as long as you define the variables you are using.

Substituting values into formulae

- To evaluate a formula, you need to know the value of all but one of its variables.
- Substitute given values to find the unknown variable.

Changing the subject of a formula

- In any formula you can 'change the subject' by rearranging the formula in the same way as you rearrange equations.

Chapter review

For additional questions on the topics in this chapter, visit GCSE Mathematics Online.

1 Make p the subject of the formula $y = 3p^2 - 4$ *(3 marks)*

©Pearson Education Ltd 2013

2 Many of the formulae you learn and prove in mathematics are for finding areas and volumes of standard 3D shapes. Research any formulae that you will need for the following questions and then do the calculations:

   a The side of a cube with a volume of $125\,\text{cm}^3$.

   b The length of a cuboid with a total surface area of $157.36\,\text{m}^2$, height $6.5\,\text{m}$ and breadth $2.2\,\text{m}$.

   c The formula

     $S = 2\pi r(r + h)$

     represents the total surface area of a cone.

     Rewrite this formula and make h the subject.

   d Find the volume of a sphere if the radius is $\sqrt{3}$. (Leave π and any surd values in your answer.)

   e The curved surface area of a hemisphere is $2\pi r^2$.

     Explain why the total surface area is $3\pi r^2$.

3 Given the following two formulae

   $A - \pi r(r + 2h)$ and $C = r + h$

   create a formula:

   a with the subject A, eliminating h

   b with the subject A, eliminating r.

Find answers at: cambridge.org/ukschools/gcsemaths-studentbookanswers

4 A runner completed a 26 km race in 4 hours. After running 15 km, his average speed decreased by 2 km/h.

Given that $t = \dfrac{d}{s}$,

where t is time in hours, d is distance covered in km and s is average speed in km/h, work out the runner's two speeds for this race.

5 A cyclic quadrilateral has all its vertices on a circle. Its area A is given by Brahmagupta's formula

$$A^2 = (s - a)(s - b)(s - c)(s - d)$$

where a, b, c and d are the side lengths of the quadrilateral and

$$s = \frac{1}{2}(a + b + c + d)$$

is the 'semi-perimeter'.

Find the area of a cyclic quadrilateral with side lengths 8 cm, 9 cm, 10 cm and 13 cm.

18 Volume and surface area

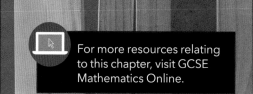

In this chapter you will learn how to ...

- calculate the volume and surface area of cuboids and prisms.
- calculate the volume and surface area of cylinders.
- calculate the volume and surface area of cones and spheres.
- calculate the volume and surface area of pyramids.
- solve volume and surface area problems involving composite shapes.

For more resources relating to this chapter, visit GCSE Mathematics Online.

Using mathematics: real-life applications

Freight costs are dependent upon the volume of material being transported. Freight rates are calculated using the container volume measured against the length of the container. The longer the container the higher the freight cost.

"To transport a container full of apples from Felixstowe, England, to Le Havre in France, I have to let the freight operator know the volume of apples I have to transport as well as the dimensions of the crates. I am then quoted a transport cost." *(Apple producer)*

Before you start ...

Chs 2 and 3	You need to be able to recognise and identify solid objects.	**1** Name each object as accurately as possible from the description. **a** A 3D object with six identical square surfaces. **b** A 3D solid with two parallel circular faces. **c** An object with a square base and triangular side faces that meet at an apex. **d** A 3D object with a circular base and one vertex. **e** A 3D object with many flat surfaces that are polygons. **f** A polyhedron with two triangular and three rectangular faces.
Ch 12	You must be able to calculate the area of plane shapes.	**2** What is the formula for the area of a circle? **3** What is the area of a right-angled triangle with sides of 3 cm, 4 cm and 5 cm?
Chs 2 and 3	You should understand and use the properties of solids.	**4** A shape has 6 faces, 8 vertices and 12 edges. **a** What could it be? **b** What additional information do you need to name the shape more accurately? Continues on next page ...

Find answers at: cambridge.org/ukschools/gcsemaths-studentbookanswers

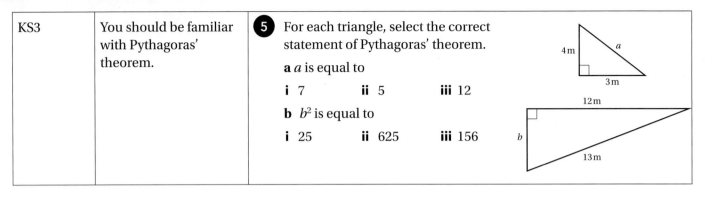

KS3	You should be familiar with Pythagoras' theorem.	**5** For each triangle, select the correct statement of Pythagoras' theorem.

5 For each triangle, select the correct statement of Pythagoras' theorem.

a *a* is equal to

i 7   **ii** 5   **iii** 12

b b^2 is equal to

i 25   **ii** 625   **iii** 156

Assess your starting point using the Launchpad

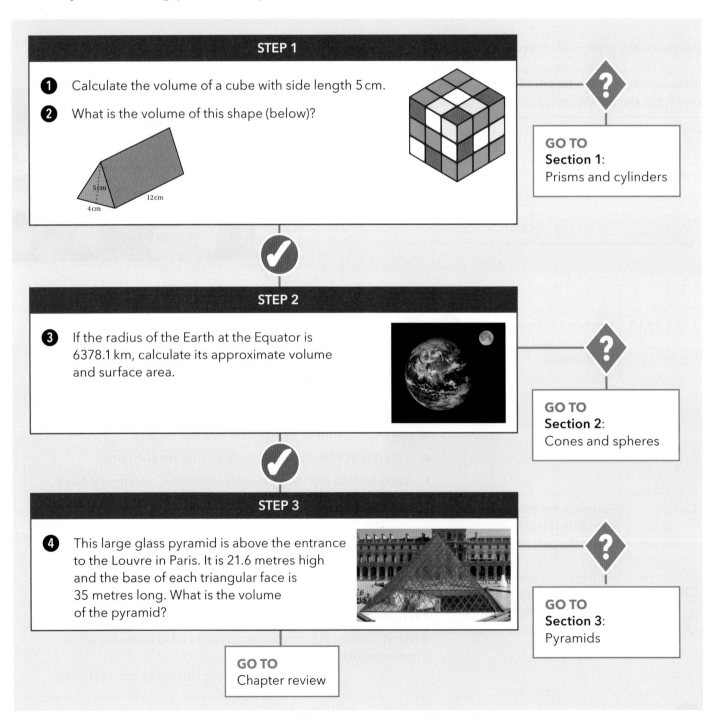

STEP 1

1 Calculate the volume of a cube with side length 5 cm.

2 What is the volume of this shape (below)?

**GO TO
Section 1:**
Prisms and cylinders

STEP 2

3 If the radius of the Earth at the Equator is 6378.1 km, calculate its approximate volume and surface area.

**GO TO
Section 2:**
Cones and spheres

STEP 3

4 This large glass pyramid is above the entrance to the Louvre in Paris. It is 21.6 metres high and the base of each triangular face is 35 metres long. What is the volume of the pyramid?

**GO TO
Section 3:**
Pyramids

GO TO
Chapter review

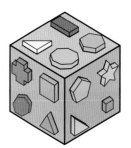

Section 1: Prisms and cylinders

A prism is a 3D object with a uniform cross-section along its length, where the cross-section is a polygon.

This shape sorter is really a prism sorter. You should be able to name the prisms sticking out of it.

This diagram shows examples of **right prisms**. One of the end faces is known as the base of the object. The sides are rectangles perpendicular to the base.

Key vocabulary

right prism: a prism with sides perpendicular to the end faces (base).

A cube (square prism)   A rectangular prism   A triangular prism

 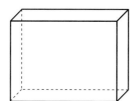 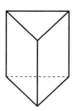

Tip

A rectangular prism is also called a cuboid.

Volume

The volume of an object is the three-dimensional space that it takes up. Volume is given in cubic units, such as mm^3, cm^3 and m^3 (for solids). For liquids, the volume of a container is referred to as capacity. Capacity is measured in litres.

You can find the volume of any right prism by finding the area of one end face (base) and multiplying this by its length or height.

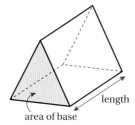

length

area of base

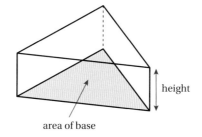

height

area of base

Surface area

Surface area is the total area of the faces of a three-dimensional object.

Sketching a rough net of the object can help you to see what faces to include when you calculate the surface area.

Tip

You learnt about nets of solids in Chapter 3. Revise that section if you need to.

Cubes and cuboids

The net of a cuboid shows that the surface area is the total area of the six faces.

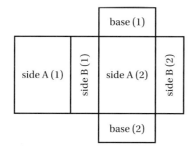

base (1)

side A (1) | side B (1) | side A (2) | side B (2)

base (2)

Find answers at: cambridge.org/ukschools/gcsemaths-studentbookanswers

The opposite faces match, so:

Surface area = 2(area of side A) + 2(area of side B) + 2(area of base)

A cube is a special case of a cuboid, it has six identical square faces. You can use the following formulae for volume and surface area:

Volume of a cube = x^3

Surface area of a cube = $6x^2$

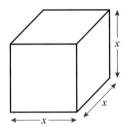

Tip

Remember to check that all measurements are in the same units, for example all cm or all m.

WORKED EXAMPLE 1

Calculate the volume and surface area of this cuboid.

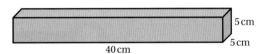

5 cm
5 cm
40 cm

Volume = lbh = 40 × 5 × 5 = 1000 cm^3

> For a cuboid, any of the surfaces could be chosen as the 'base'. The volume of a cuboid is usually calculated using the formula $V = lbh$, where l, b and h are the three different dimensions of the shape.

Surface area = 4 × (40 × 5) + 2 × (5 × 5)
= 800 + 50
= 850 cm^2

> Look for faces that are identical. This can cut down on the working you need to do.

Prisms with bases of other shapes

WORKED EXAMPLE 2

Find the volume and surface area of this triangular prism.

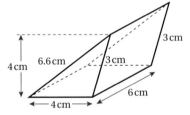

3 cm
6.6 cm
4 cm
3 cm
6 cm
4 cm

Area of the base = $\frac{1}{2}bh$ = $\frac{1}{2}$ × 4 × 4 = 8 cm^2

> The base is a triangle.

Volume = 8 × 6 = 48 cm^3

> Volume of prism = area of base × length

Surface area of the two base triangles = 8 + 8 = 16 cm^2

Surface area of side face 1 = 3 × 6 = 18 cm^2
Surface area of side face 2 = 4 × 6 = 24 cm^2
Surface area of side face 3 = 6.6 × 6 = 39.6 cm^2

> The other faces are all rectangles. Work systematically around the shape.

Total surface area = 97.6 cm^2

> Surface area of triangular prism
> = 2(area of triangular base) + area of three side faces

Prisms with bases that are trapeziums are quite common. Rubbish skips, wheelbarrows, planters and many other containers take this shape.

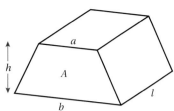

Area of the trapezium base $= \frac{1}{2}(a + b) \times h$.

Volume of prism = area of the trapezium × length

WORK IT OUT 18.1

What is the volume of soil that can be contained in this skip?

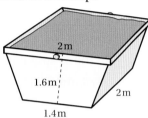

Which of the following is the correct calculation?

Calculation A	Calculation B	Calculation C
Area of the trapezium: Area $= \frac{1}{2}(a + b) \times h$ Area $= \frac{1}{2} \times 3.4 \times 1.6 = 2.72\,\text{m}^2$ Volume = area of the trapezium × length Volume $= 2.72 \times 2 = 5.44\,\text{m}^2$	Area of the trapezium: Area $= \frac{1}{2}(a - b) \times h$ Area $= \frac{1}{2} \times 0.6 \times 1.6 = 0.48\,\text{m}^2$ Volume = area of the trapezium × length Volume $= 0.48 \times 2 = 0.96\,\text{m}^3$	Area of the trapezium: Area $= \frac{1}{2} \times b \times h$ Area $= \frac{1}{2} \times 1.4 \times 1.6 = 1.12\,\text{m}^2$ Volume = area of the trapezium × length Volume $= 1.12 \times 2 = 2.24\,\text{m}^3$

Rearranging the formulae

You can change the subject of the formula to find the length of a prism if you know the volume and area of the base.

WORKED EXAMPLE 3

The volume of a triangular prism is $100\,\text{cm}^3$ and the area of the end is $25\,\text{cm}^2$. How long is the prism?

V = Area of the triangle × length   **Rearrange the formula.**
so $V \div A = L$

$L = 100 \div 25 = 4\,\text{cm}$

Problem-solving framework

You are painting a room and it needs two coats of paint. The room is 10 m long, 7 m wide and 3 m high. There is a door which is 2 m high and 1.5 m wide and a window that is 2.6 m high and 2.2 m wide. You want to colour it blue and it should takes 5 days to paint it.

Paint covers 5 m² per litre and you can buy it in 5-litre pots. Each pot costs £14.99. How many 5-litre paint pots will you need to buy?

You should add 10% into your calculations for special circumstances.

Steps for solving problems	What you would do for this example
Step 1: What have you got to do?	Paint a room with two coats of paint. Work out how many 5-litre paint pots are needed.
	A useful estimate could be calculated at first.
	The room is roughly 100 m² and the door and window are roughly 10 m². So coverage is $2 \times 90\,m^2 = 180\,m^2$.
	Plus 10% takes is roughly to 200 m².
	This means $200 \div 5 = 40$ litres.
	Eight 5-litre pots are needed.
Step 2: What information do you need?	Room dimensions are needed for surface area calculations. Door and window dimensions need to be taken away from the coverage area.
Step 3: What information don't you need?	The colour of paint, the length of time taken and the cost of the paint are not needed.
Step 4: What maths can you do?	Calculate the surface area of the room:
	Walls 1 & 3: $10 \times 3 = 30\,m^2$ Walls 2 & 4: $7 \times 3 = 21\,m^2$
	Total surface area $= 30 + 30 + 21 + 21 = 102\,m^2$
	Door area $= 2 \times 1.5 = 3\,m^2$
	Window area $= 2.6 \times 2.2 = 5.72\,m^2$
	Total surface area for painting $102 - 3 - 5.72 = 93.28\,m^2$.
	Two coats required $= 93.28 \times 2 = 186.56\,m^2$
	Add 10% $= 18.656\,m^2$
	Total paint coverage required 205.216 m²
	1 litre $= 5\,m^2$ coverage of paint
	$205.216 \div 5 = 41.0432$ litres of paint are required.
	5-litre pots of paint can be bought $41.0432 \div 5 = 8.208\,64$
	You will need to buy nine pots.
Step 5: Have you done it all?	Yes:
	room size less the door and window sizes
	two coats of paint + 10%
	total divided by the coverage of one paint pot
Step 6: Is it correct?	Yes:
	checked against estimate

Cylinders

Cylinders are not prisms, but you can find their volume and surface area in the same way as you do with prisms.

The net of a cylinder shows that the curved surface forms a rectangle when it is flattened out. The length of the rectangle is equivalent to the circumference of the circular base.

The surface area of a cylinder is calculated using the formula:

$S = 2\pi rh + 2\pi r^2$

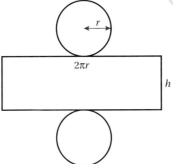

WORKED EXAMPLE 4

A road roller has a roller on the front which is filled with water to make it heavy. The tank of water in the roller has a radius of 0.95 m and a length of 2.4 m. Calculate the volume (or capacity) of the tank.

Volume of cylinder = area of the circle × length
Volume = $\pi r^2 \times l$
Volume = $3.14 \times 0.95 \times 0.95 \times 2.4 = 6.801\,24\,m^3$
$\approx 6.8\,m^3$ (1 decimal place)

EXERCISE 18A

1 Calculate the volume and surface area of each object. (Each object is a closed object.)

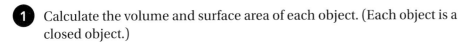

a
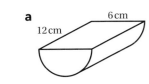

b
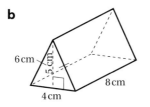

c
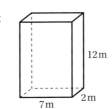

d
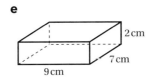

e
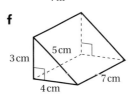

f

80 cm

50 cm

30 cm

2 What is the capacity, in litres, of the aquarium shown on the left, when filled to the top? (1 litre = 1000 cm³)

3 The volume of a cube is 144 m³. What is the length of each side?

4 The dimensions of an Olympic-sized swimming pool are 50 m long, 25 m wide, and the water is 2 m deep. What is the volume of water in an Olympic-sized swimming pool?

5 What is the volume of this triangular prism to 2 decimal places?

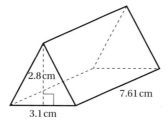

2.8 cm

7.61 cm

3.1 cm

6 A set of solar panels is being attached to a roof. What area of panels are needed to cover one side of the roof as shown (assume the panels cover the entire surface)?

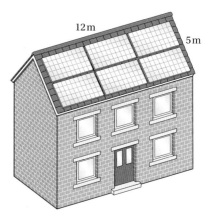

12 m

5 m

7 A cylindrical water tank with a diameter of 1.2 m and height of 1.6 m needs painting around the outside of its curved surface. What area needs to be painted?

8 You can make two types of candle – a short fat one with a radius of 4 cm and height of 5 cm or a tall thin one with a radius of 2 cm and height of 20 cm. Which one will require more candle wax?

9 **a** What is the volume of the metal in a length of a pipe with a hollow radius of 10 cm, an outer radius of 12 cm and a length of 20 cm?

b What is the volume of the hollow centre of the pipe?

10 A cube with side of x cm has a surface area of 150 cm². Calculate x.

11 Calculate the volume of the object below.

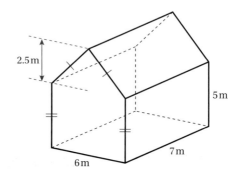

2.5 m

5 m

6 m

7 m

12 Calculate the volume of this solid piece of wood with a cylindrical hole drilled through the middle.

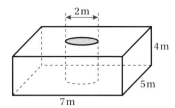

13 Find in terms of x the volume and surface area of a cuboid with sides of length x, $(x + 2)$ and $(x + 3)$.

14 Write a formula for the volume of a cube with a side equal to $a + b$.

Section 2: Cones and spheres

Cones

The formula for the volume of a cone is $\frac{1}{3} \times$ area of circular base $\times h$, where h is the perpendicular height from the base to the apex of the cone.

The area of the base can be found using the formula for the area of a circle, πr^2.

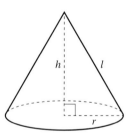

Tip

In some problems involving cones you may need to use Pythagoras' theorem to find the perpendicular height using the radius and the slant height. You will meet this in Chapter 32.

WORKED EXAMPLE 5

Find the volume of a cone of radius 12 cm with a perpendicular height of 14 cm.

$$\text{Volume} = \frac{1}{3}(\pi r^2)h = \frac{1}{3}(3.14 \times 12 \times 12) \times 14$$
$$= 2110 \text{ cm}^3 \text{ (to 3 significant figures)}$$

The area of the curved surface of a cone is πrl, where r is the radius of the base, and l is the **slant height** of the cone.

Therefore, the total surface area (S) of a cone is:

S = area of curved surface + area of base

$= \pi rl + \pi r^2$

Tip

The slant height of a cone can be calculated using Pythagoras' theorem if the dimensions of the height and base are given. The curved surface area of the cone can also be given by $\pi r\sqrt{h^2 + r^2}$

Find answers at: cambridge.org/ukschools/gcsemaths-studentbookanswers

Problem-solving framework

You are selling ice creams and need to decide on the price. With two sizes of cone available you have to decide how much to charge for each one. One cone has a radius of 3 cm and is 12 cm long; the other has a radius of 4 cm and is 16 cm long.

You are going to sell strawberry, vanilla and chocolate flavours.

The price of the small cone is £1.50. The dimensions of the smaller cone are increased by a third to get the larger cone. Show, through a comparison of the volume of ice cream, that the larger cone should not be priced at £2 and recommend a suitable price for the larger cone.

Steps for solving problems	What you would do for this example
Step 1: What have you got to do?	Compare the volume of the two cones. Recommend a price for the larger cone.
Step 2: What information do you need?	The radius and length of the small cone; the radius and length of the large cone; the formula for the volume of a cone is $\frac{1}{3} \times \pi r^2 \times h$.
Step 3: What information don't you need?	The flavours are irrelevant.
Step 4: What maths can you do?	Volume of the small cone $= \frac{1}{3} \times 3.14 \times 3 \times 3 \times 12 = 113.04 \, \text{cm}^3$ Volume of the large cone $= \frac{1}{3} \times 3.14 \times 4 \times 4 \times 16 = 267.95 \, \text{cm}^3$ Just over twice as much ice cream will fit inside the larger cone.
Step 5: Have you done it all?	No, need to suggest a suitable price. Recommended price of larger cone is £3.
Step 6: Is it correct?	Yes – double check made.

Spheres

A sphere is any perfectly round object.

Many objects include spheres or parts of spheres in their structure.

The volume of a sphere is equal to $\frac{4}{3} \pi r^3$, where r is the radius of the sphere.

The surface area of a sphere is equal to $4\pi r^2$, where r is the radius of the sphere.

WORKED EXAMPLE 6

Find the surface area and volume of a sphere with radius 3 cm. Use 3.14 as an approximate value of π. Give your answers to 2 decimal places.

Surface area $= 4 \times 3.14 \times 3 \times 3$
$= 113.04 \, \text{cm}^2$

Volume $= \frac{4}{3} \times 3.14 \times 3 \times 3 \times 3$
$= 113.04 \, \text{cm}^3$

Notice that this is numerically the same answer as for the area, so it is important that you include the correct units.

WORKED EXAMPLE 7

The radius of the Earth is approximately 6378.1 km.

a Find the approximate volume and surface area of the Earth. Use the calculator value of π. Give your answers to 4 significant figures.

b 70% of the surface of Earth is covered with water. What is the surface area of land?

a $V = \dfrac{4}{3} \times \pi \times 6378.1^3 \approx 1\,087\,000\,000\,000 \, \text{km}^3$

Surface area $= 4 \times \pi \times 6378.1^2 \approx 511\,200\,000 \, \text{km}^2$

b 30% of the Earth's surface area is land.

$0.3 \times 511\,200\,000 = 153\,400\,000 \, \text{km}^2$

> **Tip**
>
> In calculations with such large values you would normally give your answers in Standard form. You will deal with this in Chapter 29.

EXERCISE 18B

1 Calculate the volume and surface area of each object. (The objects are all closed.)

a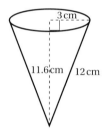

b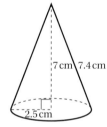

c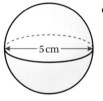

d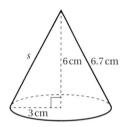

e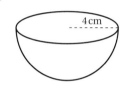

2 Earth's moon has a mean radius of 1738 km. Use the calculator value of π to find its approximate volume.

3 The table below gives some standard diameters of spherical balls used in different sports. Calculate the surface area of each ball. Assume they are round and ignore any dimples on the surface.

Give your answers to 3 significant figures.

	Sport	Standard diameter (cm)
a	snooker	5.3
b	tennis	6.5
c	football	21.6
d	golf	4.3
e	bowling	12.5
f	basketball	23.8
g	hockey	7.4
h	baseball	7.3
i	cricket	7.2

Find answers at: cambridge.org/ukschools/gcsemaths-studentbookanswers

4 A factory needs to calculate the volume and outer sloped surface area of open plastic cones which have the dimensions (in cm) given in the table. Calculate each volume and surface area.

Give your answers correct to 3 significant figures.

	Radius (*r*)	Slant height (*l*)	Perpendicular (*h*)
a	5	10	$\sqrt{75}$
b	18	34	$\sqrt{832}$
c	7	21	$\sqrt{392}$
d	16	22	$\sqrt{228}$
e	60	64	$\sqrt{496}$
f	9	26	$\sqrt{595}$
g	30	52	$\sqrt{1804}$

5 A cone and a sphere both have a diameter of 8 cm. If they have the same volume, how tall is the cone?

Composite solids

Objects in real life are very rarely composed of just one kind of geometric object. Most buildings involve a combination of solid shapes, and modern buildings often incorporate unusual shapes into their designs.

This is the winning design for the air traffic control tower at Newcastle airport. The design incorporates cut-off conical shapes around a cuboid-shaped cement tower.

This is the design of the North Gate Bus Station in Northampton. You can see that many different solids have been used in the design.

Tip

It is useful to develop a system for checking that you have included all the surfaces when you are finding the surface area of a composite shape.

When you worked with area in Chapter 12 you split composite shapes into known shapes and found the area of each shape separately. You can use the same technique to find the volume of composite solids.

To find the total surface area of a composite solid you need to find the area of each section separately. However, you cannot just automatically add the areas because the area of some faces will overlap and not form part of the 'outside' area of the solid.

WORKED EXAMPLE 8

Calculate the total volume and surface area of the object shown. Use the calculator value of π in your calculations and give final answers correct to 2 decimal places.

The object consists of a cone, cylinder and half a sphere.

Volume

Volume of cone $= \dfrac{1}{3}(\pi r^2)h$

$\qquad = \dfrac{1}{3}(\pi 3^2) \times 6$

$\qquad = 18\pi$

Volume of cylinder $= \pi r^2 h$

$\qquad = \pi 3^2 \times 9$

$\qquad = 81\pi$

Volume of half sphere $= \dfrac{2}{3}\pi r^3$

$\qquad = \dfrac{2}{3}\pi 3^3$

$\qquad = 18\pi$

Total volume $= 117\pi$

$\qquad = 367.57 \ cm^3$

Surface area

Cone:

S = area of curved surface without the area of base
(as this overlaps with the end of the cylinder)

$\qquad = \pi r l$

$\qquad = \pi \times 3 \times 6.7$

$\qquad = 20.1\pi$

Cylinder (without top and base):

$S = 2\pi r h$

$\qquad = 2 \times \pi \times 3 \times 9$

$\qquad = 54\pi$

Half sphere:

$S = 2\pi r^2$

$\qquad = 2 \times \pi \times 3^2$

$\qquad = 18\pi$

Total surface area $= 92.1\pi$

$\qquad = 289.34 \ cm^2$

EXERCISE 18C

1 Find the surface area of each solid. Give your answers correct to the nearest m² or mm² (the upper part of shape **b** is a semi-circle).

a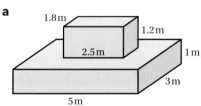

b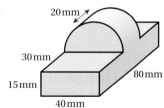

2 Calculate the volume of this capsule (the upper part of shape b and the lower parts of shape c are semi-circles).

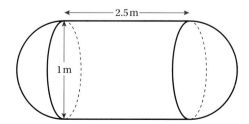

3 Calculate the volume and external surface area of this water tank. Assume the bottom section is half a cylinder and the top is a cuboid.

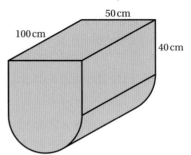

4 These metal blocks have sections cut out of them. For each block, calculate to 3 significant figures:

a the volume of the metal

b the total surface area to be coated with rust inhibitor.

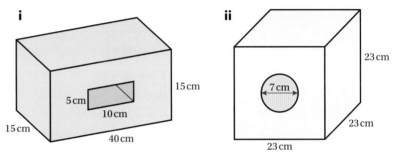

5 Determine the volume of water in a swimming pool that is 6 m wide and 30 m long. The shallow end is 2 m deep and the deep end is 3.5 m deep.

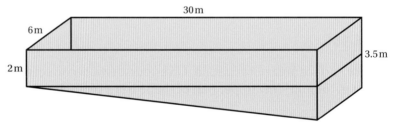

Tip

You will need Pythagoras' theorem to help with this.

6 What is the volume, to 3 significant figures, of a fish tank in the shape of a regular hexagonal prism if the hexagon has equal sides of 10 cm and the height of the tank is 30 cm?

7 Calculate the volume of the following prism. All measurements are in centimetres.

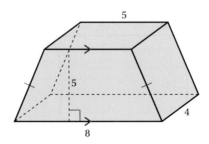

Section 3: Pyramids

Pyramids are named according to the shape of their base.

The volume of a pyramid is $\frac{1}{3}$ of the volume of a prism with the same base area and height.

Volume of a pyramid = $\frac{1}{3}$ area of base × perpendicular height.

The surface area of a pyramid is the total area of the base plus the area of each triangular side.

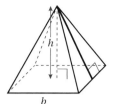

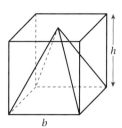

> **Tip**
>
> The slant height of a pyramid is the perpendicular height from the centre of the base of a lateral or sloping side to the top of that side

WORKED EXAMPLE 9

Calculate the volume and the surface area of this square-based pyramid.

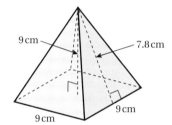

Volume $= \frac{1}{3} \times$ area of base $\times h$

$= \frac{1}{3} \times 9 \times 9 \times 9 = 243\,\text{cm}^3$

Surface area = area of square base + 4 × area of triangular sides

Surface area $= b^2 + 4 \times (\frac{1}{2} \times$ slant height $\times b)$

$= (9 \times 9) + 4 \times (\frac{1}{2} \times 7.8 \times 9)$

$= 81 + 140.4 = 221.4\,\text{cm}^2$

The perpendicular height of each triangular face can be calculated using Pythagoras' theorem

EXERCISE 18D

 These three pyramids have square bases.

Calculate the surface area and the volume of each one.

a

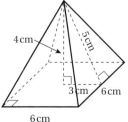

4 cm 5 cm 3 cm 6 cm 6 cm

b

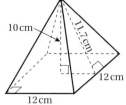

10 cm 11.7 cm 12 cm 12 cm

c

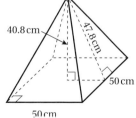

40.8 cm 47.8 cm 50 cm 50 cm

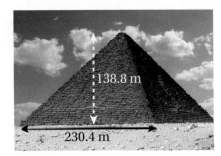

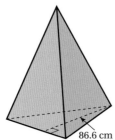

2 What is the volume of the Great Pyramid in the photograph? It has a square base.

3 What is the difference in the volumes of a pyramid with a square base of side 6 m and a pyramid with an equilateral triangle with side 6 m as a base, if both have a perpendicular height of 8 m? Take the perpendicular height of the triangular base to be 5.2 m.

4 A square-based pyramid has base sides of $6x$ and a perpendicular height of $4x$. Find, in terms of x, the volume and the surface area of the pyramid.

5 The solid wooden sculpture (left) is a triangular-based pyramid. The base is an equilateral triangle with sides of 1 m and a perpendicular height of 86.6 cm. The height of the sculpture is 2 m. Calculate the volume of wood that makes up the sculpture.

6 Ancient Egyptians used objects called obelisks in their architecture. They consisted of a square-based column with a pyramidal structure on the top.

Calculate the volume and surface area of the Obelisk of Queen Hapshetsut in the photograph. It is 30 m high, the square base has an area of 5 m² and the pyramid itself is 1.5 m high. Take the slant height of the pyramid to be 1.87 m.

7 A container must have a capacity of between 800 ml and 1 litre and the height must be 15 cm. Draw up a table to show possible dimensions, to the nearest millimetre, of a cylinder, cone and square-based pyramid that would meet these requirements.

Checklist of learning and understanding

Volume

- Volume is the amount of space a 3D object occupies.
- Volume is calculated in cubic units.
- The volume of a prism and a cylinder is the area of base × length.
- Volume of a cone $= \dfrac{1}{3} \times$ area of base × height.
- Volume of a sphere $= \dfrac{4}{3} \pi r^2$.
- Volume of a pyramid $= \dfrac{1}{3} \times$ area of base × height.
- The volumes of standard solids can be calculated by remembering only three formulae:
  - sphere – which is a 'one off'
  - prism – which is base area × height
  - pyramid – which is $\dfrac{1}{3} \times$ base area × height.
- As long as you know how to calculate the area of the relevant base, all the volume formulae fall easily into place.

Surface area

- The surface area of a solid is the total area of all the external faces.

Chapter review

For additional questions on the topics in this chapter, visit GCSE Mathematics Online.

1 How much canvas is in this tent? (Assume the shape is a triangular prism and that there is no base sheet.)

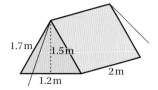

2 What is the volume of this model house?

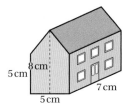

3 What is the volume of this piece of art sculpture (right)? It is made of a cube with a cylinder cut out through the middle of it.

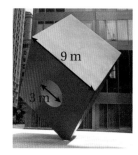

4 The volume of a room is needed in order to work out which air conditioning unit is required. Calculate the volume of a room measuring $23\,m \times 14\,m \times 13\,m$.

Diagram **NOT** accurately drawn

5 Jane has a carton of orange juice.

The carton is in the shape of a cuboid.

The depth of the orange juice in the carton is 8 cm.

Jane closes the carton.

Then she turns the carton over so that it stands on the shaded face.

Work out the depth, in cm, of the orange juice now.

(3 marks)

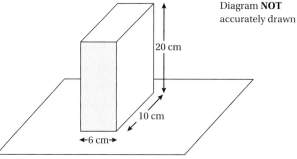

©*Pearson Education Ltd 2012*

6 The dimensions of a cube are whole numbers. If the volume of this cube is 64 cm³ which of the following whole numbers could be a side length?

A 4   **B** 10   **C** 8   **D** 16   **E** 5

7 Calculate:

a the volume of a tin of dog food.

b the surface area of the printed label.

8 How could you prove to someone sceptical, but unmathematical, that the volume of a pyramid is $\frac{1}{3}$ of the volume of a prism with the same base area and height?

Find answers at: cambridge.org/ukschools/gcsemaths-studentbookanswers

19 Percentages

In this chapter you will learn how to ...

- work interchangeably with fractions, decimals and percentages.
- calculate a percentage of an amount.
- express a quantity as a percentage of another.
- increase and decrease amounts by a given percentage.
- solve problems involving percentage change.

For more resources relating to this chapter, visit GCSE Mathematics Online.

Using mathematics: real-life applications

Percentages are often used in daily life to express fractions. For example, you might see adverts claiming that 76% of pets prefer a particular brand of food or that 90% of dentists recommend a particular type of toothpaste. Sale price-reductions, discounts and interest rates are usually given as percentages.

"Statistics in the media are often reported as percentages. This makes it easier to understand, but percentages can also be misleading – 60% sounds like a lot, but it could just mean 3 out of 5 people interviewed." *(Statistician)*

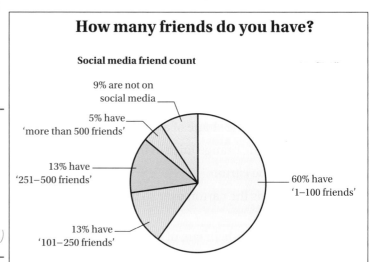

How many friends do you have?

Social media friend count

- 9% are not on social media
- 5% have 'more than 500 friends'
- 13% have '251–500 friends'
- 13% have '101–250 friends'
- 60% have '1–100 friends'

Before you start ...

Ch 7	You need to be able to multiply and divide by 100.	**1** Where should the decimal point go in each answer? **a** $210 \div 100 = 21$ **b** $21 \div 100 = 21$ **c** $0.24 \times 100 = 24$ **d** $0.024 \times 100 = 24$
Ch 6	You need to be able to cancel to express fractions in simplest terms.	**2** Match each fraction in box A to its equivalent from box B. | Box A			Box B		| |---|---|---|---|---|---| | $\frac{16}{36}$ | $\frac{15}{35}$ | $\frac{30}{36}$ | $\frac{1}{4}$ | $\frac{3}{4}$ | $\frac{1}{3}$ | | $\frac{9}{36}$ | $\frac{39}{52}$ | $\frac{13}{39}$ | $\frac{5}{6}$ | $\frac{3}{7}$ | $\frac{4}{9}$ |
Ch 7	You should be able to express any percentage as a decimal.	**3** Are the following statements true or false? **a** $20\% = 0.02$ **b** $25\% = 1.4$ **c** $3\% = 0.3$ **d** $12.5\% = 0.125$ **e** $1.25\% = 0.125$

Assess your starting point using the Launchpad

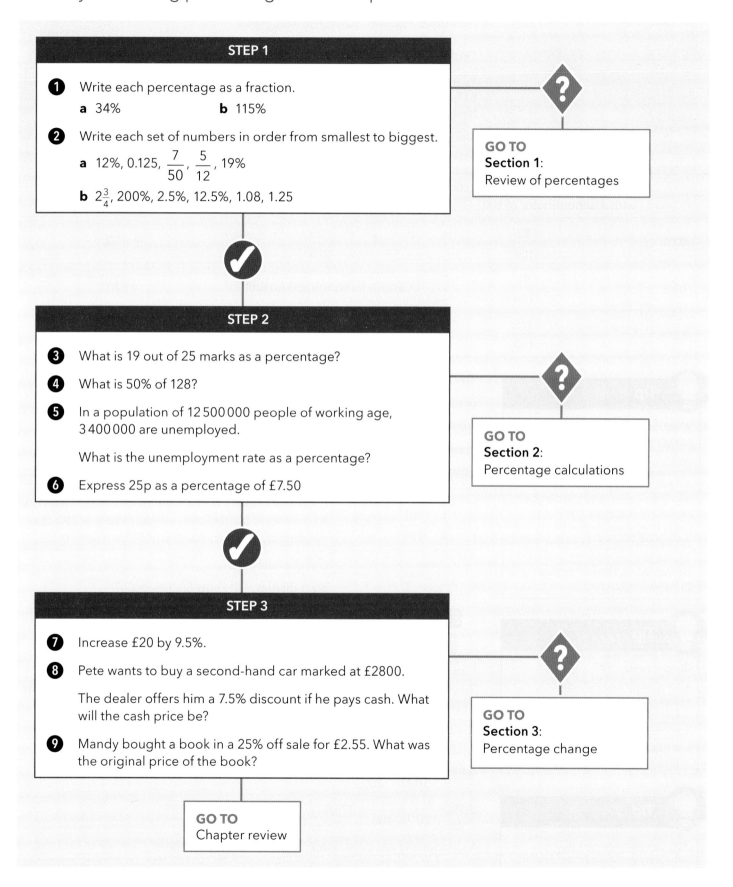

STEP 1

1 Write each percentage as a fraction.
  a 34%   **b** 115%

2 Write each set of numbers in order from smallest to biggest.
  a 12%, 0.125, $\frac{7}{50}$, $\frac{5}{12}$, 19%
  b $2\frac{3}{4}$, 200%, 2.5%, 12.5%, 1.08, 1.25

GO TO
Section 1:
Review of percentages

STEP 2

3 What is 19 out of 25 marks as a percentage?

4 What is 50% of 128?

5 In a population of 12 500 000 people of working age, 3 400 000 are unemployed.

  What is the unemployment rate as a percentage?

6 Express 25p as a percentage of £7.50

GO TO
Section 2:
Percentage calculations

STEP 3

7 Increase £20 by 9.5%.

8 Pete wants to buy a second-hand car marked at £2800.

  The dealer offers him a 7.5% discount if he pays cash. What will the cash price be?

9 Mandy bought a book in a 25% off sale for £2.55. What was the original price of the book?

GO TO
Section 3:
Percentage change

GO TO
Chapter review

Find answers at: cambridge.org/ukschools/gcsemaths-studentbookanswers

Section 1: Review of percentages

Percentages, fractions and decimals

During 2014, a mobile phone maker did a survey of 872 people.

92% of people said they would feel stressed if their phone battery ran out and 81% of people said that running out of power on their phones had led to them having a bad experience.

Since 92% means 92 out of every 100 and 81% means 81 out of every 100, percentages can be changed to fractions and to decimals.

	Write the percentage as a fraction with a denominator of 100	For a fraction, simplify if possible.	For a decimal, put the decimal point in the correct position.
92%	$= \dfrac{92}{100}$	$= \dfrac{23}{25}$	$= 0.92$
81%	$= \dfrac{81}{100}$	Cannot be simplified further	$= 0.81$
125%	$= \dfrac{125}{100}$	$= 1\frac{25}{100}$	$= 1.25$

Tip

When you use a calculator to convert a fraction to a percentage you are actually first changing $\frac{2}{3}$ to a decimal ($2 \div 3 = 0.6666666667$) and then converting the decimal to a percentage. You do not enter the percentage sign in the calculation because the values you are entering are not percentages. The percentage is the answer you get.

Tip

Simple rules:
- to change any fraction or decimal into a percentage you just multiply by 100
- to change any percentage into a fraction or decimal you just divide by 100.

Tip

You can also change all the values to decimals or equivalent fractions to compare them if the numbers are easier.

The mobile phone survey also showed that nearly $\frac{1}{2}$ of the people surveyed could remember no more than three phone numbers.

Another survey showed that $\frac{2}{3}$ of people aged 11 to 17 take an internet-connected device to bed with them every night.

Fractions can be written as percentages.

$\dfrac{1}{2} = \dfrac{50}{100} = 50\%$	If the denominator is a factor of 100, it can be written as an equivalent fraction with a denominator of 100. Do not simplify, write the fraction of 100 as a percentage.
$\dfrac{2}{3}$ ② ÷ ③ × ⑩ 66.666666667	Using a calculator. Your display will show 66.666666667 This is the percentage. Write it as 66.67% (correct to 2 decimal places).

To change a decimal to a percentage write it as a fraction with a denominator of 100, or use your calculator to multiply it by 100.

$$0.3 = \frac{3}{10} = \frac{30}{100} = 30\% \qquad\qquad 0.3 \times 100 = 30\%$$

$$0.025 = \frac{25}{1000} = \frac{2.5}{100} = 2.5\% \qquad\qquad 0.025 \times 100 = 2.5\%$$

$$3.75 = \frac{37.5}{10} = \frac{375}{100} = 375\% \qquad\qquad 3.75 \times 100 = 375\%$$

Comparing percentages, fractions and decimals

To compare a mixed set of percentages, fractions and decimals, change them all to percentages.

WORKED EXAMPLE 1

Write the following in ascending order.

$35\%, \dfrac{1}{3}, 0.38, \dfrac{2}{5}, \dfrac{2}{7}$

35%	$\dfrac{1}{3}$	0.38	$\dfrac{2}{5}$	$\dfrac{2}{7}$
35%	$\dfrac{1}{3} \times 100$ $= 33.33\%$	0.38×100 $= 38\%$	$\dfrac{2}{5} \times 100$ $= 40\%$	$\dfrac{2}{7} \times 100$ $= 28.57\%$

Convert all the fractions and decimals to percentages. Remember to round values that are not exact to a suitable level of accuracy.

The order is: $\dfrac{2}{7}, \dfrac{1}{3}, 35\%, 0.38, \dfrac{2}{5}$

Remember to use the original fractions when you write the answer, not the percentages you have changed them to.

EXERCISE 19A

1 Express the following as percentages. Use fractional ($32\frac{1}{2}\%$) or decimal (2.5%) percentages where you need to.

a $\dfrac{5}{100}$ b $\dfrac{27}{50}$ c $\dfrac{11}{25}$ d $\dfrac{17}{20}$

e $\dfrac{1}{2}$ f $\dfrac{2}{3}$ g $\dfrac{5}{8}$ h $\dfrac{92}{50}$

i 0.3 j 0.04 k 0.47 l 1.12

m 2.07 n 2.25 o 0.035 p 0.007

2 Write each of the following percentages as a common fraction in its simplest terms.

a 25% b 80% c 90% d 12.5%

e 50% f 98% g 60% h 22%

3 Write the decimal equivalent of each percentage.

a 82% b 97% c 45% d 28.6%

e 0.05% f 0.08% g 0.006% h 0.0007%

i 125% j 300% k 7.28% l 9.007%

4 a If 93.5% of the students in a school have WiFi at home, what percentage do not?

b If $\dfrac{2}{3}$ of all the SIM cards sold in a mobile phone shop are pre-paid, what percentage are not pre-paid?

c 0.325 of computer users back up their work every day. What percentage do not do this?

5 Zack spends 24.7% of a day playing computer games, 0.138 of the day doing homework and $\dfrac{3}{8}$ of the day playing sport.

What percentage of the day is spent doing other things?

6 Write each set of values in ascending order.

a $\frac{1}{20}$, 30%, 0.1, $\frac{3}{5}$, 0.8%

b 0.75, 57%, 0.88, $\frac{1}{4}$, 0.15

c $\frac{2}{3}$, 0.75, 60%, $\frac{9}{10}$, 0.25

d $\frac{3}{7}$, 0.43, 45%, 0.395, $\frac{4}{9}$

e $\frac{5}{6}$, 80%, $\frac{19}{25}$, 55%, 49.3%

7 A media company states that 83.5% of its customers read the news online every day.

What fraction of the customers is this?

8 Anna pays 0.06 of her salary into her credit card account.

What percentage of her salary is this?

9 During one shift at work, Sandy spent $\frac{9}{20}$ of her time texting on her phone.
What percentage of the shift was she not texting?

10 Angie gets the following marks for three maths assignments: $\frac{31}{40}$, $\frac{27}{30}$ and $\frac{13}{15}$.

a Which of these marks is the highest?

b What is her mean result for the three assignments as a percentage?

Section 2: Percentage calculations

WORK IT OUT 19.1

$9\frac{1}{2}$% of 400 is 38.

Which of the following methods will give you the correct answer?

Explain why the other methods won't work.

Method A	Method B	Method C	Method D	Method E
$\frac{9}{200} \times 400$	$\frac{19}{200} \times \frac{400}{1}$	$\frac{19}{2} \times 400$	9.5×400	$\frac{9.5}{400} \times 100$

To find a percentage of an amount you have to multiply by the percentage. Unless you use a calculator, you have to write the percentage as a fraction (with a denominator of 100) or a decimal.

WORKED EXAMPLE 2

What is 12% of 700?

Using fractions	Using decimals	Using a calculator
$\frac{12}{1\cancel{00}} \times 7\cancel{00}$ $= 84$	0.12×700 $= 0.12 \times 100 \times 7$ $= 12 \times 7$ $= 84$	7 0 0 × 1 2 % 84

Calculator tip

Make sure you know how to use the % button on your calculator.

You might need to enter 12% × 700 or 700 × 12% (some calculators will work both ways).

On some calculators you need to press the = but on others you might not have to.

Check how your calculator works by finding 12% of 350. The answer should be 42.

You do enter the percentage sign in these calculations because one of the values you are working with is a percentage.

EXERCISE 19B

1 Calculate.

  a 5% of 250   **b** 9% of 400   **c** 20% of 120

  d 65% of 4500   **e** 12% of 75   **f** 75% of 360

  g 32% of 50   **h** 110% of 60   **i** 150% of 90

2 Calculate, giving your answers as mixed numbers or decimals as necessary.

  a 19% of £50   **b** 60% of 70 kg   **c** 45% of 35 cm

  d 90% of 29 kg   **e** $3\frac{1}{2}$% of £400   **f** 2.6% of 80 minutes

  g 7.4% of £1000   **h** 3.8% of 180 m   **i** $9\frac{2}{3}$% of 600 litres

> **Tip**
>
> Remember your answer will have a unit not a percentage sign. You are not working out a percentage here, you are working out what a given percentage of a quantity is.

3 Annie got 85% for a test that was out of 80 marks. What was her mark out of 80?

4 A salesperson at a mobile phone shop estimates that about 3% of phones come back for some sort of repair in the first week.

If the shop sells 180 phones, how many can they expect to come back for repairs in the first week?

5 46% of residents in an area throw out the local free newspaper without even looking at it; the rest read some or all of it.

If there are 2450 residents, how many people:

a don't look at the paper

b read some or all of it?

6 Of 240 trains arriving at King's Cross, 2.5% arrived early and 13.75% arrived late.

How many trains arrived on time?

7 A tablet computer is advertised for sale for £899 excluding VAT.

Nisha wanted to buy it when VAT was 17.5% but she didn't get round to it and VAT was increased to 20% before she bought it.

How much would she have saved if she had bought it when VAT was 17.5%?

8 7.5% of a 620 m² market garden is set aside for growing tulips and the rest is used to grow vegetables.

How many square metres of land is used to grow:

a tulips   **b** vegetables?

9 The population of a town in Cornwall increases by about 24.8% each summer.

If the population of the town is normally 12 760, how many people move in during the summer?

10 Pure gold contains 24 parts (called carats) of gold in every 24 parts. $\dfrac{24}{24} = 100\%$ gold.

18 carat gold contains 18 parts pure gold per 24 parts and 9 carat gold contains 9 parts pure gold per 24 parts.

a Work out the percentage of pure gold in 9 carat and 18 carat gold.

b If Naz buys an 18 carat gold ring that weighs 7.3 grams, how much pure gold does it contain?

c If Vishnu buys a 9 carat gold pendant that has a mass of 16.3 grams, how much pure gold does it contain?

d Do you think it is accurate to label 9 carat gold as gold? Explain your answer.

EXERCISE 19C

Crime statistics are often given as percentages, but these can be misleading.

Use the following data to show how expressing values as a percentage increase can be misleading.

Location	Number of violent crimes in Year 1	Number of violent crimes in Year 2	% change in crime rate
village	12	18	50%
town	87	98	12.6%
city	1234	1230	−0.3%

1 Which place appears to have a high crime rate using these percentages? Why?

2 Which place do you think is really the most risky in terms of crime? Explain your answer.

3 What information do you think is needed to decide which location is more or less risky?

Expressing one quantity as a percentage of another

You can write one quantity as a percentage of another quantity by writing the first quantity as a fraction of the other and then multiplying by 100 to get a percentage. The two quantities must be in the same units before you write them as a fraction.

Tip

You expressed one quantity as a fraction of another in Chapter 6. Read through that work again if you cannot remember how to do this.

WORK IT OUT 19.2

Brian has run 1500 m of a 5 km race when he gets a cramp in his foot.

What percentage of the race has he completed at this stage?

Which of these two students has got the correct answer? Why is the other one wrong?

Student A	Student B
$\dfrac{1500}{5} \times 100 = 300 \times 100$ $= 300\%$	$\dfrac{1500}{5000} \times 100 = \dfrac{3}{10} \times 100$ $= 30\%$

Tip

When you convert quantities to get them to the same unit you can avoid decimal values by choosing the smaller units (for example, making both units metres in this example rather than making them both kilometres).

EXERCISE 19D

1 Express the first amount as a percentage of the second.

Give your answer correct to no more than 2 decimal places.

a 400 m of 5 km
b 45 m of 3 km
c 150 m of 1 km
d 8 cm of 2 m
e 14 mm of 4 cm
f 19 cm of 3 m
g 25p of £4
h 66p of £3.50
i 20 seconds of a minute
j 25 seconds of 1.5 minutes
k 750 g of 23 kg
l 800 g of 1.5 kg
m 4 days of a week
n 3 days of 6 weeks
o 800 kg of 3 tonnes
p 8.4 tonnes of 50 000 kg
q 500 mm of 2 m
r 90 mm of 14 cm
s 350 ml of 2 litres
t 5 ml of 0.5 litres

2 Sandra got 19 out of 24 for an assignment and Nina got 23 out of 30.

Which girl got the higher percentage mark?

3 In a local election there were 5400 registered voters. Of these, 3240 voted.

What was the percentage voter turnout?

4 Mel improved his running time for the 400 m race by 3 seconds.

If his previous running time was 50 seconds, what is his percentage improvement?

5 Kenny had a box of 40 chocolates. He ate 32 of them.

What percentage of the chocolates remain?

6 Sylvia keeps a record of how many sets she wins when she plays tennis against her sister.

In the past month she won 19 out of 27 sets. What percentage of the sets did she lose?

Find answers at: cambridge.org/ukschools/gcsemaths-studentbookanswers

Nutritional values
(Per 30 g serving)

Carbohydrates	19 g
(of which sugars)	6.2 g
Fat	3.8 g
Sodium	93 mg

7 The longest kiss lasted 58 hours, 35 minutes and 58 seconds and was achieved by Ekkachai Tiranarat and Laksana Tiranarat at an event organised by Ripley's Believe It or Not!, in Pattaya, Thailand, on 12–14 February 2013.

What percentage of the three-day event was this?

8 Read the label (left) and answer the questions.

a Calculate the combined percentage of fat and sugar in a serving.

b What percentage of a serving is sodium?

9 If x is 40% of y, what percentage of x is y?

10 $2n$ less x% of $2n$ is equivalent to n plus x% of n.

What is x%?

Section 3: Percentage change

You will often see changes (increases or decreases) in amounts expressed as percentages. For example, you might read that the price of petrol is to increase by 5.5% or that the cost of mobile broadband has decreased by 15% over the past year.

Increasing or decreasing an amount by a percentage

> **WORK IT OUT 19.3**
>
> A school population of 650 students increases by 12%.
>
> At the same time, the registration fee of £120 decreases by 15%. Work out:
>
> **a** the new student population
>
> **b** the new registration fee.
>
> Look at these examples to see how two different students solved these problems.
>
> Which method seems easier to you?
>
> Could you use your calculator to do these calculations? How?
>
> | | **Student A** | **Student B** |
> |---|---|---|
> | **a** | 650 increased by 12% $$12\% \text{ of } 650 = \frac{12}{100} \times 650$$ $$= 78$$ $$650 + 78 = 728$$ There are now 728 students. | 650 increased by 12% Old population = 100% New population = old + increase $$= 100 + 12\% = 112\%$$ $$112\% = \frac{112}{100} = 1.12$$ $$1.12 \times 650 = 728$$ The new student population is 728. |
>
> Continues on next page …

b

120 decreased by 15%	£120 decreased by 15%
15% of 120 = $\dfrac{15}{100} \times 120$ $= 18$ £120 − £18 = £102 The new registration fee is £102.	Old fee = 100% New fee = 100% − 15% = 85% $85\% = \dfrac{85}{100} = 0.85$ $0.85 \times 120 = 102$ The new registration fee is £102.

Tip

You can express any % increase or decrease as a multiplier.

To increase a number by $x\%$, multiply it by $1 + \dfrac{x}{100}$. So, to increase by 12%, multiply by 1.12.

To decrease a number by $x\%$, multiply it by $1 - \dfrac{x}{100}$. So, to decrease by 15%, multiply by 0.85.

EXERCISE 19E

1 Increase each amount by the given percentage.

a £48 increased by 14% **b** £700 increased by 35%

c £30 increased by 7.6% **d** £40 000 increased by 0.59%

e £90 increased by 9.5% **f** £80 increased by 24.6%

2 Decrease each amount by the given percentage.

a £68 decreased by 14% **b** £800 decreased by 35%

c £90 decreased by 7.6% **d** £20 000 decreased by 0.59%

e £85 decreased by 9.5% **f** £60 decreased by 24.6%

3 A building which cost £125 000 to build, increased in value by $3\frac{1}{2}\%$. What is it worth now?

4 Josh currently earns £3125 per month.

If he receives an increase of 3.8%, what will his new monthly earnings be, correct to the nearest pound?

5 Sally earns £25 per shift. Her boss says she can either have £7 more per shift or a 20% increase.

Which is the better offer?

6 The membership of a sports club increased by 26% this year.

If they had 284 members the previous year, how many will they have now?

7 Sammy bought £2500 worth of shares.

At the end of the first month their value had decreased by 4.25%.

At the end of the second month Sammy checked the value again and found it had gone up 1.5% from the previous month.

Work out the value of the shares at the end of each month.

8 Amira earns £25 000 per year plus 12% commission on any sales she generates.

Calculate her annual earnings if she sold £145 250 worth of goods.

Find answers at: cambridge.org/ukschools/gcsemaths-studentbookanswers

9 This summer, an amusement park increased its entry prices by 25% to £15.00.

This summer, the number of people entering the park dropped 8% from the previous summer to 25 530.

a What was the entry price the previous summer?

b How many visitors were there the previous summer?

c If the running costs of the amusement park remained the same as the previous summer and they made a 30% profit on the entry fees in this summer, how much was their profit amount in pounds?

10 The news media reports that the winter of 2014 was 24.5% wetter than the average winter.

Explain what this means and what data you would need to work out how much more rain fell in 2014.

11 A journalist is investigating how the price of a Eurostar train ticket varies depending on whether you buy it in London or Brussels (as a result of exchange rates).

The same ticket costs €240 in London and €225 in Brussels.

Use this information to complete the statement 'Tickets bought in London are __% more expensive than those bought in Brussels.'

Finding original values

If you know the percentage by which an amount has increased or decreased, you can use it to find the original amount. Problems involving original values are often called reverse or inverse percentages. When you work with these problems you need to remember that you are dealing with percentages of the original values.

WORKED EXAMPLE 3

A shop is offering a 10% discount on all sale goods.

Jessie bought a bike in the sale and paid £108.

What was the original price of the bike?

90% of x = £108

> If the cost is reduced by 10% then you are actually paying 90%.
>
> If you let the original amount be x, you can write an equation and solve it to find x.

$\therefore \dfrac{90}{100}x = 108$

$\therefore 90x = 100 \times 108 = 10\,800$

$\therefore x = \dfrac{10\,800}{90} = 120$

> You could write $0.9x = 108$
>
> 0.9 is a multiplying factor.
>
> Then, $x = \dfrac{108}{0.9}$

The original price was £120.

Tip

Undoing a 10% decrease is not the same as just increasing the sale price by 10%. If you add 10% to the sale price of £108 you will get £118.80 which is **NOT** the right answer.

WORKED EXAMPLE 4

Sameen sells her shares and receives £3450. This gives her a profit of 15%.
What did she pay for the shares originally?

Let the cost price be x.

$1.15x = 3450$

$x = \dfrac{3450}{1.15}$

$x = 3000$

15% profit means an increase of 15%, so the selling price = 115% of the cost.

The multiplying factor is 1.15.

She paid £3000 for the shares.

Check this by increasing 3000 by 15%.

$3000 \times 1.15 = 3450.$

EXERCISE 19F

1 Find the original value if:

 a 25% is £30

 b 8% is 120 g

 c 120% is 800 kg

 d 115% is £2000

2 VAT of 20% is added to most goods before they are sold.

Some tourists to the UK can claim back the VAT when they leave the country.

Work out the price of each of these items without VAT to see what a tourist would pay for them.

The prices given here include VAT.

 a necklace £1200

 b camera £145.50

 c painting £865

 d boots £54.99

3 Misha paid £40 for a DVD box set in a 20% off sale.

What was the original price of the DVD set?

4 In a large school 240 pupils are in Year 10. This is 20% of the school population.

 a How many pupils are there in total in the school?

 b How many pupils are in the other years at this school?

5 Susie was told that her pay had increased by 15%. Her new pay is £172.50.

What was her pay before the increase?

6 9 carat gold is 37.5% pure gold.

A piece of 9 carat gold jewellery is tested and found to contain 97.5 grams of pure gold.

What did the piece of jewellery weigh?

7 Julia is training for a marathon and she reduces her weight by 5% over a three-month period.

If she weighs 58 kg at the end of the period, what did she weigh at the start?

8 In a particularly hard ultramarathon, only 310 runners completed the course within the cut-off time.

If this represents 62% of the runners, how many runners started the race?

Checklist of learning and understanding

Review of percentages

- 'Per cent' means 'parts per hundred'.
- To convert a percentage to a fraction write the percentage with a denominator of 100 and simplify.
- To convert percentages to decimals divide by 100.
- To order a mixture of fractions, decimals and percentages change them all to percentages or decimals.

Percentage calculations

- To find a percentage of an amount, express the percentage as a fraction over 100 and then multiply the fraction by the amount.
- To express one quantity (A) as a percentage of another quantity (B), make sure the units are the same and then calculate $\dfrac{\text{quantity A}}{\text{quantity B}} \times 100$.

Percentage change

- To increase or decrease an amount by a percentage, find the percentage amount and add or subtract it from the original amount.
- Or, use a multiplier:
  - to increase an amount by $x\%$, the multiplier is $\left(1 + \dfrac{x}{100}\right)$
  - to decrease an amount by $x\%$, the multiplier is $\left(1 - \dfrac{x}{100}\right)$.
- To find an original value when you know the percentage increase or decrease and the new amount, make an equation and use reverse percentages to solve for x.

Chapter review

For additional questions on the topics in this chapter, visit GCSE Mathematics Online.

1 Write each percentage as a fraction.

   a 25%   **b** 30%   **c** 3.5%

2 Express each of these as a percentage.

   a $\dfrac{1}{20}$ **b** $\dfrac{1}{8}$ **c** $\dfrac{8}{15}$

   d 0.5   **e** 1.25   **f** 0.005

3 The value of an investment increased from £120 000 to £124 800.

What percentage increase is this?

4 The population of New Orleans was 484 674 before Hurricane Katrina.

Afterwards, the population had decreased by 53.9%.

What was the population afterwards?

5 Shaz works 30 hours per week. She wants to increase this by 12%.

How many hours will she then work per week?

6 Express as a percentage

   a 3 hours of one day   **b** 750 metres of 2 km.

7 The price of a plane ticket was reduced by 8% to £423.20.

What was the original price of the ticket?

8 Nick sold his shares for £1147.50 and made a 35% profit.

What did he pay for the shares?

9 A shop normally makes a profit of 32% on computer sales.

During a promotion, the marked selling prices of computers are reduced by 15%.

What is the cost price of a computer that sells for £980 during the promotion?

10 Mr and Mrs Adams sold their house for £168 000

They made a profit of 12% on the price they paid for the house.

Calculate how much they paid for the house.   *(3 marks)*

©*Pearson Education Ltd 2012*

 Find answers at: cambridge.org/ukschools/gcsemaths-studentbookanswers

20 Ratio

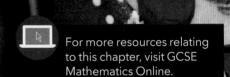

In this chapter you will learn how to …

- work with equivalent ratios.
- divide quantities in a given ratio.
- identify and work with fractions in ratio problems.
- apply ratio to real-life contexts and problems, such as those involving conversion, comparison, scaling, mixing and concentrations.

For more resources relating to this chapter, visit GCSE Mathematics Online.

Using mathematics: real-life applications

Converting between different currencies, working out which packet of crisps is the best value for money, mixing large quantities of cement and scaling up a recipe to cater for more people all involve reasoning using ratios.

"Every day customers bring me paints to match. I have to understand how changing the ratio of base colours affects the colour of the paint and how to scale the quantities up and down for larger or smaller amounts of paint. If I get it wrong, customers will have patches of different colours and their walls would look quite strange." *(Paint technician)*

Before you start …

Ch 6	You need to be able to identify and simplify fractions.	**1**	**a** In a class of 35 pupils 21 are boys. What fraction of the class are girls? **b** What fraction of this shape is shaded? Write your answer in its simplest form.
Ch 6	You need to be able to find a fraction of a quantity.	**2**	Find $\frac{2}{3}$ of 42
Ch 6	You need to be able to find an original amount given a fraction.	**3**	There are 51 parents of students in the audience at a school play. These parents make up $\frac{3}{4}$ of the audience. How many people are in the audience?

Assess your starting point using the Launchpad

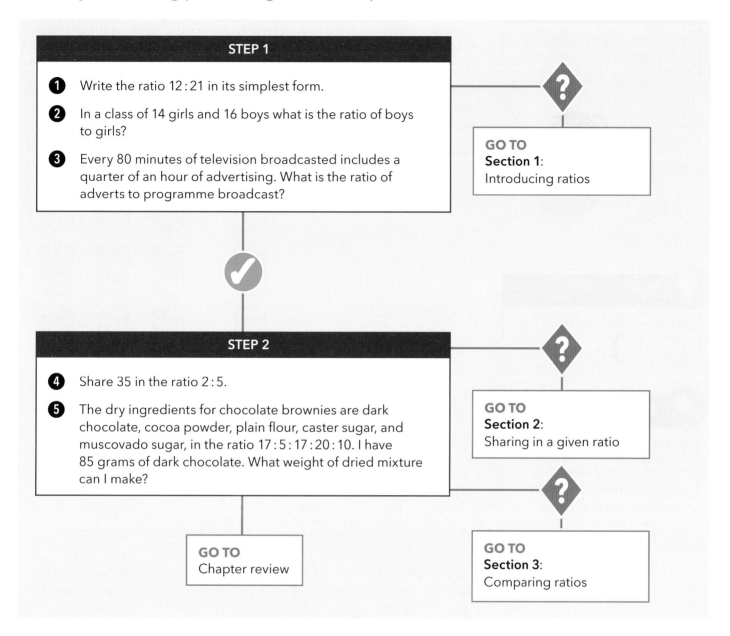

STEP 1

1 Write the ratio 12 : 21 in its simplest form.

2 In a class of 14 girls and 16 boys what is the ratio of boys to girls?

3 Every 80 minutes of television broadcasted includes a quarter of an hour of advertising. What is the ratio of adverts to programme broadcast?

GO TO
Section 1:
Introducing ratios

STEP 2

4 Share 35 in the ratio 2 : 5.

5 The dry ingredients for chocolate brownies are dark chocolate, cocoa powder, plain flour, caster sugar, and muscovado sugar, in the ratio 17 : 5 : 17 : 20 : 10. I have 85 grams of dark chocolate. What weight of dried mixture can I make?

GO TO
Section 2:
Sharing in a given ratio

GO TO
Chapter review

GO TO
Section 3:
Comparing ratios

Section 1: Introducing ratios

Most colours of paint can be mixed from the four base colours: blue, yellow, red and white.

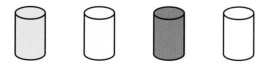

The amount of each base colour is important for getting the same shade of, say, green at different times.

Find answers at: cambridge.org/ukschools/gcsemaths-studentbookanswers

Key vocabulary

ratio: a comparison of different parts or amounts in a particular order.

Tip

With many ratio questions, drawing a picture of the situation can help you work it out.

Key vocabulary

proportion: the number or amount of a group compared to the whole, often expressed as a fraction, percentage or ratio.

equivalent: having the same value, two ratios are equivalent if one is a multiple of the other.

Paint technicians can mix the same shade of green over and over by mixing yellow and blue paints in a particular **ratio**.

Ratio describes how parts of equal size relate to each other. A ratio of yellow to blue paint of $1:3$ means one unit of yellow for every three units of blue. This would give a very dark green.

A ratio of yellow to blue paint of $5:1$ means five units of yellow for every one unit of blue. This would give a much lighter green.

The diagram below shows a ratio of yellow to blue of $3:9$.

Dividing both parts by three simplifies the ratio to give $1:3$

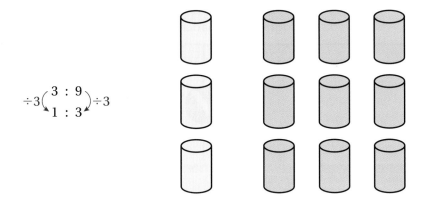

Mixing paint in the ratio $3:9$ would give the same colour as mixing it in the ratio $1:3$ because the colours are mixed in the same ratio. The yellow paint makes up the same **proportion** of the mix in both cases.

The ratios $3:9$ and $1:3$ are **equivalent** ratios.

The difference between ratio and proportion

A ratio compares two or more quantities with each other. A proportion compares a quantity to the 'whole' of which it is a part.

For example, in the dark green paint mixture, the ratio of yellow paint to blue paint is $3:9$ or $1:3$. The proportion of yellow paint in the dark green paint mixture is $\frac{3}{12}, \frac{1}{4}$ or 25%.

EXERCISE 20A

1 36 girls, 45 boys and 9 teachers went on a school trip.

   a What is the ratio of boys to girls?

   b What is the ratio of pupils to teachers?

c What is the ratio of pupils to people on the trip?

d The school policy is that each teacher can be responsible for no more than 10 pupils. Does this trip meet this requirement?

2 In each diagram, what is the ratio of shaded squares to unshaded squares? Write the answers in simplest form.

a   **b** 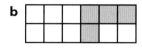 **c**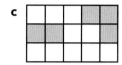

3 In each diagram, what is the ratio of shaded squares to total squares? Write the answers in simplest form.

a   **b**  **c**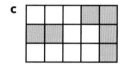

4 The ratio of shaded to unshaded squares in this diagram is 1 : 3. How many more squares need to be shaded to make the ratio 2 : 3?

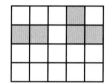

5 The distance between the post office and the bank on the local high street is represented as 5 cm on a map. In real life this distance is 20 m. What is the scale of the map (as a ratio)?

6 On a scale drawing of a cruise ship a cabin is 8 cm from the restaurant. On the actual ship the distance is 76 m. Express the distances as a ratio.

7 A natural history programme lasts 90 minutes. The crew recorded 60 hours of footage. What is the ratio of used footage to recorded footage?

Tip

Ratios do not include units. To compare measured amounts you need to make sure they are written in the same units.

8 **a** Use the diagram (right) to find the ratio of:

    i side *AB* to side *AC* **ii** side *EB* to side *DC* **iii** side *AE* to side *AD*

b What does this tell you about triangles *ABE* and *ACD*?

c What does it tell you about lines *EB* and *DC*?

d What is the ratio of angle *AEB* to angle *EDC*?

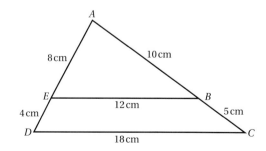

9 A jam recipe uses 55 g of fruit for every 100 g of jam. The rest is sugar. What is the ratio of fruit to sugar?

10 An adult ticket for the cinema is one and a half times the price for a child's ticket. What is the ratio of the price of an adult ticket to the price of a child's ticket?

11 According to recent statistics $\frac{3}{5}$ of 16-year-olds have a mobile phone.

What is the ratio of 16-year-olds with mobiles to those without?

12 After an increase of 20% in the number of boys in a school, the ratio of boys to girls is 3 : 4. If there are now 630 pupils in the school, how many boys were there originally?

13 If $\frac{1}{5}$ of chocolates in a box are dark chocolate, $\frac{1}{2}$ are milk and the rest are white, what is the ratio of dark : milk : white chocolate?

Tip

The box method shown in the example is useful for working out shares in a given ratio problem.

Section 2: Sharing in a given ratio

WORKED EXAMPLE 1

A group of three office workers form a lottery syndicate. Together they buy eight lottery tickets a week. Simon pays £1 a week, Oliver £3 and Lucy £4. They win £32 000.

Should they each get an equal share of the winnings? If not, how should they share their winnings? What is the fairest way?

The winnings should be distributed between Simon, Oliver and Lucy in the ratio 1 : 3 : 4.

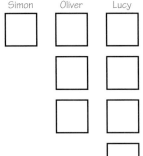

This is the fairest way, as it is in the same ratio as they bought tickets.

Every box has to have the same quantity in it. In total there are eight boxes, in which you have to share £32 000.

Each box gets £32 000 ÷ 8 = £4000

So:

Simon receives £4000.

Oliver receives 3 × £4000 = £12 000

Lucy receives 4 × £4000 = £16 000

£4000 + £12 000 + £16 000 = £32 000

Check that the shared quantities sum to the original amount.

This also shows that Simon gets $\frac{1}{8}$ of the winnings, Oliver $\frac{3}{8}$ and Lucy $\frac{1}{2}$.

EXERCISE 20B

1 Share 144 in each of the given ratios.

   a 1:3   **b** 4:5   **c** 11:1

   d 2:3:1   **e** 1:2:5   **f** 2:7:5:4

2 To make mortar you mix sand and cement in the ratio of 4:1.

   a How much sand is needed to make 25 kilograms of mortar?

   b What fraction of the mix is cement?

3 The first two-colour £2 coin was issued in 1998. The inner circle is made of cupronickel. This is copper and nickel in the ratio 3:1. The inner circle weighs 6 grams. How much copper is used to make the centres of ten £2 coins?

4 Flaky pastry is made by mixing flour, margarine and lard in the ratio 8:3:3 and then adding a drizzle of cold water.

   a How much of each ingredient is needed to make 350 g of pastry?

   b What fraction of the pastry is made up of fats (margarine and lard)?

5 The sides of a rectangle are in the ratio of 2:5. Its perimeter is 112 cm.

   a What are the dimensions of the rectangle?

   b Use these dimensions to calculate its area.

6 Orange squash is made by mixing one part cordial to five parts of water. How much squash can you make with 750 ml of cordial?

7 Two-stroke fuel is used to power small engines. It is produced by mixing oil and petrol in the ratio of 1:20. How much oil needs to be mixed with 10 litres of petrol to make two-stroke fuel?

8 Tiffin is a sweet made by crushing biscuits and mixing them with dried fruit, butter and cocoa powder. The ratio of biscuit to dried fruit to butter to cocoa powder is 5:6:2:2. How much of each ingredient is needed to make 600 g of tiffin?

9 In a music college the ratio of flute to oboe to string to percussion players is 7:2:15:1. If the college has 175 students, how many play an oboe?

10 The ratio of red to green to blue to black to white pairs of socks in a drawer is 2:3:7:1:4. If there are eight pairs of white socks, how many pairs are there altogether?

11 Potting compost is made by mixing loam, peat and sand in the ratio of 7:3:2. If a gardener has 4.5 kg of peat and plenty of loam and sand, how much potting compost can she make?

Find answers at: cambridge.org/ukschools/gcsemaths-studentbookanswers

Tip

The scale of maps is given as a ratio in the form of $1:n$. For example $1:25\,000$.

Section 3: Comparing ratios

It is often useful to write ratios in the form $1:n$ (where n represents a number) so that they are in the same form and you can compare them by size.

WORKED EXAMPLE 2

Red and white paint can be mixed to make pink paint.

Which of the mixes below will give the lightest shade of pink?

A

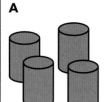 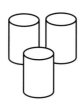

B

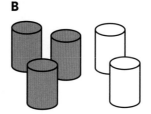

C

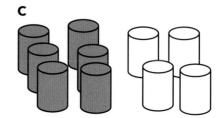

The ratios of red to white paint are:

A $4:3$ B $3:2$ C $6:4$

A $\dfrac{4}{4}:\dfrac{3}{4}=1:0.75$ B $\dfrac{3}{3}:\dfrac{2}{3}=1:0.67$ C $\dfrac{6}{6}:\dfrac{4}{6}=1:0.67$

Change these to form $1:n$ by dividing both parts of the ratio by the first part.

Give the answers as decimals to make the comparison simpler. (Round to 2 decimal places.)

Paint A has the greatest amount of white paint per unit of red paint, 0.75 tins of white for 1 tin of red, so this will make the lightest shade of pink.

Ratios in the form of $1:n$ are also useful for converting from one unit to another.

For example, the ratio of inches to centimetres is $1:2.54$.

This means that 1 inch is equivalent to 2.54 cm.

So, 2 inches = 2×2.54 cm and 12 inches = 12×2.54 cm.

This is a linear relationship and it can be shown as a straight-line graph.

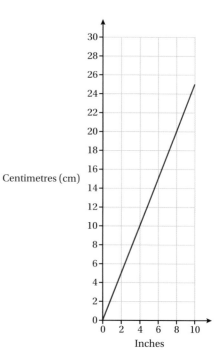

Centimetres (cm)

Inches

EXERCISE 20C

1 Different types of coffee are made by mixing espresso shots, hot water and milk in specified ratios.

Espresso	$1:0:0$
Double espresso	$2:0:0$
Flat white	$1:2:1$
Cappuccino	$1:0:2$
Latte	$1:0:4$

Put the drinks in order of strength, weakest first.

2 When Jon was going on holiday he used this graph to convert between pounds and euros.

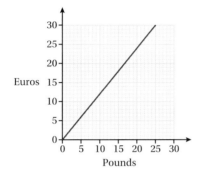

a What is the ratio of pounds to euros? Express this in the form $1:n$.

b What is the ratio of euros to pounds? Express this in the form $1:n$.

3 This graph shows the relationship between ounces and grams.

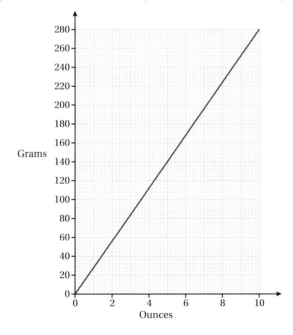

a What is the ratio of ounces to grams? Express this in the form $1:n$.

b What is the ratio of grams to ounces? Express this in the form $1:n$.

Find answers at: cambridge.org/ukschools/gcsemaths-studentbookanswers

4 Three siblings; Daisy, aged 5, Patrick, 8, and Imogen, 12, share sweets in the same ratio as their ages. Imogen gets 21 more sweets than Daisy.

  a How many sweets were there to begin with?

  b What fraction of the sweets did Patrick get?

5 The ratio of kilometres to miles is approximately 8 : 5. A car travels at 45 miles per hour for 20 minutes. How many kilometres does it travel?

6 This recipe for sausage casserole (left) serves 6.

The ratio of people to sausages is 6 : 12, this can be simplified to 1 : 2. Hence if the recipe needs adapting for 4 people, the people to sausages ratio of 1 : 2 means that you would need 8 sausages.

Using this as an example, find the quantities of ingredients needed to serve 4 people. Show all the steps in your answer.

> **Sausage casserole** (serves 6)
>
> 12 sausages
>
> 3 tins of tomatoes
>
> 450 g potatoes
>
> 9 tsp mixed herbs
>
> 600 ml vegetable stock

7 Gill and her sister Bell share a box of sweets. Bell gets $\frac{1}{3}$ of the box. Gill shares her sweets with her best friend Katy in the ratio 4 : 3. Katy gets 12 sweets. How many sweets were there in the box?

8 A box of chocolates contains white, milk and dark chocolates. A quarter of the box are white chocolate. The ratio of dark to milk chocolates is 2 : 5.

If there are seven white chocolates, how many more milk chocolates than dark chocolates are there?

9 A, B and C are three pulley wheels. For every 3 turns A makes, B makes 4 turns. For every 2 turns B makes C makes 3 turns.

  a What is the ratio of the turns A makes to the turns B makes?

  b What is the ratio of the turns C makes to the turns B makes?

  c What is the ratio of the turns A makes to the turns C makes?

  d Pulley wheel A makes 24 turns. How many turns does C make?

  e Pulley wheel C makes 36 turns. How many turns does A make?

10 A 210 cm ribbon is cut into two sections. The longer piece is 2 and a half times the length of the shorter piece.

  a What is the ratio of the longer piece to the shorter piece of ribbon?

  b How long is each piece?

11 Each month a sunflower's height increases by 40%. What was the ratio of the height of the sunflower on 1 May to its height on 1 August?

12 Which is a better deal: a 325 g jar of chocolate spread for 66p or a 1 kg tub for £1.99?

13 The ratio of Molly's height at age 3 to her height at age 4 is 15 : 16.

  a What percentage increase is this?

  b During this time Molly grew 7 cm. If Molly keeps growing with the same percentage height increase each year, how tall will she be when she is 8?

Golden ratio

The golden ratio has been studied and used for centuries. Artists, including Leonardo da Vinci and Salvador Dali often produced work using this ratio. The ratio can also be seen in buildings, such as the Acropolis in Athens. The golden ratio is said to be the most aesthetically pleasing way to space out facial features.

The diagram shows how the golden ratio can be worked out using the dimensions of a 'golden' rectangle. The large rectangle *ACDF* is similar to *BCDE*. Hence the ratio of $a : a + b$ is equivalent to $b : a$.

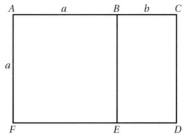

An approximate numerical value for this ratio can be found by measuring.

> **Tip**
>
> You will do more work on similar shapes in Chapter 30.

EXERCISE 20D

How golden are your hands?

Measure the distances A, B and C.

Now calculate these ratios and write them in the form $1 : n$.

> Distance B : Distance C
>
> Distance A : Distance B
>
> Length of your hand : Distance from your wrist to your elbow

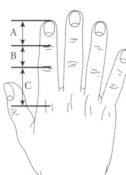

Can you see anything special about these ratios?

The closer your results are to 1.618 the more golden your hand!

> **Tip**
>
> You worked with the special sequence of Fibonacci numbers in Chapter 16. This sequence follows the golden ratio. If you calculate the ratio of consecutive numbers in the Fibonacci sequence you will find that the ratio gets closer and closer to the actual golden ratio $\dfrac{1+\sqrt{5}}{2}$ (this is equal to 1.618 to 3 decimal places) as you get further along the sequence.

EXERCISE 20E

1. What is the ratio of the diameter of a circle to its circumference in the form $1 : n$?

2. The three angles of a triangle are in the ratio $3 : 3 : 4$. What information can you give about the triangle?

3. The ratio of the five angles in a pentagon are $1 : 1 : 1 : 1 : 1$. What information does this tell you about the pentagon? How do you know this?

4. The ratio of an exterior angle to an interior angle of a regular polygon is $1 : 3$. How many sides does the polygon have?

5. The ratio of the angles in a triangle is $1 : 2 : 1$. What information can you give about the triangle? If the longest side is 10 cm, how long are its other two sides?

6. The ratio of the sides of a rectangle is $3 : 4$. After an enlargement by a scale factor of 5 what is the ratio of the same two sides?

> **Tip**
>
> To answer the questions about triangles, pentagons and rectangles you may need to look again at Chapter 2. For the question on circles, you could refer to Chapter 11, and for the questions on area and volume you may need to look again at Chapters 12 and 18.

7 Gareth and John share a box of chocolates. Gareth gets $\frac{3}{5}$ of the box. The ratio of white to milk to dark chocolates in John's share is $1:2:1$, he gets four white and dark chocolates in total. Gareth gets twice as many white chocolates as John and he has an equal number of dark and milk. How many types of each type of chocolate were in the box?

8 The ratio of the sides of two squares is $3:4$. What is the ratio of their areas?

9 The ratio of the edge of two cubes is $5:2$.

   a What is the ratio of their surface areas?

   b What is the ratio of their volumes?

 Checklist of learning and understanding

Notation

- The order in which a ratio is written is important. A ratio of $2:5$ means 2 parts to 5 parts. Each part is equal in size.

Simplifying ratios

- Two ratios are equivalent if one is a multiple of the other.
- Ratios can be simplified, by dividing both parts of the ratio by a common factor.
- Expressing ratios in the form $1:n$ makes it easy to compare ratios.

Sharing in a given ratio

- The box method can be used to tackle problems which involve sharing a quantity in a given ratio. To share quantity Q in the ratio $a:b:c$, divide the quantity evenly into $a+b+c$ boxes.

 For additional questions on the topics in this chapter, visit GCSE Mathematics Online.

 Chapter review

1 What is the ratio of vowels to consonants in the English alphabet?

2 What is the ratio of prime numbers to square numbers between (and including) 1 and 20 in its simplest form?

3 Share 360 in the ratio $3:5:1$.

4 Using the graph, express the ratio of miles to kilometres in the form $1:n$.

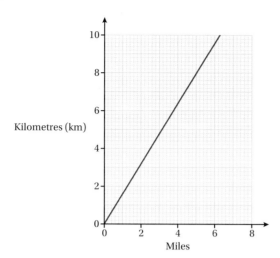

5 In a car park, three-quarters of the cars are not silver, but are blue, red, black or yellow. The proportion of blue to red to black to yellow cars is $6:2:3:1$. There are six more black cars than yellow cars. How many cars of each colour are in the car park?

Tip

Don't forget about the silver cars!

6 Mrs Jennings shares £770 between her two sons, Pete and Tim.

She shares the money in the ratio of her sons' ages.

The combined age of her two sons is 66 years.

Pete is 6 years younger than Tim.

Work out how much money each son gets.

You must show all your working. *(5 marks)*

©*Pearson Education Ltd 2011*

21 Probability basics

In this chapter you will learn how to ...

- represent and analyse outcomes of probability experiments.
- relate relative frequency to theoretical probability.
- calculate probabilities in different contexts.

For more resources relating to this chapter, visit GCSE Mathematics Online.

Using mathematics – real life applications

Software developers use probability when they build applications. Apps such as speech recognition, speech synthesis, key-word spotting and predictive text all rely on probability. In speech recognition for example, the software analyses the audio input and finds the most likely stream of text based on the audio. So, when you say a name into your phone instead of dialling, the software chooses the most likely name from your contact list.

"Knowing how to use and apply probability was one of the requirements when I was interviewed for this programming job."

(Computer programmer)

Before you start ...

Chs 6, 7, 19	You need to know how to calculate with fractions, decimals and percentages.	**1** Choose the correct answer without doing the calculations. **a** 0.13×0.24 **A** 0.312 **B** 0.0312 **C** 0.00312 **b** $0.82 + 0.18$ **A** 0.1 **B** 100 **C** 1 **c** 0.08% of 50 **A** 4 **B** 0.4 **C** 0.04
Ch 9	You need to be able to round decimals to 1, 2 or 3 places.	**2** Which answers are rounded to 3 decimal places incorrectly? Why? **a** $0.705\,882\,352 \approx 0.706$ **b** $0.316\,666\,6 \approx 0.316$ **c** $0.989\,087 \approx 1.09$
Chs 6, 7, 19	You should be able to find equivalent fractions, decimals and percentages.	**3** Match the equivalent pairs. $\dfrac{39}{52}$ 0.25 0.077 $\dfrac{13}{52}$ 50% $\dfrac{4}{52}$ $\dfrac{26}{52}$ 75%

Calculator tip

Make sure you know how to enter common fractions such as $\dfrac{17}{23}$ into your calculator and how to convert between fractions and decimals.

Assess your starting point using the Launchpad

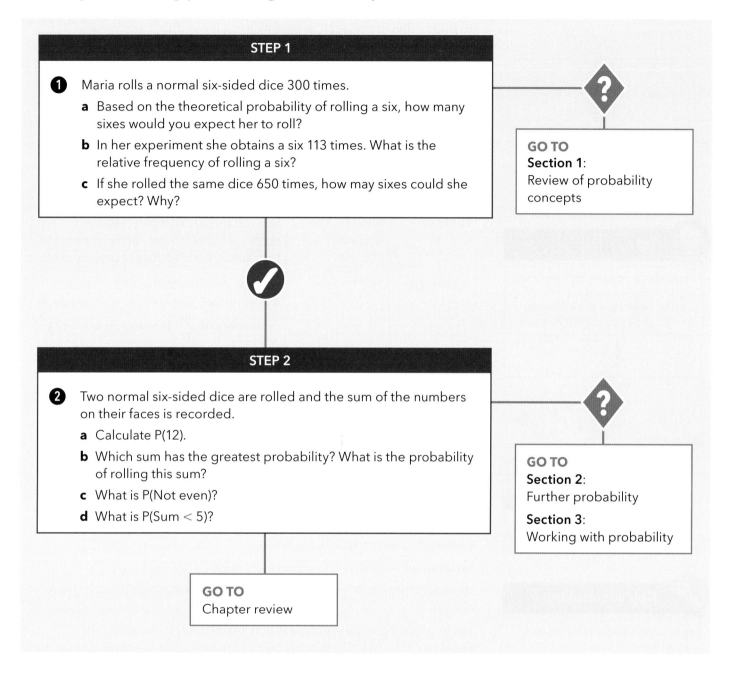

STEP 1

1 Maria rolls a normal six-sided dice 300 times.

   a Based on the theoretical probability of rolling a six, how many sixes would you expect her to roll?

   b In her experiment she obtains a six 113 times. What is the relative frequency of rolling a six?

   c If she rolled the same dice 650 times, how may sixes could she expect? Why?

GO TO
Section 1:
Review of probability concepts

STEP 2

2 Two normal six-sided dice are rolled and the sum of the numbers on their faces is recorded.

   a Calculate P(12).

   b Which sum has the greatest probability? What is the probability of rolling this sum?

   c What is P(Not even)?

   d What is P(Sum < 5)?

GO TO
Section 2:
Further probability

Section 3:
Working with probability

GO TO
Chapter review

Section 1: Review of probability concepts

Expressions of probability

Each of the following statements indicates the likelihood or probability of an **event** happening.

- I definitely didn't pass that test because I couldn't answer a single question.
- It is unlikely to rain today.
- I'm sure Sarah will be elected captain. Everyone says they will vote for her.

> **Key vocabulary**
>
> **event**: the thing to which we are trying to give a probability.

 Find answers at: cambridge.org/ukschools/gcsemaths-studentbookanswers

The likelihood of an event can be given mathematically using the probability number scale.

An impossible event (such as passing a test if you didn't answer any questions) is given a probability of 0.

A certain event (such as winning an election if you get all the votes) is given a probability of 1.

All other events are given a probability between 0 and 1.

Probabilities can be expressed as fractions, decimals or percentages.

The probability of rolling a six on a dice is:

Fraction	$\frac{1}{6}$	
Decimal	0.167 (3 decimal places)	You can quickly compare decimal values on the probability scale because you don't have to work with different denominators.
Percentage	16.7%	Percentages are often used in media reports about probability. For example, 'a probability of $\frac{28}{37}$' is not as clear or easy to read as 'a 76% chance'.

Tip

Although in real life people often say things like I have a 1 in 5 chance of getting the job, in an examination you should **not** give mathematical probabilities in the form of 1 in 5 chances, 1 to 5 or 1 : 5

Key vocabulary

outcome: a single result of an experiment or situation.

Experimental probability

You can do experiments to determine the probability that something will happen.

A class did an experiment to test whether toast always lands butter-side down. They got 30 volunteers to throw toast into the air and they recorded how many times it landed butter-side facing down. 16 out of 30 times, the toast landed butter-side facing down.

The number of trials in this experiment is 30.

There are two possible **outcomes** for each trial: butter-side down or butter-side up.

The frequency of each outcome is how many times it occurred. The frequency of butter-side down is 16 and the frequency of butter-side up is 14 (because 30 − 16 = 14).

$$\text{Relative frequency} = \frac{\text{number of favourable outcomes}}{\text{total number of outcomes}}$$

The relative frequency of butter-side down is $\frac{16}{30} \approx 0.533$

The relative frequency of butter-side up is $\frac{14}{30} \approx 0.467$

This means that the experimental probability of toast landing butter-side down is only slightly higher than it landing butter-side up.

EXERCISE 21A

1 Work with a partner. You will need two normal dice.

a Use words from the box to describe the probability of each of these outcomes when you roll two dice at the same time and add the total on the two faces.

	Outcome	Predicted probability
i	A total $\leqslant 12$	
ii	An even number	
iii	An odd number	
iv	A total of 1	
v	Exactly 12	
vi	A total > 4	

Impossible	Highly unlikely	Unlikely	Even chance
Likely	Highly likely		Certain

b Carry out an experiment in which you roll the two dice 50 times and record the frequency of each of the outcomes listed in the table. Bear in mind that one trial may meet more than one outcome.

c Compare your results with your predictions. How well did you predict the outcomes?

2 Find the experimental probability of:

a Getting heads with one toss of a coin if the coin landed heads up 96 times in 180 trials.

b Rolling a 6 with a dice given that when the dice was rolled 300 times, the frequency of rolling a 6 was 54.

c Getting an even number on a dice if an odd number was rolled 33 times in 60 trials.

3 Two dice were rolled 80 times and the total shown on the faces was recorded. This table gives the frequency of each outcome.

Total	2	3	4	5	6	7	8	9	10	11	12
Frequency	5	2	8	6	12	14	11	8	7	3	4

a Calculate the relative frequency of getting a total of 7 as a fraction and a decimal.

b What is the experimental probability of not getting a total of 7?

c What is the experimental probability of rolling a double six in this experiment?

d What is the experimental probability of getting a total less than 6?

Did you know?

The dice that are used for gambling in casinos are carefully made and checked to make sure that they are fair and unbiased. Biased dice (or coins, or spinners) will give some results more often than others. For example, confidence tricksters (con-artists) may use a coin that has been weighted to land on heads every time it is tossed, or a dice that has been manipulated to land on a six. When you are working with probability problems assume the equipment is fair and unbiased unless you are told differently.

Tip

In probability questions, a normal dice is a six-sided dice numbered from 1 to 6. Unless specifically stated, assume this is the case.

4 A market-research company did a survey to find out what brand of shampoo people bought most often. The results are given in the table.

Brand	Frequency	Relative frequency
Silk-e-shine	123	
Get knotted	105	
Goldilocks	83	
Bubbly stuff	89	
Total		

a What was the sample size for the survey?

b Calculate the relative frequency of buying each brand.

c Use the results of this survey to estimate the probability that a person chosen at random is likely to buy Silk-e-shine shampoo.

5 It is Mira's job to call customers who have had their car serviced at the dealer to check whether they are happy with the service they received. She kept this record of what happened for 200 calls made in one month.

Result	Frequency
Spoke to customer	122
Phone not answered	44
Left message on answering machine	22
Phone engaged or out of order	10
Wrong number	2

a Calculate the relative frequency of each event as a decimal fraction.

b Is it highly likely, likely, unlikely or highly unlikely that the following events will occur when Mira makes a call?

i The call will be answered by the customer.

ii The call will be answered by a machine.

iii She will dial the wrong number.

6 The results of an on-campus student council election are shown below. A total of 4000 students voted in the election.

Candidate	Votes
Alexia Adams	1445
Zunaid Darcey	1593
Amitab Smith	483
Nicky Chin	

a How many votes did Nicky Chin get?

b What is the probability that a randomly selected student voted for Zunaid Darcey?

c What is the probability that a randomly selected student did not vote for Alexia Adams?

Theoretical probability

This is where you calculate a probability based on fairness and symmetrical properties.

When you flip a fair coin there are two possible outcomes: head and tails. You have the same chance of getting heads as you have of getting tails so the outcomes are **equally likely**. This does not mean that if you flip a coin six times in a row that you will get three head and three tails. Although the outcomes are equally likely, they are also **random**. You could get six heads in a row or six tails in a row. However, the more often you flip the coin, the closer you will get to an equal number of heads and tails.

For equally likely outcomes you can calculate the probability using a formula.

probability of an event $= \dfrac{\text{number of favourable outcomes}}{\text{total number of outcomes}}$.

Key vocabulary

equally likely: having the same probability of happening.

random: not predetermined.

WORKED EXAMPLE 1

A bag of clean laundry contains 5 blue shirts, 6 red shirts, 7 green shirts and 7 white shirts. A student grabs one shirt at random from the bag. What is the probability that it is green?

$P(\text{Green}) = \dfrac{7}{25}$

There are 7 green shirts which means 7 favourable outcomes.

There are 25 shirts altogether.

$= 0.28$

Answer could be written as a fraction, decimal or percentage.

EXERCISE 21B

1 There are 19 girls and 17 boys in a classroom. The teacher puts their names into a bag and draws one at random. What is the probability that a boy's name will be selected?

2 A catering company has yellow, red and black candles which it chooses at random to put on tables. The probability of the chosen candle being yellow is 0.083. A candle is three times as likely to be red as it is to be yellow. Calculate the probability of the candle being black.

3 Nick and Vijay are playing a game in which they take turns to roll two unbiased dice with the numbers 1 to 6 on them. They find the product of the two dice. If the product is odd, Nick gets a point, if the product is even, Vijay gets a point. The first person to 20 points wins.

Predict which student is most likely to win and justify your answer.

Find answers at: cambridge.org/ukschools/gcsemaths-studentbookanswers

4 A local government agency carried out a census of 500 000 people working in the city. They collected the following data.

Qualifications	Frequency
Postgraduate diploma/degree	74 500
First degree/diploma	92 350
No post-school qualifications	333 150

Language abilities	Frequency
English only	123 000
English and one other language	209 500
Multilingual (English plus at least two other languages)	167 500

If a person included in this census is selected at random, what is the probability that the person:

a has a first degree or a diploma?

b is able to speak English only?

c has some post-school qualification?

d is able to speak a language other than English?

5 Is the reasoning in each of these statements correct? Explain why or why not.

a Since there are 26 letters in the alphabet, the probability that a name will start with X is $\frac{1}{26}$.

b My first three children were boys, so the next one must be a girl.

c There are ten teams in the tournament, so the probability of any team winning is $\frac{1}{10}$.

d The probability that a family will go on holiday in August is $\frac{1}{12}$.

e This team has won the last four matches, so they are certain to win the next one too.

Section 2: Further probability

Probability is used to predict what you expect to happen. In reality, there is no guarantee that any particular outcome will occur. The probability of getting heads when you flip a coin is $\frac{1}{2}$ and so you may expect to get heads about half of the time, but you could flip a coin 20 times and get 18 heads.

Similarly, an insurance company may use statistical data to work out that drivers between the ages of 17 and 23 are more likely to have an accident than older drivers. This does not mean that a 19-year-old driver will definitely have an accident.

A good understanding of probability and how it works will help you make sense of chance and risk in daily life.

The probability of an event not happening

The probability of Amanda scoring a goal in a netball match is 0.6. In this situation there are two possible outcomes: either Amanda scores a goal, or she does not. All probability situations can be reduced to two possible outcomes. For example, win or not win, heads or not heads, rolling a 6 or not rolling a six. When you express the outcomes in this way we say they are complementary.

When you add the probability of an event and its complement you get 1.

P(Amanda scoring) + P(Amanda not scoring) = 0.6 + 0.4 = 1

$P(\text{six}) + P(\text{not six}) = \dfrac{1}{6} + \dfrac{5}{6} = 1$ Not six is the same as rolling 1, 2, 3, 4, or 5.

In general terms, you can say that P(event occurring) + P(event not occurring) = 1

Rearranging gives: P(event not occurring) = 1 − P(event occurring)

If P(E) is the probability of an event (E) happening , and P(E′) is the probability of that event not happening then P(E′) = 1 − P(E).

WORK IT OUT 21.1

A laboratory tested 500 batches of tablets and found four to be contaminated. What is the probability that a batch of tablets produced in this laboratory would be:

a contaminated   **b** not contaminated?

Which of these answers is the correct answer to the following question? Why is the other one wrong?

Option A	Option B
a $P(\text{Contaminated}) = \dfrac{4}{500} = 0.8\%$	**a** $P(\text{Contaminated}) = \dfrac{4}{500} = 0.008$
b $P(\text{Not contaminated}) = \dfrac{496}{500} = 92\%$	**b** $P(\text{Not contaminated}) = 1 - 0.008 = 0.992$

Mutually exclusive events

Mutually exclusive events cannot happen at the same time. For example, you cannot get an even number and a three at the same time when you roll a dice and you cannot pick a vowel and a consonant if you choose one letter of the alphabet at random.

Imagine you have a bag with 3 red, 2 yellow and 5 green sweets in it and you are allowed to choose one sweet at random.

The probability of you choosing:

Red sweet	Yellow sweet	Green sweet
$\dfrac{3}{10}$	$\dfrac{2}{10}$ or $\dfrac{1}{5}$	$\dfrac{5}{10}$ or $\dfrac{1}{2}$

The sum of probabilities of the three events is 1.

You cannot pick a red sweet and a yellow sweet at the same time, so the events P(red) and P(yellow) are mutually exclusive.

You can however, work out the probability of choosing either a red or a yellow sweet.

There are 3 red and 2 yellow so $\dfrac{5}{10}$ of the sweets are either red or yellow.

Key vocabulary

mutually exclusive: events that cannot happen at the same time.

EXERCISE 21C

1 Michelle catches the C125 bus to work. Over a period of 227 working days she did not manage to get a seat on the bus 58 times.

Calculate the experimental probability of her getting a seat on the bus.

2 What is the probability that the number of a raffle ticket drawn at random from a set of tickets numbered 0 to 99 (inclusive) will be:

a divisible by 2

b not a multiple 10

c a multiple of 8

d not a multiple of 8?

3 The probability of a basketball player missing a goal is given as 0.432. What is the probability that the player will not miss?

4 A packet holds 300 sweets in five different flavours. The probability of choosing a particular flavour is given in the table.

Flavour	Strawberry	Lime	Lemon	Blackberry	Apple
P(flavour)	0.21	0.22	0.18	0.23	

a Calculate P(apple).

b What is P(not apple)?

c Calculate the probability of choosing P(not lemon and not lime).

d Calculate the number of sweets of each flavour in the packet.

5 Students in a school have five extra-curricular clubs to choose from. The probability that a student will choose each club is given in the table.

Club	Computers	Sewing	Woodwork	Choir	Chess
P(club)	0.57	0.2	0.2	0.02	0.01

a Calculate P(sewing or woodwork).

b Calculate P(not chess and not choir).

c If 55 students have to choose a club, how many would you expect to choose sewing?

d If four students chose choir, calculate how many students chose computers. (Assume the probabilities are correct.)

6 26 Scrabble tiles, each with a different letter of the alphabet, are place in a bag. A tile is drawn at random.

What is the probability of getting:

a a letter from the name Nicky or a letter from the name Sue

b a letter from the name Gary and from the name Ben?

7 A single card is drawn from a pack of standard playing cards. What is the probability that it is a club or a red card?

Organising outcomes – tables and frequency trees

There are many ways of recording and organising information to show how many favourable events there are, how many events there are in total and to find the figures you need to make decisions and calculate probabilities. Tables and simple diagrams called frequency trees are used to do this.

A doctor was interested in whether his patients knew the difference between having a cold and having the flu. One winter he kept track of 42 patients who came to see him because they thought they had a cold or the flu. Of these, 11 said they had a cold and 31 said they had the flu. Only 19 of those who said they had the flu actually had flu, and 4 of those who said they had a cold actually had the flu.

Here are two ways of organising the information from this experiment:

Two-way table

	Actual diagnosis	
Self-diagnosis	Cold	Flu
Cold	7	4
Flu	12	19

Frequency tree

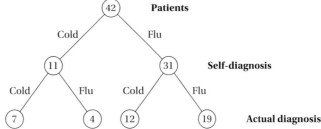

A frequency tree shows the actual frequency of different events.

The branches of the tree show the paths or decisions and the 'leaves' show the actual number of data for each path. Both the table and the frequency tree show the same information, but the frequency tree is clearer because it shows how many patients thought they had a cold or flu without you having to add the data in the table.

> **Tip**
>
> Frequency trees are organisational tools and they are often used in computer programming (they are sometimes called binary trees). They are not the same as probability tree diagrams which you will deal with in Chapter 28.

EXERCISE 21D

1 A hotel chain keeps track of which customers make use of its in-house spa facilities. Here are its results.

	Spa use	
Gender	Use the spa	Don't use the spa
Female	780	232
Male	348	640

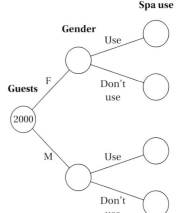

a Complete the frequency tree (right) to show this data.

b Are male or female guests more likely to use the spa?

2 After completing a multiple-choice test, Andy predicted that he got 16 of the 20 questions correct. Of the 16 he predicted that he'd answered correctly, he got 3 wrong. Altogether he got 17 out of 20.

a Draw a frequency tree to show this information.

b Comment on how well he predicted the outcomes of the test.

 Find answers at: cambridge.org/ukschools/gcsemaths-studentbookanswers

3 Of 60 patients visiting a GP's surgery, 42 are convinced they will need prescription medication, the others think they probably won't need a prescription. Of those who think they will need a prescription 13 do not. Altogether 36 patients do need a prescription.

a Complete the frequency tree to show the actual numbers.

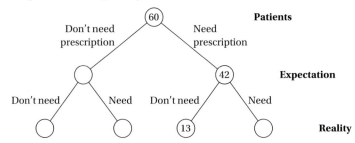

b Assuming this is a representative situation, what is the probability that a patient that thinks they need a prescription will actually need one?

c What percentage of patients who thought they would not need a prescription actually needed one?

4 80 volunteers take an HIV-test to help the medical researchers work out how accurate the test is. Of the volunteers 17 people are HIV-positive, the others are not. The results show that one of the HIV-positive people gets a negative result on the test and two of the HIV-negative people get a positive result.

Draw a frequency tree to show the actual results.

Section 3: Working with probability

In real life, probability is used quite informally to explain things and to predict what will happen in the future. You may have heard people say things like:

- You must drive carefully on this bend because there are always accidents here.
- It is never sunny here in February.
- If it rains on match day the other team has a better chance of winning.
- We are only selling 10 000 tickets so you have an excellent chance of winning the car.
- Young people who haven't had a driving licence for very long have more accidents than older drivers.

But, each statement can be untrue in individual cases. For example, Pete might say, 'You must drive carefully on this bend because there are often accidents here.' His friend Ahmed might say, 'I don't agree, I drive along that road all the time and I have never seen an accident there.'

Both statements can be true. In reality, the traffic department would want to know the relative frequency of accidents $\left(\dfrac{\text{number of cars involved in accidents}}{\text{total number of cars using the road}} \right)$ before they make decisions about the safety of the bend.

Understanding probability allows you to think more critically about statements like the ones above and to work out more accurately what the chance is of different things happening.

WORKED EXAMPLE 2

A consumer organisation commissioned a series of tests to determine the average lifetime of a locally produced solar garden lamp. The results of the tests are shown in the table:

Lifetime of solar lamp, L (hours)	$0 \leqslant L < 1000$	$1000 \leqslant L < 2000$	$2000 \leqslant L < 3000$	$3000 \leqslant L$
Frequency	30	75	160	35

a Use the results of the tests to estimate the probability that a solar lamp will last for less than 3000 hours but more than 1000 hours.

b If the hardware depot orders 2000 solar lamps, how many of them can they expect to last for more than 3000 hours?

a
$$P(1000 \leq L < 3000 \text{ hours}) = \frac{75}{300} + \frac{160}{300} = \frac{235}{300}$$
$$= 0.783$$

Add the frequencies for the two class intervals.

b $P(\text{lasts more than 3000 hours}) = \dfrac{35}{300}$

Find the test probability.

$\dfrac{35}{300} \times 2000 = 233$

Multiply the probability by the number of lamps ordered.

If these statistics are correct, 233 of the solar lamps should last more than 3000 hours.

Tip

The lifetimes are shown as class intervals. You can find out more about these in Chapter 37.

Problem-solving framework

Nick is throwing a ball randomly at a wall on the side of a building. The side of the building is 2 m high and 10 m wide. There are three windows on the side of the building, each window is 2 m wide and 1 m high. Assuming that Nick hits the wall each time he throws, what is the probability that Nick will hit a window when he throws the ball at the wall? Express your answer as a percentage.

Steps for solving problems	What you would do for this example
Step 1: What are you trying to work out?	The probability of hitting any of the windows.
Step 2: What do you need to work out before you can find this?	The area of the wall and the area of the windows.
	Area of wall = 10 m × 2 m = 20 m²
	Area of windows = 3 × (2 m × 1 m) = 3 × 2 m² = 6 m²
Step 3: Apply the formula and calculate the probability. Convert the answer to a percentage.	$P(\text{Hits window}) = \dfrac{6}{20} = \dfrac{3}{10}$
	$\dfrac{3}{10} \times 100 = 30\%$
	There is a 30% probability that Nick will hit a window.

EXERCISE 21E

1 Nina and Maria made up a game with an eight-sided dice. The sides of the dice are labelled 6, 24, 9, 29, 15, 7, 18 and 12.

They take turns to roll the dice. Nina wins the roll if the dice shows a multiple of 2. Maria wins the roll if the dice shows a multiple of 3.

a Is this a fair game? Give a reason for your answer.

b What is the theoretical probability that the dice will show a multiple of 3?

2 During a netball competition, the same coin was tossed 20 times. Busi claimed the coin was unfair because it landed on tails only 5 out of the 20 times.

She says the probability of getting tails when you toss a coin is 0.5, so if you toss the coin 20 times you should get $20 \times 0.5 = 10$ tails.

Was she correct? Explain your answer.

3 A local educational authority wants to introduce random drug testing in secondary schools. It claims the tests have a very small false-positive rate of one half of one per cent.

a Express one half of one per cent as a decimal.

b The parents at a school with 800 students object to the test. They claim that four students could incorrectly test positive for drug use and that this could ruin their futures. Are the parents concerns valid? Explain why or why not.

c There were 3 831 937 secondary school students under this authority in the year they wanted to do the drug testing. If they were all tested for drug use, how many of them would you expect to be incorrectly accused of being drug users?

4 Professional athletes are routinely tested for prohibited performance enhancing drugs. The testing authority estimates only 1% of the athletes tested are actually using prohibited drugs. If an athlete is using prohibited drugs, 90% of the time he or she will test positive in the test (in other words, fail the drug test). But, 10% of the athletes who are not using prohibited drugs will also test positive (in other words, fail the drug test even though they are not using drugs).

Status	Test positive (i.e. fail drug test)	Test negative (i.e. pass drug test)	Total
Athletes who are using illegal substances			10
Athletes who are not using illegal substances			990
Total			1000

a Complete this table to show how many athletes will pass or fail the drug test for every 1000 athletes tested.

b Represent the same information on a frequency tree.

c If an athlete tests positive for the illegal substance, what is the chance that he or she is not actually using the substance? Give your answer as a percentage.

d If an athlete tests negative for the substances is it certain that he or she is not using them? Explain your answer.

5 Amit designed a round spinner out of plastic to be used in a game at a school fund-raising event. The spinner was divided into quarters coloured red, green, yellow and white. His friend Nick said the spinner might be biased because Amit didn't sand it down smoothly. Amit disagreed, but they decided to test whether it was fair or not by spinning it 1000 times and recording the outcomes. These are the results.

Does the evidence suggest the spinner is biased?

Outcome	Frequency
Red	295
Green	248
Yellow	238
White	219

6 A shopkeeper did a survey to find out which customers buy fresh fish at his shop every week.

Age group	Females Buy fish	Females Don't buy fish	Males Buy fish	Males Don't buy fish
20–50 years old	23	56	19	25
Over 50 years old	45	26	13	5

a How many people were surveyed?

b How many people over 50 were surveyed?

c A customer from the survey is chosen at random. What is the probability that the customer is:

  i male?   **ii** male or over 50?   **iii** over 50 and buys fish?

d How could this information help the shopkeeper plan advertising and marketing campaigns?

7 There are four main blood groups: A, B, AB and O. The data on the right was collected by a blood bank based on the blood types of 500 donors.

a What percentage of donors belongs to group O?

b What is the probability of a donor having blood type AB?

c People with blood type O negative are often called universal donors because their blood can usually be given to people of any blood type without any bad reaction. Only about 7% of the population are O negative. How many of these donors would you expect to have O negative blood?

d Given these statistics, what is the probability that a baby will be born with blood type AB?

e Why is theoretical probability not very useful for predicting blood type?

Blood type	Number of donors
A	220
B	49
AB	21
O	210

8 80 people are asked if they can tell the difference between butter and margarine. 37 say they can, 24 say no and 19 say they are not sure. The interviewer then carries out a blind taste test. Of those who said they could tell the difference, 14 got it wrong, of those who said no, 9 got it right and 14 of those who said they were not sure got it wrong. Draw a frequency tree to show the outcomes of this experiment.

Find answers at: cambridge.org/ukschools/gcsemaths-studentbookanswers

Checklist of learning and understanding

Range of probabilities

- The probability scale ranges from 0 to 1. Impossible events have a probability of 0 and certain events have a probability of 1. It is not possible to have a negative probability (< 0) or a probability greater than 1.

- Probabilities between 0 and 1 should be expressed as fractions, decimals or percentages.

Theoretical probability

- Probability of an event $= \dfrac{\text{number of favourable outcomes}}{\text{number of possible outcomes}}$

- The greater the number of trials, the closer the relative frequency is likely to be to the theoretical probability.

Sum of probabilities and complementary events

- The sum of probabilities will always total 1.

- The probability of an event not happening is equal to 1 minus the probability that the event will happen. So, P(Not E) = 1 – P(E).

Experimental probability and relative frequency

- Experimental probability tells you how often a favourable outcome occurs in an experiment. Experimental probability = $\dfrac{\text{relative frequency of a favourable outcome}}{\text{number of possible outcomes}}$

- Tables and frequency trees can be used to organise the outcomes of different experiments.

- Statistical data can also be used to give the relative frequency of particular events. The relative frequency of an event can be used to predict future outcomes.

Mutually exclusive events

- Mutually exclusive events cannot happen at the same time. For example, you cannot throw a 1 and a 5 at the same time when you roll a dice.

For additional questions on the topics in this chapter, visit GCSE Mathematics Online.

Chapter review

 1 A coin is flipped a number of times giving the following results.

Heads: 4083

Tails: 5917

- **a** How many times was the coin tossed?

- **b** Calculate the relative frequency of each outcome.

- **c** What is the probability that the next toss will result in heads?

- **d** Jess says she thinks the results show that the coin is biased. Do you agree? Give a reason for your answer.

2 A bag contains 10 red, 8 green and 2 white counters. Each counter has an equal chance of being chosen. Calculate:

  a the probability of choosing a red ball.

  b the probability of choosing a red or a green ball.

  c the probability of not choosing a white ball.

  d P(ball is not red).

3 Here is a four-sided spinner.

The spinner is biased.

The table shows the probabilities that the spinner will land on 1 or on 3

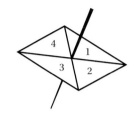

Number	1	2	3	4
Probability	0.2		0.1	

The probability that the spinner will land on 2 is the same as the probability that the spinner will land on 4

  a Work out the probability that the spinner will land on 4   *(3 marks)*

Shunya is going to spin the spinner 200 times.

  b Work out an estimate for the number of times the spinner will land on 3   *(2 marks)*

©Pearson Education Ltd 2013

4 Research shows that the probability of a person being left-handed is 0.23. How many left-handed people would you expect in a population of 25 000?

5 The probability of a sim card for a mobile phone being faulty is found to be 0.0265. What percentage of sim cards are not faulty?

6 Jill interviews 64 people to get their opinions about sending texts when in company. 44 of those interviewed say it is rude to send texts in company. Jill then observes the people at a large event. Of those who said it was rude to send texts in company 13 sent texts when at the table with others. Of those who said it was acceptable, 9 did not send texts when in company. Complete the frequency tree (right) to show this data.

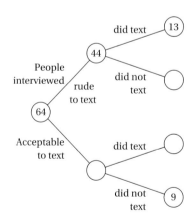

7 Mina used a computer program to simulate drawing a playing card at random from a shuffled pack. She recorded the suit of each card drawn. These are her results for 1000 trials.

Suit drawn	Hearts	Diamonds	Spades	Clubs
Frequency	238	240	264	258

  a Calculate the relative frequency of each outcome.

  b Do these results indicate that the simulation is fair and unbiased? Give a reason for your answer.

Find answers at: cambridge.org/ukschools/gcsemaths-studentbookanswers

22 Construction and loci

In this chapter you will learn how to ...

- use a ruler, protractor and pair of compasses effectively.
- use a ruler and a pair of compasses to bisect lines and angles and construct perpendiculars.
- accurately construct geometrical figures.
- construct accurate diagrams to solve problems involving loci.

 For more resources relating to this chapter, visit GCSE Mathematics Online.

Using mathematics: real-life applications

Draughtspeople and architects need to draw accurate scaled diagrams of the buildings and other structures they are working on.

Although the drawings are complicated, they still use ordinary mathematical instruments like pencils, rulers and pairs of compasses to draw them.

"I prepare technical drawings and plans that are given to me by an architect.

I use a CAD program, but I always start with a drawing board and plans that I draw using my ruler, set square and pair of compasses."

(Draughtsperson)

Before you start ...

KS3	You need to be able to measure and draw angles accurately using a protractor.	**1** Choose the correct measurement for each angle. **a** **b** **2** Use a ruler and a protractor to draw a reflex angle the same size as this one.
KS3	You should be able to convert between units of length.	**3** Choose the correct answers. **a** 1 m is equivalent to: **A** 10 mm **B** 100 mm **C** 1000 mm **D** none of these measurements **b** Half of 8.7 cm is: **A** 43 mm **B** 435 mm **C** 43.5 mm **D** none of these measurements
Ch 2	You must know and be able to use the correct names for parts of shapes, including circles.	**4** Match the letters **a** to **e** with the correct mathematical names from the box below. vertex centre radius side diameter

Assess your starting point using the Launchpad

STEP 1

1 Which of the following statements are true of this angle?

A It is an acute angle.

B It measures 120°.

C It is called *QRP*.

D If you extend arm *QR*, the size of the angle will increase.

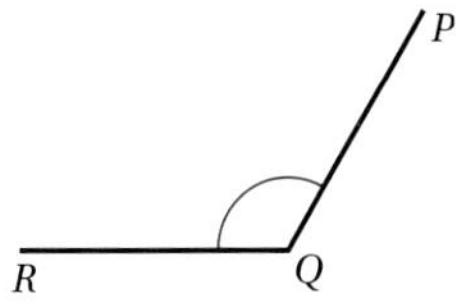

2 Which of the following statements are **not** true of this circle?

A It has a radius of 5 cm.

B It has a diameter of 5 cm.

C $OC \perp AB$

D $OC = \dfrac{1}{2}(AB)$

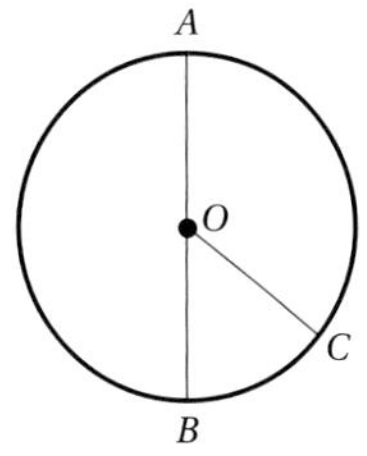

GO TO
Section 1:
Using geometrical instruments

STEP 2

3 Niresh did the construction shown here.

a What do you call line *BR*?

b What did Niresh do to produce points *P* and *Q*?

c Given that angle *ABC* = 24°, state the size of angle *ABR* without measuring it.

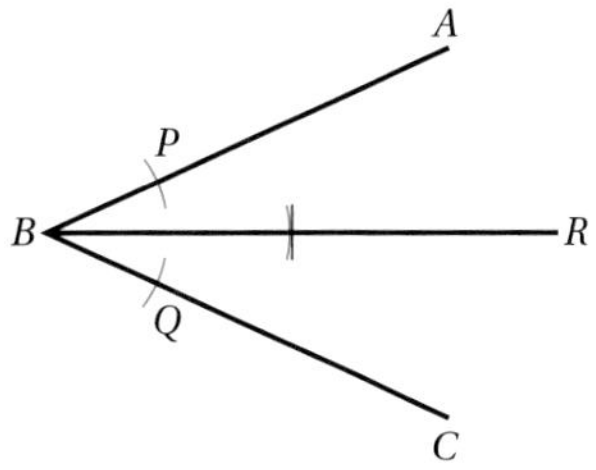

GO TO
Section 2:
Ruler and compass constructions

STEP 3

4 Simone is going camping.

She wants to pitch her tent less than 50 m from the river and no further than 50 m from the showers.

A = showers

She drew this diagram to help her decide where to camp.

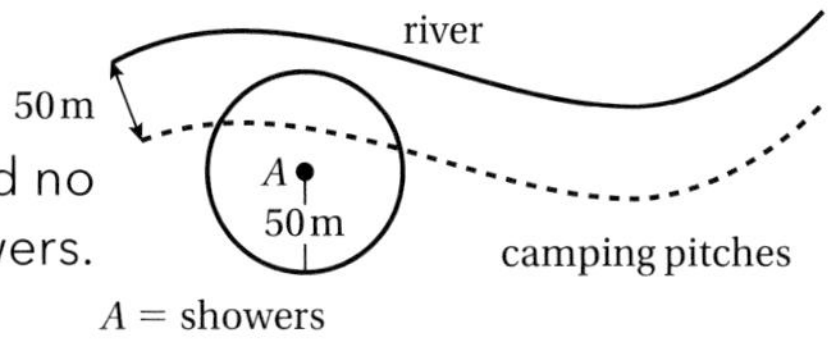

Copy the diagram and shade the area which satisfies Simone's conditions to show where she could camp.

GO TO
Section 3:
Loci

Section 4:
Applying your skills

GO TO
Chapter review

Section 1: Using geometrical instruments

Measuring and drawing angles

You use a protractor to measure and draw angles.

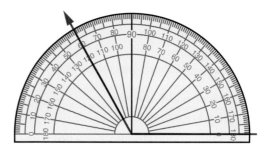

Protractors like the one above have two scales.

To avoid reading the wrong scale, estimate the size of the angle before you measure.

Use your knowledge of acute, right and obtuse angles to estimate as accurately as possible.

WORKED EXAMPLE 1

Estimate and then measure the size of each red angle.

a

b

a

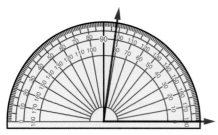

This is an acute angle but it is close to 90°. Estimate about 80°.

Use the inner scale to measure because this is the scale that has 0 on the arm of the angle.

$ABC = 82°$

b

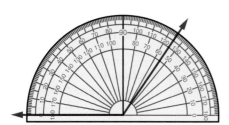

This is an obtuse angle. It is about one-third bigger than a right angle.

Estimate about 120°

Use the outer scale to measure because now this is the scale that has 0 on the arm of the angle.

$DEF = 125°$

WORKED EXAMPLE 2

Use your protractor to draw angle ABC = 76°.

Draw a straight line using your ruler and mark the points *B* and *C*.

B is the vertex in angle *ABC*.

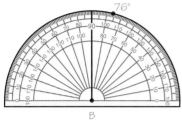
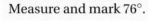

Place your protractor with its centre on *B* and baseline on the line you drew.

Measure and mark 76°.

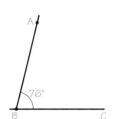

Remove the protractor.

Draw a line from *B* through the 76° marking.

Label the angle correctly.

76° is an acute angle. Look at your angle and check that it looks less than 90°. If it does not, you have used the wrong scale on your protractor.

Using a pair of compasses

A pair of compasses (sometimes just called compasses) is useful for marking accurate line lengths in figures, for drawing circles, and for constructing some angles without measuring them with a protractor.

Make sure your pencil point is sharp and that the compasses are not too loose.

Parts of a circle

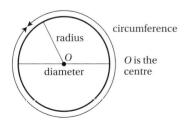

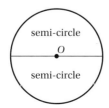

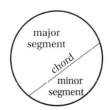

 Find answers at: cambridge.org/ukschools/gcsemaths-studentbookanswers

WORKED EXAMPLE 3

Draw a circle with a **radius** of 4.5 cm.

Place the pair of compasses alongside a ruler and open it to 4.5 cm.

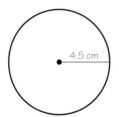

Draw a circle.

💡 **Tip**

Using a pair of compasses effectively takes practice.

WORKED EXAMPLE 4

Make an accurate copy of this figure.

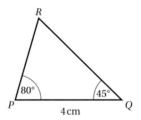

First draw the base line of 4 cm and label this *PQ*.

Use a protractor to measure the angle 80° from point *P* and draw a line.

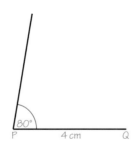

From point *Q* measure the angle 45° and draw a line from *Q* extending out so that it crosses the other line.

Where the two lines cross is point *R*. This is the apex of the triangle.

 Tip

Draw the lines in faintly first. Then go over them to show the final triangle. Never rub out your construction lines.

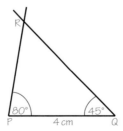

WORKED EXAMPLE 5

Construct an equilateral triangle with side lengths 6 cm.

First draw the base line of 6 cm with a ruler and label it *AB*.

Then set your compasses to 6 cm and draw an arc above that line, setting the point of your compasses at *A*.

Repeat this from the other side at point *B*.

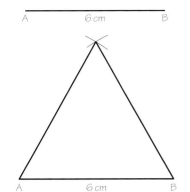

Where the two arcs join is the apex of the triangle. Use this point to complete the triangle.

You have constructed a triangle with three equal side lengths, so this is an equilateral triangle with three equal angles of 60°.

Tip

Leave the construction markings (arcs made using your pair of compasses) on your diagrams as this shows the method you used to construct them.

This method can be used for triangles with sides of different lengths by setting your pair of compasses to whatever the lengths of the sides are.

EXERCISE 22A

1 Use a ruler and protractor to draw and label the following angles.

    a $PQR = 25°$ **b** $DEF = 149°$ **c** $XYZ = 90°$

2 How could you use a protractor marked from 0° to 180° to measure an angle of 238°?

3 **a** Draw line *MN* which is 8.4 cm long.

      At *M*, measure and draw angle $NMR = 45°$.

      At *N*, measure and draw angle $RNM = 98°$ so that it forms a triangle *MNR*.

    b Explain why it is not necessary to know the lengths of *MR* and *NR* in order to construct the triangle accurately.

 Find answers at: cambridge.org/ukschools/gcsemaths-studentbookanswers

4 Use a pair of compasses to construct:

    a a circle of radius 4 cm

    b a circle of diameter 12 cm

    c a circle of diameter 2 cm which shares a centre, *O*, with another circle of radius 5 cm.

5 Draw a line *AB* which is 70 mm long. Construct the circle for which this line is the diameter.

6 **a** Draw a circle of radius 3.5 cm and centre *O*.

    Use a ruler to draw any two radii of the circle. Label them *OA* and *OB*.

    Join point *A* to point *B* to form triangle *AOB*.

    Measure angles *AOB*, *OBA* and *BAO*. Write the measurements on your diagram.

    b What type of triangle is triangle *AOB*?

7 Accurately copy the following diagrams using only a ruler and pair of compasses.

a 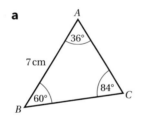   **b**   **c**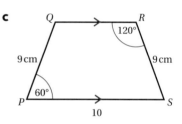

8 Prepare a step-by-step set of instructions for using **only** a ruler and a pair of compasses to construct:

    a an equilateral triangle *ABC* with sides of 6.4 cm

    b a semi-circle with a radius of 30 mm.

9 Use a ruler, a pair of compasses and a protractor to construct 1/9th of a circle of diameter 82 mm.

Section 2: Ruler and compass constructions

Bisecting a line

 Key vocabulary

bisect: divide exactly into two equal halves.

You can use a ruler and a pair of compasses to **bisect** any line **without** measuring it.

WORKED EXAMPLE 6

Bisect line *AB* by construction.

A ——————— B

Open the pair of compasses to any width that is greater than half the line.

Continues on next page …

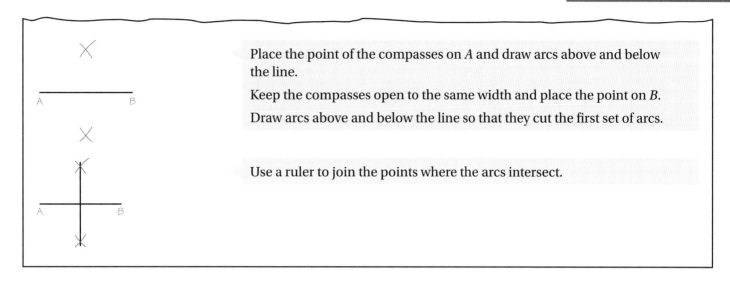

Place the point of the compasses on *A* and draw arcs above and below the line.

Keep the compasses open to the same width and place the point on *B*.

Draw arcs above and below the line so that they cut the first set of arcs.

Use a ruler to join the points where the arcs intersect.

The point where the constructed line cuts *AB* is called the **midpoint** of *AB*.

The distance from A to this point is equal to the distance from *B* to this point.

The constructed line is perpendicular to *AB*, so it is called the **perpendicular bisector** of *AB*. All points along the constructed line are an equal distance from both point *A* and point *B*.

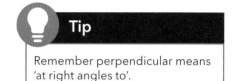

Tip

Remember perpendicular means 'at right angles to'.

Key vocabulary

midpoint: the centre of a line; the point that divides the line into two equal halves.

perpendicular bisector: a line perpendicular to another that also cuts it in half.

Constructing perpendiculars

Construct a perpendicular at a given point on a line

WORKED EXAMPLE 7

Construct $XY \perp AB$ at point *X*.

Tip

Remember, ⊥ is the symbol which means 'perpendicular to'.

Draw and label a line, *AB*, about 12 cm long and mark on it point *X*, about 5 cm from *A*.

Open your compasses to a width of about 4 cm.

Place the point of your compasses on *X*.

Draw two arcs to cut *AB* on either side of *X*.

Continues on next page …

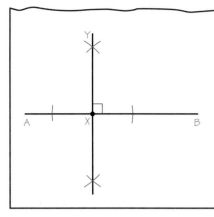

Construct the perpendicular bisector of the line segment between the arcs.

Draw a line through the intersecting arcs.

Label one end of it *Y* to produce *XY*.

Construct a perpendicular from a point to a line

WORKED EXAMPLE 8

Construct *PX* perpendicular to line *AB* from point *P*.

🔆 **Tip**

The shortest distance from any point to a line is a perpendicular from that point to the line.

Draw and label a line, *AB*, about 12 cm long and mark on it point *P*, about 5 cm above the line.

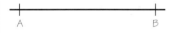

Place the point of your compasses on *P*.

Draw an arc that cuts *AB* in two places.

Label these places *C* and *D*.

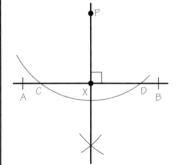

Open the pair of compasses to a width more than half the distance between *C* and *D*.

Place the point on *C* and draw an arc on the opposite side of the line to point *P*.

Place the point on *D* and draw an arc which intersects the one you just drew.

Draw a line from the intersecting arcs to *P*.

Label *PX* and mark the perpendicular.

Tip

Remember, if you bisect a 90° angle you will then have two angles of 45°.

Bisecting an angle

An angle bisector divides any angle into two equal halves.

WORKED EXAMPLE 9

Use a protractor to draw an angle *PQR* of 70°.

Construct the angle bisector of this angle without measuring.

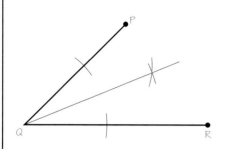

Place the pair of compasses on the vertex of the angle, *Q*.

Open your compasses a few centimetres and draw arcs that cut each arm of the angle.

Place the point of your compasses on each arc where it cuts the arm of the angle in turn and, keeping the width the same, draw arcs between the arms of the angle.

Draw a line from the vertex of the angle through the intersection of the arcs.

This is the angle bisector.

EXERCISE 22B

1 Measure and draw the following lines segments. Find the midpoint of each by construction.

a *AB* = 9 cm   **b** *MN* = 48 mm   **c** *PQ* = 6.5 cm

2 **a** Draw any three acute angles. Bisect each angle without measuring.

b How could you check the accuracy of your constructions?

3 Draw the angles shown and then, using only a ruler and pair of compasses, bisect each angle.

4 Draw any triangle *ABC*.

a Construct the perpendicular bisector of each side of the triangle.

b Use the point where the perpendicular bisectors meet as the centre and vertex *A* as a radius and draw a circle.

c What do you notice about this circle?

5 Construct equilateral triangle *DEF* with sides of 7 cm.

a Bisect each angle of the triangle by construction. Label the point where the angle bisectors meet as *O*.

b Measure *DO*, *EO* and *FO*. What do you notice?

6 Draw *MN* = 80 mm. Insert any point *A* above *MN*.

a Construct *AX* ⊥ *MN*.   **b** Draw *AB* ∥ *MN*.

7 Draw line segments *PQ* and *ST* that intersect at point *O*.

a Bisect *SOQ*.

b If you continue your line in **a** through *O*, is the angle bisector of *SOQ* also the bisector of *POT*?

Explain your answer.

Find answers at: cambridge.org/ukschools/gcsemaths-studentbookanswers

8 Draw any circle and use a ruler to draw in two chords.

   a Construct the perpendicular bisector of each chord.

   b Describe where they meet.

   Repeat parts **a** and **b** for a different circle with two different chords.

   c What can you deduce from this?

Section 3: Loci

A **locus** is a set of points that all meet a given condition or set of conditions.

The locus can be a single point, a line, a curve or a shaded region of points that overlap because they meet the same conditions in a particular area.

Some of the rules for loci produce shapes and lines (paths) that you are already familiar with from your work on constructions.

> ### 🔑 Key vocabulary
>
> **locus** (plural **loci**): a set of points that satisfy the same rule.

> ### 💡 Tip
>
> The locus of points at a fixed distance from a given point is a circle. The given point is at the centre of the circle, and the fixed distance is the radius.

> ### 💡 Tip
>
> If a line is included in the locus you draw it as a solid line. If the line is not included, but just shows the edge of the locus you draw it as a broken, or dashed, line.

WORKED EXAMPLE 10

A tap is located at point X.

Draw the locus of points that are exactly 50 metres from the tap.

(Your diagram does not need to be to scale.)

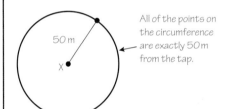

All of the points on the circumference are exactly 50 m from the tap.

Use compasses to draw a circle. Label the centre X and mark the radius.

Using Worked example 10, the locus of points that are less than 50 m from the tap is the region inside the circle.

If you were asked to construct this locus, you would shade the interior of the circle to show that all the points inside the circumference meet the conditions of the locus.

You would show the circumference as a broken line to indicate that it is **not** included in the locus.

WORKED EXAMPLE 11

Anna lives at point A. Josie lives at point B.

They want to meet exactly midway between their homes.

Draw a diagram to show where they could meet.

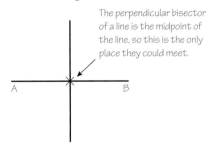

The perpendicular bisector of a line is the midpoint of the line, so this is the only place they could meet.

Draw a line to join the points.

Construct the perpendicular bisector of this line.

The point where the lines cross is exactly midway between their homes.

In Worked example 11 you can take any point on the perpendicular bisector and it will be the same distance from *A* and *B*.

If the girls wanted to meet at any point that was the same distance from their home, they could meet anywhere along that line.

However, the question asked you to find the point exactly midway between *A* and *B*, and the midpoint of line *AB* is the only point that meets that condition.

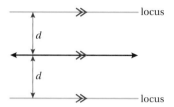

A line segment has a fixed length.

The locus of points equidistant from a line segment has to be the same distance from the line and also the same distance from its end point.

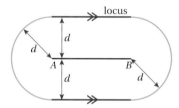

This produces an oval 'racing track' shape with all points the same distance (*d*) from the line segment.

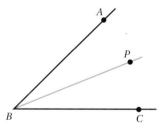

EXERCISE 22C

1 Loci are common in architecture and also in the line markings on sports fields.

Try to identify and describe some of the loci in the two photographs.

2 Without drawing them, describe the point, path or area that each locus will produce.

a Points that are 200 km from a shop at point *X*.

b Points that are more than 2 km but less than 3 km from a straight fence 1 km long.

c Points that are equidistant from the two baselines of a tennis court.

d Points that are equidistant from the four corners of a soccer field.

e Points that are within 1 km of a railway line.

3 Accurately construct the locus of points 4 cm from a point D.

4 Draw angle $MNO = 50°$.

Accurately construct the locus of points equidistant from MN and NO.

5 Draw PQ 4 cm long.

Construct the locus of points 1 cm from PQ.

6 PQ is a line segment of 5 cm.

X is a point exactly 4 cm from P and exactly 2.5 cm from Q.

Show by construction the possible locations of point X.

7 Draw a rectangle $ABCD$ with $AB = 6$ cm and $BC = 4$ cm.

a Construct the locus of points that are equidistant from AB and BC.

b Shade the locus of points that are less than 1 cm from the centre of the rectangle.

c Construct the locus of points that are exactly 1 cm outside the perimeter of the rectangle.

8 $MNOP$ is a square with sides of 5 cm.

Show by construction the locus of all points that are less than 1 cm from the sides of the square.

9 Draw a diagram to show:

a the locus of the valve on the rim of a bicycle wheel as it moves along a flat road surface.

b the locus of the centre of the same wheel as it moves along the road.

Section 4: Applying your skills

Questions that require the accurate drawing of shapes and loci may be given in a real world context.

You will need to decide which construction technique to use.

You may be asked to draw scaled diagrams to solve these problems.

Tip

Scale was covered in Chapter 10.

If you are not given a scale, always state the scale that you have used.

Problem-solving framework

A, B and C represent three towns.

A mobile phone tower is to be erected in the area.

The tower is to be equidistant from towns A and B and within 30 km of town C.

Show by accurate construction on a scale diagram all possible sites for the tower.

Use a scale of 1 cm : 10 km.

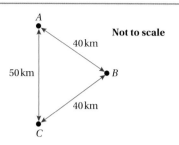

Not to scale

Steps for solving problems	What you would do for this example
Step 1: Work out what you have to do. Start by reading the question carefully.	Although it doesn't say so, this is a locus problem. You have to find the locus of points equidistant from A and B and the locus of points that are less than 30 km from C. The solution is where these loci overlap.
Step 2: What information do you need? Have you got it all?	You have to draw a scale diagram. The distances and the scale are given. The conditions for the loci are given.
Step 3: Decide what maths you can do.	First work out the lengths you have to construct using the scale. The scale is 1 cm : 10 km. So: $\dfrac{40\text{ km}}{10} = 4\text{ cm} \qquad \dfrac{50\text{ km}}{10} = 5\text{ cm}$ Use these lengths to construct a triangle using your ruler and pair of compasses. Once you have the triangle you can find the loci by construction.
Step 4: Set out your solution clearly. Check your working and that your answer is reasonable.	points equidistant from A and B possible location for the tower points 30 km from C The tower could be built at any position along the thick red line.
Step 5: Check that you've answered the question.	You have shown the overlapping loci and written a statement to answer the question.

EXERCISE 22D

1 Draw line $AB = 5.2$ cm.

Construct DE, the perpendicular bisector of AB. Draw DE so that it is 44 mm long.

Mark the intersection point of line AB and DE as C.

Mark point F on DE such that $DF = FC = 11$ mm.

Construct $MN \parallel AB$ and passing through point F.

2 Construct a parallelogram with sides of 46 mm and 28 mm and a longest diagonal of length 60 mm. Measure and write in the length of the other diagonal.

3 Accurately construct a square of side 45 mm.

4 Construct quadrilateral $ABCD$ such that $ABC = 90°$, $AB = DC = 2.2$ cm and $AD = BC = 5$ cm.

What kind of quadrilateral is this?

5 On a treasure map, the position of buried treasure is known to be 10 metres from the castle at point Y and 12 metres from the cave at point Z.

Y and Z are 15 metres apart.

Draw a scale diagram and mark with an X all the places where the treasure might be buried.

Use a scale of 1 cm to 2 m.

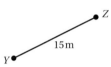

6 A monkey is in a rectangular enclosure which is 10 m by 17.5 m.

The monkey is able to stretch through the fence around its enclosure and reach a distance of 25 cm.

a Draw a scale diagram to show the locus of points that the monkey can reach outside its enclosure.

b Show on your diagram where you would place a safety barrier to make sure that people cannot touch the monkey.

Give a reason for your choice.

7 A garden has a semi-circular lawn surrounded by fencing.

If the semi-circle has a diameter of 10 m and the distance from the lawn to the fence is consistently 1 m, draw an accurate scaled diagram of the lawn and fence.

8 $MNOP$ is a rectangular field 150 m by 400 m.

A fence is to be built across the field so that it is equidistant from points M and O.

Draw a scale plan of the field and indicate on it the position in which the fence is to be built.

9 To prevent theft, a small museum plans to put motion sensors at points *A* and *B* as shown on the plan of the building.

Each motion sensor can pick up any movement within the building up to a range of 8 m, as long as the distance is a straight line.

a Determine by scale drawing and construction any areas not protected by the motion sensors.

b Are these the optimal positions for the sensors?

If not, suggest where they might be located to ensure better coverage and security.

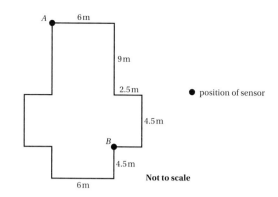

Checklist of learning and understanding

Geometry constructions

- A protractor is used to measure and draw angles.
- You can use a ruler and pair of compasses to construct perpendicular lines and to bisect lines and angles.
- The perpendicular bisector of any line cuts the line at its midpoint.
- The shortest distance from a point to a line is always the perpendicular distance.

Loci

- A locus is a set of points that obey a certain rule.
- The locus of points can be a single point, a line, a curve or a shaded area.
- Loci can be used to solve problems involving equal distances and overlapping areas.

Chapter review

For additional questions on the topics in this chapter, visit GCSE Mathematics Online.

1 **a** Use a protractor to measure angles *a* and *b* on this clock face.

b Draw two angles which are the same size as *a* and *b*.

c Bisect the two angles you have drawn by construction.

2 Draw a line *AB* of length 6.5 cm and find its midpoint by construction.

Indicate the locus of points that are equidistant from *A* and *B* on your diagram.

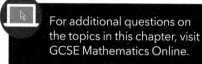

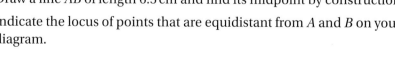

3 Town *X* is due north of Town *Y* and they are 20 km apart.

Town *Z* is 25 km from Town *X* and 35 km from Town *Y* and lies to the east of both towns.

a Draw a scale diagram to show the location of Town *Z* in relation to the other two towns.

Use a scale of 1 cm : 5 km.

b A railway runs between towns *X* and *Y* such that it is equidistant from both towns.

Indicate the position of the railway on your drawing.

c The electricity supply from town *X* is carried on a cable that is the same distance from *XZ* and *XY* along its length.

Indicate where this cable would be.

d Salman wants to live within 10 km of town *Y*, but no more than 30 km from town *Z*.

Show by shading the area that meets these conditions.

4 Here is a scale drawing of a rectangular garden *ABCD*.

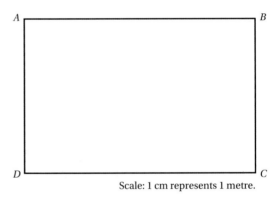

Scale: 1 cm represents 1 metre.

Jane wants to plant a tree in the garden

    at least 5 m from point *C*,

    nearer to *AB* than to *AD*

and less than 3 m from *DC*.

On the diagram, shade the region where Jane can plant the tree.

(4 marks)

©*Pearson Education Ltd 2013*

5 Make an accurate drawing to show the loci of all points that are within 1 cm of the circumference of a circle of radius 2.5 cm.

6 Construct a parallelogram with diagonals 46 mm and 80 mm and one side of 60 mm.

Measure and fill in the sizes of the internal angles and the length of the other side.

23 Vectors

In this chapter you will learn how to ...

- represent vectors as a diagram or column vector.
- add and subtract vectors.
- multiply vectors by a scalar.
- use vectors to construct geometric arguments and proofs.

For more resources relating to this chapter, visit GCSE Mathematics Online.

Using mathematics: real-life applications

Vectors have huge applications in the physical world. For example, mathematical modelling of objects sliding down slopes with varying amounts of friction, working out how far objects can tilt before they tip over and making sure two ships don't crash in the night. All these problems involve the use of vectors.

"When landing at any airport I have to consider how the wind will blow me off course. Over a set amount of time I expect to travel through a particular vector but I have to add on the effect the wind has on my flight path. If I don't do this accurately I would struggle to land the plane safely." *(Pilot)*

Before you start ...

KS3	You need to be able to plot coordinates in all four quadrants.	**1** Draw a set of axes going from -6 to 6 in both directions. Plot the points $A(2, 3)$, $B(-3, 4)$ and $C(-2, -3)$.
KS3	You need to be able to add, subtract and multiply negative numbers.	**2** Calculate. **a** $3 - 7$ **b** $-4 + 11$ **c** $-5 - 18$ **d** -4×7 **e** -3×-9
Ch 15	You need to be able to solve simple linear equations.	**3** Solve. **a** $12 = 4m - 36$ **b** $2k + 15 = 7$ **c** $-6 + 5d = -41$
Ch 15	You need to be able to solve simultaneous linear equations.	**4** Solve. $3x + 2y = 8$ and $4x - 3y = 5$

Find answers at: cambridge.org/ukschools/gcsemaths-studentbookanswers

Assess your starting point using the Launchpad

STEP 1

1 Give the column vector for $\overrightarrow{HG}$.

2 Draw the triangle ABC where $\overrightarrow{AB} = \begin{pmatrix} 3 \\ -5 \end{pmatrix}$ and $\overrightarrow{CA} = \begin{pmatrix} 2 \\ 7 \end{pmatrix}$.

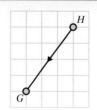

**GO TO
Section 1:**
Vector notation and representation

STEP 2

3 $\mathbf{j} = \begin{pmatrix} -1 \\ 3 \end{pmatrix}$ $\qquad \mathbf{k} = \begin{pmatrix} 2 \\ 1 \end{pmatrix}$ $\qquad \mathbf{l} = \begin{pmatrix} -4 \\ -2 \end{pmatrix}$

Write the following as single vectors.

a $\mathbf{j} + \mathbf{k}$ $\qquad$ **b** $2\mathbf{k} - \mathbf{l}$

4 Find the values of f and g.
$$\begin{pmatrix} 10 \\ g \end{pmatrix} - 4 \begin{pmatrix} f \\ -3 \end{pmatrix} = \begin{pmatrix} -2 \\ 18 \end{pmatrix}$$

5 In the diagram to the right
$\overrightarrow{AC} = \begin{pmatrix} 14 \\ 2 \end{pmatrix}$ and $\overrightarrow{AB} = \begin{pmatrix} 9 \\ 12 \end{pmatrix}$
Find:

a $\overrightarrow{CA}$ $\qquad$ **b** $\overrightarrow{CA} + \overrightarrow{AB}$.

6 Which of these vectors are parallel?
$$\begin{pmatrix} -3 \\ 4 \end{pmatrix} \begin{pmatrix} 9 \\ 16 \end{pmatrix} \begin{pmatrix} 15 \\ 20 \end{pmatrix} \begin{pmatrix} -3 \\ 2 \end{pmatrix}$$

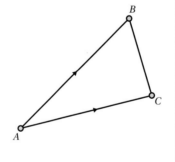

**GO TO
Section 2:**
Vector arithmetic

STEP 3

7 ABCD is a square.

$\overrightarrow{AB} = \mathbf{x}$, $\overrightarrow{BC} = \mathbf{y}$

If the ratio of $AB:BE$ is $1:2$, find

a $\overrightarrow{BE}$ $\qquad$ **b** $\overrightarrow{AF}$

M is the midpoint of EF.

c Find $\overrightarrow{AM}$

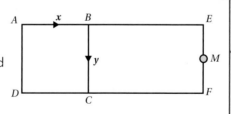

**GO TO
Section 3:**
Using vectors in geometric proofs

GO TO
Chapter review

Section 1: Vector notation and representation

A **vector** describes movement from one point to another, it has a direction and a magnitude (size).

Vectors can be used to describe many different kinds of movement. For example: **displacement** of a shape following translation, displacement of a boat during its journey, the velocity of an object, and the acceleration of an object.

A vector that describes the movement from A to B can be represented by:

- an arrow in a diagram
- $\overrightarrow{AB}$ (arrow indicates direction)
- **a** (if handwritten this would be underlined, <u>a</u>)
- a column vector $\begin{pmatrix} x \\ y \end{pmatrix}$

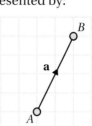

If you were to travel along this vector in the opposite direction, from B to A, you would represent this vector as:

- $\overrightarrow{BA}$
- **-a**
- $\begin{pmatrix} -2 \\ -4 \end{pmatrix}$

Column vectors

In a column vector x represents the **horizontal** movement; y represents the **vertical** movement.

	Movement	
	x	y
positive	right	up
negative	left	down

In the diagram, $\overrightarrow{AB} = \begin{pmatrix} 2 \\ 4 \end{pmatrix}$.

EXERCISE 23A

1 Match up equivalent representations of the vectors.

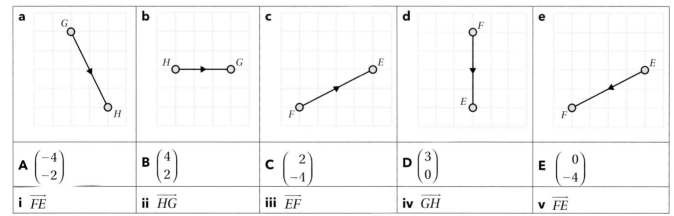

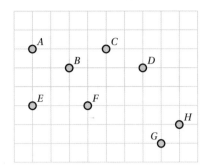

2 Use the diagram (left) to answer the following questions.

Find each of the column vectors.

a $\overrightarrow{AB}$ **b** $\overrightarrow{DC}$ **c** $\overrightarrow{BC}$

d $\overrightarrow{DF}$ **e** $\overrightarrow{HF}$ **f** $\overrightarrow{BH}$

g What do you notice about $\overrightarrow{AB}$ and $\overrightarrow{DC}$?

h What do you notice about $\overrightarrow{AB}$ and $\overrightarrow{BH}$?

3 Draw a pair of axes where x and y vary from -8 to 8.

Plot the point A $(2, -1)$.

Then plot points B, C, D, E, F and G where:

$$\overrightarrow{AB} = \begin{pmatrix} 2 \\ 7 \end{pmatrix} \qquad \overrightarrow{AC} = \begin{pmatrix} -3 \\ 7 \end{pmatrix} \qquad \overrightarrow{AD} = \begin{pmatrix} -6 \\ 3 \end{pmatrix}$$

$$\overrightarrow{AE} = \begin{pmatrix} 5 \\ 3 \end{pmatrix} \qquad \overrightarrow{AF} = \begin{pmatrix} -3 \\ -1 \end{pmatrix} \qquad \overrightarrow{AG} = \begin{pmatrix} 2 \\ -1 \end{pmatrix}$$

4 **a** Find the vector from point A with coordinates $(3, -4)$ to point B with coordinates $(-1, 2)$.

b Give the coordinates of two more points E and F where the vector from E to F is the same as $\overrightarrow{AB}$.

5 **a** Find the vector from point K with coordinates $(-2, -1)$ to point L with coordinates $(-8, 9)$.

b Use your answer to find the coordinates of the midpoint of KL.

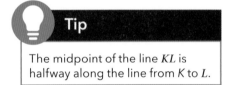

Tip

The midpoint of the line KL is halfway along the line from K to L.

6 These vectors describe how to move between points A, B, C and D.

$$\overrightarrow{AB} = \begin{pmatrix} 2 \\ 1 \end{pmatrix} \qquad \overrightarrow{BC} = \begin{pmatrix} 1 \\ 0 \end{pmatrix} \qquad \overrightarrow{DA} = \begin{pmatrix} -1 \\ 2 \end{pmatrix}$$

Draw a diagram showing how the points are positioned to form the quadrilateral $ABCD$.

7 In a game of chess, different pieces move in different ways.

- A king can move one square in any direction (including diagonals).
- A bishop can move any number of squares diagonally.
- A knight moves two squares horizontally and one square vertically or two squares vertically and one horizontally.

A chessboard is eight squares wide and eight squares long.

What vectors can the following pieces move?

a Bishop   **b** King   **c** Knight

For part **a**, you will need to think algebraically

8 How would you find the length (magnitude) of a vector?

How could you describe its direction?

Use these diagrams and your knowledge of Pythagoras and trigonometry to help design a method.

vector $\begin{pmatrix} 2 \\ -4 \end{pmatrix}$ vector $\begin{pmatrix} 3 \\ 5 \end{pmatrix}$

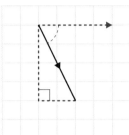 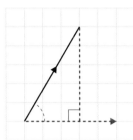

Tip

See Chapters 32 and 33 if you need a reminder.

Section 2: Vector arithmetic

Addition and subtraction

The diagram shows $\overrightarrow{AB} = \begin{pmatrix} 2 \\ 4 \end{pmatrix}$, $\overrightarrow{BC} = \begin{pmatrix} 4 \\ -2 \end{pmatrix}$,

and $\overrightarrow{AC} = \begin{pmatrix} 6 \\ 2 \end{pmatrix}$

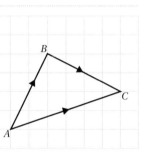

Moving from A to B and then from B to C is the same as moving directly from A to C. In other words, you can take a 'shortcut' from A to C by adding together $\overrightarrow{AB}$ and $\overrightarrow{BC}$.

$\overrightarrow{AC}$ is known as the **resultant** of $\overrightarrow{AB}$ and $\overrightarrow{BC}$.

$$\overrightarrow{AB} + \overrightarrow{BC} = \overrightarrow{AC}$$

$$\begin{pmatrix} 2 \\ 4 \end{pmatrix} + \begin{pmatrix} 4 \\ -2 \end{pmatrix} = \begin{pmatrix} 6 \\ 2 \end{pmatrix}$$

The diagram shows $\overrightarrow{AB}$ and $\overrightarrow{CB}$.

To find $\overrightarrow{AC}$ you need to travel along $\overrightarrow{CB}$ in the opposite direction.

So, **subtract** $\overrightarrow{CB}$.

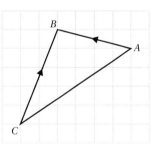

$$\overrightarrow{AB} - \overrightarrow{CB} = \overrightarrow{AC}$$

$$\begin{pmatrix} -4 \\ 1 \end{pmatrix} - \begin{pmatrix} 2 \\ 5 \end{pmatrix} = \begin{pmatrix} -4 - 2 \\ 1 - 5 \end{pmatrix} = \begin{pmatrix} -6 \\ -4 \end{pmatrix}$$

Multiplying by a scalar

Multiplying a vector by a **scalar** results in repeated addition.

This is the same as multiplying the x-component by the scalar, k, and the y-component by the same scalar, k.

Key vocabulary

scalar: a numerical quantity (it has no direction).

Find answers at: cambridge.org/ukschools/gcsemaths-studentbookanswers

$$\overrightarrow{AB} = \begin{pmatrix} 4 \\ -1 \end{pmatrix} \text{ and } \overrightarrow{CD} = \begin{pmatrix} 12 \\ -3 \end{pmatrix}$$

$$CD = 3\overrightarrow{AB}$$

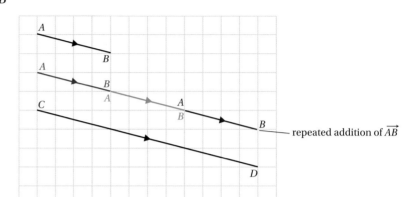

repeated addition of $\overrightarrow{AB}$

$$3 \times \begin{pmatrix} 4 \\ -1 \end{pmatrix} = \begin{pmatrix} 4 \\ -1 \end{pmatrix} + \begin{pmatrix} 4 \\ -1 \end{pmatrix} + \begin{pmatrix} 4 \\ -1 \end{pmatrix} \quad\text{—— repeated addition}$$

$$= \begin{pmatrix} 3 \times 4 \\ 3 \times -1 \end{pmatrix} \quad\text{—— multiplying the } x\text{-component by the scalar } k$$

$$\text{—— multiplying the } y\text{-component by the scalar } k$$

$$= \begin{pmatrix} 12 \\ -3 \end{pmatrix}$$

Key vocabulary

parallel vectors: occur when one vector is a multiple of the other.

Multiplying a vector by a scalar k results in a **parallel vector** with a magnitude multiplied by k.

Vectors are parallel if one is a multiple of the other.

WORK IT OUT 22.1

Which of the following vectors are parallel?

$$\mathbf{a} = \begin{pmatrix} 3 \\ -1 \end{pmatrix} \qquad \mathbf{b} = \begin{pmatrix} 4 \\ -3 \end{pmatrix} \qquad \mathbf{c} = \begin{pmatrix} 9 \\ -3 \end{pmatrix} \qquad \mathbf{d} = \begin{pmatrix} 6 \\ 2 \end{pmatrix} \qquad \mathbf{e} = \begin{pmatrix} -6 \\ 2 \end{pmatrix}$$

Option A	Option B	Option C
Vectors **a** and **c**	Vectors **d** and **e**	Vectors **a**, **c** and **e**

EXERCISE 23B

1 $\mathbf{p} = \begin{pmatrix} -3 \\ 2 \end{pmatrix} \qquad \mathbf{q} = \begin{pmatrix} 5 \\ -1 \end{pmatrix} \qquad \mathbf{r} = \begin{pmatrix} -3 \\ -2 \end{pmatrix} \qquad \mathbf{s} = \begin{pmatrix} 4 \\ -7 \end{pmatrix}$

Write each of these as a single vector.

    a $\mathbf{p} + \mathbf{q}$ **b** $\mathbf{s} - \mathbf{r}$ **c** $4\mathbf{p}$

    d $-3\mathbf{s}$ **e** $\mathbf{p} + \mathbf{q} + \mathbf{r}$ **f** $2\mathbf{p} + \mathbf{q} - 2\mathbf{s}$

    g Which of the results from parts **a** to **f** are parallel to the vector $\begin{pmatrix} 3 \\ -2 \end{pmatrix}$?

2 Give three vectors parallel to $\begin{pmatrix} 2 \\ -3 \end{pmatrix}$.

3 Find x, y, z and t in each of the following vector calculations.

a $\begin{pmatrix} x \\ 3 \end{pmatrix} + \begin{pmatrix} 5 \\ y \end{pmatrix} = \begin{pmatrix} 9 \\ 3 \end{pmatrix}$

b $\begin{pmatrix} 10 \\ y \end{pmatrix} - \begin{pmatrix} x \\ -3 \end{pmatrix} = \begin{pmatrix} -2 \\ 8 \end{pmatrix}$

c $\begin{pmatrix} x \\ -3 \end{pmatrix} + \begin{pmatrix} -6 \\ y \end{pmatrix} = \begin{pmatrix} 11 \\ -8 \end{pmatrix}$

d $z\begin{pmatrix} x \\ 12 \end{pmatrix} = \begin{pmatrix} 7 \\ -24 \end{pmatrix}$

e $z\begin{pmatrix} 12 \\ y \end{pmatrix} = \begin{pmatrix} 3 \\ 8 \end{pmatrix}$

f $\begin{pmatrix} 2 \\ -4 \end{pmatrix} + z\begin{pmatrix} 5 \\ y \end{pmatrix} = \begin{pmatrix} 17 \\ 14 \end{pmatrix}$

g $\begin{pmatrix} x \\ -4 \end{pmatrix} - z\begin{pmatrix} -5 \\ -3 \end{pmatrix} = \begin{pmatrix} 20 \\ 5 \end{pmatrix}$

h $z\begin{pmatrix} 3 \\ 4 \end{pmatrix} + t\begin{pmatrix} 2 \\ -2 \end{pmatrix} = \begin{pmatrix} 18 \\ 10 \end{pmatrix}$

4 In the diagram, $\overrightarrow{AB} = \begin{pmatrix} 20 \\ 16 \end{pmatrix}$. C lies on the line AB.

The ratio of $AC : CB$ is $1 : 3$.

a Find $\overrightarrow{AC}$.

b Find $\overrightarrow{BC}$.

5 These vectors describe how to move between points E, F, G and H, which are four vertices of a quadrilateral.

$$\overrightarrow{EF} = \begin{pmatrix} 3 \\ -1 \end{pmatrix} \qquad \overrightarrow{HG} = \begin{pmatrix} 6 \\ -2 \end{pmatrix} \qquad \overrightarrow{EH} = \begin{pmatrix} 0 \\ 1 \end{pmatrix}$$

a What can you say about sides EF and HG?

b Predict what kind of quadrilateral $EFGH$ is.

c Draw the quadrilateral and find $\overrightarrow{GF}$.

6 $ABCD$ is a quadrilateral. $\overrightarrow{AB} = \overrightarrow{DC}$ and $\overrightarrow{DA} = \overrightarrow{CB}$.

What kind of quadrilateral is ABCD? How do you know this?

Section 3: Using vectors in geometric proofs

Vectors can be used to prove geometric results. You can use them to:

- identify parallel lines
- find midpoints
- share lines in a given ratio.

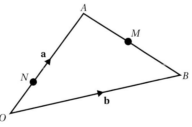

For example, in this triangle $\overrightarrow{AB} = -\mathbf{a} + \mathbf{b}$

$$= \mathbf{b} - \mathbf{a}$$

M is the midpoint of AB.

The ratio of $ON : NA$ is $1 : 2$

- You can use what you know about vectors to find $\overrightarrow{AM}$.

  You know that AM is half of AB, so it follows that $\overrightarrow{AM}$ is half of the journey from A to B, so

$$\overrightarrow{AM} = \frac{1}{2}(\mathbf{b} - \mathbf{a})$$

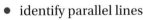

Find answers at: cambridge.org/ukschools/gcsemaths-studentbookanswers

- You can use what you know about the effect of scalars on vectors to calculate $\overrightarrow{ON}$.

  You know that the ratio of $\overrightarrow{ON} : \overrightarrow{NA}$ is $1 : 2$.

  So, you know that the point N is such that $2\overrightarrow{ON} = \overrightarrow{NA}$, so

  $$\overrightarrow{ON} = \frac{1}{3}\mathbf{a}$$

Tip

If you're struggling with a question, highlight sides that are labelled with vectors or that are parallel to any given vectors. Then identify the journey between your two points by using these highlighted lines.

WORKED EXAMPLE 1

In this parallelogram, M is the midpoint of AC, and N is the midpoint of BC. Prove that $\overrightarrow{MN}$ is parallel to $\overrightarrow{AB}$.

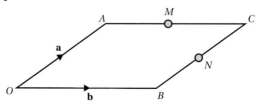

$\overrightarrow{AB} = \mathbf{b} - \mathbf{a}$

$\overrightarrow{MN} = \overrightarrow{MA} + \overrightarrow{AO} + \overrightarrow{OB} + \overrightarrow{BN}$

$= -\dfrac{1}{2}\mathbf{b} - \mathbf{a} + \mathbf{b} + \dfrac{1}{2}\mathbf{a}$

$= \dfrac{1}{2}(\mathbf{b} - \mathbf{a})$

Since $\overrightarrow{MN}$ is a multiple of $\overrightarrow{AB}$, they are parallel.

WORKED EXAMPLE 2

In the regular hexagon shown, $\overrightarrow{EF} = \mathbf{e}$ and $\overrightarrow{JI} = \mathbf{j}$

It is possible to move between any two vertices of the regular hexagon using combinations of vectors $\mathbf{e}$ and $\mathbf{j}$.

Find the vector that describes each journey.

a $\overrightarrow{EG}$ **b** $\overrightarrow{HJ}$ **c** $\overrightarrow{EJ}$

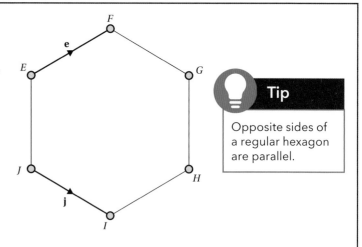

Tip

Opposite sides of a regular hexagon are parallel.

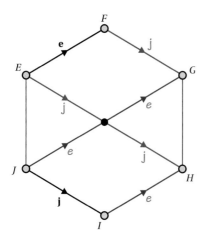

Drawing a few additional lines parallel to the vectors given can help you to see a solution.

Write these in terms of $\mathbf{e}$ and $\mathbf{j}$.

Continues on next page ...

a $\overrightarrow{EG} = \overrightarrow{EF} + \overrightarrow{FG}$

Using addition of vectors, $\overrightarrow{EG}$ is the resultant vector.

$\overrightarrow{FG} = \mathbf{j}$

$\overrightarrow{EG} = \mathbf{e} + \mathbf{j}$

Using the properties of a regular hexagon, the line *FG* is parallel to *JI*. Parallel vectors are a multiple of each other, in this case the scalar is 1.

b $\overrightarrow{HJ} = \overrightarrow{HI} + \overrightarrow{IJ}$

Using addition of vectors, $\overrightarrow{HJ}$ is the resultant vector.

$\overrightarrow{HI} + - \mathbf{e}$

Using the properties of a regular hexagon, the line *IH* is parallel to *EF*. Parallel vectors are a multiple of each other, in this case the scalar is 1. You are travelling from *H* to *I*, in the opposite direction of **e**, so need the negative of **e**.

$\overrightarrow{HJ} = -\mathbf{e} - \mathbf{j}$

$\overrightarrow{JI}$ is the opposite direction to $\overrightarrow{JI}$.

c $\overrightarrow{EJ} = \overrightarrow{EH} + \overrightarrow{HI} + \overrightarrow{IJ}$

Using addition of vectors $\overrightarrow{EJ}$ is the resultant vector.

$\overrightarrow{EH} = 2\mathbf{j}$

Using the helpful additional lines, *EH* is parallel to *IJ* and twice its length. It is moving in the same direction.

$\overrightarrow{HI} = -\mathbf{e}$

$\overrightarrow{HI}$ is the opposite direction to $\overrightarrow{IH}$.

$\overrightarrow{IJ} = -\mathbf{j}$

$\overrightarrow{JI}$ is the opposite direction to $\overrightarrow{JI}$.

$\overrightarrow{EH} = 2\mathbf{j} - \mathbf{e} - \mathbf{j} = \mathbf{j} - \mathbf{e}$

EXERCISE 23C

1 In the diagram, $\overrightarrow{AC} = \begin{pmatrix} 10 \\ 2 \end{pmatrix}$ and $\overrightarrow{AB} = \begin{pmatrix} 8 \\ 14 \end{pmatrix}$

M is the midpoint of *BC*.

Find:

a $\overrightarrow{CA}$ **b** $\overrightarrow{CA} + \overrightarrow{AB}$

c $\overrightarrow{CM}$.

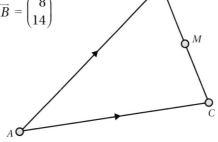

2 Two triangles have vertices *ABC* and *DEF*:

A(0, 0), *B*(3, 2), *C*(2, 5)

D(1, 1), *E*(7, 5), *F*(5, 11)

Compare the vectors:

a $\overrightarrow{AB}$ and $\overrightarrow{DE}$

b $\overrightarrow{AC}$ and $\overrightarrow{DF}$.

c What does this tell you about the triangles *ABC* and *DEF*?

Find answers at: cambridge.org/ukschools/gcsemaths-studentbookanswers

3 MNOP is a square.

Find the vectors. Explain your answers.

a $\overrightarrow{NO}$ **b** $\overrightarrow{OP}$

c $\overrightarrow{MO}$ **d** $\overrightarrow{PN}$

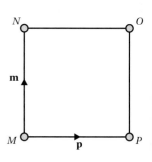

4 ABCD is a parallelogram.

M is the midpoint of side BC, N the midpoint of CD.

$\overrightarrow{AB} = \mathbf{p}$ and $\overrightarrow{BM} = \mathbf{q}$

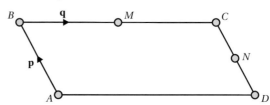

Find the vectors. Explain your answers.

a $\overrightarrow{AC}$ **b** $\overrightarrow{DB}$

c $\overrightarrow{MD}$ **d** Show that $\overrightarrow{NM}$ is parallel to $\overrightarrow{DB}$.

5 The diagram shows four congruent triangles forming a tessellating pattern, and vectors **m** and **n**.

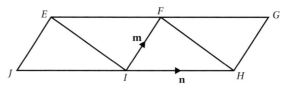

Find the vectors

a $\overrightarrow{JI}$ **b** $\overrightarrow{EJ}$ **c** $\overrightarrow{JF}$ **d** $\overrightarrow{EH}$

6 EFG is an equilateral triangle.

Points H, I and J are the midpoints of each side.

$\overrightarrow{EF} = \mathbf{e}$ and $\overrightarrow{EG} = \mathbf{g}$.

Find the vectors

a $\overrightarrow{EH}$ **b** $\overrightarrow{JE}$ **c** $\overrightarrow{FG}$

d $\overrightarrow{HI}$ **e** $\overrightarrow{JI}$

What can you say about triangle HIJ?

7 EFG is an equilateral triangle.

Points H and I are the midpoints of sides EF and FG.

JI is a straight line with midpoint H.

$\overrightarrow{EF} = \mathbf{e}$ and $\overrightarrow{EG} = \mathbf{g}$.

Find the vectors

a $\overrightarrow{FH}$ **b** $\overrightarrow{IG}$ **c** $\overrightarrow{HI}$ **d** $\overrightarrow{JI}$ **e** $\overrightarrow{JE}$

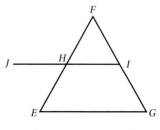

8 In the diagram, V is the midpoint of TR and W the midpoint of RS.

The ratio of $TU : US$ is $1 : 4$.

$\overrightarrow{SR} = \mathbf{r}$ and $\overrightarrow{TU} = \mathbf{t}$.

Find the vectors

a $\overrightarrow{TS}$ **b** $\overrightarrow{UR}$

c $\overrightarrow{VR}$ **d** $\overrightarrow{WV}$

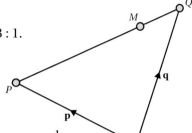

9 In the diagram, the ratio of $PM : MQ$ is $3 : 1$.

a Find $\overrightarrow{PQ}$

b Find $\overrightarrow{PM}$

c Show $\overrightarrow{OM} = \dfrac{1}{4}(3\mathbf{q} + \mathbf{p})$

10 A river runs from east to west at 3 m every second.

It is 12 m wide.

James can swim at 1.5 m every second.

He sets off to cross the river.

How far off course is he when he reaches the other river bank?

How far does he actually swim?

Checklist of learning and understanding

Notation

- Vectors can be written in a variety of ways: $\overrightarrow{AB}$, $\mathbf{a}$, $\begin{pmatrix} 1 \\ 2 \end{pmatrix}$.

Addition and subtraction

- To add or subtract vectors simply add or subtract the x- and y-components.

$$\begin{pmatrix} 3 \\ 2 \end{pmatrix} + \begin{pmatrix} 2 \\ -4 \end{pmatrix} = \begin{pmatrix} 5 \\ -2 \end{pmatrix} \qquad \begin{pmatrix} -1 \\ 4 \end{pmatrix} - \begin{pmatrix} 5 \\ -6 \end{pmatrix} = \begin{pmatrix} -6 \\ 10 \end{pmatrix}$$

Multiplication by a scalar

- To multiply by a scalar you can use repeated addition, or multiply the x-component by the scalar and the y-component by the scalar.

$$3\begin{pmatrix} -2 \\ 1 \end{pmatrix} = \begin{pmatrix} -2 \\ 1 \end{pmatrix} + \begin{pmatrix} -2 \\ 1 \end{pmatrix} + \begin{pmatrix} -2 \\ 1 \end{pmatrix} = \begin{pmatrix} -6 \\ 3 \end{pmatrix}$$

$$3\begin{pmatrix} -2 \\ 1 \end{pmatrix} = \begin{pmatrix} -6 \\ 3 \end{pmatrix}$$

- Multiplying a vector by a scalar quantity produces a parallel vector; you can identify that vectors are parallel if one vector is a multiple of the other. Parallel vectors can be part of the same line and described using a ratio.

Using vectors in geometric proofs

- You can use vectors to identify parallel lines, find midpoints and share lines in a given ratio.

Find answers at: cambridge.org/ukschools/gcsemaths-studentbookanswers

For additional questions on the topics in this chapter, visit GCSE Mathematics Online.

 Chapter review

1 What is the difference between coordinate $(-2, 3)$ and vector $\begin{pmatrix} -2 \\ 3 \end{pmatrix}$?

2 Match the parallel vectors.

$\mathbf{a} = \begin{pmatrix} -6 \\ 2 \end{pmatrix}$ $\mathbf{b} = \begin{pmatrix} 1 \\ 3 \end{pmatrix}$ $\mathbf{c} = \begin{pmatrix} 3 \\ -1 \end{pmatrix}$ $\mathbf{d} = \begin{pmatrix} 7 \\ 21 \end{pmatrix}$

$\mathbf{e} = \begin{pmatrix} -2 \\ 4 \end{pmatrix}$ $\mathbf{f} = \begin{pmatrix} -6 \\ 12 \end{pmatrix}$ $\mathbf{g} = \begin{pmatrix} -1 \\ 2 \end{pmatrix}$

3 Calculate.

a $\begin{pmatrix} 1 \\ -2 \end{pmatrix} + \begin{pmatrix} -2 \\ -1 \end{pmatrix}$ **b** $\begin{pmatrix} 0 \\ -3 \end{pmatrix} - \begin{pmatrix} -2 \\ 4 \end{pmatrix}$ **c** $-3\begin{pmatrix} 2 \\ -1 \end{pmatrix}$

4 *EFG* is a straight line.

$EF : FG = 2 : 3$

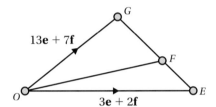

Find.

a $\overrightarrow{EG}$ **b** $\overrightarrow{FG}$ **c** $\overrightarrow{OF}$

5 The points *G* and *H* lie on line *EF*.

$\overrightarrow{EF} = 12\mathbf{e} - 18\mathbf{f}$

The ratio of $EG : GH : HF$ is $1 : 3 : 2$.

a Draw a sketch of this situation.

b Find the vectors

  i $\overrightarrow{GH}$ **ii** $\overrightarrow{HE}$

 6 *PQRS* is a parallelogram.

N is the point on *SQ* such that $SN : NQ = 3 : 2$

$\overrightarrow{PQ} = \mathbf{a}$

$\overrightarrow{PS} = \mathbf{b}$

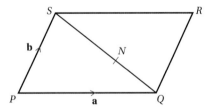

a Write down, in terms of **a** and **b**, an expression for $\overrightarrow{SQ}$ *(1 mark)*

b Express $\overrightarrow{NR}$ in terms of **a** and **b**.   *(3 marks)*

24 Straight-line graphs

$\phi\,981,4$
$\phi\,965,8$
$\phi\,960,0$
$\phi\,941,4$
$\phi\,919,1$

In this chapter you will learn how to ...

- use a table of values to plot graphs of linear functions.
- identify the main features of straight-line graphs and use them to sketch graphs.
- sketch graphs from linear equations in the form $y = mx + c$.
- find the equation of a line parallel to a given line.
- find the equation of a straight line using the gradient and points on the line.
- find the equation of a tangent that touches a circle with centre $(0, 0)$.

 For more resources relating to this chapter, visit GCSE Mathematics Online.

Using mathematics: real-life applications

This is a photograph of a building nicknamed "The Gherkin", in London. The curves and lines of the building were designed using complex equations and their graphs. Architecture is just one of many professions in which people plot and use graphs in their work.

"When designing a new building, I use graphs to help identify and describe the structural properties the building needs to have."

(Architect)

Before you start ...

Ch 16	You should remember how to generate terms in a sequence using a rule.	**1** Use the rule $T(n) = 3n - 2$ to complete this table.

Term number	1	3	5	10
Term				

KS3	You should be able to give the coordinates of points on a grid.	**2** Use the grid. **a** Write down the coordinates of points A, D and E. **b** What point has the following coordinates? **i** $(-2, 2)$ **ii** $(0, -6)$ **c** What is the name given to the point $(0, 0)$?

Ch 15	You must be able to manipulate and solve equations.	**3** Solve for x.
		   a $4 - 3x = 13$ **b** $\dfrac{x}{7} = 6$ **c** $-3(5x + 2) = 0$
		
		 4 If $y = 2x + 5$:
		   a find y when $x = -2$ **b** find x when $y = 8$

Ch 17	You should remember how to change the subject of a formula.	**5** Make y the subject of each equation. **a** $-2x - y + 1 = 0$ **b** $2x + 3y = 6$ **c** $x - 2y = -2$

Find answers at: cambridge.org/ukschools/gcsemaths-studentbookanswers

Assess your starting point using the Launchpad

STEP 1

1 Complete the table of values for each function.

a $x - y = 2$

x	−2	−1	0	1
y				

b $x + y = 4$

x	−2	0	1	2
y				

c $2x + y + 2 = 0$

x	−3	−2	0	1
y				

d $x - 2y + 2 = 0$

x	−2	0	2	4
y				

2 The graphs of two of the functions from Question **1** are shown here.

Match each graph to its equation.

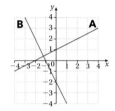

GO TO
Section 1:
Plotting graphs

STEP 2

3 **a** Sketch the graph of $y = 2x + 4$ without plotting a table of values.
   b Find the gradient and y-intercept of the resulting straight line.

4 Find the equation of the straight line that passes through the points (1, 4) and (3, 7).

5 A line cuts the x-axis at 4 and the y-axis at 5. What is its gradient?

GO TO
Section 2:
Gradient and intercepts of straight-line graphs

GO TO
Step 3:
The Launchpad continues on the next page …

Launchpad continued ...

STEP 3

6 Which of these lines are parallel to each other?

    a $y = -3x + 3$ **b** $y = 7 - 3x$ **c** $y = 3x + 7$

    d $y = \frac{1}{3}x + 3$ **e** $y = 7 - 2x$

7 A line is parallel to the line $y = \frac{1}{2}x$ and passes through the point (2, 4). What is its equation?

8 How do you know $y = \frac{1}{2}x + 3$ crosses the line $y = 5 - 2x$ at right angles?

9 Find the tangent to the circle $x^2 + y^2 = 25$ that passes through point (−3, 4).

GO TO
Section 3:
Parallel lines, perpendicular lines and tangents
Section 4:
Working with straight-line graphs

GO TO
Chapter review

Section 1: Plotting graphs

You can draw straight-line and curved graphs to show **functions**.

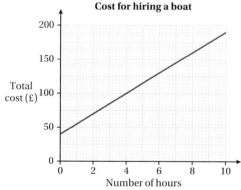

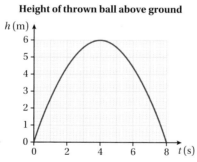

Key vocabulary

function: a set of instructions for changing one number (the input) into another number (the output).

coordinates: an ordered pair (x, y) identifying position on a grid.

Functions that produce straight lines when you plot matching x- and y-values (**coordinates**) are called linear functions.

Plotting linear functions

You can plot the graph of a function by drawing up a table of values.

Tip

When you worked with functions and sequences in Chapter 16 you used a rule to find the terms in a pattern or sequence. You will apply these skills again in this section.

Tip

When you draw a graph, continue the line in both directions through the points. Don't just join the three plotted points together; they are just three of the infinite number of points on the line.

Tip

If the points you have plotted do not line up, then check your calculations for the y-values and/or check that you have plotted the points correctly.

WORKED EXAMPLE 1

Draw up a table of values and plot the graph of $y = 2x + 1$.

x	-1	0	1	2
y	-1	1	3	5

Choose some values for x.

Substitute each x-value into the equation to find the matching y-value.

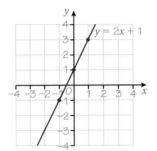

Plot at least three points using the coordinates.

Points $(-1, -1)$, $(0, 1)$ and $(1, 3)$ have been plotted here.

Draw a straight line through the points.

Label the graph with the equation.

EXERCISE 24A

1 Complete a table of values for each function. Plot the graphs.

a $y = x$ **b** $y = x + 2$ **c** $y = 3x - 5$

d $y = 6 - x$ **e** $y = 2x + 1$ **f** $y = x - 1$

g $y = -2x + 3$ **h** $y = 4 - x$ **i** $y = 3x - 2$

2 What is the minimum number of points you need to plot a straight line accurately? Why?

Section 2: Gradient and intercepts of straight-line graphs

You can use the characteristics of straight-line graphs and their equations to sketch graphs without drawing up a table of values.

The main characteristics of a straight-line graph are:

- the **gradient**, or slope of the graph
- the **x-intercept** (where it crosses the x-axis)
- the **y-intercept** (where it crosses the y-axis).

Gradient

On the following graph of $y = 2x + 4$, a right-angled triangle has been drawn on the graph so you can measure the gradient.

Key vocabulary

gradient: a measure of the steepness of a line.

$$\text{gradient} = \frac{\text{change in } y}{\text{change in } x}$$

x-intercept: the point where a line crosses the x-axis when $y = 0$.

y-intercept: the point where a line crosses the y-axis when $x = 0$.

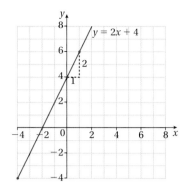

On a graph, the gradient is the vertical distance travelled (difference between the y-coordinates) divided by the horizontal distance (difference between the x-coordinates):

$$\text{Gradient of a line} = \frac{\text{difference in } y\text{-values}}{\text{difference in } x\text{-values}}$$

$$\text{Or, more simply, gradient} = \frac{\text{vertical rise}}{\text{horizontal run}}$$

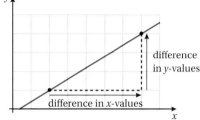

The graph of the linear equation $y = 2x + 4$ shown above slopes up to the right. This is described as a **positive** gradient.

$$\text{Gradient} = \frac{\text{vertical rise}}{\text{horizontal run}} = \frac{2}{1} = 2$$

WORKED EXAMPLE 2

Calculate the gradient of each line.

a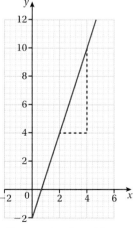

Movement up is positive

b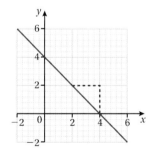

Movement down is negative

a $\text{Gradient} = \dfrac{\text{change in } y}{\text{change in } x} = \dfrac{6}{2} = 3$

b $\text{Gradient} = \dfrac{\text{change in } y}{\text{change in } x} = \dfrac{-2}{2} = -1$

This line slopes from top left to bottom right.

This is described as a **negative** gradient.

You don't need to draw the graph to find the gradient of a line.

You can calculate the gradient if you know the coordinates of any two points on the line.

WORKED EXAMPLE 3

Calculate the gradient of the line that passes through the points $(1, 4)$ and $(3, 8)$.

$$\frac{\text{difference in } y\text{-values}}{\text{difference in } x\text{-values}} = \frac{(y_2 - y_1)}{(x_2 - x_1)}$$

$$= \frac{(8 - 4)}{(3 - 1)}$$

$$= \frac{4}{2}$$

$$= 2$$

Let the coordinates be (x_1, y_1) and (x_2, y_2) and substitute the values to find the gradient.

The gradient of the line that passes through the points $(1, 4)$ and $(3, 8)$ is 2.

EXERCISE 24B

1 Calculate the gradient of each line. Leave your answer as a fraction in lowest terms if necessary.

a
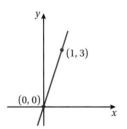

b
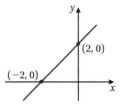

c
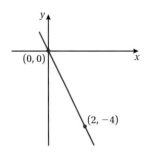

d
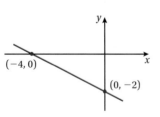

e
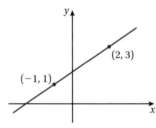

f
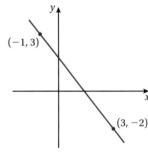

2 Find the gradient of the line that passes through points A and B in each case.

    a $A(1, 2)$ and $B(3, 8)$ **b** $A(0, 6)$ and $B(3, 9)$

    c $A(-1, -4)$ and $B(-3, 2)$ **d** $A(3, 5)$ and $B(7, 12)$

Using the gradient and y-intercept to sketch graphs

This is the graph of $y = -x + 2$.

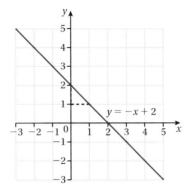

The graph slopes down to the right so it has a **negative** gradient. For every one unit it moves right it goes one unit down. The gradient of the line is $\dfrac{-1}{1} = -1$.

The line crosses the y-axis at the point $(0, 2)$. This is the y-intercept.

In the equation $y = -x + 2$, the coefficient of x is -1 and the constant is 2.

The general form of a linear equation is $y = mx + c$.

In this form:

- The value of the coefficient m is the gradient of the graph.
- The value of the constant c is the y-intercept.

Key vocabulary

coefficient: the number before a variable.

constant: a number on its own.

Tip

$y = mx + c$, it is known as the **gradient-intercept** form of a straight line.

WORK IT OUT 24.1

Without plotting a graph, find the gradient and y-intercept of the linear function $y = -2x + 4$.

In which direction does the line move across the page?

Which of the answers below is correct?

Option A	Option B	Option C
$y = -2x + 4$	$y = -2x + 4$	$y = -2x + 4$
2 is the coefficient of x.	-2 is the coefficient of x.	-2 is the coefficient of x.
4 is the constant.	4 is the constant.	4 is the constant.
So, the gradient is 2 and the y-intercept is 4.	So, the gradient is -2 and the y-intercept is 4.	So, the gradient is -2 and the y-intercept is 4.
The graph goes up to the right.	The graph goes down to the right.	The graph goes down to the left.

You can use the values of m and c to sketch a graph.

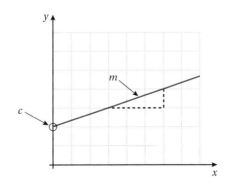

Find answers at: cambridge.org/ukschools/gcsemaths-studentbookanswers

Using the *x*-intercept and *y*-intercept to sketch a graph

If you know where the graph cuts the axes you can sketch the graph of the line.

You can find the *x*-intercept by substituting $y = 0$ into the equation and you can find the *y*-intercept by substituting $x = 0$ into the equation.

Consider these two lines.

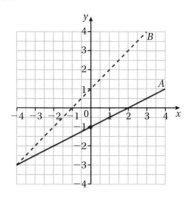

Line A has an *x*-intercept at $(2, 0)$ and a *y*-intercept at $(0, -1)$.

Line B has an *x*-intercept at $(-1, 0)$ and a *y*-intercept at $(0, 1)$.

WORKED EXAMPLE 4

Find the *x*- and *y*-intercepts and use them to sketch the graph of $y + 2x = 6$.

When $x = 0$
$y + 2(0) = 6$
The *y*-intercept is $(0, 6)$.
When $y = 0$
$0 + 2x = 6$
$2x = 6$
$x = 3$
The *x*-intercept is $(3, 0)$.

First find the intercepts.

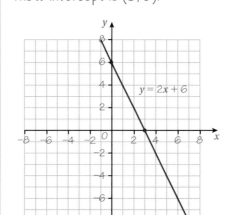

$y = 2x + 6$

Plot the two points and join them to draw the graph. Label the line.

This method of sketching graphs is called the intercept-intercept method. It is useful when the equation is in the general form $ax + by = c$. You don't need to rearrange the equation to find the intercepts.

EXERCISE 24C

1 Plot the graph of each function. Write a description of each one, giving the y-intercept and gradient, stating whether this is positive or negative.

a $y = 3x - 2$ **b** $y = -2x + 3$ **c** $y = \dfrac{1}{2}x - 1$ **d** $y = x - 1$

2 Rearrange each equation so it is in the gradient-intercept form ($y = mx + c$). Sketch each of the lines.

a $3x - 2y = 6$ **b** $6x + 2y + 10 = 0$ **c** $3y - 6x + 12 = 0$

d $2y - x + 18 = 0$ **e** $6y - 2x + 18 = 0$ **f** $2x - 3y + 12 = 0$

3 Match each graph to the correct linear equation.

a $y = x + 1$ **b** $y = 3 - x$ **c** $y = 9 - 3x$

d $y = x + 4$ **e** $y = -2x + 20$

A

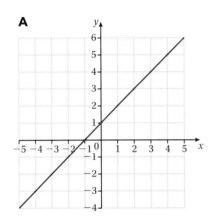

B

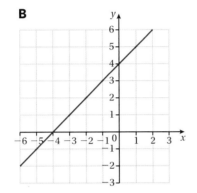

C

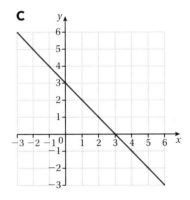

D

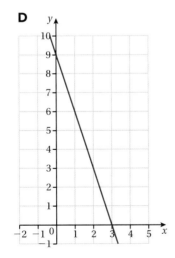

E

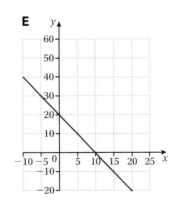

4 Sketch the graph of each line by calculating the coordinates of the x- and y-intercepts. Write down the gradient of each graph.

a $2x + y = 4$ **b** $3x + 4y = 12$ **c** $x + 2y = 1$

d $3x + y = 2$ **e** $x - y = 4$ **f** $x - y = 1$

g $4x - 2y = 8$ **h** $3x - 4y = 12$

Find answers at: cambridge.org/ukschools/gcsemaths-studentbookanswers

Finding the equation of a line using two points on the line

If you have the coordinates of two points on a line you can use them to find the gradient.

Once you have the gradient, you can find the y-intercept by substituting the (x, y) values of one of the points on the line into the equation and solving it to find c.

You can then write the equation of the line in the gradient-intercept form: $y = mx + c$

WORKED EXAMPLE 5

Find the equation of the line passing through points $(3, 11)$ and $(6, 7)$.

$$\text{Gradient} = \frac{change\ in\ y}{change\ in\ x} = \frac{y_2 - y_1}{x_2 - x_1} = \frac{7 - 11}{6 - 3} = -\frac{4}{3}$$

> Find the gradient first.
>
> Let the points be (x_1, y_1) and (x_2, y_2).

$$y = -\frac{4}{3}x + c$$

$$\text{So, } 7 = -\frac{4}{3} \times 6 + c$$

$$7 = -8 + c$$

$$15 = c$$

> Use either of the points on the line to calculate c. Here we substitute the point $(6, 7)$.

The equation is $y = -\dfrac{4}{3}x + 15$

> This equation could be written $3y = -4x + 45$

WORKED EXAMPLE 6

Find the equation of a line that has the same gradient as the line $y = \dfrac{1}{2}x - 3$ and passes through the point $(-1, 2)$.

$$y = mx + c$$

$$y = \frac{1}{2}x + c$$

$$2 = (\frac{1}{2} \times -1) + c$$

> Substitute the values you know into the equation to find the value of c.

$$c = \frac{5}{2}$$

The equation is $y = \dfrac{1}{2}x + \dfrac{5}{2}$

> This equation could be written $2y = x + 5$

EXERCISE 24D

1 For each equation, find c if the given point is on the line.

    a $y = 3x + c$ $(1, 5)$ **b** $y = 6x + c$ $(1, 2)$

    c $y = -2x + c$ $(-3, -3)$ **d** $y = \dfrac{3}{4}x + c$ $(4, -5)$

2 Find the equation of the line passing through each pair of points.

    a $(0, 0)$ and $(6, -2)$ **b** $(0, 0)$ and $(-2, -3)$

    c $(-2, -5)$ and $(-4, -1)$ **d** $(-2, 9)$ and $(3, -1)$

3   **a** A line passes through the point $(2, 4)$ and has gradient 2. Find the y-coordinate of the point on the line when $x = 3$.

    b A line passes through the point $(4, 8)$ and has gradient $\dfrac{1}{2}$. Find the y-coordinate of the point on the line when $x = 8$.

    c A line passes through the point $(-1, 6)$ and has gradient -1. Find the y-coordinate of the point on the line when $x = 4$.

Tip

Find the equation of the line before you try to find the coordinates of points on it.

Section 3: Parallel lines, perpendicular lines and tangents

Parallel lines

Tip

You learned about parallel lines in Chapter 2.

These three graphs are parallel to each other.

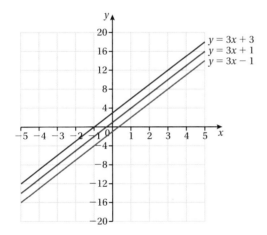

Look at the equations of each line, you can see that they all have the same gradient. Lines with equal gradients are parallel to each other.

These three graphs are members of a family of parallel lines with a gradient of positive 3. Each line in the family can be defined by the equation $y = 3x + c$.

WORK IT OUT 24.2

In which option have parallel lines been correctly grouped together?

Option A	Option B	Option C
$y = 4 - 2x$	$y = \frac{1}{3}x + 1$	$y = x - 1$
$y + 2x = 5$	$3y + x = 1$	$y + x = 1$
$y = -2x + 1$	$y = 3x + 1$	$y = 1 - x$
$y = 3x + 1$	$2y = x + 1$	$x = y + 1$
$y - 3x = -1$	$2y - x = 3$	$x - y = 1$
$y = 2 + 3x$	$y = \frac{1}{2}x - 1$	$x = 1 - y$

In mathematics one way to prove a statement is true is to follow a series of statements that end in a valid conclusion. You can use this method to prove that lines are parallel.

Steps for approaching a proof	What would you do to prove lines are parallel?
Step 1: Draw a diagram?	A diagram might take too long, especially if you are working with many different lines.
Step 2: Identify what you have to do.	Compare the gradients to see if they are the same or not.
Step 3: Test the problem with what you know.	If lines are parallel they will have an identical value for the gradient. The gradient is the coefficient of x in the equation (the value of m).
Step 4: What maths can you do?	Rearrange the equations so they are all in the form $y = mx + c$ to compare the gradients (m). If there are identical values for m then you have proved that the lines are parallel lines.

EXERCISE 24E

 a If $y = (2a - 3)x + 1$ is parallel to $y = 3x - 4$, find the value of a.

    b If $y = (3a + 2)x - 1$ is parallel to $y = ax - 4$, find the value of a.

2 Find the equation of the blue line.

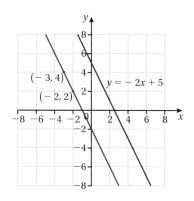

3 The vertices (corners) of a quadrilateral have coordinates $A(1, 6)$, $B(3, 14)$, $C(15, 16)$ and $D(13, 8)$.

a Find the gradient of the line AB.

b Find the equation of the line AB.

c Prove that $ABCD$ is a parallelogram.

Tip

You learned about the properties of quadrilaterals in Chapter 2.

4 Investigate lines that are parallel to the axes. How are the equations for these graphs different to those for slanted graphs? Why?

Perpendicular lines

If two lines are perpendicular, the product of their gradients is -1.

Conversely, if the product of their gradients is -1, then two lines are perpendicular.

Tip

In order for two graphs to be perpendicular, in general one must have a negative gradient and the other must have a positive gradient. Exceptions are lines parallel to the axes, such as $y = k$ and $x = m$, which are perpendicular.

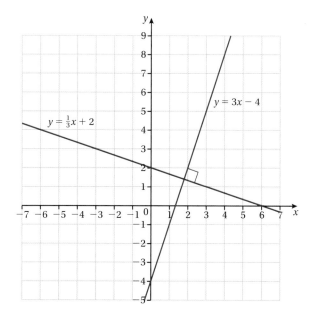

Graph $y = \dfrac{-1}{3}x + 2$ has negative gradient $m = \dfrac{-1}{3}$.

Graph $y = 3x - 4$ has positive gradient $m = 3$.

Tip

Remember that $\dfrac{1}{3}$ is the reciprocal of 3 and that for any value,

$x \times \dfrac{1}{x} = \dfrac{x}{x} = 1$.

When one value of x is negative, the product will also be negative.

The product of the gradients $\dfrac{-1}{3} \times 3 = -1$.

The graphs are perpendicular to each other.

WORKED EXAMPLE 7

What is the gradient of a linear graph which is perpendicular to $y = \dfrac{-4}{5}x - 2$?

$$\dfrac{-4}{5} \times \dfrac{5}{4} = \dfrac{-20}{20} = -1$$

So the gradient of a graph perpendicular to this $\dfrac{5}{4}$.

> In this graph, $m = \dfrac{-4}{5}$.

WORKED EXAMPLE 8

Given that $y = \dfrac{2}{3}x + 2$, determine the equation of the straight line that is:

a perpendicular to this line and which passes through the origin.

b perpendicular to this line and which passes though the point $(-3, 1)$.

a $y = mx + c$

$$m = \dfrac{-3}{2}$$

> Perpendicular gradients have a product of -1.

$$c = 0$$

> The line passes through the origin.

The equation of the line is

$$y = \dfrac{-3}{2}x.$$

b $y = \dfrac{-3}{2}x + c \qquad m = \dfrac{-3}{2}$

$$1 = \dfrac{-3}{2}(-3) + c$$

> Substitute $x = -3$ and $y = 1$ and solve for c.

$$1 = \dfrac{9}{2} + c$$

$$c = -3\dfrac{1}{2}$$

The equation of the line is

$$y = \dfrac{-3}{2}x - 3\dfrac{1}{2}$$

> This equation could be written $2y = -3x - 7$

EXERCISE 24F

1 Which of the lines $y = 4x$, $y = 3x + 2$ and $y = x$ is perpendicular to the line $4y + x = -2$?

2 The graph shows a pair of parallel lines. Determine the equation of the line perpendicular to both lines and passing through:

a the origin   **b** $(0, 4)$ **c** $(2, -3)$

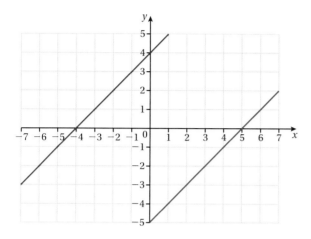

3 Show that the line through the points $A(6, 0)$ and $B(0, 12)$ is:

a perpendicular to the line through $P(8, 10)$ and $Q(4, 8)$.

b perpendicular to the line through $M(-4, -8)$ and $N(-1, -6\frac{1}{2})$.

4 $A(3, 6)$ and $B(4, 7)$ are two adjacent vertices of a square $ABCD$.

a Determine the gradient of AB.

b What is the gradient of CD?

5 Write the equations of these two lines from information in the graph and prove that the lines are perpendicular.

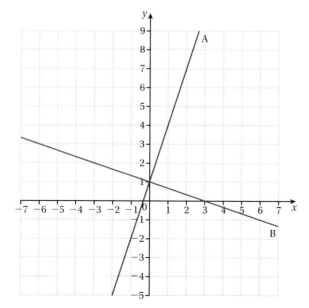

Find answers at: cambridge.org/ukschools/gcsemaths-studentbookanswers

6 Given points $X(2, -1)$, $Y(3, -2)$ and $Z(4, -1)$, prove that XY is perpendicular to YZ.

7 Is the triangle formed by joining $P(-1, 3)$, $Q(5, 1)$ and $R(-2, 0)$ right-angled?

Finding the equation of a tangent to a circle

A circle with its centre on the origin $(0, 0)$ and radius r, has the equation $x^2 + y^2 = r^2$.

A **tangent** to a circle will meet the radius at a right angle.

Key vocabulary

tangent: a line that makes contact with a curve at one point; it does not cut the curve, it just touches the curve.

Tip

You will learn more about tangents in Chapter 27.

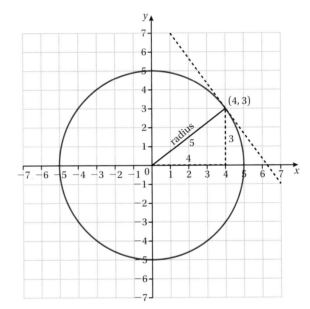

Tip

With a circle centred at the origin, the gradient of the radius to a point (x, y) on the circumference is always $\frac{y}{x}$.

In the diagram, a tangent touches the circle at the point $(4, 3)$.

You can use $m_{\text{tangent}} \times m_{\text{radius}} = -1$ to calculate the gradient of the tangent.

The gradient of the radius is $\frac{3}{4}$.

$$m_{\text{tangent}} \times m_{\text{radius}} = -1$$

$$m_{\text{tangent}} \times \frac{3}{4} = -1$$

$$m_{\text{tangent}} = -\frac{4}{3}$$

To work out the equation of the tangent, you need the y-intercept.

Substitute the values into the gradient-intercept equation of a line, $y = mx + c$. The tangent passes through the point $(4, 3)$. So, $y = 3$ when $x = 4$.

$$3 = 4 \times -\frac{4}{3} + c$$

$$c = 3 + \frac{16}{3} = \frac{25}{3}$$

The equation of the tangent to the circle at $(4, 3)$ is $y = \frac{16}{3}x + \frac{25}{3}$.

This is better expressed as $3y = -4x + 25$

EXERCISE 24G

1 This diagram shows the circle $x^2 + y^2 = 25$. The tangent touches the circle at $(3, -4)$.

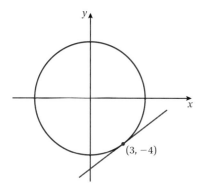

 a Copy the diagram. Draw in a radius from $(0, 0)$ to the point $(3, -4)$.

 b What is the gradient of the line of this radius?

 c What is the gradient of the tangent to the circle at point $(3, -4)$?

 d Find the equation of this tangent.

2 The point at which a tangent touches each circle is given. Determine the equation of each tangent.

 a $x^2 + y^2 = 5$ $(2, 1)$

 b $x^2 + y^2 = 80$ $(-4, 8)$

 c $x^2 + y^2 = 90$ $(3, 9)$

3 Determine the equations of the tangents to the circle $x^2 + y^2 = 81$ at the points $(0, 9)$ and $(9, 0)$.

Section 4: Working with straight-line graphs

You need to be able to interpret straight-line graphs. This means you can:

- determine the equation of the graph
- calculate the gradient of a line using given information
- use graphs to model and solve problems, including solving simultaneous equations.

The point of intersection of any two graphs is the solution to the simultaneous equations (of the graphs).

WORKED EXAMPLE 9

a Sketch the graphs of $x + 3y = 6$ and $y = 2x - 5$.

b What are the coordinates of the point of intersection of the two graphs?

c Show by substitution that these values are the simultaneous solution to the equations
$x + 3y = 6$ and $y = 2x - 5$.

a Sketch the graphs.

$x + 3y = 6$ Let $y = 0$
  Let $x = 0$ $x = 6$
     $3y = 6$ Plot $(0, 2)$ and $(6, 0)$
      $y = 2$

> Use the intercept-intercept method for $x + 3y = 6$

$y = 2x - 5$
y-intercept $= -5$
gradient $= 2$

> Use the gradient-intercept method for $y = 2x - 5$

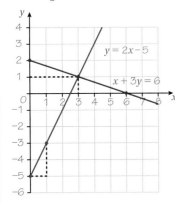

b The point of intersection is $(3, 1)$

> Read this from the graph.

c Let $x = 3$ and $y = 1$
   Substitute in $x + 3y = 6$:
         $3 + 3(1) = 6$
   Substitute in $y = 2x - 5$:
         $1 = 2(3) - 5$
         $1 = 6 - 5$
         $1 = 1$

> The solutions work for both equations.

EXERCISE 24H

1 Each table of values has been generated from a function.

i

x	-2	-1	0	1	2	3
y	-4	-3	-2	-1	0	1

ii

x	-2	-1	0	1	2	3
y	4	3	2	1	0	-1

a Which of these functions would produce each set of values?

$y = -x + 2,$ $y = 2x - 1,$ $y = -2x + 4,$ $y = x - 2$

b Plot the graph of each function in part **a** on a separate grid.

c On each grid, draw a line parallel to the graph which crosses the y-axis at $(0, 3)$ and write its equation.

d Determine the gradient of lines perpendicular to each pair of parallel lines.

2 Find and write in gradient-intercept form $y = mx + c$ equations which satisfy the following statements.

   a A linear equation that does not pass through the first quadrant.

   b Two lines whose gradients differ by 2.

   c An equation of a straight line that passes through $(2, 3)$ and has a gradient of 3.

   d An equation of a vertical line and a horizontal line.

3 Given the graph $2x + 5y = 20$:

   a Write the equation of the line parallel to this one, that crosses the y-axis at -2.

   b Give the equation of a graph which intersects this graph at the x-axis and which passes through the point $(6, -4)$.

4 Calculate the gradient of the line shown in the diagram and write down the equation of the line.

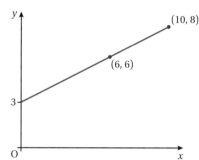

Tip

Sketch means draw a basic diagram to represent each equation showing the direction and intercept on the y-axis.

5 Sketch each of the following graphs.

   a $y = 3x + 2$ **b** $y = -2x - 1$ **c** $2y = x + 8$

   d $x - y = -3$ **e** $y + 4 = x$ **f** $3x + 4y = 12$

6 Find the equation of the line that passes through each pair of points.

   a $(5, 6)$ and $(-4, 10)$ **b** $(3, 4)$ and $(-2, 8)$ **c** $(-2, 6)$ and $(1, 10)$

7 **a** Find the equation of the line with gradient -4 that passes through the point $(0, -6)$.

   b Find the equation of the line with gradient -4 that passes through the point $(3, 8)$.

   c Find the equation of the line that passes through the points $(-4, 8)$ and $(-6, -2)$.

8 The line passing through the points $(-1, 6)$ and $(4, b)$ has gradient -2. Find the value of b.

Find answers at: cambridge.org/ukschools/gcsemaths-studentbookanswers

9 **a** Is the gradient of this straight line 2 or −2? Write down the equation of the line.

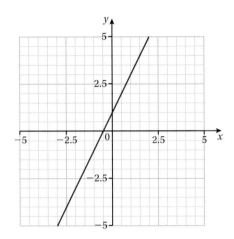

b Write the equation of this line.

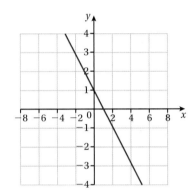

10 Find the equations of the four straight lines that make this square.

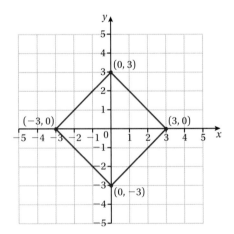

11 Show that the points $A(1, 1)$, $B(3, 11)$ and $C(-2, -14)$ all lie on the same line (are collinear) and find the equation of this line.

12 Given the circle $x^2 + y^2 = 25$, determine the equation of the tangent that touches the circle at $(-1, -2\sqrt{6})$.

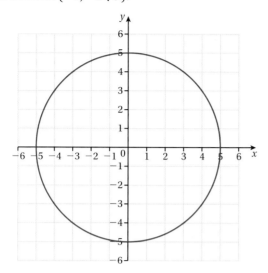

 Checklist of learning and understanding

Plotting straight-line graphs

- You can use the equation of a line to generate a table of x- and y-values.
- Choose any three (x, y) values, plot them and join the points to draw the graph.

Characteristics of straight-line graphs

- The general form of a straight-line graph is represented by $y = mx + c$, where m is the gradient and c is the point where the line cuts the y-axis (y-intercept).
- You can find the equation of a straight line if you have two points on it or one point and the gradient.
- You can sketch graphs using the gradient and y-intercept or using the x- and y-intercepts.

Parallel and perpendicular lines

- Parallel lines have the same gradient so the value of m is equal when their equation is written in the form $y = mx + c$.
- The product of the gradients of two perpendicular lines is -1.
- A tangent to a circle touches it at one point only. A tangent is perpendicular to a radius where it touches the circle, so $m_{\text{tangent}} \times m_{\text{radius}} = -1$. Once you have the value of the gradient, you can use the point of contact to calculate the value of c. You can substitute these values into the gradient-intercept form to write the equation of the tangent.

For additional questions on the topics in this chapter, visit GCSE Mathematics Online.

 Chapter review

1 **i** Write the equation of each line.

ii Determine the equation of the line parallel to line **b** passing through point $(0, -1)$.

iii Is the line $2y + 6 = 2x$ perpendicular to graph **d**?

a
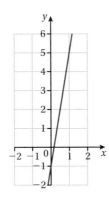

b
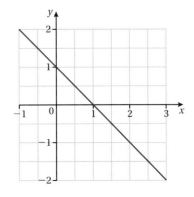

c
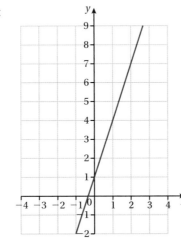

d
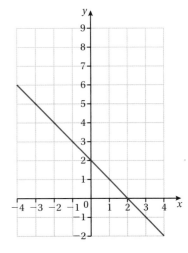

2 Find the equation of the line that passes through the two points $(2, 4)$ and $(6, -12)$.

3 **a** Draw a graph of the two lines $y = 3x - 2$ and $y + 2x = 3$ and find their point of intersection.

b Show by substitution that this is the simultaneous solution to the two equations.

 4 **a** Write down an equation of a straight line that is parallel to the straight line $y = 3x - 5$ *(1 mark)*

A straight line, L, is perpendicular to the straight line $y = 3x - 5$ and passes through the point $(6, 5)$

b Find an equation of L. *(3 marks)*

©Pearson Education Ltd 2013

5

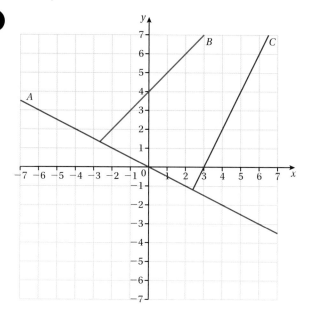

a Find the equation of each line *A*, *B* and *C*.

b Show that *A* is perpendicular to *C*.

c Show that *B* and *C* are not parallel.

d Determine the *x*-intercept of *B* algebraically.

e Determine the *y*-intercept of *C* algebraically.

f Determine the equation of a line passing through (2, 3) such that the four lines on the graph form a trapezium with its base passing through the origin.

25 Graphs of functions and equation

Using mathematics: real-life applications

Graphs are used to process information, make predictions and generalise patterns from sets of data. The nature of the data and the relationship between values determines the shape and form of the graph.

"I study the Earth using gravity, magnetic, electrical, and seismic methods. I used this graph in a study of the Pacific and Atlantic oceans. I need to be able to understand equations and recognise the features of graphs to understand and interpret it."

(Geophysicist)

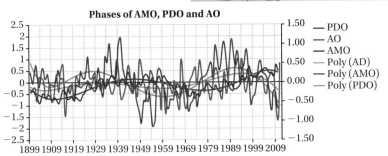

Before you start ...

Ch 24	You should be able to interpret equations of linear graphs.	**1** For the graph $y = 3x + 1$: **a** Identify the gradient of the graph. **b** Give the coordinates of the y-intercept. **c** Find the value of x when $y = -14$. **d** Show that it is parallel to the graph $2y - 6x = -4$.
Ch 24	You must be able to generate a table of values from a function.	**2** Given $y = 3x^2 + 1$, complete the table of values. | x	-2	-1	0	1	2
---	---	---	---	---	---
y						
Ch 15	You need to be able to find the roots of a quadratic equation algebraically.	**3** What are the roots of: **a** $x^2 + 2x - 8 = 0$? **b** $x^2 + 5x = -4$?
Ch 15	You need to be able to find the roots of a quadratic equation by completing the square.	**4** Complete the square to find the solution of $x^2 + 4x - 6 = 0$.

Assess your starting point using the Launchpad

STEP 1

1 How many points do you need to calculate to plot the graph of a linear equation?

2 Sketch the graph of the linear equation $y = 2x + 1$.

GO TO
Section 1:
Review of linear graphs

STEP 2

3 **a** Is this the graph of $y = x^2 + 1$ or $y = -x^2 + 1$?
  b How can you tell?

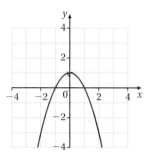

GO TO
Section 2:
Quadratic functions

  c Is the turning point a maximum or a minimum?
  d What are the coordinates of the vertex?
  e For what values of x is $y = 0$?

STEP 3

4 **a** What type of equation is $y = x^3$?
  b How many points do you need to calculate to plot the graph of $y = x^3$?

5 Given $y = \dfrac{1}{x}$:
  a Explain what happens when $x = 0$.
  b What happens to the value of y as the value of x increases?
  c When $x = 60$, what is the value of y?

GO TO
Section 3:
Other polynomials and reciprocals

GO TO
Step 4:
The Launchpad continues on the next page …

Find answers at: cambridge.org/ukschools/gcsemaths-studentbookanswers

Launchpad continued ...

STEP 4

6 Sketch the graph of $y = 2^x$.

7 Which of these graphs is $y = \sin x$ and which one is $y = \cos x$?

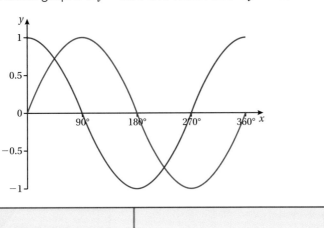

GO TO
Section 4:
Exponential and trigonometric functions

Section 5:
Circles and their equations

GO TO
Chapter review

Section 1: Review of linear graphs

Graphs in the form of $y = mx$

In the general form of a linear function, $y = mx + c$, m is the gradient of the line and the value of c tells you where the line cuts the y-axis. When $c = 0$, you get an equation in the form of $y = mx$.

WORK IT OUT 25.1

These are three linear functions.

$$y = 3x \qquad y = -3x \qquad y = \frac{1}{3}x$$

There is a common point which all the graphs pass through.

What is that point? How do you know?

Option A	Option B	Option C
$(0, 3)$	$(-3, 0)$	$(0, 0)$

Any linear equation of the form $y = mx$ passes through the origin.

The graphs of $y = mx$ and $y = -mx$ are shown on the left.

If $m = 1$ the equation is written as $y = x$. If $m = -1$, the equation is written as $y = -x$.

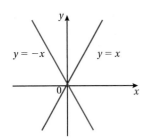

$y = x$ is the line that passes through the origin going up from left to right at an angle of 45°.

$y = -x$ is the line that passes through the origin going down from left to right making an angle of 45°.

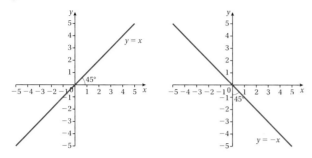

Sketching $y = ax$ ...	Examples	Notes
if a is greater than 1.	$y = 3x$ $y = 7x$	The line still passes through the origin but is steeper than $y = x$.
if a is a value between 0 and 1.	$y = \frac{1}{2}x$ $y = \frac{1}{5}x$	The line still passes through the origin but is less steep than $y = x$.
if a is a negative value.	$y = -3x$ $y = -\frac{1}{2}x$	The line still passes through the origin, but will go down from left to right like $y = -x$.

Vertical and horizontal lines

Consider the equation $x = 7$.

The graph of this equation passes through the point $(7, 0)$. It also passes through all points on the grid with an x-coordinate of 7. For example: $(7, -4)$, $(7, -1)$, $(7, 3)$, $(7, 50)$.

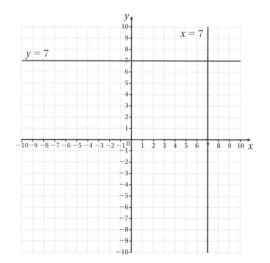

Now consider the equation $y = 7$.

This graph would need to pass through the point $(0, 7)$ and all other points with a y-coordinate of 7. For example: $(3, 7)$, $(-2, 7)$, $(7, 7)$, $(50, 7)$.

- Any graph in the form of $x = a$ is parallel to the y-axis and passes through a on the x-axis.

- Any graph in the form of $y = b$ is parallel to the x-axis and passes through b on the y-axis.

- The values of a and b can be positive or negative.

The axes themselves are straight lines and can be described using equations.

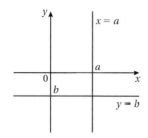

Tip

You should be able to recognise and sketch the graphs of any line in the form $x = a$ or $y = b$.

The x-axis is the line $y = 0$ and the y-axis is the line $x = 0$.

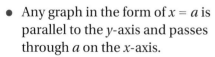 **Find answers at: cambridge.org/ukschools/gcsemaths-studentbookanswers**

EXERCISE 25A

1 Write down which of the graphs on the grid to the right can be described in each of the following ways.

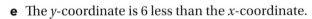

a The x-coordinate of each point is equal to the y-coordinate.

b The gradient is negative.

c The general form of the graph is $y = mx$.

d The y-coordinate is 6 times the x-coordinate.

e The y-coordinate is 6 less than the x-coordinate.

2 Give the equation of each line on the grid in question **1**.

3 **a** Write down the equation of each line A to F on the grid to the right.

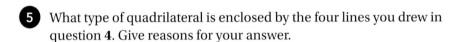

b Determine the equation of the line parallel to D which passes through point $(0, 2)$.

4 Draw the following graphs on a grid numbered from -6 to 6 on each axis.

a $x = -3$ **b** $y = 5$ **c** $y = -3$ **d** $x = 5$

5 What type of quadrilateral is enclosed by the four lines you drew in question **4**. Give reasons for your answer.

6 **a** Write the equations of two lines which would divide the quadrilateral formed in question **4** into two identical rectangles.

b What is the mathematical name for lines which divide shapes into two identical halves?

c It is possible to draw two other lines that divide the quadrilateral into two equal halves.

    i Draw these lines on your diagram.

    ii Determine the equation of each line.

7 Sketch the graph of each linear equation.

a $y = 2x$ **b** $y = -8x$ **c** $y = -\dfrac{1}{4}x$

d $y = x + 7$ **e** $y = -2x - 1$

Key vocabulary

quadratic: an expression with a variable to the power of 2 but no higher power.

Section 2: Quadratic functions

A **quadratic** expression has the form $ax^2 + bx + c$, where $a \neq 0$.

$2x^2 + 4x - 1$ and $3x^2 + 7$ are quadratic expressions.

The path of moving objects such as this basketball can be modelled as a curved graph called a parabola.

The graph of a quadratic function is a curve called a **parabola**.

The simplest equation of a parabola is $y = x^2$.

You can plot the graph of a quadratic function by drawing up a table of values.

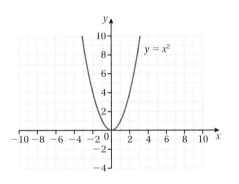

Tip

In Chapter 15 you learned how to solve quadratic equations by writing them as the product of two factors equal to 0. Revise that chapter if you have forgotten how to do this.

Key vocabulary

parabola: the symmetrical curve produced by the graph of a quadratic function.

Tip

The shape of a parabola can extend downwards to a minimum, $y = x^2$, or upwards to a maximum, $y = -x^2$. The equation of the graph tells you which of these shapes it will be.

WORKED EXAMPLE 1

Plot the graph of $y = x^2 - 2x - 8$.

x	−3	−2	−1	0	1	2	3	4	5
y	7	0	−5	−8	−9	−8	−5	0	7

Draw up a table of points that satisfy the equation $y = x^2 - 2x - 8$.

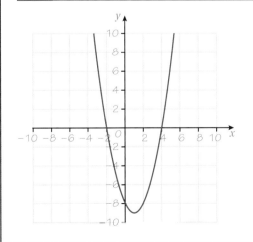

Plot all these points to draw the graph and produce a smooth curve drawing through and beyond the points calculated.

EXERCISE 25B

1 Plot the graph of each of these equations for $-3 \leqslant x \leqslant 3$ on the same grid.

a $y = x^2$ **b** $y = -x^2$

c $y = x^2 + 1$ **d** $y = x^2 - 4$

2 Plot the graph of each quadratic equation for whole number values of x in the given range:

a $y = x^2 + 2x - 3$ $-4 \leqslant x \leqslant 2$

b $y = x^2 + x - 2$ $-3 \leqslant x \leqslant 2$

c $y = x^2 + 3x$ $-4 \leqslant x \leqslant 1$

3 You may need to plot some more graphs to answer these questions.

a If the coefficient of x^2 is greater than 1, what impact does it have on the shape of the parabola?

b If the coefficient of x^2 is a value between 1 and 0, what impact does it have on the shape of the parabola?

c What happens to the graph of the parabola if a constant value is added? Consider the difference between the graph of an equation such as $y = ax^2$ and $y = ax^2 + b$.

d How does the graph of the parabola differ from the basic $y = x^2$ graph when the coefficient of x^2 is negative?

4 Plot the graph of $y = x^2 - x - 2$ for $-2 \leqslant x \leqslant 3$.

a Solve the equation $x^2 - x - 2 = 0$.

b How would you read the solution to the equation $x^2 - x - 2 = 0$ from the graph?

Tip

You might find it useful to use ICT to investigate further examples of quadratic graphs to confirm your thinking.

Features of graphs of quadratic equations

Quadratic graphs have characteristics that you can use to sketch and interpret them.

- The axis of symmetry – a line which divides the parabola into two symmetrical halves.
- The y-intercept where the curve cuts the y-axis – a parabola can only have one y-intercept.
- The turning point or vertex of the graph – this is the point at which the graph changes direction.
- The x-intercepts where the graph cuts the x-axis – a parabola can have 0, 1 or 2 x-intercepts depending on the position of the graph.

The graph either has a minimum turning point or a maximum turning point.

If the x^2 term is positive, the turning point will be a minimum (this is the lowest point of the graph).

If the x^2 term is negative, the turning point will be a maximum (this is the highest point of the graph).

The diagram below shows the main features of a parabola.

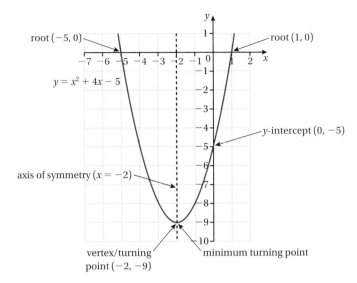

The curve is symmetrical, the axis of symmetry is $x = -2$ (the x-value of the vertex).

The y-intercept, where the graph cuts the y-axis, is the point $(0, -5)$.

The vertex is $(-2, -9)$ and is a minimum turning point.

The curve cuts the x-axis at the points $(-5, 0)$ and $(1, 0)$.

The values of x for which the quadratic function equals 0 are known as the roots of the quadratic equation. By sketching or plotting a quadratic equation, you can find the roots as these are the points where it crosses the x-axis (when $y = 0$). In the example above, the roots of the equation are $x = -5$ and $x = 1$

Alternatively if you can identify the roots from the graph of a parabola you can establish the equation of the parabola.

$\therefore (x + 5)(x - 1) = 0$

$x^2 + 4x - 5 = 0$

This is the graph of $y = x^2 + 4x - 5$.

Identifying the turning point

You can complete the square of an equation to find the turning point algebraically.

Completing the square for $y = x^2 + 4x - 5$, gives $y = (x + 2)^2 - 9$

As a square number cannot be negative, $(x + 2)^2 \geqslant 0$, so the minimum value of y is when $(x + 2)^2 = 0$.

This is when $x = -2$ and $y = -9$. So the turning point is the point $(-2, -9)$.

The axis of symmetry goes through the turning point, so the axis of symmetry of this graph is the line $x = -2$.

All parabolas are symmetrical and will have an axis of symmetry. Not all parabolas will cross the x-axis and have real roots.

Tip

The roots can be established algebraically by solving
$x^2 + 4x - 5 = 0$
$(x + 5)(x - 1) = 0$

Either $x + 5 = 0$ or $x - 1 = 0$.
$x = -5$ or $x = 1$

The y-intercept can be found algebraically. It is the value of y when $x = 0$:

$y = x^2 + 4x - 5$

$= 0^2 + (4 \times 0) - 5 = -5$

So the y-intercept is the point $(0, -5)$.

WORK IT OUT 25.2

What are the main features of this parabola?

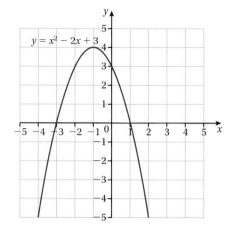

$y = x^2 - 2x + 3$

Option A

y-intercept $(0, 3)$

vertex $(-1, -4)$ is a minimum turning point.

axis of symmetry $x = 1$

x-intercepts $(-3, 0)$ and $(1, 0)$

roots $x = -3$ and $x = 1$

Option B	Option C
y-intercept $(0, 3)$	y-intercept $(0, 3)$
vertex $(-1, 4)$ is a maximum turning point.	vertex $(-1, 4)$ is a maximum turning point.
axis of symmetry $x = 1$	axis of symmetry $x = -1$
x-intercepts $(-3, 1)$ and $(1, 1)$	x-intercepts $(-3, 0)$ and $(1, 0)$
no roots	roots $x = -3$ and $x = 1$

EXERCISE 25C

1 For each parabola determine:

i the turning point and whether it is a minimum or maximum

ii the axis of symmetry

iii the y-intercept

iv the x-intercepts

v the roots of the equation used to generate the graph.

a

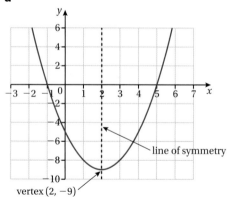

line of symmetry

vertex $(2, -9)$

b

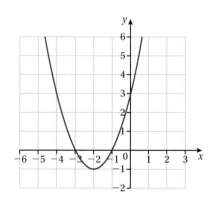

c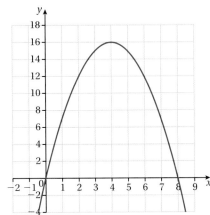

d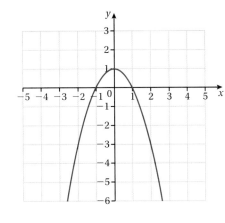

2 Rewrite the equation $y = 3x^2 + 6x + 3$ in the form $y = a(x + h)^2 + k$.

a Determine the y-intercept.

b Find the axis of symmetry and the vertex.

c Determine the x-intercepts.

d Sketch the graph of the equation labelling the main features.

Sketching quadratic graphs

You can use the characteristics of a parabola to sketch graphs without drawing up a table of values. Remember, a sketch shows the general features of a graph but it does not have to be drawn on graph paper.

To sketch a parabola of the general form $y = ax^2 + bx + c$ (where a is the **coefficient** of x^2, b is the coefficient of x and c is a constant):

- Check the sign of a to determine whether the graph goes up to a maximum turning point or down to a minimum turning point.
- Work out the y-intercept (this is given by c in the equation).
- Calculate the x-intercepts by substituting $y = 0$ and solving for x. If there are no x-intercepts or only one when the graph only touches the x-axis, you will have to find the coordinates of one point on the graph to help you draw an accurate sketch.
- Mark the y-intercept and x-intercepts (if they exist) and use the shape of the graph as a guide to draw a smooth curve.
- Label your graph.

> **Key vocabulary**
>
> **coefficient**: a number used to multiply a variable.

WORKED EXAMPLE 2

Sketch the graph of $y = 3x^2$

- 3 is positive so the graph goes down to a minimum turning point.
- There is no constant, so the graph goes through the origin $(0, 0)$.
- When $y = 0$, $x = 0$ so there is only one solution for x. You need to find a point on the graph.
  When $x = 1$
  $y = 3(1)^2 = 3$
  So, $(1, 3)$ is a point on the curve.
- Sketch and label the graph.

 Find answers at: cambridge.org/ukschools/gcsemaths-studentbookanswers

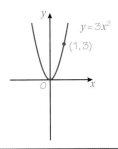

Tip

Draw a smooth curve to join the points and try to make your graph as symmetrical as possible.

WORKED EXAMPLE 3

Sketch the graph of $y = -x^2 + 4$

- Coefficient of x is -1, so graph goes up to a maximum turning point.
- Constant is 4, so y-intercept is $(0, 4)$.
- x-intercepts when $y = 0$
  $0 = -x^2 + 4$
  $\therefore x^2 - 4 = 0$
  This is a difference of squares
  $(x + 2)(x - 2) = 0$
  $x + 2 = 0$ or $x - 2 = 0$
  $x = -2$ or $x = 2$
  So, intercepts are $(-2, 0)$ and $(2, 0)$.
- Sketch and label the graph.

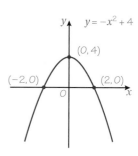

EXERCISE 25D

1 Noor sketched these quadratic graphs but she didn't write the equations on them. Use the features of each graph to work out what the correct equations are.

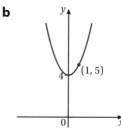

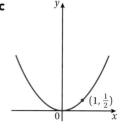

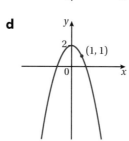

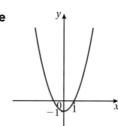

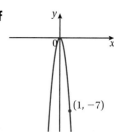

2 Sketch the graph of each of these quadratic equations on the same grid.

$y = x^2 \qquad y = x^2 + 2 \qquad y = 3x^2 \qquad y = \dfrac{1}{2}x^2 - 2 \qquad y = -x^2 + 2$

3 For each equation, determine:

   i   the y-intercept   **ii**   the x-intercept(s)

   iii   the axis of symmetry   **iv**   the turning point.

Use the results to sketch and label each graph.

a $y = x^2 + 2x - 3$ **b** $y = 2x^2 + 4x + 3$

c $y = 4x - x^2$ **d** $y = x^2 + 2x - 8$

e $y = x^2 - 8x + 12$ **f** $y = -x^2 - 6x - 10$

g $y = 2(x - 3)(x + 5)$ **h** $y = 4x^2 + 16x + 7$

i $x^2 + 3x - 6 = y$ **j** $2x^2 + x = 8 + y$

Section 3: Other polynomials and reciprocals

A **polynomial** is an expression with many terms. If the highest power of x is 3, the expression is called a cubic expression. For example, $2x^3$ and $2x^3 + x^2 + 3$ are both cubics.

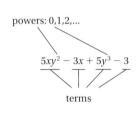

powers: 0,1,2,...

$5xy^2 - 3x + 5y^3 - 3$

terms

a polynomial

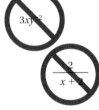

$3xy^{-2}$

$\dfrac{2}{x + 2}$

not polynomials

Key vocabulary

polynomial: an expression made up of many terms with positive powers for the variables.

You can use a table of values to plot the graph of a cubic equation. The simplest equation of a cubic graph is $y = x^3$.

The diagram below shows the basic shape of cubic graphs in the form of $y = ax^3$.

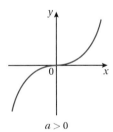

$a > 0$

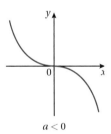

$a < 0$

The shape on the left occurs when a is positive. This is an increasing curve.

The shape on the right occurs when a is negative. This is a decreasing curve.

The larger the value of a, the steeper the curve.

This is a table of values for $y = x^3$ for values of x from -3 to 3.

x	-3	-2	-1	0	1	2	3
y	-27	-8	-1	0	1	8	27

Tip

Remember that when you cube a negative number you will get a negative result.

For example,
$(-1)^3 = -1 \times -1 \times -1$
$= (-1 \times -1) \times -1$
$= +1 \times -1 = -1$

To draw an accurate graph you plot all of the calculated points and draw a smooth curve through and beyond them.

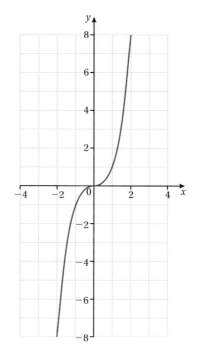

For more complicated cubic equations with two or more terms, you should work out whole number and half number values to make sure you plot the graph as accurately as possible.

You may find it easier to evaluate each term separately in the table and add them to find y-values.

WORKED EXAMPLE 4

Draw the graph of the equation $y = x^3 - 6x$ for $-3 \leqslant x \leqslant 3$

x	-3	-2	-1	0	1	2	3
x^3	-27	-8	-1	0	1	8	27
$-6x$	18	12	6	0	-6	-12	-18
y	-9	4	5	0	-5	-4	9

Determine whole number values first.

x	-2.5	-1.5	-0.5	0.5	1.5	2.5
x^3	-15.625	-3.375	-0.125	0.125	3.375	15.625
$-6x$	15	9	3	-3	-9	-15
y	-0.625	5.625	2.875	-2.875	-5.625	0.625

Construct a separate table for in-between values of x.

Continues on next page …

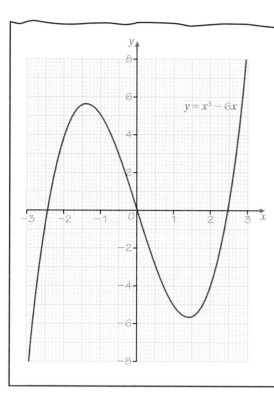

$y = x^3 - 6x$

Plot the points against the axes and join them with a smooth curve.

EXERCISE 25E

1 Complete a table of values for whole number values of x from -3 to 3 for $y = -x^3$. Draw the graph $y = -x^3$. How does this graph differ from the graph of $y = x^3$?

2 Use a table of values to sketch the following pairs of cubic graphs. Plot each pair on the same grid, but use a separate grid for each pair.

a $y = -2x^3$ and $y = 2x^3$ **b** $y = \dfrac{1}{2}x^3$ and $y = -\dfrac{1}{2}x^3$

3 Work with a partner to compare the pairs of graphs you drew in question **2**. Discuss how you could sketch the graph of $y = -4x^3$ if you were given the graph of $y = 4x^3$.

4 Complete a table of values for whole number values of x from -3 to 3 for these equations and draw a graph of each curve.

a $y = x^3 + 1$ **b** $y = x^3 - 2$

5 Look at the graphs and their equations in question **4**. What information does the constant give you about the graph?

6 The red line on the diagram (right) is the graph $y = x^3$. What are the equations of graphs A and B?

7 Plot the graph of each cubic equation for the given values of x.

a $y = x^3 + 3x^2$ $-3 \leqslant x \leqslant 3$

b $y = x^3 - 3x + 1$ $-3 \leqslant x \leqslant 4$

 Find answers at: cambridge.org/ukschools/gcsemaths-studentbookanswers

Reciprocal functions

The product of a number and its **reciprocal** is 1.

$$8 \times \frac{1}{8} = 1 \qquad \frac{2}{5} \times \frac{5}{2} = 1$$

Every number has a reciprocal except for 0, as $\frac{1}{0}$ cannot be defined.

The reciprocal of a is $\frac{1}{a}$: $\qquad a \times \frac{1}{a} = 1$

The general equation of a reciprocal function is $y = \frac{a}{x}$, where a is a constant value. This equation can be re-arranged to give $xy = a$.

The graphs of reciprocal functions have a characteristic shape. Each graph is made of two curves which are mirror images in diagonally opposite quadrants of the grid.

Key vocabulary

reciprocal: the value obtained by inverting a fraction. Any number multiplied by its reciprocal is 1. Note that any number can be written as $\frac{a}{1}$. For example, 8 can be written as $\frac{8}{1}$, and therefore $\frac{1}{8}$ is the reciprocal of 8.

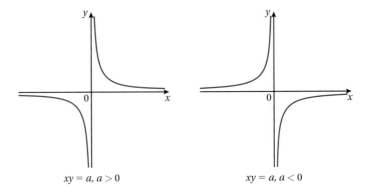

$xy = a, a > 0$ $\qquad\qquad\qquad$ $xy = a, a < 0$

This is the table of values for the equation of $y = \frac{1}{x}$.

x	-3	-2	-1	$-\frac{1}{2}$	$-\frac{1}{3}$	0	$\frac{1}{2}$	$\frac{1}{3}$	1	2	3
y	$-\frac{1}{3}$	$-\frac{1}{2}$	-1	-2	-3	undefined	2	3	1	$\frac{1}{2}$	$\frac{1}{3}$

In order to draw a reciprocal graph accurately you need to work with some non-integer values of x.

Note that there is no y-value when $x = 0$ because division by 0 is undefined.

To draw the graph:

* Plot the (x, y) values from the table.

* Join the points with a smooth curve.

* Write the equation on both parts of the graph.

Note that as the value for x gets bigger, the value for y gets closer and closer to 0 but the graph never actually meets the y-axis.

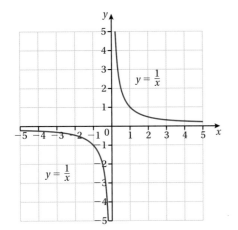

EXERCISE 25F

1 Copy and complete each table for the given values of x. Plot the graphs on the same grid.

a $y = \dfrac{2}{x}$

x	-4	-2	-1	1	2	4
y						

b $y = \dfrac{6}{x}$

x	-6	-3	-1	1	3	6
y						

c $xy = -12$

x	-10	-8	-6	-4	-2	2	4	6	8
y									

d $y = \dfrac{8}{x}$

x	-8	-6	-4	-2	1	2	4	6	8
y									

2 Compare the graphs that you have drawn for question **1**. How does the value of the constant in the equation affect the position of the graph?

3 Plot each of the following graphs on the same grid using x-values from -5 to 5.

a $y = \dfrac{1}{x}$ **b** $y = \dfrac{1}{x} + 1$ **c** $y = \dfrac{1}{x} + 3$

4 Use your graphs from question **4** to describe how the constant c in the equation $y = \dfrac{a}{x} + c$ changes the reciprocal graph of $y = \dfrac{a}{x}$.

5 Neo says that the line $y = x$ is the line of symmetry of the graph $y = \dfrac{1}{x}$. Is he correct? Explain your answer.

6 Plot the graphs for each of the reciprocal equations for the given values of x.

a $y = \dfrac{5}{x}$ $-5 \leqslant x \leqslant 4$

b $y = \dfrac{3}{x + 2}$ $x = -16, -12, -8, -4, 0, 4, 8, 12, 16$

c $y = \dfrac{1}{x - 2}$ $-4 \leqslant x \leqslant 6$

Find answers at: cambridge.org/ukschools/gcsemaths-studentbookanswers

7 Use what you now know about the shape of the graphs of the basic cubic and reciprocal from questions **1** and **2** to sketch diagrams of these equations:

a $y = x^3 + 2$ **b** $y = -x^3$ **c** $y = \dfrac{2}{x}$ **d** $y = \dfrac{1}{x} - 1$

e $y = -\dfrac{1}{x}$ **f** $y = \dfrac{1}{x} + 2$

Use ICT to check your answers and try some more versions of a basic cubic and a reciprocal by changing the value of the constant numbers in the equations.

8 The equation of graph A is $y = \dfrac{1}{x}$. What is the equation of graph B?

A
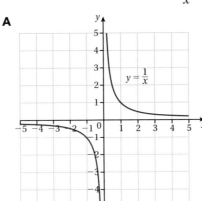

B
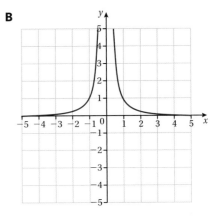

Section 4: Exponential and trigonometric functions

Exponential functions are used to model situations involving growth or decay.

An **exponential function** has a number as the base and a variable as the exponent. For example, $y = 2^x$.

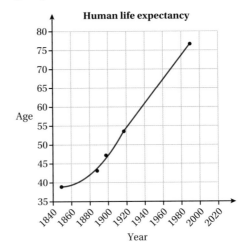

Population growth and compound interest are both examples of exponential growth.

The general form of the exponential function $y = k^x$ (where k is positive) produces a graph called an exponential curve.

Key vocabulary

exponential function: a function of the form $y = k^x$.

exponent: the number that says how many times a base number multiplies: exponent 2 means the number is squared (5×5), exponent 3 means it is cubed ($5 \times 5 \times 5$).

WORKED EXAMPLE 5

Complete a table of values for $y = 2^x$ for $-4 \leqslant x \leqslant 4$ and draw the graph.

x	-4	-3	-2	-1	0	1	2	3	4
y	$\dfrac{1}{16}$	$\dfrac{1}{8}$	$\dfrac{1}{4}$	$\dfrac{1}{2}$	1	2	4	8	16

Plot all of the calculated points and draw a smooth curve through and beyond the points plotted.

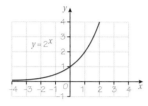

You can see from the example that the curve rises rapidly towards the right. This is the typical shape of graphs of exponential growth.

As the value of x decreases the curve gets closer and closer to the x-axis without ever touching it. This is because there is no defined value for x when $y = 0$.

Note also that the curve has a y-intercept at $(0, 1)$. When $x = 0$, $y = k^0 = 1$, so **all** graphs in the form $y = k^x$ will pass through the point $(0, 1)$.

Exponential curves do not pass through the origin and they are not symmetrical.

If $k = 1$ we get $1^x = 1$ and the equation becomes $y = 1$, which is a straight line.

k cannot be a negative value because the y-value might not be defined.

Because k^x is always positive, the curve will never extend below the x-axis.

The graph $y = k^{-x}$ is the reciprocal of $y = k^x$.

Graphing $y = 2^{-x}$ produces a reflection of the graph $y = 2^x$ about the y-axis.

From the laws of indices, you should remember that $2^{-x} = \left(\dfrac{1}{2}\right)^x$

So $y = 2^{-x}$ is equivalent to $y = \left(\dfrac{1}{2}\right)^x$. So, if x is negative then $0 < k < 1$. (k is a fractional value).

Whether the curve slopes up to the right (increases) or down to the right (decreases) depends on the value of k.

Where $k > 1$, the graph is increasing.

Where $0 < k < 1$, the graph is decreasing.

The value of k affects the steepness of the curve. The graphs of $y = 2^x$, $y = 3^x$ and $y = 5^x$ are shown here on the same grid.

Note that they all have a y-intercept at $(0, 1)$ and they all approach the x-axis to the left. The graph of $y = 5^x$ is much steeper than $y = 2^x$ and $y = 3^x$ because powers of 5 (5, 25, 125, 625) increase in value faster than powers of 2 and 3.

In many real-life applications, exponential functions are multiplied by a fixed value. For example, radioactivity levels in a sample of radioactive material

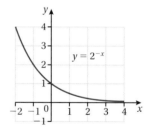

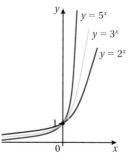

> **Tip**
>
> Remember that any value raised to a power of 0 is equal to 1.
> $k^0 = 1$

Find answers at: cambridge.org/ukschools/gcsemaths-studentbookanswers

with initial activity 80 decrease exponentially over time at a rate of $R = 80 \times 0.55^t$, where R is the level of radioactivity and t is the time in hours. The initial value of 80 is the multiplying constant for the particular sample. The base value 0.55 is fixed for the particular radioactive material.

The general form of exponential functions like these is $y = ak^x$, where a is also a constant value and $a > 0$.

The constant value (a) determines the y-intercept of the graph.

WORKED EXAMPLE 6

Plot a table of values and draw the graphs of $y = 3^x$, $y = \dfrac{1}{2} \times 3^x$ and $y = 2 \times 3^x$ on the same grid.

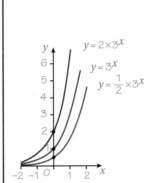

x	-2	-1	0	1	2
3^x	$\dfrac{1}{9}$	$\dfrac{1}{3}$	1	3	9
$\dfrac{1}{2} \times 3^x$	$\dfrac{1}{18}$	$\dfrac{1}{6}$	$\dfrac{1}{2}$	$\dfrac{3}{2}$	$\dfrac{9}{2}$
2×3^x	$\dfrac{2}{9}$	$\dfrac{2}{3}$	2	6	18

The curve of $y = ak^x$ can be an increasing curve or a decreasing curve.

EXERCISE 25G

1 Produce a table of values and draw the graph of each equation for the given values of x.

Draw each set of graphs on the same axes.

a i $y = 3^x$ **ii** $y = 1.1 \times 3^x$ **iii** $y = 2.5 \times 3^x$ values: $-2 \leqslant x \leqslant 3$

b i $y = 5^x$ **ii** $y = 2 \times 5^x$ **iii** $y = \dfrac{1}{2} \times 5^x$ values: $-1 \leqslant x \leqslant 2$

2 a Plot the graph of the equation $y = 2^x$ on a grid. (Use the table of values from Worked example 5 to do this.)

b Sketch the graphs of $y = 4^x$ and $y = 2^{-x}$ in relation to $y = 2^x$.

3 Complete a table of values, plot the points and draw the graph for $y = \left(\dfrac{1}{4}\right)^x$ for $-3 \leqslant x \leqslant 3$.

4 Draw a sketch graph of the following equations.

a $y = 3^x$ **b** $y = 1^x$

5 Consider the equation $P = 5 \times (0.85)^a$

a Will this equation result in an increasing or decreasing curve? Give a reason for your answer.

b Where will this graph cut the y-axis?

c Use the information to draw a sketch of this graph.

Trigonometric functions

In Chapter 11 you did some calculations involving angles and dimensions of the London Eye. Consider what happens to one capsule on the Eye as it rotates through 360°.

As the Eye turns, the angle of the capsule in relation to the vertical and its distance above the ground changes. Each time the capsule passes the same point in its rotation, it will be at the same angle and the same height again and again.

The graph of this movement has a wave shape.

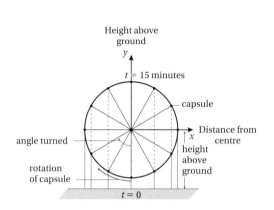

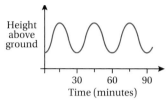

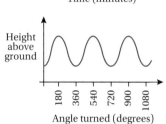

The graph of the movement over time is a **periodic graph** because the same y-values repeat at regular intervals. The graph shows that the capsule completes a rotation every 30 minutes.

The sin function ($y = \sin x$)

The table of values below shows the positive values of $y = \sin x$ for angles from 0° to 360°.

x	0°	30°	90°	180°	270°	360°
$y = \sin x$	0	$\dfrac{1}{2}$	1	0	−1	0

The x-axis for this graph needs to be labelled in degrees as the values of the x-coordinates are angles.

Plotting these values produces this graph (right).

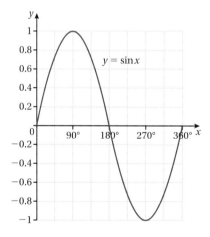

This graph only shows the values of $y = \sin x$ between 0° and 360° but the graph is not restricted to these values. Working out values from $-270°$ to 720° would produce this graph (below).

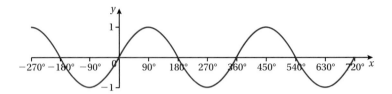

Notice that the graph repeats itself every 360° and that it intercepts the x-axis every 180°.

The cos function ($y = \cos x$)

In a similar way to $y = \sin x$, the graph of $y = \cos x$ can be generated from a table of values. This is the resulting graph for $-360° \leqslant x \leqslant 360°$.

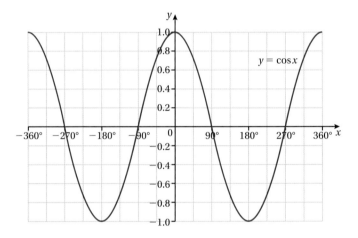

The graph of $y = \cos x$ has the same shape as the graph of $y = \sin x$ with minimum and maximum values at -1 and 1. However, it does not go through the origin because $\cos 0° = 1$.

The graph repeats every 360° and it intercepts the x-axis every 180° after 90°.

If you don't recognise the curve by sight, you can work out whether it is a sin or cos graph by finding values of y for different values of x. One set of values does not allow for a conclusive identification of the function, but consider when $x = 0°$ and $x = 90°$.

$x = 0°$ $x = 90°$

$\sin 0° = 0$ $\sin 90° = 1$

$\cos 0° = 1$ $\cos 90° = 0$

The tan function ($y = \tan x$)

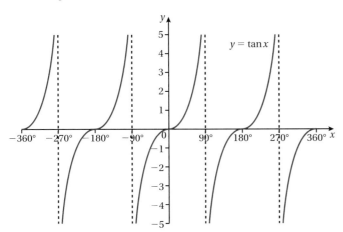

Tip

You will learn more about graphs of trigonometric functions when you deal with transformation of curved graphs in Chapter 41.

The tan function is periodic, repeating every 180°, but it is not a wave function. The graph is discontinuous and it has no minimum or maximum turning points.

Notice also that the tan function approaches but never crosses the lines $x = -270°$, $x = -90°$, $x = 90°$ and $x = 270°$. The function $\tan x$ is undefined for these values.

EXERCISE 25H

1 Plot the graphs of $y = \sin x$, $y = \cos x$ and $y = \tan x$ for $-360° \leqslant x \leqslant 360°$.

   a Label the minimum and maximum (if it exists) on each graph and state the period over which it repeats.

   b Use the graphs to determine the value of x for which $\sin x = \cos x$ between 0° and 90°.

Tip

These graphs are useful for solving trigonometric equations. You will refer to them again when dealing with trigonometry in Chapter 33.

2 Graph A shows how voltage varies over time in mains electricity. Graph B shows the electronic signal when an AC signal is added to a DC voltage source.

Which trigonometric function does each graph most resemble? Why?

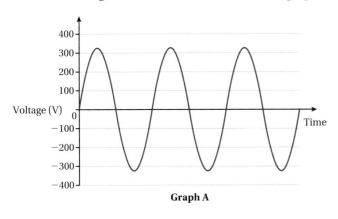

Graph A

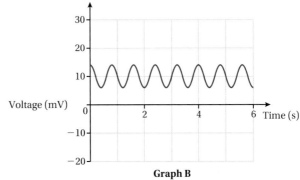

Graph B

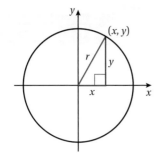

Section 5: Circles and their equations

The equation of a circle is based on the fact that every point on the circumference is the same distance from the centre.

Any circle that has its centre on the origin and a radius of r can be defined by the equation:

$x^2 + y^2 = r^2$

WORK IT OUT 25.3

What is the equation of a circle centre on the origin with a radius of 4 units?

Option A	Option B	Option C
$(x + y)^2 = 4$	$x^2 + y^2 = 16$	$x^2 + y^2 = 4$

EXERCISE 25I

1 $x^2 + y^2 = 25$ is a circle centre on the origin.

   a What is the value of the radius?

   b Verify that the following points lie on the circle: $(3, 4)$, $(-3, 4)$.

   c List the coordinates of four other points that would also lie on this circle.

2 Sketch the graph of each circle, marking the intercepts on each of the axes.

   a $x^2 + y^2 = 25$ **b** $x^2 + y^2 = 1$ **c** $x^2 + y^2 = 2$
   d $x^2 + y^2 = \dfrac{9}{4}$ **e** $x^2 = 5 - y^2$

3 **a** Which of these points lie on the circle $x^2 + y^2 = 100$?

   $(6, 8)$ $(10, 10)$ $(20, 80)$ $(-6, 8)$ $(5\sqrt{2}, 5\sqrt{2})$ $(10, 0)$

   b Which of these points lie on the circle $x^2 + y^2 = 169$?

   $(5, 12)$ $(100, 69)$ $(-5, -12)$ $(-5, 12)$ $(-13\sqrt{2}, 13\sqrt{2})$ $(0, 13)$

4 Write the equation of each of the circles in the diagram on the left.

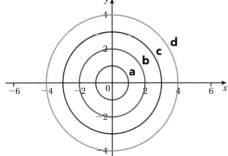

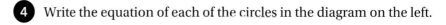

Checklist of learning and understanding

Linear functions

- Linear functions produce straight-line graphs.
- The general form of the linear function is $y = mx + c$.
- Graphs $x = a$ are vertical lines parallel to the y-axis.
- Graphs $y = a$ are horizontal lines parallel to the x-axis.
- Lines of the form $y = mx$ go through the origin.

Quadratic functions

- The graphs of quadratic equations such as $y = ax^2$, $y = ax^2 + c$, $y = ax^2 + bx + c$ are called parabolas.

- When a is positive the graph goes down to a minimum point. When a is negative the graph goes up to a maximum point. The y-intercept is given by c.

- A parabola has a turning point which can be a minimum or maximum depending on the shape of the graph.

Polynomials and reciprocals

- To draw graphs of polynomials first calculate a table of values that satisfy the equation for a range of values for x.

- $y = ax^3$ is an example of a cubic function.

- A reciprocal function is a graph made of two curves in diagonally opposite quadrants defined by $y = \dfrac{a}{x}$ or $xy = a$.

Other curved graphs

- An exponential function is a steeply increasing or decreasing curve defined by $y = k^x$.

- The graphs of trigonometric functions are periodic graphs with particular shapes and characteristics.

- Any circle with a centre of $(0, 0)$ and radius r, can be defined by $x^2 + y^2 = r^2$.

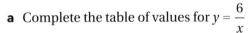

Chapter review

For additional questions on the topics in this chapter, visit GCSE Mathematics Online.

1 **a** Complete the table of values for $y = \dfrac{6}{x}$ *(2 marks)*

x	0.5	1	2	3	4	5	6
y		6	3		1.5		1

b On a copy of the grid, draw the graph of $y = \dfrac{6}{x}$ for $0.5 \leqslant x \leqslant 6$ *(2 marks)*

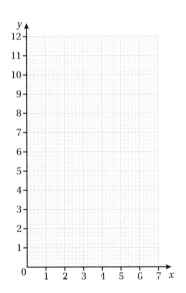

©Pearson Education Ltd 2012

2 Draw the graphs of the straight lines $y = 2x - 5$ and $2y - x = 5$. What is the point of intersection of these two lines?

3 **a** What are the roots of the quadratic equation represented by this graph?

b Show that the equation of the graph is $y = -x^2 + 2x + 3$.

c Complete the square for $x^2 - 2x - 3 = 0$ to find the coordinates of the turning point and the axis of symmetry for the graph of $y = -x^2 + 2x + 3$.

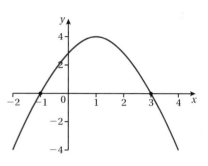

4 **a** Identify and give the equation of the red and blue curves on this grid.

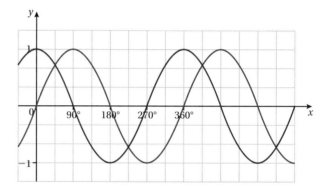

b For what values of x in the range $0° \leqslant x \leqslant 270°$ are the values of $\sin x$ and $\cos x$ equal?

5 Draw a sketch diagram of the circle $x^2 + y^2 = 25$.

On the same diagram, sketch the two linear functions represented by the equations $y = 2x - 2$ and $y = -\frac{3}{4}x + 6\frac{1}{4}$ to verify that one of the lines will intersect with the circle at two points and the other line will be a tangent to the circle.

What are the coordinates of the point of contact of the tangent with the circle?

6 Determine the equation of each graph using what you know about the features of different graphs.

a
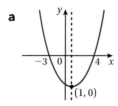

b
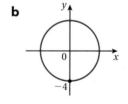

c
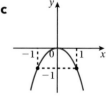

d
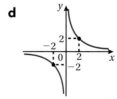

e
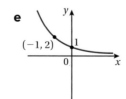

f
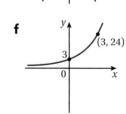

26 Angles

For more resources relating to this chapter, visit GCSE Mathematics Online.

Using mathematics: real-life applications

Many people rely on an understanding of angles and spatial relationships in their daily work. These include designers, architects, opticians and tree surgeons.

"I had to work quite carefully with the 360 degrees around the centre to place each of the 32 pods correctly on the London Eye." *(Structural engineer)*

Before you start …

Ch 1	You should be able to use inverse operations to make 180 and 360.	**1** Copy and complete. **a** $180 - 96 = \square$ **b** $180 - 116 = \square$ **c** $360 - 173 = \square$ **d** $360 - 55 - 97 = \square$
Ch 2	You need to know and apply the basic properties of triangles and quadrilaterals.	**2** Use the marked properties to name each polygon as accurately as possible. **a** 45° 45° **b** **c** x y **3** What can you say about angles x and y in figure **c**? Why?
Ch 22	You need to know how to use a protractor to measure angles.	**4** Measure the following angles. **a** **b**

Find answers at: cambridge.org/ukschools/gcsemaths-studentbookanswers

Assess your starting point using the Launchpad

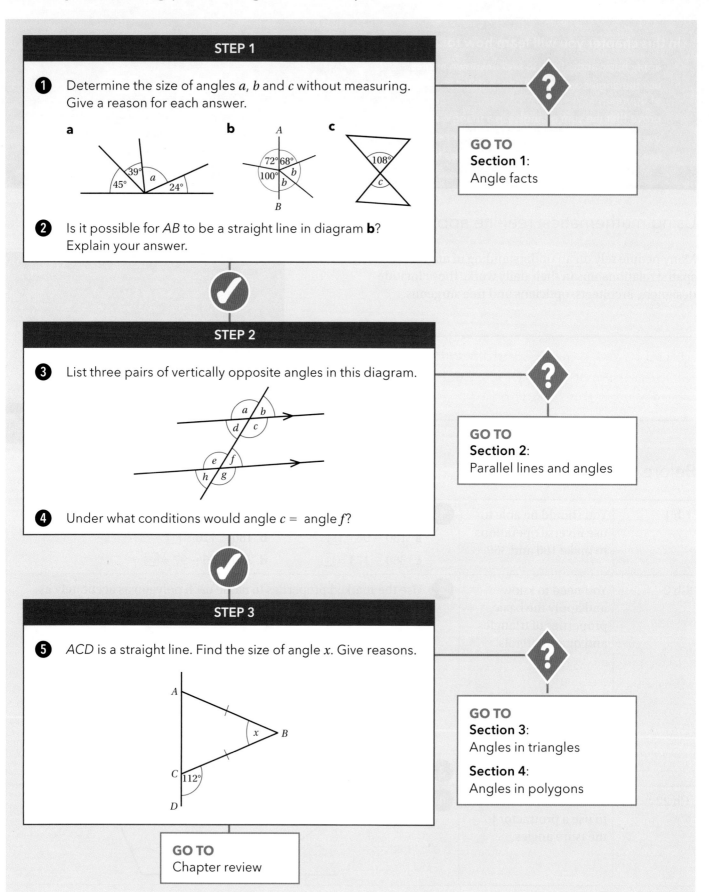

STEP 1

1 Determine the size of angles *a*, *b* and *c* without measuring. Give a reason for each answer.

a

39°
45° *a* 24°

b

A
72° 68°
100° *b*
b
B

c

108°
c

GO TO
Section 1:
Angle facts

2 Is it possible for *AB* to be a straight line in diagram **b**? Explain your answer.

STEP 2

3 List three pairs of vertically opposite angles in this diagram.

a *b*
d *c*

e *f*
h *g*

GO TO
Section 2:
Parallel lines and angles

4 Under what conditions would angle *c* = angle *f*?

STEP 3

5 *ACD* is a straight line. Find the size of angle *x*. Give reasons.

A
x B
C 112°
D

GO TO
Section 3:
Angles in triangles

Section 4:
Angles in polygons

GO TO
Chapter review

Section 1: Angle facts

Angles around a point

A 90° angle is one quarter of a turn, two 90° angles are half a turn and so on.

There are four quarter turns around a point.
$4 \times 90° = 360°$

The sum of angles around a point is 360°.

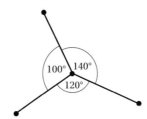

Find the size of x.

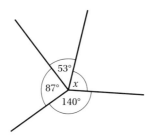

$87° + 53° + x + 140° = 360°$

Use the angles round a point fact to form an equation in x.

$x = 360° - 140° - 53° - 87°$
$\quad = 360° - 280°$
$\quad = 80°$

Solve the equation.

Angles on a straight line

Angles on a straight line add up to 180°.

This is true for any number of angles which meet at a point on a line.

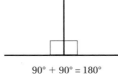

$90° + 90° = 180°$

$a + b = 180°$

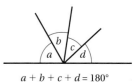

$a + b + c + d = 180°$

Determine the size of x.

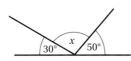

$30 + x + 50 = 180°$

Use the angles on a straight line fact to form an equation in x.

$x = 180° - 30° - 50°$
$\quad = 100°$

Solve the equation.

Find answers at: cambridge.org/ukschools/gcsemaths-studentbookanswers

Vertically opposite angles

When two lines cross, or intersect, they form four angles.

The angles a and b are vertically opposite each other, i.e. they share the same vertex, as do angles x and y.

Vertically opposite angles are equal.

$a = b$ and $x = y$

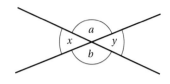

EXERCISE 26A

1 Calculate the size of the missing angles.

a

b

c

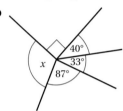

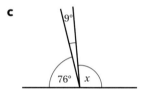

d What type of angle is x in each case?

2 Find the value of the lettered angles in each diagram. Give reasons for any deductions you make.

a Find x and y.   **b** Find x.   **c** Find p.

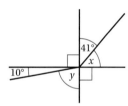

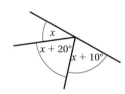

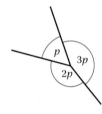

3 Explain why AE in the diagram on the left cannot be a straight line.

4 Calculate the size of the marked angles in each of the two figures below. The lines are straight lines but the diagrams are not to scale.

Show your working and give reasons for any deductions you make.

a

b

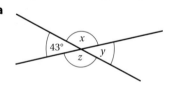

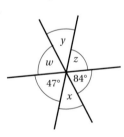

5 Given that $x = 50°$, find the size of angle z.

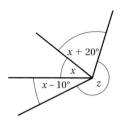

6 Use the diagram to calculate the size of each angle given the following information.

a $x = 69°$ **b** $x = b$ **c** $2b = 112°$ **d** $a = 2x$

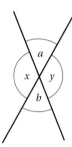

7 Find the value of the variables in each figure.

a

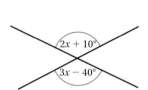

b

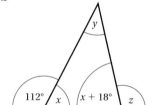

c

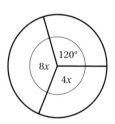

"When I'm designing and making clothes I need to be able to cut on the bias (at a given angle) and also bisect angles to add darts and fit sleeves."

(Fashion designer)

Section 2: Parallel lines and angles

A line intersecting two or more parallel lines is called a **transversal**.

When a transversal intersects with parallel lines, some pairs of angles have useful properties.

 Find answers at: cambridge.org/ukschools/gcsemaths-studentbookanswers

Vertically opposite angles are equal, so in the diagram on the left:

$$a = c \qquad b = d \qquad e = g \qquad f = h$$

Angles on a straight line add up to 180° so:

$$a + d = 180° \quad b + c = 180° \quad a + b = 180° \quad c + d = 180° \text{ and so on ...}$$

Corresponding angles

Corresponding angles, formed between a transversal and each parallel line, are equal.

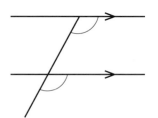

Key vocabulary

corresponding angles: angles that are created at the same point of the intersection when a transversal crosses a pair of parallel lines.

In the diagram on the right, there are four pairs of corresponding angles.

The corresponding angle pairs are:

$$a = b$$
$$c = d$$
$$e = f$$
$$g = h$$

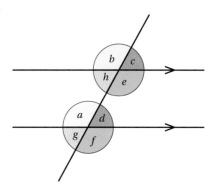

Alternate angles

Key vocabulary

alternate angles: the angles on parallel lines on opposite sides of a transversal.

Alternate angles, on opposite sides of the transversal and between the parallel lines, are equal.

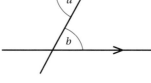
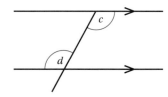

Co-interior angles

The angles inside the parallel lines and on the same side of the transversal are called **co-interior angles.** They add up to 180°.

Co-interior angles are therefore **supplementary**.

Key vocabulary

co-interior angles: the angles within the parallel lines on the same side of the transversal. Co-interior angles are sometimes referred to as 'allied angles'.

supplementary angles: two angles are supplementary angles if they add up to 180°.

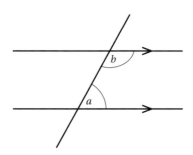

Read through this proof to see why co-interior angles are supplementary.

Prove that ∠BEF + ∠EFD = 180°

Let ∠BEF = x

∴ ∠EFC = x   Alternate angles are equal.

∠EFC + ∠EFD = 180°   Angles on a line sum to 180°.

∴ ∠EFD = 180° − x

∠BEF + ∠EFD = x + 180° − x = 180°

So, ∠BEF + ∠EFD = 180°

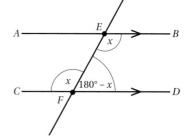

EXERCISE 26B

1 Find the size of the missing angles *a*, *b*, *c* and *d*.

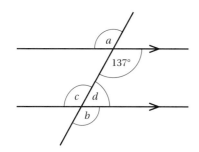

2 Given that the two poles are parallel to each other, find the angle *x* that the second pole makes with the incline upwards.

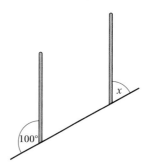

3 Find the size of the missing angles *a*, *b* and *c*.

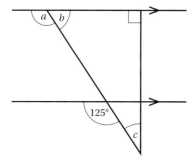

4 Find the size of angles *x* and *y*.

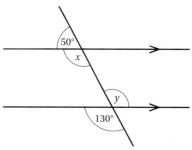

5 Find the size of each missing angle.

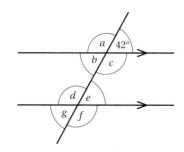

6 Find the size of ∠CEG.

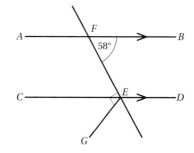

7 Find the size of ∠DCF.

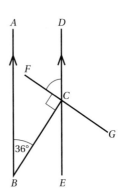

8 Find the value of x.

a

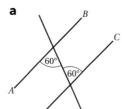

b

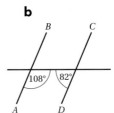

9 Decide whether $AB||DC$ in each of the following. Give a reason for your answer.

a

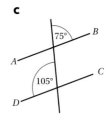

b

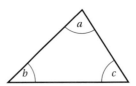

c

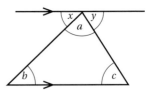

Section 3: Angles in triangles

Angle sum of a triangle

Tip

Make sure you know the differences between an equilateral triangle, a right-angled triangle, an isosceles triangle and a scalene triangle. Look back at Chapter 2 if you need to revise the properties of these triangles.

To prove that the angles in a triangle add up to 180°, you have to construct a line parallel to one side of the triangle like this:

Once you have done that, you can prove that $a + b + c = 180°$ using mathematical principles.

$x + a + y = 180°$ Angles on a straight line sum to 180°.

But, $x = b$ and $y = c$ Alternate angles are equal.

Substitute b for x and c for y and you prove that $a + b + c = 180°$.

The exterior angle is equal to the sum of the opposite interior angles

WORKED EXAMPLE 3

Show that $a + b = x$, and hence prove that the exterior angle of any triangle is equal to the sum of the opposite interior angles (see pages 465 and 467 for a definition of interior and exterior angles).

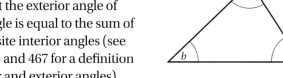

$c + x = 180°$
$\therefore c = 180° - x$ Angles on a straight line sum to 180°.

$a + b + c = 180°$
$\therefore c = 180° - (a + b)$ Angle sum of triangle.

But, $c = 180° - x$ From above.

So, $180° - (a + b) = 180° - x$
$\therefore a + b = x$

You can now combine basic angle facts, angle facts related to parallel lines and angle facts about triangles to find unknown angles in different figures.

Always give reasons for any statements you make based on known facts.

EXERCISE 26C

1 Calculate the size of each missing angle.

2 Find the size of angles x and y.

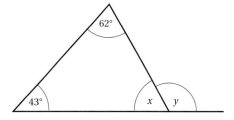

3 Find the size of angles a and b.

4 Find the size of angles x, y and z.

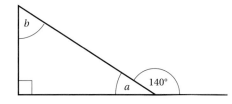

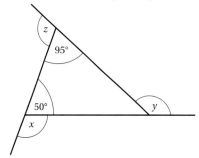

Find answers at: cambridge.org/ukschools/gcsemaths-studentbookanswers

5 Work out the size of the angles marked *a*, *b* and *c*. Give reasons to justify your answers.

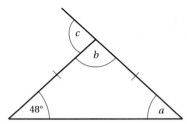

6 Calculate the value of *x*.

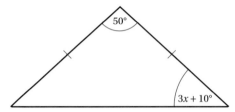

7 With reference to the figure below, show how you can prove that the exterior angle of a triangle is equal to the sum of the opposite interior angles by construction of $CE \parallel AB$.

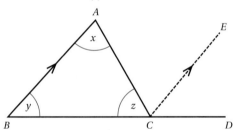

8 Find the value of the angles marked with variables in each diagram. Give reasons.

a
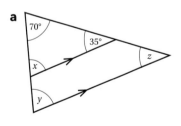

b
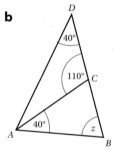

c
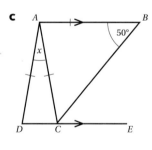

d
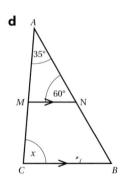

e
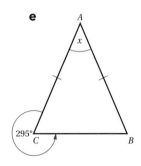

Section 4: Angles in polygons

Remember that:

- A polygon is a plane shape with three or more straight sides.
- Polygons are regular if all their sides and angles are equal.
- Polygons are named according to how many sides they have: triangle (3), quadrilateral (4), pentagon (5), hexagon (6), heptagon (7) and octagon (8).

These basalt columns are formed naturally when lava cools. The end faces are almost perfectly hexagonal.

The angle sum of a polygon

You can divide any polygon into triangles by drawing in the diagonals from one vertex.

This allows you to use the angle sum of triangles to work out the sum of the interior angles in a polygon.

This regular hexagon has six **interior angles** which are all equal.

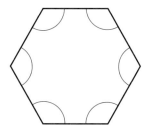

> **Key vocabulary**
>
> **interior angles**: angles inside a two-dimensional shape at the vertices or corners.

The diagonals divide the hexagon into four triangles.

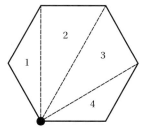

So, the sum of the interior angles of a hexagon is $4 \times 180° = 720°$.

$720° \div 6 = 120°$. So, each interior angle is 120°.

Work through the investigation in Exercise 26D to develop a rule for finding the angle sum of any polygon.

EXERCISE 26D

1. Draw the following polygons and divide them into triangles by drawing diagonals from one vertex as with the hexagon above.

2 Predict how many triangles you could form if you did the same for a 10-sided and 20-sided polygon.

3 Copy and complete this table using your results from questions **1** and **2**.

Number of sides in a polygon	3	4	5	6	7	8	10	20
Number of triangles	1			4				
Angle sum of interior angles	180°			720°				

4 What is the relationship between the number of sides in a polygon and the number of triangles you can form in this way?

5 If a polygon has *n* sides, how many triangles can you form in this way?

6 Write a rule for finding the angle sum of a polygon:

a in words

b in general algebraic terms for a polygon of *n* sides.

7 Use your rule to find the angle sum of a polygon with 12 sides.

8 How could you find the size of each interior and exterior angle of a regular 12-sided polygon?

WORK IT OUT 26.1

Three students attempted to calculate the size of interior angles in a regular pentagon.

Which is the correct solution?

What mistakes have been made by the other students?

Option A	Option B	Option 3
There are three triangles within the pentagon.	There are five triangles in a pentagon.	There is a trapezium and a triangle inside the pentagon.
$3 \times 180° = 540°$	$5 \times 180° = 900°$	$360° + 180° = 540°$
Five angles in a pentagon.	$900° \div 5 = 180°$	There are five angles inside the pentagon including the central 360° which gives a total of 900°.
$540° \div 5 = 108°$	Interior angle = 180°.	
Each interior angle = 108°.		Interior angle = $900° \div 5 = 180°$.

The sum of exterior angles of a polygon

Look at the regular hexagon again.

You know that each interior angle is 120°.

By extending each side, you can form six **exterior angles** as shown in the diagram on the right.

There are six sides, so this produces six pairs of angles (one interior and one exterior per pair) on straight lines.

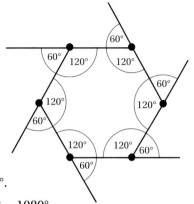

> 🔑 **Key vocabulary**
>
> **exterior angles**: angles produced by extending the sides of a polygon.

The sum of the angles on a straight line is 180°.

So, the sum of these six angle pairs is $6 \times 180° = 1080°$.

But, you already know that the sum of just the interior angles is $180°(n - 2) = 180° \times 4 = 720°$.

So, the sum of the exterior angles of the hexagon is $1080° - 720° = 360°$.

Now consider any polygon with n sides.

The sum of interior plus exterior angles can be found using $180n$, where n is the number of sides.

The sum of the interior angles can be found using $180(n - 2)$ where n is the number of sides.

So, for a pentagon, the sum of the exterior and interior angles would be $180° \times 5 = 900°$ because there are five sides.

The sum of interior angles is $180(5 - 2) = 180° \times 3 = 540°$.

The sum of the exterior angles

= the sum of the interior and exterior angles − the sum of the interior angles

= 900° − 540°

= 360°

You can express this relationship in general terms as follows:

Let I be the sum of interior angles.

Let E be the sum of exterior angles.

$I = 180(n - 2)$

$I + E = 180n$

$E = 180n - 180(n - 2)$

$= 180n - 180n + 360$

$= 360$

The sum of the exterior angles of any polygon is always 360°.

You can use these rules to find the angle sum of any polygon.

WORKED EXAMPLE 4

For a regular 10-sided polygon, find:

a the sum of the interior angles   **b** the size of each interior angle.

a Angle sum = $180(n - 2) = 180(8)$ In a 10-sided figure $n = 10$.
$$= 1440°$$

b One interior angle = $\dfrac{1440}{10} = 144°$ There are 10 interior angles.

If the polygon is regular, you can also calculate the size of each interior and exterior angle.

WORKED EXAMPLE 5

A regular polygon has an exterior angle of 18°. How many sides does it have?

Sum of exterior angles = 360

Number of angles = $\dfrac{360}{18} = 20$

∴ Number of sides = 20   The number of sides equals the number of angles.

WORKED EXAMPLE 6

A polygon has an angle sum of 2340°. How many sides does it have?

$2340 = 180(n - 2)$ Using the angle sum rule.

$\dfrac{2340}{180} = n - 2$

$13 = n - 2$

$15 = n$

The polygon has 15 sides.

EXERCISE 26E

1 Calculate the sum of interior angles of a polygon with:

   a 9 sides   **b** 12 sides   **c** 25 sides.

2 A regular polygon has 15 sides. Find:

   a the sum of the interior angles

   b the sum of the exterior angles

   c the size of an interior angle

   d the size of an exterior angle.

3 A regular polygon has an interior angle that is three times the size of the exterior angle.

   a What is the size of each exterior angle?

   b What is the size of each interior angle?

   c What is the name of the regular polygon?

4 Find the size of the missing interior and exterior angles x, y and z in this irregular pentagon.

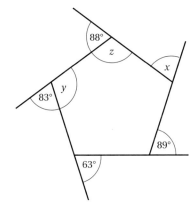

5 A pentagon has three angles that add up to 266° and two other angles that are equal in size. Determine the size of each of the other two angles.

6 A hexagon has four angles with a sum of 555° and two unknown angles.

Given that one of the unknown angles is twice the size of the other, what are their sizes?

7 Could a regular polygon have interior angles of 125°? Justify your answer.

8 How many sides does a polygon have if the sum of its interior angles is:

   a 1620°   **b** 3060°?

9 The exterior angle of a regular polygon is 40°. What is the sum of its interior angles?

Checklist of learning and understanding

Basic angle facts

- Angles around a point sum to 360°.
- Angles on a straight line sum to 180°.
- Vertically opposite angles are equal.

Angles associated with parallel lines

- Corresponding angles are equal.
- Alternate angles are equal.
- Co interior angles sum to 180°.

Find answers at: cambridge.org/ukschools/gcsemaths-studentbookanswers

Geometric proofs

- Using properties of alternate and corresponding angles, you can show that the three interior angles of any triangle sum to 180°.
- Using the angle sum of triangles and properties of angles at a line and at a point, you can find the interior and exterior angles of any polygon.

For additional questions on the topics in this chapter, visit GCSE Mathematics Online.

 Chapter review

1 Select from the box below the correct size for the marked angle in each diagram.

| 270° | 92° | 120° | 162° | 61° | 55° |

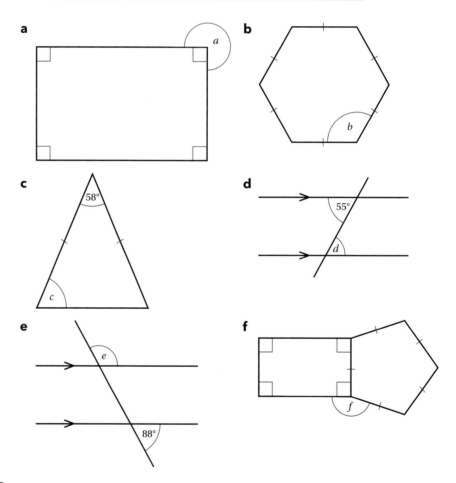

2 If the interior angle of a regular polygon is 108°, what type of polygon is it?

3 Calculate the value of $p + q + r + s + t$.

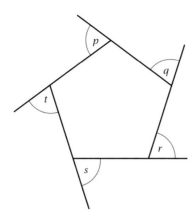

4 In this irregular hexagon, calculate the value of z.

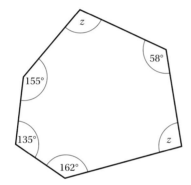

5 This diagram shows part of a regular polygon. The interior angle is 144°.

Calculate the number of sides of the polygon.

What is the name given to this polygon?

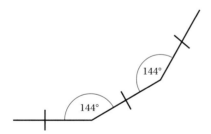

6 Calculate the exterior angle of a regular nine-sided polygon.

7 Explain mathematically why the sum of the exterior angles of any polygon is 360°.

Find answers at: cambridge.org/ukschools/gcsemaths-studentbookanswers

8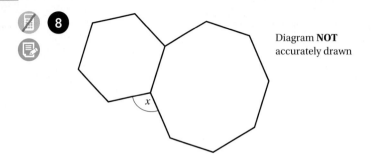

Diagram **NOT** accurately drawn

The diagram shows a regular hexagon and a regular octagon.

Calculate the size of the angle marked x.

You must show all your working.

(4 marks)

©*Pearson Education Ltd 2012*

9 Find the values of x and y.

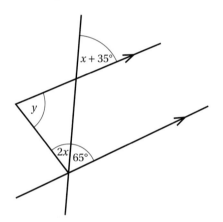

10 Prove that quadrilateral *ABCD* is a trapezium.

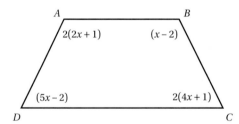

11 The sum of interior angles of an irregular polygon is 3600°.

  a Determine the number of sides.

  b Determine x, if half the angles in the polygon are size x and the other half are size $2x$.

27 Circles

In this chapter you will learn how to...

- use and apply circle definitions and understand their properties.
- prove and apply the standard circle theorems, using them to find related results.

For more resources relating to this chapter, visit GCSE Mathematics Online.

Using mathematics: real-life applications

Circle theorems are a set of proofs that have been developed over hundreds of years by mathematicians who wondered about, and investigated, the properties of circles. Learning about them allows you to appreciate some of the surprising properties of circles and the angles within them.

"I use circle theorems on board the ship to calculate the visible distance to the horizon. I use the tangent properties to give me a right-angled triangle, which I then use with Pythagoras' theorem to do my calculations."   *Navigation officer*

Before you start ...

Chs 2 and 26	You should be able to calculate the sizes of missing angles in geometry problems.	**1** Decide whether each statement is true or false. **a** $c = 120°$ **b** $a = 120°$ **c** $d = b$ **d** $b = c = 60°$
Chs 2, 11 and 12	You should know how to find the circumference and area of circles and parts of circles.	**2** For each of these circle sectors, calculate the length of the arc and the area of the sector: **a** **b** **c** 3 cm, 72° 25 mm, 45° 150°, 12 cm
Chs 2 and 26	You should be able to use given facts in geometry problems to write proofs.	**3** You need to write a proof that angle $BAD = 50°$. Which of these proofs is **not** correct? **A** Angle $CED = 50°$ (the sum of angles of a triangle is 180°) Angle $BAD = 50°$ (corresponding angle to angle CED, $AB \parallel EC$) **B** Angle $CEA = 100°$ (alternate angle to angle ECD) Angle $BAD = 50°$ ($180° - 30° - 100° = 50°$) **C** Angle $DBA = 100°$ (corresponding angle to angle ECD, $AB \parallel EC$) Angle $BAD = 50°$ (the sum of angles of a triangle is 180°)

Assess your starting point using the Launchpad

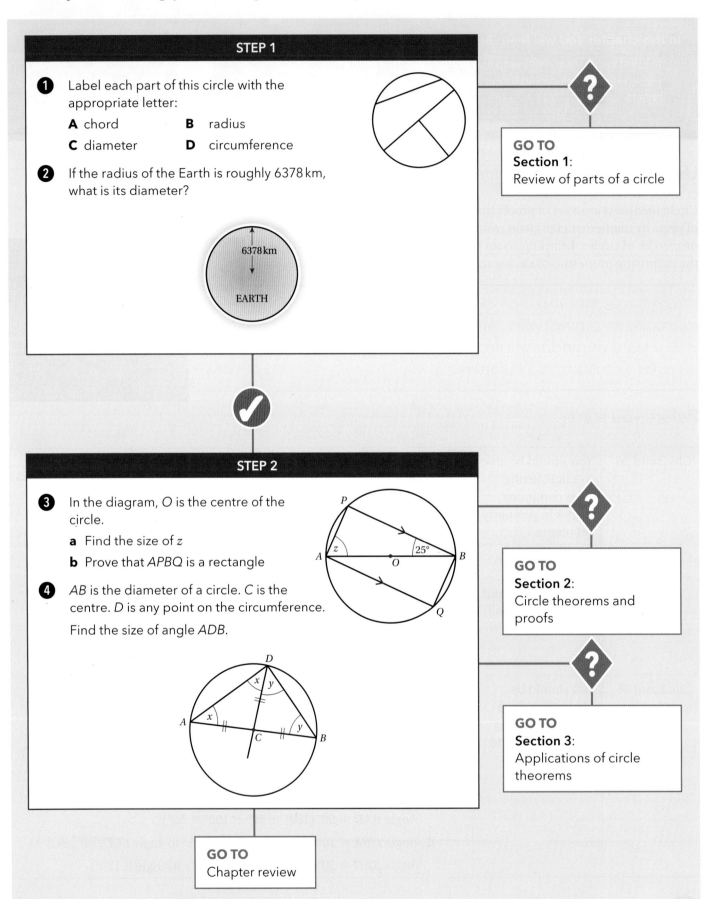

STEP 1

1 Label each part of this circle with the appropriate letter:

A chord **B** radius

C diameter **D** circumference

2 If the radius of the Earth is roughly 6378 km, what is its diameter?

6378 km

EARTH

GO TO
Section 1:
Review of parts of a circle

STEP 2

3 In the diagram, O is the centre of the circle.

a Find the size of z

b Prove that $APBQ$ is a rectangle

4 AB is the diameter of a circle. C is the centre. D is any point on the circumference.

Find the size of angle ADB.

GO TO
Section 2:
Circle theorems and proofs

GO TO
Section 3:
Applications of circle theorems

GO TO
Chapter review

Section 1: Review of parts of a circle

The basic terminology

Any line drawn from the centre to the circumference of a circle is called a radius.

If you take any two points on the circumference and join them, you get a line called a chord. If the chord passes through the centre, then it is called the diameter and it is equal in length to two radii ($d = 2r$).

A chord splits a circle into minor and major segments.

An arc is part of the circumference.

A tangent to a circle is a straight line which just touches a curve at one point.

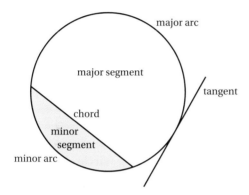

Tip

Refer back to Chapter 11 and Chapter 12 if you've forgotten the names of circle parts.

Naming angles in circles

Angles can be formed at the centre of the circle or at the circumference.

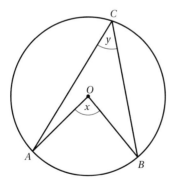

AOB is the angle at the centre.

ACB is the angle at the circumference.

The arms of both these angles are 'standing' on the minor arc AB.

Angles that stand on an arc are said to be **subtended** by the arc.

Tip

The straight line joining *A* to *B* is a chord, so the angles could also be referred to as being subtended by a chord.

Find answers at: cambridge.org/ukschools/gcsemaths-studentbookanswers

EXERCISE 27A

1 Read the clues and identify the circle parts correctly.

a half the diameter

b the larger part of a circle when it is divided into two parts by a chord

c formed by two radii and an arc

d a line outside a circle that touches the circumference at one point only

e the locus of a point at a fixed distance from another point

f the smaller part of the circumference when a circle is divided by a chord

A sector

B tangent

C minor arc

D circle

E radius

F major segment

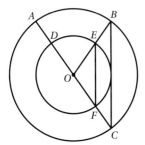

2 In the diagram (left), *O* is the centre of both circles. Complete the sentences using the correct mathematical terms.

a *DF* is the _____ of the smaller circle.

b *AO* is a _____ of the larger circle.

c *AC* is the diameter of the _____ circle.

d *ED* is a _____ _____ of the smaller circle.

e *AOB* is a _____ of the larger circle.

f *EF* is a _____ of the smaller circle.

g Angle *FOE* is the angle at the _____ subtended by arc ___.

h Angle *ACB* is subtended by ___ at the circumference.

3 Look again at the diagram in the previous question.

a What can you say about angles *OFE* and *OEF*? Why?

b How can you prove that angle *OEF* = *OFE* = *OCB* = *OBC*?

Section 2: Circle theorems and proofs

Being able to find and use angles in and around circles has applications in fields such as engineering and computer-aided design. Designing cogs and camshafts, plotting navigation charts and working out angles in astronomy all use or apply circle theorems.

Angles subtended at centre and circumference

In the diagram (right), the minor arc *DE* (or chord *DE*):

● subtends angle *DOE* at the centre *O*

● subtends angle *F* at point *F* on the circumference.

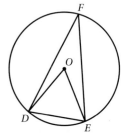

> **Tip**
>
> Think of *DE* forming a base for the angle at the centre or at the circumference of the circle to stand on. Angle *DOE* and angle *DFE* stand on the chord *DE*.

The theorem states that the angle subtended by an arc at the centre of a circle is twice the angle subtended by the same arc at the circumference.

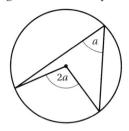

Proof

Angle *AOB* and angle *ACB* are both subtended by arc *AB*.

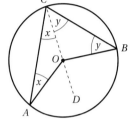

Drawing a line segment joining the centre *O* to *C* forms two isosceles triangles: triangle *AOC* and triangle *BOC*. The equal sides of each triangle are the radii of the circle.

Angle $ACB = x + y$

Angle $AOC = (180 - 2x)$ (because the angles in a triangle sum to 180°)

Angle $BOC = (180 - 2y)$ (because the angles in a triangle sum to 180°)

$360 = AOB + (180 - 2x) + (180 - 2y)$ (angles round a point sum to 360°)

$0 = AOB - 2x - 2y$

Angle $AOB = 2x + 2y$ (add 2x and 2y to both sides)

$2x + 2y = 2(x + y)$

So, angle $AOB = 2 \times$ angle ACB

Therefore, the angle subtended by *AB* at the centre is twice the angle subtended by *AB* at the circumference.

The theorem that the angle subtended at the centre is twice the angle subtended at the circumference by the same arc, will be used in the proof of other theorems. You can accept that it is true when proving other theorems.

Angle in a semicircle

This theorem states that the angle subtended by a diameter at the circumference of a circle is a right angle.

In this diagram, *AB* is a diameter, and *ACB* is called an angle in a semicircle.

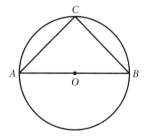

Arc *AB* subtends an angle of 180° at the centre (a straight line), and it subtends angle *ACB* on the circumference.

>
> **Tip**
>
> When using this result for other proofs, simply write 'angle in a semicircle' as a reason.

Using the first theorem, you know that the angle subtended at the centre is twice the angle subtended by the same arc at the circumference.

So, *ACB* angle $ACB = \frac{1}{2} \times 180° = 90°$

Angles in the same segment

This theorem states that two angles in the same segment are equal. This theorem also follows easily from the first theorem.

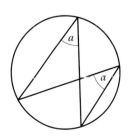

 Find answers at: cambridge.org/ukschools/gcsemaths-studentbookanswers

Two angles in the same segment refers to two angles at the circumference that are subtended by the same arc or chord.

Proof

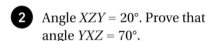

Angles C and D are in the same segment, because they are both subtended at the circumference by arc AB.

Let x be the size of angle ACB.

The arc AB also subtends angle AOB at the centre. $AOB = 2x$ (using the result of first theorem). We can state the reason as 'angles subtended at centre and circumference'.

Angle ADB is also equal to x, using the same reason: angles subtended at centre and circumference.

So angle ACB = angle $ADB = x$, as required.

> **Tip**
>
> Simply write 'angles in the same segment' as a reason in your proofs.

EXERCISE 27B

1 Angle $CAB = 40°$. Prove that angle $CBO = 50°$.

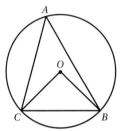

2 Angle $XZY = 20°$. Prove that angle $YXZ = 70°$.

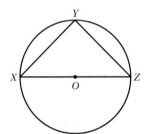

3 Prove that $y = 25°$.

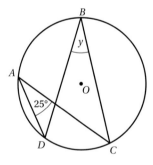

4 What is the size of angle POQ?

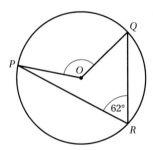

5 In triangle ABC, angle $ABC = 55°$ and angle $BAC = 35°$. State, with reasons, the property of line AB.

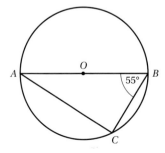

6 The angle CAB is twice the angle CBA.

What is the size of each angle?

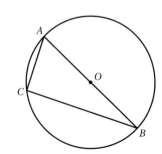

Angle between radius and chord

This theorem states that a radius or diameter bisects a chord if and only if it is perpendicular to the chord.

Another way of looking at this is that the perpendicular bisector of a chord will pass through the centre of a circle.

The phrase 'if and only if' means that the radius will not bisect the chord if it is not perpendicular to the chord.

Proof

Draw a radius from the centre of the circle that goes through the midpoint of the chord (M).

Triangles OAM and OBM have three sides the same:

$OA = OB$ (radii)

$MA = MB$ (since M is the midpoint)

OM is common to both triangles.

Triangles that are exactly the same size are called congruent. They have equal angles.

Angle OAM = angle OBM (base angles isosceles triangle)

This means that angle OMA = angle OMB. Since these two angles are on a straight line, they must each be 90°.

So, a radius does bisect a chord at right angles, as required.

> ### Tip
>
> Congruent means exactly the same size. You will learn more about congruence in Chapter 31.

> ### Tip
>
> State it in short as 'angle between radius and chord'.

Angle between the radius and tangent

This theorem states that for a point P on the circumference, the radius or diameter through P is perpendicular to the tangent at P.

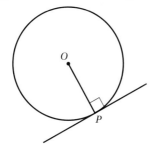

A tangent is a line that touches the circle only once.

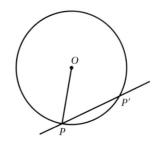

The line through PP' is not a tangent.

Triangle OPP' is isosceles, so angle OPP' = angle $OP'P$.

As the chord moves further away from the centre of the circle, the distance PP' reduces, the angle POP' reduces and each of the angles OPP' and $OP'P$ increases (getting closer to 90°).

In the limit that P and P' coincide, the chord becomes a tangent (it touches the circle only once), the angle POP' becomes 0° and the angle at P = 90°.

Two tangent theorem

This theorem states that two tangents from a given point outside the circle are equal in length.

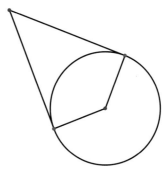

WORKED EXAMPLE 1

We are given a circle with centre O and tangents TA and TB touching the circle at A and B.

We need to prove that $TA = TB$.

Draw radii OA and OB. Join OT.

Angle TAO = angle TBO = 90° (the tangent is perpendicular to the radius).

OA and OB are radii, so $OA = OB$.

Side TO is common to both and is the hypotenuse.

Triangle OAT is congruent to triangle OBT (RHS).

This means the third sides of each triangle are equal, so $TA = TB$, as required.

EXERCISE 27C

1 *PQ* is a chord of a circle centre *O*. Radius *OS* is perpendicular to *PQ*, and cuts *PQ* at *R*. Radius *OQ* = 25 units and *PQ* = 48 units.

Calculate the length of *SR*.

2 *PQ* is a chord of a circle with centre *O*. *OR* is perpendicular to *PQ*. *OR* = 6 units and *PQ* = 16 units.

Calculate the length of *OQ*.

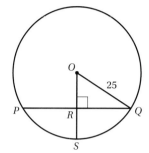

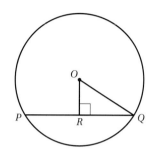

3 In the diagram below, *COE* is a diameter of the circle centre *O* and *NT* is parallel to *CD*. *NAT* is a tangent to the circle at point *A*. Given that angle *NAC* is 66°, what is the size of angle *ECD*?

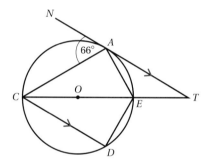

Alternate segment theorem

This theorem states that for a point *P* on the circumference, the angle between the tangent and a chord through *P* equals the angle subtended by the chord in the alternate segment.

Consider what the term 'alternate segment' means. Remember from the parts of a circle that a chord divides a circle into a minor segment and a major segment. So we are looking at one angle in a minor segment and one angle in the major segment. So for the diagram on the right, angle *TPR* = angle *PQR*.

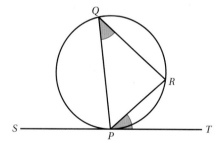

Proof

We are given a circle with centre *O* which has a tangent at *P*.

PR is a chord with *W* on the minor arc and *Q* on the major arc.

Prove that angle *TPR* = *PQR* and also that angle *SPR* = *PWR*.

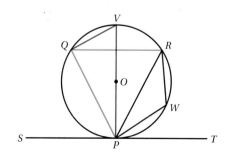

- To prove angle *TPR* = angle *PQR*:

  Draw diameter *VP*. Join points *V* and *Q*.

  Angle *PQV* = 90° (*VP* is the diameter, so angle *PQV* is the angle in a semicircle)

  Angle *TPV* = 90° (angle between the radius and tangent)

  So angle *PQV* = angle *TPV*

  But angle *RPV* = angle *RQV* (angles in the same segment)

  So, angle *TPR* = *PQR*, as required.

- To prove angle *TPR* = angle *PQR*:

  Join line segment *VW*.

  Angle *SPV* = 90° (angle between radius and tangent)

  Angle *PWV* = 90° (angle in a semicircle)

  Now notice that angle *RPV* = *RWV* (angles in the same segment subtended by *VR*)

  Angle *SPV* + *RPV* = angle *PWV* + *RWV*

  So, angle *SPR* = *PWR*, as required.

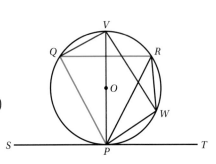

Angles in cyclic quadrilaterals

A **cyclic quadrilateral** is a quadrilateral which has all four vertices touching the circumference of a circle.

This theorem states that the opposite angles in a cyclic quadrilateral add up to 180°.

Proof

ABCD is a cyclic quadrilateral. *BO* and *DO* are radii of the circle.

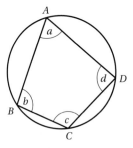 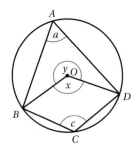

$x = 2a$ (angle at centre theorem, minor arc *BD*)

$y = 2c$ (angle at centre theorem, major arc *BD*)

$\therefore x + y = 2a + 2c$

But $x + y = 360°$ (angles at a point add up to 360°)

$\therefore 2a + 2c = 360°$

$\therefore a + c = 180°$

Since the sum of the angles in any quadrilateral is 180°, and $a + c = 180°$, then $b + d = 360 - 180 = 180°$

Key vocabulary

cyclic quadrilateral: any quadrilateral with all four vertices on the circumference of a circle.

Did you know?

Squares and rectangles and some kites and trapezia can be cyclic quadrilaterals, but a rhombus or parallelogram cannot ever be a cyclic quadrilateral.

Tip

ABCO is not a cyclic quadrilateral.

For a quadrilateral to be a cyclic quadrilateral all four vertices must sit on the circumference. Make sure you check this carefully when you are applying the theorems.

EXERCISE 27D

1 Opposite angles in a cyclic quadrilateral have special properties. Which is the correct statement?

   A Opposite angles are corresponding and are therefore equal.

   B Opposite angles add up to 180°.

   C Opposite angles are equal as they are vertically opposite.

   D Opposite angles are alternate angles and are therefore equal.

2 In the diagram on the right *TAN* is a tangent to the circle and angle *TAC* = angle *BAN*.

   Prove that:

   a *CB* is parallel to *TN*

   b *AC* = *AB*

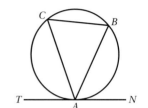

3 In the diagram on the right *APB* is a tangent at *P* to the circle, centre *S*. Angle *APR* = *x*.

   Write the following angles in terms of *x*:

   a angle *SQP*   **b** angle *QSP*

   c angle *RSP*   **d** angle *RPS*

   e angle *QPB*

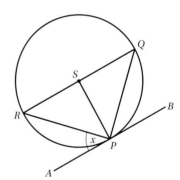

4 Calculate the value of each lettered angle. Give reasons for your statements.

   a

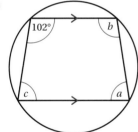

   b

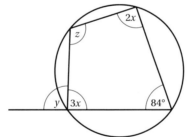

   c

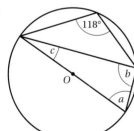

   d

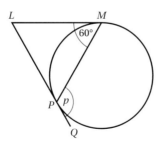

Section 3: Applications of circle theorems

To solve problems in geometry, you need to apply your knowledge correctly. You will often not see the solution immediately, but you can start to identify a pathway towards the final solution by building on the information step by step.

Problem-solving framework

Look at the diagram below. AOB and COD are diameters of circle with centre O.
Angle ACD = 33°.

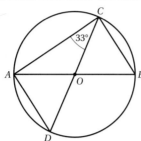

Calculate the sizes of:

a angle AOD

b angle D

c angle B

Steps for approaching a problem-solving question	What you would do for this example
Step 1: What do you have to do?	Calculate the size of various angles using one known angle and circle theorems.
Step 2: If a diagram is useful, draw one.	You have been given a diagram but it would be useful to mark on any additional information that you can work out.
	Angles *DAC* and *ACB* are right angles (angles in a semicircle). Lines *AB* = *CD* (both are diameters of the circle).
	Label angle *OCB* as x. Then, using angles in the same segment or isosceles triangles formed by radii, label other angles that also equal x. Angles *AOD* and *COB* = $(180° - x)$ because angles in a triangle sum to 180°, also vertically opposite angles are equal. Angle *AOC* = $2x$ (angles on a straight line sum to 180°). Same applies for angle *BOC* (also, vertically opposite angles are equal).
Step 3: What maths can you do?	Use this information to decide what method you will use. This may not be obvious immediately. You may need to spend some time studying the problem. Write out all your working and include reasoning. Even if you've already applied this reasoning to mark up your diagram, you still need to state it as part of your working. You can use the theorems as accepted facts. You can also use facts that you have proved.
	a angle *ACB* = 90° (angle in a semicircle) angle *OCB* = 90° − 33° = 57° angle *DAO* = angle *OCB* = 57° (angles in the same segment) angle *ODA* = angle *DAO* = 57° (triangle *OAD* is isosceles) angle *AOD* = 180° − 2(57°) = 66° (sum of angles in a triangle)
	b angle *D* = 57° (already proved in part a)
	b angle *B* = angle *OCB* = 57° (triangle *OBC* is isosceles)
Step 4: Have you answered the question? Do your answers seem reasonable? Check your answers.	Answers seem reasonable given the angle of 33° supplied. Checked all calculations. ✓

WORK IT OUT 27.1

Rose needs to solve the following problem.

P, Q and T are points on the circumference of a circle, centre O.

The line ATB is the tangent to the circle at T.

$PQ = TQ$

Angle $ATP = 58°$

Calculate the size of angle OTQ.

Give a reason for each stage in your working.

Which of her answers below is the correct answer?

Where have her other answers gone wrong?

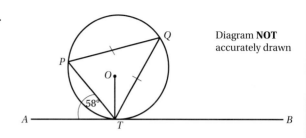

Diagram **NOT** accurately drawn

Option A	Option B	Option C
angle $PQT = 58°$ (angles in alternate segments)	angle $PQT = 58°$ (angles in alternate segments)	angle $PQT = 58°$ (angles in alternate segments)
angle OTQ = angle PQT (radii of circle are equal, isosceles triangle)	Triangle QPT is isosceles ($QP = QT$) So angle QPT = angle QTP	Triangle QPT is isosceles ($QP = QT$)
angle $OTQ = 58°$	angle $QTP = \frac{1}{2} \times (180° - 58°)$ (the sum of angles in a triangle is 180°) angle $QPT = 61°$	angle QPT = angle OTQ (triangle QPT is isosceles)
	angle OTA = angle $OTB = 90°$ (angle between radius and tangent)	angle $OTQ = \frac{1}{2} \times (180° - 58°)$ (the sum of angles in a triangle is 180°)
	$OTP = 90° - 58° = 32°$	angle $OTQ = \frac{1}{2} \times 122°$
	$QTP - OTP$ = angle OTQ $OTQ = 61° - 32° = 29°$	angle $OTQ = 61°$

EXERCISE 27E

 1 AB is a chord of a circle, centre P, with D the midpoint of AB.
  $PA = 50$ units and $AB = 96$ units.

  Calculate the length of:

  a PD **b** DE **c** DF **d** BF **e** BE.

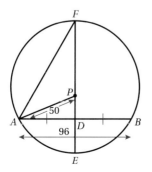

2 *ABC* is a tangent to a circle, with centre *O*, at *B*. *FOB* is a diameter. *GF* ∥ *BD*, *EH* = *HD* and angle *ABG* = 62°.

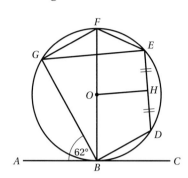

Write down the size of each angle. Give reasons in each case.

a angle *EHO*   **b** angle *GFB*   **c** angle *GBF*

d angle *FEG*   **e** angle *DBF*   **f** angle *GEH*

3 Find the size of angle *PLM* in terms of *x*.

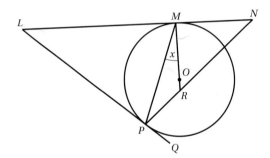

4 In the diagram, *TA* and *TB* are the tangents from *T* to the circle with centre *O*. *AC* is a diameter of the circle and angle *ACB* = *x*.

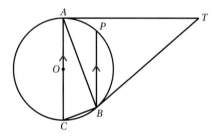

a Find angle *CAB* in terms of *x*.

b Find angle *ATB* in terms of *x*.

c The point *P* on the circumference of the circle is such that *BP* is parallel to *CA*. Express angle *PBT* in terms of *x*.

Checklist of learning and understanding

Circle theorems

- The angle subtended by an arc or chord at the centre is twice the angle at the circumference.

- The angle on the circumference subtended by a diameter is a right angle.

- Two angles in the same segment are equal.

- A radius or diameter bisects a chord if and only if it is perpendicular to the chord.

- For a point P on the circumference, the radius or diameter through P is perpendicular to the tangent at P.

- For a point P on the circumference, the angle between the tangent and a chord through P equals the angle subtended by the chord in the alternate segment.

- The opposite angles of a cyclic quadrilateral are supplementary.

Chapter review

For additional questions on the topics in this chapter, visit GCSE Mathematics Online.

1 AC is the diameter of a circle centre O.

AT and BT are tangents to the circle and AC is parallel to PB.

If angle PBA is 32°, what is the size of angle BCA?

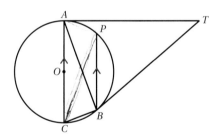

A 32°   **B** 58°   **C** 60°   **D** 122°

2 A, B, C and D are points on the circumference of a circle.
Angle $ABD = 54°$. Angle $BAC = 28°$.

Find the size of angle ACD. Give a reason for your answer.

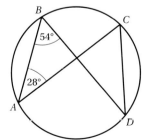

Not to scale

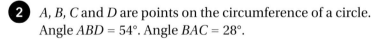

Find answers at: cambridge.org/ukschools/gcsemaths-studentbookanswers

3 In the diagram, A, B, C and D are points on the circumference of a circle, centre O. Angle $BAD = 70°$. Angle $BOD = x°$. Angle $BCD = y°$.

a Work out the value of x. Give a reason for your answer.

b Work out the value of y.

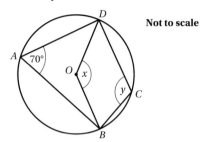

Not to scale

4 B, C and D are points on the circumference of a circle, centre O.

AB and AD are tangents to the circle.

Angle $DAB = 50°$

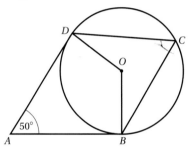

Diagram **NOT** accurately drawn

Work out the size of angle BCD.

Give a reason for each stage in your working. *(4 marks)*

28 Probability – combined events

In this chapter you will learn how to ...

- use a range of diagrams to list outcomes of combined events.
- apply the product, addition and multiplication rules.
- use various representations to solve probability problems.
- understand conditional probability and solve problems involving conditional probability.

For more resources relating to this chapter, visit GCSE Mathematics Online.

Using mathematics: real-life applications

Medical researchers have developed a range of tests to detect drug use, blood-alcohol levels, disease markers and genetic and birth defects in unborn children. The probability that the test results are accurate is very high, but it is seldom 100%.

"An incorrect test result can be devastating. People can be convicted of drink-driving or more serious crimes, be expelled from competitive sports, risk surgery or decide to terminate a pregnancy based on test results, so it is really important to understand the probability of a good test giving a bad result." *(Medical statistician)*

Before you start ...

Chs 6 and 7	You'll need to be able to calculate effectively with fractions and decimals.	**1** These calculations are all incorrect. What should the answers be? **a** $\frac{1}{8} + \frac{1}{4} = \frac{1}{12}$ **b** $\frac{2}{3} + \frac{1}{5} = \frac{2}{15}$ **c** $1 - \frac{3}{5} = -\frac{2}{5}$ **d** $\frac{2}{3} \times \frac{2}{5} = \frac{2}{15}$ **e** $0.3 \times 0.6 = 1.8$
Ch 21	Check that you can list all the possible outcomes of an experiment.	**2** Complete each list of possible outcomes. **a** Two students are to be chosen at random from a group of males and females: FF, FM, ... **b** Two coins are to be flipped at the same time: HH, ... **c** Two cards are selected from a set of three cards labelled A, B and C and placed next to each other in the order they are drawn: AB, AC, ...

Find answers at: cambridge.org/ukschools/gcsemaths-studentbookanswers

Assess your starting point using the Launchpad

STEP 1

1 The Venn diagram shows the different sports chosen by students from one particular class. T represents students who play tennis and S represents those who take swimming.

a How many students are in the class?

b How many students play tennis?

c How many students play tennis and swim?

d If a student is chosen at random from the class, what is the probability that he or she will take swimming?

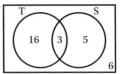

GO TO
Section 1:
Representing combined events

STEP 2

2 The diagram is used to find the probability of drawing hearts or twos at random from a normal pack of 52 playing cards.

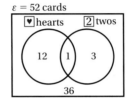

What is the probability that a card drawn at random will be:

a both a heart and a two   **b** either a heart or a two

c neither a heart nor a two?

GO TO
Section 2:
Theoretical probability of combined events

3 A black (B) or white (W) counter is drawn at random from a box containing both black and white counters. The counter is replaced before a second counter is drawn. The possible outcomes and the probabilities of each outcome are shown on the right.

What is the probability of:

a drawing a black counter on the first draw

b drawing two counters the same colour

c drawing a white counter first and a black counter second?

GO TO
Section 3:
Conditional probability

4 **a** Draw a tree diagram to show the sample space for the genders of the children in a two-child family. (The chances of a child being a boy or a girl are equal.)

b If the older child is a girl, calculate the probability that the younger child is a boy.

GO TO
Chapter review

Section 1: Representing combined events

Lists and tables are useful for showing the sample space of possible outcomes. For example, you can list the sample space for rolling a six-sided dice (1, 2, 3, 4, 5, 6).

For more complex sample spaces, where more than one action is taking place, tables are more useful than lists. In some cases you don't have to list all the possible outcomes. For example, let's say you want to know how many ways there are to get a total score of 7 when you roll two ordinary dice. You can draw up a table like this one:

Number on dice	1	2	3	4	5	6
1	2	3	4	5	6	7
2	3	4	5	6	7	
3	4	5	6	7		
4	4	6	7			
5	6	7				
6	7					

> **Tip**
>
> Once you get to a sum of 7 you can stop because the next sum will be greater than that.

The table shows there are six ways of getting a score of 7: (1, 6), (2, 5), (3, 4), (4, 3), (5, 2) and (6, 1).

Even though you haven't filled in the empty blocks, you can still see that there are 36 possible outcomes. So the probability of getting 7 is $\frac{6}{36}$ or $\frac{1}{6}$.

Tables and grids

WORKED EXAMPLE 1

Represent the sample space for flipping a coin and rolling a dice using:

a a table.　　**b** a grid.

a Table

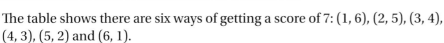

Dice / Coin	1	2	3	4	5	6
Heads	H1	H2	H3	H4	H5	H6
Tails	T1	T2	T3	T4	T5	T6

b Grid

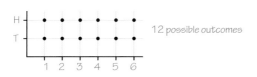

12 possible outcomes

> **Tip**
>
> You can check that you have recorded all the combinations. There are two possible outcomes for flipping a coin and six for rolling a dice. Combining these gives a total of 2 × 6 = 12.

Tree diagrams

A tree diagram is a branching diagram that shows all the possible outcomes (sample space) of one or more activities.

To draw a tree diagram:

- Make a dot to represent the first activity.
- Draw branches from the dot to show all possible outcomes of that activity only.
- Write the outcomes at the end of each branch.
- Draw a dot at the end of each branch to represent the next activity.
- Draw branches from this point to show all possible outcomes of that activity.
- Write the outcomes at the end of the branches.

These two diagrams both show the possible outcomes for throwing a dice and flipping a coin at the same time. Both diagrams are correct.

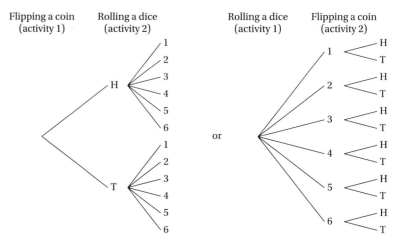

Did you know?

The tree diagram in Worked example 2 assumes that each pregnancy is equally likely to result in a boy as a girl. In reality the probability of having a boy or a girl varies by family and by country.

Once you've drawn a tree diagram you can list the possible outcomes by following the paths along the branches. Listing the combinations lets you work out the probability of different events.

WORKED EXAMPLE 2

Draw a tree diagram to find how many possible combinations of boys and girls there are in a three-child family if the probability of having a boy or a girl is equal.

Use your diagram to find:

a the probability of three girls

b the probability of three children with the same gender.

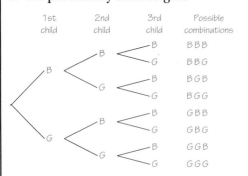

Draw a dot for the first-born child.

Draw and label two branches, one B and one G.

Repeat this at the end of each branch for the second and third child.

List the possible combinations.

Continues on next page …

There are eight combinations.

As all the branches have equal probability, you can see from the diagram there are eight, equally likely, possible combinations of boys and girls.

a $P(3 \text{ girls}) = \dfrac{1}{8}$

There is only one outcome that produces three girls.

b $P(\text{all the same gender}) = \dfrac{2}{8} = \dfrac{1}{4}$

Same gender is all girls or all boys. There are two outcomes that satisfy this, GGG and BBB.

EXERCISE 28A

1 Use a grid to represent the sample space for:

  a flipping two coins

  b choosing a letter at random from the word DOG and flipping a coin

  c drawing a counter from each of two bags containing one red, one blue and one yellow counter.

2 **a** Draw a table to show:

  i all possible combinations of scores when you roll two dice

  ii the sample space for flipping a coin and spinning a spinner with equal sectors A, B, C and D.

  b For each table above, make up five probability questions that could be answered from the tables. Exchange questions with a partner and try to answer each other's questions.

3 Draw a tree diagram to show the sample space when three coins are flipped one after the other.

4 Sandy has a bag containing a red, a blue and a green pen. Copy and complete this tree diagram to show the sample space when she takes a pen from the bag at random, replaces it, and then takes another pen.

5 In a knockout quiz, the winner goes on to the next round. Naresh takes part in a four-round quiz and he estimates that he has an equal chance of winning or losing each round.

  a Using W to represent win and L to represent loss, draw a tree diagram to show all possible outcomes for Naresh.

  b How many possible outcomes are there?

  c What is the probability that he will win the first round given his own estimate of his chances?

6 Here are two groups of jelly beans.

  a Draw a tree diagram to show the sample space for taking a jelly bean at random from each group of jelly beans.

  b Based on this, does it seem that any particular combination of colours has a higher probability than another? Is that the reality? Explain your reasoning.

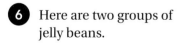 Find answers at: cambridge.org/ukschools/gcsemaths-studentbookanswers

Tip

In all exercises in this chapter, assume that all dice and coins are 'fair', i.e. that there is an equal chance of landing on any of the sides of the dice, or either side of the coin.

Venn diagrams

Venn diagrams show the mathematical relationships between sets of data. Different events (sets of outcomes) are represented by circles inside a rectangular frame which in turn represents the sample space (universal set).

Look at the Venn diagram below and read through the information to revise the main features of Venn diagrams.

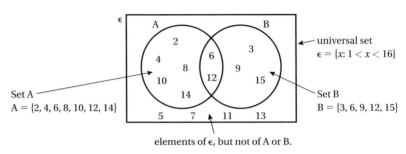

elements of ϵ, but not of A or B.

> ### Tip
>
> $\mathcal{E}$ can also be written as:
> $\mathcal{E}$ = {set of numbers between 1 and 16}.

> ### Tip
>
> The curly brackets { } are used to show you are describing a set. The numbers between the brackets are elements of the set (for example 2 ∈ A). The symbol ∉ means 'not an element of a set'. 3 ∉ A.

ε is the universal set. In this case it is the whole numbers between 1 and 16 (not 1 and not 16).

The circles A and B represent sets.

Set A is the set of even numbers between 1 and 16: A = {2, 4, 6, 8, 10, 12, 14}.

Set B is the set of multiples of three between 1 and 16: B = {3, 6, 9, 12, 15}.

There are seven elements in Set A. This can be written as n(A) = 7.

There are five elements in Set B, so n(B) = 5.

The numbers 5, 7, 11 and 13 are not elements of A or B but they are elements of the universal set, so they are written inside the rectangle, but outside the circles.

Intersection, union and complement of sets

Venn diagrams can also represent operations between sets.

Set A and Set B have two elements in common. The numbers 6 and 12 are written in the overlapping section of the circles.

This is the **intersection** between A and B.

$A \cap B$ = {6, 12}

$n(A \cap B)$ = 2

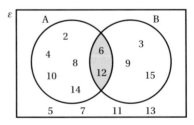

The shaded area on the left represents the **union** of A and B. This is the combined elements of both sets with no elements repeated.

$A \cup B$ = {2, 3, 4, 6, 8, 9, 10, 12, 14, 15}

$n(A \cup B)$ = 10

The **complement** of a set refers to all the members of the universal set not in the given set. In the diagram on the right, the complement of Set A is shaded.

A′ = {3, 5, 7, 9, 11, 13, 15}

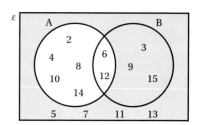

WORKED EXAMPLE 3

Given that ε = {x: x is a letter from a to h inclusive}, A = {a, b, c, e} and B = {c, d, e, f, g}, draw a Venn diagram to represent this information.

c and e are elements of A and B, so A ∩ B = {c, e}

> Look for elements that are common to both sets. These will go in the intersection.

h is not in A or B, so (A ∪ B)′ = h

> Look for any elements which are in the universal set but which are not in A or B (the complement of A and B or (A ∪ B)′).

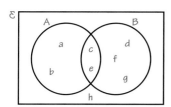

> Draw the diagram and label it correctly.

In some problems you might be given information and have to define the sets yourself. In some cases you can't list the separate elements of the sets so you write the number of elements in each set.

WORKED EXAMPLE 4

In a survey of 25 people it was found that they all liked either chocolate or ice cream or both. 15 people said they liked ice cream and 18 said they liked chocolate.

Draw a Venn diagram and use it to work out the probability that a person chosen at random from this group will like both chocolate and ice cream.

ε = {number of people surveyed}, so, n(ε) = 25
C = {people who like chocolate}, so, n(C) = 15
I = {people who like ice cream}, so, n(I) = 18

> Start by defining the sets and writing the information in set language.

n(C) + n(I) = 15 + 18 = 33,
n(C ∩ I) = 33 − 25 = 8

> But there were only 25 people surveyed, so eight people must have said they liked both chocolate and ice cream.

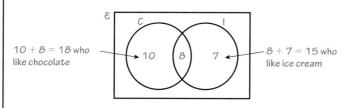

10 + 8 = 18 who like chocolate

8 + 7 = 15 who like ice cream

> Use the figures to draw your Venn diagram.

P(person likes both)

$= \dfrac{\text{number of people who like both}}{\text{number of people surveyed}} = \dfrac{8}{25} = 0.32$

> Finally, calculate the probability.

Find answers at: cambridge.org/ukschools/gcsemaths-studentbookanswers

Tip

You don't know the names of the people surveyed in Worked example 4, so you can't list them in the diagram. You do know how many of each response there was, so you can just write the number of people in the diagram.

EXERCISE 28B

1 ε = {integers from 1 to 20 inclusive}, A = {6, 7, 8, 9, 10, 11, 12} and B = {factors of 24}.

   a Draw a Venn diagram to show this information.

   b Use your Venn diagram to find:

      i $A \cap B$ **ii** $A \cup B$ **iii** n(A)   **iv** n(A′)   **v** n(B′).

2 Nadia has 20 pairs of shoes. Six pairs are sports shoes, four pairs are red and only one of the pairs of sports shoes is red.

   Draw a Venn diagram to show this information and work out the probability that a pair of shoes chosen at random from her shoe collection will be neither red nor sports shoes.

3 A factory employs 100 people. 47 of the employees have to work with moving machinery so if they have long hair they have to tie it back. 35 employees have long hair, and of these, some work with moving machinery. 23 employees neither have long hair nor work with moving machinery.

   Draw a Venn diagram to show this information and use it to work out the probability of a random employee having to tie his or her hair back at work.

4 Of the first 20 students to walk into a classroom, 13 were wearing headphones and 15 were sending texts. Four students were not wearing headphones or sending texts.

   Represent this information on a Venn diagram and state how many students were wearing headphones while sending texts when they walked into class.

5 A group of 200 people at a function were questioned to find out about their food preferences. It was found that 110 people ate red meat, 135 ate chicken, and 15 ate neither.

   Calculate the probability that a person chosen at random will eat:

   a red meat and chicken

   b only red meat

   c only chicken.

6 A health-policy researcher asked 500 shoppers in one morning which of three items they bought at their local supermarket.

   Of these 500 shoppers, 224 bought ready-made meals, 213 shoppers bought fresh produce (fruit or vegetables) and 198 bought dairy products.

137 of the shoppers bought only ready-made meals.

43 of them bought both fresh produce and ready-made meals, but no dairy products.

32 of them bought only ready-made meals and dairy products.

122 of them bought only fresh produce.

Represent this information on a Venn diagram. Use the diagram to find out:

a how many of the shoppers bought all three of the items

b how many bought only fresh produce and dairy products, but no ready-made meals

c how many bought only dairy.

Section 2: Theoretical probability of combined events

Once you have identified all the possible outcomes you can mark the ones that are favourable and use these to find the probability of different events.

The formula, P(event happens) = $\dfrac{\text{number of favourable outcomes}}{\text{number of possible outcomes}}$, can still be used to work this out.

WORKED EXAMPLE 5

Jay has six cards with the numbers 0, 0, 2, 2, 3 and 7 on them. He picks a card, returns it and then picks another at random.

a Draw a grid to show the sample space

b Use the grid to find the probability that Jay will pick:

  i two numbers that are the same   **ii** two numbers that add up to 7.

a

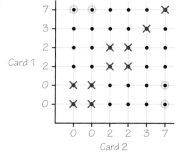

The grid shows there are 36 possible outcomes.

b i P(two numbers the same) = $\dfrac{10}{36}$

$= \dfrac{5}{18}$

or 0.28 (correct to 2 decimal places)

The successful outcomes are marked with a cross on the grid.

ii P(sum of 7) = $\dfrac{4}{36}$

$= \dfrac{1}{9}$

The successful outcomes are circled on the grid.

The product rule for counting

In Worked example 5, the number of possible outcomes is 36. You can count the dots on the grid, but you can also find the total by multiplying: $6 \times 6 = 36$.

WORK IT OUT 28.1

A tube station has two entrance turnstiles and three exit turnstiles. How many possible options are there to leave and enter the station?

Which answer is correct? List all the possible outcomes to show this.

Option A	Option B
Two entrances = 2 ways in Three exits = 3 ways out Total number of ways in and out = $2 + 3 = 5$	For each of the two ways in there are three ways out. $2 \times 3 = 6$ possible options.

The problem above can also be solved by drawing a tree diagram or grid.

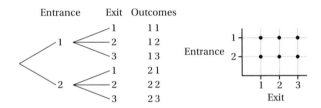

The product rule is useful for quickly solving probability problems like the one above without drawing the sample space.

WORKED EXAMPLE 6

How many three-digit numbers can be made from the digits 2, 3, 4 and 5 without repeating any digits?

☐ ☐ ☐

You need three digits. One way to look at this is to draw three empty boxes.

There are four options for the first digit.

$4 \times 3 \times 2$
$= 24$ ways of arranging the digits.

Once you have chosen the first digit, there are only three options for the second digit, and once that is chosen, there are only two options for the third digit.

 Tip

If the digits can be repeated, then y͟ ͟ ͟ ͟ ͟ ͟ ͟ ͟ $4 \times 4 = ?$ ͟ ͟ he number of options doesn't reduc͟ ͟ ͟

EXERCISE 28C

1 In a class of 28 students, 12 take physics, 15 take chemistry and eight take neither physics nor chemistry.

   a Draw a Venn diagram to represent this information.

   b What is the probability that a student chosen at random from this class:

     i takes physics but not chemistry

     ii takes physics or chemistry

     iii takes physics and chemistry?

2 Sunil has to choose a six-character password for his phone. He decides to choose two letters and four numbers, in that order, with no repetition of letter or digits (there are 26 letters in the alphabet, and numbers are from 0–9). How many password options does he have?

3 What is the probability of winning the jackpot in a lottery if there are 49 numbers to choose from and you need to match six (different) numbers to win?

4 Anna wants to buy running shoes from a specialist running shop. She wants to choose:

- either neutral, cushioned or stability shoes
- from three top brands
- one of five trendy colours.

How many different shoes can she choose between?

5 How many combinations are possible for a four-digit code number made from digits 1 to 9? The digits cannot be repeated.

6 There are five questions in a multiple-choice test and the answers for each are A, B, C or D. A hacker uses a computer to generate answers. How many sets of answers must she generate to make sure that one of the sets is 100% correct?

7 You can choose from eight different fillings for a wrap. How many different combinations are there if you order a wrap with three fillings?

8 Three dice are rolled. How many outcomes are possible?

Different types of events

The type of event determines whether you add or multiply the probabilities.

Mutually exclusive events and the addition rule

Imagine you have a bag with 3 red, 2 yellow and 5 green sweets in it and you are allowed to choose one sweet at random. You cannot pick a red sweet and a yellow sweet at the same time, so the events P(red) and P(yellow) are mutually exclusive.

Tip

You should remember from Chapter 21 that mutually exclusive events cannot happen at the same time.

Tip

Questions involving 'either–or' events usually involve mutually exclusive events so they can usually be solved by adding the probabilities.

You can work out the probability of choosing *either* a red *or* a yellow sweet. There are 3 red and 2 yellow sweets, so $\frac{5}{10}$ of the sweets are either red or yellow.

$$P(\text{red or yellow}) = P(\text{red}) + P(\text{yellow}) = \frac{3}{10} + \frac{2}{10} = \frac{5}{10} = \frac{1}{2}$$

You can say that P(A or B) = P(A) + P(B) where A and B are mutually exclusive events.

This is called the addition rule for mutually exclusive events.

Events that are not mutually exclusive

When you list the elements in the union of sets you do not repeat shared elements (those in the intersection).

In set language, you can write this as $n(A \cup B) = n(A) + n(B) - n(A \cap B)$. The elements in the intersection of sets are not mutually exclusive and this affects your probability calculations.

Tip

The word 'or' means it belongs in one set or the other, so you need to deal with the union of the sets.

WORKED EXAMPLE 7

The Venn diagram shows the possible outcomes when a six-sided dice is rolled. Set A = {prime numbers} and Set B = {odd numbers}. Use the diagram to find the probability of rolling a number that is either odd or prime.

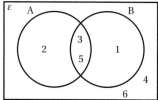

$P(A \text{ or } B) = P(A) + P(B) - P(A \text{ and } B)$

> You don't want to add the numbers that fall into the intersecting part twice, which is why you subtract $n(A \cap B)$ in the formula.

$P(A) = \dfrac{3}{6}$

$P(B) = \dfrac{3}{6}$

$P(A \text{ and } B) = \dfrac{2}{6}$

> The total number of outcomes is the denominator, and it's easier to add and subtract the fractions if you don't simplify the fractions first.

So, $P(A \text{ or } B) = \dfrac{3}{6} + \dfrac{3}{6} - \dfrac{2}{6} = \dfrac{4}{6} = \dfrac{2}{3}$

> You can see this is true by looking at the diagram. The combined elements of A and B are 1, 2, 3 and 5, giving you $\dfrac{4}{6}$ numbers falling into one or the other of these sets.

Independent events

When the outcome of one event does not affect the outcome of the others, the events are **independent**.

Rolling a dice and flipping a coin are independent events. The score (outcome) on the dice doesn't affect whether you get heads or tails.

The probability of combined events on a tree diagram

This tree diagram shows the possible outcomes for throwing a dice and flipping a coin at the same time (H is used for head and T is used for tail).

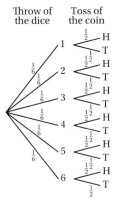

To find the probability of one particular combination of outcomes, multiply the probabilities on consecutive branches, for example, the probability of throwing a 5 and getting heads is $\frac{1}{6} \times \frac{1}{2} = \frac{1}{12}$.

This is called the multiplication rule and it works for independent events only.

$P(A \text{ and } B) = P(A) \times P(B)$

Tip

It can be helpful to use a colour to mark the route along the branches to show which events you are dealing with.

Combining the rules

To find the probability when there is more than one favourable combination or when the events are mutually exclusive:

- multiply the probabilities on consecutive branches

- add the probabilities (of each favourable combination) obtained by multiplication, for example, throwing 1 or 2 and getting an H

is $\left(\frac{1}{6} \times \frac{1}{2}\right) + \left(\frac{1}{6} \times \frac{1}{2}\right) = \frac{1}{12} + \frac{1}{12} = \frac{2}{12} = \frac{1}{6}$.

WORKED EXAMPLE 8

Two coins are flipped together. Draw a tree diagram to find the probability of getting:

a two tails.   **b** one head and one tail.

a $P(TT) = P(T \text{ on 1st flip}) \times P(T \text{ on 2nd flip})$

$= \frac{1}{2} \times \frac{1}{2} = \frac{1}{4}$

b $P(HT \text{ or } TH) = P(HT) + P(TH)$

$= \left(\frac{1}{2} \times \frac{1}{2}\right) + \left(\frac{1}{2} \times \frac{1}{2}\right) = \frac{1}{4} + \frac{1}{4} = \frac{1}{2}$

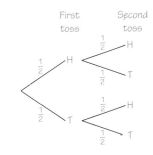

Key vocabulary

dependent events: events in which the outcome is affected by what happened before.

Dependent events

When the outcome of one event affects the outcome of another the events are said to be **dependent**.

Here are 4 red and 2 yellow sweets.

Suppose you choose one sweet at random and eat it before you select a second sweet. What is the probability of the second sweet being red?

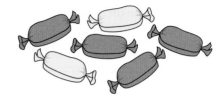

The answer to this depends on what colour the first sweet was. If the first sweet was red then the probability on the branch to the second red is $\frac{3}{5}$ because there are only 5 sweets left and only 3 of those are red.

1 red eaten

If the first sweet was yellow then the probability on the branch to the second one being red is $\frac{4}{5}$. There are still only five sweets left to choose from, but this time four of them are red.

1 yellow eaten

For dependent events you can find the probability by adapting the multiplication rule to accommodate the dependent event.

P(*A and* then B) = P(A) × P(*B given* that A has occurred)

Tree diagrams can be useful for showing dependent events.

WORKED EXAMPLE 9

A box contains three yellow, four red and two purple marbles. A marble is chosen at random and not replaced before choosing the next one. If three marbles are chosen (without replacement), what is the probability of choosing:

a three red marbles?

b a yellow, red and purple marble in that order?

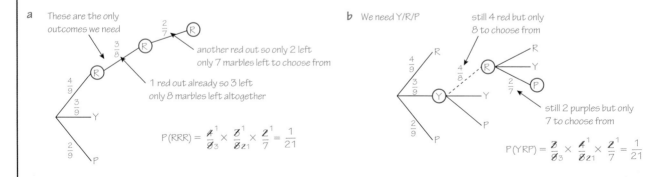

502

The product rule for counting is also useful for solving some types of problems without drawing the sample space.

WORKED EXAMPLE 10

Josh has four cards labelled 1, 2, 3 and 4. He draws two cards at random to make a 2-digit number, with the first card drawn being used to make the tens digit.

a How many possible outcomes are there?

b What is the probability of making 32?

a ☐☐

$4 \times 3 = 12$ possible outcomes

Draw two empty boxes to represent the 2-digit number.

4 options for first digit leaves 3 for the second.

b $P(32) = \dfrac{1}{12}$

Given the digits don't repeat you should be able to tell straight away that there is only one option.

$P(3 \text{ then } 2) = P(3) \times P(2, \text{given } 3 \text{ has occurred})$

$$= \frac{1}{4} \times \frac{1}{3} = \frac{1}{12}$$

You can also work this out using probabilities.

Tip

You need to understand the difference between independent and dependent events to make sense of conditional probability in Section 3.

EXERCISE 28D

1 Nico is on a bus and he is bored. He passes the time by choosing a consonant and a vowel at random from the names of towns on road signs. The next road sign is DUNDEE.

    a Draw up a sample space diagram to list all the options that Nico has.

    b Calculate P(D and E).

    c Calculate P(D and E or U).

    d Calculate P(not N and not U).

2 A bag contains 3 red counters, 4 green counters, 2 yellow counters and 1 white counter. Two counters are drawn at random from the bag, one after the other, without being replaced. Calculate:

    a P(2 red counters)

    b P(2 green counters)

    c P(2 yellow counters)

    d P(white and then red)

    e P(white or yellow, but not both)

    f P(white or red, but not both)

    g P(white or yellow first and then any other colour).

 Find answers at: cambridge.org/ukschools/gcsemaths-studentbookanswers

3 A card is randomly selected from a pack of 52 playing cards and its suit is noted. The card is not replaced. Then a second card is chosen.

    a Draw a tree diagram to represent this situation.

    b Use the tree diagram to find the probability that:

       i both cards are hearts

       ii neither of the cards are clubs

       iii the first card is red and the second card is black.

4 Mohammed has four Scrabble tiles with the letters A, B, C and D on them. He draws a letter at random and places it on the table, then he draws a second letter and a third, placing them down next to the previously drawn letter.

    a What is the probability that the letters he has drawn spell the words:

       i CAD   **ii** BAD   **iii** DAD?

    b What is the probability that he will not draw the letter B?

    c What is Mohammed's chance of drawing the letters in alphabetical order?

5 In a standard pack of cards, A = {hearts} and B = {kings}. If a card is picked at random, determine:

    a P(A)   **b** P(B)   **c** P(A and B)   **d** P(A or B).

6 During January in Manchester it rained on 16 days and the temperature fell below 6 °C on 25 days. There were no days when it either did not rain or did not fall below 6 °C .

Draw a Venn diagram to determine the number of days in January that were below 6 °C and rainy.

Section 3: Conditional probability

Conditional probability is used when you need to work out the probability of one event happening when you already know that another has happened. The information about the first event changes the sample space and affects the calculation. For two events A and B, the notation P(B|A) is used to refer to the conditional probability of B happening given that A has already happened. We read B|A as 'B given A' .

The way that you work out the conditional probability depends on whether the events are independent or not.

Consider rolling two normal six-sided dice. What is the probability of getting double sixes?

Consider that the first dice has already landed on a six. What is the probability of the second dice being a six?

These two events are independent. The score on the second dice is not dependent on, or affected by, the outcome of the first. In this case, the probability of it landing on a six is still $\frac{1}{6}$.

$$P(6 \text{ then } 6) = \frac{1}{6} \times \frac{1}{6} = \frac{1}{36}$$

You can see this by following the upper the branches of the tree diagram.

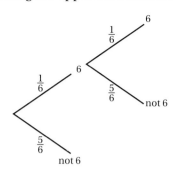

For independent events, P(B|A) = P(B). In other words, the probability of the second event occurring, given that the first has already occurred is simply the probability of the second event.

If two events A and B are independent, you will find that it is always true that P(B|A) = P(B).

WORKED EXAMPLE 11

Two coins are flipped. One lands on the table heads up, the other rolls under the table and cannot be seen. What is the probability that the second coin is also heads up?

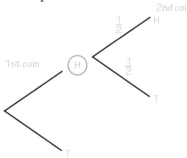

$$P(\text{second coin is H} | \text{first coin is H}) = \frac{1}{2}$$

The actions are independent so conditional probability is the same as P(H) for a single coin.

For dependent events, the outcome of the first event affects the probability of the second. In Section 2, you used the formula P(A and B) = P(A) × P(B given that A has occurred).

To find P(B|A), you can adapt the rule to get $P(B|A) = \dfrac{P(A \text{ and } B)}{P(A)}$.

Tip

When you deal with Venn diagrams, this rule can be written in set language as

$$P(B|A) = \frac{P(A \cap B)}{P(A)}$$

Tip

When the problem states that the items are 'replaced' then the events are independent and the probabilities don't change. When the item is not replaced, the outcome of the second depends on the outcome first event and the probabilities change.

 Find answers at: cambridge.org/ukschools/gcsemaths-studentbookanswers

WORKED EXAMPLE 12

What is the probability of drawing two queens if you draw one card and then another at random from a 52-card pack without replacing the first card?

The probability that the first card is a queen is $\frac{4}{52}$ or $\frac{1}{13}$.

$$P(A \text{ and } B) = \frac{1}{13} \times \frac{3}{51} = \frac{3}{663} = \frac{1}{221}$$

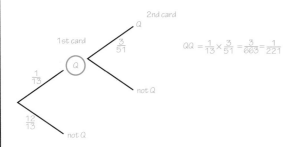

The second probability is dependent on the first. You can only draw two queens if the first and the second card are queens.

Once you remove a card, there are only 51 cards left to choose from. As the first card was a queen there are only three queens left in the pack.

You can also use a partial probability tree to work this out. You don't need to draw the branches for not getting a queen with the first card. You are only interested in the branches that give you two queens.

WORKED EXAMPLE 13

A card is drawn at random from a normal 52-card pack and not replaced, then a second card is drawn. What is the probability that the second card is a king, given that the first card is not a king?

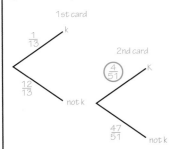

You don't need the paths that follow from drawing a king first; you know the first card is not a king.

The probability of drawing a king is now $\frac{4}{51}$. There are still four kings, but there are only 51 cards.

47 cards are not kings, so the probability of not drawing a king is now $\frac{47}{51}$.

$$P(\text{2nd card is king} \mid \text{1st card is not a king}) = \frac{4}{51}.$$

Tip

In a test or exam, you may need to work out which type of diagram and which method or combination of methods is most useful for solving the particular problem.

For some conditional probability problems it is easier to use Venn diagrams.

Tip

When a problem asks for the probability of at least one event. you can either list all the possible outcomes or you can use the fact that P(at least one happens) = 1 − P(none of the events happen).

WORKED EXAMPLE 14

In a group of 50 students, 36 students work on tablet computers, 20 work on laptops and 12 work on neither of these. If a student is chosen at random, what is the probability that he or she:

a works on a tablet and a laptop computer

b works on at least one type of these types of computer

c works on a tablet given that he or she works on a laptop

d doesn't work on a laptop, given that he or shc works on a tablet.

a $P(\text{works on both}) = P(T \cap L) = \dfrac{18}{50} = \dfrac{9}{25}$

b $P(\text{works on at least one}) = 1 - P(\text{works on neither})$

$$= 1 - \dfrac{12}{50} = \dfrac{38}{50} = \dfrac{19}{25}.$$

c $P(T|L) = \dfrac{P(L \text{ and } T)}{P(L)} = \dfrac{18}{20} = \dfrac{9}{10}$

d $P(L'|T) = \dfrac{P(T \text{ and } L')}{P(T)} = \dfrac{18}{36} = \dfrac{1}{2}$

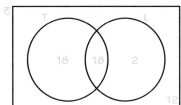

$50 - 12 = 38$
$T = 36$ students
$L = \dfrac{20}{56}$ students
$\dfrac{-38}{18}$ ← like both

Problem-solving framework

When you use Venn diagrams to solve problems it is important to choose the correct operation to solve the problem. The wording of the problem normally gives you clues about which operation you need.

Given that Set A = {x: x is an even number} and Set B = {x: x is a multiple of 3}, you may be asked questions like the ones in the first column of the table.

Question: What is the probability of a number …	Which operation is involved in finding the solution?	Why?
being even?	No operations	The probability will only involve the elements of one set.
being even and a multiple of 3?	Intersection	The word 'and' tells you to look for numbers that are elements of both sets (i.e. those in the overlapping section).
being even or a multiple of 3?	Union	The word 'or' tells you it can be in either of the two sets, so you need to include all the elements of both sets – without repeating any in the intersection.
not being even?	Complement	All numbers that are outside the set of even numbers must be included. These are the numbers outside the circles and also the numbers in the multiples of three, but not in the overlap.
being neither even nor a multiple of 3?	Complement	'Neither, nor' tells you that two sets have to be excluded, you are looking for the elements outside the circles in this case.

EXERCISE 28E

1 There are 21 students in a class. 12 are boys and nine are girls. The teacher chooses two different students at random to answer questions.

  a Draw a tree diagram to represent this information.

  b Find the probability that:

   i both students chosen are boys

   ii both students are girls

   iii the second student is a girl given that the first student was a boy.

  c The teacher chooses a third student at random. What is the probability that:

   i all three students chosen are girls

   ii at least one student is a girl

   iii the third student is a girl, given that the first two students were boys?

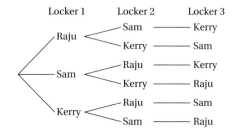

Locker 1 Locker 2 Locker 3

2 A cleaner accidentally knocked the name labels off three students' lockers. The labels say Raju, Sam and Kerry. The tree diagram (left) shows the possible ways of replacing the labels.

  a Copy the diagram and write the probabilities next to each branch.

  b Are these events dependent or independent? Why?

  c How many correct ways are there to match the name labels to the lockers?

  d How many possible ways are there for the cleaner to label the lockers?

  e If the cleaner randomly stuck the names back onto the lockers, what is the chance of getting the names correct?

  f What is the probability of getting the labels on Lockers 2 and 3 correct given that the first one is correctly labelled Kerry?

3 A climatologist reports that the probability of rain on Friday is 0.21. If it rains on Friday, there is a 0.83 chance of rain on Saturday; if it doesn't rain on Friday, the chance of rain on Saturday is only 0.3

  a Draw a tree diagram to represent this situation.

  b Use your diagram to work out the probability of rain on:

   i Friday and Saturday

   ii Saturday given that it was sunny on Friday.

4 In a group of 25 people, 15 like cappuccino (C), 17 like latte (L) and two people like neither. Using an appropriate sample space diagram, calculate the probability that a person will:

  a like cappuccino

  b like cappuccino given that he or she likes latte.

5 100 teenagers went on a summer camp during which 80 of them went hiking, 42 went sailing and each student did at least one of these activities.

a Draw a Venn diagram to show how many teenagers did both activities.

b If a teenager is randomly selected, find the probability that he or she:

i went hiking but not sailing

ii went sailing given that he or she went hiking.

6 In a group of 120 students, 25 are in the sixth form, 15 attend maths tutorials and four of the students are sixth formers who attend maths tutorials. What is the probability that a randomly chosen student who attends maths tutorials will be a sixth former?

7 Three counters are removed at random one at a time from a bag containing two red and six yellow counters and not replaced. Find the probability that:

a the three counters are the same colour

b at least one counter is red

c you get exactly one red counter

d the second counter is red given that the first is yellow.

Tip

Think carefully about question 7; it involves conditional probability.

8 When Nadia takes the train from Monday to Thursday the probability that she gets a seat is 95%. When she takes the train on a Friday or Saturday, the probability that she gets a seat is 70%. Assuming that she is equally likely to take the train on any day from Monday to Saturday, determine the probability that:

a she gets a seat

b it is Saturday and she gets a seat.

9 a Explain how you can know whether two events A and B are dependent or independent, given the probability of A and the probability of A given B.

b The probability of drawing a red marble from a bag is $\frac{1}{8}$.

The probability of drawing a blue and then a red marble from a bag is $\frac{2}{15}$. Is the marble returned to the bag after the first draw? Explain.

 Checklist of learning and understanding

Representing combined events

- The sample space of an event is all the possible outcomes of the event.

- When an event has two or more stages it is called a combined event.

- Lists, tables, grids, tree diagrams and Venn diagrams can be used to represent combined events.

Find answers at: cambridge.org/ukschools/gcsemaths-studentbookanswers

Calculating probabilities for combined events

- For mutually exclusive events P(A or B) = P(A) + P(B).
- For independent events P(A and then B) = P(A) × P(B).
- When independent events are mutually exclusive, you need to add the probabilities obtained by multiplication.
- For dependent events P(A and then B) = P(A) × P(B given that A has happened).

Conditional probability

- For independent events, P(B|A) = P(B).
- For dependent events, $P(B|A) = \dfrac{P(A \text{ and } B)}{P(A)}$
- For 'at least' problems P(at least A) = 1 − (not A)

 For additional questions on the topics in this chapter, visit GCSE Mathematics Online.

 Chapter review

1 Choose the most appropriate method and use it to represent the sample space in each of the following.

   a A coin is flipped and an octagonal dice with faces numbered 0 to 7 is rolled at the same time.

   b Boxes A, B and C contain pink and yellow tickets. One box is selected at random and a ticket is drawn from it.

   c The number of ways in which three letters P, A and N can be arranged to form a three-letter sequence.

   d In a class of 24 students, 10 take art, 12 take music and five take neither.

2 Two normal six-sided dice are rolled simultaneously. Draw a sample space for this information and hence calculate the probability of rolling:

   a double 2   **b** at least one 4

   c a total greater than 9   **d** a total of 6 or 7.

3 The letters from the word MANCHESTER are written on cards and placed in a bag.

   a What is the probability of drawing a vowel if one letter is drawn at random?

   b Copy and complete the tree diagram (left) to show all probabilities for when a letter is drawn from the bag, noted and replaced and then another letter is drawn.

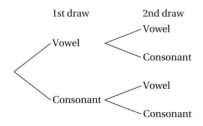

   c Use the tree diagram to determine the probability of drawing:

     i two vowels   **ii** two consonants

     iii a vowel and a consonant   **iv** at least one consonant.

   d Explain why drawing the letters can be considered independent events in this case.

   e How could you change the experiment to make the events dependent?

4 There are 50 students in a year group. 30 have brown eyes, nine have fair hair and three have both brown eyes and fair hair. Represent this information on a Venn diagram and use it to determine the probability that a student chosen at random from this group:

a has neither brown eyes nor fair hair

b has brown eyes but not fair hair

c has fair hair given that he or she has brown eyes

d does not have brown eyes given that he or she does not have fair hair.

5 The probability that it will rain on Monday is 0.6

When it rains on Monday, the probability that it will rain on Tuesday is 0.8

When it does not rain on Monday, the probability that it will rain on Tuesday is 0.5

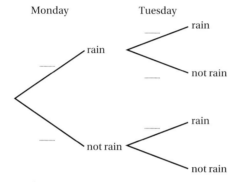

a Copy and complete the probability tree diagram. *(2 marks)*

b Work out the probability that it will rain on both Monday and Tuesday. *(2 marks)*

c Work out the probability that it will rain on at least one of the two days. *(3 marks)*

©Pearson Education Ltd 2011

6 The vowels and the consonants from the word PROBABILITY are placed in separate piles. A vowel and a consonant, in that order, are chosen at random.

Find:

a the number of different ways of getting a vowel and a consonant

b the probability that you get an I and a B.

29 Standard form

For more resources relating to this chapter, visit GCSE Mathematics Online.

Using mathematics: real-life applications

The study of stars, moons and planets involves huge numbers. Astronomers use standard form to make it easier to write or type very large quantities, to make them easier to compare and to allow them to calculate with and without calculators. The Sun has a mass of 1.988×10^{30} kg. This is a number with 27 zeros and it would be clumsy and impractical to have to write it out each time you wanted to use it.

Calculator tip

Make sure you know how your calculator deals with powers and that you have it in the correct mode to do calculations involving powers.

"In astronomy we work with very large and very small numbers. There are 100 000 000 000 000 000 000 000 known stars alone! Imagine having to write this number out in full every time you wanted to use it! It is much easier to write 1×10^{23}." *(Astronomy student)*

Before you start …

Ch 7	You should be able to calculate efficiently with decimals.	**1** Evaluate these without using a calculator. **a** $2.9 + 5.8$ **b** $12.5 - 3.8$ **c** 4.5×1.5 **d** $4.5 \div 0.3$

Ch 9	You need to be able to round numbers to a given number of significant figures.	**2** Choose the correct answer.
		a 507 000 000 rounded to 2 significant figures.
		   A 50 700 **B** 510 000 000
		b 1.098 rounded to 3 significant figures.
		   A 1.10 **B** 1.09
		c 0.006 25 rounded to 1 significant figure.
		   A 0.6 **B** 0.006

Ch 8	You should know how to apply the laws of indices.	**3** State whether the following are true or false. **a** $3^2 \times 3^3 = 3^6$ **b** $x^5 \times x^3 = x^8$ **c** $x^{-3} \times x^4 = x$ **d** $\dfrac{x^4}{x^5} = x$ **e** $\dfrac{x^{-4}}{x^2} = x^{-6}$

Assess your starting point using the Launchpad ...

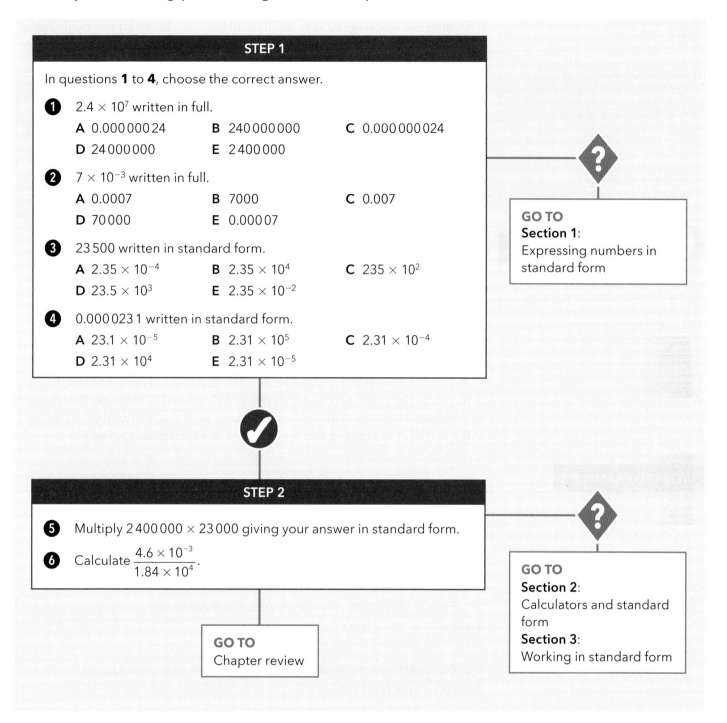

STEP 1

In questions **1** to **4**, choose the correct answer.

1 2.4×10^7 written in full.
    A 0.000 000 24   **B** 240 000 000   **C** 0.000 000 024
    D 24 000 000   **E** 2 400 000

2 7×10^{-3} written in full.
    A 0.0007   **B** 7000   **C** 0.007
    D 70 000   **E** 0.000 07

3 23 500 written in standard form.
    A 2.35×10^{-4} **B** 2.35×10^4 **C** 235×10^2
    D 23.5×10^3 **E** 2.35×10^{-2}

4 0.000 023 1 written in standard form.
    A 23.1×10^{-5} **B** 2.31×10^5 **C** 2.31×10^{-4}
    D 2.31×10^4 **E** 2.31×10^{-5}

GO TO
Section 1:
Expressing numbers in standard form

STEP 2

5 Multiply $2\,400\,000 \times 23\,000$ giving your answer in standard form.

6 Calculate $\dfrac{4.6 \times 10^{-3}}{1.84 \times 10^4}$.

GO TO
Chapter review

GO TO
Section 2:
Calculators and standard form
Section 3:
Working in standard form

Find answers at: cambridge.org/ukschools/gcsemaths-studentbookanswers

Section 1: Expressing numbers in standard form

Writing out very large or very small numbers takes time and you might make mistakes and skip zeros when you do calculations. You use standard form to write these numbers in a simpler way using powers of 10.

> Algebraically, we can say that any number (x) can be expressed in the form of:
>
> $A \times 10^n$, where $1 \leqslant A < 10$ and n is an integer.

2×10^2 and 1.2×10^{-2} are both in standard form but 32×10^3 and 0.47×10^8 are not.

Consider $3 \times 10^4 = 30\,000$ and $3 \times 10^{-4} = 0.0003$.

The index (power of 10) gives you important information.

- Multiplying by 10^4 moves the digits four places to the left.
- Multiplying by 10^{-4} moves the digits four places to the right.

Writing a number in standard form

To write a number in standard form, place the decimal point after the first non–zero digit and then find the power of 10 needed to move the first digit back to its original position. In other words, work out the number of places the first digit has moved and the direction in which it has moved.

Tip

In the UK we use the term standard form for numbers in the form $A \times 10^n$, where $1 \leqslant A < 10$. This notation is also called scientific notation.

WORKED EXAMPLE 1

Express these numbers in standard form.

a 416 000   **b** 0.0037

a 416000
    4.16
    4 1 6 0 0 0

Write the number with the decimal point after the first non-zero digit, to get the number between 1 and 10.

Work out how many decimal places the first digit needs to move to get back to its original place value.

$416000 = 4.16 \times 10^5$

The first digit needs to move five places to the left. This gives a larger number, so the power is 5.

b 0.0037
    3.7
    0.0 0 3 7

Write the number with the decimal point after the first non-zero digit, to get the number between 1 and 10.

Work out how many decimal places the first digit needs to move to get back to its original place value.

$0.0037 = 3.7 \times 10^{-3}$

The first digit needs to move three places to the right. This gives a smaller number, so the power is -3.

Converting from standard form to ordinary numbers

To convert numbers from standard form to ordinary numbers or decimals you need to look at the powers and move the digits the correct number of decimal places to the left or right.

WORKED EXAMPLE 2

Write as ordinary numbers.

a 3.25×10^5 **b** 2.07×10^{-5}

a 3.25×10^5

$3.2\,5$

$3\,2\,5\,\_\,\_\,\_.$

| The digits need to move five decimal places to the left. |

$3\,2\,5\,0\,0\,0$

$3.25 \times 10^5 = 325\,000$

| Fill in the correct number of zeros. |

b 2.07×10^{-5}

2.07

$\_.\_\,\_\,\_\,\_\,\_\,2\,0\,7$

| The digits need to move five decimal places to the right. |

$0.0\,0\,0\,0\,2\,0\,7$

| Fill in the correct number of zeros. |

$2.07 \times 10^{-5} = 0.000020\,7$

| Remember to write the 0 before the decimal point as well. |

EXERCISE 29A

1 Express each of the following in standard form.

    a $321\,000$ **b** 1340 **c** $3\,010\,000$ **d** 0.08

    e 0.0001 **f** $32\,000\,000$ **g** $910\,000$ **h** $0.000\,031\,255$

    i $0.000\,000\,241\,52$ **j** $0.003\,05$ **k** 0.201 **l** $0.000\,34$

    m 0.009 **n** 2.45 **o** $0.000\,426$ **p** 0.426

2 Express each of the following as an ordinary number.

    a 1.4×10^2 **b** 4.8×10^4 **c** 2.9×10^3

    d 3.25×10^2 **e** 3.25×10^{-1} **f** 3.67×10^5

    g 4.5×10^7 **h** 2.13×10^{-2} **i** 3.209×10^4

    j 3.46×10^{-3} **k** 1.89×10^{-4} **l** 7×10^{-7}

    m 1.03×10^{-2} **n** 1.025×10^{-3} **o** 2.09×10^{-5}

3 Express each of the following quantities in standard form.

   a In 2011 the population of the Earth reached 7 000 000 000.

   b The distance from the Earth to the Moon is approximately 240 000 miles.

   c There are about 37 000 000 000 000 cells in your body.

   d Some cells are about 0.000 000 2 metres in diameter.

   e The surface area of the Earth's oceans is about 140 million square miles.

   f An angstrom is a unit of measure. One angstrom is equivalent to 0.000 000 000 1 metre.

   g Humans blink on average about 6 250 000 times per year.

   h A dust particle has a mass of about 0.000 000 000 753 kg.

4 Write each quantity out in full as an ordinary number.

   a The surface area of the Atlantic Ocean is 3.18×10^7 square miles.

   b The space between tracks on a DVD disk is 7.4×10^{-4} mm.

   c The diameter of the silk used to weave a spider's web is 1.24×10^{-6} mm.

   d There are 3×10^9 possible ways to play the first four moves in a game of chess.

   e A sheet of paper is about 1.2×10^{-4} m thick.

   f The distance between the Sun and Jupiter is about 7.78×10^8 km.

   g The Earth is about 1.5×10^{11} km from the Sun.

   h The mass of an electron is about $9.109 382 2 \times 10^{-31}$ kg.

Section 2: Calculators and standard form

You can use a modern scientific calculator to enter calculations in standard form. The calculator will also give you an answer in standard form if it has too many digits to display on the screen.

Entering standard form calculations

You will need to use the $\boxed{\times 10^x}$, $\boxed{\text{Exp}}$ or $\boxed{\text{EE}}$ button on your calculator.

These are known as the exponent keys and they all work in the same way, even though they might look different on different calculators.

When you are using the exponent function key of your calculator you don't enter the $\times 10$ part of the calculation because the calculator function automatically includes that part.

Use your own calculator to work through this example. You should get the same result even if your function key is different to those in the example.

WORKED EXAMPLE 3

Enter these into your calculator.

a 2.134×10^4 **b** 3.124×10^{-6}

a

Enter the figures using your calculator's key for the exponent.

21 340

You should get this. If not, check that you are using the exponent key correctly.

b $\boxed{3}\ \boxed{.}\ \boxed{1}\ \boxed{2}\ \boxed{4}\ \boxed{\text{Exp}}\ \boxed{+/-}\ \boxed{6}\ \boxed{=}$

Use the correct key for your calculator to enter the negative 6.

0.000 003 124

 Calculator tip

Calculators work in different ways and you need to understand how your own calculator works. Make sure you know which buttons to use to enter standard form calculations, how to read and make sense of the display and how to convert your calculator answer into decimal form.

Making sense of the calculator display

How your calculator displays an answer will depend on the calculator you use.

5.98^E-06

This is 5.98×10^{-6}

2.56ε24

This is 2.56×10^{24}

To give the answer in standard form, read the display and write the answer correctly.

EXERCISE 29B

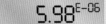

1 Enter each of these numbers into your calculator using the correct function key and write down what appears on the display.

    a 4.2×10^{12} **b** 1.8×10^{-5} **c** 2.7×10^6

    d 1.34×10^{-2} **e** 1.87×10^{-9} **f** 4.23×10^7

    g 3.102×10^{-4} **h** 3.098×10^9 **i** 2.076×10^{-23}

 Find answers at: cambridge.org/ukschools/gcsemaths-studentbookanswers

2 Here are nine different calculator displays giving answers in exponential form. Write each answer correctly in standard form.

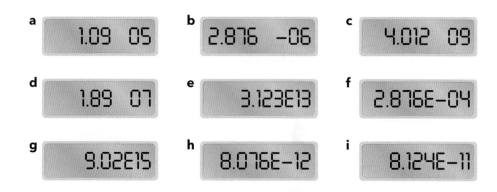

a   1.09   05

b   2.876   −06

c   4.012   09

d   1.89   07

e   3.123E13

f   2.876E−04

g   9.02E15

h   8.076E−12

i   8.124E−11

Significant figures

When you work with standard form, you will often be asked to give the answers in standard form correct to a given number of significant figures.

When working with decimal values, remember that none of the zeros before a non-zero digit are significant.

- 0.003   is correct to 1 significant figure.
- 0.01   is correct to 1 significant figure.
- 0.10   is correct to 2 significant figures.

A zero after a non-zero digit is significant.

> **Tip**
>
> You rounded numbers in Chapter 9.

EXERCISE 29C

Use your calculator to do these calculations. Give your answers in standard form correct to 3 significant figures.

1   a 4216^6 b $(0.00009)^4$

     c $0.0002 \div 2500^3$ d $65\,000\,000 \div 0.000\,0045$

2   a $(0.0029)^3 \times (0.003\,65)^5$ b $(48 \times 987)^4$

3   a $\dfrac{4525 \times 8760}{0.000\,020}$ b $\dfrac{9500}{0.0005^4}$

     c $\sqrt{5.25} \times 10^8$ d $3\sqrt{9.1} \times 10^{-8}$

4   Work out the following using your calculator. Give the answers in standard form correct to 5 significant figures.

     a $0.0008 \div 9200^3$ b $(1.009)^5$ c $123\,000\,000 \div 0.00076$ d $(97 \times 876)^4$

     e $(0.0098)^4 \times (0.0032)^3$ f $\dfrac{8543 \times 9210}{0.000\,034}$ g $\dfrac{9745}{(0.0004)^4}$ h $\sqrt[3]{4.2 \times 10^{-8}}$

Section 3: Working in standard form

Writing numbers in standard form allows you to use the laws of indices to calculate quickly without using a calculator.

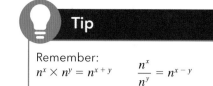

Multiplying and dividing numbers in standard form

WORKED EXAMPLE 4

Do these calculations without using a calculator. Give your answers in standard form.

a $(3 \times 10^5) \times (2 \times 10^6)$ **b** $(2 \times 10^{-3}) \times (3 \times 10^{-7})$

c $(2 \times 10^3) \times (8 \times 10^7)$ **d** $\dfrac{2.8 \times 10^6}{1.4 \times 10^4}$ **e** $\dfrac{4 \times 10^8}{9 \times 10^5}$

a $(3 \times 10^5) \times (2 \times 10^6)$

This is the same as: $3 \times 2 \times 10^5 \times 10^6$

$\quad = 6 \times 10^{5+6}$ Simplify 3×2 and add the indices.

$\quad = 6 \times 10^{11}$ Write the answer in standard form.

b $(2 \times 10^{-3}) \times (3 \times 10^{-7})$

This is the same as: $2 \times 3 \times 10^{-3} \times 10^{-7}$

$\quad = 6 \times 10^{-3 + -7}$

$\quad = 6 \times 10^{-10}$

c $(2 \times 10^3) \times (8 \times 10^7)$

This is the same as: $2 \times 8 \times 10^3 \times 10^7$

$\quad = 16 \times 10^{3+7}$

$\quad = 16 \times 10^{10}$ But 16 is greater than 10 so this is not in standard form.

$\quad = 1.6 \times 10 \times 10^{10}$ If you think of 16 as 1.6×10 you can change it to standard form.

$\quad = 1.6 \times 10^{11}$

d $\dfrac{2.8 \times 10^6}{1.4 \times 10^4} = \dfrac{2.8}{1.4} \times \dfrac{10^6}{10^4}$

$\quad = 2 \times 10^{6-4}$ Subtract the indices to divide the powers.

$\quad = 2 \times 10^2$

e $\dfrac{4 \times 10^8}{9 \times 10^5} = \dfrac{4}{9} \times \dfrac{10^8}{10^5}$

$\quad = 0.44 \times 10^3$ (to 2 significant figures)   0.44 is smaller than 1 so this is not standard form.

$\quad = 4.4 \times 10^{-1} \times 10^3$

$\quad = 4.4 \times 10^2$ (to 2 significant figures)   If you think of 0.44 as 4.4×10^{-1} you can change it to standard form.

EXERCISE 29D

1 Simplify, giving the answers in standard form.

a $(2 \times 10^{13}) \times (4 \times 10^{17})$

b $(1.4 \times 10^8) \times (3 \times 10^4)$

c $(1.5 \times 10^{13}) \times (1.5 \times 10^{13})$

d $(0.2 \times 10^{17}) \times (0.7 \times 10^{16})$

e $(9 \times 10^{17}) \div (3 \times 10^{16})$

f $(8 \times 10^{17}) \div (4 \times 10^{16})$

g $(1.5 \times 10^8) \div (5 \times 10^4)$

h $(2.4 \times 10^{64}) \div (8 \times 10^{21})$

2 Simplify, giving the answers in standard form.

a $(2 \times 10^{-4}) \times (4 \times 10^{-16})$

b $(1.6 \times 10^{-8}) \times (4 \times 10^{-4})$

c $(1.5 \times 10^{-6}) \times (2.1 \times 10^{-3})$

d $(11 \times 10^{-5}) \times (3 \times 10^2)$

e $(9 \times 10^{17}) \div (4.5 \times 10^{-16})$

f $(7 \times 10^{-21}) \div (1 \times 10^{16})$

g $(4.5 \times 10^8) \div (0.9 \times 10^{-4})$

h $(11 \times 10^{-5}) \times (3 \times 10^2) \div (2 \times 10^{-3})$

 3 Carry out these calculations without using your calculator. Leave the answers in standard form.

a $(3 \times 10^{12}) \times (4 \times 10^{18})$

b $(1.5 \times 10^6) \times (3 \times 10^5)$

c $(1.5 \times 10^{12})^3$

d $(1.2 \times 10^{-5}) \times (1.1 \times 10^{-6})$

e $(0.4 \times 10^{15}) \times (0.5 \times 10^{12})$

f $(8 \times 10^{17}) \div (3 \times 10^{12})$

g $(1.44 \times 10^8) \div (1.2 \times 10^6)$

h $(8 \times 10^{-15}) \div (4 \times 10^{-12})$

4 The speed of light is approximately 3×10^8 metres per second. How far will the light travel in:

a 10 seconds?

b 20 seconds?

c 10^2 seconds?

d 2×10^3 seconds?

5 A human being blinks approximately 6.25×10^6 times per year.

a How often will you blink in 5 years? Give the answer in standard form and as an ordinary number.

b If there were 7.2×10^9 people on the planet, how many blinks would there be in a year?

Adding and subtracting in standard form

You already know from algebra that you can add or subtract like terms and that you cannot add or subtract unlike terms. The same rules apply to powers of 10. You can only add or subtract powers of 10 if the powers are identical. This means that you sometimes have to manipulate the expressions to get like terms that you can add or subtract.

For example, you can change 3×10^6 into $3 \times 10^4 \times 10^2$ because $10^4 \times 10^2 = 10^6$.

You can also manipulate the number by multiplying it or dividing it by 10 to increase or decrease the powers. For example, you can change 1.6×10^3 into 16×10^2 or into 0.16×10^4.

Calculator tip

If you are using a calculator you don't need to manipulate the terms. You just need to enter them correctly.

WORKED EXAMPLE 5

Simplify and give the answers in standard form.

a $(2.5 \times 10^6) + (3.2 \times 10^8)$ **b** $6 \times 10^{-3} - 3 \times 10^{-4}$

a $(2.5 \times 10^6) + (3.2 \times 10^8)$

$= 2.5 \times 10^6 + 3.2 \times 10^6 \times 10^2$ | Rewrite the second power as its factors to get like powers.

$= 10^6(2.5 + 3.2 \times 10^2)$ | Remove the common factor.

$= 10^6(2.5 + 320)$ | $3.2 \times 10^2 = 320$

$= 10^6(322.5)$ | Add the numbers.

$= 3.225 \times 10^8$ | Rewrite the answer in standard form.

b $6 \times 10^{-3} - 3 \times 10^{-4}$

$= 60 \times 10^{-4} - 3 \times 10^{-4}$ | 6×10^{-3} is the same as 60×10^{-4}.

$= 57 \times 10^{-4}$ | This is not yet in standard form.

$= 5.7 \times 10^{-3}$

You can also convert the standard form expressions to ordinary numbers and add or subtract them. You can then write the answer back in standard form.

EXERCISE 29E

1 Carry out these calculations without using a calculator. Give your answers in standard form.

a $(3 \times 10^8) + (2 \times 10^8)$ **b** $(3 \times 10^{-3}) - (1.5 \times 10^{-3})$

c $(1.5 \times 10^5) + (3 \times 10^6)$ **d** $(6 \times 10^7) - (4 \times 10^6)$

e $(4 \times 10^{-4}) + (3 \times 10^{-3})$ **f** $(5 \times 10^{-3}) - (2.5 \times 10^{-2})$

2 The Pacific Ocean has a surface area of approximately $1.65 \times 10^8 \, \text{km}^2$ and the Atlantic Ocean has a surface area of approximately $1.06 \times 10^8 \, \text{km}^2$.

a Which ocean has the greater surface area?

b How much larger is it?

c If the total surface area of the world's oceans is $361\,000\,000 \, \text{km}^2$, work out the combined surface area of the other three oceans (the Indian, Southern and Arctic), giving the answer in standard form.

Find answers at: cambridge.org/ukschools/gcsemaths-studentbookanswers

3 The Earth is approximately 9.3×10^7 miles from the Sun and 2.4×10^5 miles from the Moon. How much further is it from the Earth to the Sun than from the Earth to the Moon?

4 A scientist studying viruses finds that Virus A has a diameter of 3×10^{-8} m and Virus B has a diameter of 3×10^{-7} m.

  a Which has the smaller diameter?

  b What is the difference in diameter between the two viruses?

  c If the two viruses were placed alongside each other, what would the length of their combined diameters be in millimetres?

Solving problems using standard form

Problems involving the modelling of growth rates of bacteria in biology, population growth and decline in ecology and future values in economics are often best solved using functions that rely on expressing values in standard form.

Computer engineering problems often involve very small values as engineers try to fit more and more hardware into smaller and smaller devices.

WORKED EXAMPLE 6

Naresh has worked out that he has a space $0.000\,003\,27$ m wide, $0.000\,000\,2$ m long and $0.000\,116$ m high into which he must fit a similarly shaped component with a volume of 8.034×10^{-17}. Will it fit?

$0.000\,003\,27 = 3.27 \times 10^{-6}$ $0.000\,000\,2 = 2 \times 10^{-7}$ $0.000\,116 = 1.16 \times 10^{-4}$	Convert the dimensions to standard form.
$3.27 \times 2 \times 1.16 = 7.5864$	Multiply the numbers.
$10^{-6} \times 10^{-7} \times 10^{-4} = 10^{-17}$	Combine the powers by adding the indices.
7.5864×10^{-17}	Combine the results to get the volume of the space.
$7.5864 \times 10^{-17} < 8.034 \times 10^{-17}$ $\therefore$ the component will not fit.	Use your result of the volume of the space to answer the original question.

EXERCISE 29F

1 Data storage in computers is measured in gigabytes. One gigabyte is 2^{30} bytes.

a Write 2^{30} in standard form correct to 3 significant figures.

b There are 1024 gigabytes in a terabyte. How many bytes is this? Give your answer in standard form correct to 3 significant figures.

2 The display on a mobile phone screen is made up of small rectangular areas called pixels. The density of pixels per unit determines the image quality – the more pixels in an area, the clearer the picture. Most mobile phone manufacturers talk about pixels per inch (ppi). This is the number of pixels on one side of a square inch. You can see this in the image below.

10 ppi

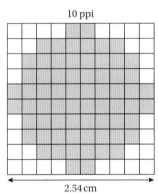

2.54 cm

20 ppi

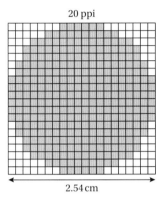

2.54 cm

a How many pixels are there in a 2.54 cm × 2.54 cm area of the screen on the right?

b Calculate the area (in cm²) covered by one pixel at a density of 20 ppi. Give your answer in standard form correct to 3 significant figures.

c At a density of 20 ppi, how many pixels would you have on a 4 inch by 3 inch rectangular screen?

d On a particular phone, one pixel is 1×10^{-3} cm wide and 4×10^{-5} cm long. What is the area of a pixel?

e What is the total area of 2.5×10^2 pixels of that size?

Calculator tip

An inch is an imperial unit of length measurement. It is equivalent to 2.54 cm.

3 A nanometre (nm) is a very small unit of measure. One nanometre is 1.0×10^{-9} m. Express the following measurements in nanometres.

    a 33 m   **b** 21 mm

4 Light travels at a speed of 3×10^8 metres per second. The Sun is an average distance of 1.5×10^{11} m from Earth, and Pluto is an average 5.9×10^{12} m from the Sun.

a Work out how long it takes light from the Sun to reach Earth (in seconds). Give your answer in both ordinary numbers and standard form.

b How much longer does it take for the light to reach Pluto? Give your answer in both ordinary numbers and standard form correct to 3 significant figures.

Find answers at: cambridge.org/ukschools/gcsemaths-studentbookanswers

5 An immunologist cultures two sets of bacteria. Culture X contains 5.8×10^{11} bacterial cells and Culture Y contains 4.8×10^9 bacterial cells. She combines the two cultures in one incubation flask.

    a How many cells are there when she combines the two cultures?

    b The bacteria numbers double every 8 hours. How many cells will there be after two days?

6 Use the dimensions given in questions **3** and **4** of Exercise 29A to construct five mixed standard form problems. (Work out the solutions as well.) Exchange these with another student and try to solve each other's problems.

 Checklist of learning and understanding

Standard form

- Very large and very small numbers can be written in standard form by expressing them as the product of a value greater or equal to 1 and less than 10, and a power of 10.

- Positive powers of 10 indicate large numbers and negative powers of 10 indicate decimal fractions (small numbers).

Using a calculator

- The exponent function of the calculator allows you to enter calculations in standard form without entering the $\times 10$ part of the calculation.

- When a number has too many digits to display, the calculator will give the answer in exponent form.

Calculations in standard form

- You can multiply and divide numbers in standard form by applying the laws of indices.

- You can manipulate expressions to get like terms so that you can add or subtract numbers in standard form without a calculator.

 For additional questions on the topics in this chapter, visit GCSE Mathematics Online.

 Chapter review

1 Express the following numbers in standard form.

    a 45 000   **b** 80   **c** 2 345 000

    d 32 000 000 000   **e** 0.0065   **f** 0.009

2 Write the following as ordinary numbers.

    a 2.5×10^3 **b** 3.9×10^4

    c 4.265×10^5 **d** 1.045×10^{-5}

3 Use a calculator and give the answers in standard form.

a $5 \times 10^4 + 9 \times 10^6$ **b** $3.27 \times 10^{-3} \times 2.4 \times 10^2$

c $5(8.1 \times 10^9 - 2 \times 10^7)$ **d** $(3.2 \times 10^{-1}) - (2.33 \times 10^{-6})$ (to 3 s.f.)

e $\dfrac{4.22 \times 10^7 \times 3.25 \times 10^6}{4 \times 10^5}$ **f** $2.13 \times 10^6 \div (5.67 \times 10^{-5})$

4 Simplify the following without using a calculator and give the answers in standard form.

a $(1.44 \times 10^7) + (4.3 \times 10^7)$ **b** $(4.9 \times 10^5) \times (3.6 \times 10^9)$

c $(3 \times 10^4) + (4 \times 10^3)$ **d** $(4 \times 10^6) \div (3 \times 10^5)$

5 $p^2 = \dfrac{x-y}{xy}$

$x = 8.5 \times 10^9$

$y = 4 \times 10^8$

Find the value of p.

Give your answer in standard form correct to 2 significant figures.

(3 marks)

©*Pearson Education Ltd 2012*

6 The distance between interconnecting lines on a silicon chip used in computer processing is 4×10^{28} m. What is:

a twice this distance?   **b** a quarter of this distance?

c 10 times this distance?

7 The Sun has a mass of approximately 1.998×10^{27} tonnes. The planet Mercury has a mass of approximately 3.302×10^{20} tonnes.

a Which has the greater mass?

b How many times heavier is the greater than the smaller mass? Give your answer to 3 significant figures.

8 The diameter of the Earth (at the equator) is approximately 1.27×10^4 km.

a What is the approximate radius of the Earth at the equator? Give this answer in standard form.

b Given that $C = 2\pi r$, calculate the approximate distance around the Earth at the equator in kilometres.

c If the volume of a sphere is $V = \dfrac{4}{3}\pi r^3$, where r is the radius, calculate the approximate volume of the Earth correct to 2 decimal places. (The Earth is not a perfect sphere, but assume that it is for your calculation.)

Find answers at: cambridge.org/ukschools/gcsemaths-studentbookanswers

30 Similarity

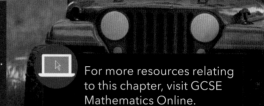

In this chapter you will learn how to …

- identify similar triangles and prove that two triangles are similar.
- work with positive, fractional and negative scale factors to enlarge shapes on a grid.
- find the scale factor and centre of enlargement of a transformation.
- understand the relationship between lengths, areas and volumes of similar objects.

For more resources relating to this chapter, visit GCSE Mathematics Online.

Using mathematics: real-life applications

When you enlarge a photo, project an image onto a screen or make scale models you are dealing with similarity. Many toys and other objects are scaled, but similar, versions of larger objects.

"I work with scale drawings and scale models all the time. The models are mathematically similar to the real planes so the clients can see what they are buying. We made these scaled models to display at an international air show." *(Aircraft designer)*

Before you start …

Ch 26	You need to be able to label angles correctly.	**1** a Which angle is a right angle? b What size is the acute angle BOA? c What size is the obtuse angle BOD?	
Ch 15	You need to know how to solve simple equations using inverse operations.	**2** Solve a $3x = 24$ b $16 = \dfrac{h}{4}$ c $6.25 = 25k$	
Ch 20	You need to be able to recognise numbers in equivalent ratios.	**3** Which pairs of numbers are in the same ratio as $3:2$? A $6:5$ B $4:6$ C $0.15:0.1$ **4** Given that $\dfrac{x}{15} = \dfrac{4}{90}$, find x.	
Chs 4 and 8	You need to be able to find powers of whole numbers, fractions and decimals.	**5** Calculate the following: a $\left(\dfrac{1}{2}\right)^3$ b 4.5^2 c 15^3	

Find your starting point using the Launchpad

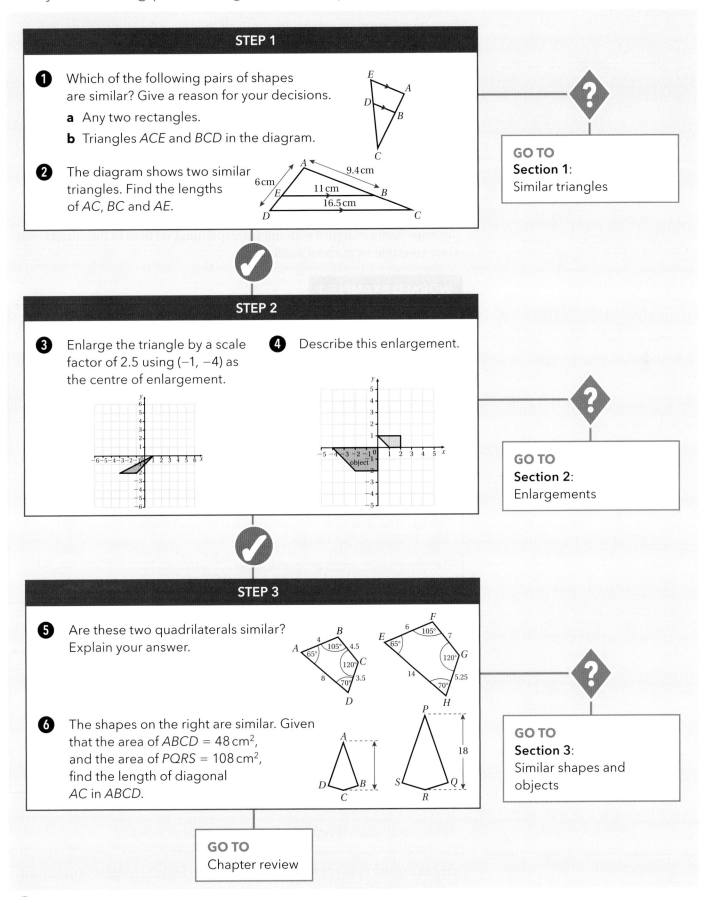

STEP 1

1 Which of the following pairs of shapes are similar? Give a reason for your decisions.

   a Any two rectangles.

   b Triangles *ACE* and *BCD* in the diagram.

2 The diagram shows two similar triangles. Find the lengths of *AC*, *BC* and *AE*.

GO TO
Section 1:
Similar triangles

STEP 2

3 Enlarge the triangle by a scale factor of 2.5 using (−1, −4) as the centre of enlargement.

4 Describe this enlargement.

GO TO
Section 2:
Enlargements

STEP 3

5 Are these two quadrilaterals similar? Explain your answer.

6 The shapes on the right are similar. Given that the area of *ABCD* = 48 cm², and the area of *PQRS* = 108 cm², find the length of diagonal *AC* in *ABCD*.

GO TO
Section 3:
Similar shapes and objects

GO TO
Chapter review

Section 1: Similar triangles

Two shapes are mathematically similar if they have the same shape and proportions but are different in size.

If the corresponding angles in two triangles are equal, then the corresponding sides will be in proportion, and the triangles will be similar.

To prove that two triangles are similar, you have to show that one of these statements is true:

- All the corresponding angles are equal.
- The three sides are in proportion.
- Two sides are in proportion and the included angle (between these two sides) are equal.

You must name triangles with the corresponding vertices in the correct order when you state facts about similarity.

WORKED EXAMPLE 1

Prove that the triangles *ABC* and *RTS* are similar.

State which angles are equal and which sides are in proportion.

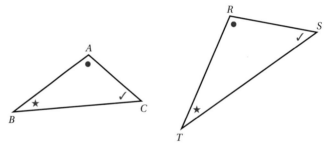

Triangle *ABC* is similar to triangle *RTS* because angle *A* = angle *R*, angle *B* = angle *T* and angle *C* = angle *S*.

The three sides are in proportion, so $\dfrac{AB}{RT} = \dfrac{AC}{RS} = \dfrac{BC}{TS}$.

WORKED EXAMPLE 2

Given that the following relationship exists between the sides of triangle *PQR* and triangle *WXY*, write down which angles are equal.

$$\frac{PQ}{WY} = \frac{PR}{WX} = \frac{QR}{YX}$$

Triangle *PQR* is similar to triangle *WYX*.

Therefore, $\angle P = \angle W$; $\angle Q = \angle Y$ and $\angle R = \angle X$.

Finding unknown lengths using proportional sides

You can use the ratio of corresponding sides to find the lengths of unknown sides in similar figures.

Problem-solving framework

In the figure, triangle *ABC* is similar to triangle *QRP*. Find the length of *x*.

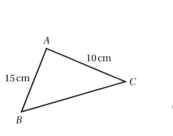
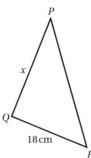

Steps for approaching a problem-solving question	What you would do for this example
Step 1: Identify the similar triangles in the problem and write down with the vertices in the correct order.	Triangle *ABC* is similar to triangle *QRP*.
Step 2: Write down what you know.	That the triangles are similar. Two sides of triangle *ABC*. One side of triangle *QRP*.
Step 3: Find the ratio between the sides.	*AB* corresponds to *QR* so the ratio is 15 : 18.
Step 4: Write a proportion with the unknown side.	$\dfrac{AB}{QR} = \dfrac{15}{18} = \dfrac{10}{x}$
Step 5: Solve the proportion equation.	$x = \dfrac{18 \times 10}{15} = 12\,\text{cm}$
Step 6: Have you answered the question?	$x = 12\,\text{cm}$

EXERCISE 30A

1 Each diagram below contains a pair of similar triangles. Identify the matching angles and the sides that are in proportion. Explain your reasoning using the correct angle vocabulary.

a 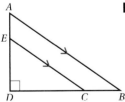   **b** 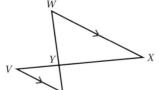   **c** 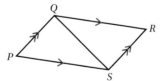   **d**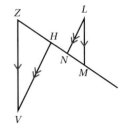

Find answers at: cambridge.org/ukschools/gcsemaths-studentbookanswers

2 Are the following pairs of triangles similar? Explain your answers.

a

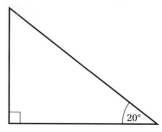

b

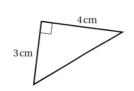
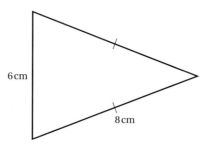

c

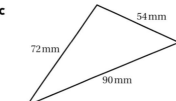
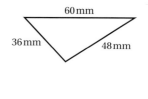

3 Are the statements below true or false? Explain your reasoning, give a counter-example for any statement you believe is false.

a All isosceles triangles are similar.

b All equilateral triangles are similar.

c All right-angled triangles are similar.

d All right-angled triangles with an angle of 30° are similar.

e All right-angled isosceles triangles are similar.

f No pair of scalene triangles are ever similar.

4 Each diagram below contains three similar triangles. Identify the matching angles and sides in each group of triangles, explaining your reasoning.

a

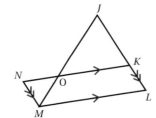

b

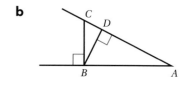

5 The two shapes below are similar. Find the missing lengths *c* and *d*.

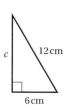

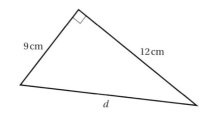

6 The two shapes below are similar. Find the missing lengths *e* and *f*.

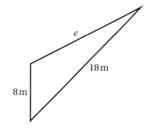

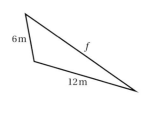

7 **a** Explain why triangles *EDC* and *ADB* are similar.

  b Find the lengths of *AE, CE* and *AB*.

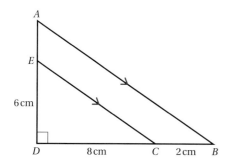

8 Find the lengths of *YZ* and *XY*.

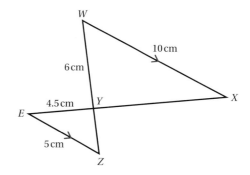

9 The diagram shows part of a children's climbing frame. Find the length of *BC*.

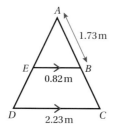

10 Swimmer A and boat B, shown in the diagram, are 80 m apart. Boat B is 1200 m from the lighthouse C. The height of the boat is 12 m and the swimmer can just see the top of the lighthouse at the top of the boat's mast when her head lies at sea level. What is the height of the lighthouse?

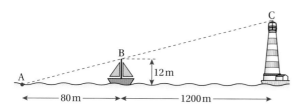

Find answers at: cambridge.org/ukschools/gcsemaths-studentbookanswers

Section 2: Enlargements

An enlargement is a transformation that changes the size of a shape as well as its position. Under enlargement, an object and its image are similar shapes.

In mathematics, the word enlargement is used for all transformations that produce similar images even if the image is smaller than the original object. When you take a photo, the image you see on your screen is considered to be an enlargement of the scene in front of you even though it is smaller.

To construct an enlargement of a shape, you multiply the length of each side by the scale factor.

Before you enlarge a shape, consider its new dimensions.

Has it got bigger?	Has it stayed the same size?	Has it got smaller?

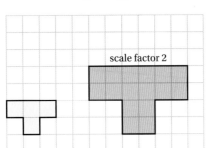

scale factor 2

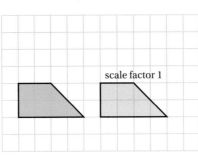

scale factor 1

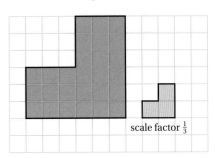

scale factor $\frac{1}{3}$

The object and its image are similar under enlargement. Sides are in the ratio $1:k$, where k is the scale factor.

WORKED EXAMPLE 3

Draw an enlargement of triangle ABC by a scale factor of 2.

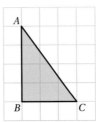

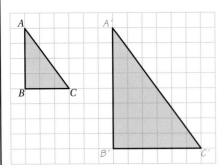

AB is 4 squares long so $A'B'$ is $2 \times 4 = 8$ squares long.

BC is 3 squares long so $B'C'$ is 6 squares long.

The angle at B is 90°.

Draw lines $A'B'$ and $B'C'$ at right angles to each other and join A' to C'.

Notice that triangle ABC is similar to triangle $A'B'C'$ and that the sides are in proportion.

EXERCISE 30B

 1 Enlarge each shape as directed.

a Enlarge A by a scale factor of 3.

b Enlarge B by a scale factor of 0.5.

c Enlarge C by a scale factor of $1\frac{1}{2}$.

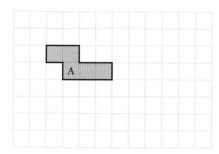
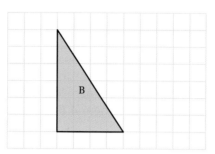
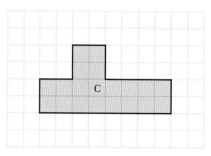

The centre of enlargement

You need two pieces of information to accurately draw an enlargement.

- The scale factor.
- The centre of enlargement.

The centre of enlargement is the point from where the enlargement is measured. In Worked example 3, you drew the enlargements at any convenient position on the grid. When you use a centre of enlargement, you draw the enlargement in a certain position in relation to the original object.

WORKED EXAMPLE 4

Enlarge the rectangle *ABCD* from the given centre by a scale factor 2.

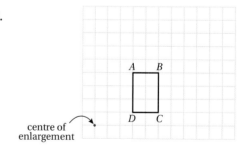

Find the distance from the centre of enlargement to a point on the object. You can draw a ray from the centre to the point.

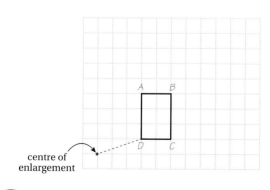

Continues on next page …

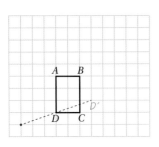

The original ray is three units to the right and one unit up. Double the distance of the ray to find the image of point D. Label it D'.

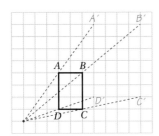

Follow the same process of drawing rays and extending them to find the images of all the vertices $ABCD$. Label them $A'B'C'D'$.

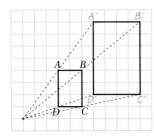

Draw in the image. Check that the lengths of the image are correct.

Note that lines from the corresponding vertices of the object and its image will meet at the centre of enlargement.

The procedure is the same for a centre of enlargement in any position, even for a centre of enlargement inside the shape itself.

The centre of enlargement can be anywhere: inside the object, on a vertex or side of the object or outside the object.

WORK IT OUT 30.1

This triangle is enlarged from centre $(-3, 4)$ scale factor 2. Draw its image.

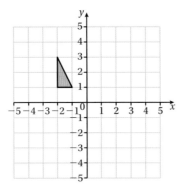

Which one of these answers is correct? Why are the others wrong?

How many marks would you give the incorrect answers if you were the teacher? Why?

Continues on next page …

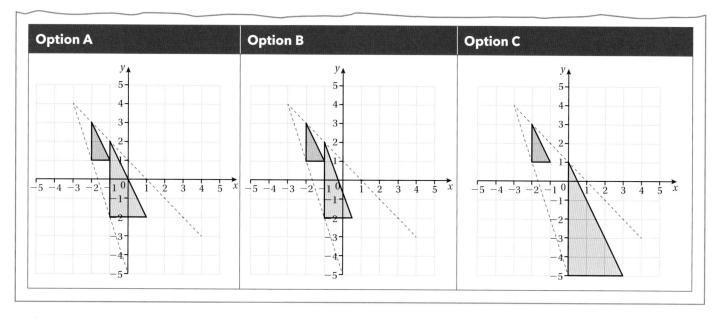

Option A	Option B	Option C

Tip

Sketch the new shape before you construct the enlargement. Draw one ray to identify the new position of the shape. After drawing the enlargement add in additional rays to check that it is in the correct position.

A fractional scale factor

If the scale factor is a fraction, the image will be smaller than the object.

A scale factor greater than 1 will enlarge the object. A scale factor smaller than 1 will reduce the size of the object although this is still called an enlargement.

WORKED EXAMPLE 5

Enlarge the triangle on the grid by a scale factor of $\frac{1}{2}$ through the given centre of enlargement.

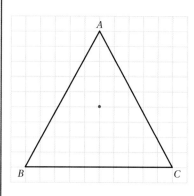
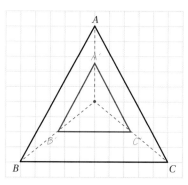

In this case, the rays from each vertex of the object are halved to find the position of the image.

EXERCISE 30C

1 Enlarge each shape as directed using the point C as the centre of enlargement.

    a Enlarge shape R by a scale factor of 3.

    b Enlarge shape S by a scale factor of 2.

    c Enlarge shape T by a scale factor of $\frac{1}{2}$.

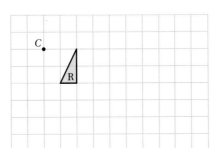 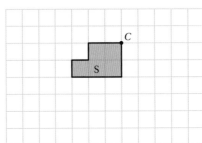 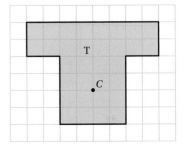

2 Enlarge the given shape by a scale factor of 3 using the origin as the centre of enlargement.

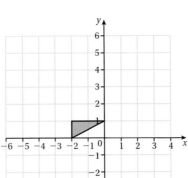

3 Enlarge the given shape by a scale factor of 2 using $(-4, 3)$ as the centre of enlargement.

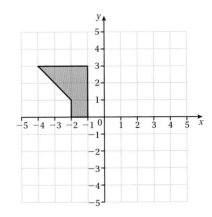

4 Enlarge the given shape by a scale factor of $\frac{1}{3}$ using $(-5, 2)$ as the centre of enlargement.

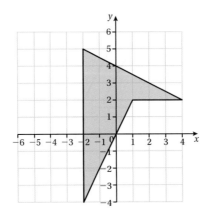

5 Enlarge the given shape by a scale factor of $1\frac{1}{2}$ using $(0, 1)$ as the centre of enlargement.

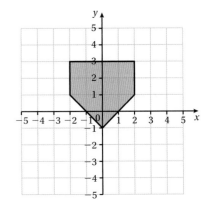

Negative scale factors

A negative scale factor has additional effects on the image.

The points of the image remain on their ray but they are located on the **other side** of the centre of enlargement in an inverted position.

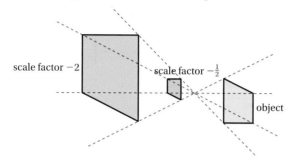

scale factor -2 scale factor $-\frac{1}{2}$ object

WORKED EXAMPLE 6

Enlarge the rectangle *PQRS* by a scale factor of -2 using the origin as the centre of enlargment.

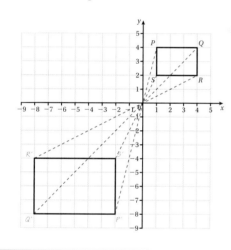

For each vertex, the distance to the centre is multiplied by -2, so the image appears on the opposite side of the centre to the original shape.

EXERCISE 30D

1 Enlarge the given shape by a scale factor of -1 using the origin as the centre of enlargement.

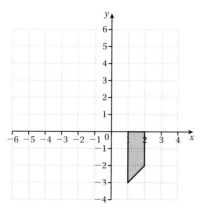

2 Enlarge the given shape by a scale factor of -2 using $(-2, 2)$ as the centre of enlargement.

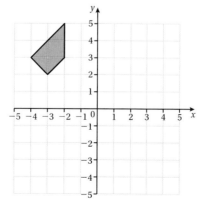

3 Enlarge the given shape by a scale factor of $-\frac{1}{2}$ using $(-3, 0)$ as the centre of enlargement.

4 Enlarge the given shape by a scale factor of $-1\frac{1}{2}$ using $(-1, 1)$ as the centre of enlargement.

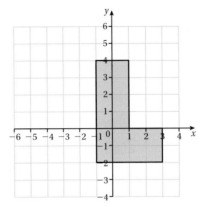

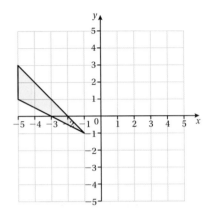

Describing enlargements

Tip

The ratio of sides gives the scale factor.

To describe an enlargement you need to give:

- the scale factor.
- the centre of enlargement.

To find the centre of enlargement you need to draw lines from corresponding vertices of the object and its image to find the point where they meet.

WORK IT OUT 30.2

What scale factors have been used to enlarge this shape?

Which one of these students' answers is correct?

What feedback would you give each student to make sure they don't make the same mistakes again?

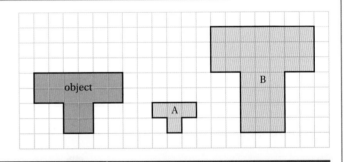

Ben	Ellie	Rosie
A scale factor of 2 has been used to produce shape A.	Since the sides have halved in length to get A, the scale factor is $\frac{1}{2}$.	To get shape A you have to take away one square along the bottom and along each side edge. So the scale factor is -1.
The top of shape A is 3 squares across, multiply this by 2 to get 6, the length of the top of the object.	Shape B isn't an enlargement. The sides have been increased by different numbers of squares.	Shape B is a scale factor of $1\frac{1}{2}$ because 2 squares have become 3 squares.
B can't be an enlargement. Its top is 7 squares and the object is 6. You can't do that using multiplication. Maybe it's -1?		

EXERCISE 30E

1 Which of the following houses are enlargements of house A? For each enlargement state the scale factor.

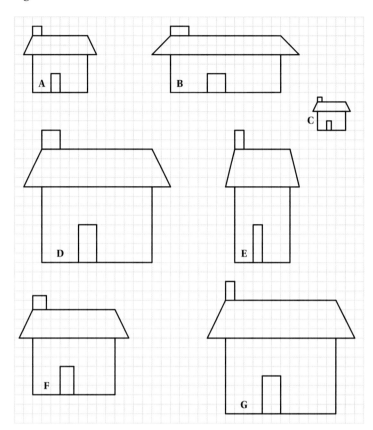

2 These diagrams each show an object and its image after an enlargement. Describe each of these enlargements by giving both the scale factor and the coordinates of the centre of enlargement. In each case the object is labelled.

a

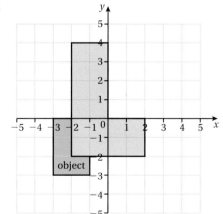

b

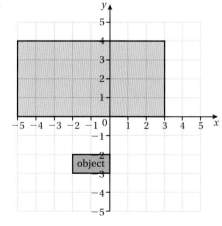

c

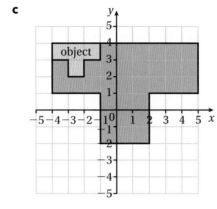

d

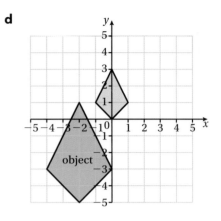

e

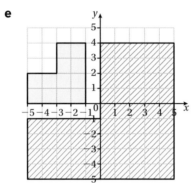

3 Describe each of these enlargements. In each case the object is labelled.

a

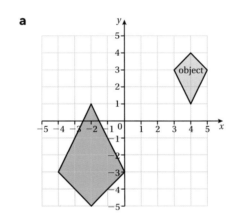

b

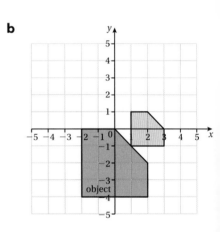

Section 3: Similar shapes and objects

A polygon is similar to another polygon if it is an enlargement of the original polygon. So two polygons will be similar if the angles in one polygon are equal to the angles in the other polygon, **and** the ratio of the sides from the one polygon to the other is kept the same.

For polygons other than triangles, equal angles alone are not sufficient to prove similarity.

WORKED EXAMPLE 7

Compare each of the quadrilaterals B to D below to the first quadrilateral, A. Which of them are similar to A?

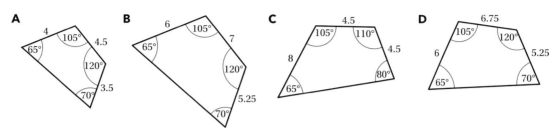

B has the same size angles as A, but the sides are not in proportion. For example, $\dfrac{4}{6} \neq \dfrac{4.5}{7}$. So, B is not similar to A.

The angles in C are different to the angles in A, so C is not similar to A.

D has corresponding angles equal to those in A. Test to see whether the sides are in the same proportion:

$\dfrac{4}{6} = \dfrac{4.5}{6.75} = \dfrac{3.5}{5.25}$. So, D is similar to A.

D is an enlargement of A with a scale factor of 1.5.

Areas and volumes of similar shapes

You know that if two shapes are similar their corresponding sides are in the same ratio, and their corresponding angles are equal.

Consider the following set of similar triangles.

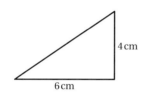

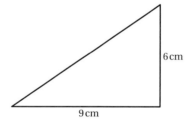

enlargement scale factor 1

area = 3 cm²

enlargement scale factor 2

area = 12 cm²

enlargement scale factor 3

area = 27 cm²

You should notice the following:

Scale factor 2   area scale factor $2^2 = 4$

Scale factor 3   area scale factor $3^2 = 9$

Scale factor n area scale factor n^2

Consider the following set of similar cuboids.

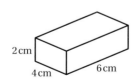

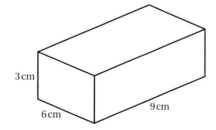

enlargement scale factor 1

volume = 6 cm³

enlargement scale factor 2

volume = 48 cm³

enlargement scale factor 3

volume = 162 cm³

 Find answers at: cambridge.org/ukschools/gcsemaths-studentbookanswers

You should notice the following;

Scale factor 2   volume scale factor $2^3 = 8$

Scale factor 3   volume scale factor $3^3 = 27$

Scale factor n volume scale factor n^3

If a 2D shape is enlarged, a similar shape is created. All of the dimensions of the image will be enlarged by the same scale factor. If the scale factor is a, then the ratio of the area of the image to the area of the original shape will be a^2.

If a 3D object is enlarged by a scale factor of a, then the ratio of the volume of the enlarged object will be a^3.

The scale factor of enlargement can be a whole number or a fraction. It can't be a negative number, as measurements cannot take on negative values.

WORKED EXAMPLE 8

The triangle below is enlarged by a factor of 3.

a What will the new dimensions and the area be?

b Calculate the ratio of the new area to the original area.

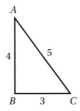

a $3AB = 12$
$3AC = 15$
$3BC = 9$

> Each side of the triangle will be enlarged by a factor of 3.

Area of enlarged triangle $= \dfrac{1}{2} \times$ base $\times$ height

$= \dfrac{1}{2} \times 9 \times 12$

$= 54$ square units

b Area of original triangle $= \dfrac{1}{2} \times$ base $\times$ height

$= \dfrac{1}{2} \times 3 \times 4$

$= 6$ square units

The ratio of the enlargement is 54 to $6 = 9 : 1^2$

> Notice that this is equal to the square of the scale factor: $3^2 = 9$

WORKED EXAMPLE 9

A triangular prism has a height of 10 cm. The triangular cross-section of the prism is the same as triangle *ABC* in Worked example 8. The whole prism is enlarged by a scale factor of 3.

a Calculate the new surface area of the triangular prism.

b What is the ratio of the new surface area to the original surface area?

c Calculate the new volume of the prism.

d What is the ratio of the new volume to the original volume?

a Surface area = 2(area of base) + area of 3 rectangles
$$= 2(54) + (9 \times 30) + (12 \times 30) + (15 \times 30)$$
$$= 1188 \text{ square units}$$

b Original surface area = 2(area of base) + area of 3 rectangles
$$= 2(6) + (3 \times 10) + (4 \times 10) + (5 \times 10)$$
$$= 132 \text{ square units}$$
Ratio is 1188 : 132 = 9 : 1   This is $3^2 : 1$

c Volume = area of base × height
$$= 54 \times \text{new height}$$
$$= 54 \times 30 = 1620 \text{ cubic units}$$

d Original volume = 6 × 10
$$= 60$$
Ratio is 1620 : 60 = 27 : 1   This is $3^3 : 1$

EXERCISE 30F

1 Decide whether each statement below is true or false. Explain your reasoning.

    a All squares are similar.

    b All hexagons are similar.

    c All rectangles are similar.

    d All regular octagons are similar.

2 Sketch the following pairs of shapes and decide if they are similar. Explain your reasoning.

    a Rectangle *ABCD* with *AB* = 5 cm and *BC* = 3 cm.

       Rectangle *EFGH* with *EF* = 10 cm and *FG* = 6 cm.

    b Rectangle *ABCD* with *AB* = 5 cm and *BC* = 3 cm.

       Rectangle *EFGH* with *EF* = 10 cm and *FG* = 9 cm.

    c Square *ABCD* with *AB* = 4 cm.

       Square *EFGH* with *EF* = 6 cm.

3 The two shapes below are similar. Find the missing lengths *a* and *b*.

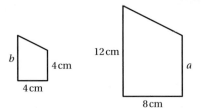

4 The two shapes below are similar. Find the lengths of the missing sides in the second shape.

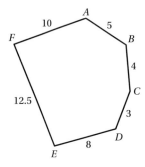
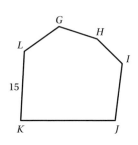

5 The first shape below has been enlarged by a scale factor of 1.5 to create the image *GHIJKL*. *AB* = 5 cm and *BC* = 7 cm. Find the lengths of sides *JK* and *GL* in the second shape.

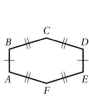
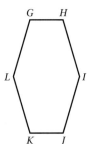

6 Two similar shapes have volumes in the ratio 1 : 512. What is the ratio of their surface areas?

7 Triangles A and B are similar. Triangle A has an area of 48 square units. Triangle B has an area of 588 square units.

   a What is the scale factor of enlargement?

   b If triangle A has a base of 8 units, what are the dimensions of the base of triangle B?

8 A canned food producer makes tins of radius 2.5 cm, and similar tins that have a radius of 7 cm. The smaller tin has a volume of 157 ml (or 157 cm^3).

   a What is the height of the smaller tin?

   b What will the height and the volume of the larger tin be?

9 A cone has a radius of 4 cm and a height of 8 cm.

   a Calculate the volume and surface area of the cone.

   b If each measurement is increased by a factor of 3 calculate the new volume and surface area.

10 A sphere of radius 13 units is enlarged by a factor of 4.

   a Determine the surface area of the original as well as the enlarged sphere.

   b Determine the volume of the original as well as the enlarged sphere.

Checklist of learning and understanding

Similar triangles

- Two triangles are similar if all three corresponding angles are equal. Similar triangles are the same shape, and their corresponding sides are in proportion.

- The proportion between corresponding sides of similar triangles can be used to solve problems in geometry.

Enlargements

- An enlargement is a transformation that changes the position and size of a shape.

- Enlargements are described by a scale factor and centre of enlargement.

Similar shapes

- If shapes are enlarged, similar shapes are created with all their sides in proportion. The proportionality between lengths can be used to solve geometry problems.

- If a 2D shape is enlarged a similar shape is created. All of the dimensions of the image will be enlarged by the same scale factor. If the scale factor is a, then the ratio of the area of the image to the area of the original shape will be a^2.

- If a 3D object is enlarged by a scale factor of a, then the ratio of the volume of the enlarged object will be a^3.

Chapter review

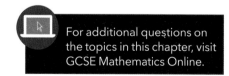
For additional questions on the topics in this chapter, visit GCSE Mathematics Online.

1 **a** Prove that triangle *VWX* is similar to triangle *VYZ*.

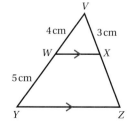

   b Find the length of *XZ*.

2 A tree which is 3 m high has a shadow length of 7.5 m. At the same time of day, a building casts a shadow that is 16.25 m long. Use similar triangles to calculate the height of the building.

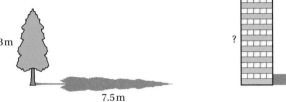
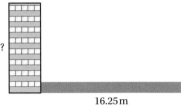

3 Draw an enlargement of $ABCD$ by $\frac{1}{3}$, using the given point as the centre of enlargement.

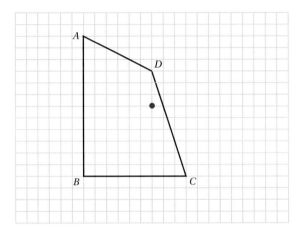

4 Draw an enlargement of this shape by 1.5, using the origin as the centre of enlargement.

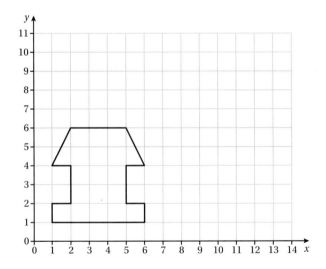

5 Are any two regular hexagons similar shapes? Explain.

6 Are any two rhombuses similar shapes? Explain.

7 Two similar shapes have areas of $90\,\text{cm}^2$ and $62.5\,\text{cm}^2$. The perimeter of the smaller shape is $40\,\text{cm}$. What is the perimeter of the larger shape?

8 A square-based pyramid has a base length of $10\,\text{cm}$ and a perpendicular height of $12\,\text{cm}$. If the pyramid is enlarged by a factor of $\dfrac{1}{2}$, calculate the new volume.

9 The diagram shows two similar solids, A and B.

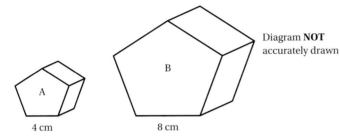

Diagram **NOT** accurately drawn

4 cm   8 cm

Solid A has a volume of $80\,\text{cm}^3$.

a Work out the volume of solid B.   *(2 marks)*

Solid B has a total surface area of $160\,\text{cm}^2$.

b Work out the total surface area of solid A.   *(2 marks)*

©*Pearson Education Ltd 2012*

10 Describe this enlargement. The object is labelled.

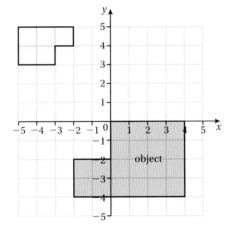

Congruence

In this chapter you will learn how to ...

- prove that two triangles are congruent using the cases SSS, ASA, SAS, RHS.
- apply congruency in calculations and simple proofs.

For more resources relating to this chapter, visit GCSE Mathematics Online.

Using mathematics: real-life applications

Congruent triangles are used in construction to reinforce structures that need to be strong and stable.

"When designing any bridge I have to allow for reinforcement. This ensures that the bridge stays strong and doesn't collapse under heavy traffic. Any bridge I design has many congruent triangles." *(Structural engineer)*

Before you start ...

Ch 2	You need to know how to label angles and shapes that are equal.	**1** Here are two identical triangles. **a** Write down a pair of sides that are equal in length. **b** What angle is equal in size to angle *BAC*? **c** Write down another pair of angles that are equal in size.
Chs 2 and 26	You need to know basic angle facts.	**2** Match up the correct statement with the correct diagram. **a** Vertically opposite angles are equal. **b** Alternate angles are equal. **c** Corresponding angles are equal.
Chs 2 and 26	You should be able to apply angle facts to find angles in figures and to justify results in simple proofs.	**3** Decide whether each statement is true or false. **a** Angle *DBE* = 40° (alternate to angle *ADB*). **b** Angle *BEC* = 50° (complementary to angle *ADB*). **c** Triangle *ABD*, triangle *BDE* and triangle *BCE* are equilateral. **d** Angle *BDE* = angle *BED* = 70°.
Ch 2	You need to know and be able to apply the properties of triangles and quadrilaterals.	**4** What is the value of *x*? Choose the correct answer. **A** 60°　　**B** 30° **C** 45°　　**D** 50°

Assess your starting point using the Launchpad

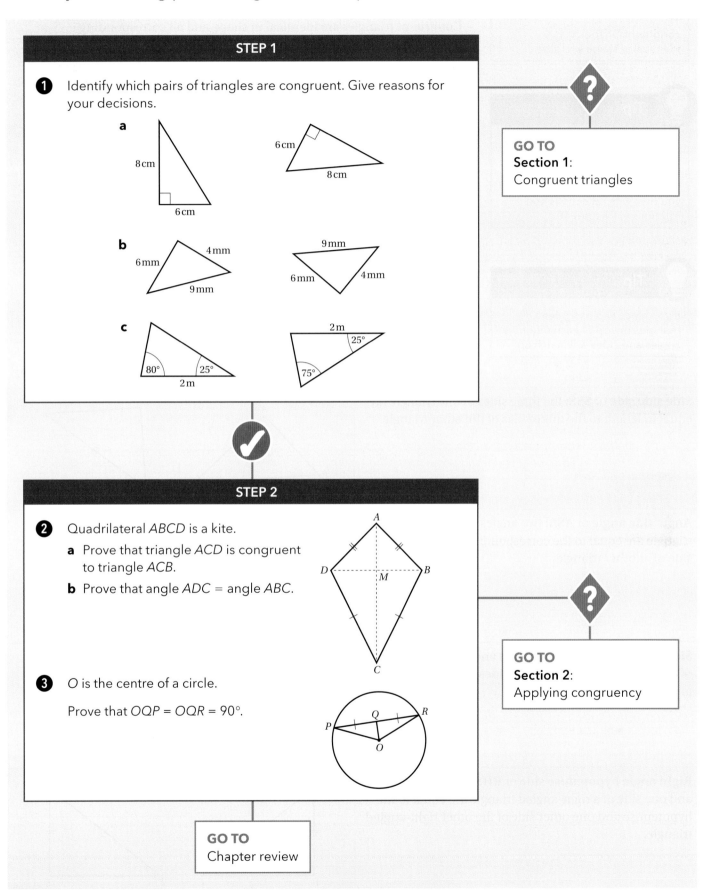

STEP 1

1 Identify which pairs of triangles are congruent. Give reasons for your decisions.

a   8cm   6cm
     6cm   8cm

b   6mm   4mm   9mm
     9mm   6mm   4mm

c   80°   25°   2m
     2m   75°   25°

GO TO
Section 1:
Congruent triangles

STEP 2

2 Quadrilateral *ABCD* is a kite.
  a Prove that triangle *ACD* is congruent to triangle *ACB*.
  b Prove that angle *ADC* = angle *ABC*.

3 *O* is the centre of a circle.

  Prove that *OQP* = *OQR* = 90°.

GO TO
Section 2:
Applying congruency

GO TO
Chapter review

Key vocabulary

congruent: shapes that are identical in shape and size.

Tip

You learned about congruent shapes in Chapter 2. You will work with congruent shapes in different orientations when you deal with reflections and rotations in Chapter 40.

Tip

If you place two congruent triangles on top of each other the angles and sides will match up.

Section 1: Congruent triangles

Congruent triangles are identical in shape and all corresponding measurements (lengths and angles) are equal.

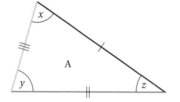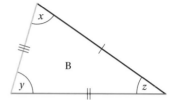

Congruent triangles can have different orientations.

When the triangles are in different orientations you need to think carefully about the corresponding sides and angles.

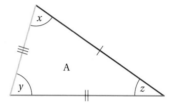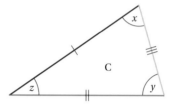

Two triangles are congruent if one of the following sets of conditions is true.

Side side side or **SSS:** the three sides of one triangle are equal in length to the three sides of the other triangle.	
Angle side angle or **ASA:** two angles and one side of one triangle are equal to the corresponding two angles and side of another triangle.	
Side angle side or **SAS:** two sides and the included angle of one triangle are equal to two sides and the included angle of the other triangle.	
Right angle hypotenuse side or **RHS:** the hypotenuse and one side of a right-angled triangle are equal to the hypotenuse and one other side of the other right-angled triangle.	

The conditions in the table are the minimum conditions for proving that triangles are congruent. No other combinations of side and angle facts are sufficient to tell you whether a triangle is congruent or not.

For example:

Two triangles with all their angles equal can still be very different sizes.

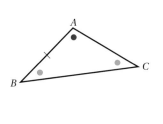
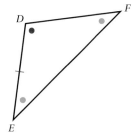

> **Tip**
>
> It is important to write the letters of the vertices of the two triangles in the correct order.
>
> When you write that triangle *ABC* is congruent to triangle *DEF*, it means that:
>
> angle *A* = angle *D*, angle *B* = angle *E*, angle *C* = angle *F*
>
> and
>
> *AB* = *DE*; *AC* = *DF* and *BC* = *EF*.

If you are given two triangles that have two equal sides and one equal angle, but where the equal angle is not included (between the two given sides), you do not know if they are congruent or not. The third side may have a different length in the two triangles.

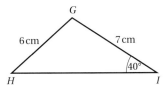
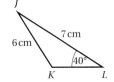

> **Tip**
>
> If two congruent shapes are drawn in different orientations it is sometimes hard to see which angles and sides match each other. To help you, trace one shape onto tracing paper and label its vertices, then rotate and/ or flip the paper over to help see which sides and angles match up.

Although a pair of triangles with two sides and one angle matching might actually be congruent, there is not enough evidence to prove that they are.

WORK IT OUT 31.1

Here are three proofs for congruence for the pair of triangles.

Which one uses the correct reasoning?

Why are the others incorrect?

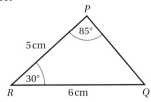
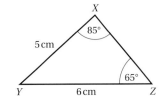

Option A	Option B	Option C
In triangle *PQR* and triangle *XYZ*:	In triangle *PRQ* and triangle *XYZ*:	In triangle *PRQ* and triangle *XYZ*:
PR = *XY* = 5 cm	In triangle *PRQ*, angle *Q* = 65° (sum of angles in a triangle)	*PR* = *XY* = 5 cm
angle *P* = angle *X* = 85°	angle *Q* = angle *Z* = 65°	*RQ* = *YZ* = 6 cm
RQ = *YZ* = 6 cm	*RQ* = *YZ*	In triangle *XYZ*, angle *Y* = 30° (sum of angles in a triangle)
so triangle *PQR* is congruent to triangle *XYZ* (SAS).	so the triangles are congruent.	so triangle *PRQ* is congruent to triangle *XYZ* (SAS).

EXERCISE 31A

1 Match up each of the congruency descriptions (SSS, ASA, SAS, RHS) with each pair of triangles below:

a
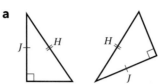

b
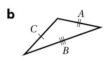

c
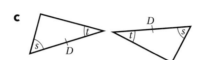

d
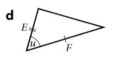

2 State whether each pair of triangles is congruent or not. For those that are, state the conditions that make them congruent.

a
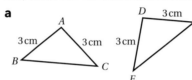

b
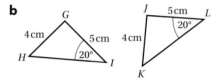

c
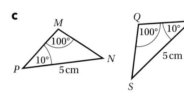

d
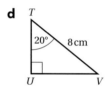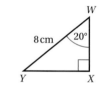

e
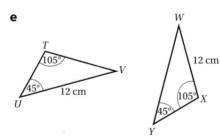

3 Prove that triangle *ABC* is congruent to triangle *DCE*.

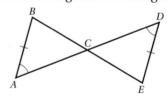

4 *EFG* is a straight line. Write down two different proofs for congruence of triangles *DEF* and *DGF*.

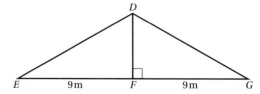

5 In the diagram, *PQ* is parallel to *SR* and *QT* = *TR* = 2 cm.

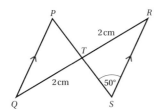

Prove that triangle *PQT* is congruent to triangle *SRT*.

6 Prove that triangles *ABE* and *CBD* in the figure are congruent, giving full reasons.

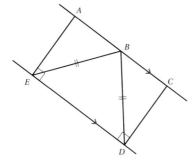

7 Triangle *ABD* is isosceles. *AC* is the perpendicular height. Prove that triangle *ABC* is congruent to triangle *ADC*.

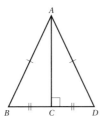

8 In the figure below, *PR* = *SU* and angle *PUT* = angle *SRT*. Prove that triangle *PQR* is congruent to triangle *SQU*.

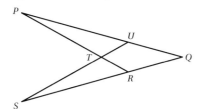

9 *ABCD* in the figure is a kite.

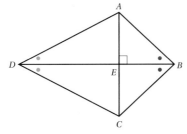

Prove that:

a triangle *ADB* is congruent to triangle *CDB*

b triangle *AED* is congruent to triangle *CED*.

Find answers at: cambridge.org/ukschools/gcsemaths-studentbookanswers

10 Quadrilateral *ABCD* is a rhombus.

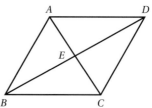

Write down three sets of congruent triangles in this diagram and write down the cases of congruence.

11 *O* is the centre of two concentric circles. Prove that triangle *MPO* is congruent to triangle *NQO* giving reasons.

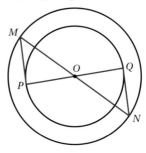

Section 2: Applying congruency

Problem-solving framework

The following steps are useful for solving geometry problems:

In the diagram, *AM* = *BM* and *PM* = *QM*.

a Prove that triangle *AMP* is congruent to triangle *BMQ*.

b Prove that *AP* is parallel to *BQ*.

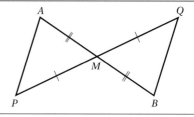

Steps for approaching a problem-solving question	What you would do for this example
Step 1: Read the question carefully to decide what you have to find.	**a** Prove that triangle *AMP* is congruent to triangle *BMQ*. **b** Prove that $AP \parallel BQ$.
Step 2: Write down any further information that might be useful.	The two triangles also have vertically opposite angles, which are equal.
Step 3: Decide what method you'll use.	You are given two equal sides and you can see that the included angle is also equal, so use SAS to prove congruence.

Step 4: Set out your working clearly.	**a** In triangles *AMP* and *BMQ*:
	    AM = *BM* (given).
	    PM = *QM* (given).
	    angle *AMP* = angle *BMQ* (vertically opposite angles at *M*).
	    So triangle *AMP* is congruent to triangle *BMQ* (SAS).
	b Angle *APM* = *BQM* (matching angles of congruent triangles).
	    So $AP \parallel BQ$ (alternate angles are equal).

WORKED EXAMPLE 1

Triangle *DEF* is divided by *GF* into two smaller triangles. Prove that *FG* is perpendicular to *DE*.

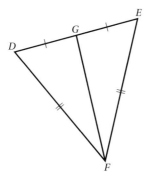

In triangle *FGD* and triangle *FGE*:

Side *FG* is common to both triangles.

DG = *GE*

DF = *EF*

So the triangles are congruent (SSS).

Angle *DGF* = angle *EGF* and the two angles lie on a straight line.

So each angle = 90°, and *FG* is perpendicular to *DE*.

Tip

'Common' means included in both triangles.

EXERCISE 31B

1 In the diagram, prove that *KL* = *ML*.

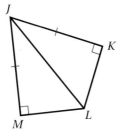

2 Use the facts given in the diagram to:
  a prove that angle *ABE* = angle *EDC*
  b prove that quadrilateral *ABCD* is a parallelogram.

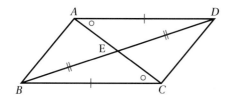

Find answers at: cambridge.org/ukschools/gcsemaths-studentbookanswers

3 In the quadrilateral, $SP = SR$, $QP = QR$ and $QP \parallel RS$. Angle $QRP = 56°$.

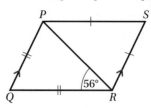

  a Calculate the size of angle PSR and give reasons.

  b What does this tell you about quadrilateral $PQRS$?

4 In the diagram, $PQ = PT$ and $QR = ST$. Prove that triangle PRS is isosceles.

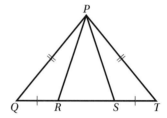

5 In the figure, prove that angle EAD = angle ECD.

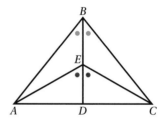

6 Prove that the diagonals of a rectangle are equal in length. Use the diagram below to help if needed.

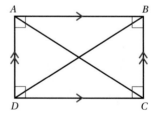

7 In the parallelogram $ABCD$, the points X and Y are on the diagonal such that $DX = DA$ and $BY = BC$. Angle $ADX = 40°$.

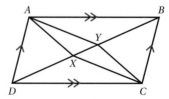

  a Find angle XYC.

  b Prove that $AY = CX$.

  c Prove that triangles AYX and CXY are congruent.

  d Prove that $AYCX$ is a parallelogram.

8 **a** The points *P* and *Q* are chosen on the diagonal *BD* of the square *ABCD* so that *BP* = *DQ*.

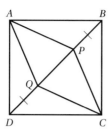

   i Prove that the triangles *ABP*, *CBP*, *ADQ* and *CDQ* are all congruent.

   ii Hence prove that *APCQ* is a rhombus.

 Checklist of learning and understanding

Congruent triangles

- You can prove that two triangles are congruent using one of the four cases of congruence:

  ○ Side side side or SSS: the three sides of one triangle are equal in length to the three sides of the other triangle.

  ○ Angle side angle or ASA: two angles and one side of one triangle are equal to the corresponding two angles and side of another triangle.

  ○ Side angle side or SAS: two sides and the **included** angle of one triangle are equal to two sides and the **included** angle of the other triangle.

  ○ Right angle hypotenuse side or RHS: the hypotenuse and one side of a right-angled triangle are equal to the hypotenuse and one other side of the other right-angled triangle.

 Chapter review

 For additional questions on the topics in this chapter, visit GCSE Mathematics Online.

1 State whether these pairs of triangles are congruent. Give reasons for your answers and give the vertices of the triangles in the correct order.

a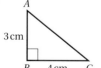

b

c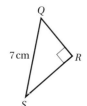

d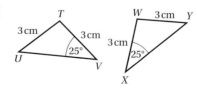

  Find answers at: cambridge.org/ukschools/gcsemaths-studentbookanswers

2 Use triangle congruence to prove that triangle *EBA* is congruent to triangle *ECD*.

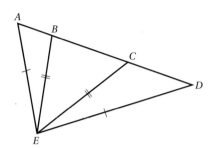

3 *ABCD* is a parallelogram. *CD* is produced to *E* such that when *E* is joined to *B*, it bisects *AD* at *F*. Prove that triangle *ABF* is congruent to triangle *DEF*.

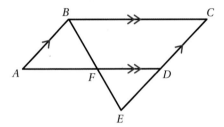

4 Triangle *UVW* is congruent to triangle *UZY*.

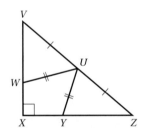

Prove that quadrilateral *UWXY* is a kite.

5 Given that triangle *MNP* is congruent to triangle *NPQ*, prove that quadrilateral *MNPQ* is a square.

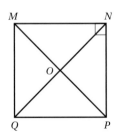

6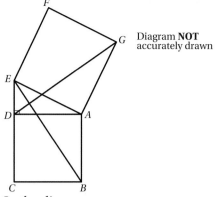

Diagram **NOT**
accurately drawn

In the diagram,

ADE is a right-angled triangle,

ABCD and *AEFG* are squares.

Prove that triangle *ABE* is congruent to triangle *ADG*. *(3 marks)*

©Pearson Education Ltd 2013

32 Pythagoras' theorem

In this chapter you will learn how to:

- develop full knowledge and understanding of Pythagoras' theorem.
- apply Pythagoras in 2D and 3D contexts.
- link the maths to real-life situations.

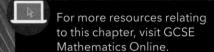

For more resources relating to this chapter, visit GCSE Mathematics Online.

Using mathematics: real-life applications

Builders, carpenters, garden designers, and navigators all use Pythagoras' theorem. It is a method based on right-angled triangles which helps them to work out unknown lengths and to test that angles are right angles.

Calculator tip

Make sure you know how to work with surds on your calculator and that you can round numbers to given levels of accuracy using decimal places and significant figures.

"I use Pythagoras' theorem to help me prepare floor plans and do calculations for footings and heights of buildings. Any building surveyor will have a range of tools to help them make and check calculations on site." *(Building surveyor)*

Before you start …

Ch 14	You must be able to work with exact and approximate values of surds.	**1** **a** Which are correct? **i** $\sqrt{19} = \pm 4.36$ (2 decimal places) **ii** $\sqrt{19} = \pm 361$ **iii** $\sqrt{361} = \pm 19$ **iv** $19^2 = 361$ **b** Which give the correct answer to 2 decimal places? **i** $\sqrt{7} = 2.64575… = \pm 2.64$ **ii** $1.95^2 = 3.8025 = 3.80$ **iii** $\sqrt{3} = 1.73205… = 1.73$ **iv** $3.14^2 = 9.8596 = 9.85$
Ch 26	You need to recognise and define different types of angle.	**2** Which is a right angle? Identify the other angles. **i** **ii** **iii** **iv** **v** Continues on next page …

Ch 2	You'll need to apply the properties of different types of triangle to solve problems.	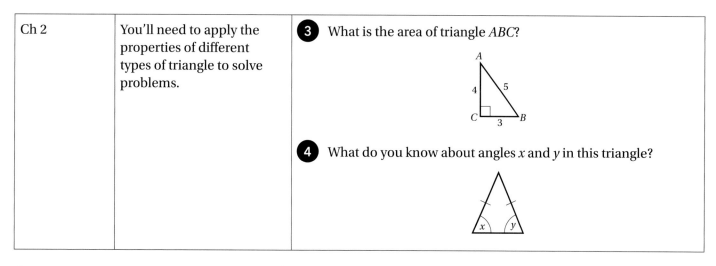

3 What is the area of triangle *ABC*?

4 What do you know about angles *x* and *y* in this triangle?

Assess your starting point using the Launchpad

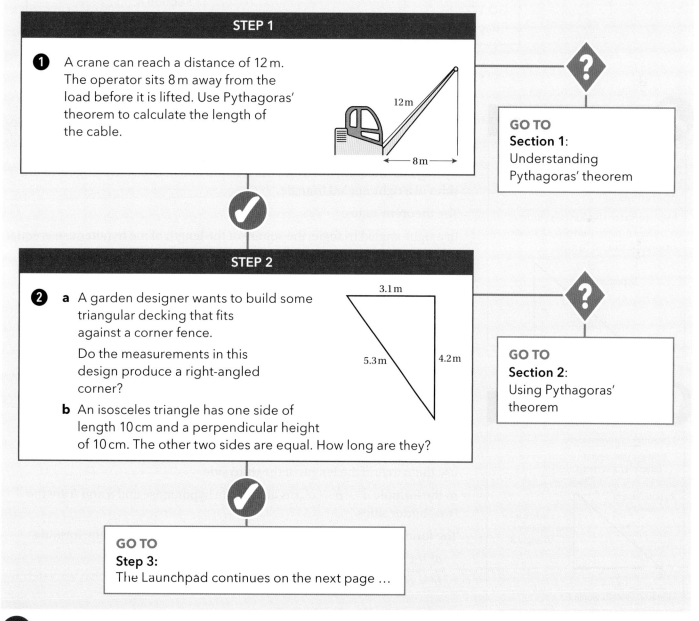

STEP 1

1 A crane can reach a distance of 12 m. The operator sits 8 m away from the load before it is lifted. Use Pythagoras' theorem to calculate the length of the cable.

12 m

8 m

GO TO
Section 1:
Understanding Pythagoras' theorem

STEP 2

2 a A garden designer wants to build some triangular decking that fits against a corner fence.

Do the measurements in this design produce a right-angled corner?

3.1 m

5.3 m   4.2 m

b An isosceles triangle has one side of length 10 cm and a perpendicular height of 10 cm. The other two sides are equal. How long are they?

GO TO
Section 2:
Using Pythagoras' theorem

GO TO
Step 3:
The Launchpad continues on the next page …

Find answers at: cambridge.org/ukschools/gcsemaths-studentbookanswers

Launchpad continued ...

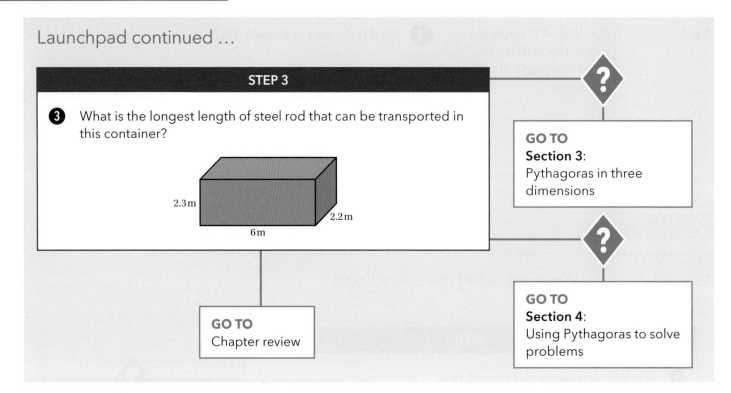

STEP 3

❸ What is the longest length of steel rod that can be transported in this container?

2.3 m
2.2 m
6 m

GO TO
Section 3: Pythagoras in three dimensions

?

GO TO
Section 4: Using Pythagoras to solve problems

?

GO TO
Chapter review

Section 1: Understanding Pythagoras' theorem

What is Pythagoras' theorem?

Pythagoras' theorem describes the relationship between the lengths of the sides of a right-angled triangle.

The **theorem** states:

In a right-angled triangle, the square of the length of the **hypotenuse** is equal to the sum of the squares of the two shorter sides.

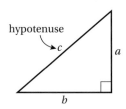

hypotenuse
c
a
b

For this triangle, the theorem can be expressed using the formula:

$$a^2 + b^2 = c^2$$

If you know the lengths of any two sides of a right-angled triangle, you can use them to find the length of the third side.

In the formula $a^2 + b^2 = c^2$, c is always the hypotenuse and a and b are the two shorter sides.

The formula can be rearranged to make a or b the subject of the formula.

$$a^2 = c^2 - b^2$$
$$b^2 = c^2 - a^2$$

Key vocabulary

theorem: a statement that can be demonstrated to be true by accepted mathematical operations.

hypotenuse: the longest side of a right-angled triangle; the side opposite the 90° angle.

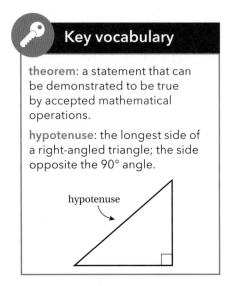

hypotenuse

Tip

Naming conventions:

always use capital letters for a vertex

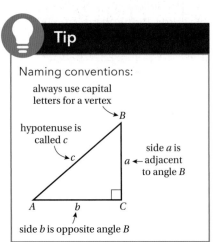

hypotenuse is called c

B

c

side a is
a ← adjacent to angle B

A b C

side b is opposite angle B

WORK IT OUT 32.1

This is the design of an access ramp for the front entrance to a building.
What is the vertical height of the step?

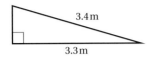

3.4 m

3.3 m

Which of these calculations is correct for this design? Why are the others wrong?

Calculation A	Calculation B	Calculation C
$c^2 - b^2 = a^2$	$c^2 - b^2 = a^2$	$c^2 - b^2 = a^2$
$3.4^2 - 3.3^2 = a^2$	$3.3^2 + 3.4^2 = c^2$	$3.4^2 - 3.3^2 = a^2$
$3.4 \times 2 = 6.8$	$3.3 \times 3.3 = 10.89$	$3.4 \times 3.4 = 11.56$
$3.3 \times 2 = 6.6$	$3.4 \times 3.4 = 11.56$	$3.3 \times 3.3 = 10.89$
$6.8 - 6.6 = a^2$	$10.89 + 11.56 = c^2$	$11.56 - 10.89 = a^2$
$0.2 = a^2$	$22.45 = c^2$	$a^2 = 0.67$
$a = 0.2 \div 2$	$a = \sqrt{22.45}\,\text{m} = 4.74\,\text{m}$	$a = \sqrt{0.67}\,\text{m} = 0.82\,\text{m}$
$a = 0.1\,\text{m}$	(to 2 decimal places)	(to 2 decimal places)

EXERCISE 32A

1 Find the length of the hypotenuse in each of the following triangles:

a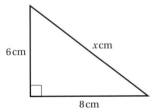

6 cm

x cm

8 cm

b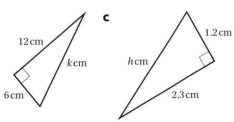

12 cm

k cm

6 cm

c

h cm

1.2 cm

2.3 cm

d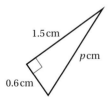

1.5 cm

p cm

0.6 cm

e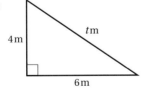

4 m

t m

6 m

Tip

The five rules for exam success when working with Pythagoras' theorem:
● Always write the formula.
● Always include a sketch of the problem.
● Show full workings.
● Show the final answer to a given degree of accuracy. This could be 2 decimal places or several significant figures, depending on the detail of the problem.
● In practical questions, always make sure you use consistent units.

Find answers at: cambridge.org/ukschools/gcsemaths-studentbookanswers

2 Find the missing length in each of these triangles.

a

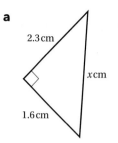

2.3 cm

1.6 cm

x cm

b

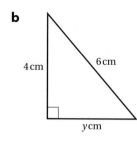

4 cm

6 cm

y cm

c

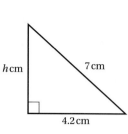

h cm

7 cm

4.2 cm

d

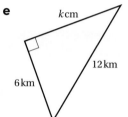

p cm

3 km

8 km

e

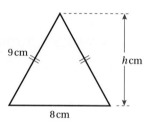

k cm

12 km

6 km

f

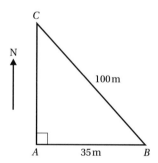

9 cm

h cm

8 cm

3 Points *A*, *B* and *C* are markers on a building site, at ground level.

Point *B* is 35 m east of point *A*. Point *C* is due north of point *A* and 100 m from point *B*.

Calculate the distance *AC*, giving your answer to 2 decimal places.

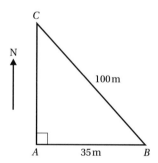

C

N

100 m

A   35 m   *B*

4 Find the value of *x* in each of the following triangles correct to 2 decimal places.

a

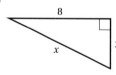

8

x

3

b

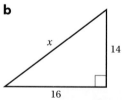

x

14

16

c

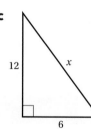

12

x

6

d

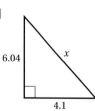

6.04

x

4.1

e

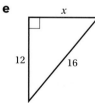

x

12

16

f

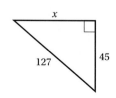

x

127

45

Section 2: Using Pythagoras' theorem

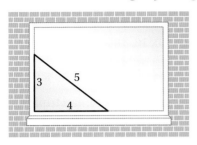

"I use 'Pythagorean triples' in my job. I measure 3 units up and 4 across the corner of a frame and check that the line that joins the end points is 5 units long. If the rule applies, then I know the frame is a right angle and that the window will fit properly." (Window fitter)

Pythagorean triples

Carpenters need to make rectangular window frames. If the frames don't have right angles at the corners then the window won't fit. If the sides of the triangle at the corner of the frame have lengths in the ratio of $3:4:5$, then the carpenter knows the angle is a right angle because $3^2 + 4^2 = 5^2$. Carpenters call this the '3, 4, 5 rule'.

Any set of three whole numbers that satisfy Pythagoras' theorem are called **Pythagorean triples**. One such triple is 3, 4, 5; so are any multiples of that, for example, 6, 8, 10 and 9, 12, 15. Other common triples are 5, 12, 13 and 7, 24, 25.

> **🔑 Key vocabulary**
>
> **Pythagorean triple:** three non-zero integers (a, b, c) for which $a^2 + b^2 = c^2$.

The converse of Pythagoras' theorem

The converse of Pythagoras' theorem states that:

If the square on the longest side of any triangle is equal to the sum of the squares of the other two sides, then the triangle is right-angled.

WORK IT OUT 32.2

Is this triangle right-angled?

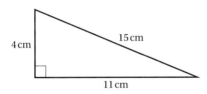

Which of these answers is correct?

Where have the others gone wrong?

Option A	Option B	Option C
$4 + 11 = 15$	$a^2 + b^2 = 4^2 + 11^2$	$a^2 + b^2 = 4^2 + 11^2$
So $a^2 + b^2 = c^2$	$\quad = 4 \times 2 + 11 \times 2$	$\quad = 16 + 121 = 137$
Yes, the triangle is right-angled!	$\quad = 8 + 22 = 30$	$c^2 = 15 \times 15 = 225$
	$c^2 = 15^2 = 15 \times 2 = 30$	$a^2 + b^2 \neq c^2$
	$a^2 + b^2 = c^2$	No, the triangle is not right-angled!
	Yes, the triangle is right-angled!	

> **ℹ️ Did you know?**
>
> To measure right angles, builders used to carry a coil of rope 12 feet long with knots tied at each 1-foot length. They would put a peg in the ground and then hold the rope taught around it so that there were three knots on one side, four knots on the second side and the remaining five knots on the third side. Putting in pegs at the ends they would then mark out a perfect right angle.

Find answers at: cambridge.org/ukschools/gcsemaths-studentbookanswers

EXERCISE 32B

1 Determine which of these sets of lengths are Pythagorean triples.

    a 6, 8, 10   **b** 24, 45, 51   **c** 10, 16, 18

    d 20, 48, 52   **e** 9, 40, 41   **f** 12, 35, 37

2 Why is 3, 4, 5 the smallest possible whole number Pythagorean triple?

3 Is there a limit to the number of Pythagorean triples there are? Explain why or why not.

4 Which of the following triangles are right-angled?

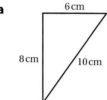

a

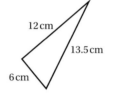

b

c

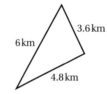

d

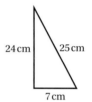

e

5 Determine which of the following are rectangles.

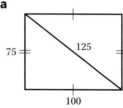

a

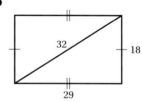

b

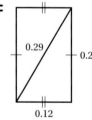

c

Pythagoras in polygons

Pythagoras' theorem is very useful for solving many geometrical problems involving polygons and composite figures, particularly when you need to find the lengths of unknown sides.

WORKED EXAMPLE 1

Find the length of side x and then calculate the perimeter of this composite shape.

All dimensions are shown in centimetres.

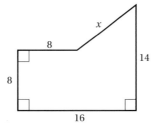

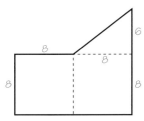

Divide the shape to make a right-angled triangle.

$8^2 + 6^2 = x^2$
$64 + 36 = x^2$
$100 = x^2$
$x = 10\,\text{cm}$

Now you can use Pythagoras to find x.

Perimeter $= 16 + 14 + 8 + 8 + 10$
$= 56\,\text{cm}$

WORKED EXAMPLE 2

Rhombus $ABCD$ has diagonals $BD = 12\,\text{cm}$ and $AC = 8\,\text{cm}$ which intersect at E. What is the exact side length of the rhombus? Give your answer in simplified surd form.

Tip

Remember, a surd is a number left in square root form.

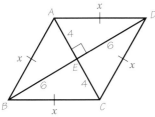

Start by doing a rough sketch and marking what you know.

$AE = 4\,\text{cm}$ and $BE = 6\,\text{cm}$

Diagonals of a rhombus bisect at right angles.

$x^2 = 4^2 + 6^2$
$x^2 = 52$
$x = \sqrt{52}$

Now you can use Pythagoras.

$x = 2\sqrt{13}$

Simplify but leave your answer in surd form. This is what was asked for.

EXERCISE 32C

1 What is the perpendicular height of an equilateral triangle of side length 5 cm?

2 What is the perpendicular height of an isosceles triangle of side lengths 8 cm and base length 6 cm?

3 What is the length of the sides in this square?

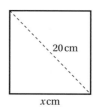

4 A scalene triangle has lengths 14 cm, 10.5 cm and 17.5 cm. Is it a right-angled scalene triangle?

Tip

Note that there are different types of right-angled triangle:

Scalene right-angled triangle
- one right angle
- two other unequal angles
- no equal sides.

Isosceles right-angled triangle
- one right angle
- two other equal angles, always 45°
- two equal sides.

You can apply Pythagoras' theorem to both types of right-angled triangle.

---

5 **a** Show that the length of the hypotenuse of this triangle is 20.0 cm to 1 decimal place.

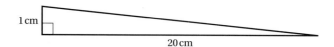

b Is it an isosceles triangle?

6 Find the length of *AB* in this figure.

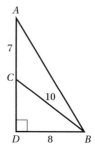

7 Calculate the length of:

   a *AC*   **b** *BC*   **c** *EC*

8 For the isosceles trapezium *ABCD*, find the area of the figure.

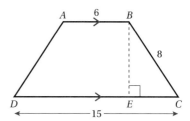

9 Find the length of side *AD* and calculate the perimeter of this shape.

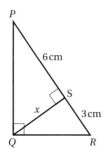

10 The area of square *ACDE* is 50 mm². Determine the length of *AB*.

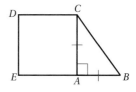

11 Find the value of *x*. Leave your answer as a surd in simplified form.

12 Prove that in this figure, $BN^2 + CM^2 = 5BC^2$

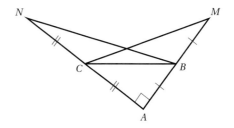

Section 3: Pythagoras in three dimensions

So far you have used Pythagoras to solve problems involving plane shapes in two dimensions. In reality, many problems involve three-dimensional objects or spaces.

When you work with three-dimensional shapes it is important to draw careful diagrams. In most cases, you will need to separate out triangles to work with them.

The first step in working with three-dimensional objects is to find the right-angled triangle in the plane which has the length you need to work out. Once you've identified the correct triangle, you can draw it on its own and add all the necessary information.

WORKED EXAMPLE 3

The height of a box is 7 cm, its length is 4 cm and its depth is 3 cm. Find the length of the diagonal *SB*.

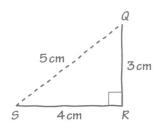

> Find the length of the diagonal *QS* first.
>
> It is the hypotenuse of right-angled triangle *QRS* on the base of the box.

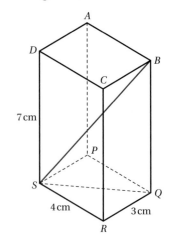

$QS = \sqrt{4^2 + 3^2} = \sqrt{25} = 5\,cm$

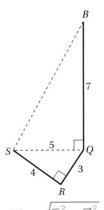

> Draw the upright right-angled triangle with a base of 5 cm.
>
> Find *SB*, the hypotenuse of this triangle.

$SB = \sqrt{5^2 + 7^2} = \sqrt{74} = 8.60\,cm$ (2 decimal places)

EXERCISE 32D

1 This symmetrical pyramid has a rectangular base. Find the perpendicular height of the pyramid.

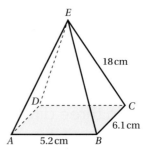

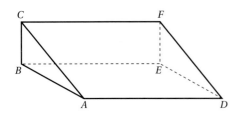

2 The diagram (left) shows a wedge used to get trolleys through a doorway.

The face *ABED* is a rectangle and is at right angles to *CBEF*, which is another rectangle.

AB = 50 cm, *AF* = 65 cm and *BE* = 30 cm.

Calculate whether the wedge will fit under the lip of a door measuring 30.5 cm high.

3 An office block is the shape of a cuboid with a rectangular-based pyramid fitting exactly on the top. How tall is the building?

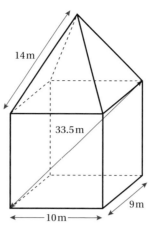

14 m

33.5 m

9 m

10 m

4 A spaghetti jar is the shape of a cylinder with a radius of 8 cm and a height of 0.35 m. Will dried spaghetti that is 40 cm long fit into the jar?

5 The slant height of a cone with a circular base is 100 mm and the diameter of its base is 60 mm. Determine the perpendicular height of the cone.

Section 4: Using Pythagoras to solve problems

Pythagoras' theorem is useful for solving problems such as shortest and longest routes.

Problem-solving framework

You want to cross a 100 metre by 60 metre rectangular football field diagonally from one corner to the other but there is a game playing so you have to go round the edge. Calculate how much further you have to walk.

Steps for approaching a problem-solving question	What you would do for this example
Step 1: If it is useful to have a diagram, sketch one and add the information. This may help you visualise the problem.	60 m 100 m
Step 2: Identify what you have to do.	Find the difference between the length of the diagonal and the length of the two sides added together.
Step 3: Test the problem with what you know. Can I use a ruler? What type of angle is it?	You could use a ruler, but you would have to draw a very accurate diagram to scale. As you have a right-angled triangle and side lengths you can use Pythagoras' theorem.
Step 4: What maths can I do?	Use Pythagoras' theorem to work out the length of the diagonal: $100^2 + 60^2 = c^2$ $10\,000 + 3600 = c^2$ $13\,600 = c^2$ $c = \sqrt{13\,600} = 116.6\,\text{m}$

Continues on next page …

	If you walked straight across the diagonal the distance would be 116.6 m. You have to go round the outside which is 160 m (100 + 60), so you must walk 43.4 m further.
Step 5: Check your workings and that your answer is reasonable.	A diagonal pitch length of 116.6 m seems reasonable given the sides are 60 m and 100 m.
Step 6: Have you answered the question?	You were asked to find how much further you would have to walk. You have found this to be 43.4 m.

EXERCISE 32E

1 Computer gaming designers use *x*- and *y*-coordinates to place characters or objects in a game. They need to know distances between characters or how far players are apart.

If one player is at coordinate (30, 10) and the other at (15, 4), how far apart are they?

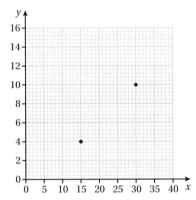

2 You are going to buy a new television. It is an 80-inch television (measured along its diagonal).

Your current television is a 52-inch television.

Both are the same height, 40 inches.

a How much wider is your new television than your current one?

b More importantly, will it fit in the 58-inch gap between the chimney breast and wall?

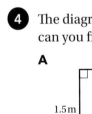

3 A cuboid metal storage container (left) measures 6 metres by 4 metres by 3 metres.

Will a boat mast 7 metres long fit inside?

4 The diagrams show the plan view of two storage boxes. In which box can you fit the longest pole, laid flat on the floor of the box?

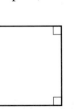
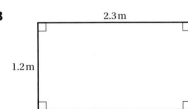

A 2 m 1.5 m   **B** 2.3 m 1.2 m

5 Find the length of the hypotenuse of the largest triangle.

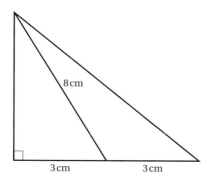

6 Here is a square frame with a brace across it. Is it constructed correctly as a perfect square, within reasonable bounds?

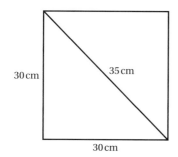

7 Calculate the length of *AB* in this trapezium.

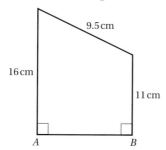

8 A plumber carries piping on the roof of his van in a cylindrical canister that is 4.6 m long. The longest pipe the tube can carry is 4.65 m (assume the pipe is narrow so that its width is insignificant).

What is the diameter of the tube, in centimetres, to 2 decimal places?

Find answers at: cambridge.org/ukschools/gcsemaths-studentbookanswers

9 A hotel has a square courtyard with sides 12 metres long. The hotel owners want to construct a circular fountain with diameter 1.2 m in the middle of the courtyard.

   a What is the length of each of the courtyard's diagonals?

   b How many metres along each diagonal should the fountain be placed?

Tip

When facing more complex questions involving triangles remember the problem-solving steps. There are some key questions to ask yourself.

1 What information do I have? Sketch it onto a diagram if there isn't one. If the question is about a three-dimensional object, you need to draw a separate diagram for every calculation you do.

2 What information do I need to find out? Is it lengths of sides?

3 What can I do? Is there a right angle somewhere or could one be created?

4 What maths can I do to find more information? Can I use Pythagoras' formula? Do I need to rearrange it?

5 Check your working. What roughly is the length I need to find? Is the result roughly what I had estimated? Is the hypotenuse the longest side of any right-angled triangles? If not, then you've definitely made a mistake!

6 Double check you've answered the question.

10 A horse paddock is the shape of a rectangle with a diagonal of 20 m and a shorter side of 10 m.

   a What is the perimeter and the area of the paddock?

   b How many laps of the paddock would a horse have to trot to cover a kilometre, to the nearest whole lap?

11 When tiling a bathroom a plumber uses tiles that are isosceles triangles of side length 15 cm and base 10 cm.

   a What would the height of 10 rows of tiles be?

   b How many rows of tiles would fit below a shelf which sits 90 cm from the floor?

12 A piece of artwork has been designed with the dimensions shown in the diagram on the left.

It is three right-angled triangles welded together. The hypotenuse of the top triangle is perpendicular to the ground.

It is to be displayed in an alcove in which is 3 m high. Will it fit in the alcove?

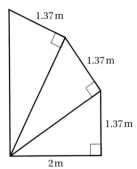

Checklist of learning and understanding

Pythagoras' theorem

- Pythagoras' theorem only applies to right-angled triangles.

- In a right-angled triangle, the square of the hypotenuse (longest side) equals the sum of the squares of the other two sides. It can be written as:

  $a^2 + b^2 = c^2$

- Rearrange the formula to find either of the other two sides:

  $a^2 = c^2 - b^2$

  $b^2 = c^2 - a^2$

- You can use the theorem to find an unknown length, or to prove there is a right angle within a triangle.

- Always draw a diagram and label it; also write out the formula you are using to fully explain what you have done.

- Pythagorean triples are three whole-number lengths that satisfy the formula and therefore prove you have a right angle; learn the common ones, such as 3, 4, 5 and 5, 12, 13.

- A Pythagorean triple can also be expressed as three non-zero integers (a, b, c) for which $a^2 + b^2 = c^2$

Chapter review

For additional questions on the topics in this chapter, visit GCSE Mathematics Online.

1 Find the length of x and y in this figure giving your answers correct to 2 decimal places.

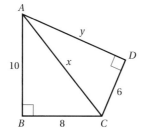

2 *XYZ* is a right-angled triangle.

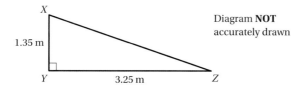

Diagram **NOT** accurately drawn

Calculate the length of *XZ*.

Give your answer correct to 3 significant figures.   *(3 marks)*

©*Pearson Education Ltd 2013*

Find answers at: cambridge.org/ukschools/gcsemaths-studentbookanswers

3 What is the perimeter of this kite?

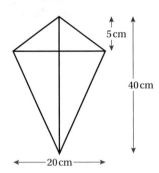

4 Find the length of *FG*.

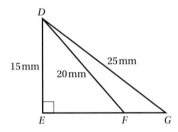

5 The base of a pyramid of height 1.6 m is a square with a diagonal of 2.4 m.

Calculate the length of the sloping edge of the pyramid.

6 A gardener is laying a rectangular patio from a conservatory that is 9 m wide. To make sure that the angles are right angles and that the edges of the patio are parallel, she measures the diagonal from either end of the conservatory to make sure the length is the same.

If the patio is to be 12 m long, what will the lengths of the diagonals be?

7 On his journey to work, Andrew used to take a shortcut along a farm track.

The farm track started 250 m from a crossroads and was 400 m long. The farmer decided to close the track.

a How much further does Andrew now have to travel on his journey (answer to the nearest cm)?

b Andrew did this journey twice each day for five days. How many kilometres extra does he travel in this time (answer to the nearest tenth of a km)?

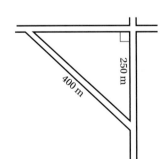

33 Trigonometry

In this chapter you will learn how to ...

- use trigonometric ratios to find lengths and angles in right-angled triangles.
- find and use exact values of important trigonometric ratios.
- use the sine and cosine rules to calculate unknown sides or angles in any triangle.
- use the area rule to calculate the area of a triangle.
- solve trigonometry problems in two- and three-dimensional figures.

For more resources relating to this chapter, visit GCSE Mathematics Online.

Using mathematics: real-life applications

Trigonometry means 'triangle measurements' and it is very useful for finding the lengths of sides and sizes of angles. Trigonometry is used to determine lengths and angles in navigation, surveying, astronomy, engineering, construction and even in the placement of satellites and satellite receivers.

"I use a theodolite to work out the height of mountains. You basically point it at the top of the mountain. The theodolite uses the principles of trigonometry to measure angles and distances." *(Geologist)*

Before you start ...

Ch 32	You should be able to use Pythagoras' theorem to find lengths in triangles.	**1** Find the length of x in each triangle: **a** (triangle with sides 7, 16, hypotenuse x) **b** (triangle with sides x, 7, base 5)
Ch 9	You must be able to work with approximate values and round to a specified number of places.	**2** What is $\sqrt{53}$ correct to 2 decimal places? **3** If $c^2 = 94.34$, what is c correct to 3 significant figures?
Ch 20	You need to be able to use ratio and proportion to calculate sides in similar triangles.	**4** Find the length of AC if the ratio of sides $\dfrac{AB}{AC} = \dfrac{5}{3}$ and $AB = 35\,\text{cm}$.

Find answers at: cambridge.org/ukschools/gcsemaths-studentbookanswers

Assess your starting point using the Launchpad

STEP 1

1 Find the length of the diagonal x in this rectangle.

3.4 cm

36°

2 One end of a wheelchair ramp is placed on a step 24 cm above the horizontal floor. From the bottom of the ramp to the step is a distance of 90 cm.

Calculate the angle between the ramp and the floor. Give your answer correct to 2 decimal places.

24 cm

90 cm

GO TO
Section 1:
Trigonometry in right-angled triangles

STEP 2

3 Write down the exact value of:

   a sin 45°   **b** cos 0°   **c** tan 60°

4 Without using a calculator, show that $(\sin 60°)^2 + (\cos 60°)^2 = 1$

GO TO
Section 2:
Exact values of trigonometric ratios

STEP 3

5 What is angle C if $c = 4$ cm, $B = 46°$ and b is 7 cm?

6 In triangle PQR, $R = 100°$, $PR = 8$ cm and $PQ = 5$ cm.

   a Calculate the length of PQ.

   b Calculate, correct to the nearest degree, the size of angles P and Q.

B

c a

A b C

GO TO
Section 3:
The sine, cosine and area rules

GO TO
Step 4:
The Launchpad continues on the next page …

Launchpad continued ...

STEP 4

7 A girl is standing looking at a chimney. Use the dimensions in the diagram to find the height of the chimney.

35°

12m

1.5m

8 A pyramid, *VPQRS*, has a square base, *PQRS*, with sides of length 8 cm. Each sloping edge is 9 cm long.

a Calculate the perpendicular height of the pyramid.

b Calculate the angle the sloping edge *VP* makes with the base.

V

9 cm

S

R

P   8 cm   *Q*

?

GO TO
Section 4:
Using trigonometry to solve problems

GO TO
Chapter review

Section 1: Trigonometry in right-angled triangles

There are special relationships between the lengths of the sides of right-angled triangles and you can use Pythagoras' theorem to find missing sides when two sides are known. In similar triangles, the ratio of corresponding pairs of sides is always the same.

These facts are important in understanding and using trigonometry.

Naming the sides of right-angled triangles

The hypotenuse is the longest side of a right-angled triangle, opposite the right angle.

The other two (shorter) sides are named in relation to the acute angles (marked θ) in the triangle.

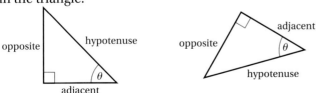

Make sure you understand this system of naming the sides and how it works for triangles in any orientation (triangles shown any way up).

The ratio of sides in similar triangles

This diagram shows three similar right-angled triangles. The green sides are opposite angle θ and the orange sides are adjacent to it. You can see that the ratio of $\dfrac{\text{opposite}}{\text{adjacent}}$ sides is $\dfrac{1}{2}$ for all the similar triangles.

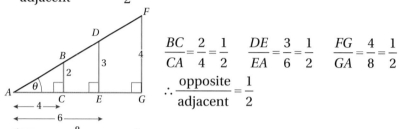

$$\frac{BC}{CA} = \frac{2}{4} = \frac{1}{2} \qquad \frac{DE}{EA} = \frac{3}{6} = \frac{1}{2} \qquad \frac{FG}{GA} = \frac{4}{8} = \frac{1}{2}$$

$$\therefore \frac{\text{opposite}}{\text{adjacent}} = \frac{1}{2}$$

You can extend the diagram forever, but the ratio is always the same for the similar triangles. Depending on which sides you compare, the ratio is given a special name. You will work with three ratios: sine, cosine and tangent.

The trigonometric ratios

The trigonometric ratios (shortened to trig ratios) are named as follows:

- The sine ratio ($\sin \theta$) is the ratio of the side opposite the angle to the hypotenuse.
- The cosine ratio ($\cos \theta$) is the ratio of the side adjacent to the angle to the hypotenuse.
- The tangent ratio ($\tan \theta$) is the ratio of the side opposite the angle to the side adjacent to the angle.

$$\sin \theta = \frac{a}{c} = \frac{\text{opposite}}{\text{hypotenuse}}$$

$$\cos \theta = \frac{b}{c} = \frac{\text{adjacent}}{\text{hypotenuse}}$$

$$\tan \theta = \frac{a}{b} = \frac{\text{opposite}}{\text{adjacent}}$$

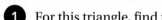

The three ratios have the same value for a particular angle, no matter how long the sides are.

WORKED EXAMPLE 1

1 For this triangle, find the value of:

a $\sin A$

b $\cos A$

c $\tan A$

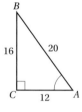

a $\sin A = \dfrac{\text{opposite}}{\text{hypotenuse}} = \dfrac{16}{20} = \dfrac{4}{5}$

> You can write this as $\dfrac{\text{opp}}{\text{hyp}}$ for short.

b $\cos A = \dfrac{\text{adjacent}}{\text{hypotenuse}} = \dfrac{12}{20} = \dfrac{3}{5}$

> Remember to simplify your answer.

c $\tan A = \dfrac{\text{opposite}}{\text{adjacent}} = \dfrac{16}{12} = \dfrac{4}{3}$

You can find the ratio for any angle using your calculator. Make sure you know how to find and use the trig function keys.

Solving triangles

Finding unknown sides or angles is called solving the triangle. You can use the three trigonometric ratios to do this.

Finding unknown sides

If you know an angle (other than the right angle) and one side in a right-angled triangle, you can use the ratios to form equations that you solve to find the missing lengths.

You will not be told which ratio to use. You have to pick the right one based on the information that you have about the triangle.

You can remember the ratios using the mnemonic SOH-CAH-TOA and the formula triangles.

> **Tip**
>
> If you have two sides of a right-angled triangle you can find the other side using Pythagoras' theorem. If you have one side and at least one of the acute angles, you will need to use the trigonometric ratios.

  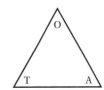

SOH: $\text{Sin} = \dfrac{\text{Opposite}}{\text{Hypotenuse}}$ CAH: $\text{Cos} = \dfrac{\text{Adjacent}}{\text{Hypotenuse}}$ TOA: $\text{Tan} = \dfrac{\text{Opposite}}{\text{Adjacent}}$

> **Tip**
>
> Circle the angle you are working with and mark the sides H, A and O to help you see which values you have and which you need.

WORKED EXAMPLE 2

In triangle ABC, angle $B = 90°$, $AC = 15$ cm and angle $C = 35°$.

Calculate the length of AB correct to 1 decimal place.

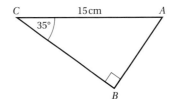

You have angle C.
You want side AB which is opposite to C.
You have CA, which is the hypotenuse.

Identify which sides you have and want in relation to the acute angle.

Use the ratio with O and H, which is SOH.

Choose the correct trig ratio.

$\sin 35° = \dfrac{opposite}{hypotenuse}$

$\sin 35° = \dfrac{AB}{15}$

$AB = \sin 35° \times 15$

Multiply both sides by 15 to get AB on its own.

$AB = 8.603646545$

Use your calculator to find this value.

$AB = 8.6$ cm (to 1 decimal place)

Round your answer to the required number of decimal places.

WORKED EXAMPLE 3

In triangle *XYZ*, angle *Z* is a right angle and angle *X* = 71°. Side *YZ* = 7.9 cm.

Calculate the length of *XZ* correct to 1 decimal place.

You have angle *X*.
You want *XZ* which is adjacent to *X*.
You have *YZ* which is opposite to *X*.
Use the ratio with OA which is TOA.

$$\tan = \frac{opposite}{adjacent}$$

$$\tan 71° = \frac{7.9}{XZ}$$

$7.9 = XZ \times \tan 71°$

Multiply both sides by *XZ* to get rid of the fraction.

$$\frac{7.9}{\tan 71°} = XZ$$

Divide by tan 71° to get *XZ* on its own.

$XZ = 2.720188145$

Do the calculation on your calculator.

$XZ = 2.7$ cm (to 1 decimal place)

Round your answer to the required number of decimal places.

EXERCISE 33A

1 Use your calculator to give the value of each ratio correct to 3 decimal places if necessary.

a sin 32°	**b** cos 90°	**c** tan 24°
d sin 30°	**e** tan 87°	**f** cos 49°
g sin 0°	**h** cos 32°	**i** tan 45°

Calculator tip

Most calculators have different angle modes. Make sure yours is set for degrees.

2 Select the correct trigonometric ratio and use it to find the length of the side marked with a variable in each triangle.

a

b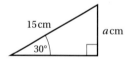

c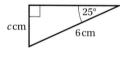

d

e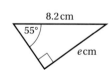

f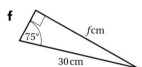

g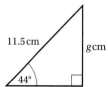

h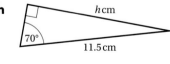

582

3 Determine the length of the side marked with a variable in each triangle. Give your answers correct to 2 decimal places.

a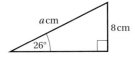

b

c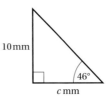

d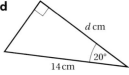

e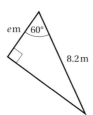

f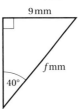

Finding unknown angles

You can use the trig ratios to find the size of missing angles.

To find the size of unknown angles using the trig ratios you need to use the inverse function of each ratio. On most calculators these are the second functions of the sin, cos and tan buttons. They are usually marked $\sin^{-1}$, $\cos^{-1}$ and $\tan^{-1}$.

> **Calculator tip**
>
> Your calculator can 'work backwards' to find the size of the unknown angle associated with a particular trigonometric ratio.
>
> To find the angle if you have the ratio, key in the inverse trigonometric function on your calculator, i.e. $\sin^{-1}$, $\cos^{-1}$ or $\tan^{-1}$.

WORKED EXAMPLE 4

Given that $\tan x$ is 5, what is the size of angle x (to 1 decimal place)?

   78.69006753   Using your calculator.

Angle x is 78.7°

WORKED EXAMPLE 5

Find the size of angle x in each triangle. Give your answers correct to 1 decimal place.

a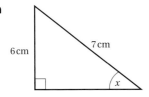

b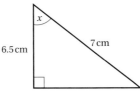

c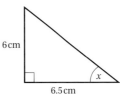

a $\sin x = \dfrac{\text{opposite}}{\text{hypotenuse}} = \dfrac{6}{7} = 0.857\ldots$

Choose the correct trig ratio. You have the side opposite to angle x and also the hypotenuse.

$x = \sin^{-1} 0.857\ldots = 59.0°$

b $\cos x = \dfrac{\text{adjacent}}{\text{hypotenuse}} = \dfrac{6.5}{7} = 0.928\ldots$

Use the second function button on your calculator.

$x = \cos^{-1} 0.928\ldots = 21.8°$

c $\tan x = \dfrac{\text{opposite}}{\text{adjacent}} = \dfrac{6}{6.5} = 0.923\ldots$

$x = \tan^{-1} 0.923\ldots = 42.7°$

WORK IT OUT 33.1

For a ladder to be safe it must be inclined at an angle between 70° and 80° to the ground.

The diagram shows a ladder resting against a wall.

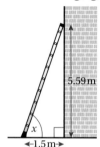

Not to scale

5.59 m

x

←1.5 m→

Is the ladder positioned safely? Which of these calculations gives you the answer that you need?

Option A	Option B	Option C
$\sin x = \dfrac{1.5}{5.59} = 0.268...$	$\cos x = \dfrac{1.5}{5.59} = 0.268...$	$\tan x = \dfrac{5.59}{1.5} = 3.726...$
$\sin^{-1} 0.268... = 15.57°$	$\cos^{-1} 0.268... = 74.43°$	$\tan^{-1} 3.726... = 74.98°$
Ladder is not safe.	Ladder is safe.	Ladder is safe.

EXERCISE 33B

1 Determine, correct to the nearest degree:

    a $\sin^{-1} 0.7$ **b** $\cos^{-1} 0.713$ **c** $\tan^{-1} 0.1$

    d $\sin^{-1} 0.732$ **e** $\cos^{-1} 0.1234$ **f** $\tan^{-1} 12$

2 Calculate the size of θ, correct to the nearest degree.

    a $\sin \theta = 0.682$ **b** $\cos \theta = 0.891$ **c** $\tan \theta = 2.4751$

    d $\sin \theta = 0.2588$ **e** $\tan \theta = 3.9469$ **f** $\cos \theta = 0.7847$

3 Find the size of each marked angle. Give your answers correct to 1 decimal place.

a
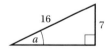

b

c

d

e
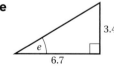

f

4 PQR is a right-angled triangle; $PQ = 11$ cm and $QR = 24$ cm.

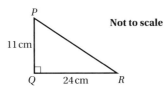

Not to scale

Calculate the size of angle PRQ.

5 What is the size of angle x in the triangle on the right?

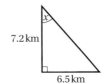

6 For each of these, sketch the triangle and calculate the missing value.

a In triangle ABC, angle $B = 90°$, $BC = 45$ units and angle $C = 23°$.
Calculate the length of AB.

b In triangle PQR, angle $R = 90°$, $PQ = 12.2$ cm and angle $P = 57°$.
Calculate the length of QR.

c In triangle EFG, angle $G = 90°$, $EG = 8.7$ cm and angle $E = 49°$.
Calculate the length of FG.

d In triangle XYZ, angle $Y = 90°$, $XZ = 36$ units and angle X is $25°$.
Calculate the length of:

i XY **ii** YZ.

7 For each triangle, draw a sketch and then calculate the required values.

a In triangle ABC, angle $C = 90°$, $BC = 6.7$ units and $AB = 9.8$ units.
Calculate angle A.

b In triangle DEF, angle $D = 90°$, $DF = 13$ units and $EF = 17$ units.
Calculate angle F.

c In triangle GHI, angle $I = 90°$, $HI = 8.2$ cm and $GI = 13.7$ cm.
Calculate the size of:

i angle G **ii** angle H.

d In triangle JKL, angle $J = 90°$, $JK = 85$ mm and $KL = 113$ mm.
Calculate the size of:

i angle K **ii** angle L.

e In triangle MNO, angle $M = 90°$, $NO = 29.8$ cm and $MN = 20.6$ cm.
Calculate:

i angle N **ii** angle O **iii** MO.

f In triangle PQR, angle $Q = 90°$, $PQ = 57.3$ mm and $QR = 45.1$ mm.
Calculate:

i angle P **ii** angle R **iii** PR.

Find answers at: cambridge.org/ukschools/gcsemaths-studentbookanswers

Section 2: Exact values of trigonometric ratios

When you work out trigonometric ratios on your calculator you often get approximate (or truncated) values.

If left as fractions (or sometimes as square roots) then these ratios are said to be expressed **exactly**.

You need to know the exact values of the sin, cos and tan ratios for the angles 0°, 30°, 60° and 45°, as well as the values of sin and cos for 90°. There is no tan ratio for 90°.

Sine, cosine and tangent ratios for 30° and 60°

An equilateral triangle has all angles equal to 60°. Dividing the triangle in half gives two right-angled triangles, each with one 30° angle and one 60° angle.

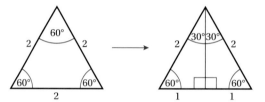

Using Pythagoras' theorem you can find the height h of the right-angled triangle.

$$2^2 = 1^2 + h^2$$

$$4 = 1 + h^2$$

$$h^2 = 3 \quad \text{so} \quad h = \sqrt{3}$$

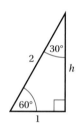

You cannot write the square root of 3 as an exact decimal number, so leave it in surd form. This right-angled triangle with angles of 30° and 60° can be used to work out the values of the trig ratios for these angles.

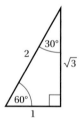

$$\sin 30° = \frac{\text{opposite}}{\text{hypotenuse}} = \frac{1}{2} \qquad\qquad \sin 60° = \frac{\text{opposite}}{\text{hypotenuse}} = \frac{\sqrt{3}}{2}$$

$$\cos 30° = \frac{\text{adjacent}}{\text{hypotenuse}} = \frac{\sqrt{3}}{2} \qquad\qquad \cos 60° = \frac{\text{adjacent}}{\text{hypotenuse}} = \frac{1}{2}$$

$$\tan 30° = \frac{\text{opposite}}{\text{adjacent}} = \frac{1}{\sqrt{3}} \qquad\qquad \tan 60° = \frac{\text{opposite}}{\text{adjacent}} = \frac{\sqrt{3}}{1} = \sqrt{3}$$

Sine, cosine and tangent ratios for 45°

The diagram below shows a right-angled isosceles triangle with equal sides, 1 cm long.

The hypotenuse is $\sqrt{2}$ cm long.

The acute angles are both 45°.

$\sin 45° = \dfrac{\text{opposite}}{\text{hypotenuse}} = \dfrac{1}{\sqrt{2}}$

$\cos 45° = \dfrac{\text{adjacent}}{\text{hypotenuse}} = \dfrac{1}{\sqrt{2}}$

$\tan 45° = \dfrac{\text{opposite}}{\text{adjacent}} = \dfrac{1}{1} = 1$

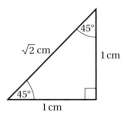

You will find the exact values of the ratios for 0° and 90° as part of the next exercise.

EXERCISE 33C

1 Copy this table and complete it. Use it to help you memorise the exact values of the trigonometric ratios for the different angles.

Angle θ	$\sin \theta$	$\cos \theta$	$\tan \theta$
0°			
30°			
45°			
60°			
90°			$\tan 90°$ is undefined

2 Without using your calculator, find:

a $\sin 30° + \cos 60°$ **b** $\sin 45° + \cos 45°$ **c** $\cos 30° + \sin 60°$.

d Explain your results with reference to complementary angles.

3 Find the exact value of the letters in each triangle.

a

b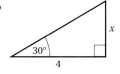

c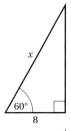

d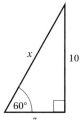

e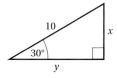

f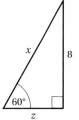

Find answers at: cambridge.org/ukschools/gcsemaths-studentbookanswers

Section 3: The sine, cosine and area rules

So far you have worked only with right-angled triangles. However, trigonometry can be used to solve any triangle. There are two important formulae for finding lengths and angles in any triangle: the sine rule and the cosine rule.

The sine rule

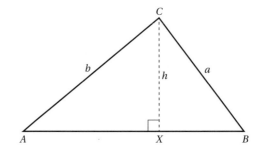

> **Tip**
>
> The sine rule works for right-angled triangles too, but SOH-CAH-TOA is quicker to use.

In triangle CAX the sine of the base angle at $A = \dfrac{h}{b}$

Rearranged, this becomes $h = b \sin A$

In triangle CBX the sine of base angle at $B = \dfrac{h}{a}$

Rearranged, this becomes $h = a \sin B$

Since h is the same value for both triangles, $b \sin A = a \sin B$

This can be rearranged to:

$$\frac{a}{\sin A} = \frac{b}{\sin B} = \frac{c}{\sin C}$$

This is the sine rule.

This rule means that any side of the triangle divided by the sine of its opposite angle is equal to any other side divided by the sine of its opposite angle. So, the rule actually shows three possible relationships.

This version of the sine rule, with the sine ratios as the denominator, is usually used to calculate lengths.

> **Tip**
>
> The sine rule is used when you are dealing with pairs of opposite sides and angles.

You can invert the ratios to calculate the size of unknown angles:

$$\frac{\sin A}{a} = \frac{\sin B}{b} = \frac{\sin C}{c}$$

WORKED EXAMPLE 6

Calculate length AB. Give your answer correct to 1 decimal place.

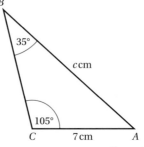

Continues on next page …

$$\frac{b}{\sin B} = \frac{c}{\sin C}$$

Choose the pair of ratios for what you know and what you want.

$$\frac{7}{\sin 35°} = \frac{c}{\sin 105°}$$

$$\frac{7 \times \sin 105°}{\sin 35°} = c$$

$$c = 11.788...$$

$$c = 11.8 \text{ cm}$$

WORKED EXAMPLE 7

Find the size of angle θ correct to the nearest degree.

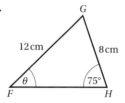

$$\frac{\sin F}{f} = \frac{\sin H}{h}$$

Choose the angle form of the sine rule. Use the letters given in the diagram.

$$\frac{\sin \theta}{8} = \frac{\sin 75°}{12}$$

$$\sin \theta = \frac{8 \sin 75°}{12} = 0.64395...$$

$$\therefore \theta = 40° \text{ (to the nearest degree)}$$

Use $\sin^{-1}$ to find the angle.

EXERCISE 33D

1 Find the value of x in each of the following equations.

a $\dfrac{x}{\sin 50°} = \dfrac{9}{\sin 38°}$ **b** $\dfrac{x}{\sin 25°} = \dfrac{20}{\sin 100°}$ **c** $\dfrac{20.6}{\sin 50°} = \dfrac{x}{\sin 70°}$

2 Find the length of the side marked x in each triangle.

a

b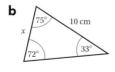

c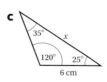

d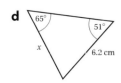

e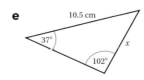

f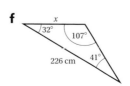

3 Find the size of the angle marked θ in each triangle. Give your answers correct to 1 decimal place.

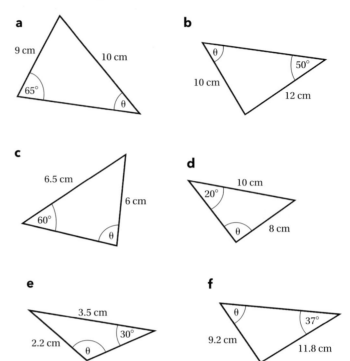

4 In triangle *XYZ*, angle *X* = 40°, side *XZ* = 12 cm and side *YZ* = 15 cm.

  a Explain why angle *Y* must be less than 40°.

  b Calculate the size of angle *Y* and angle *Z*.

  c Determine the length of side *XY*.

5 *ABCD* is a parallelogram with *AB* = 32 mm and *AD* = 40 mm. Angle *BAC* = 77°.

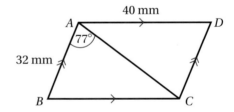

  a Find the size of angle *BCA* to the nearest degree.

  b Find the size of *ABC* to the nearest degree.

  c What is the length of the diagonal *AC* in this figure? Give your answer correct to 2 decimal places.

The cosine rule

You can use the sine rule when you know the size of an angle and the length of the side opposite the angle. If you do not have this information, you may be able to use another formula called the cosine rule.

The cosine rule is based on Pythagoras' theorem and it applies to any triangle.

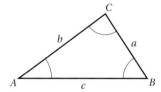

The cosine rule states that:

$$a^2 = b^2 + c^2 - 2bc \cos A$$

Notice that all three sides are used in the cosine rule but only one angle.

The side whose square is used as the subject of the formula is opposite the known angle. This form of the cosine rule is used to find unknown sides.

The formula can be rearranged to make the square of any side the subject.

$$b^2 = a^2 + c^2 - 2ac \cos B \quad c^2 = a^2 + b^2 - 2ab \cos C$$

You can also make the cosine ratio the subject of the formula in order to calculate unknown angles.

WORKED EXAMPLE 8

In triangle ABC, angle $B = 50°$, $AB = 9$ cm and $BC = 18$ cm.

Find the length of AC correct to 3 significant figures.

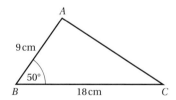

$b^2 = 9^2 + 18^2 - (2 \times 9 \times 18 \times \cos 50°)$
$b^2 = 81 + 324 - (208.2631\ldots)$
$b^2 = 196.7368\ldots$
$\therefore b = \sqrt{196.7368\ldots}$
$b = 14.0262\ldots$

$AC = 14.0$ cm (3 significant figures)

$AC = b$ and you know that $B = 50°$, so use the cosine rule in the form:
$b^2 = a^2 + c^2 - 2ac \cos B$

WORKED EXAMPLE 9

Calculate the size of angle C. Give your answer correct to 1 decimal place.

$a^2 + b^2 - 2ab \cos C = c^2$
$9^2 + 5^2 - 2 \times 9 \times 5 \cos C = 64$
$81 + 25 - 90 \cos C = 64$
$106 - 64 - 90 \cos C = 0$
$42 - 90 \cos C = 0$
$42 = 90 \cos C$
$\dfrac{42}{90} = \cos C$
$\therefore C = \cos^{-1}\left(\dfrac{42}{90}\right) = 62.181\ldots$
angle $C = 62.2°$

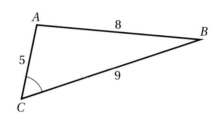

EXERCISE 33E

1 Find the size of the side marked x in each triangle. Give answers correct to 3 significant figures.

a

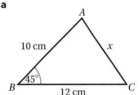

b

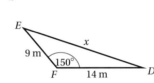

2 In triangle PQR, side $PQ = 11$ cm, side $QR = 9$ cm and side $RP = 8$ cm. Find the size of angle RPQ giving your answer correct to 3 significant figures.

3 In triangle STU, angle $S = 95°$, $ST = 10$ m and $SU = 15$ m.

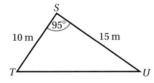

a Calculate the length of TU.

b Find the size of angles U and T.

4 Determine the size of each angle in this triangle.

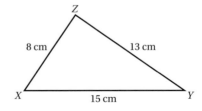

5 A boat sails in a straight line from Aardvark Island on a bearing of 060°. When the boat has sailed 8 km it reaches Beaver Island and it turns to sail on a bearing of 160°. The boat remains on this bearing until it reaches Crow Island, 12 km from Beaver Island. From Crow Island, the boat sails directly back to Aardvark Island.

Calculate:

a the length of the return journey

b the bearing on which the boat must sail to return directly to Aardvark Island.

The area rule

You already know that the area of a triangle can be found using the formula

$$A = \frac{1}{2}bh$$

If you do not know the length of the base or the perpendicular height, you can calculate the area of any triangle using trigonometry.

Look at triangle *ABC*.

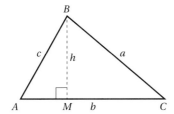

The perpendicular height (*h*) creates a right-angled triangle *BMC*.

In triangle *BMC*, the height (*h*) is the side opposite angle C and the hypotenuse is side *a*.

Using the sine ratio, $\sin C = \frac{h}{a}$, so $h = a \sin C$.

This means that you have a way of determining the perpendicular height (whether it is drawn in the triangle or not) and you can use it with the base length to find the area.

$$\text{area} = \frac{1}{2} \times \text{base} \times \text{height}$$

$$= \frac{1}{2}b \times a \sin C$$

This gives a formula for finding the area of any triangle.

To use the area formula you need two sides and their included angle.

When you find the area of a triangle, you can use any side as the base. This means that the formula can be rearranged to suit the information you have.

$$\text{area} = \frac{1}{2}ac \sin B \qquad \text{area} = \frac{1}{2}bc \sin A$$

Learn this formula

$$\text{Area} = \frac{1}{2}ab \sin C$$

Find answers at: cambridge.org/ukschools/gcsemaths-studentbookanswers

Problem-solving framework

1 Calculate the area of triangle ABC, to 2 decimal places, if angle $A = 48°$, $c = 5$ cm and $b = 7$ cm.

Steps for solving problems	What you would do for this example
Step 1: What information have you been given?	You have been given the measurements of two sides and the included angle and so you can use the area rule.
Step 2: Draw a diagram to show the information.	 ![triangle ABC with B at top, c=5, angle 48° at A, b=7 at base from A to C]
Step 3: Choose the formula and write it down correctly.	Since you are given the size of angle A, use the formula: area of triangle $ABC = \dfrac{1}{2}bc \sin A$
Step 4: Do the calculation.	$= \dfrac{1}{2} \times 7 \times 5 \sin 48°$ $= 13.0 \text{ cm}^2$
Step 5: Check the answer.	

WORKED EXAMPLE 10

In triangle PQR, angle $P = 125°$, $q = 48.1$ cm and $r = 32.7$ cm.

Determine the area of the triangle, correct to 2 decimal places.

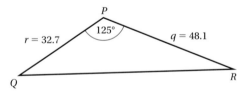

Area PQR $= \dfrac{1}{2}qr \sin P$

> Use this version as you know the size of angle P.

$= \dfrac{1}{2} \times 48.1 \times 32.7 \times \sin 125°$

$= 644.21 \text{ cm}^2$

EXERCISE 33F

1 Calculate the area of each triangle. Give your answers correct to 2 decimal places.

a

b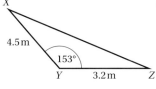

c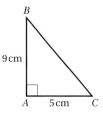

d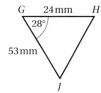

e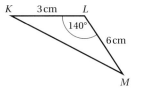

f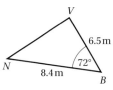

2 Calculate the area of each triangle ABC with the following measurements.

a $a = 3$ cm, $b = 6$ cm and angle $C = 65°$

b $b = 5.2$ cm, $c = 7.7$ cm and angle $A = 105°$

c $a = 6.1$ cm, $c = 5.3$ cm and angle $B = 98°$

d $b = 8$ cm, $c = 12$ cm and angle $A = 39°$.

3 Triangle XYZ has an area of 50 cm^2.

Calculate the length of XZ.

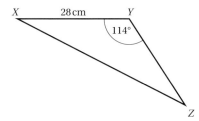

Section 4: Using trigonometry to solve problems

The trigonometric ratios together with the sine, cosine and area rules can be applied to many different types of measurement problems in both two- and three-dimensional figures.

If trigonometry problems do not include a sketch, it is useful to draw one. Make it large and clear and mark what you know on it. This will help you to identify the correct ratio or rule to use to solve the problem.

Angles of elevation and depression

Many trigonometry problems involve lines of sight.

Problems that involve looking up to an object can be described in terms of an **angle of elevation**. This is the angle between an observer's line of sight and a horizontal line.

 Key vocabulary

angle of elevation: when looking up, the angle between the line of sight and the horizontal.

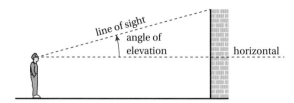

When an observer is looking down, the **angle of depression** is the angle between the observer's line of sight and a horizontal line.

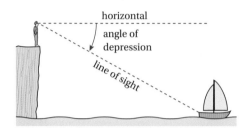

WORKED EXAMPLE 11

From the top of a lighthouse 105 m above sea level, the angle of depression of a boat is 5°.

How far is the boat from the shore? Give the answer to the nearest metre.

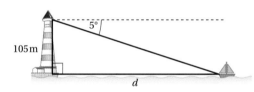

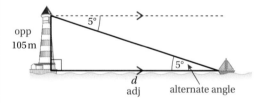

Mark on the diagram what you know.

The angle of depression is alternate to the angle of elevation from the boat.

Choose the correct trigonometric ratio.

d is the side adjacent to 5° and the height to the lighthouse is opposite.

You need the ratio with OA, which is TOA.

$$\tan 5° = \frac{105}{d}$$

$$\tan 5° \times d = 105$$

$$d = \frac{105}{\tan 5°} = 1200.155492$$

$$d = 1200 \text{ m}$$

Problem-solving framework

A ship is laying cable along the sea bed.

The angle of the cable to the sea bed is 40° and the length of cable to the sea bed is 40 metres.

The ship is 50 miles offshore and travelling northwest.

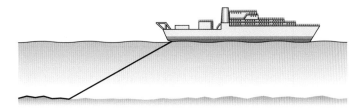

What is the depth of the seabed?

Steps for solving problems	What you would do for this example
Step 1: What have you got to do?	Use Pythagoras' theorem or trigonometry to find the depth of water.
Step 2: What information do you need?	Angle 40° and length of cable as the hypotenuse is 40 m.
Step 3: What information don't you need?	50 miles offshore and the direction of travel.
Step 4: What maths can you do?	Use a right-angled triangle. Cannot use Pythagoras as you do not know two lengths, so use trig. Decide which trigonometry function – sin, cos or tan? One angle and the hypotenuse are known – need to find the opposite length. $\sin 40° = \dfrac{\text{opp}}{\text{hyp}} = \dfrac{\text{opp}}{40}$ $\sin 40° \times 40 = \text{opposite length} = 25.7 \text{ m}$
Step 5: Have you done it all?	Yes
Step 6: Is it correct?	Yes – double-checked and estimated. The length must be less than 40 m. $\sin 30° = 0.5$ so half of 40 m would be 20 m.

Three-dimensional problems

To solve problems related to three-dimensional objects you need to visualise two different flat planes and how they meet at right angles. Then you think of the problem in terms of 2D triangles. One of the 2D triangles will give you the information you need to solve the other.

Tip

It often helps to sketch the 2D triangles from a 3D problem. Then solve each triangle in turn.

WORKED EXAMPLE 12

The diagram shows a door wedge with a rectangular horizontal base *PQRS*.

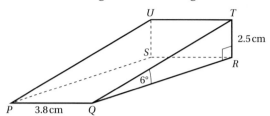

The sloping face *PQTU* is also rectangular. *PQ* = 3.8 cm and angle *TQR* = 6°.

The height TR is 2.5 cm.

What is the length of the diagonal *PT*?

$$\sin 6° = \frac{2.5}{QT}$$

Using trigonometry in triangle *TQR*.

$$QT = \frac{2.5}{\sin 6°} = 23.9169... \text{ cm}$$

Keep the full value in your calculator and use that for the next step.

$$PQ^2 + QT^2 = PT^2$$
$$3.8^2 + 23.9169...^2 = PT^2$$
$$14.44 + 572.0195... = PT^2$$
$$586.45695... = PT^2$$
$$PT = \sqrt{586.45695...}$$
$$= 24.2 \text{ cm}$$

Using Pythagoras' theorem for triangle *PQT*.

Round the final answer to 1 decimal place.

EXERCISE 33G

1 A child's playground slide is 4.2 m long and makes an angle of 33° with the horizontal.

Calculate the height of the slide.

2 Carol is in a hot air balloon at point *C* in the sky. *CG* is the vertical height of the hot air balloon above the ground. David is standing on the ground at point *D*. The distance between points *D* and *G* is 27 m. The angle of elevation from David to the hot air balloon is 53°.

Calculate the height, *CG*.

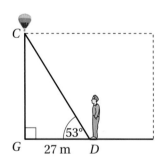

3 Two boats are sailing out at sea a distance of 25 m apart. The angle of depression from the top of a lighthouse to one boat is 35° and to the other boat is 55°. How tall is the lighthouse?

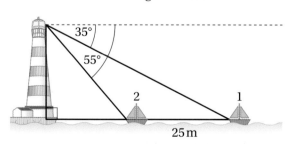

4 Mike is standing 15 m away from a flagpole. His eye level is 1.6 m above the ground. The angle of elevation from his line of sight to the top of the flagpole is 60°.

  a How tall is the flagpole?

  b If he moves another 10 m further away from the flagpole, how will the angle of elevation to the top of the flagpole change?

5 Two observers in different positions at *A* and *B* are watching a rare bird on a tree at *C*. The angle of elevation from *A* to *C* is 56° and the angle of elevation from *B* to *C* is 25°.

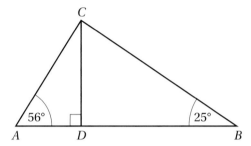

  a If person *B* is standing 15 m from *D* (the base of the tree), calculate the height of the bird above the ground (the length of *CD*).

  b Calculate the distance of person *A* from *D*.

6 A person is standing at a point *P*, 30 m away from a signal tower for a mobile phone operator. The angle of depression from the top of the tower to *P* is 56°.

Calculate the height of the tower.

7 A tree surgeon uses an instrument to measure that the angle of elevation from her line of sight to the top of a tree is 20°. She is standing 10 m away from the tree. Her eye level is 1.5 m above the ground.

  a If she assumes that the tree is perfectly perpendicular to the ground, how would she calculate the height of the tree?

  b To check her calculation, she moves another 10 m away from the tree in a straight line along flat ground, and measures the angle of elevation again. What should the angle measurement be now if her first measurement and calculation were correct?

8 The sketch represents a field *PQRS* on level ground. The sides *PQ* and *SR* run due east.

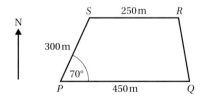

  a Determine the bearing of *S* from *P*.

  b Calculate the shortest distance between *SR* and *PQ*.

  c Calculate the area of the field in square metres.

Find answers at: cambridge.org/ukschools/gcsemaths-studentbookanswers

9 Find the area of a regular pentagon with sides $2a$ metres long.

10 The diagram represents a room in the shape of a cuboid.
$AB = 6\,m$, $AD = 4\,m$ and $AP = 2\,m$.

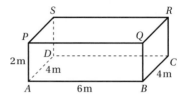

Calculate the angle between the diagonal BS and the floor $ABCD$.

11 $ABCDE$ is a square-based pyramid. $AB = BC = CD = AD = 5.6\,cm$. N is the centre of the square $ABCD$. E is directly above N.

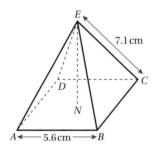

a Calculate the distance BD.

b Calculate angle EBN.

12 The Great Pyramid at Giza in Egypt has a square base with sides of $232.6\,m$ long.

The distance from the top of the pyramid to each corner of the base was originally $221.2\,m$.

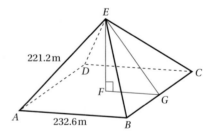

a Determine the angle each face makes with the base.

b Determine the size of the apex angle of an edge of the pyramid (angle BEF).

Checklist of learning and understanding

Trigonometric ratios

- In a right-angled triangle, the longest side is the hypotenuse. For a given angle θ, the other two sides can be labelled opposite (to angle θ) and adjacent (to angle θ).

- The sine, cosine and tangent ratios can be used to find unknown sides and angles in right-angled triangles.

   o $\sin \theta = \dfrac{\text{opposite}}{\text{hypotenuse}}$

   o $\cos \theta = \dfrac{\text{adjacent}}{\text{hypotenuse}}$

   o $\tan \theta = \dfrac{\text{opposite}}{\text{adjacent}}$

- You can find the value of a ratio using the sin, cos and tan buttons on your calculator. To find the size of an angle, use the inverse functions.

Exact values

- You can find the exact values of sin, cos and tan for special angles. Some exact values contain square roots.

Sine, cosine and area rules

- The sine and cosine rules can be used to calculate unknown sides and angles in triangles that are not right-angled.

- The sine rule is used for calculating an angle from another angle and two sides, or a side from another side and two known angles. The sides and angles must be arranged in opposite pairs.

- The cosine rule is used for calculating an angle from three known sides, or a side from a known angle and two known sides.

- You can calculate the area of any triangle by using the sine ratio (the area rule).

Chapter review

For additional questions on the topics in this chapter, visit GCSE Mathematics Online.

1 The diagram shows a triangle ABC. Angle $A = 20°$ and angle $C = 90°$; $AB = 32\,\text{m}$.

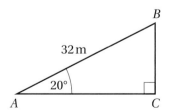

Calculate the height BC.

Find answers at: cambridge.org/ukschools/gcsemaths-studentbookanswers

2 A ladder leans against the side of a house. The ladder is 4.5 m in length, and makes an angle of 74° with the ground.

How high up the wall will it reach? (This length is marked x in the diagram.)

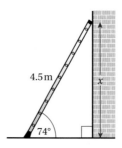

Not drawn accurately

3 The same ladder is now placed 0.9 m away from the side of the house.

What angle does the ladder now make with the ground? (This angle is marked y in the diagram.)

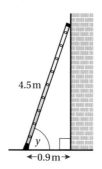

Not drawn accurately

4 Triangles ABC and PQR are similar. $AC = 3.2$ cm, $AB = 4$ cm and $PR = 4.8$ cm.

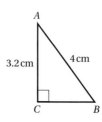 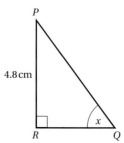

Explain why $\sin x = 0.8$

5 What would be the round trip starting at point A all the way round, to the nearest mile?

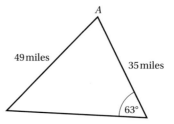

6 Determine the length, correct to 1 decimal place, of a side of an equilateral triangle with an area of 24 cm².

7 If the area of triangle *FGH* is 804 cm², with *FG* = 43.2 cm and *GH* = 38.7 cm, calculate two possible values for angle *G*, correct to 1 decimal place.

8 If the area of triangle *ABC* is 18 cm², with angle *B* = 30° and *AB* = 8 cm, calculate the length of *BC*.

9 *ABC* is a triangle.

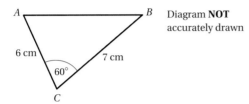

Diagram **NOT** accurately drawn

a Work out the area of triangle *ABC*.

Give your answer correct to 3 significant figures. *(2 marks)*

b Work out the length of the side *AB*. *(3 marks)*

Give your answer correct to 3 significant figures.

©Pearson Education Ltd 2013

10 In triangle *OAB*, angle *AOB* = 15°, *OA* = 3m and *OB* = 8 m. Calculate:

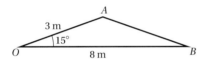

a the length of *AB*

b the area of triangle *OAB*.

11 A cuboid is 15 cm long, 5 cm wide and 3 cm high. Calculate:

a the length of the diagonal on its base

b the length of its longest diagonal

c the angle between the base and the longest diagonal.

34 Growth and decay

In this chapter you will learn how to ...

- solve problems involving depreciation and decay. including simple and compound interest.
- express exponential growth or decay as a formula.

For more resources relating to this chapter, visit GCSE Mathematics Online.

Using mathematics: real-life applications

Many real-life situations involve growth (increase) or decay (decrease) as time passes. Population numbers, growth of bacteria, disease infection rates, world temperature patterns and the value of money or possessions may all increase or decrease over time.

"My computer program calculates interest on a daily basis. This means whatever is in the account gains interest, not just the initial investment."   *(Investment broker)*

Before you start …

Chs 7 and 19	You must be able to convert percentages to decimals.	**1** Write each of the following as a decimal: **a** 5% **b** 190% **c** 0.4% **d** 12.5%
Ch 19	You must be able to increase or decrease a quantity by a given percentage by multiplying by a suitable decimal.	**2** Carry out the following increases and decreases using only multiplication: **a** Increase $44 by 22% **b** Increase £35 by 5.5% **c** Decrease £13 by 44% **d** Decrease $170 by 8%
Ch 25	You should remember how to plot and interpret functions in the form of $y = ab^x$.	**3** The graph shows the growth rate of bacteria in cheese. **a** How many bacteria were there to start with? **b** What happens to the number of bacteria each hour? **4** The function for this graph is $n = 100(b)^t$, where n is the number of bacteria and t is the time period in hours. **a** Where does the constant value of 100 come from? **b** Why is $b = 2$?

Assess your starting point using the Launchpad

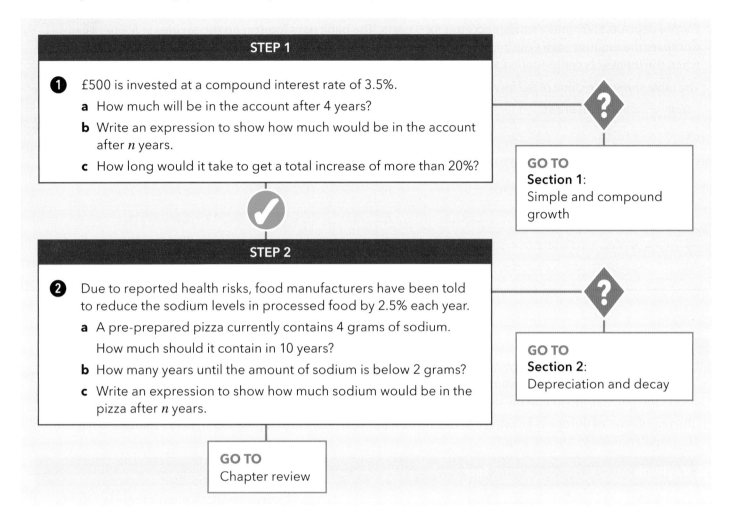

STEP 1

1 £500 is invested at a compound interest rate of 3.5%.

   a How much will be in the account after 4 years?

   b Write an expression to show how much would be in the account after n years.

   c How long would it take to get a total increase of more than 20%?

GO TO
Section 1:
Simple and compound growth

STEP 2

2 Due to reported health risks, food manufacturers have been told to reduce the sodium levels in processed food by 2.5% each year.

   a A pre-prepared pizza currently contains 4 grams of sodium. How much should it contain in 10 years?

   b How many years until the amount of sodium is below 2 grams?

   c Write an expression to show how much sodium would be in the pizza after n years.

GO TO
Section 2:
Depreciation and decay

GO TO
Chapter review

Section 1: Simple and compound growth

Simple interest

When you borrow money, or buy things on credit, you are normally charged interest for the use of the money. When you invest or save money, you are paid interest by the bank or other institution in return for leaving your money with them.

The amount of money you invest or borrow is called the principal (P).

Simple interest (I) is interest paid on the original principal. The same interest is paid for each time period (T). The rate of interest (R) is given as a percentage.

Simple interest can be worked out using a formula:

$I = PRT$

Compound interest

When using compound interest, the interest earned in the first time period is added to the principal so in the next time period you calculate the interest on the principal amount plus any interest that has been added to it.

Tip

The total simple interest could be found using the formula:
$I = PRT$
$= 500 \times 0.05 \times 6 = 150$
So, final value $= 500 + 150 = £650$

Find answers at: cambridge.org/ukschools/gcsemaths-studentbookanswers

WORKED EXAMPLE 1

Fatima deposits £500 into a savings account for 6 years. The bank pays interest on the savings at 5% per year. Compare the amount each year for 6 years when the interest is calculated using simple interest to the amount when the interest is compounded annually.

The table shows the value of the investment over the 6 years when using both simple interest and compound interest.

Year	Simple interest	Compound interest
1	£500 + 5% = £525	£500 + 5% = £525
2	£525 + (5% of £500) = £550	£525 + (5% of £525) = £551.25
3	£550 + (5% of £500) = £575	£551.25 + (5% of £551.25) = £578.81
4	£575 + (5% of £500) = £600	£578.81 + (5% of £578.81) = £607.75...
5	£600 + (5% of £500) = £625	£607.75... + (5% of £607.75...) = £638.14...
6	£625 + (5% of £500) = £650	£638.14... + (5% of £638.14...) = £670.04...

WORK IT OUT 34.1

Three students attempt the question below. In pairs, decide who has got not only the correct answer but also the most efficient method to find the answer.

The population of Europe is growing at a rate of 0.2% per year. The current population is 739 million. What will the population be in 3 years' time?

Kayleigh	Tom	Zac
Find 0.2%:	Year 1:	Increase by 0.2% means there is 100.2%, do this three times in a row.
0.2% of 739 000 000	Find 0.2% of 739 000 000	$739\,000\,000 \times 1.002 \times 1.002 \times 1.002$
$= 0.002 \times 739\,000\,000$	$= 0.002 \times 739\,000\,000$	$= 739\,000\,000 \times 1.002^3$
$= 1\,478\,000$	$= 1\,478\,000$	$= 743\,442\,874$
The same growth for 3 years:	Add it on: 740 478 000	
$3 \times 1\,478\,000 = 4\,434\,000$	Year 2:	
Add it on:	Find 0.2% of 740 478 000	
$739\,000\,000 + 4\,434\,000$	$= 0.002 \times 740\,478\,000$	
$= 743\,434\,000$	$= 1\,480\,956$	
	Add it on: 741 958 956	
	Year 3:	
	Find 0.2% and add it on	
	1 483 918 + 741 958 956	
	$= 743\,442\,874$	

Working with compound interest and growth rates is very much like working with function machines. Each time an output is produced it goes back to becoming an input and the process is repeated. This keeps going for the allotted period of time. This kind of process is called iterative – it iterates or repeats.

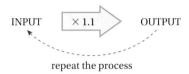

repeat the process

WORKED EXAMPLE 2

The population of starlings in a park increases at a rate of 10% per year. If the population started with 80 starlings, how many would there be in 5 years' time?

$80 \times 1.1 = 88$

The first input would be 80.

To increase a quantity by 10%, you multiply by 1.1

$88 \times 1.1 = 96.8$

Use the output from year 1 as the input for year 2.

(Notice that if you stop here, you would round sensibly. However, you use the unrounded value in the next stage and only round at the end.)

$96.8 \times 1.1 = 106.48$
$106.48 \times 1.1 = 117.128$
$117.128 \times 1.1 = 128.8408$
≈ 129 starlings in 5 years' time.

Instead of rewriting the output each time, this could be written as:

$80 \times 1.1 \times 1.1 \times 1.1 \times 1.1 \times 1.1$ or $80 \times 1.1^5 = 128.8408$.

This can be generalised for n years as 80×1.1^n.

Exponential growth

When a quantity increases (grows) in a fixed proportion (normally a percentage) at regular intervals the growth is said to be exponential.

You should remember from Chapter 25 that increasing exponential functions produce curved graphs that slope steeply up to the right. The general function for these graphs is $y = ka^x$, where $k > 0$ and $a > 1$.

This function can be used to express compound growth as a formula:

$y = a(1 + r)^n$

where a is the principal (original value),

r is the growth rate (expressed as a decimal),

and n is the number of time periods.

WORKED EXAMPLE 3

£100 is invested subject to compound interest at a rate of 8% per annum. Find the value of the investment after a period of 15 years.

$\text{Value} = a(1 + r)^n$
$\quad\quad = 100(1.08)^{15}$
$\quad\quad = 317.2169114$
Value is £317.22 (correct to the nearest pence).

EXERCISE 34A

1 £300 is invested for 3 years with interest compounded annually at a rate of 2%. How much is in the account after:

   a 1 year   **b** 3 years   **c** 8 years   **d** n years?

2 Copy and complete this table. The interest is compounded annually.

Investment	Interest rate	1 year	2 years	$5\frac{1}{2}$ years	n years
£250	2%				
£1500	4.5%				
	3%	£51.50			

3 £1000 is invested subject to compound interest at a rate of 3% per annum.

Plot a graph showing how much money is in the account over the first 10 years of the investment.

4 A colony of bacteria grows by 4% every hour. At first the colony has 100 bacteria.

   a How many bacteria will there be after 24 hours if the colony grows at this rate?

   b Write a formula to calculate the number of bacteria after n hours.

5 The population of Ireland is growing at an annual rate of 1.7%. In 2014 the population was 4.6 million.

   a If this growth rate remains constant, what will the population of Ireland be in 2024?

   b How many more people is this?

   c Using this model, determine how many people lived in Ireland in 2012? Comment on the likely validity of your answers.

6 The Bank of England's target inflation rate is 2%. This tells you how much the cost of living, food, fuel and rent is likely to go up each year. In 1999 a month's rent was assumed to be £450.

   a Assuming that the target is met, how much is this likely to be 20 years later in 2018?

   b What will rent be in n years' time?

7 Gavin is saving for a new bike. The model he wants costs £255. So far he has saved £200. Gavin's dad has offered to pay him 8% interest on the total of his saving for every month that Gavin does his homework, cleans his room and loads the dishwasher.

How long is he going to have to wait for the bike? Show clear working to explain your answer.

8 Population growth models help predict the spread of invasive species. Zebra mussels are one such species. Their population can increase by 1900% each year. Two mussels are found in a fresh water lake.

Should biologists be worried that this will have a significant impact over the next 10 years? Give details to explain your response.

9 Two investors are having an argument. They want to maximise their profit. They are investing for 5 years and have a choice. They can either have 6% simple interest or 5.5% compound.

   a Which should they choose?

   b Would their answer change if they were investing for 4 years?

10 Copy and complete this table:

Investment	Rate	1 year	2 years	3 years	n years
					$\$600 \times 1.015^{n}$
£500		£530			
$6000			$7260		
£750				£1296	

11 Jenny is saving for her first car. She needs a deposit of £2775. Each month she saves £200 in an account offering 1% interest a month.

   a Will Jenny have enough money after a year to buy a car?

   b If not, how much extra money does she need?

   c How many more months will this take her to save?

Find answers at: cambridge.org/ukschools/gcsemaths-studentbookanswers

12 Between 1980 and 2010 the price of a chocolate bar went from 25p to 65p.

   a By what percentage did the cost rise overall?

   b What annual percentage increase is this?

   c If the cost of the bar keeps going at the same rate, how much will it cost in 2040?

   d If the cost of the bar keeps going at the same rate, how much will it cost in 2070?

   e When will the chocolate bar first cost more than £1?

13 $100 000 is invested at a rate of 5% for 10 years.

   a How much more money is earned using compound interest compared to simple interest?

   b What simple interest rate would be needed to achieve the same earnings?

14 House prices are rising. A two-bedroomed house cost £195 000 last year and now costs £216 450.

   If the price keeps rising at the same rate, how much will this house cost in 3 years' time?

15 Which of the following investment models gives the highest earnings?

Model 1	Model 2	Model 3
Year 1: 5% interest	Years 1–3	Years 1–3
Year 2: 4% interest	4% compound interest	3.9% simple interest
Year 3: 3% interest		

16 A colony of bacteria grows by 5% every hour.

   How long does it take for the colony to double in size?

Key vocabulary

depreciation: the loss in value of an object over a period of time.

Section 2: Depreciation and decay

When the value of something goes down, you say it has depreciated. For example, a new car will show a **depreciation** in value of about 30% in the first year of ownership alone.

WORKED EXAMPLE 4

A new computer depreciates by 30% per year. If it cost £1200 new, what will it be worth in 2 years' time?

Method 1	Method 2

Value after 1 year = £1200 – (30% of £1200)
          = £1200 – £360
          = £840
	Value after 1 year = 70% of £1200 = £840
	Value after 2 years = 70% of £840 = £588

Value after 2 years = £840 – (30% of £840)
          = £840 – £252
          = £588	

When the number of items in a population declines over time, or a physical measure such as atmospheric pressure declines over a distance, is called **decay** rather than depreciation.

For example, if the population of squirrels is in decay, it means that each year there are fewer and fewer animals in the population. If the rate of decline is 10%, each year 10% of the squirrels disappear, leaving 90%. So from one year to the next the number of animals is $n \times 0.9$.

Key vocabulary

decay: the reduction in a quantity over time or some other measure such as distance. The opposite of growth.

WORK IT OUT 34.2

Three students attempt the question below. In pairs, decide who has got not only the correct answer but also the most efficient method to find the answer.

For every 1000 metres you climb, the atmospheric pressure decreases by 12% of the sea-level value. If the sea-level atmospheric pressure is 100 300 pascal (Pa), what would the pressure be for a skydiver at an altitude of 4000 metres?

Belle	Jordan	Ethan
12% of 100 300	Decrease by 12% leaves 88%	Decrease by 12% leaves 88%, do this four times in a row.
$= 0.12 \times 100\,300$	88% of 100 300	$100\,300 \times 0.88 \times 0.88 \times 0.88 \times 0.88$
$= 12\,036$	$= 0.88 \times 100\,300$	$= 100\,300 \times 0.88^4$
$4 \times 12\,036 = 48\,144$	$= 88\,264$	$= 60\,149.444\,608\,\text{Pa}$
$100\,300 - 48\,144$	88% of 88 264	$= 60\,149.4\,\text{Pa}$ (1 d.p.)
$= 52\,156\,\text{Pa}$	$= 77\,672.32$	
	88% of 77 672.32	
	$= 68\,351.6416$	
	88% of 68 351.6416	
	$= 60\,149.444\,608\,\text{Pa}$	

Exponential decay

When a quantity decreases by a fixed percentage over regular periods of time it is called exponential decay. The graph of exponential decay is a curve that slopes down steeply towards the right.

The general function of such decreasing exponential graphs is $y = ka^x$, where $k > 0$ and $0 < a < 1$.

The general formula for exponential decay is therefore:

$y = a(1 - r)^n$

where a is the original value/quantity,

   r is the rate of decay (as a decimal),

and n is the number of time periods.

EXERCISE 34B

1   A car depreciates in value each year by 8%. A new Compact car costs £11 000. How much will this be worth in:

   a 1 year   **b** 3 years   **c** 8 years   **d** n years?

 Find answers at: cambridge.org/ukschools/gcsemaths-studentbookanswers

2 Copy and complete this table:

Initial cost	Depreciation rate	1 year	2 years	6 years	n years
£400	2%				
£2500	15%				
£50 000	3.5%				

3 The pesticide DDT was banned after being discovered to be dangerous. It remains in the soil for many years. It decays by being absorbed by the soil at a rate of 7% a year.

   a If a farmer used 2 kg of DDT in a field in 1970, how much remains in the field in 2014?

   b Will there ever be 0 g of DDT left in the field? Explain.

4 The rate at which water flows out of a tank with an opening at the bottom depends on the amount of water left in the tank. For one particular tank, every 5 minutes the height of the water left reduces by 15% of its value at the start of the 5-minute period. Which of the following graphs depicts this?

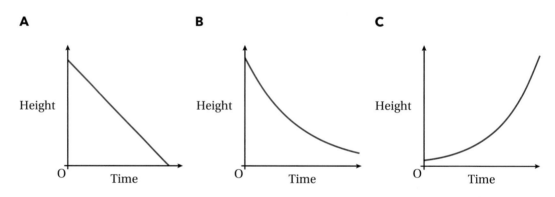

5 At the start of an experiment there are 8000 bacteria. A lethal pathogen is introduced to the population causing a reduction of 1600 in the population in an hour.

   a What percentage decrease in population is this?

   b Assuming the same rate of decrease, how many bacteria would you expect to be alive after 8 hours?

   c How long until fewer than 100 bacteria are alive?

6 For every 1000 m that you climb, the atmospheric pressure decreases by 12% from its sea-level value. If the sea-level atmospheric pressure is 100 300 pascal (Pa), what was the pressure for world record holder Felix Baumgartner, who jumped off a balloon flying 39 km above sea level?

7 The population of Bulgaria is decreasing at a rate of 0.6% per year. In 2014 the population was 7.4 million people.

   a How many people are expected to be living in Bulgaria in 2020?

   b How many years until the population dips below 7 million?

8 Copy and complete this table:

Initial cost	Depreciation rate	1 year	2 years	6 years	n years
					$\$7500 \times 0.925^n$
£650		£617.50			
	11%	$\$30\,260$			
£12 million			£10 267 500		

9 The cost of mobile phones has been falling. Three years ago the latest model cost £400 with no contract; now the latest model costs £342.95.

If the price keeps falling at the same rate, how long until the current model costs less than two-thirds of today's price?

 ## Checklist of learning and understanding

Simple and compound growth

- Simple growth, such as interest, is a fixed rate of growth, calculated on the original amount.

- The formula $I = PRT$ can be used to calculate simple interest.

- Compound growth, such as compound interest, is calculated on the principal for the first period and then compounded by calculating it on the principal plus any interest paid or due for each previous period.

- You can work out compound growth using a multiplier for each period or by applying the formula $y = a(1 + r)^n$.

Depreciation and decay

- A drop in value of an object over time is called depreciation.

- A decline in a population or physical quantity is called decay.

- Simple and compound decay can be found by repeated subtraction, by working out the percentage remaining, or by applying the formula for exponential decay: $y = a(1 - r)^n$.

Chapter review

 For additional questions on the topics in this chapter, visit GCSE Mathematics Online.

1 A camera has a cash price of £850. Nasief buys it on credit and pays a 10% deposit, with the balance to be paid over 2 years at a simple interest rate of 10%. Calculate:

a the amount of his deposit

b the balance owing after deducting the deposit

c the amount of interest paid in total over 2 years

d the monthly payment amount for 24 equal monthly instalments

e the difference between the cash price and what Nasief actually paid in the end.

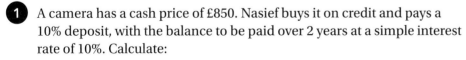 Find answers at: cambridge.org/ukschools/gcsemaths-studentbookanswers

2 Salma invests her money in an account that pays 6% interest compounded half-yearly.

If she puts £2300 in the account and leaves it there for 2 years, how much money will she have at the end of the period?

3 A car valued at £8500 depreciates by 30% in the first year, 20% in the second year and a further 12% in the third year.

How much is it worth after 3 years?

4 Each year the education department arranges a quiz. There are 128 students in the competition to start with. During each round, half of the quiz contestants are eliminated.

How many students will still be participating after round 4?

5 Due to pollution in an estuary, the number of freshwater shrimp is declining. In 2012, it was estimated that there were 15 000 shrimp in the estuary, and in 2013, 14 100.

a What is the percentage depreciation?

b At the same rate, what will the population be in 2020?

c During which year will the population have halved?

6 Here are two schemes for investing £2500 for 2 years.

Scheme A

gives 4% **simple** interest each year.

Scheme B

gives 3.9% **compound** interest each year.

Which scheme gives the most total interest over 2 years?

You must show all your working. *(4 marks)*

©*Pearson Education Ltd 2013*

7 The population of elephants in a natural park in southern Africa increased exponentially from just 40 elephants in 1963 to 640 in 2013 as a result of conservation efforts.

Determine the growth rate *r* of the elephant population.

35 Proportion

In this chapter you will learn how to …

- understand proportion and the equality of ratios.
- solve problems involving direct and inverse proportion, including graphical and algebraic representations.
- understand that x is inversely proportional to y is equivalent to x is proportional to $\frac{1}{y}$.
- interpret equations that describe direct and inverse proportion.

For more resources relating to this chapter, visit GCSE Mathematics Online.

Using mathematics: real-life applications

Proportional reasoning is very common in daily life. You use proportional reasoning when you mix ingredients for a recipe, convert between units of measurement or work out costs per unit. It is an area of maths where you can use many different methods to solve particular problems.

> **Tip**
>
> Review the sections in Chapter 20 on equivalent ratios and fractions to prepare for this chapter.

"I test out new dishes on my family. Then I have to scale up the recipes in proportion so that they taste just as good. Sometimes it may be for just a few people at one table in my restaurant; at other times it may be for a whole room of wedding guests."

(Chef and restaurant owner)

Before you start …

Chs 6 and 11	You need to know how many minutes there are in fractions of an hour.	**1** How many minutes in **a** half an hour? **b** a quarter of an hour? **c** a third of an hour? **d** a fifth of an hour?
Chs 6 and 10	You need to be able to find what fraction of an hour a given time is.	**2** What fraction of an hour is **a** 5 minutes? **b** 24 minutes? **c** 54 minutes?
Chs 5 and 17	You should know how to substitute values into formulae.	**3** $g = 3b$ **a** What is the value of g when $b = 7$? **b** What is the value of b when $g = 72$? **c** What is b when $g = 1.2$?

Find answers at: cambridge.org/ukschools/gcsemaths-studentbookanswers

Assess your starting point using the Launchpad

STEP 1

1
a A recipe for blueberry muffins makes 12 muffins. It uses 180 g of blueberries.

What weight of blueberries is needed to make 30 muffins?

b A car is travelling at 80 km per hour.

How far would it travel in 75 minutes?

c €1 = $1.40

How many euros is a t-shirt that costs $24.50?

GO TO
Section 1:
Direct proportion

STEP 2

2 The cost of carpeting a hallway is proportional to the area of the hall. One hallway measuring 15 m² costs £97.50.

a Find a formula for the cost, c, of carpeting a hallway with area, a.

b How much would it cost to carpet an area of 32 m²?

c What area can be carpeted for £328.90?

GO TO
Section 2:
Algebraic and graphical representations

STEP 3

3 The cost of putting new soundproofing on a square dance floor is directly proportional to the square of the length of the side of the floor. A dance floor with a side length of 8 metres costs £976.

a Find a formula for the cost, c, of soundproofing a dance floor with side length s.

b How much would it cost to lay flooring on a dance floor with side length 7.5 m?

c To the nearest 10 centimetres, what size floor can be soundproofed for £645?

GO TO
Section 3:
Directly proportional to the square, square root and other expressions

GO TO
Step 4:
The Launchpad continues on the next page …

Launchpad continued …

STEP 4

4 Ten people have enough food for a 6-day camping trip.
  a How long would the food last if there were only five people?
  b Two more people join the group unexpectedly.
    How long would the food last if there were 12 people?

GO TO
Chapter review

GO TO
Section 4:
Inverse proportion

Section 1: Direct proportion

When two quantities vary but remain in the same **ratio** they are said to be in **direct proportion**. A simple example would be the quantity and price of petrol. The more petrol a driver puts into the car, the more it costs.

Scaling up recipe ingredients also involves direct proportion. If you want to make double the amount of food, you need to use double the amount of ingredients. Other examples are the number of hours someone works and the amount they get paid at an hourly rate, and exchange rates between two currencies.

In direct proportion problems, you might be given a rate such as price per litre. If not, it might be helpful to find this rate.

Key vocabulary

ratio: a comparison of different parts or amounts in a particular order.

direct proportion: two values that both increase in the same ratio.

WORKED EXAMPLE 1

A car travels 12 miles in 15 minutes at a constant speed.

a At what speed is the car travelling?

b How far would the car go in 75 minutes?

c How long would it take the car to travel 80 miles?

a $12 \times 4 = 48$ miles per hour

15 minutes is $\frac{1}{4}$ of an hour, so multiply 12 by 4 to get the speed in mph.

b $\frac{75}{15} \times 12 = 60$ miles

How many 15s in 75 minutes? Use this to multiply by 12.

c $80 \div 48 = 1.66...$ hours
This is 100 minutes or 1 hour 40 minutes

Time = distance ÷ speed.

Here it is sensible to give the final answer in hours and minutes.

Tip

Often it helps to write down a proportion fact you know and consider what would happen if one side is halved, doubled, multiplied by 10 and so on. For example, if you know that six eggs make two cakes then half the number of eggs, three, will make just one cake.

1 A bluefin tuna fish can travel 3 km in just 20 minutes.

List some other distance–time facts about the fish assuming that it always travels at a constant rate.

2 Patrick works for 4 hours and gets paid £22.

What is his rate of pay per hour?

3 Jelly beans cost £1.20 for 100 g.

a How much would 50 g cost?

b How much would 300 g cost?

c How much would 1 kg cost?

d What weight of jelly beans could you buy with £4.20?

4 On holiday Ben uses his mobile to call home. A 12-minute call costs £4.20.

a How much would it cost to ring home for 18 minutes?

b Danny calls home for 20 minutes and it costs him £6.40.

Whose phone is better value, Ben's or Danny's? Why?

5 Look at this pancake recipe. It serves eight people.

100 g plain flour

2 eggs

300 ml semi-skimmed milk

If you have 2 litres of milk, 500 g of plain flour and nine eggs and make as much pancake mixture as possible, how many will it serve?

6 The fastest train in Europe is the French TGV from Paris to Le Mans. It travels at 320 kilometres per hour. Assume that the train is going at its full speed.

a How far does it travel in 2 hours?

b How far does it travel in 30 minutes?

c How far does it travel in 15 minutes?

d How far does it travel in 1 minute?

e How far does it travel in 10 seconds?

f The Equator is approximately 40 000 km long.

If it were possible, how long would it take to travel around the Equator in a TGV train?

7 The fastest animal on land is the cheetah. It can reach speeds of up to 120 kilometres per hour but for only a short burst of time.

How far would it travel at this speed in 15 seconds?

Unitary method

Sometimes, scaling up or down by an easy figure, halving, trebling, and so on is not possible. In these cases, you use the given relationships to find the value of one item.

WORKED EXAMPLE 2

While in Florida, Danny bought a t-shirt for $18. He paid using a debit card. When Danny returned home the charge on his debit card statement was £10.71. He also bought a pair of jeans for $32. Assuming the bank uses the same exchange rate, what would this charge appear as on his debit card statement?

$18 = £10.71   Divide both sides by 18

$1 = £0.595

Using the information for $18, you need to find the equivalent information for $1.

$32 = £0.595 × 32 = £19.04

The charge on Danny's debit card statement should say £19.04

$1 = £0.595 is the exchange rate of dollars to pounds. You can use this to convert any number of dollars to pounds.

EXERCISE 35B

1 Before going to Australia, Finley exchanges £175 into Australian dollars. He gets an exchange rate of £1 = AU$1.81.

How many dollars does he get?

2 When returning from her holiday, Amber exchanges her $44 back into pounds. The exchange rate is £1 = $1.68.

How many pounds does she receive?

3 Paint is sold in a variety of tins. However, the price per litre remains unchanged. Find the cost of each of these tins of paint:

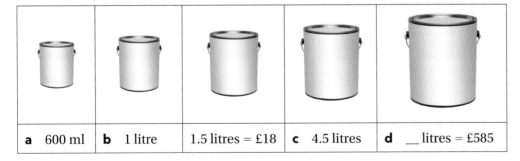

a 600 ml	**b** 1 litre	1.5 litres = £18	**c** 4.5 litres	**d** __ litres = £585

4 Lucy exchanges £50 for €60.50.
   a What is the exchange rate from pounds to euros?
   b What is the exchange rate from euros to pounds?

 Find answers at: cambridge.org/ukschools/gcsemaths-studentbookanswers

5 When planning a skiing holiday in Switzerland, Ethan compares two resorts. The exchange rate from pounds to Swiss Francs is £1 = CHF1.48

Which resort is a better deal? How many pounds cheaper is it?

Resort	Accommodation	Food	Ski rental	Flights
Bun di Scuol	£340	CHF96.20	£300	CHF102.12
Flims-Laax-Falera	CHF444	£100	CHF164.28	£144

6 The graph shows how to convert between pounds and Bulgarian lev (ЛВ).

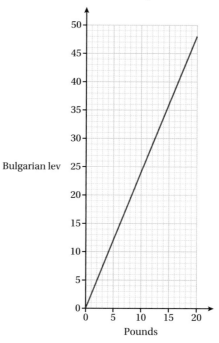

a What is the exchange rate from pounds to lev?

b What is the exchange rate from lev to pounds?

7 During his gap year Aaron had to change currencies on a regular basis. Use the following exchange information to answer the questions below.

UK pound	Euro	Kenyan shilling	Indian rupee	Mongolian tughrik	New Zealand dollar	Brazilian real
£1	€1.21	KSh145	₹102	₮3000	$1.95	R$3.77

a Aaron exchanged £350 into euros.

How many euros did he get?

b When in Kenya, Aaron went on a safari drive. He had booked this before going out at a cost of £185. He paid in Kenyan shillings.

How many Kenyan shillings did it cost?

c When he left India Aaron exchanged 5202 Indian rupees into Mongolian tughrik.

How many tughrik did he receive?

d Aaron paid €11 for a hostel in France, 1305 shillings in Kenya, 500 rupees in India, 6500 tughrik in Mongolia, 15 dollars in New Zealand and 20 real in Brazil.

Put these prices in order of expense, cheapest first.

8 On a recent holiday to Spain, Megan compares the price of saffron. In the UK 35 g of saffron can be bought for £2.69. In Spain it costs €11.80 for 125 g.

Which is the better deal, given that £1 = €1.21? Explain your answer clearly.

9 What information would you need to collect to compare the 'crowdedness' of two school playing fields? How would you carry out the comparison?

Section 2: Algebraic and graphical representations

Direct proportion problems can also be represented graphically or generalised through the use of algebra. This allows you to solve problems concerning the same relationship, either by reading information off a graph or by using an algebraic formula.

The graph of a directly proportional relationship has a fixed gradient and goes through the origin.

The mathematical symbol $\propto$ is used to indicate that two values are proportional.

If you pay per minute to use your mobile phone, the cost of the call, c, is proportional to the time you speak, t. This can be written algebraically as: $c \propto t$.

This means that for some fixed value k (called the constant of proportionality), you can write a formula:

$c = kt$

WORK IT OUT 35.1

Which of these graphs show a pair of variables that are directly proportional to each other?

Explain your choice. How can you tell that the variables in the other graphs are not directly proportional to each other?

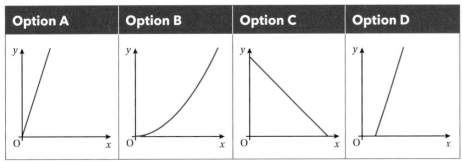

Option A	Option B	Option C	Option D

WORKED EXAMPLE 3

If you pay 75p for a 15 minute call, find:

a the value of the constant of proportionality

b a formula connecting cost and time of call

c the cost of a call taking 13 minutes.

a $c \propto t$

The cost (c) is proportional to the time (t) of the call.

$c = kt$

Rewrite as a formula, replacing the $\propto$ symbol with $=$ and introducing the constant of proportionality.

$75 = k \times 15$
$k = 5$

Substitute the values you know and solve for k.

b $c = 5t$

Replace k with 5 in the formula.

c $c = 5 \times 13 = 65p$

Substitute $t = 13$ into the formula.

Tip

Be careful with units in questions. In Worked example 3, the cost is in pence and time in minutes. To use the formula you would need to make sure all quantities were in pence and minutes and convert any that were not.

WORK IT OUT 35.2

Which of these formulae represent variables that are directly proportional to each other? Why or why not?

Option A	Option B	Option C	Option D
$y = 3x + 5$	$10w = h$	$\dfrac{s}{t} = 7$	$d^2 = 4f$

EXERCISE 35C

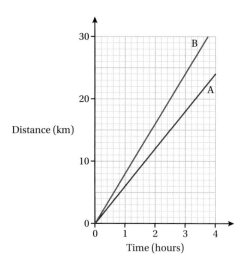

Distance (km)

Time (hours)

1 On the left is a time–distance graph for two runners.

    a How far had runner A travelled after 30 minutes?

    b How long did it take runner B to travel 18 km?

    c Which runner is going faster?

    d What is the speed of each runner?

    e What assumptions have been made when drawing this graph?

2 The graph on the right shows the cost of telephone cable.

Write a formula linking the cost, in pounds (c) and length, in metres, of wire (l).

3 The length of an object's shadow is directly proportional to the object's height. Use the diagram below to help explain why this is true.

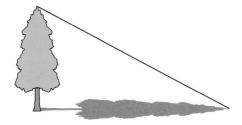

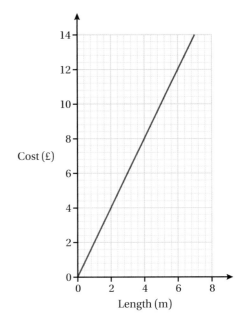

At one specific time in the day a man of height 1.8 metres has a shadow of 1.35 m.

a Find a formula for the length of an object's shadow (s) in terms of its height (h).

b The Angel of the North in Gateshead is 20 m tall. How long would its shadow be at the same specific time?

c The shadow of the tallest upright stone at Stonehenge at this specific time is 502.5 cm. How tall is the stone?

d Measure your height and use the method of comparing shadows to find the height of your school building.

4 Two variables p and q are directly proportional. When $p = 6.5$, q is 52.

a Find a formula for q in terms of p.

b Find the value of q when p is 3.8

c Find the value of p when q is 14.8

5 Wheelchair ramps have to be designed with a specific steepness allowing their safe use. One such, well-designed, ramp has a horizontal distance of 4 metres and a height gain of 60 cm.

Find a formula for the horizontal distance (d) in terms of the height gain (h).

Section 3: Directly proportional to the square, square root and other expressions

An object dropped from rest does not travel at a constant velocity; it accelerates. This means the distance it travels is not directly proportional to the time it has been falling.

In fact the distance travelled, d, by an object dropped from rest is proportional to the square of the time, t, for which it has been falling. So, if you double the time you quadruple the distance travelled; if you triple the time you multiply the distance travelled by 9, and so on.

WORKED EXAMPLE 4

An object is dropped from rest and after 3 seconds has travelled a distance of 44.1 metres. The distance travelled is proportional to the square of the time taken.

a How far will it have gone after 7 seconds?

b How long will it take to travel 100 metres?

a $d \propto t^2$

> Write the proportionality.

$d = kt^2$

> Rewrite as a formula.

$44.1 = k \times 3^2$
$k = 4.9$

> Substitute in the given values.

$d = 4.9t^2$

> Rewrite the formula with the found value of k.

$4.9 \times 7^2 = 240.1 \text{ m}$

> Substitute $t = 7$.

b $t = \sqrt{\dfrac{d}{4.9}}$

> Change the subject of the formula.

$\sqrt{\dfrac{100}{4.9}} = 4.52 \text{ seconds (2 decimal places)}$

> Substitute $d = 100$.

EXERCISE 35D

1 w is directly proportional to the cube of m. When $m = 3$, $w = 108$.

    a Find a formula for w in terms of m.

    b Find the value of w when $m = 5$.

    c Find the value of m when $w = 62.5$.

2 r is directly proportional to the square root of s. When $r = \dfrac{1}{2}$, $s = \dfrac{1}{16}$.

    a Find a formula for r in terms of s.

    b Find the value of r when $s = 20$.

    c Find the value of s when $r = 12$.

3 The rate at which a toaster produces heat, J (joules), is proportional to the square of the current, I (amps) in the circuit (Joule's first law). A toaster using 3.5 amps produces 857.5 joules of heat.

    a Find a formula for the heat produced, J, in terms of the current, I.

    b Another toaster produces 400 joules of heat.

       What current does this toaster draw?

4 The time it takes a pendulum to complete one full swing (from left to right and back again) is directly proportional to the square root of its length. A pendulum of length 16 cm takes 1.28 seconds to complete a full swing.

   a Find a formula for the time taken, t, in terms of the length of the pendulum, l.

   b How long is a pendulum that takes 2 seconds to complete one full swing?

5 The mass of a cube of gold, m, is directly proportional to the cube of its side length, s. A cube with side length 2 cm has a mass of 154.4 grams.

   a Find a formula for the mass of a cube of gold in terms of its side length.

   b A gold ingot has a mass of 12.4 kg. What size cube would this bar make?

Section 4: Inverse proportion

If you increase your speed, the time it takes to travel a fixed distance is reduced. If you add more workers, the time it takes to complete the job goes down. In these examples, one quantity decreases as the other one increases. These types of relationship are inversely proportional.

The graph of a pair of inversely proportional variables never quite touches the x- or y-axis, but comes closer and closer to them.

WORK IT OUT 35.3

A rectangle has a fixed area of 24 cm². Its length, x, and height, y, can vary. Which of the graphs below represents this situation? How did you come to your decision?

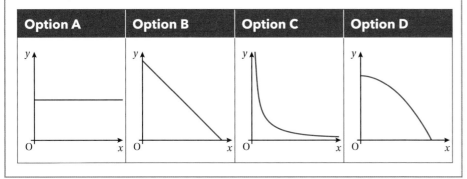

Option A	Option B	Option C	Option D

In the example of a rectangle with a fixed area, the length, x, and height, h, are in **inverse proportion**. When one is multiplied the other is divided. Hence:

$$y \propto \frac{1}{x}$$

$$y = \frac{k}{x}$$

Substituting related values for x and y allows you to find the value of the constant of proportionality, as for direct proportion.

Key vocabulary

inverse proportion: a relation between two quantities such that one increases at a rate that is equal to the rate that the other decreases.

 Find answers at: cambridge.org/ukschools/gcsemaths-studentbookanswers

EXERCISE 35E

1 It takes four people three days to paint the school hall.

a How many person-days is this?

b How long would it take two people?

c How long would it take six people?

d The job needs to be completed in a day.

How many people are needed?

e What assumptions are being made?

2 While on holiday you budget to buy five souvenirs at $2.40 each.

a How much money do you intend to spend?

b How many souvenirs costing $0.80 each could you buy with your budget?

c If you need eight souvenirs of equal value, how much should you pay for each souvenir to keep within your budget?

3 Speed (s miles per hour) and travel time (t hours) are inversely proportional. The faster you travel the less time a journey takes. A journey between Cambridge and Manchester takes 3 hours when travelling at 60 miles per hour.

a Find a formula for the time taken, t, in terms of the speed s.

b It takes 4 hours to make the journey.

What speed is this?

c How long will it take to do the journey at 75 miles per hour?

d It takes 2 hours 15 minutes to make the journey.

What speed is this?

4 A group of friends play a lucky draw game. The more friends they get the more tickets they can buy but the more people they have to share the prize with. The graph (left) shows the relationship between the number of people in the group and their share of the winnings.

a If 10 people buy tickets how much do they each win?

b How much is in the prize fund?

c Find a formula for the winnings, w, in terms of the number of people buying the winning ticket, n.

5 A water tap is running at a constant rate (r litres per minute), filling a pond in m minutes. The greater the flow of water the less time it takes to fill the pond. Copy and complete the table below and then draw a graph to represent this situation.

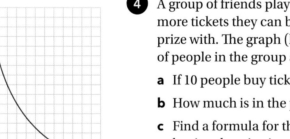

Winnings (£)

Number of people

m minutes	10	20	30	40	50	60	70	80	90	100
r litres per minute						10				

Find a formula for r in terms of m.

6 The variable a is inversely proportional to the square of b. When $b = 5$, $a = 2$.

   a Find a formula for a in terms of b.

   b Find the value of a when $b = 2$.

   c Find the value of b when $a = 0.5$.

7 The rate, r, at which a gas diffuses is inversely proportional to the square root of its molecular mass, m (Graham's law of diffusion). Carbon dioxide diffuses at 1 m/s (metre per second) and has molecular mass 44 g/mol (gram per mole).

Find a formula for r in terms of m.

8 In 1963 the land speed record of 407 miles per hour was held by American Craig Breedlove. In 1997 this record was held by British driver Andy Green. His recorded speed was 340 metres per second. What was the difference, in minutes, between the times it took the two drivers to travel a mile?

Checklist of learning and understanding

Direct proportion

- If two quantities are directly proportional to each other they increase and decrease at the same rate. For example, if one is tripled so is the other, if one is halved so is the other.

- A formula for a direct proportion relationship between two variables x and y is $y = kx$, where k is the constant of proportionality and can be found by substituting in known values.

- The graph of two directly proportional variables is a straight-line graph of the form $y = mx$, where m is positive.

Inverse proportion

- If two quantities are inversely proportional to each other, when one increases the other decreases. For example, if one is tripled the other is divided by three, if one is halved the other is doubled.

- A formula for an inverse proportion relationship between two variables x and y is $y = \dfrac{k}{x}$, where k is the constant of proportionality and can be found by substituting in known values.

- The graph on the right of two inversely proportional variables is of the form $y = \dfrac{m}{x}$, where m is positive.

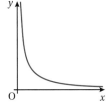

Chapter review

For additional questions on the topics in this chapter, visit GCSE Mathematics Online.

1 Wine gums cost 90p for 200 grams.

   a How much would 800 grams cost?

   b What weight of wine gums would you get for £2.70?

 Find answers at: cambridge.org/ukschools/gcsemaths-studentbookanswers

2 Look at this stir-fry recipe. It serves six people.

120 g chicken

300 g vegetables

15 tbsp of soy sauce

If you have 300 g of chicken, 500 g of vegetables, and 60 tbsp of soy sauce and make the most stir-fry possible, how many will it serve?

3 The graph shows the cost of buying electrical wire.

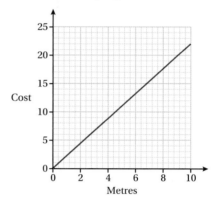

Write a formula for the cost, *c*, in terms of the number of metres bought, *m*.

4 *F* is directly proportional to the cube root of *g*. When *g* = 64, *F* = 12.

a Find a formula for *F* in terms of *g*.

b When *g* = 125, what is *F*?

c When *F* = 21, what is *g*?

5 It takes three hairdressers an hour to style the hair of models for a fashion show.

How long would it take nine hairdressers?

6 The rate at which water flows into a pond is inversely proportional to the time it takes to fill up. It takes 2 hours for the pond to fill when water flows in at a rate of 50 litres an hour.

Find a formula for the time in hours, *t*, in terms of the flow rate of the water, *w*.

7 *h* is inversely proportional to the square of *r*.

When *r* = 5, *h* = 3.4.

Find the value of *h* when *r* = 8. *(3 marks)*

©Pearson Education Ltd 2013

8 The variable *d* is inversely proportional to the cube of *e*. When *d* = 3, *e* = 2.

a Find a formula for *d* in terms of *e*.

b Find the value of *d* when *e* = 3.

c Find the value of *e* when *d* = 0.5.

36 Algebraic inequalities

In this chapter you will learn how to ...

- use the correct symbols to express inequalities.
- solve linear and quadratic inequalities in one variable and represent the solution set on a number line and in set notation.
- solve (several) linear inequalities in two variables, representing the solution set on a graph.

 For more resources relating to this chapter, visit GCSE Mathematics Online.

Using mathematics: real-life applications

Inequalities can be used to model and solve problems where a range of answers are possible, for example, all distances less than 2 m from the edge of a road. Linear programming is used in logistic and project management. It involves graphing constraints for a project to find a region of feasibility and identify the best solution.

"Civil engineering projects involve a great deal of planning. We need to work with limits on time and budget. Inequalities are one way of expressing the range of values that have to be met and considered together."

(Civil engineer)

Before you start …

Ch 15	You need to be able to solve linear equations.	**1** **a** If $3x + 2 = 2x + 5$, $x = ?$ **b** If $4(n + 3) = 6(n - 1)$, $n = ?$ **c** If $6(5 - 3x) = 5(2x - 5)$, $x = ?$ **d** If $\dfrac{3a - 2}{4} = \dfrac{a - 5}{2}$, $a = ?$
Ch 15	You should remember how to solve quadratic equations.	**2** $x^2 - 2x - 3 = 0$. $x = 3$ is one of the roots of this equation. What is the other root?
Ch 24	You should be confident using linear (straight line) graphs.	**3** The equation of the red line is $y = -\dfrac{1}{3}x + 1$. **a** What is the gradient of the line that is perpendicular to this line? **b** What is the equation of that line if it cuts the given line at (3, 0)?

Find answers at: cambridge.org/ukschools/gcsemaths-studentbookanswers

Assess your starting point using the Launchpad

STEP 1

1 Use mathematical symbols to express the following:

a p is less than 0.45   **b** x is greater or equal to -4

c y lies between the values of 11 and 18

2 List the whole numbers that satisfy each inequality:

a $2 < x < 5$ **b** $12 \geqslant x > -2$ **c** $2 \leqslant x - 1 < 5$

GO TO
Section 1:
Expressing inequalities

STEP 2

3 Draw a number line to represent each of the following:

a $x > -1$ **b** $x \leqslant 2$ **c** $-3 \leqslant x \leqslant 4$

4 Say whether each statement is true or false.

a A graph of $\{x : x \leqslant -3\}$ would be a number line starting at and including -3 and pointing in a negative direction.

b A graph of $\{x : x > 2\frac{1}{2}\}$ would be a number line starting at $2\frac{1}{2}$ and including $2\frac{1}{2}$ and pointing in a positive direction.

GO TO
Section 2:
Number lines and set notation

STEP 3

5 Solve these inequalities.

a $4x - 5 < 3$ **b** $3(x + 5) \geqslant 9$

GO TO
Section 3:
Solving linear inequalities

STEP 4

6 Solve $x^2 - 4x - 5 = 0$.

7 Produce a graph of the equation $y = x^2 - 4x - 5$ and represent the solution set for the inequality $x^2 - 4x - 5 > 0$.

Use the graph to identify the range of values that would satisfy this inequality.

GO TO
Section 4:
Solving quadratic inequalities

Section 5:
Graphing linear inequalities

GO TO
Chapter review

Section 1: Expressing inequalities

An **inequality** is a mathematical sentence that uses symbols such as $<$, $\leqslant$, $\neq$, $>$ or $\geqslant$ in place of an equals sign. The expressions on either side of the symbol are not equal.

The most common inequality symbols are:

>	greater than	$x > 5$ means x can have any value bigger than (but not including) 5.
<	less than	$x < 8$ means x can have any value less than (but not including) 8.
$\geqslant$	greater than or equal to	$x \geqslant 4$ means x can equal 4 or any value bigger than 4.
$\leqslant$	less than or equal to	$x \leqslant 7$ means x can equal 7 or any value smaller than 7.

Two inequality symbols can be used to give a limited range of values. For example, the following means 2 is *less than x* and *x* is *less than* 6:

$2 < x < 6$

Another way to read this statement is to say x lies between 2 and 6.

Sometimes, whole number (integer) values of x are asked for. In the above example, the integer values that satisfy the expression are 3, 4 and 5. If values other than integer values can be considered, there will be an infinite number of values between 2 and 6.

Addition and subtraction

If you add or subtract the same number to both sides of an inequality, then the resulting inequality is true.

$x > 3$ $x + 4 > 3 + 4$ $x + 4 > 7$	$x > 7$ $x - 6 > 7 - 6$ $x - 6 > 1$
For example, if $x = 10$ $10 > 3$ $10 + 4 > 3 + 4$ $14 > 7$	For example, if $x = 8$ $8 > 7$ $8 - 6 > 1$ $2 > 1$

Multiplication and division

If you multiply or divide both sides of an inequality by a positive number, then the resulting inequality is true.

$3x \leqslant 15$ $\dfrac{3x}{3} \leqslant \dfrac{15}{3}$ (Divide by 3) $x \leqslant 5$	$\dfrac{x}{2} > 5$ $\dfrac{x}{2} \times 2 > 5 \times 2$ (Multiply by 2) $x > 10$ Continues on next page ...

Find answers at: cambridge.org/ukschools/gcsemaths-studentbookanswers

For example, if $x = 4$, then $3x = 12$	For example, if $x = 18$, then $\dfrac{x}{2} = 9$
$12 \leqslant 15$ (Divide by 3)	$9 > 5$ (Multiply by 2)
$4 \leqslant 5$	$18 > 10$

If you multiply or divide both sides of an inequality by a negative number, then you must **reverse** the inequality sign to make the resulting inequality true.

$$7 > 3 \qquad \text{(Multiply both sides by } -2\text{)}$$
$$-14 < -6 \qquad \text{(Reverse the inequality sign)}$$

This result is useful if you need x and not $-x$. For example,

$$-x < 3 \qquad \text{(Multiply or divide both sides by } -1\text{)}$$
$$x > -3 \qquad \text{(Remember to reverse the inequality sign)}$$

EXERCISE 36A

Tip

Remember that we read inequalities from left to right.

1 Complete the statements with the correct inequality symbol:

     a $7 > 3$, then $4 + 7 \,\square\, 4 + 3$ **b** $8 < 13$, then $8 - 5 \,\square\, 13 - 5$

     c $-5 < -1$, then $-5 + 3 \,\square\, -1 + 3$ **d** $-4 > -11$, then $-4 - 6 \,\square\, -11 - 6$

2 Complete the statements with the correct inequality symbol:

     a $7 > 3$, then $2 \times 7 \,\square\, 2 \times 3$ **b** $8 < 13$, then $2 \times 8 \,\square\, 2 \times 13$

     c $7 > 3$, then $7 \div 2 \,\square\, 3 \div 2$ **d** $8 < 13$, then $8 \div 2 \,\square\, 13 \div 2$

3 Complete the statements with the correct inequality symbol:

     a $7 > 3$, then $-2 \times 7 \,\square\, -2 \times 3$ **b** $8 < 13$, then $-2 \times 8 \,\square\, -2 \times 13$

     c $7 > 3$, then $7 \div -2 \,\square\, 3 \div -2$ **d** $8 < 13$, then $8 \div -2 \,\square\, 13 \div -2$

4 List four whole numbers that satisfy the following inequalities:

     a $x > 14$ **b** $x \geqslant 6$ **c** $x \leqslant -2$

     d $x + 3 \geqslant 7$ **e** $x - 4 \leqslant 5$

5 If $x > 6$, how many values can x take?

6 If $3 < x < 8$, how many whole number (integer) values can x take? How many values can x take if we include decimal values or fractions?

7 List the whole number values given by $6 > x > 2$.

Section 2: Number lines and set notation

You can use a number line to illustrate an inequality.

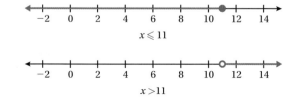

$$x \leqslant 11$$

$$x > 11$$

The expression $x \leqslant 11$ means numbers less than 11 and including 11. So a number line representing $x \leqslant 11$ shows values starting from and including 11 with a **solid** dot at 11.

The expression $x > 11$ means numbers greater than 11. So a number line representing $x > 11$ starts at 11 but with an **open** dot to show that 11 is not included.

Set notation

Another way to write statements about inequalities and the range of numbers that have been identified is to use **set** notation.

$\{x: x \leqslant 11\}$ This is the set of numbers that are equal to or less than 11.

$\{x: x > 11\}$ This is the set of numbers that are greater than 11.

This set $\{x: 3 \leqslant x < 6\}$ can be shown on a number line.

EXERCISE 36B

1 Use set notation to describe the range of values shown on each number line:

a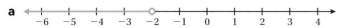

b

c

d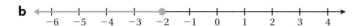

2 Show each set on a number line

  a $\{x: x > 8\}$ **b** $\{x: x \leqslant 0\}$ **c** $\{x: x < -5\}$

  d $\{x: x > -1\}$ **e** $\{x: x \leqslant -2\frac{1}{2}\}$

3 Using set notation write a statement for each of the sets identified in these number lines in two different ways.

a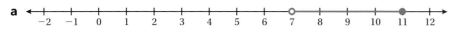

b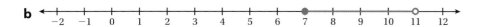

c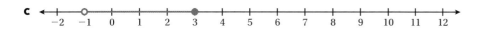

d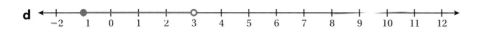

Tip

When drawing inequalities on a number line, the convention is to use an open dot (small circle) if the starting value is not included and a solid dot if the starting point is included.

Key vocabulary

set: a collection. The brackets { } are shorthand for 'the set of'. For example, {2, 4, 6, 8} is the set of the numbers 2, 4, 6, 8, which represents the even numbers between 1 and 9.

Tip

Number lines are a good way of checking you have identified the correct range of numbers in a set.

4 Draw a number line for each of the following sets using conventional notation.

    a $\{x: -5 \leqslant x \leqslant 1\}$ **b** $\{x: 6 > x > -1\}$

Section 3: Solving linear inequalities

Solving the linear inequality $4x - 5 < 3$ means finding all of the values for x that satisfy that inequality.

You can solve inequalities using the same methods that you used for linear equations.

However, you must also apply the rules that you learned in Section 1.

WORKED EXAMPLE 1

Solve for x. Show your solutions on a number line.

a $4x - 5 < 3$ **b** $\dfrac{5x-3}{2} \geqslant 11$ **c** $-5 \leqslant 3x + 4 \leqslant 13$ **d** $8 - 3x > 14$ **e** $2(5x - 2) > 6$ **f** $4(7 - x) \leqslant 3$

a $4x - 5 < 3$

    $4x < 8$ Add 5 to both sides.

    $x < 2$ Divide both sides by 4.

b $\dfrac{5x - 3}{2}$

    $5x - 3 \geqslant 11 \times 2$ Multiply both sides by 2.

    $5x \geqslant 22 + 3$ Add 3 to both sides.

    $5x \geqslant 25$

    $x \geqslant 5$ Divide both sides by 5.

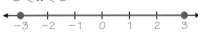

c $-5 \leqslant 3x + 4 \leqslant 13$

    $-5 - 4 \leqslant 3x \leqslant 13 - 4$ Subtract 4 from **each** expression.

    $-9 \leqslant 3x \leqslant 9$

    $-3 \leqslant x \leqslant 3$ Divide all the terms by 3.

d $8 - 3x > 14$

    $-3x > 14 - 8$ Subtract 8 from both sides.

    $-3x > 6$

    $x < \dfrac{6}{-3}$ Divide both sides by −3.

                Don't forget to reverse the direction of the inequality.

    $x < -2$

                You can check your answer by choosing a suitable value and substituting in the original inequality.

Continues on next page …

e $2(5x - 2) > 6$
$10x - 4 > 6$ Expand the brackets.

$10x > 10$ Add 4 to both sides.

$x > 1$ Divide both sides by 10.

f $4(7 - x) \leqslant 3$
$28 - 4x \leqslant 3$ Expand the brackets.

$25 \leqslant 4x$ Add $4x$ to both sides and subtract 3 from both sides.

$6.25 \leqslant x$ Divide both sides by 4.

$x \geqslant 6.25$ It is usually preferred to have the variable on the left. If you swap sides the inequality will reverse.

Tip

You can substitute your solution in the inequality to check that it is correct in the same way you can check solutions to equations.

EXERCISE 36C

1 Solve these inequalities, making sure you have the correct symbol in your answer.

    a $4x \leqslant 20$ **b** $-10x \geqslant 130$ **c** $-12x > -42$

    d $\dfrac{-x}{2} \leqslant 5$ **e** $\dfrac{-x}{5} > 4$ **f** $3 - 2x > 5$

2 Solve each inequality. Leave fractional answers as fractions in simplest form.

    a $3(h - 4) > 5(h - 10)$ **b** $\dfrac{y + 6}{4} < 9$

    c $\dfrac{1}{2}(x + 50) \leqslant 2$ **d** $3 - 7h \leqslant 6 - 5h$

    e $2(y - 7) + 6 \leqslant 5(y + 3) + 21$ **f** $6(n - 4) - 2(n + 1) < 3(n + 7) + 1$

    g $5(2v - 3) - 2(4v - 5) \geqslant 8(v + 1)$ **h** $\dfrac{z - 2}{3} - 7 > 13$

    i $\dfrac{3k - 1}{7} - 7 > 7$ **j** $\dfrac{2e + 1}{9} > 7 - 6e$

3 When 5 is added to twice p, the result is greater than 17. What values can p take?

4 When 16 is subtracted from half of q, the result is less than 18. What values can q take?

Find answers at: cambridge.org/ukschools/gcsemaths-studentbookanswers

5 When $2p$ is subtracted from 10, the result is greater than or equal to 4. What values can p take?

6 The sum of $4d$ and 6 is greater than the sum of $2d$ and 18. What values can d take?

7 A number a is increased by 3 and this amount is then doubled. If the result of this is greater than a, what values can a take?

8 At a certain school, the mark out of 100 for the Term 1 exam and twice the mark out of 100 for the Term 3 exam are added together. The students must obtain at least 150 marks to achieve a satisfactory grade. A student obtains x marks in the Term 1 exam.

  a Write an appropriate inequality to show the mark, y, that the student must obtain in the Term 3 exam in order to pass.

  b Solve this inequality for:

     i $x = 35$ **ii** $x = 49$

Section 4: Solving quadratic inequalities

A quadratic inequality contains at least one term with a squared variable and no terms with any powers higher than 2.

You can solve quadratic inequalities using the methods you applied to quadratic equations.

WORKED EXAMPLE 2

Find the values of x that satisfy $x^2 - 4x > 5$.

$x^2 - 4x - 5 > 0$	Rewrite the inequality to make the right-hand side 0.
$(x - 5)(x + 1) > 0$	Factorise.
Either both brackets are positive (in other words > 0), **or** both brackets are negative (in other words < 0).	The inequality 'greater than 0' means the product of the brackets is positive.
Either $(x - 5) > 0$ and $(x + 1) > 0 \rightarrow x > 5$ and $x > -1$; this results in $x > 5$ **Or** $(x - 5) < 0$ and $(x + 1) < 0 \rightarrow x < 5$ and $x < -1$; this results in $x < -1$	This could mean two things.

Continues on next page …

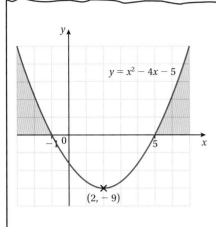

The graph of $y = x^2 - 4x - 5$ is useful to check this result (it can also be used to find the result).

For $x^2 - 4x - 5 > 0$, this means $y > 0$, which is the parts of the graph **above** the x-axis.

From the graph, you can see that these are the two regions, $x > 5$ or $x < -1$.

WORKED EXAMPLE 3

Find the values of x that satisfy $x^2 - 4x < 5$.

Notice that this is similar to Worked example 2 but the direction of the inequality has been reversed.

$x^2 - 4x - 5 < 0$

Rewrite the inequality to make the right-hand side 0.

$(x - 5)(x + 1) < 0$

Factorise.

Either $(x - 5) > 0$
and $(x + 1) < 1 \rightarrow x > 5$
and $x < -1$,
but this is a contradiction, as x cannot satisfy both conditions at the same time,
Or $(x - 5) < 0$
and $(x + 1) > 0 \rightarrow x < 5$
and $x > -1$.

This time the product is less than zero. One of the brackets most be > 0 and the other < 0.

$\{x: -1 < x < 5\}$

This can be written using set notation.

Tip

If you are solving a quadratic inequality algebraically, be sure to include all the steps involved in the solution to help you apply the correct reasoning.

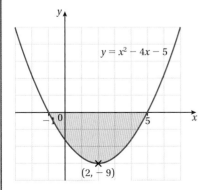

You can use the same graph as in Worked example 2 to see this result.

For $x^2 - 4x - 5 < 0$, this means $y < 0$, which is the parts of the graph **below** the x-axis.

From the graph you can see that this is just one enclosed region, $-1 < x < 5$.

EXERCISE 36D

1 **a** For what values of x is $x^2 - 3x - 3 \geqslant 0$?

b For what values of x is $x^2 - 3x - 3 < 0$?

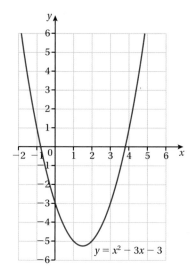

2 **a** For what values of x is $-2x^2 + 16x - 24 \geqslant 0$?

b For what values of x is $-2x^2 + 16x - 24 \leqslant 0$?

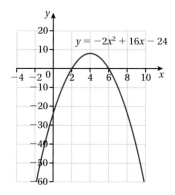

3 Sketch a graph and find all values of x such that:

a $(x - 3)(x + 2) > 0$ **b** $(x + 1)(x + 4) \leqslant 0$

c $(x - 5)(x - 2) \geqslant 0$ **d** $x(x + 3) < 0$

4 Solve for x. Sketch the graphs if you need to.

a $-2x^2 - 5x + 12 > 0$ **b** $x^2 - 5x < 0$ **c** $8 + 2x - x^2 \leqslant 0$

d $12 - 5x - 2x^2 < 0$

5 Write the quadratic inequalities that are represented by the values on these number line graphs.

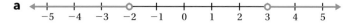

Section 5: Graphing linear inequalities

So far you have dealt with inequalities with one variable and solutions that can be shown on a number line. Inequalities such as $y > x + 1$ have two variables connected to them (x, y). The solution to such an inequality is a region on a plane. You need to understand how to represent inequalities on a number plane so that you can use graphs to find and/or represent the solution to two or more simultaneous inequalities.

Regions on a plane

Simple equations like $y = 3$ and $x = -2$ can also be called **equalities**.

On a number plane, all the points that satisfy an equality lie on one straight line.

Key vocabulary

equalities: having the same amount or value.

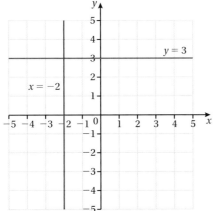

All the points that satisfy the inequality $x > 2$ lie on one side of the line $x = 2$.

The region into which these points fall is shaded on the graph below.

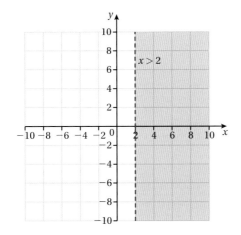

All points on the other side of the line satisfy the inequality $x < 2$.

The line itself is not included in the region $x > 2$, so it is shown as a broken line.

This diagram shows the inequality $y \leqslant 2x + 1$.

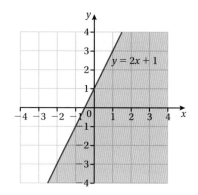

Tip

For inequalities linked by $<$ or $>$ symbols, the boundary line of the region is a broken line.

For inequalities linked by $\leqslant$ or $\geqslant$ symbols, the boundary line of the region is a solid line.

In this case, the points on the line are included in the region so the line is shown as a solid line.

WORKED EXAMPLE 4

Draw a set of x- and y-axes from -4 to 4. Shade the region on the diagram that satisfies both statements $y > 3$ and $x < -2$. Give two points in the identified (shaded) region.

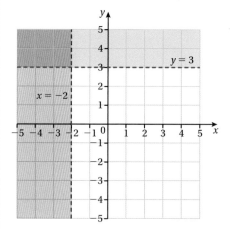

For example, $(-3, 4)$ and $(-5, 5)$.

Draw the lines $y = 3$ and $x = -2$; make sure the lines are dashed as $y = 3$ and $x = -2$ are not included in their respective inequality.

Shade in the graph **above** the line $y = 3$ (you should still see the squared grid through the shading); shade in the graph to the **left** of the line $x = -2$ in a different colour.

You can choose any two points within the shaded region, **except** for those that contain an x-coordinate of -2 or those with a y-coordinate of 3.

Verifying solutions

This is the graph of $y = -x + 3$.

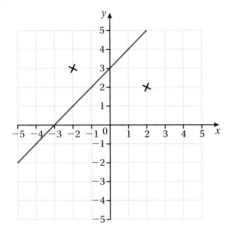

In order to identify the region that is $y \geqslant -x + 3$, test a point either side of the line, for example $(-2, 3) \rightarrow 3 \geqslant -(-2) + 3$, but 3 is not greater than or equal to 5. Try $(2, 2)$ on the other side of the line $\rightarrow 2 \geqslant -2 + 3$, 2 is greater than 1 so the region to the right represents $y \geqslant -x + 3$.

EXERCISE 36E

1 Sketch a graph for each of the following linear equations and on each graph shade the region defined by the inequality.

a $y = x + 1, y \geqslant x + 1$ **b** $y = -2x + 4, y \leqslant -2x + 4$

c $y = \dfrac{1}{2}x + 3, y > \dfrac{1}{2}x + 3$ **d** $x - y = 2, x - y < 2$

2 Draw the following vertical and horizontal lines on a graph:
$x = -4, x = 1, y = 5$ and $y = -3$.

Shade in the regions defined by the inequalities $x \geqslant 1, y \leqslant -3$.

State the coordinates of two points in the region where the two inequalities overlap.

3 Is the region shaded in this diagram $y \geqslant \dfrac{1}{3}x - 2$ or is it $y \leqslant \dfrac{1}{3}x - 2$? How do you know?

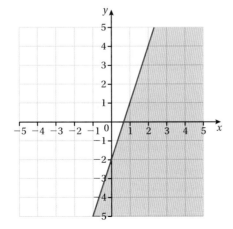

> ### Tip
>
> A quick way to check which side of a line to shade for a given inequality is to use the origin $(0, 0)$. Substitute $x = 0$ and $y = 0$ into the inequality. If the resulting statement is true, then the origin is in the correct area to be shaded. If it is not true, then shade the other side of the line.

4 For each of the diagrams below, find the equation of the line and write an inequality to define the shaded region.

a

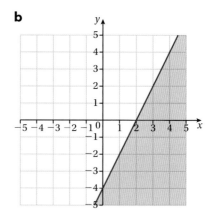

b

c

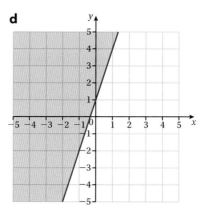

d

5 Check that the inequalities that define each region of the diagram are correct by substituting a point from the region.

Write a pair of inequalities which define the unshaded region.

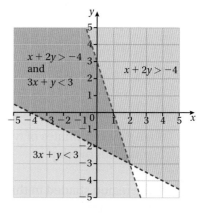

6 Study this diagram and then answer the questions that follow.

a Find the equation of the blue line.

b Find the equation of the broken red line.

c Using the inequality symbols, describe the:

i pink region   **ii** blue region

iii purple region where the two regions overlap.

Verify your answers using a point from each of the regions.

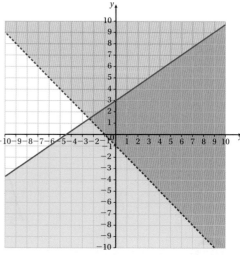

Graphing several inequalities

Many problems involving two or more inequalities can be solved by a graphical method.

A company had to decide which of two different storage cabinets to buy.

They had to consider some restrictions on price and floor space.

They wrote and graphed inequalities so that they could find feasible solutions. These are shown on the diagram.

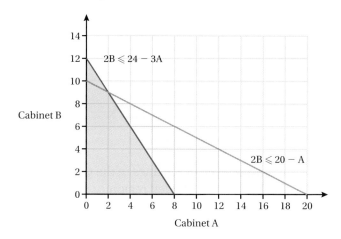

The green area represents the overlap region where all the restrictions on cost and area are met.

Point (2, 9) represents the maximum number of cabinets (11) that can be purchased to meet the restrictions, i.e. two of cabinet A and nine of cabinet B.

Only whole number solutions are valid to solve this problem – it would not be possible to purchase a fraction of a cabinet.

EXERCISE 36F

1 Draw a sketch diagram of the two linear equations $y = -4x + 8$ and $y = x + 1$.

Identify and shade the region satisfied by the inequalities $y > x + 1$ and $y \leqslant -4x + 8$.

2 Plot the following linear equations:

$y = 2x - 3$

$y = -\dfrac{5}{4}x + \dfrac{5}{2}$

$y = -3$

Identify and shade the region defined by:

$y \geqslant 2x - 3, y > -3, y \leqslant -\dfrac{5}{4}x + \dfrac{5}{2}$

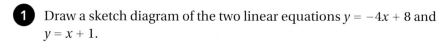

Find answers at: cambridge.org/ukschools/gcsemaths-studentbookanswers

3 Write the equations of the two lines and identify the inequalities that represent the shaded area. Verify your answer with a point in the shaded region.

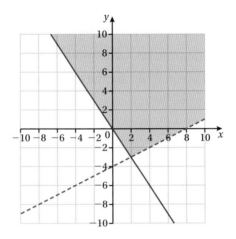

4 Write the equations of each of the lines in the graph. Write the three inequalities that identify the shaded region.

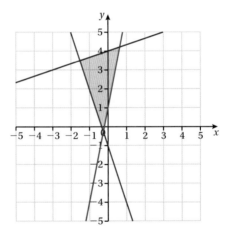

5 List the three inequalities that identify the shaded region and verify your answer with a point in the region.

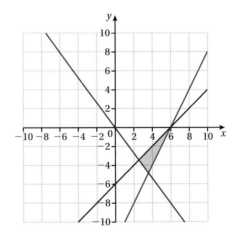

6 Solve the simultaneous equations

$4x - 5y = 20$

$7x - 2y = 14$

Draw a sketch graph of the two lines and shade the region defined by:
$4x - 5y < 20$ and $7x - 2y \geqslant 14$.

 Checklist of learning and understanding

Inequalities

- Inequalities indicate a range of values to be considered. $a \leqslant x \leqslant b$: x is a value that lies between the values of a and b and can be equal to a and b. This statement can also be written in the form $b \geqslant x \geqslant a$.

- An inequality will have a finite number of integer solutions but an infinite number of real solutions. Solutions can be shown on a number line.

Solving inequalities

- Linear inequalities can be solved using techniques similar to those for solving linear equations, but any multiplication or division by a negative will reverse the sign. For example, $4 > 3$ but $-4 < -3$; if $x > y$, then $-x < -y$. If you are not sure, verify by substituting numbers.

- If a solution to an inequality is $3 > x$ you can write this with x on the left-hand side: $x < 3$.

- Solutions can be written using set notation: $\{x: x < 3\}$ means the set of numbers x such that the value of x is less than 3. For example, integer solutions for $\{x: 2 < x \leqslant 5\} = \{5, 4, 3\}$.

- Quadratic inequalities are best solved by considering values on a graph. The shaded area in this graph represents the values of x for $y > x^2 - 1$.

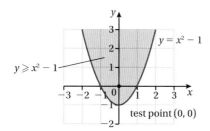

Graphing inequalities

- Problems that require more than one linear inequality can be solved by graphing and identifying the area that is the solution set.

For additional questions on the topics in this chapter, visit GCSE Mathematics Online.

 Chapter review

1 On a graph, identify the three integral values of x and y which satisfy all these four inequalities:

$4x + 3y < 12 \quad y < 3x \quad y > 0 \quad x > 0$

2 On a diagram, draw straight lines and use shading to show the region R that satisfies the inequalities $x \geqslant 2$, $y \geqslant x$, $x + y \leqslant 6$.

3 Write a list of the three inequalities which identify the values in the shaded area.

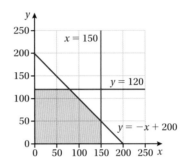

4 The shaded area in this diagram represents $x^2 - x - 12 > 0$.

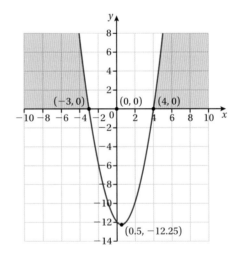

Verify that the shaded area is correct by solving the quadratic inequality $x^2 - x - 12 > 0$ and stating the solution sets for x.

5 m is an integer such that $-2 < m \leqslant 3$.

a Write down all the possible values of m. *(2 marks)*

b Solve $7x - 9 < 3x + 4$. *(2 marks)*

37 Sampling and representing data

Using mathematics: real-life applications

We live in a very information-rich world. Knowing how to construct accurate graphs and how to interpret the graphs we see is important. Many graphs in print and other media are carefully designed to influence what we think by displaying the data in particular ways.

"When we have data, we need to display it so that our message has the maximum impact."

(Newspaper editor)

> **Tip**
>
> The key to displaying data is to choose the graph or chart that clearly shows what the data tells us without the reader having to work too hard.

> **Tip**
>
> Getting the scale and labelling right makes a big difference when creating graphs and charts.

Before you start…

KS3	You need to be able to sort and categorise data.	**1** What would be suitable categories for a set of adult heights ranging from 1.39 m to 1.85 m?
Chs 9 and 10	You need to be able to use scales properly.	**2** **a** What is each division on this scale? **b** A scale between 0 and 100 has five divisions. Which numbers should go alongside each division?
Chs 22 and 26	You need to be able to measure and draw angles to create pie charts.	**3** **a** Measure these angles: **b** Draw an angle of 72° accurately.

Assess your starting point using the Launchpad

STEP 1

1 You want to find out what is the most popular music in the school, but you don't have time to ask everybody.

   a How can you do this?

   b How will you make sure your data is reliable?

GO TO
Section 1:
Populations and samples

STEP 2

2 **a** Who scored the fewest goals in qualifying for the 2014 football World Cup tournament?

   b Which teams scored the same number of goals?

   c Given this graph, which teams would you have chosen to be in the top four of the tournament?

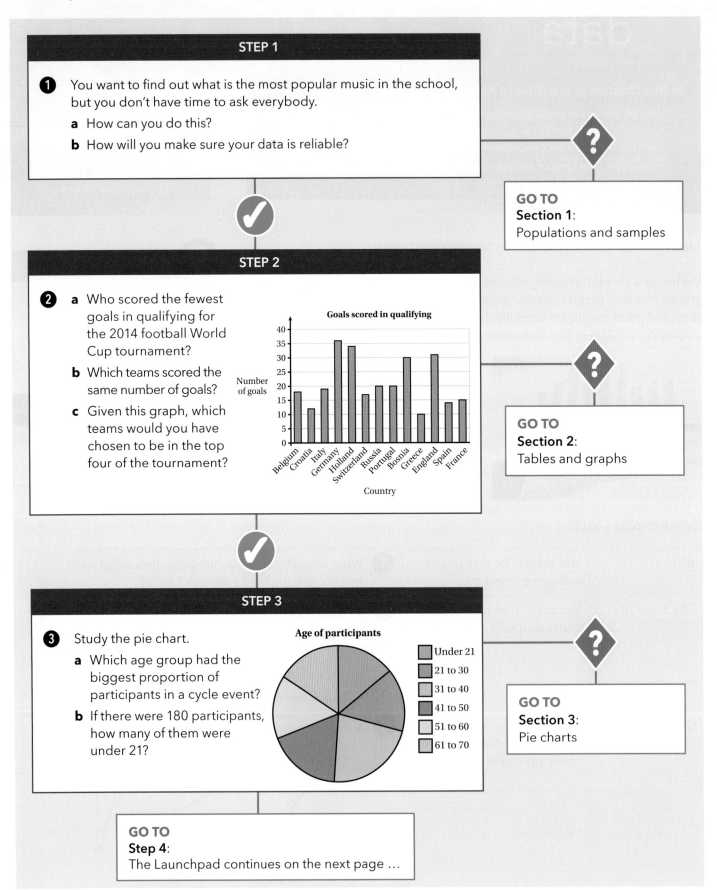

GO TO
Section 2:
Tables and graphs

STEP 3

3 Study the pie chart.

   a Which age group had the biggest proportion of participants in a cycle event?

   b If there were 180 participants, how many of them were under 21?

GO TO
Section 3:
Pie charts

GO TO
Step 4:
The Launchpad continues on the next page …

Launchpad continued ...

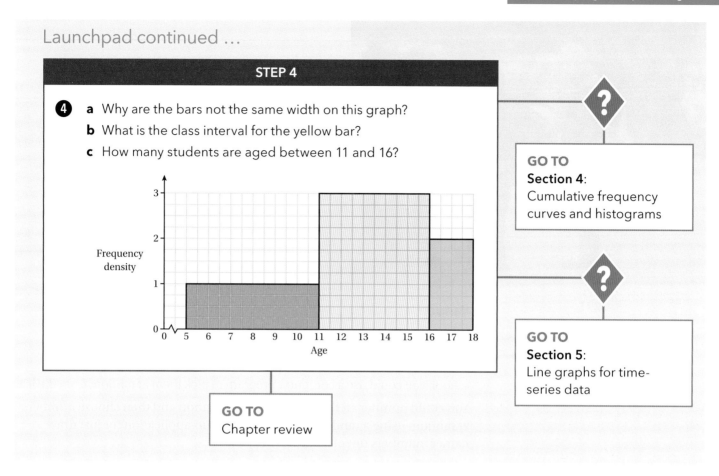

STEP 4

4
   a Why are the bars not the same width on this graph?
   b What is the class interval for the yellow bar?
   c How many students are aged between 11 and 16?

GO TO
Section 4: Cumulative frequency curves and histograms

GO TO
Section 5: Line graphs for time-series data

GO TO
Chapter review

Section 1: Populations and samples

A statistical **population** is a set of individuals or objects of interest.

A school might want to find the mean height of students to decide what size of equipment to buy for the gymnasium. In this example, the population would be all the students in the school.

In a large school it would be impractical to measure each student's height. Instead, a **sample** of the students (population) would be used. The sample needs to be a **representative sample** to provide useful data.

A representative sample would come from a mix of male and female students from different years. It would not be a good idea to measure just the Year 7 students.

A representative sample can be created by taking a factor that is unrelated to age or gender, for example, all the students whose first name begins with a letter drawn at random.

As the starting letter of your name has no effect on your height, this should give you a representative sample.

Although the sample cannot guarantee you will get the heights of the biggest and smallest students, it should make sure that you get a good idea of the spread of the data.

 Key vocabulary

population: the name given to a data set.

sample: a set of data collected from a population.

representative sample: a smaller quantity of data that represents the characteristics of a larger population.

"I collect data on behalf of my company so that they can find out
how likely people are to buy new products. We use quota sampling in our work. This involves choosing people with particular characteristics. For example, I may only be interested in collecting data on teenagers who play video games.

(Market researcher)

Random sampling

In a random sample, each member of the population is equally likely to be chosen. If you wanted a 10% sample and had a list of all the students in the school, you could use a computer program to pick them at random from the list.

You could number all the items in the population and then choose numbers at random using a random number generation application (or just draw names/numbers out of a hat).

In reality, it is often difficult to choose a genuinely random sample. If you are doing a survey for a school project, you are likely to use convenience sampling because you would probably survey friends and family members. This method could result in a biased sample.

In statistics, the population may be divided into groups using a particular system. Stratified sampling is quite common. This involves dividing the sample into groups (strata) and then choosing a random sample from each group. The size of the sample chosen from each group should be in proportion to the size of the group within the population.

For example, in a school population you could use the year groups as strata. If the Year 9 students make up 30% of the school population, then 30% of the sample should come from that group.

WORK IT OUT 37.1

A market researcher has been asked to survey a random sample of shoppers at a shopping centre. She suggests the following four options.

a Which is the only option that would produce a random sample?

b Explain why each of the other three options does not produce a random sample.

Option A	Option B	Option C	Option D
Ask all the women with children.	Ask people between 8 a.m. and 8.30 a.m.	Stand outside a book shop and ask everyone who comes out.	Stop and ask every 10th person who walks by the researcher.

EXERCISE 37A

1 Which of these methods are likely to give a random sample?

  a Selecting all the odd numbered houses in a street.

  b Calling people on their home telephones during the day.

  c Selecting everybody who is wearing trainers.

  d Calling the person whose name is at the top of each page of the phone book.

  e Drawing a series of names from a hat.

  Give reasons for your answers.

2 A market research company wants to find out how many people are likely to buy a new baby food.

  a Suggest a good place to conduct a survey of young parents.

  b 35 of the 50 parents asked said they would be interested. How many parents would you expect to be interested in a population of 1000 parents?

3 A gym owner wants to know how many running machines to buy. She asks every member whose surname begins with an 'S' whether they will use a running machine.

  a If 15 of the 28 in her sample say 'yes', what would be a sensible number of machines to buy if there are 300 members overall?

  b Does she really need this many machines?

  c Is there a better way of sampling her members to make sure she gets a realistic number of machines?

4 At the end of 2012 there were 28.7 million cars on the roads of Great Britain.

  Surjay and his friends conduct a random survey of the cars passing the school and discover that of the 50 cars recorded, three had no sun roof, one had a faulty exhaust and four had chips on the windscreen.

  Use this information to estimate how many cars in Great Britain have:

  a no sun roof   **b** faulty exhausts   **c** chips in the windscreen.

5 A building firm employs joiners (30), electricians (40), plumbers (20) and bricklayers (10). For a survey, they want a 10% representative sample in proportion to the different trades. How many of each trade will be in the survey?

6 A survey of 100 people who live on the same street in a town showed that the radio stations in the table are listened to for at least an hour per day.

  a Suggest one reason why the sample may not be representative.

  b If the population of the town is 4550, and the sample is representative, estimate how many people listen to each of the radio stations.

Radio station	Number of listeners
Radio Uno	25
Ears on	12
Hip and happening	11
Classic Numbers	6
R Town radio	23

Find answers at: cambridge.org/ukschools/gcsemaths-studentbookanswers

Section 2: Tables and graphs

Using tables to organise data

A frequency table is a table used to organise data and show the 'frequency' of an event, or how often it happens. For example, the number of goals scored by each of the 20 premiership teams one weekend was:

| 5 | 1 | 3 | 0 | 1 | 2 | 4 | 1 | 1 | 2 |
| 0 | 3 | 1 | 0 | 0 | 4 | 0 | 1 | 3 | 0 |

In a frequency table these results would look like this:

Number of goals scored	Tally	Frequency
0	Ж||	6
1	Ж||	6
2				2
3					3
4				2
5			1

Using bar charts to display data

The data in the frequency table above can be shown on a bar chart.

Number of goals scored by each team

The chart has a title, a scale on the left and accurately drawn bars (of the same width).

Note that there is an equal gap between each bar and each one is labelled.

Bar charts are used to display **discrete data**. The number of goals scored by each team is discrete data because it can only have certain values. It must be a whole number – you can't score $\frac{1}{2}$ a goal or 2.34 goals.

Sometimes it is helpful to sort data into categories. Pairs of shoes in a cupboard could be categorised into 'brown shoes', 'black shoes', and so. Each piece of data can only be in one category. This is known as **categorical data**.

Tip

Tally marks are used as you work systematically through the data. Adding the tallies gives you the frequency.

Key vocabulary

discrete data: data that can be counted and can only take certain values.

categorical data: data that has been arranged in categories.

A vertical line graph is very similar to a bar graph but the number of items in each category is represented by a line rather than a bar.

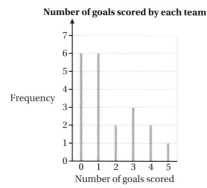

This data could also be shown using a pictogram.

In a pictogram, a symbol is used to represent either each team or a number of teams.

In this example each ball represents two teams:

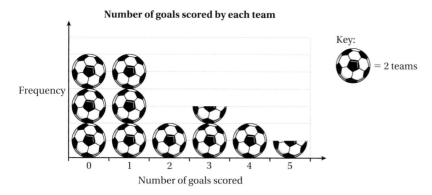

Note that a pictogram should also have a key to indicate what the symbol represents.

WORK IT OUT 37.2

Ramiz records the number of mistakes he makes in a series of maths tests.

2 3 1 3 4 2 0 3 2 6 1 1 3 2 4 2

Which graph or chart best shows this data? What is wrong with the other two?

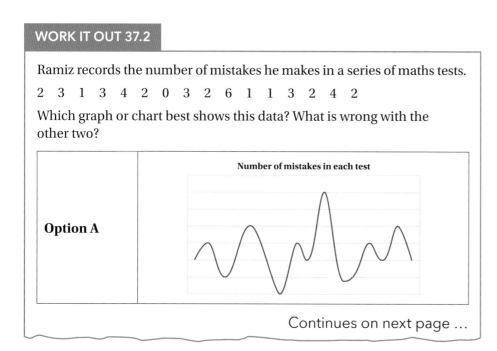

Continues on next page …

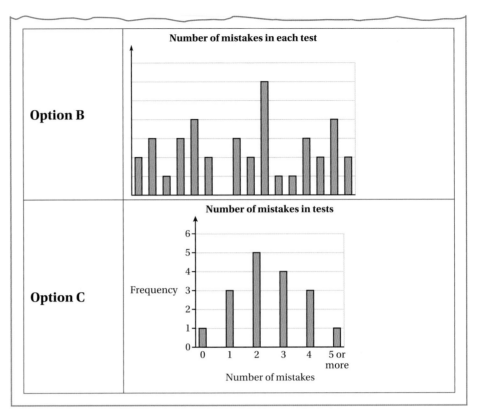

It is not always possible to say that one type of graph is better than another.

These guidelines can help you choose an appropriate graph for different kinds of data:

- Use bar graphs or vertical line charts for discrete data that can be categorised.
- Use a pie graph or a composite bar graph if you want to compare different parts of the whole or show proportions in the data.
- Use a line graph for numerical data when you want to show trends (changes over time).
- Use scatter diagrams when you want to show relationships between different sets of data (you will deal with these in Chapter 38).
- Use histograms for continuous data with equal or unequal class intervals.

EXERCISE 37B

1 In an extended family of 30 members, 10 have blond hair, nine have black hair, six have brown hair and five have grey hair.

Draw a vertical line graph to show this information.

2 This table (right) shows the percentages of people who use a particular mode of transport to get to work in a factory.

Show this information in a bar chart.

Mode of transport	Percentage
car	36
bus	27
cycle	19
walk	18

3 30 students were asked how many times in the last week they had visited the snack shop. Their responses were:

1 2 1 2 1 5 1 3 2 1 2 1 3 2 1 2 0 2 3 2 0 2 0 1 2 0 0 3 1 2

a Draw a frequency table for this data.

b Present this information on a suitable graph.

4 Construct a bar chart for the data in this table.

Favourite holiday destination	UK	Spain	France	USA	Greece
Frequency	9	15	17	12	8

5 A group of students were asked to choose their favourite snacks.
The results are in the table below.

Favourite snack	Number of students
fruit	6
crisps	8
chocolate bar	9
pizza slice	12
cookie	7

Draw a pictogram to show these results.

6 The graph below shows the monthly rainfall in Lowestoft in 2012.

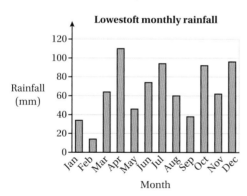

a In which month was the rainfall heaviest?

b Estimate the amount of rain that fell in April.

c Which was the driest month?

d Spring is March, April and May. Estimate how much rain fell in the spring.

e The average annual rainfall for Lowestoft is approximately 575 mm.

Was 2012 a wetter or drier year than average?

Find answers at: cambridge.org/ukschools/gcsemaths-studentbookanswers

Jenny is carrying out a survey of what sort of snacks are bought from a shop outside her school.

She writes down the items that people buy:

Chocobar	Apple	NRG drink	Juicebar	Crisps	NRG drink	Chocobar	NRG drink	Juicebar
Juicebar	Crisps	Cheese puffs	Gum	Cheese puffs	Fruit chews	NRG drink	NRG drink	Chocobar
Chocobar	Juicebar	Chocobar	Crisps	Chocobar	Gum	Chocobar	Cheese puffs	Crisps
Cheese puffs	Crisps	NRG drink	Fruit chews	NRG drink	Cheese puffs	NRG drink	Juicebar	Gum
NRG drink	Chocobar	Apple	NRG drink	Chocobar	Juicebar	Crisps	Chocobar	Cheese puffs
Gum	Fruit chews	Gum	Crisps	Apple	Crisps	Fruit chews	Fruit chews	Fruit chews
Juicebar	Crisps	Cheese puffs	Fruit chews	Gum	Cheese puffs	Fruit chews	Crisps	Cheese puffs

a How could Jenny have been better organised before she started her survey?

b Use Jenny's data to create a table to show what was bought in the shop.

c Jenny will get extra credit if she can categorise her data. Adjust your table so that the data is classified in an appropriate way.

Multiple and composite bar charts

A multiple bar chart is useful when you want to compare data for two or more groups. For example, to compare shoe sizes of male and female students in Year 9 you would show the data for male and female students in matching pairs of bars like this:

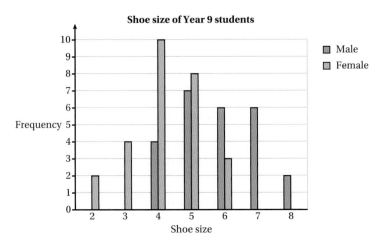

Notice that:

- The graph has a key to show what each colour bar represents.
- The two bars for male and female students who wear each size touch each other, but there is an equal space between each pair of bars.

Composite bar graphs are used to show parts of a whole. The total height of each bar represents a total amount. The length of the bar is divided into parts that show each category's share of the total amount.

To interpret a composite bar chart you need to work out what each bar represents and then do a calculation to find the fraction or percentage of the total that each part represents.

WORKED EXAMPLE 1

This composite bar chart shows the amount of water used by three different households over a 4-month period.

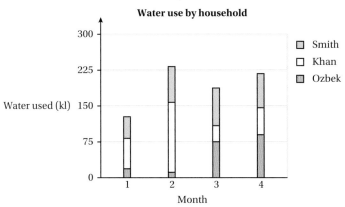

a What does each bar show?

The top of each bar shows the total water used by three households in a month. Each coloured segment shows the proportion of the total used by each household.

b Which household used the greatest amount of water in month 1?

The Khan household. The yellow section is bigger than the other two.

c Describe the trend in water use for the Ozbek household over this period.

In months 1 and 2 they used very little water. In month 3 the amount of water used increased quite dramatically and in month 4 it went up a little more.

d One household had a leaking pipe in this period. Can you work out from the graph who this was and when it happened?

It is most likely the Khan household as they had a massive jump in consumption in month 2. However, it could be the Ozbeks as well. If their water pipe started leaking in month 3 and wasn't fixed, it could account for the big increase in their consumption.

EXERCISE 37C

1

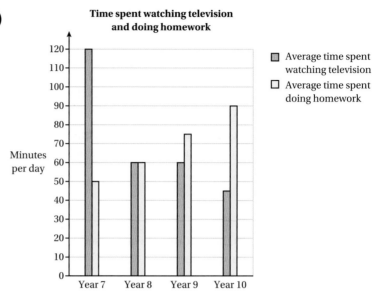

Time spent watching television and doing homework

Minutes per day

Year 7 Year 8 Year 9 Year 10

- Average time spent watching television
- Average time spent doing homework

a What two sets of data are shown on this graph?

b Describe the trend in the amount of time spent watching TV as students move into higher years.

c What happens to the amount of time spent on homework as TV watching time decreases?

d How much time do Year 10 students spend on average each day on

   i homework   **ii** watching TV?

2 Naresh runs a computer company. He keeps a record of his costs and his income for four large projects in a year.

He drew this graph to compare his costs and his income for each project.

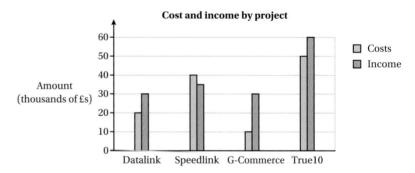

Cost and income by project

Amount (thousands of £s)

Datalink   Speedlink   G-Commerce   True10

- Costs
- Income

a Which project brought in most money?

b Which project brought in least money?

c Which project had the highest costs?

d Which project had the lowest costs?

e Which project gave Naresh the biggest profit? (Remember, profit = income − cost.)

f On which project did Naresh lose money? How can you tell?

g How much profit did Naresh make altogether?

3 This composite bar graph (right) shows the proportion of total sales and how they are made for four different companies.

a Can you work out the value of each company's total sales from this graph? Explain your answer.

b Which company does most of its sales direct from the shop?

c Which company makes the least of its sales through agents?

d Which company makes 40% of its sales through agents?

e What percentage of Company A's sales are by catalogue mail order?

f Describe the breakdown of sales by type for Company D.

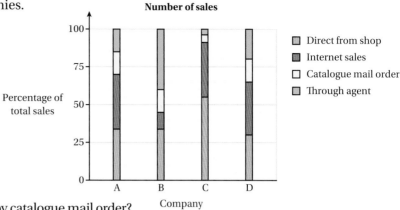

Number of sales

Percentage of total sales

Company

Legend:
- Direct from shop
- Internet sales
- Catalogue mail order
- Through agent

4 The World Health Organization (WHO) reported the following malaria data for different regions of the world in 2010.

a What percentage of the population of Africa had or were suspected of having malaria?

b In South East Asia what percentage of the population were suspected of having malaria?

c Were any of the suspected cases in the Eastern Mediterranean confirmed? How can you tell?

d Which region of the world has the biggest problem with malaria?

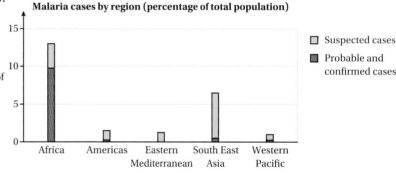

Malaria cases by region (percentage of total population)

Percentage of population

Africa, Americas, Eastern Mediterranean, South East Asia, Western Pacific

Legend:
- Suspected cases
- Probable and confirmed cases

5 The table on the right shows exam grades for boys and girls in a Year 11 group.

Construct a bar chart to show both sets of data.

Grade	Boys	Girls
A*	12	6
A	15	9
B	17	22
C	13	15
D	8	6

Section 3: Pie charts

A pie chart is useful for displaying data when you are interested in the relative sizes or the proportions of the data.

Pie charts are always circular, and so the sum of the angles at the centre must always be 360°.

When drawing pie charts that have data as percentages, each 1% will be represented by 3.6° because 360 ÷ 100 = 3.6

This data shows the area in which students in a class live:

Area	Frequency	Percentage	Angle
Reepham	12	40.0%	144°
Whitwell	6	20.0%	72°
Booton	3	10.0%	36°
Cawston	2	6.7%	24°
Salle	7	23.3%	84°

Tip

Each percentage is worked out by dividing the number of students by the total number of students and multiplying by 100; for example, $\frac{12}{30} \times 100 = 40\%$

There are 30 students altogether.

The pie chart below shows this data:

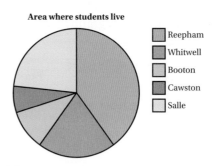

Area where students live

■ Reepham
■ Whitwell
□ Booton
■ Cawston
□ Salle

WORK IT OUT 37.3

A survey of how late 20 trains are in minutes gives the following results:

1 0 2 0 3 1 5 4 1 3 6 4 3 5 2 4 3 2 2 4

Which of the pie charts best shows this information? Explain what is wrong with the other two pie charts.

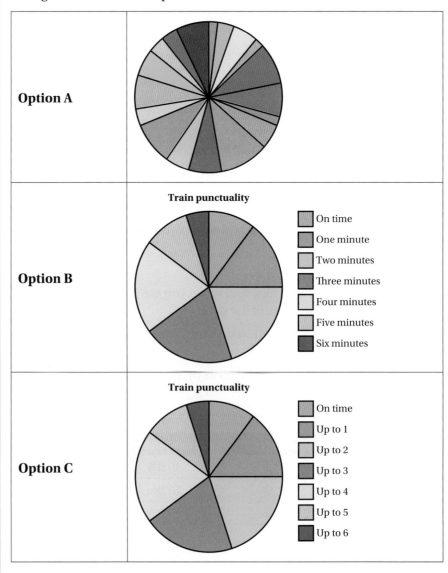

Option A	
Option B	**Train punctuality** — On time, One minute, Two minutes, Three minutes, Four minutes, Five minutes, Six minutes
Option C	**Train punctuality** — On time, Up to 1, Up to 2, Up to 3, Up to 4, Up to 5, Up to 6

EXERCISE 37D

1 Create a pie chart to represent this data:

Electricity generation	Proportion used
Gas	28%
Other fuels	2.6%
Coal	39%
Nuclear	19%
Renewables	11.4%

2 The pie charts below show the population of two different countries by age.

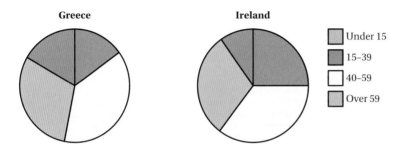

a Write down two differences between Greece and Ireland.

b Which country has the bigger number of over 59s?

c There are more under 15s in Ireland than Greece.

Is this statement true?

3 This pie chart shows the favourite leisure activity of 72 students.

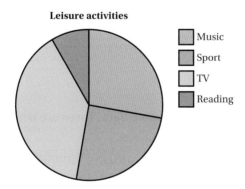

a Use a protractor to measure the sector for music. Use this measurement to work out how many students prefer music.

b Which is the most popular activity?

c How many students prefer reading?

Find answers at: cambridge.org/ukschools/gcsemaths-studentbookanswers

4 This data shows the destinations of students leaving a sixth form college:

Destination	College A	College B
Higher education	32	46
Further education	45	72
Employment	28	31
Gap year	12	24
Unemployment	15	22

Create two pie charts and use them to argue that one college is more successful than the other.

5 The department of transport maintains data for the different types of vehicles on the road in the UK. Data for vehicles other than cars is shown for 1994 and 2013.

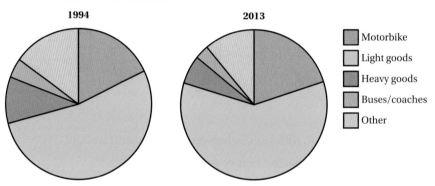

a Give two differences between the proportions for 1994 and 2013.

b If there were 6.075 million vehicles other than cars on the road in 2013, calculate the number of light goods vehicles there were.

c What percentage of vehicles other than cars were motorbikes in 2013?

Section 4: Cumulative frequency curves and histograms

Grouped and continuous data

In Section 1 you worked with discrete data. These are whole number values for data that can be counted.

In this section you are going to work with **continuous data**. These are data collected by measurement, so the data can take on any fractional value. Height, mass and age are all examples of continuous data.

You are also going to work with grouped data. When you collect data with a lot of different possible values, it makes sense to group the values. For example, if you are collecting test percentages the data values could range from 0 to 100. In this case you might group the data in tens, listing scores from 0 to 10, 11 to 20 and so on.

The groups are called **class intervals**. The top value in each interval is called the class boundary.

Key vocabulary

continuous data: data that can have any value.

class intervals: the sizes of the groups that data has been grouped into.

Generally, class intervals are equal and they do not overlap. For discrete data the intervals may be given in the form of a range such as 11–20. For continuous data the interval is often given in inequality notation. For example, heights between 25 and 30 metres might be given as $25 \leqslant h < 30$.

The class size is normally chosen to give between 5 and 10 class intervals in the data set.

Cumulative frequency

Questions can be answered using cumulative frequencies. For example:

How many cars were travelling above 30 miles per hour?

How many students scored higher than 60% on a test?

How many of the strawberries in your garden weighed at least 24 grams?

A cumulative frequency is a running total of the frequencies for each class interval. Adding the frequencies up to a particular value allows you to work out how many values were below or above that level.

This frequency table shows the masses of strawberries picked from a garden.

Mass (m) in grams	Frequency	Cumulative frequency
$12 \leqslant m < 16$	3	3
$16 \leqslant m < 20$	5	3 + 5 = 8
$20 \leqslant m < 24$	9	3 + 5 + 9 = 17
$24 \leqslant m < 28$	7	24
$28 \leqslant m < 32$	2	26

The data has been **grouped** into equal class intervals, and the **cumulative frequency** calculated as a 'running total'.

Now you can see quite quickly that 17 of the strawberries have a mass of less than 24 grams.

Cumulative frequencies can be plotted against the upper boundaries of each class interval to produce a curved graph.

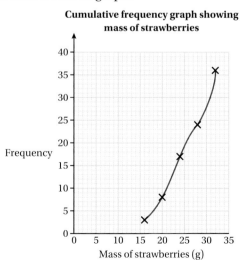

Cumulative frequency graph showing mass of strawberries

Key vocabulary

cumulative frequency: the sum total of all the frequencies up to a given value.

grouped data: data that has been put into groups.

Tip

You plot the point for each cumulative frequency **at the upper end** of the class interval. The graphs are called cumulative frequency curves, so you must join them with a smooth curved line and not broken straight lines.

Key vocabulary

histogram: a graph with bars whose area is proportional to the frequency of a variable and whose width is equal to the class interval.

Cumulative frequency curves are called ogives (oh-jives) because they take the shape of narrow pointed architectural arches (called ogees) like these ones on the Royal Pavilion in Brighton.

Histograms

Grouped continuous data can also be plotted on a graph called a **histogram**. This histogram shows the ages of members visiting a gym:

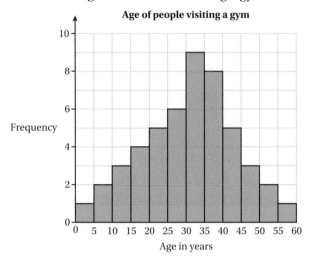

Histograms look like bar charts but there are important differences between them:

- The horizontal scale is continuous and each 'bar' is drawn above a particular class interval. For example, the first bar shows ages from 0 to 5.

- The frequency of the data is shown by the area of the bars.

- There are no spaces between the bars because the horizontal scale is continuous.

In this example, the class intervals are equal so the bars are the same width. When the class intervals are equal you can read the frequency off the vertical axis and you do not need to determine the area of the bars.

Histograms with unequal class intervals

When the class intervals in the data are not the same you cannot use the height of the bars to give the frequency. Instead, the vertical scale gives the frequency density:

$$\text{frequency density} = \frac{\text{frequency }(f)}{\text{class width}}$$

The frequency is the area of each bar, found from:

frequency = frequency density × class width

WORKED EXAMPLE 2

The ages of young people visiting a park are shown in the frequency table.

Draw a histogram to show these results.

Age in years	Frequency
$5 \leqslant \text{age} < 10$	10
$10 \leqslant \text{age} < 16$	24
$16 \leqslant \text{age} < 18$	6
$18 \leqslant \text{age}$	0

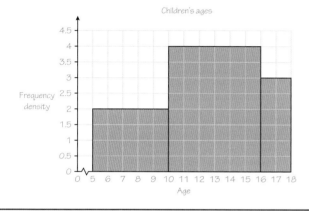

Find the class boundaries first (5, 10, 16 and 18 are the lowest values that could be in each class).

Then determine the class widths:
$10 - 5 = 5$, $16 - 10 = 6$, $18 - 16 = 2$.

In the histogram the area of the block represents the frequency, so the first group has a frequency density of 2 because 2×5 (class width) = 10 (frequency).

As there are 24 children in the group $10 \leqslant \text{age} < 16$ the density is 4 because 24 (frequency) ÷ 6 (class width) = 4.

Problem-solving framework

The heights of sunflowers grown by a class of children are measured and recorded.

85.4	114.9	99.6	81.6	105	114.7
88	99.2	107	123.8	104.5	121.4
116.7	79.4	118.5	115.8	103.8	113.6
77.5	89.9	113.6	100.7	120.3	103.5
75.9	99	104.1	99	101.8	98.7

Group the data into suitable class intervals and draw a cumulative frequency curve and a histogram to represent the data.

Steps for approaching a problem-solving question	What you would do for this example	
Step 1: Choose a class interval that allows for between 5 and 10 classes. Put the data into a frequency table.	**Class interval**	**Frequency**
	$75 \leqslant h < 95$	7
	$95 \leqslant h < 105$	11
	$105 \leqslant h < 115$	6
	$115 \leqslant h < 120$	3
	$120 \leqslant h < 125$	3

Continues on next page …

Step 2: Identify what you have to do.	You need to choose a suitable means of displaying the data and then draw it. As you have grouped data, either a cumulative frequency graph or a histogram would be appropriate. You need a cumulative frequency table.
Step 3: Start working on the problem using what you know.	

Class interval	Frequency	Cumulative frequency
$75 \leqslant h < 95$	7	7
$95 \leqslant h < 105$	11	18
$105 \leqslant h < 115$	6	24
$115 \leqslant h < 120$	3	27
$120 \leqslant h < 125$	3	30

Construct a cumulative frequency graph, remembering to use the upper boundary of each class interval.

Cumulative frequency graph showing sunflower heights

The histogram is plotted using the area of each rectangle to represent the frequency, and will look like this:

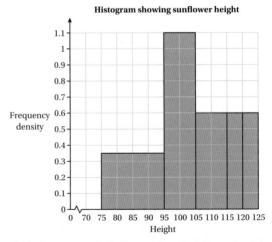

Histogram showing sunflower height

The area of each rectangle is found by dividing the frequency by the class width. The first rectangle has a frequency density of 7 (frequency) divided by 20 (class width) = 0.35

Continues on next page …

Step 4: Check your working and that your answer is reasonable.	Check the shape of the graphs. Does the cumulative frequency graph resemble an ogive curve? Do the areas of the rectangles match the numbers in each class interval?
Step 5: Have you answered the question?	Yes, the data is correctly displayed.

EXERCISE 37E

1 The number of ice creams sold on a series of days is recorded:

193	210	265	203	246	216	236
343	242	208	294	229	287	266
343	223	308	235	166	231	241
255	196	230	276	247	296	266

Tip

Too few class intervals can oversimplify, and too many can negate the effect of grouping. Aim for between 5 and 10 groups.

Group the data into suitable equal-sized class intervals, and create a cumulative frequency curve.

Use your curve to estimate:

a On how many days were less than 230 ice creams sold?

b On how many days were more than 300 ice creams sold?

2 The maximum daily temperature is measured every day for 25 days:

18.5	19.6	18.6	23.5	17.2
19	17.1	23	17.5	15
22.4	24.6	24.1	15.3	18.3
15.1	19.7	19.3	17.9	20.5
16	18.5	18.3	15.8	15.3

Group the data into suitable equal-sized class intervals, and create a cumulative frequency curve.

Use your graph to estimate:

a how many days the temperature was less than 20 °C

b how many days the temperature was above 22 °C

c how many days the temperature was between 20 °C and 22 °C.

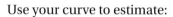 Find answers at: cambridge.org/ukschools/gcsemaths-studentbookanswers

3 The timed results from a 5 km race are given below:

20:48	18:39	26:09	23:36	21:20	26:07
23:46	23:31	20:03	21:45	23:20	22:55
24:38	25:16	22:24	18:26	21:27	21:04
17:33	22:14	20:57	24:00	19:14	24:38
19:32	26:39	17:31	23:25	22:50	21:27
25:08	22:57	23:55	20:25	25:30	24:45
21:43	19:04	18:19	17:36	22:31	25:14
22:40	21:07	24:11	21:34	25:41	23:45
25:42	24:01	20:19	26:17	20:13	25:10
20:14	24:44	26:21	23:48	22:52	24:14

Group the data into suitable equal-sized class intervals, and create a cumulative frequency curve.

Use your graph to estimate:

a how many runners completed the course in more than 25 minutes

b how many completed the course in less than 20 minutes

c how many runners finished in less than 19 minutes.

4 In a medical test, a group of students had the distance from hip to heel measured. The measurements were made correct to the nearest centimetre. The results were as follows:

85 86 91 87 77 88 83 86 74 89 85 85 80

94 82 84 89 84 94 84 76 93 86 84 94 84

Present this information in a histogram using the classes:

a $70 \leqslant d < 80$ $80 \leqslant d < 90$ $90 \leqslant d \leqslant 99$

b $70 \leqslant d < 75$ $75 \leqslant d < 80$ $80 \leqslant d < 85$ $85 \leqslant d < 90$ $90 \leqslant d \leqslant 94$

Section 5: Line graphs for time-series data

Some data that you collect change with time. For example, the average temperature each month for a year, the number of cars that pass through a junction each hour, or the amount of credit you have left on your mobile each week.

Line graphs are useful for showing how data changes over time.

When time is one of the variables it is always plotted on the horizontal axis of the graph.

The maximum temperature at a weather station is recorded at noon every day. Data which shows change over time like this is called time-series data.

Monday	Tuesday	Wednesday	Thursday	Friday	Saturday	Sunday
15 °C	17 °C	18 °C	21 °C	16 °C	20 °C	14 °C

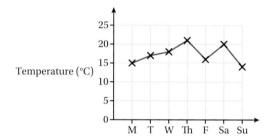

Each of the points on the line (for example, Monday, 15 °C) is joined by a straight line. This type of graph is used when you want to show trends over time.

Problem-solving framework

The average temperature each month in Alicante is as follows:

Jan 17 °C	Feb 18 °C	Mar 20 °C	Apr 21 °C	May 24 °C	Jun 28 °C
Jul 30 °C	Aug 31 °C	Sep 29 °C	Oct 25 °C	Nov 20 °C	Dec 18 °C

How can we display this data to show how the temperature changes?

Steps for approaching a problem-solving question	What you would do for this example
Step 1: If it is useful to have a table draw one.	<table><tr><td>J</td><td>F</td><td>M</td><td>A</td><td>M</td><td>J</td><td>J</td><td>A</td><td>S</td><td>O</td><td>N</td><td>D</td></tr><tr><td>17 °C</td><td>18 °C</td><td>20 °C</td><td>21 °C</td><td>24 °C</td><td>28 °C</td><td>30 °C</td><td>31 °C</td><td>29 °C</td><td>25 °C</td><td>20 °C</td><td>18 °C</td></tr></table>
Step 2: Identify what you have to do.	You need to choose a suitable means of displaying the data and then draw it.

Continues on next page …

Steps for approaching a problem-solving question	What you would do for this example
Step 3: Start working on the problem using what you know.	You know that a time-series graph shows changes over time, so it will be a good visual way of showing how the temperature varies. Choose a suitable scale and plot each point on the axes using the table. Join the points to make a line.
Step 4: Check your working and that your answer is reasonable.	Check the shape of the graph. Does it get warmer in the summer and colder in the winter? Are there any unexpected sharp increases or decreases?
Step 5: Have you answered the question?	Yes, the graph shows how the temperature changes through the year.

EXERCISE 37F

1   **a**   Construct a time-series graph for the average temperature (in °C) in a particular city, which is given in the table below.

Month	Jan	Feb	Mar	Apr	May	Jun	Jul	Aug	Sep	Oct	Nov	Dec
Average Temp (°C)	15.2	16.5	17.2	19.1	19.6	20.1	22.2	24.1	21.3	19.3	17.6	16.6

    b   Use the time-series line graph to write a brief description of how the average temperature varies in this particular city.

2   The table below gives the annual profit (in £million) of a company over a 10-year period. Construct a time-series graph of the information.

Year	Year 1	Year 2	Year 3	Year 4	Year 5	Year 6	Year 7	Year 8	Year 9	Year 10
Profit (£million)	2.2	1.8	2.3	1.2	0.6	1.1	2.2	3.1	3.7	4.2

3   The table below gives the number of teeth extracted at a dentist's surgery each month for a year.

Month	Jan	Feb	Mar	Apr	May	Jun	Jul	Aug	Sep	Oct	Nov	Dec
Number of teeth	54	47	49	60	41	45	36	11	38	42	32	22

a Represent this information on a time-series graph.

b Briefly describe how the number of teeth extracted each month changed over the year.

c Why might the number of teeth extracted fall during August?

4 The table below gives the position of a particular five-a-side football team in a league of 10 teams at the completion of each week throughout the season.

Round	1	2	3	4	5	6	7	8	9
Position	2	3	5	7	6	5	6	7	5
Round	10	11	12	13	14	15	16	17	18
Position	5	4	5	3	4	3	3	4	3

a Represent this information on a time-series graph.

b Describe the progress of the team throughout the season.

5 The data below shows the value of sales at a service station on a main road over a period of 3 years. Each quarter represents 3 months (a quarter) of the year. The quarters are labelled 1-12 in the corresponding time-series graph.

Sales quarter	Sales £thousand
Quarter 1	64
Quarter 2	82
Quarter 3	83
Quarter 4	65
Quarter 5	77
Quarter 6	89
Quarter 7	96
Quarter 8	58
Quarter 9	79
Quarter 10	92
Quarter 11	101
Quarter 12	66

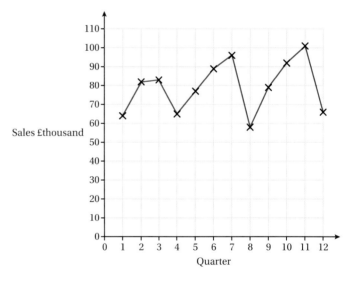

a In which quarter of each year is the value of sales highest?

b In which quarter of each year is the value of sales lowest?

c Compare the sales figures for the first quarter of each year. Are the sales figures improving from one year to the next?

6 The table below gives the numbers of garden sheds sold each quarter during 2012–2014.

Number of sales	Q1	Q2	Q3	Q4
2012	27	32	56	41
2013	33	35	65	45
2014	38	41	72	51

a Represent this information on a time-series graph.

b Describe how the shed sales have altered over the given time period.

c Does it appear that shed sales are seasonal?

7 Study the following graph.

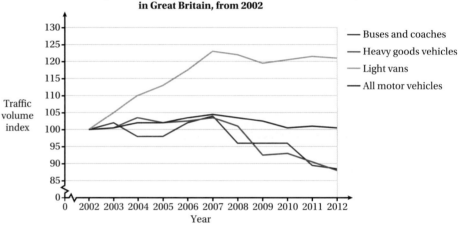

Road traffic by vehicle type (commercial and public service vehicles) in Great Britain, from 2002

a Describe the trend in numbers of light vans.

b What has happened to the number of all motor vehicles?

c Suggest why the number of heavy goods vehicles might have decreased. Can you answer this by just using the graph?

8 This graph (left) shows how the water level in a pond varies from month to month.

a When is the depth of water lowest?

b What do you think might have happened in July?

c When does the water level drop most rapidly?

d How much water is in the pond in May?

e What is the difference in depth between August and September?

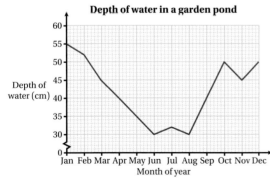

Depth of water in a garden pond

Checklist of learning and understanding

Sampling

- A sample is a representative group chosen from a population.
- In a random sample, each member of the population is equally likely to be chosen for the sample.

Tables and graphs

- A frequency table is a method of organising data by showing how often a result appears in the data.
- Data can be displayed using a number of different graphs and charts.
- All graphs should be clearly labelled and scaled, and include a title.
- Vertical line graphs and bar charts are good ways of showing discrete data, where the height of each bar, or line, determines the frequency.
- Pictograms are an interesting visual way of displaying discrete data.
- Pie charts are used to compare categories of the same data set.

Cumulative frequency curves and histograms

- Cumulative frequency curves are used to display grouped continuous numerical data.
- Histograms are specialised bar graphs that can be used to show grouped continuous data for equal and unequal class intervals. There are no gaps between the bars (unless a class interval has no data) and the area of each bar gives the frequency density of the data.

Line graphs

- Line graphs for time-series data show trends and changes over time.

Chapter review

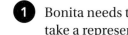

For additional questions on the topics in this chapter, visit GCSE Mathematics Online.

1 Bonita needs to find out how students travel to school, so she decides to take a representative sample.

  a Suggest two ways in which she could do this.

  b Bonita asks a representative sample of 50 students and gets results shown in the table:

Car	15
Walk	17
Bus	6
Taxi	7
Bike	5

If there are 600 students in the school, what is a sensible estimate of the number of students who walk to school?

 Find answers at: cambridge.org/ukschools/gcsemaths-studentbookanswers

2 A business employs 18 office workers and 63 factory floor workers. The manager wants nine workers for a survey.

   a What would be wrong with a simple random survey?

   b How many should be chosen from each group of workers?

   c How could the workers be chosen from each group?

3 Two adults are comparing how much money they spend each month.

Expenditure per month (£)	Josh	Ben
Rent	840	450
Food	250	300
Transport	350	160
Savings	250	40
Entertainment	110	250

   a Draw suitable graphs to enable you to compare the proportions of money they spend.

   b Write two sentences comparing their spending habits.

4 The profits for two companies are given for each quarter of a 2-year period below:

Company profits (£)	Company A	Company B
1st quarter 2013	134 820	125 912
2nd quarter 2013	138 429	189 355
3rd quarter 2013	140 721	130 969
4th quarter 2013	131 717	156 548
1st quarter 2014	103 746	219 357
2nd quarter 2014	197 028	151 296
3rd quarter 2014	187 883	249 216
4th quarter 2014	168 414	102 158

Use the data to plot a suitable graph to compare how profits change.

   a Which company is more successful?

   b Which is the biggest change between quarters?

5 The histogram gives information about the areas of 285 farms.

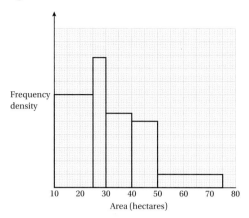

Work out an estimate for the number of these farms with
an area greater than 38 hectares. *(3 marks)*

©Pearson Education Ltd 2012

6 Two machines are used in a factory to pack crisps into packets of 65 g.

A random sample of the mass of 30 bags packed by each machine is
given in the tables below:

Machine A				
65.4	64.8	65.4	64.3	64.2
64.4	65.3	65.1	64.7	64.7
64.6	65	65.5	64.1	65
64.9	64.5	64.6	64.2	64.7
65.3	64.9	64.5	64.6	65.4
65.5	64.5	65.5	64.6	64.2

Machine B				
64	65.5	63.6	63.9	65.8
64.3	65.2	64.7	64.7	64.4
65.4	64.2	65.7	65.2	63.9
64.4	65.6	63.9	65.9	65
65.6	65.7	64	64.2	66
65	65.7	64.8	64.8	64.7

a Use class intervals of 0.5 and draw a histogram for each machine.

b Which machine is more reliable?

38 Data analysis

For more resources relatin to this chapter, visit GCSE Mathematics Online.

In this chapter you will learn to …

- calculate and compare summary statistics for ungrouped and grouped data and compare distributions.
- draw and interpret box plots.
- recognise when data is being misrepresented.
- plot and interpret scatter diagrams and lines of best fit and use them to describe correlation and predict results.
- identify outliers and understand how they can indicate errors in data.

Using mathematics: real-life applications

Analysing large sets of data enables financial and insurance companies to make predictions about what might happen in the future. Car insurance premiums are worked out according to typical or 'average' behaviour of large groups of people.

"We group drivers together by age and gender and use statistics to find typical driving behaviour for each group. Young drivers have more accidents, so their insurance costs more."

(Insurance broker)

Tip

Knowing how to calculate averages and measures of spread gives you tools to compare different sets of data. Make sure you know what these are and when to use the different measures.

Before you start…

KS3	You should remember how to find the mean, median, mode and range of a set of data.	**1**	Find the mean, median, mode and range of the following sets of data. Give your answers correct to 1 decimal place. **a** 2 4 2 7 3 5 4 2 3 1 **b** 40 20 30 60 50 10
Ch 24	You should be able to plot coordinates on a set of axes.	**2**	Write down the coordinates of points A, B and C on the line.
Ch 24	You should be able to recognise whether a gradient is positive or negative.	**3**	Use the graph above. **a** What is the gradient of the graph? **b** What is the equation of the line?

Assess your starting point using the Launchpad

STEP 1

1 The table shows how many cups of coffee a group of office workers drank in a particular week.

Number of cups of coffee	Frequency
0–5	16
6–10	5
11–15	5
16–20	4
21–25	5
26–30	3

a What is the modal class of the data?

b Estimate the median number of cups consumed per week.

c Estimate the mean number of cups of coffee consumed per week.

d How many people drink 10 or fewer cups of coffee per week?

**GO TO
Section 1**:
Summary statistics

2 These box plots compare the distribution of a class's marks in March and June of the same year.

a Comment on the differences in the data.

b Did the class's performance improve in June?

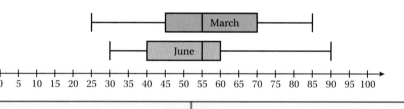

STEP 2

3 This graph appeared in a newspaper article. Explain how this graph could be misleading.

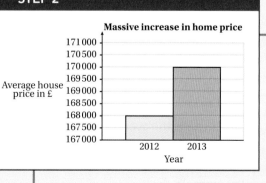

**GO TO
Section 2**:
Misleading graphs

**GO TO
Step 3**:
The Launchpad continues on the next page …

Find answers at: cambridge.org/ukschools/gcsemaths-studentbookanswers

Launchpad continued …

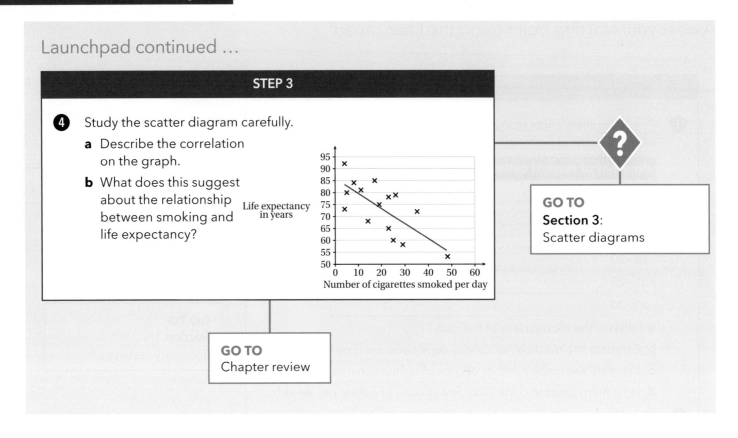

STEP 3

4 Study the scatter diagram carefully.

a Describe the correlation on the graph.

b What does this suggest about the relationship between smoking and life expectancy?

Life expectancy in years

Number of cigarettes smoked per day

GO TO
Section 3:
Scatter diagrams

GO TO
Chapter review

Section 1: Summary statistics

The mean, median and mode are all types of averages, or measures of central tendency.

The range is a measure of spread or dispersion. The range is useful for determining whether the mean is distorted or not.

- the mean: $\dfrac{\text{sum of values}}{\text{number of values}}$

- the mode: the value with the highest frequency

- the median: the middle value when the values are arranged in size order

- the range: the difference between the highest value and the lowest value.

To describe and compare two sets of data, calculate the averages and range and write sentences to summarise what you notice.

Choosing the correct average

The type of average that you choose depends on the situation and what you want to know.

The mean is the average that is used most often. The mean is useful when you want to know a typical value. If the data is very spread out (it has a big range) then the mean will not be typical.

For example, the boss in a company earns £20 000 per month. Her nine employees earn £2000 each. This gives a mean salary of £3800, which is not typical.

In this situation, the median salary is £2000 and the modal salary is £2000. Both are more representative than the mean.

When the data is not numerical, you have to use the mode as the average.

The mode is most useful when you need to know which item is most common or most popular.

You would use the mode when you wanted to show:

- which clothing size was bought most often
- which shoe size is most common
- which brand of mobile phone is the most popular.

The average you choose can affect how you see the data.

Quartiles and interquartile range

Quartiles and the interquartile range are summary statistics that give more information about the spread of data.

The median, which is the middle data item in an ordered set of data values, divides the data into two halves, with 50% of the data to the left of the median, and 50% of the data to the right of the median.

The quartiles divide an ordered data set into quarters. You work out the value of the quartiles in a similar way to the median.

The first quartile (Q_1) is the data value one quarter of the way along the data set.

So 25% of the values are smaller than the first quartile, and three-quarters (75%) lie to the right of the first quartile.

The second quartile (Q_2) is the same as the median.

The third quartile (Q_3) is the value that lies three-quarters of the way along the data set. So 75% of the values are smaller than this value.

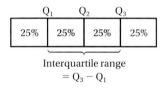

The interquartile range (IQR) is the difference between the values of the upper and lower quartiles.

IQR = third quartile − first quartile

The IQR tells you where the middle 50% of the data occurs. This is important to know, because it gives us information about whether the data is spread out far away from the median, or clustered close to the median value.

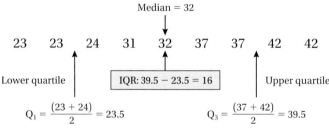

WORKED EXAMPLE 1

Josh has developed a website and is monitoring how many hits it receives per hour.

In the first two days (48 hours) it receives the following numbers of hits per hour (arranged in numerical order):

100	105	106	106	107	107	108	110	117	118
135	137	145	148	148	148	153	155	157	159
162	171	171	179	183	183	185	185	189	199
201	203	204	209	216	220	223	224	224	227
229	230	231	233	234	235	237	238		

Continues on next page …

a Find the following summary statistics:

  i the mean, median and mode

  ii the range.

    i Mean of the data: $8394 \div 48 = 174.88$ hits.

     Median of the data is halfway between the 24th and the 25th data values

$$= \frac{179 + 183}{2} = 181 \text{ hits.}$$

     The value 148 is the mode because it occurs three times.

    ii The range $= 238 - 100 = 138$.

b Josh is trying to sell advertising on his website.

Write a mathematical sentence he could use about the number of hits his site is receiving.

There is a consistent hit rate of over 100 hits per hour with 175 hits per hour on average.

c Josh compares his data to a similar website run by Delia. Delia's data set has the following data values:

mean = 180 hits

median = 140 hits

mode = 135 hits

range = 200

What can Josh say to compare the two sets?

Although the mean of the hits is a bit higher for Delia's set, the median is much lower. This indicates that the mean of Delia's hits is influenced by a few high values, but usually the number of hits is lower. Delia's data shows a wider range, showing that the data is more spread out and therefore less consistent.

Analysing grouped data

Data is sometimes grouped together before it is analysed. The groups are known as **class intervals**. Note that they do not overlap.

For example:

Marks scored	Frequency
0−9	6
10−19	6
20−29	4
30−39	5
40−50	9
Total	30

When you only have the grouped data in a frequency table, it is not possible to calculate precise values for the mean, median, mode and range because you don't know the individual values.

You can identify the modal and median classes from the previous table.

- The modal class is the class interval that has the most elements, not the individual value that appears the most. In this table the modal class is 40–50 marks.
- To estimate the median of grouped data, find the class interval in which the middle value occurs. It is only possible to say that the median is within that group. In the table there are 30 values, the middle value is between the 15th and 16th values, so it must fall into the class 20–29 marks.

Estimating the mean of a frequency distribution

To estimate the mean of grouped data find the midpoint of each class interval. The midpoint is found by adding the lowest and highest possible values for each class interval and dividing by 2. Multiply each midpoint by the frequency for each class interval. Find the total of these values, and divide by the total number of values you have.

WORKED EXAMPLE 2

Ben goes fishing and records the masses of the fish he catches in the table below:

Mass (m) in kg	Frequency	Midpoint	Midpoint × frequency
$2 \leqslant m < 4$	5		
$4 \leqslant m < 6$	8		
$6 \leqslant m < 8$	4		
$8 \leqslant m < 10$	9		
$10 \leqslant m < 12$	3		

a Copy and complete the table.

b Find the modal class.

c Estimate the mean, median and range.

a *Completed table:*

Mass (m) in kg	Frequency	Midpoint	Midpoint × frequency
$2 \leqslant m < 4$	5	3	15
$4 \leqslant m < 6$	8	5	40
$6 \leqslant m < 8$	4	7	28
$8 \leqslant m < 10$	9	9	81
$10 \leqslant m < 12$	3	11	33

Continues on next page …

Find answers at: cambridge.org/ukschools/gcsemaths-studentbookanswers

b The modal class is $8 \leqslant m < 10$ kg.

c Estimating the mean:
Total of the midpoint × frequency values is 197.
Estimated mean is 197 ÷ 29 = 6.79 kg.
The median class:
There are 29 values, so the middle value is value number 15. This occurs in the interval $6 \leqslant m < 8$ kg.
The range is 12 − 2 = 10 kg.

EXERCISE 38A

1 A large company has kept a record of how many days each employee is absent from work each year.

The results are in the table below:

Days absent (d)	Frequency	Midpoint	Midpoint × frequency
$0 \leqslant d < 5$	15		
$5 \leqslant d < 10$	23		
$10 \leqslant d < 15$	19		
$15 \leqslant d < 20$	12		
$20 \leqslant d < 25$	6		
Total			

a Copy and complete the table.

b Use the information to find the modal class.

c Estimate the mean, median and range.

2 For a charity event, several students are throwing darts at a dart board while blindfolded.

The scores they achieve are given on the right:

89	11	57	25	55	78
28	35	15	90	83	38
57	37	28	14	36	40
74	59	57	9	18	70
25	18	22	2	37	53
74	61	79	53	87	46
30	29	4	90	83	77

a Choose suitable class intervals and group the data.

b Estimate the mean, the median and the range of the scores.

c Is it sensible to estimate the range?

d What is the modal group?

3 A health club has measured its members' heights (in metres) before buying some new gym equipment. The data is given on the right:

a Use group intervals of every 5 cm, starting with the group $1.45 \leqslant h < 1.50$

Estimate the mean and the median.

b What is the modal class?

c Use class intervals of every 10 cm, starting with the class $1.40 \leqslant h < 1.50$

What difference does this make to your estimates of the mean and median?

1.68	1.68	1.58	1.72	1.58	1.75	1.89
1.84	1.55	1.65	1.66	1.84	1.55	1.81
1.47	1.55	1.58	1.66	1.55	1.61	1.68
1.57	1.57	1.69	1.65	1.75	1.55	1.73
1.64	1.85	1.53	1.65	1.77	1.66	1.75
1.75	1.59	1.88	1.82	1.62	1.69	1.67
1.63	1.66	1.84	1.77	1.52	1.84	1.53

4 30 runners complete a marathon race. Their times are given below (to the nearest minute):

2 h 45 min, 3 h 25 min, 3 h 46 min, 4 h 15 min, 5 h 8 min, 4 h 49 min,
4 h 18 min, 3 h 38 min, 3 h 43 min, 3 h 5 min, 2 h 55 min, 4 h 23 min,
4 h 25 min, 3 h 39 min, 3 h 20 min, 4 h 1 min, 3 h 33 min, 4 h 6 min,
5 h 11 min, 2 h 51 min, 4 h 35 min, 3 h 19 min, 4 h 47 min, 4 h 28 min,
5 h 5 min, 4 h 19 min, 2 h 46 min, 3 h 18 min, 3 h 53 min, 4 h 35 min.

a Group the data into suitable class intervals.

b Find the modal class.

c Estimate the mean, median and range.

5 The mass of fruit harvested in a week from an orchard is recorded in the table below.

Mass (m) of fruit in kg	Frequency	Midpoint of class interval	Midpoint × frequency
$2000 \leqslant m < 2500$	15		
$2500 \leqslant m < 3000$	11		
$3000 \leqslant m < 3500$	13		
$3500 \leqslant m < 4000$	7		
$4000 \leqslant m < 4500$	2		
$4500 \leqslant m < 5000$	2		
$5000 \leqslant m < 5500$	2		
Total			

a Calculate an estimate of the mean mass of the fruit harvested in a week.

b In which interval does the median lie?

6 11 Year 10 students were asked how long they chatted on their mobile phones one evening. Their times, in minutes, were:

18, 22, 30, 36, 40, 42, 45, 50, 50, 55, 60

a What are the values of Q_1, Q_2 and Q_3?

b What is the interquartile range?

Tip

Tip

Remember that cumulative frequency graphs are drawn from grouped data and are plotted at the upper end of the class interval.

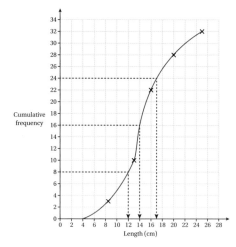

Estimating values from cumulative frequency graphs

It is possible to find summary statistics about grouped data from a cumulative frequency curve.

In the graph shown below left there are 32 pieces of data, as the maximum cumulative frequency is 32.

The median of the data is therefore halfway up the vertical scale (16). Draw a line across to the curve and down to the horizontal scale giving a value of 14. (This is an estimate of the median as the data is grouped.)

Q_1 is the value $\frac{1}{4}$ of the total frequency. $\frac{1}{4}$ of 32 is 8, making 12 an estimate of Q_1.

Q_3 is the value $\frac{3}{4}$ of the total frequency. $\frac{3}{4}$ of 32 is 24, so 17 is an estimate of the upper quartile.

The interquartile range is upper quartile − lower quartile, and is a way of measuring how spread out the middle 50% of the data values are.

In this example, the interquartile range (IQR) is $17 - 12 = 5$ (although this is an estimate).

WORKED EXAMPLE 3

24 dogs are weighed and their masses recorded:

46	41	44	38	49	30
27	49	43	30	37	48
30	28	46	51	43	36
47	52	37	29	38	40

a Group the data into suitable equal-sized class intervals and draw a cumulative frequency graph.

b Use the cumulative frequency graph to estimate the median and the interquartile range.

a *Grouped data*

Class intervals	Frequency	Cumulative frequency
$25 \leqslant m < 30$	3	3
$30 \leqslant m < 35$	3	6
$35 \leqslant m < 40$	5	11
$40 \leqslant m < 45$	5	16
$45 \leqslant m < 50$	6	22
$50 \leqslant m < 55$	2	24

Continues on next page …

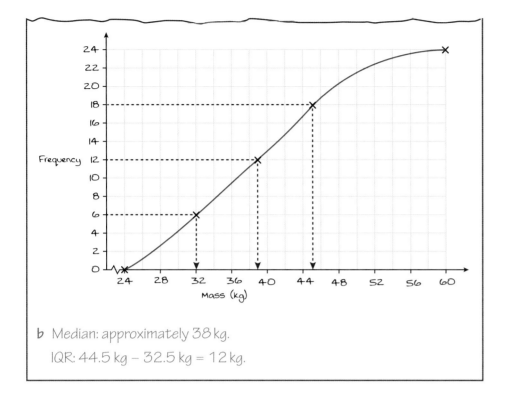

b Median: approximately 38 kg.

IQR: 44.5 kg – 32.5 kg = 12 kg.

EXERCISE 38B

1 The graph below shows the cumulative frequency of the ages of 30 members of a bingo club.

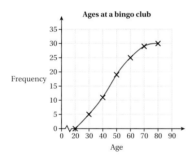

Use the graph to estimate the median and interquartile range of the ages.

2 The graph below shows the prices of 25 cars in a second-hand car shop.

Use the graph to estimate the median and the interquartile range of the prices.

Find answers at: cambridge.org/ukschools/gcsemaths-studentbookanswers

3 The graph below shows the time taken for the same train journey on 32 different occasions.

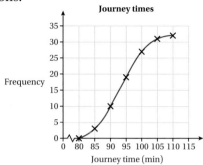

Use the graph to estimate the median and the interquartile range of the journey times.

Using box plots to compare two sets of data

A **box plot** shows five summary statistics: the lowest and highest values (range), the first and third quartiles (the interquartile range) and the median. The box plot gives an instant impression of how the data set is distributed.

It is especially useful for comparing data for two different populations, by aligning the box plots on the same number line.

WORKED EXAMPLE 4

The masses in kilograms of 20 students are (in order): 48, 52, 54, 55, 55, 58, 58, 61, 62, 63, 63, 64, 65, 66, 66, 67, 69, 70, 72, 79.

Draw a box plot to show these data.

There are 20 data values, so the median will be halfway between the 10th and the 11th data values. In this case they are both 63, so the median is 63 kg.

To find Q_1, consider the data values that are lower than the median. Q_1 is halfway between the 5th and 6th data values,

so $Q_1 = \dfrac{55 + 58}{2} = 56.5$ kg.

To find Q_3, consider the data values that are higher than the median. Q_3 is halfway between the 15th and 16th data values,

so $Q_3 = \dfrac{66 + 67}{2} = 66.7$ kg.

To draw a box plot, use a horizontal scale that allows the highest and lowest values.

Mark the median, and the upper (Q_3) and lower (Q_1) quartiles.

Create a rectangle from the upper and lower quartiles as shown.

Extend a horizontal line to the highest and lowest values.

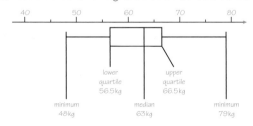

Tip

When comparing box plots, plot them on the same scale so that you can compare the IQR, median and range.

686

WORKED EXAMPLE 5

There are 10 boys and 10 girls in a Year 7 class.

Their heights (in cm) are:

Girls	137	133	141	137	138	134	149	144	144	131
Boys	145	142	146	139	138	148	138	147	142	146

a Use calculations of the mean, median and range to describe and compare these populations.

b Draw a box plot for both sets of data, and compare the interquartile ranges.

a Arrange data in order:

Girls: 131   133   134   137   137   138   141   144   144   149

Girls: mean = 138.8 cm, median = 137.5 cm and range = 18 cm.

Boys: 138   138   139   142   142   145   146   146   147   148

Boys: mean = 143.1 cm, median = 143.5 cm and range = 10 cm.

The boys' averages are higher than the girls'. The girls' range is bigger than the boys'.

b Box plot:

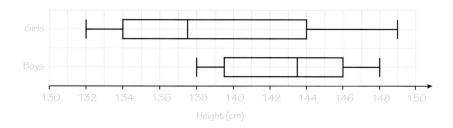

The IQR for girls (10 cm) is wider than that for boys (7 cm), showing that the data is more varied and spread out.

EXERCISE 38C

1 The results from two maths tests are given.

A	35	68	55	52	49	63	61	69	35	53
B	47	34	71	41	60	44	57	74	67	64

Describe and compare the results.

2 Two cricketers are having an argument about who has had the better season.

They have both batted 16 times, and the number of runs they have scored in each innings is as follows:

Ahmed   27 16 36 27 55 35 51 38 44 17 41 53 7 43 48 49

Bill   2 30 44 11 26 32 13 46 40 44 0 45 15 34 14 24

a Compare and describe their records.

b Who do you think has had the better season?

3 Yusuf has recorded the time in minutes it takes him to get home on two different buses.

Which bus route should he use?

Bus 127   17 17 21 23 19 20 19 18 21 22 19 22 21 20

Bus 362   23 26 20 15 15 20 26 19 18 15 16

Explain your answer. Does it matter that he has more data about the 127 bus?

4 A factory needs to choose between two machines that are both capable of bottling soft drinks.

Both manufacturers have provided data about how many bottles each machine fills per hour.

Machine A		Machine B	
Bottles (b)	**Frequency**	**Bottles (b)**	**Frequency**
$200 < b \leqslant 250$	36	$200 < b \leqslant 250$	16
$250 < b \leqslant 300$	48	$250 < b \leqslant 300$	58
$300 < b \leqslant 350$	59	$300 < b \leqslant 350$	63
$350 < b \leqslant 400$	61	$350 < b \leqslant 400$	78
$400 < b \leqslant 450$	21	$400 < b \leqslant 450$	15

Use estimates of the mean, median and the range along with the modal group to decide which machine to choose.

5 a The median, rather than the mean, is usually given when discussing ages, house prices and incomes. Why do you think this is the case?

b Give other examples in which it would be appropriate to use the median as the measure of the centre rather than the mean.

c Give examples in which it would be appropriate to use the mean as the measure of the centre rather than the median.

6 The heights, measured in centimetres, of 25 students in a class are:

170   175   133   153   164   189   143   133   167   145

150   164   169   159   177   186   173   164   177   168

142   155   153   167   166

a Find Q_1, the median and Q_3.

b Find the interquartile range.

c Draw a box plot to display the data.

7 The annual incomes of 30 people, given correct to the nearest £1000, are:

54 000	67 000	92 000	78 000	54 000	87 000
102 000	112 000	132 000	45 000	256 000	89 000
78 000	98 000	34 000	75 000	65 000	100 000
34 000	68 000	79 000	81 000	82 000	103 000
21 000	345 000	98 000	67 000	105 000	98 000

a Find Q_1, the median and Q_3.

b Find the interquartile range.

c Draw a box plot to display the data.

8 Two teams of friends have recorded their scores on a game and created a pair of box plots.

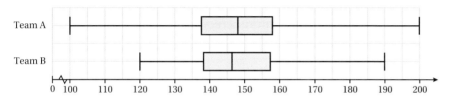

a What is the interquartile range for Team A?

b What is the interquartile range for Team B?

c Which team has the most consistent scores?

d To stay in the game you must score at least 120. Which team seems most likely to stay in?

e Which team gets the highest scores?

f Explain your reasons for part **e**.

Section 2: Misleading graphs

One of the advantages of using graphs is that they show information at a glance. But graphs can also be misleading because most people do not look at them very closely.

When you look carefully at a graph you might find that it has been drawn in a way that gives a misleading impression. Sometimes this is intentional, sometimes it is not. You need to be able to look at graphs and know if they are misleading or wrong.

When you look at a graph, you have to think about:

- the scale and whether or not it has been exaggerated in any way to give a particular impression
- whether or not the scale starts at 0 – this can affect the information shown and give a misleading impression
- whether bars or pie diagrams have sections that look three-dimensional, which make some parts look much bigger than others
- whether the scales are labelled and whether or not the graph has a title
- whether the source of the data is given.

Find answers at: cambridge.org/ukschools/gcsemaths-studentbookanswers

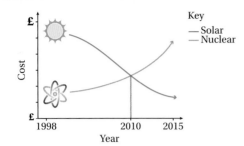

Here are some examples of misleading graphs.

This graph (left) seems to suggest that the price of solar energy is dropping quickly while the cost of nuclear power is increasing.

There are no values on the scale, so it is not possible to decide whether that is really true and no source is given for the information. The scale could be £5 million at the bottom and £10 million at the top, in which case the graph would be very misleading.

You also don't know which costs are being compared. The graph could be comparing the cost of building a nuclear power station (very expensive) and the cost of installing 25 solar panels (much less expensive).

The graph below is suggesting that recycling has increased dramatically from 1975. The graph uses proportion to mislead. If you look at the scale, you will see that the amount of recycled material has increased from 100 kg to 250 kg, so 2.5 times more material is recycled. The bin, however, is about six times bigger, so it looks like much more is recycled.

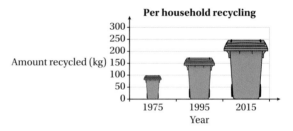

By drawing the pie chart (on the left) in this orientation and making the sectors appear 3D, it looks as if raisins are just as popular as peanuts and that popcorn is more popular than crisps. The real figures show that only 5% chose raisins and 11% chose peanuts, so the ▇ sector that sticks out represents less than half of the ▇ sector. The other two sectors each represent 42% but they do not look the same size in this graph.

WORKED EXAMPLE 6

What is wrong with this graph?

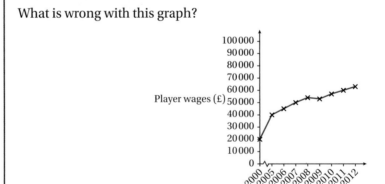

The scale of the vertical axis goes as high as £100 000, which makes the increases in wages from year to year appear to be less significant. The small scale makes the slope appear flatter. The years 2001–2004 are omitted, making the increase between 2000 and 2005 seem more significant.

EXERCISE 38D

1 Identify the error in this graph.

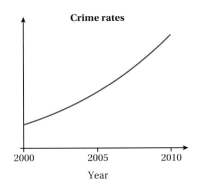

2 How is this graph misleading?

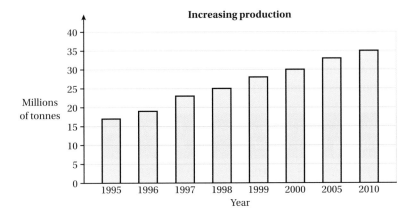

Why might someone have drawn the graph like this?

3 Look carefully at the graph below.

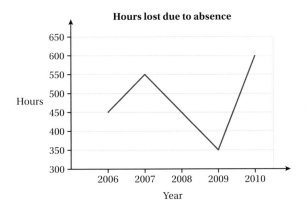

a What is misleading about this graph?

b Why do you think it has been drawn this way?

4 The same data as in question **3** has been presented in this 3D graph.

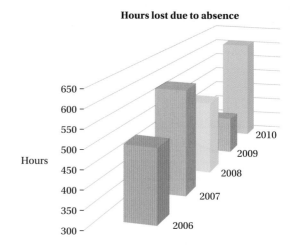

Hours lost due to absence

a Which year has the most hours lost, 2006 or 2008?

b Why is it hard to tell?

5 You are given the following data showing viewing figures for various TV programmes (in millions).

Week beginning	*Britain's Got Talent*	*The Crimson Field*	*Gogglebox*
7/4/14	10.03	6.89	2.75
14/4/14	8.45	6.31	3.37
21/4/14	8.63	6.25	3.48
28/4/14	8.45	6.01	3.47
5/5/14	8.58	6.33	3.54

Choose one of the TV programmes and create a graph which shows how well it has performed. You can use any type of graph, but you must not change the numbers.

Section 3: Scatter diagrams

A scatter diagram is used to show whether or not there is a relationship between two sets of data collected in pairs. Data that is collected in pairs is called **bivariate data**.

For example, you could record the number of hours different students spend studying and the results they get in a test. This would give two pieces of data for each learner: time spent studying and results. You can think of these as a pair of number coordinates (x, y).

In bivariate data, both sets of data are numerical, so each pair of data can be plotted as a point using coordinates on a pair of axes.

Key vocabulary

bivariate data: data that is collected in pairs.

correlation: relationship or connection between data items.

Once you have plotted the data, you can look for a pattern to see whether there is a relationship or correlation between the two variables or not. The diagrams below show the typical patterns of correlation and what they mean.

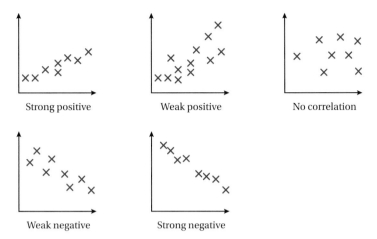

Strong positive   Weak positive   No correlation

Weak negative   Strong negative

WORKED EXAMPLE 7

Nick says people who are good at maths are also good at science.

Use this data to draw a scatter diagram and comment on whether Nick is correct or not.

	Maths average (%)	Science average (%)
Student A	20	22
Student B	32	30
Student C	45	39
Student D	38	40
Student E	60	60
Student F	80	70
Student G	80	72
Student H	90	90
Student I	80	25
Student J	60	65

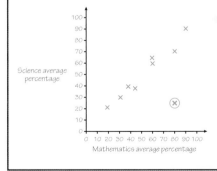

The points slope up towards the right, so it seems there is a positive correlation between maths achievement and science achievement. Nick seems to be correct.

Key vocabulary

outlier: data value that is much larger or smaller than others in the same data set.

dependent variable: data that is measured in an experiment.

interpolation: using two known values to estimate an unknown value.

extrapolation: using values within a known range to estimate an unknown value that lies outside of that range.

Look at the graph in Worked example 7.

Note that maths is on the horizontal axis and science on the vertical axis.

Science is the **dependent variable** in this case. Nick's statement is that science achievement is dependent on whether or not you are good at maths. Maths is the independent variable so it goes on the horizontal axis.

The pattern of points is used to decide whether there is a relationship. In this case, the points are grouped fairly closely and they form a thick line that slopes up to the right, so you can say there is a positive correlation between the scores.

One point is far away from the others and doesn't seem to fit the pattern (shown circled). It shows a student with a high mark for maths but a low mark for science. This point is an **outlier** in this set of data.

It is important to note that *correlation is not causation*. This means that although there might be a relationship between two variables, the change in one cannot be said to be the definite reason for the change in the other; one does not necessarily cause the other.

Lines of best fit

A line of best fit is used to show a general trend on a scatter diagram.

This is a line drawn on the graph passing as close to as many points as possible.

This is a line of best fit for the scatter diagram in Worked example 7.

You can use a line of best fit to make predictions based on the collected data.

For example, if you wanted to predict the science results for a student who got 90% (or any other value) for maths, you could find this is 85% using the line. This is shown by the dotted line on the diagram (left).

Estimating a value in this way is known as **interpolation**, but can only be used as a safe estimate if the values lie within the range of the original data. **Extrapolation** is a similar process but here the line of best fit is used to predict a result whose values lie outside the range of the original data. Results from extrapolation should be treated with care as they can be unreliable.

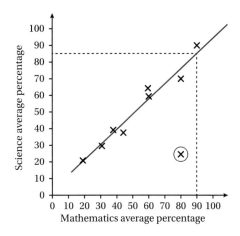

EXERCISE 38E

1 Draw a scatter diagram for the following data and draw a line of best fit:

Homework (minutes)	10	25	38	65	84	105	135	158
TV viewing (minutes)	60	55	50	20	30	15	10	8

What kind of correlation is this?

2

Miles per gallon	64	60	59	58	55	49	47	42
Car engine size (litres)	1.1	1.3	1.4	1.6	1.8	2	2.5	3

a Draw a scatter diagram to show the relationship between car engine size and fuel economy (miles per gallon).

b Draw a line of best fit for this data.

c Use the line of best fit to estimate the fuel economy of a car with a 1.5-litre engine.

d Why would it not be a good idea to use the line of best fit to estimate the economy of a car with a 6-litre engine?

3 Mike has an ice cream stall in the local park.

He writes down the number of ice creams he sells and the maximum temperature each day for a week.

Ice creams sold	86	89	45	69	84	25	78
Maximum temperature	25 °C	26 °C	19 °C	23 °C	25 °C	15 °C	21 °C

a Draw a scatter diagram to show the correlation between ice cream sales and the temperature.

b Can you suggest any other factors that might affect sales?

4 During a census the number of people living in each house is recorded.

House number	1	3	5	7	9	11	13	15	17	19	21
Number of residents	1	5	1	4	2	5	6	3	5	3	6

a Draw a scatter diagram to show this data.

b What kind of correlation is this?

5 The table below shows the athlete's height and the height jumped by the last 10 men's high jump world record holders.

Athlete	Athlete height (m)	Height jumped (m)
Sotomayor	1.95	2.45
Sjoberg	2.00	2.42
Paklin	1.91	2.41
Povarnitsyn	2.01	2.40
Jianhua	1.93	2.39
Wessig	2.00	2.36
Mogenburg	2.01	2.35
Wszola	1.90	2.35
Yashchenko	1.93	2.34
Stones	1.96	2.32

a Draw a scatter diagram showing this data.

b Is there a correlation between the height of the jumper and the height he jumped?

Find answers at: cambridge.org/ukschools/gcsemaths-studentbookanswers

Outliers

Outliers are data values that lie outside the normal range for a set of data. In science experiments they might be 'freak' results or the result of inaccurate measurements. It can be difficult to decide when it is reasonable to disregard an outlier, but if it is an obvious error then the value is usually just ignored.

Outliers can't be ignored just because they spoil a pattern. Outliers will have an impact on calculating the mean and the range of a set of data, but less so when finding the median and the mode.

On a scatter diagram an outlier will be a point that is away from the main scatter of points, or might fit the line of best fit but be at an extreme value.

WORKED EXAMPLE 8

A coach records the 100 m times of her 10 athletes at the start and the end of a week of intense training.

Nine of the athletes improve by a mean of 0.2 seconds, but one athlete is 2 seconds slower.

Can the coach claim to be making an impact on her athletes?

Yes, the coach is making an impact on the athletes, although the mean would show a reduced performance, because the single athlete's performance has reduced by much more than the others have improved. The athlete with reduced performance is an outlier, and her performance may be affected by ill health.

EXERCISE 38F

1 Several students sit a maths test and their scores are given below:

| 54 | 50 | 47 | 42 | 54 | 44 | 36 | 37 | 45 | 36 | 55 | 55 | 52 | 85 | 39 |

  a What is the mean score in the test?

  b What is the range?

  c What is the median score?

  d What is the median without the outlier?

  e What is the mean without the outlier?

2 Several students sit a maths and an English exam. Their scores are given below:

| English | 49 | 42 | 46 | 44 | 53 | 41 | 64 | 14 | 44 | 53 | 55 | 42 |
| Maths | 46 | 47 | 43 | 45 | 49 | 48 | 69 | 39 | 33 | 46 | 53 | 44 |

  a Plot their scores on a scatter diagram.

  b Draw a line of best fit on your scatter diagram.

  c Are any of the points outliers?

3 The time taken to travel by train from Norwich to London in minutes is recorded for 20 journeys:

109	129	98	106	109	156	128	98	99	113
126	99	105	110	126	98	106	114	122	107

On a normal day the journey should take between 95 and 115 minutes, depending on the number of stops at stations.

a What is the mean journey time?

b The train company claim that the mean journey time is 111 minutes on a normal day.

Is this right?

Checklist of learning and understanding

Summary statistics

- The mean, median and mode are all measures of central tendency, which are often called 'averages'. They can be found precisely for populations that are ungrouped, and estimated for grouped data.

- The range is a measure of spread. It can be found precisely for ungrouped data and estimated for grouped data.

- Quartiles are the values that divide an ordered set of data into quarters.

- The interquartile range is the range between the upper and lower quartiles, and is a measure of spread.

- Box plots show the range, the quartiles and the median value and are a good way of comparing data sets.

Misleading graphs

- The way that data is presented in graphs can be misleading. Watch out for uneven scales on the axes and graphs that show comparisons using areas, which exaggerate increases.

Scatter diagrams and correlation

- Scatter diagrams can be used to look for correlations in bivariate data. A correlation is a relationship, such as one quantity increasing as another decreases. Some bivariate data has no correlation.

- Correlation does not mean causation; in other words, identifying a relationship does not necessarily mean that a change in one data set is causing the change in the other.

- Outliers are pieces of data that sit outside the pattern or expected result. They can be ignored if an obvious error, but otherwise should be considered and explained.

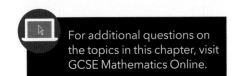

For additional questions on the topics in this chapter, visit GCSE Mathematics Online.

Chapter review

1 Windsurfers need a certain amount of wind to surf, but too much can be dangerous.

A learner would typically surf in a speed of 7–18 knots, but an expert would prefer to surf at above 30 knots.

Use the data on wind speed in knots measured at the same time each day for the two lakes below to decide which lake is better for beginners and which for experts. Use measures of central tendency and spread to support your argument.

First lake (knots)	0	21	33	13	20	11	35	3	5	3	31
	28	19	19	22	26	40	40	4	25	21	26
Second lake (knots)	15	11	19	11	10	19	23	25	10	18	10
	16	23	15	15	20	22	10	13	11	18	18

2 The box plot shows the height of 30 Year 10 students in centimetres.

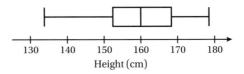

Height (cm)

a What information is shown on the box plot?

b How does this help you make sense of the data?

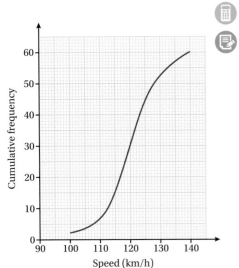

3 The cumulative frequency graph shows information about the speeds of 60 cars on a motorway one Sunday morning.

a Use the graph to find an estimate for the median speed. *(1 mark)*

The speed limit on this motorway is 130 km/h.

The traffic police say that more than 20% of cars travelling on the motorway break the speed limit.

b Comment on what the traffic police say. *(3 marks)*

For these 60 cars the minimum speed was 97 km/h and the maximum speed was 138 km/h.

c Use the cumulative frequency graph and the information above to draw a box plot showing information about the speeds of the cars. *(3 marks)*

©Pearson Education Ltd 2010

4 Study the two line graphs.

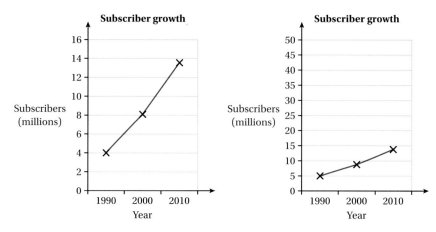

a These two graphs show the same data. Explain why they look different.

b Which graph would you use if you were a mobile phone service provider who wanted to suggest that there had been a huge increase in subscribers over this period? Why?

c Who might find the other graph useful? Why?

5 Data for the price of chocolate bars and their mass is given:

Price	45p	80p	£1.50	£3.00	£5.00	£10
Mass	35 g	80 g	175 g	320 g	540 g	1 kg

a Plot the data on a scatter diagram and draw a line of best fit.

b State what type of correlation there is.

39 Interpretation of graphs

In this chapter you will learn how to ...

- construct and interpret graphs in real-world contexts.
- interpret the gradient of a straight-line graph as a rate of change.
- find and interpret the gradient at a point on a curve as the instantaneous rate of change.
- measure the area under a graph in order to find further information.

For more resources relating to this chapter, visit GCSE Mathematics Online.

Using mathematics: real-life applications

All sorts of information can be obtained from graphs in real-life contexts. The shape of a graph, its gradient and the area underneath it can tell us about speed, time, acceleration, prices, earnings, break-even points or the values of one currency against another, among other things.

"My car needs to perform at its optimum limits. We generate and analyse diagnostic graphs to calculate the slight changes that would increase power, acceleration and top speed." *(Racing driver)*

Before you start ...

Ch 35	You will need to be able to distinguish between direct and inverse proportion.	**1** Which of these graphs shows an inverse proportion? How do you know this? 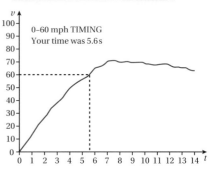
Ch 24	You'll need to be able to calculate the gradient of a straight line.	**2** Calculate the gradient of *AB*.
Ch 12	You'll need to be able to work with the area of composite shapes.	**3** *ABCD* is a rectangle of area $63\,\text{cm}^2$. Given that *CD* = 7 cm, determine the area of trapezium *BCDE*.

Assess your starting point using the Launchpad

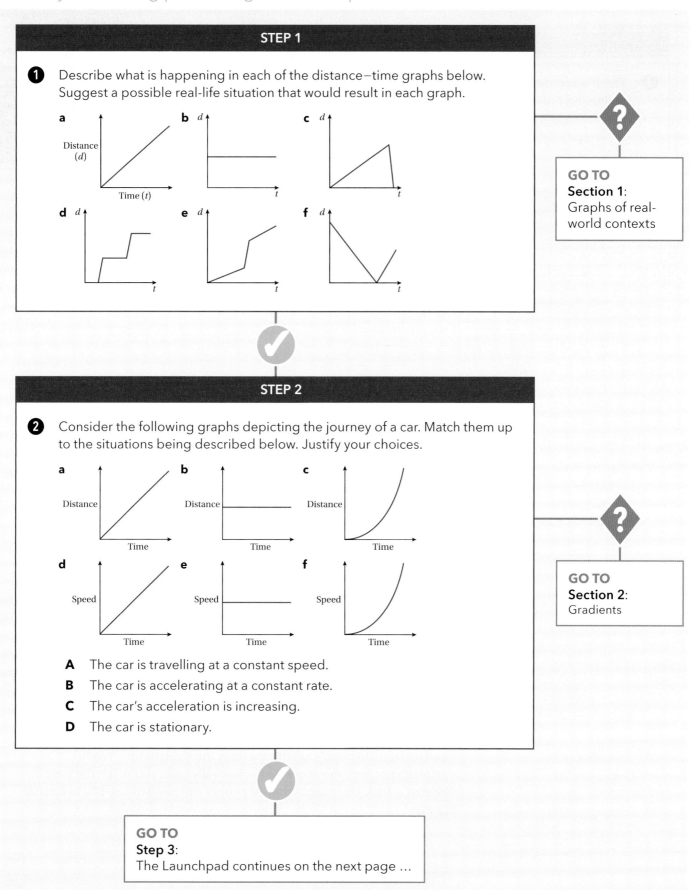

STEP 1

❶ Describe what is happening in each of the distance–time graphs below. Suggest a possible real-life situation that would result in each graph.

a

Distance (*d*)

Time (*t*)

b *d*

t

c *d*

t

d *d*

t

e *d*

t

f *d*

t

?

GO TO
Section 1:
Graphs of real-world contexts

STEP 2

❷ Consider the following graphs depicting the journey of a car. Match them up to the situations being described below. Justify your choices.

a

Distance

Time

b

Distance

Time

c

Distance

Time

d

Speed

Time

e

Speed

Time

f

Speed

Time

A The car is travelling at a constant speed.

B The car is accelerating at a constant rate.

C The car's acceleration is increasing.

D The car is stationary.

?

GO TO
Section 2:
Gradients

GO TO
Step 3:
The Launchpad continues on the next page …

Find answers at: cambridge.org/ukschools/gcsemaths-studentbookanswers

Launchpad continued …

STEP 3

3 The shaded part of one of these graphs represents the amount of water in a swimming pool after 4 hours. Which graph is it? Explain your answer.

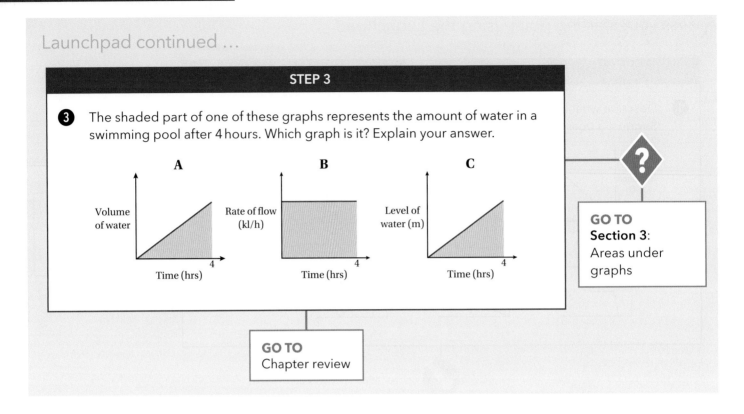

GO TO
Section 3:
Areas under graphs

GO TO
Chapter review

Section 1: Graphs of real-world contexts

Graphs are useful for visually representing the relationships between quantities.

The ticket and transport costs for a group of people to attend a play are shown in the graph.

The horizontal axis (or x-axis) shows the number of people attending. The vertical axis (or y-axis) shows the total cost.

The cost depends on the number of people attending (with a fixed minimum charge of £10).

There are six marked points on the graph.

This graph is a linear graph, but it does not show direct proportion because it does not go through the origin.

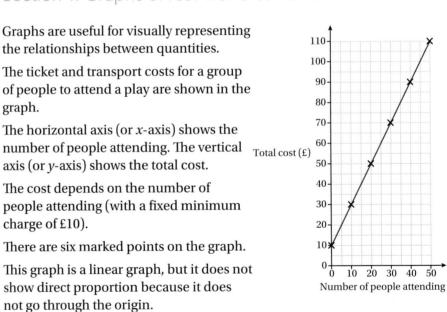

Read up from 10 people on the x-axis to the straight line. When you reach the line, move across horizontally until you reach the y-axis. The cost is £30. This means that 10 people will need to pay £30 to attend the play.

WORKED EXAMPLE 1

This graph shows the relationship between the length and the breadth of different rooms, all of which have the same area.

Find the formula for this relationship.

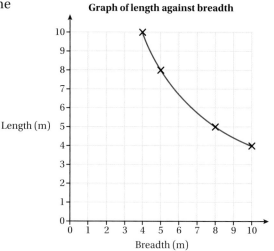

Graph of length against breadth

Length (m)

Breadth (m)

The area of the rooms are constant, $40\,m^2$

Reading the points off the graph, you have $(4, 10)$, $(5, 8)$, $(8, 5)$ and $(10, 4)$.
$4 \times 10 = 5 \times 8 = 40$

The formula is $length = \dfrac{40}{breadth}$

This graph shows an inverse proportion.

Because it shows a real-world context, the graph in the example above is only valid for that particular range of values.

Graphs are also useful in the real world for reading off values quickly without having to do the whole calculation. They can serve as conversion charts.

WORKED EXAMPLE 2

This graph shows the number of Indian rupees you would get for different numbers of US dollars at an exchange rate of US\$1 : Rs45. This relationship is a direct proportion.

a Use the graph to estimate the dollar value of Rs250.

b Use the graph to estimate how many rupees you could get for US\$9.

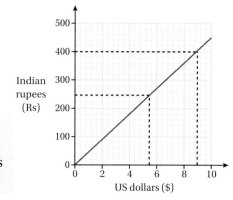

Indian rupees (Rs)

US dollars (\$)

a Rs250 is worth about \$5.50.

Follow across from Rs250 on the vertical axis to reach the graph. Drop down to the dollars axis to find \$5.50.

b You could get about Rs400 for \$9.

Go straight up from US\$9 on the horizontal axis to reach the graph. Then move left to the rupees axis to find Rs400.

Distance–time graphs

Graphs that show the connection between the distance an object has travelled and the time taken to travel that distance are called distance–time graphs or travel graphs.

Time is always shown along the horizontal axis and distance on the vertical.

The graphs normally start at the origin because at the beginning no time has elapsed (passed) and no distance has been covered.

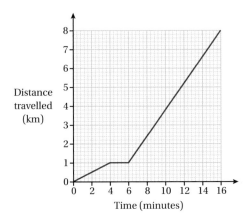

This graph shows the following journey:

- a cycle ride for 4 minutes from home to a bus stop 1 km away

- a 2 minute wait for the bus

- a 7 km journey on the bus that takes 10 minutes.

The line of the graph remains horizontal while the person is not moving (waiting for the bus) because no distance is being travelled at this time. The steeper the line, the faster the person is travelling.

EXERCISE 39A

1 This graph shows the movement of a taxi during a 4-hour period.

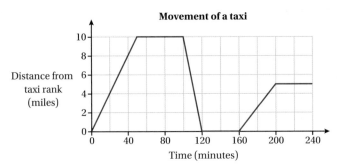

a Clearly and concisely describe the taxi's journey.

b For how many minutes was the taxi waiting for passengers in this period?

How can you tell this?

c What was the total distance travelled?

2 This distance–time graph (right) represents Monica's journey from home to a supermarket and back again.

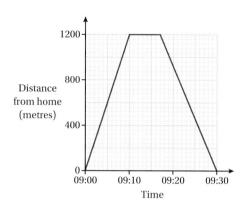

  a How far was Monica from home at 09:06 hours?

  b How many minutes did she spend at the supermarket?

  c At what times was Monica 800 m from home?

  d On which part of the journey did Monica travel faster, going to the supermarket or returning home?

3 A swimming pool is 25 m long. Jasmine swims from one end to the other in 20 seconds.

  She rests for 10 seconds and then swims back to the starting point. It takes her 30 seconds to swim the second length.

  a Draw a distance–time graph for Jasmine's swim.

  b How far was Jasmine from her starting point after 12 seconds?

  c How far was Jasmine from her starting point after 54 seconds?

4 A hurricane disaster centre has a certain amount of clean water. The length of time the water will last depends on the number of people who come to the centre.

  a Calculate the missing values in this table.

  b Plot a graph of this relationship.

No. of people	120	150	200	300	400
Days the water will last	40	32			

Section 2: Gradients

Speed in distance–time graphs

The steepness (slope) of a graph gives an indication of speed. A straight-line graph indicates a constant speed.

The steeper the graph is, the greater the speed.

An upward slope and a downward slope represent movement in opposite directions.

The distance–time graph shown is for a person who walks, cycles and then drives for three equal periods of time.

For each period, speed is given by the formula:

$$\text{speed} = \frac{\text{distance travelled}}{\text{time taken}}$$

The average speed for the whole journey $= \dfrac{\text{total distance travelled}}{\text{total time taken}}$

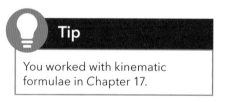

> **Tip**
>
> You worked with kinematic formulae in Chapter 17.

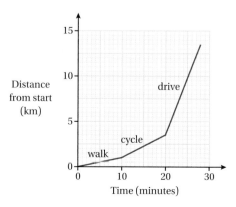

Find answers at: cambridge.org/ukschools/gcsemaths-studentbookanswers

Using gradient triangles to interpret changing gradients

The gradient of a graph, along with the axis labels, gives a large amount of detail – even when, as in the following case, there is no scale given.

Consider these graphs:

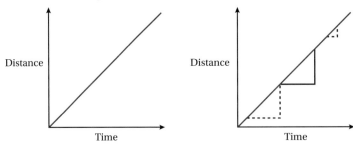

What happens as time moves on? In this case, as time moves on the distance covered increases. So the car is moving.

Look at the gradient triangles drawn on the second copy of the graph. It doesn't matter where these triangles are drawn or how large they are; all the triangles are similar to each other. The ratio of the rise/run is the same for each similar triangle, so the gradient is the same.

This shows that the car is moving at a constant speed.

The graph on the left also shows that, as time moves on the distance covered increases. So the car is moving.

Now consider the gradient triangles drawn on the graph; each has the same base (unit of time).

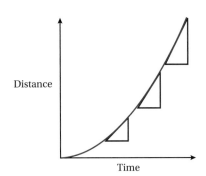

This time the gradient triangles don't fit the graph as it is not a straight line. Instead, they have been laid against the graph at different places so that the hypotenuse of each forms a tangent to the graph.

You can see by the slope of each triangle's hypotenuse that the speed is changing along the graph. Moving up the slope, the hypotenuse of each triangle is steeper than the one before. The gradient of the graph is increasing. This shows that the car is speeding up, or accelerating.

EXERCISE 39B

1 The following graphs show what is happening to the level of water in a tank.

Describe what is happening in each case. Justify your answers using gradient triangles.

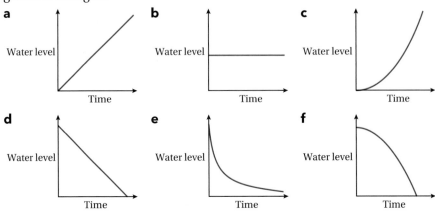

2 The following graphs show what is happening to the price of oil.

Describe what is happening in each case, justifying your answers using gradient triangles.

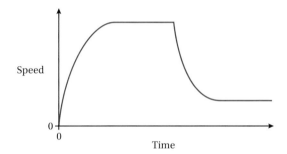

a
Price
Time

b
Price
Time

c
Price
Time

d
Price
Time

e
Price
Time

f
Price
Time

3 The following is a speed–time graph of a parachute jump.

Speed

0
0
Time

Describe what is happening to the speed and acceleration of the parachutist throughout the jump.

4 This graph (from Exercise 39A) shows the movement of a taxi in city traffic during a 4-hour period.

Calculate the taxi's average speed:

a during the first 20 minutes

b during the first hour

c from 160 to 210 minutes

d for the full period of the graph.

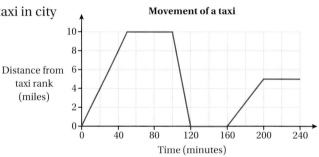

Movement of a taxi

Distance from taxi rank (miles)

Time (minutes)

Finding the gradient of a curve using a tangent line

This graph of height against distance shows the route followed by a mountain biker on a trail.

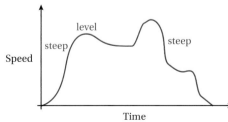

Speed

steep
level
steep

Time

Tip

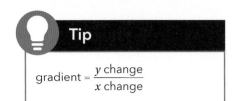

$$\text{gradient} = \frac{y \text{ change}}{x \text{ change}}$$

Some parts of the trail have a steep positive gradient, some have a gradual positive gradient, some parts are level and other parts have a negative gradient. It should be clear from this graph that a curved graph never has a single gradient like a straight line has.

You cannot find the gradient of a whole curve but you can find the gradient at a point on the curve by drawing a tangent to it.

Once you have drawn the tangent to a curve, you can work out the gradient of the tangent just as you would for a straight-line gradient:

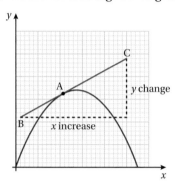

How to draw the tangent

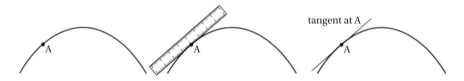

| Mark a point on the curve (A). | Place your ruler against the curve so that it touches only at point A. | Position the ruler so that the angle on either side of the point is more or less equal. Use a pencil to draw the tangent. |

Calculating the gradient to a tangent

Mark two points, P and Q, on the tangent. Try to make the horizontal distance between P and Q a whole number of units (measured on the x-axis scale).

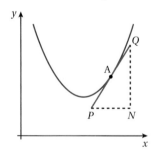

Tip

Remember that a tangent sloping from top left to bottom right will have a negative gradient.

Draw a horizontal line through P and a vertical line through Q to form a right-angled triangle PNQ.

gradient of the curve at A = gradient of the tangent PAQ

$$= \frac{\text{distance } NQ \text{ (measured on the } y\text{-axis scale)}}{\text{distance } PN \text{ (measured on the } x\text{-axis scale)}}$$

WORKED EXAMPLE 3

The graph shows the height of a tree (y metres) plotted against the age of the tree (x years).

Estimate the rate at which the tree was growing when it was 4 years old.

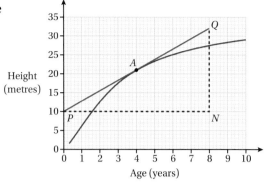

Gradient at $A = \dfrac{NQ}{PN} = \dfrac{22}{8} = 2.75$

The rate at which the tree was growing when it was 4 years old is equal to the gradient of the curve at the point where $x = 4$.

Draw the tangent at this point (A).

The tree was growing at a rate of 2.8 metres per year (to 1 decimal place).

EXERCISE 39C

1 The following graph is a distance–time graph for a drag-racing car.

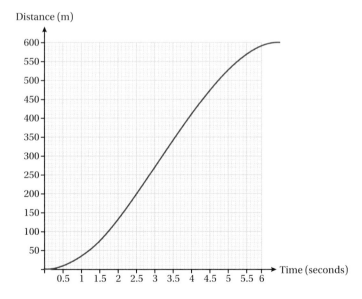

a How far had the car travelled after 2 seconds?

b How long did it take the car to travel the first 50 metres?

c When was the car going at its fastest speed?

d How fast was the car going after

   i 0.5 seconds   **ii** 3.5 seconds?

2 The following graph shows the predicted height of the tide at Milford Haven.

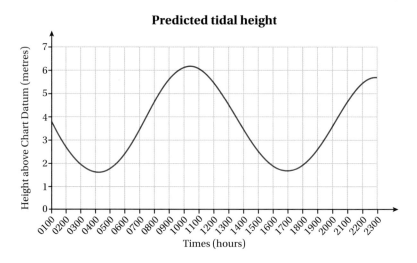

Predicted tidal height

a When is the tide coming in at its fastest rate?

b When is the tide fully in?

c How fast is the tide going out at

   i 4 p.m.   **ii** 2 p.m.?

d Why would this kind of information by useful?

3 A walker in the Lake District is training for a mountain climb.

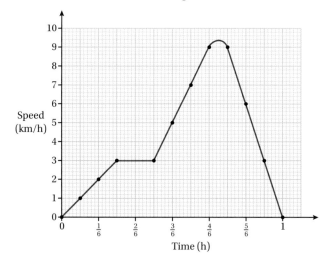

a Describe the speed changes on the route that this person is taking. Pay particular attention to the four sections of the graph.

b What is the speed of the person after 30 minutes?

c What is happening after 43 minutes?

d What is the acceleration of the person after 10 minutes?

e At what rate is the person decelerating after 50 minutes?

4 The graph of $y = x^2$ is shown in the diagram.

   a Copy the graph using tracing paper and find the gradient of the graph at the points:

     i $(2, 4)$ **ii** $(-1, 1)$

   b The gradient of the graph at the point $(1.5, 2.25)$ is 3.

     Write down the coordinates of the point at which the gradient is -3.

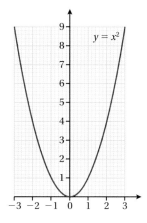

Section 3: Areas under graphs

WORKED EXAMPLE 4

The graph on the right shows a car travelling at a constant speed of 40 km/h.

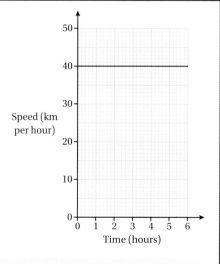

a Find the area under the graph after 2 hours, 3 hours, 4 hours.

b What do you notice?

   a $2 \times 40 = 80$ units
      $3 \times 40 = 120$ units
      $4 \times 40 = 160$ units

                         The shape for each period is a rectangle.
                         Area = length × width.

   b The results in part (a) increase by 40 every hour. The units of one side of the rectangle are time and of the other sides are speed,

      which is $\dfrac{\text{distance}}{\text{time}}$.

      So, if you multiply:

      $\text{speed} \times \text{time} = \dfrac{\text{distance}}{\text{time}} \times \text{time} = \text{distance}$

      The area under the graph equals the distance travelled.

The same works if the car is accelerating or decelerating. The area under a speed–time graph is equal to the distance travelled.

EXERCISE 39D

1 Find the distance travelled for each of the following vehicles in their first 4 hours (for graph d provide an estimate):

a
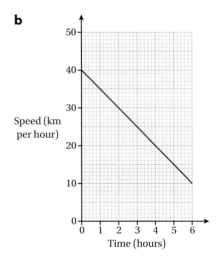

b

c
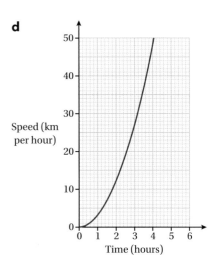

d

2 The following graph shows the rate of water flow in a river throughout the day.

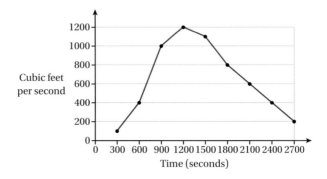

a What would the area under the graph represent?

b How much water had flowed down the river in the first 5 minutes?

c How much flowed between 10 and 15 minutes?

d How much less water flowed between 35 and 40 minutes compared to 15 and 20 minutes?

e Why might a river's flow change like this?

Checklist of learning and understanding

Graphs of real-world contexts

- Real-world graphs show the relationship between variables.

Gradient

- Distance–time graphs show the connection between the distance an object has travelled and the time taken to travel that distance. If speed is constant the gradient is constant.

- Curved graphs have gradients that change along the graph continually.

- Gradient triangles can be used to estimate the changes in the gradient.

- The gradient at a point on a distance–time graph will give the instantaneous speed. This can be calculated by drawing a tangent at the point and finding the gradient of the tangent.

Area under a graph

- The area under a graph can be used to calculate other values. For example, the area under a speed–time graph gives the distance covered.

Chapter review

For additional questions on the topics in this chapter, visit GCSE Mathematics Online.

1 Debbie drove from Junction 12 to Junction 13 on a motorway.

The travel graph shows Debbie's journey.

Ian also drove from Junction 12 to Junction 13 on the same motorway.

He drove at an average speed of 66 km/hour.

Who had the faster average speed, Debbie or Ian?

You must explain your answer.

(4 marks)

©*Pearson Education Ltd 2013*

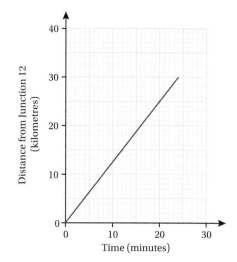

 Find answers at: cambridge.org/ukschools/gcsemaths-studentbookanswers

2 This speed–time graph represents the journey of a train between two stations. The train slowed down and stopped after 15 minutes because of engineering work on the railway line.

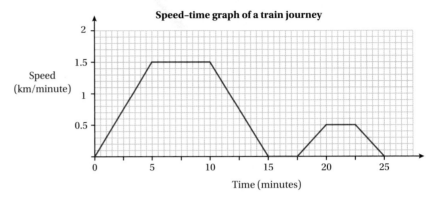

Speed–time graph of a train journey

a Calculate the greatest speed, in km/h, which the train reached.

b Calculate the deceleration of the train as it approached the place where there was engineering work.

c Calculate the distance the train travelled in the first 15 minutes.

d For how long was the train stopped at the place where there was engineering work?

e What was the speed of the train after 19 minutes?

f Calculate the distance between the two stations.

3 The graph shows how the population of a village has changed since 1930.

a Copy the graph using tracing paper and find the gradient of the graph at the point (1950, 170).

b What does this gradient represent?

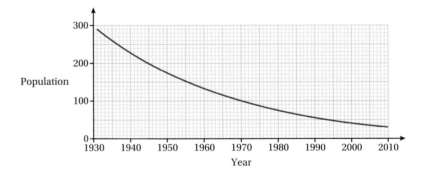

40 Transformations

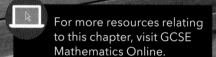

For more resources relating to this chapter, visit GCSE Mathematics Online.

Using mathematics: real-life applications

You can see examples of reflections, rotations and translations all around you. Patterns in wallpaper and fabric are often translations, images reflected in water are reflections and the blades of a wind turbine are a good example of rotation.

"I use transformations all the time when I program computer graphics. Transformations allow me to position objects, shape them and change the view I have of them. I can even change the type of perspective that is used to show something." *(Computer programmer)*

Before you start ...

Ch 26	You need to know what angles of 90°, 180° and 270° look like and also the directions clockwise and anti-clockwise.	**1**	How many degrees is each angle? State whether each arrow is showing clockwise or anti-clockwise movement. **a** **b** **c**
Ch 24	You need to know how to plot straight-line graphs in the form $x = a$, $y = a$ and $y = x$.	**2**	Find the equation of each of these lines. 
Ch 23	You need to know what a vector is and how they describe movement.	**3**	**a** What is the difference between the coordinate (3, 2) and the vector $\begin{pmatrix} 3 \\ 2 \end{pmatrix}$? **b** What is the difference between the vectors $\begin{pmatrix} -1 \\ 3 \end{pmatrix}$ and $\begin{pmatrix} 3 \\ 1 \end{pmatrix}$?

Assess your starting point using the Launchpad

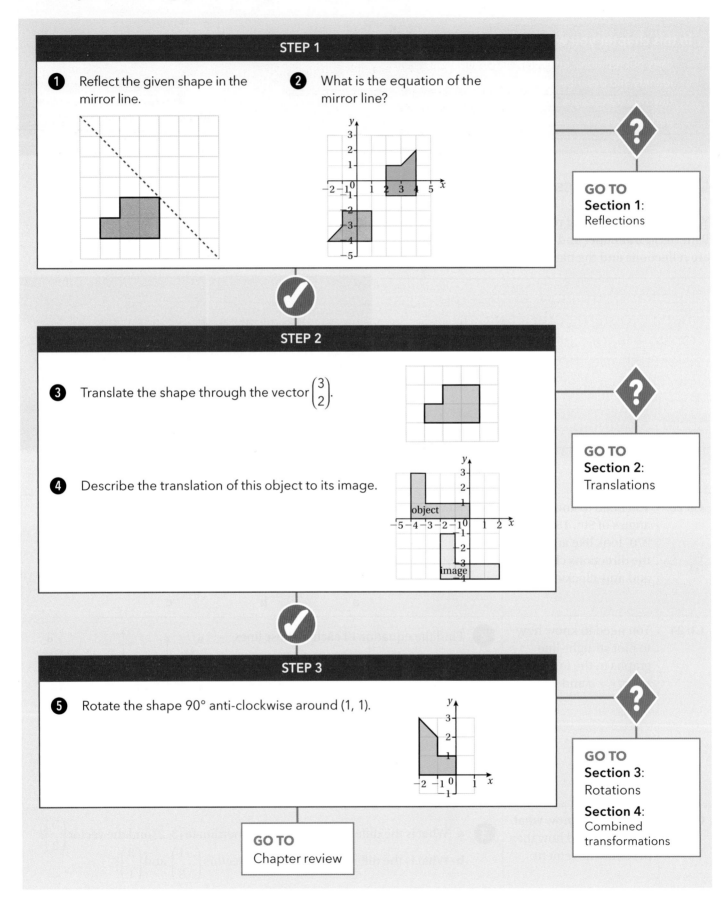

STEP 1

1 Reflect the given shape in the mirror line.

2 What is the equation of the mirror line?

GO TO
Section 1:
Reflections

STEP 2

3 Translate the shape through the vector $\begin{pmatrix} 3 \\ 2 \end{pmatrix}$.

4 Describe the translation of this object to its image.

GO TO
Section 2:
Translations

STEP 3

5 Rotate the shape 90° anti-clockwise around (1, 1).

GO TO
Section 3:
Rotations

Section 4:
Combined transformations

GO TO
Chapter review

Section 1: Reflections

A transformation is a change in the position of a point, line or shape. When you transform a shape you change its position or its size, or both.

The original point, line or shape is called the **object**. For example, a triangle *ABC*.

The transformation is called the **image**. The symbol ′ is used to label the image. For example, the image of triangle *ABC* is *A′B′C′*.

Reflection, rotation and translation change the position of an object, but not its size. Under these three transformations an object and its image will be congruent.

Mirrors, windows and water surfaces all reflect objects. You can see the reflection of clouds and trees clearly in the photograph. If you draw a line horizontally across the centre of the image and fold it, the top half will fit exactly onto the bottom half. The fold line is called a **mirror line**.

Mathematically, when a shape is reflected it is 'flipped' over a mirror line to give its image. The object and the image are the same distance from the mirror line.

Key vocabulary

object: the original shape (before it has been transformed).

image: the new shape (once the object has been transformed.

mirror line: line equidistant from all corresponding points on a shape and its reflection).

Tip

You worked with congruent triangles in Chapter 31.

Enlargement is also a transformation. Enlargement changes the position of an object and also its size. This was covered in Chapter 30.

EXERCISE 40A

1 Reflect the triangle in the line $x = 1$, and then reflect the triangle and the resultant image in the line $y = -1$.

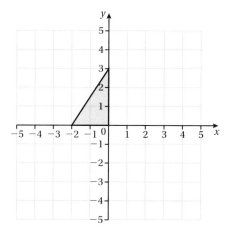

 Find answers at: cambridge.org/ukschools/gcsemaths-studentbookanswers

2 Reflect this shape in the line $y = x$, and then reflect the shape and the resultant image in the line $y = 1 - x$.

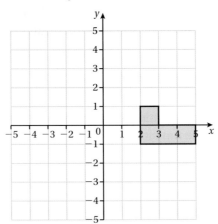

3 Copy the grid and shapes below. Carry out the 10 reflections on your grid to reveal the picture.

Shape A in the line $y = x$ Shape E in the line $x = 7$ Shape I in the line $y = 6$

Shape B in the x-axis   Shape F in the line $y = -x$ Shape J in the line $y = x$

Shape C in the line $y = -2$ Shape G in the line $x = -4$

Shape D in the line $y = 4$ Shape H in the line $x = 1.5$

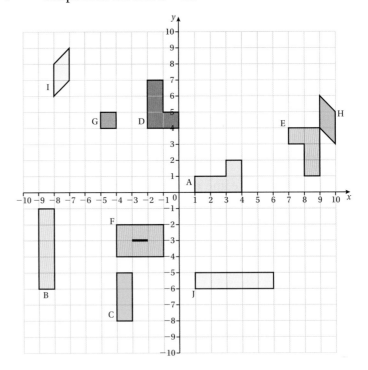

4 Draw a pair of axis going from -10 to 10 in both directions. Draw two line segments, the first with ends at $(0, 0)$ and $(1, 1)$ and the second with ends at $(1, 1)$ and $(2, 1)$. Show how this shape can be made into:

a a hexagon with two successive reflections.

b an octagon with three successive reflections.

5 Make up your own reflection puzzle for another student to solve.

Under reflection corresponding points on the object and the image are the same distance from the mirror line. If you join a pair of corresponding points the line formed is cut in half by the mirror line and they meet at 90°. The mirror line is the **perpendicular bisector** of any pair of corresponding points.

Tip

You learned about perpendicular bisectors in Chapter 22.

Tip

You can turn your book around so that diagonal mirror lines look vertical or horizontal. Often our brains find this easier than working diagonally.

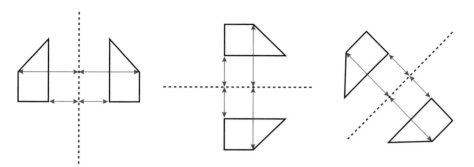

WORK IT OUT 40.1

This Z shape is reflected in the line $y = -1$. What is its image?

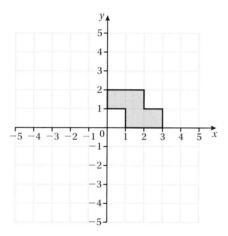

Which one of these answers is correct? What has gone wrong in each of the others?

Option A	Option B	Option C

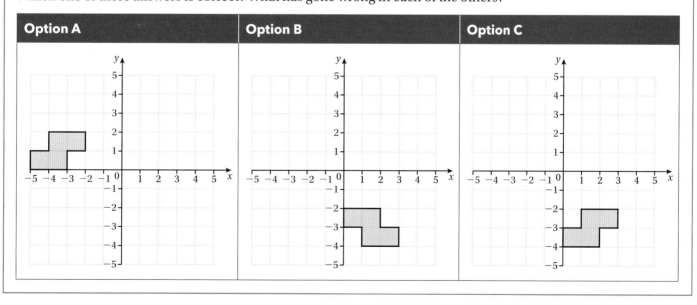

Describing reflections

Since the mirror line is the perpendicular bisector of two corresponding points in a reflection, if you can't 'spot' a mirror line you can join two corresponding points and construct the perpendicular bisector to find it.

You must also be able to give the equation of the mirror line when the reflection is shown on a coordinate grid.

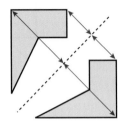

EXERCISE 40B

1 Find the equation of the mirror line in each reflection.

a

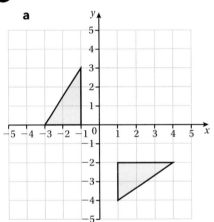

b

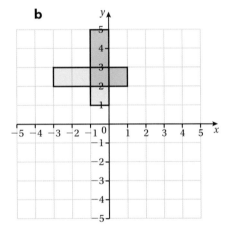

c

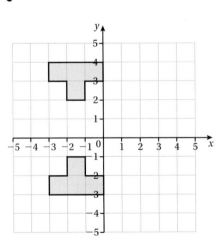

d

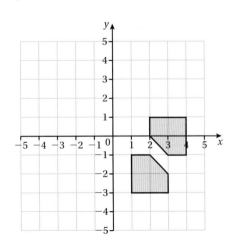

2 **a** Describe fully each of the following reflections.

    i **S**hape A to shape E.

    ii Shape C to shape G.

    iii Shape G to shape E.

    iv Shape B to shape F.

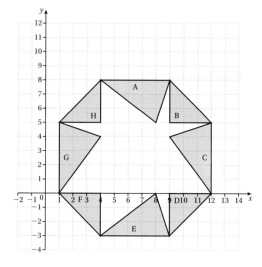

b Challenge another student to describe a reflection of two triangles you choose.

3 Trace each pair of shapes and construct the mirror line for the reflection.

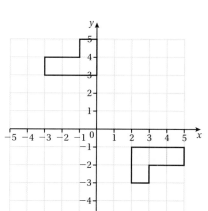

    a

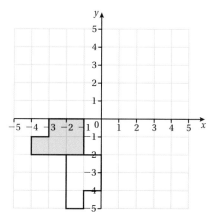

    b   **c**

4 **a** In each diagram below describe the multiple reflections that take the original shaded shape to its image.

    i   **ii**

b Is there more than one answer?

c Does the order of the reflections matter?

d Is there any easy way to tell the minimum number of reflections needed?

Tip

You will do more on multiple transformations in *Section 4*.

Section 2: Translations

A translation is a 'slide' along a straight line. (Think about pushing a box across a floor.) The translation can be from left to right (horizontal), up or down (vertical) or both (horizontal and vertical, i.e. diagonal).

The image is in the same **orientation** as the object and every point on the shape moves exactly the same distance in exactly the same direction. Translated shapes are congruent to each other.

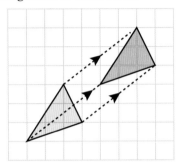

> ### 🔑 Key vocabulary
>
> orientation: the position of a shape relative to the grid.

> ### 💡 Tip
>
> Remember, shapes that are congruent are exactly the same size and shape.

You can describe translations on a coordinate grid using column vectors. Remember, a column vector shows horizontal displacement over vertical displacement.

WORKED EXAMPLE 1

Describe the translation ABC to $A'B'C'$ by means of a column vector.

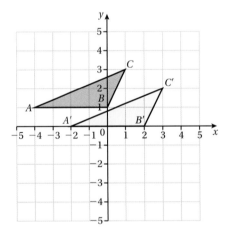

Look at point C and point C'.

> Take any point on the object and find the corresponding point on the image.

To get from C to C' move:
2 units to the right = +2
1 unit down = −1

> Work out how the point has been translated horizontally and vertically.

The translation is $\begin{pmatrix} 2 \\ -1 \end{pmatrix}$

> Write this as a vector.

Tip

Drawing on the grid to show the movements can help you to avoid unnecessary mistakes.

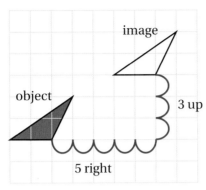

WORK IT OUT 40.2

This T shape is translated through a vector of $\begin{pmatrix} -2 \\ 4 \end{pmatrix}$. Draw its image.

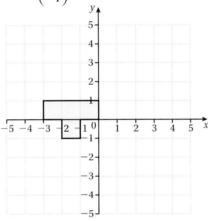

Which one of these answers is correct? What has gone wrong in each of the others?

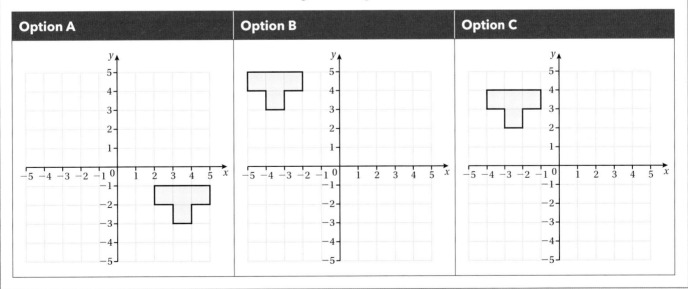

Option A	Option B	Option C

EXERCISE 40C

1 Translate each shape using the given vector.

a $\begin{pmatrix} 3 \\ -2 \end{pmatrix}$ **b** $\begin{pmatrix} -1 \\ 2 \end{pmatrix}$ **c** $\begin{pmatrix} 0 \\ 4 \end{pmatrix}$

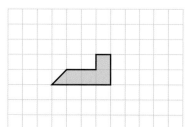 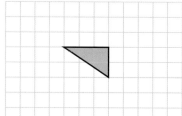 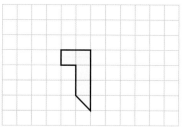

2 Translate each shape by the given vector. Then give the name of the shape you have put together.

a Translate shape A $\begin{pmatrix} -1 \\ -3 \end{pmatrix}$.

b Translate shape B $\begin{pmatrix} 1 \\ 5 \end{pmatrix}$.

c Translate shape C $\begin{pmatrix} 2 \\ -1 \end{pmatrix}$.

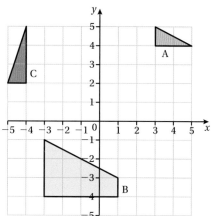

3 Translate each piece of this jigsaw using the vectors on the right.

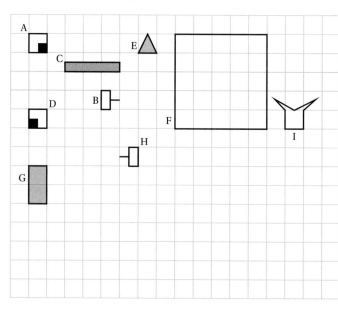

A $\begin{pmatrix} 12 \\ -8 \end{pmatrix}$

B $\begin{pmatrix} 12 \\ -5 \end{pmatrix}$

C $\begin{pmatrix} 10 \\ -9 \end{pmatrix}$

D $\begin{pmatrix} 14 \\ -4 \end{pmatrix}$

E $\begin{pmatrix} 7 \\ -9 \end{pmatrix}$

F $\begin{pmatrix} 3 \\ -7 \end{pmatrix}$

G $\begin{pmatrix} 13 \\ -5 \end{pmatrix}$

H $\begin{pmatrix} 5 \\ -2 \end{pmatrix}$

I $\begin{pmatrix} -1 \\ -2 \end{pmatrix}$

Describing translations

You should be able to use vectors to describe a translation. Remember to count between corresponding points on the two shapes.

Tip

Make sure you count from the object to the image and write this as a column vector (not a coordinate!).

WORK IT OUT 40.3

Which transformations below are reflections and which are translations? How did you make your decision? Describe the translations as vectors.

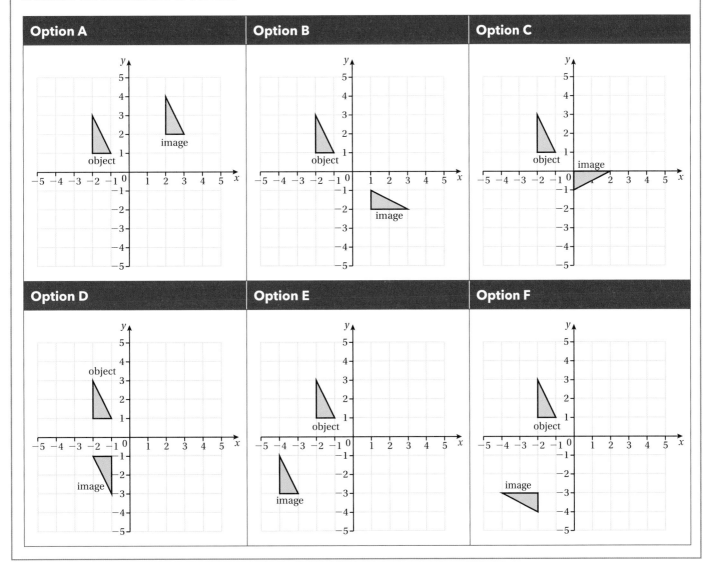

EXERCISE 40D

1 Here are some completed translations. The objects are shown in grey and the images are in colour. Write column vectors to describe the translation from each object to its image.

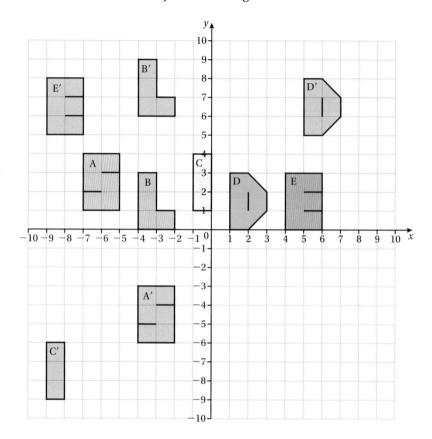

2 Work on a grid. Draw the four objects (A–D) used to make this image in any position on the grid. Make up translation instructions for moving the four objects to form the image. Exchange with a partner and perform the translations to make sure their instructions are correct.

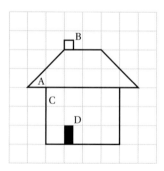

Section 3: Rotations

A rotation is a turn. An object can turn clockwise or anti-clockwise around a fixed point called the centre of rotation. The centre of rotation can be inside, on the edge of or outside the object.

A rotation changes the orientation of a shape, but the object and its image remain congruent.

When you rotate a shape the distance from the centre of rotation to any point on the object remains the same. Each point travels in a circle around the centre. Think about the tip of a blade on a wind turbine or a child sitting on a roundabout. When they rotate, the paths they trace out are circles.

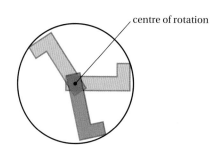

centre of rotation

To carry out a rotation you need to know the centre of rotation as well as the angle and direction of rotation. At this level, all rotations will be in multiples of 90°.

WORK IT OUT 40.4

This L shape is rotated anti-clockwise with centre of rotation (0, 1) through an angle of 90°. What is its image?

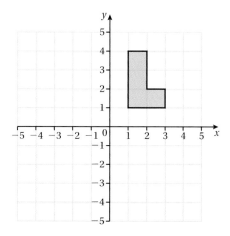

Which one of these answers is correct? What has gone wrong in each of the others?

Option A	Option B	Option C
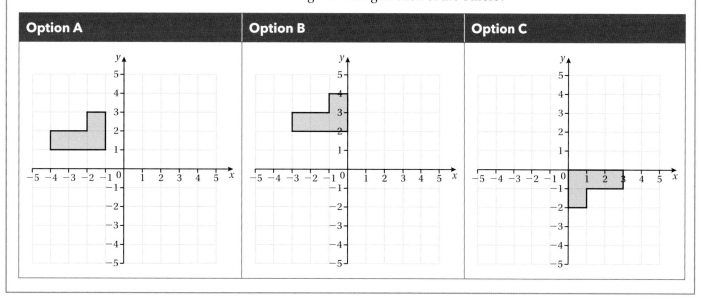		

EXERCISE 40E

1 Rotate the triangle 180° about the origin.

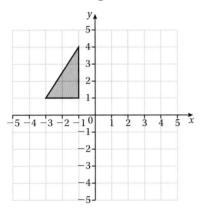

2 Rotate the shape 90° clockwise around the point (1, 1).

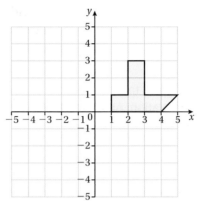

3 Rotate the shape 90° anti-clockwise around the point (−2, 1).

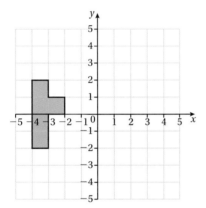

4 Rotate the shape 90° anti clockwise around the point (2, 1).

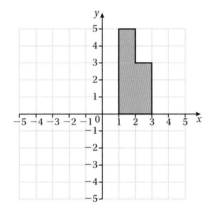

5 Rotate each shape as directed.

Shape A: 90° anti-clockwise around the point (−1, −1).

Shape B: 180° around the point (2, 3).

Shape C: 90° clockwise around the point (1, 0). Label this D.

Shape D: 180° around the point (−3.5, 2).

Shape E: 180° around the point (3, 1).

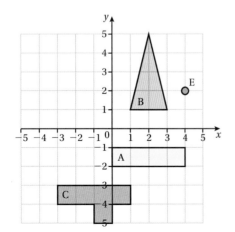

6 The image below was designed by drawing a triangle and rotating this around the origin in multiples of 90°. What do you notice about the coordinates of the vertices of the triangle? Would this work if you rotated an image around a different point? Why?

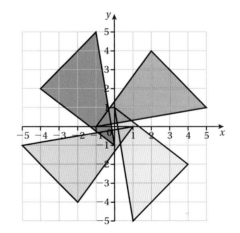

Describing rotations

To describe a rotation you give a centre, angle and direction. Very often you can find the centre using tracing paper and trial and error. Trace the object and rotate the tracing paper using different centres of rotation. Spotting the centres improves with practice.

You can use construction to find the centre of rotation. Corresponding points on an object and its image under rotation lie on the circumference of a circle. If you join these to make a chord, its perpendicular bisector will go through the centre of the circle. So by drawing two perpendicular bisectors you can determine the centre.

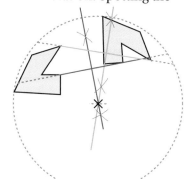

Tip

Always give the direction and angle from the object to the image.

WORK IT OUT 40.5

Which of these transformations are reflections, which are rotations and which are translations? How did you make your decision?

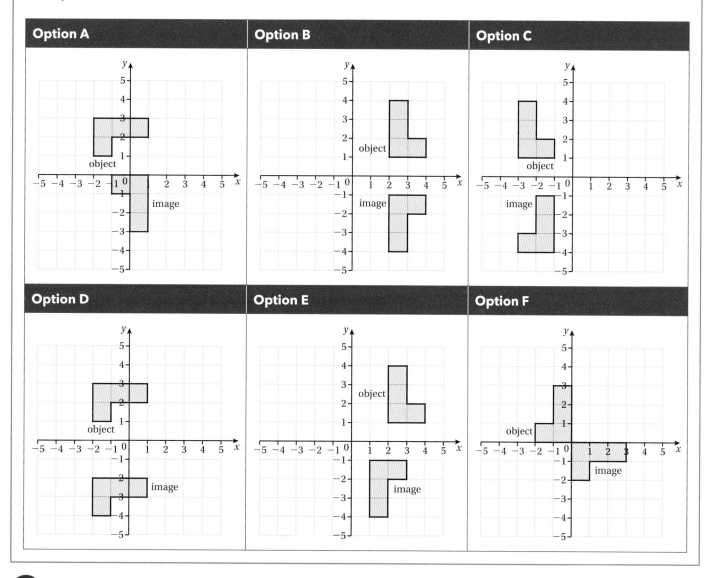

Find answers at: cambridge.org/ukschools/gcsemaths-studentbookanswers

Tip

Tracing paper is very useful for work with transformations. Don't be afraid to ask for it in an exam.

EXERCISE 40F

1 Describe each of the following rotations.

a

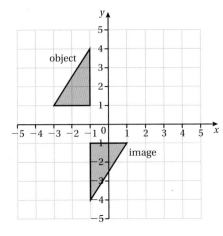

b

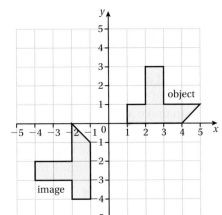

c

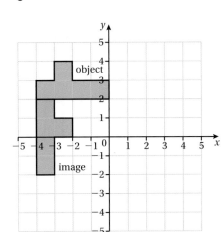

d

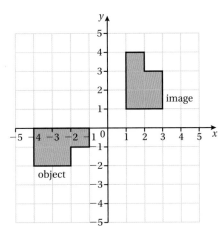

2 This section of wallpaper has been designed using rotations. A **coordinate** grid has been overlaid. Identify as many different rotations as you can.

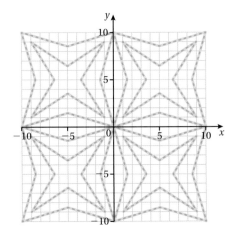

3 Use construction to locate the centres of rotation for each pair of shapes.

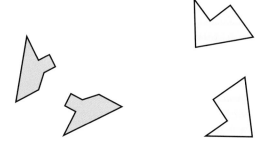

Section 4: Combined transformations

An object can undergo two (or more) transformations in a row. For example, it could be reflected in the line $y = 0$ and then rotated clockwise through $90°$ about a vertex. Sometimes a combined transformation can be described by a single, equivalent transformation.

WORKED EXAMPLE 2

a Reflect triangle A in the y-axis and label the image B. Rotate image B by $180°$ about the origin and label this image C.

b What single transformation of A would also give the image C?

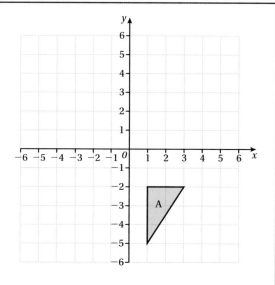

First reflect A in the y-axis.

a

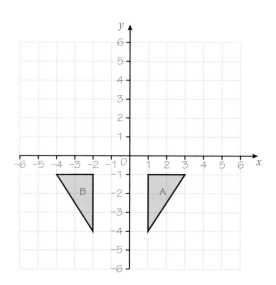

Continues on next page ...

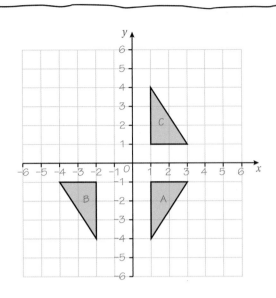

Rotate image B by 180° about the origin.

b A single reflection of A in the *x*-axis would also produce image C.

Some combinations of transformations can return an object to its original position. In Worked example 2, if image C is reflected in the *x*-axis, then the final image is the starting image, A.

EXERCISE 40G

1 Make a copy of this diagram. Reflect the object A in the line *x* = 2 and label it A′.

Rotate shape A′ 90° anti-clockwise around the point (2, −2) and label it A″.

Describe the single transformation that maps shape A on to shape A″.

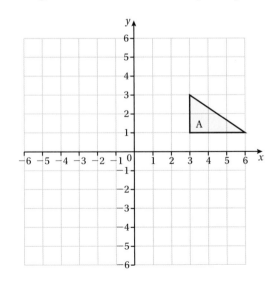

2 Make a copy of this diagram. Translate F through a vector of $\begin{pmatrix} -3 \\ 2 \end{pmatrix}$ and label it F′.

Rotate F′ 180° around the point $(-3, 0)$ and label it F″.

Describe the single transformation that maps shape F onto shape F″.

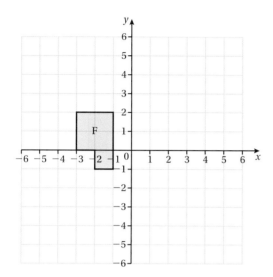

3 Make a copy of this diagram. Reflect K in the y-axis and label it K′.

Rotate K′ 90° clockwise around the point $(2, -1)$ and label if K″.

Reflect K″ in the line $x = 0$, label it K‴.

Describe the single transformation that maps shape K onto shape K‴.

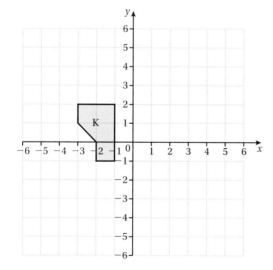

4 **a** Describe fully the combined transformation from shape A to A'.

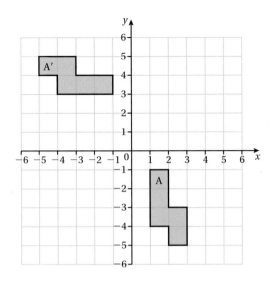

b Does the order of the transformations matter?

c Find another solution.

5 A shape is transformed by carrying out a reflection in the x-axis followed by a reflection in the y-axis. What single transformation has the same effect?

6 What two transformations would have the same effect as rotating the following shape 90° anti-clockwise around the point $(-2, 0)$?

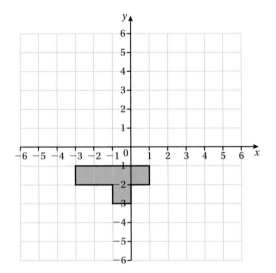

7 Perform the following transformations on the shape given.

Translate A $\begin{pmatrix} 4 \\ -2 \end{pmatrix}$ to A′.

Reflect A′ in the x-axis to A″.

Reflect A″ in the line $x = -1$ to A‴.

Rotate A‴ 180° about the point $(-3, 1)$ to A⁗.

What do you notice about the final image?

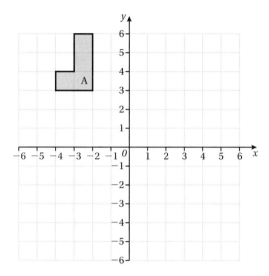

Checklist of learning and understanding

Reflections

- Reflections change the orientation of a shape but the image remains congruent.

- To describe a reflection the equation of the mirror line needs to be given.

- The mirror line is the perpendicular bisector of any two corresponding points on the image and object.

Translations

- Translations leave the orientation of the shape unchanged but move it horizontally and/or vertically.

- Translations are described using vectors.

Rotations

- A rotation is a turn around a centre. Rotations are described by giving the coordinates of the centre of rotation, angle and direction of the rotation.

Combined transformations

- Transformations can be combined by completing one after another.

Find answers at: cambridge.org/ukschools/gcsemaths-studentbookanswers

For additional questions on the topics in this chapter, visit GCSE Mathematics Online.

Chapter review

1   Which of the following statements are true? Explain your reasoning.

  a The images constructed by reflecting, rotating, or translating are congruent to the objects you started with.

  b The images constructed by reflecting, rotating, or translating are similar to the objects you started with.

  c The images constructed by reflecting, rotating, or translating are in the same orientation as the objects you started with.

  d The images constructed by reflecting, rotating, or translating have the same angles as the objects you started with.

2   Describe fully the transformation from:

  a shape A to shape B   **b** shape B to shape C   **c** shape C to shape A.

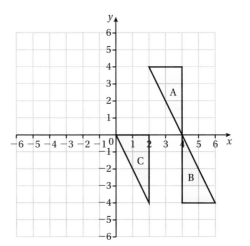

 3   **a** Translate shape P by the vector $\begin{pmatrix} 5 \\ -2 \end{pmatrix}$ *(2 marks)*

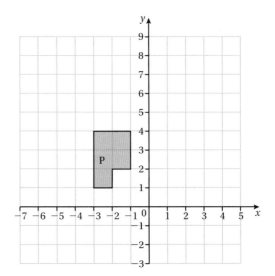

b Describe fully the single transformation that maps shape A onto shape B.

(3 marks)

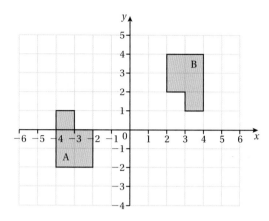

4 The triangle below is used to create a tessellating pattern. This is produced using multiple translations and one rotation. Explain how this could be done.

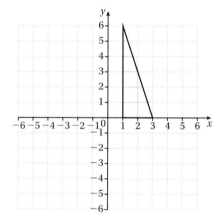

5 Rotate shape A 90° clockwise around the point (1, 2), label it B.

Reflect shape B in the line $y = x$, label it C.

Translate shape C through the vector $\begin{pmatrix} -1 \\ 1 \end{pmatrix}$, label it D.

Describe the single transformation that maps shape A onto shape D.

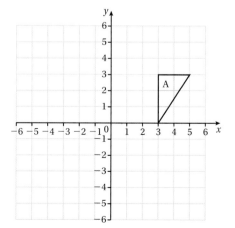

Find answers at: cambridge.org/ukschools/gcsemaths-studentbookanswers

6 Look at the dancing figure below. Describe how the figure can be drawn using only transformations of shapes A, B, C, and D.

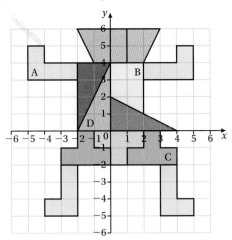

7 For each part, start with a fresh copy of this shape and carry out the multiple transformations.

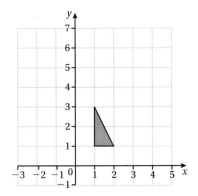

a Rotation 180° about the origin followed by a reflection in the line $y = -x$.

b Reflection in the line $y = -x$ followed by a rotation, 180° about the origin.

c Reflection in the line $y = 2 - x$ followed by a rotation, 180° about the point $(1, 1)$.

d What do you notice about your answers to parts **a**–**c**?

41 Transforming curves

For more resources relating to this chapter, visit GCSE Mathematics Online.

Using mathematics: real-life applications

Many people study the graphs of curves in the course of their work. Sound engineers are a good example. They mix and balance sounds by looking at curves made by sound waves.

Tip

Use ICT when studying this chapter. This allows you to generate graphs so you can study them quickly and experiment with changing values and comparing results.

"Sound engineers in today's music industry need to be talented in both the arts and the sciences." *(Sound engineer)*

Lower pitch

Higher pitch

Before you start ...

Chs 24 and 25	You should recognise the graphs of standard functions: $y = mx + c$ $y = x^2$ $y = ax^2 + bx + c$ $y = \dfrac{1}{x}$	**1**	Which of these functions would result in a graph as a curve and which would produce a graph as a line? **a** $y = x^2 + 9$ **b** $5y + x = 10$ **c** $y = \dfrac{2}{x}$ **d** $y = (x + 7)^2 - 2$ Sketch each function to show its general shape.
Ch 25	You should be able to sketch the trigonometric functions: $y = \sin x$ $y = \cos x$ $y = \tan x$	**2**	Which trigonometric functions are represented by these graphs? **a** **b** **c** Sketch and label the third trigonometric function.
Ch 13	You should be able to complete the square on a quadratic equation.	**3**	Rewrite $y = 3x^2 + 6x + 7$ in the form: $a(x - h)^2 + k$

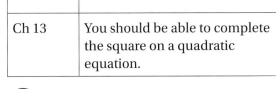

Assess your starting point using the Launchpad

STEP 1

① This is a graph of $y = x^2$.

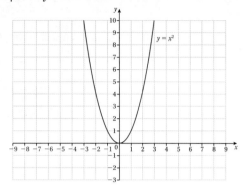

Sketch:

a $y = x^2 + 2$ **b** $y = x^2 - 2$

c Write the equation of the reflection of this graph in the x-axis.

GO TO
Section 1:
Quadratic functions and parabolas

STEP 2

② **a** What are the values of sin 90° and cos 90°?
For what values of θ does cos $\theta = 1$?

b Sketch graphs of $y = \sin x + 2$ and $y = \cos (x + 90°)$.

GO TO
Section 2:
Trigonometric functions

STEP 3

③ **a** What is the equation of this function, $y = x^3$ or $y = -x^3$?

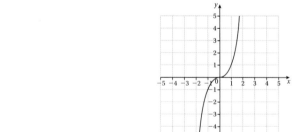

b Draw its reflection about the x-axis and give the equation of the function.

c Sketch the graph of $y = \dfrac{1}{x}$.

GO TO
Chapter review

GO TO
Section 4:
Translation and reflection problems

GO TO
Section 3:
Other functions

Section 1: Quadratic functions and parabolas

The general form of a quadratic function is:

$y = ax^2 + bx + c$

The graph of a quadratic equation is called a parabola.

WORK IT OUT 41.1

Quadratic equations can have two different solutions, a single solution or no **real** solutions. Which of these three graphs has two real solutions.

What can you say about the other two equations based on the graphs?

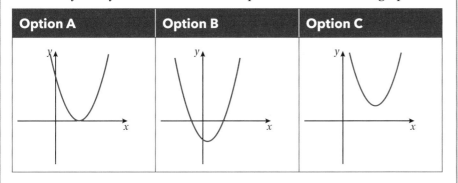

Option A	Option B	Option C

Did you know?

Parabolas are curves that can be observed in many places in the natural and built environment.

 Key vocabulary

real numbers: these are all the numbers that can be placed on a number line.

 Tip

Look back at Chapters 15 and 25 to make sure you understand the main features of quadratic equations. You should be able to solve quadratic equations and understand what is meant by the terms turning point, vertex and roots.

Vertical translations

This is a graph of the function $f(x) = x^2$. The axis of symmetry is the y-axis (the line $x = 0$). The minimum turning point is the origin $(0, 0)$, and this is called the vertex of the function $f(x) = x^2$.

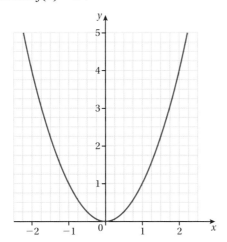

Consider what happens to the graph $y = x^2$ if you add three units to the function and get $y = x^2 + 3$.

The vertex $(0, 0)$, and every other point on the graph, moves up three positions. The graph $y = x^2 + 3$ cuts the y-axis at $(0, 3)$, the new minimum value.

Now consider the axis of symmetry. $x^2 = (-x)^2$ and $x^2 + 3 = (-x)^2 + 3$, so y has the same value for + and − values of x. The axis of symmetry is still the y-axis.

 Find answers at: cambridge.org/ukschools/gcsemaths-studentbookanswers

741

Adding a positive constant moves the curve up and subtracting a constant will move the curve down. The axis of symmetry is unchanged in a vertical translation.

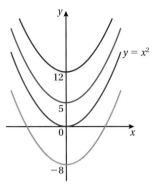

The graphs shown on the right are all vertical translations of $y = x^2$, and are all members of the family of curves $y = x^2 + c$. The axis of symmetry is $x = 0$ in each case.

EXERCISE 41A

1 Sketch the graphs of the following quadratic functions and state the coordinates of the vertex:

a $y = x^2 + 1$ **b** $y = x^2 - 1$ **c** $y = x^2 - 4$

d $y = x^2 + 2$ **e** $y = x^2 - 3$ **f** $y = x^2 + 3$

2 Sketch the graph of $y = -x^2$. This is an image of the graph $y = x^2$.

What word can you use to describe the transformation?

3 Using your sketch for $y = -x^2$, complete this sentence:

As x increases and decreases in value, y ...

4 Draw a sketch graph for each of the quadratic functions in question **1** if x^2 is now replaced by $(-)x^2$.

What word can you use to describe the transformations to the original curves?

Horizontal translations

When graphs are translated in a horizontal direction, they shift to the left or right.

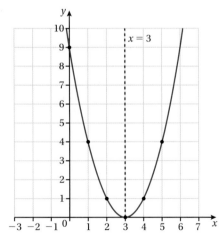

Every point on the basic parabola $y = x^2$ has coordinates (p, p^2).

If you translate the parabola three units to the right, then the vertex $(0, 0)$ goes to $(3, 0)$, and the axis of symmetry, $x = 0$, goes to $x = 3$.

For a horizontal translation of three units, the general point (p, p^2) goes to the point $(p + 3, p^2)$.

This means that $x = p + 3$ and $y = p^2$.

Rearranging to get $p = x - 3$ and substituting into $y = p^2$ gives:

$$y = (x - 3)^2$$

So a translation of three units to the right results in the function $y = (x - 3)^2$.

If you translate three units to the left, a similar argument would produce the result $y = (x + 3)^2$. The axis of symmetry for $y = (x + 3)^2$ is $x = -3$.

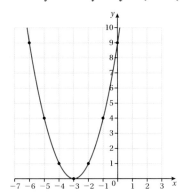

For the general parabola, $y = x^2$:

	Equation of translated curve	Axis of symmetry	Vertex
Vertical translations	$y = x^2 + a$	$x = 0$	$(0, a)$
	$y = x^2 - a$	$x = 0$	$(0, -a)$
Horizontal translations	$y = (x + a)^2$	$x = -a$	$(-a, 0)$
	$y = (x - a)^2$	$x = a$	$(a, 0)$

Tip

To draw a sketch of a graph from a translation of a quadratic function, you need to check for vertical and horizontal moves. Identify the axis of symmetry and the vertex (the turning point).

WORKED EXAMPLE 1

Sketch $y = (x - 2)^2 - 4$.

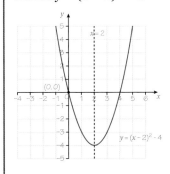

The graph of $y = (x - 2)^2 - 4$ is obtained by translating the graph of $y = x^2$ two units to the right and four units down.

The axis of symmetry is $x = 2$. The vertex is at $(2, -4)$.

When $x = 0$, $y = (-2)^2 - 4 = 0$, so the y-intercept is $(0, 0)$, the origin.

Tip

Learning rules can be useful but it is always best if these rules are based on understanding, so that you can go back and establish the rule if you forget it.

Reflection in the x-axis

When you reflect a positive quadratic in the form $y = ax^2 + bx + c$ (where $a > 0$) over the x-axis, you will get a negative quadratic function, $y = \times(ax^2 + bx + c)$ (where $a > 0$), that is, there is a reversal of signs for all the values of a, b and c. For example, $y = 2x^2 + 4x + 1$ has a reflection in the x-axis represented by the equation $y = -2x^2 - 4x - 1$, not $y = -2x^2 + 4x + 1$.

 Find answers at: cambridge.org/ukschools/gcsemaths-studentbookanswers

The vertex becomes a maximum turning point and not a minimum turning point (where $a < 0$) the vertex becomes a minimum turning point and not a maximum point.

The graph of the equation $y = 2x^2$ is the image of $y = x^2$ reflected in the x-axis.

If $y = x^2$ and $y = 2x^2$ are reflected about the y-axis the graphs remains the same because the y-axis is the axis of symmetry.

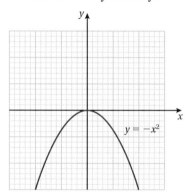

$y = -x^2$

Reflection in the y-axis

When you reflect a quadratic in the form $y = ax^2 + bx + c$ about the y-axis, the line of symmetry and the x-coordinate reverse their sign.

Using the equation in Worked example 1, if $y = (x - 2)^2 - 4$ is reflected about the y-axis the axis of symmetry becomes $x = -2$ and the vertex $(-2, 4)$.

The equation that represents this reflection is $y = (x + 2)^2 - 4$. The y-intercept remains the same, in this case $(0,0)$.

The equation of the reflection of $y = x^2 + 4x - 5$ about the y-axis becomes $y = x^2 - 4x - 5$.

Tip

A reflection about the y-axis represents a horizontal translation.

WORKED EXAMPLE 2

Sketch the graph of the equation $y = x^2 + 4x - 5$ reflected about the y-axis.

Write the equation of the resulting graph.

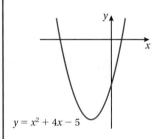

$y = x^2 + 4x - 5$

$y = x^2 + 4x - 5$

By completing the square $y = (x + 2)^2 - 9$

The axis of symmetry is $x = -2$. The vertex is at $(-2, -9)$.

When $x = 0$, $y = -5$, so the y-intercept is $(0, -5)$.

If this graph is reflected about the y-axis the axis of symmetry becomes $x = 2$ and the vertex is $(2, -9)$. The y-intercept remains $(0, -5)$

The equation is $y = (x - 2)^2 - 9$, which gives the equation $y = x^2 - 4x - 5$.

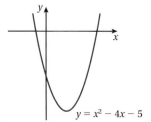

$y = x^2 - 4x - 5$

In Worked example 2 the graph is translated 4 units to the right.

EXERCISE 41B

1 Find the axis of symmetry, the vertex and the y-intercept of these equations:

a $y = (x - 5)^2$ **b** $y = (x - 2)^2 + 9$

c $y = (x + 6)^2 - 7$ **d** $y = (x - 3)^2 - 10$

2 Sketch the graphs of:

a $y = (x - 5)^2$ **b** $y = (x - 1)^2 - 3$ **c** $y = (x + 2)^2 + 3$

d $y = (x - 4)^2 - 3$ **e** $y = (x - 1)^2 + 6$ **f** $y = (x - 4)^2 - 4$

3 $y = x^2$ is the equation of the basic parabola that passes through the origin and is symmetrical about the y-axis.

Write the equation when this parabola is:

a translated 5 units to the left.

b translated b units to the right

c translated 3 units up

d translated c units down

4 What is the equation of the resulting curve when the graph of $y = x^2 + 4x - 21$ is reflected about the y-axis?

Sketching quadratic functions by completing the square

Writing a quadratic equation in the completing the square form, $y = a(x + b)^2 \pm c$, can give you all the information you need to sketch the resulting parabola:

$(x = -b)$ is the axis of symmetry,

$(-b, \pm c)$ is the vertex

$(0, b^2 \pm c)$ is the y-intercept

In a negative quadratic function $y = -ax^2 + bx + c$ (where $a > 0$), the vertex becomes a maximum turning point and not a minimum turning point.

The graph of the equation $y = -x^2$ is the image of $y = x^2$ reflected in the x-axis.

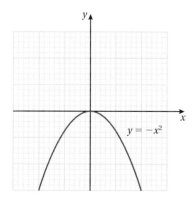

WORKED EXAMPLE 3

Sketch the parabola $y = -x^2 - 6x + 7$

$y = -x^2 - 6x + 7 = -(x+3)^2 + 16$

> Complete the square to rewrite this in the form $y = a(x - b)^2 + c$. (Look back at the section on completing the square in Chapter 13)

The axis of symmetry of $x = -3$, the y-intercept is $(0, 7)$ and the vertex is $(-3, 16)$.

> Identify key features of the curve.

$-(x+3)^2 + 16 = 0$
$-(x+3)^2 = -16$
$(x+3)^2 = 16$
$(x+3) = \pm 4$

So $x = 1$ or $x = -7$: the parabola crosses the x-axis at $(1, 0)$ and $(-7, 0)$.

> Solve $y = 0$ to find the x-intercepts.

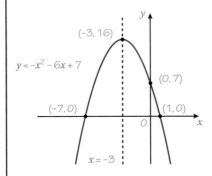

> Use what you have found to sketch the curve.

EXERCISE 41C

1 Complete the square to find the information you need to sketch the following graphs.

  a $y = x^2 + 6x - 5$ **b** $x^2 + 8x + 4 = y$ **c** $y = x^2 - 4x + 2$

  d $(x - 1)(x + 2) - 1 = y$

2 Complete the square to sketch each parabola. Show the y-intercept, the axis of symmetry, the vertex and the x-intercepts.

  a $y = -x^2 + 3$ **b** $y = -x^2 - 2x$ **c** $y = -x^2 + 6x + 13$

  d $y = -x^2 + 8x - 7$ **e** $y = -x^2 + 8x + 7$

Section 2: Trigonometric functions

This diagram shows the graphs of $y = \sin x$ and $y = \cos x$ for a range of values for angles from 0° to 360°. The maximum and minimum values of the two functions are 1 and -1, respectively. The graphs are called wave functions and continue in both directions, repeating the same pattern at set intervals.

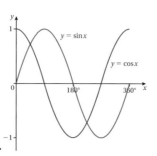

EXERCISE 41D

1 Investigate these graphs using ICT and write an explanation of what you find.

    a $y = \sin x + 2$, $y = \sin x - 2$ **b** $y = \cos x + 2$, $y = \cos x - 2$

2 Investigate these graphs using ICT and write an explanation of what you find.

    a $y = \sin(x + 90°)$, $y = \sin(x - 90°)$ **b** $y = \cos(x + 90°)$, $y = \cos(x - 90°)$

3 Without using ICT, describe the following transformations of the trigonometric functions.

    a $y = \sin x + 1$ **b** $y = \sin(x + 45°)$

    c $y = \cos(x - 45°)$ **d** $y = \cos x - 1$

4 What happens to the graph of $y = -\sin x$ and what is its relationship to $y = \sin x$?

5 What happens to the graph of $y = -\cos x$ and what is its relationship to $y = \cos x$?

Transformations of trigonometric functions

Your investigation in Exercise 41D should have helped you reach these conclusions.

Action	Transformation	Resultant image
Adding or subtracting a numerical value to a trigonometric function. Example: $y = \sin x + a$	Vertical translation	The graph of the transformed function follows a parallel path to the original.
Adding or subtracting an angle to the argument of a trigonometric function. Example: $y = \sin(x + a°)$	Horizontal translation	The graph of the transformed function moves left for an addition to the angle and right for a subtraction.
Taking the negative of a trigonometric function. Example: $y = -\sin x$	Reflection	The graph of the transformed function is a reflection of the original in the x-axis ($y = 0$).

Tip

Remember that some parabolas will not cut the x-axis.

Section 3: Other functions

You can apply what you have learned about transformations of curves to some of the other functions you have studied in this course.

In the next exercise you can use ICT to produce graphs of the functions, but use the findings from earlier in the chapter to predict what you expect to see before you use ICT to look at the graphs of the transformations.

EXERCISE 41E

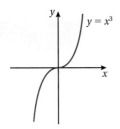

1 This is the basic cubic equation (highest power of x is 3).

Sketch:

a $y = x^3 + 2$ and $y = x^3 - 2$ 　　　　**b** $y = (x + 2)^3$ and $y = (x - 2)^3$

c $y = -x^3$.

About what line is $y = x^3$ reflected to become $y = -x^3$?

2 This is a graph of a reciprocal function.

Why do you think it has two sections? What happens when $x = 0$? Why?

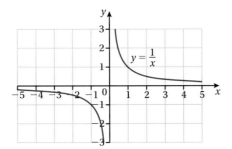

Sketch:

a $y = \dfrac{1}{x} + 3$ 　　　　**b** $y = \dfrac{1}{x} - 3$ 　　　　**c** $y = -\dfrac{1}{x}$

3 This is an exponential function.

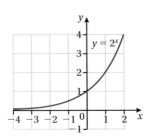

Sketch these exponential functions:

a $y = -2^x$ 　　　　**b** $y = 2^x + 3$ 　　　　**c** $y = 2^{-x}$

Section 4: Translation and reflection problems

You have seen that changing the **parameters** of a function can change the position and orientation of a graph. In this section you are going to use the general principles you learned to solve problems related to shifting graphs.

Key vocabulary

parameter: a value built into a function.

EXERCISE 41F

1 Sketch the parabola $y = (x + 3)^2 - 8$. What is the equation of the resulting image if it is:

  a translated units up and 3 units to the right

  b translated units to the left and 3 units down?

2 Consider the parabola $y = (x - 1)^2 + a$. Find the value of a if the y-intercept is:

  a 1 **b** 3 **c** 0 **d** −7

Sketch the graph in each case.

3 Sketch the graph of each quadratic, clearly labelling the x - and y-intercepts, the axis of symmetry and the vertex:

  a $y = x^2 - 6x + 5$ **b** $y = x^2 - 4x - 12$

Tip

Congruent means exactly the same as. In geometry it means the same shape and size. Two shapes are congruent if you can move one shape so it fits exactly on the other by turning, reflecting or sliding (translating).

4 What is the translation of $y = \sin x$ that would result in $y = \sin x$ merging with $y = \cos x$?

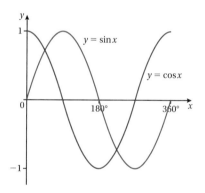

5 Draw a sketch of:

  a $y = x^3 + 2$

  b the reflection of $y = x^3 + 2$ about the y-axis and about the x-axis.

6 The diagram shows the graph of $y = 2^x$ shifted horizontally to the right.

What is the equation of the image?

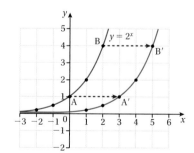

7 A basic curve has been shifted to form each of the graphs below. Decide how the graph was shifted and write the equation of the graph shown. Substitute the coordinates of the given points into the equation to check that your answers are correct.

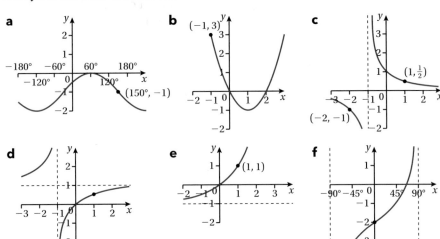

8 If you shift the graph of $y = \sin x$ to the right by 40° and down by two units, what will the equation of the new graph be?

Checklist of learning and understanding

Quadratic functions

- Vertical translations of the basic parabola $y = x^2$ are represented by the family of curves $y = x^2 \pm a$. The vertex is $(0, \pm a)$ and the axis of symmetry is the y-axis, $x = 0$.

- $y = -x^2 \pm a$ represents the family of curves with a maximum turning point, which are reflections of the curves $y = x^2 \pm a$ about the x-axis.

- Horizontal translations of $y = x^2$ are represented by $y = (x \pm a)^2$.

- The axis of symmetry for $y = (x + a)^2$ is $x = -a$ and the vertex is $(-a, 0)$.

- The axis of symmetry for $y = (x - a)^2$ is $x = a$ and the vertex is $(a, 0)$.

- Completing the square: $y = (x + a)^2 \pm b$ gives the axis of symmetry $x = -a$, vertex $(-a, \pm b)$, y-intercept $(0, a^2 \pm b)$

Trigonometric functions

- $y = \sin x \pm a$ and $y = \cos x \pm a$ represent vertical translations of the functions $y = \sin x$ and $y = \cos x$.

- $y = \sin(x \pm a°)$ and $y = \cos(x \pm a°)$ represents a horizontal translation of the functions $y = \sin x$ and $y = \cos x$, $+a°$ to the left and $-a°$ to the right.

Chapter review

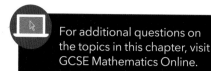For additional questions on the topics in this chapter, visit GCSE Mathematics Online.

1 Sketch the following graphs on the same set of axes and describe the transformation that changes graph *a* to graphs *b*, *c* and *d*.

a $y = x^2$

b $y = x^2 - 5$

c $y = -x^2$

d $y = (x - 5)^2$

2 What translation of the trigonometric function $y = \sin x$ has resulted in this shift to the right?

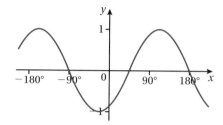

Draw a sketch of:

a $y = \sin(x - 90°) + 1$

b $y = \cos(x - 45°)$

3 Sketch the graph of:

a $y = \dfrac{1}{x} - 1$

b $y = 2^x$ reflected in the line $y = 0$

4 The diagram shows a sketch of the graph of $y = \cos x°$

a Write down the coordinates of the point A. *(1 mark)*

b On the same diagram, draw a sketch of the graph of $y = 2\cos x°$. *(1 mark)*

©Pearson Education Ltd 2013

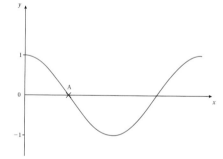

5 The reciprocal function $y = \dfrac{1}{x} + 2$ is changed and the new function is $y = \dfrac{1}{x + 1} + 2$.

What effect would this change have on the graph?

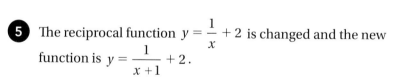

Glossary

A

Adjacent: next to each other; sides that meet at a common vertex.

Alternate angles: the angles on parallel lines on opposite sides of a transversal.

Angle of depression: when looking down, the angle between the line of sight and the horizontal.

Angle of elevation: when looking up, the angle between the line of sight and the horizontal.

Arithmetic sequence: a sequence where the difference between each term is constant.

B

Binomial: an expression consisting of two terms.

Binomial product: the product of two binomial expressions; for example, $(x + 2)(x + 3)$.

Bisect: to divide exactly into two equal halves.

Bivariate data: data that is collected in pairs.

C

Categorical data: data that has been arranged in categories.

Chord: a straight line that joins one point on the circumference of a circle to another point on its circumference. The diameter is a chord that goes through the centre of the circle.

Circumference: distance round the outside of a circle.

Class intervals: the sizes of the groups that data has been grouped into.

Coefficient: the number before a variable in a mathematical expression, which multiplies the variable. In the term $5x^2$, 5 is the coefficient and x^2 is the variable.

Co-interior angles: the angles within the parallel lines on the same side of the transversal. Co-interior angles are sometimes referred to as 'allied angles'.

Combined events: one event followed by another event producing two or more outcomes.

Common denominator: a number into which all the denominators of a set of fractions divide exactly.

Composite function: a function created by combining two or more functions.

Congruent: identical in shape and size.

Conjugate: binomial expressions with the same terms but opposite signs.

Consecutive: following each other in order. For example 1, 2, 3.

Consecutive terms: terms that follow each other in a sequence.

Constant: in algebra, a constant is a value that does not change. It is usually a number. It could be a letter with a fixed value, like π.

Continuous data: data that can have any value.

Continuous quantities: measurements that can take any value in a range.

Conversion factor: the number that you multiply or divide by to convert one measure into another smaller or larger unit.

Coordinates: an ordered pair (x, y) identifying a position on a grid.

Correlation: a relationship or connection between data items.

Corresponding angles: angles that are created at the same point of the intersection when a transversal crosses a pair of parallel lines.

Cumulative frequency: the sum total of frequencies up to a given value.

Cyclic quadrilateral: any quadrilateral with all four vertices on the circumference of a circle.

D

Decay: the reduction in a quantity over time. The opposite of growth.

Degree of accuracy: the number of places to which you round a number.

Dependent events: events in which the outcome is affected by what happened before.

Dependent variable: data that is measured in an experiment.

Depreciation: the loss in value of an object over a period of time.

Direct proportion: two values that both increase in the same ratio.

Discrete data: data that can be counted and can only take certain values.

Discrete quantities: countable values using whole numbers.

Displacement: a change in position.

E

Elevation view: a view of an object from the front, side or back (front elevation, side elevation or back elevation).

Equalities: having the same amount or value.

Equally likely: having the same probability of happening.

Equivalent: having the same value, two ratios are equivalent if one is a multiple of the other.

Error interval: the difference between the upper and lower bounds.

Estimate: an approximate answer or rough calculation.

Evaluate: to calculate the numerical value of something.

Event: the thing to which you are trying to give a probability.

Exchange rate: the value of one currency used to convert that currency to an equivalent value in another currency.

Expanding: multiplying out an expression to get rid of the brackets.

Exponent: the number that says how many times a base number multiplies: exponent 2 means the number is squared (5×5), exponent 3 means it is cubed ($5 \times 5 \times 5$).

Exponential function: a function of the form $y = kx$.

Expression: a group of numbers and letters linked by operation signs.

Exterior angles: angles produced by extending the sides of a polygon.

Extrapolation: using values within a known range to estimate an unknown value that lies outside of that range.

F

First difference: the result of subtracting a term from the next term.

Formula: a general rule or equation showing the relationship between unknown quantities; the plural is formulae.

Function: a set of instructions for changing one number (the input) into another number (the output).

G

Geometric sequence: a sequence where the ratio between each term is constant.

Gradient: a measure of the steepness of a line.

$$\text{gradient} = \frac{\text{change in } y}{\text{change in } x}.$$

Grouped data: data that has been put into groups.

H

Histogram: a graph with bars whose area is proportional to the frequency of a variable and whose width is equal to the class interval.

Hypotenuse: the longest side of a right-angled triangle; the side opposite the 90° angle.

I

Identity: an equation that is true no matter what values are chosen for the variables.

Image: the new shape (once the object has been transformed).

Independent events: events that are not affected by what happened before.

Index: a power or exponent indicating how many times a base number multiplies: index 2 means the number is squared (5×5); index 3 means it is cubed ($5 \times 5 \times 5$).

Index notation: writing a number as a base and index, for example 2^3.

Inequality: a mathematical sentence in which the left side is not equal to the right side.

Integers: whole numbers belonging to the set $\{... -3, -2, -1, 0, 1, 2, 3, ...\}$; they are sometimes called directed numbers because they have a negative or positive sign.

Interior angles: angles inside a two-dimensional shape at the vertices or corners.

Interpolation: using two known values to estimate an unknown value.

Inverse function: a function that reverses another function.

Inverse proportion: a relation between two quantities such that one increases at a rate that is equal to the rate that the other decreases.

Irrational number: a number that cannot be written in the form of $\frac{a}{b}$ or as a terminating or repeating decimal.

Irregular polygon: a polygon that does not have equal sides or equal angles.

Isometric grid: special drawing paper based on an arrangement of equilateral triangles.

L

Line of symmetry: a line that divides a plane shape into two identical halves, each the reflection of the other.

Linear equation: an equation where highest power of the unknown is 1 for example $x + 3 = 7$ (x means x^1, but you don't need to write the '1').

Locus (plural loci): a set of points that satisfy the same rule.

Lower bound: the smallest value that a number (given to a specified accuracy) can be.

M

Mathematical model: a representation of a real-life problem; assumptions are used to simplify the situation so that it can be solved mathematically.

Midpoint: the centre of a line; the point that divides the line into two equal halves.

Mirror line: a line equidistant from all corresponding points on a shape and its reflection.

Mutually exclusive: events that cannot happen at the same time.

N

Number line: a line marked with positions of numbers showing the valid values of a variable.

O

Object: the original shape (before it has been transformed).

Orientation: the position of a shape relative to the grid.

Outcome: a single result of an experiment or situation.

Outlier: data value that is much larger or smaller than others in the same data set.

P

Parabola: the symmetrical curve produced by the graph of a quadratic function.

Parallel vectors: vectors with the same direction. When drawn next to each other they are parallel lines, even if they go in opposite directions.

Parameter: a value built into a function.

Perfect square: a binomial product of the form $(a \pm b)^2$.

Periodic graph: a graph that repeats itself in a regular way.

Perimeter: the distance around the boundaries (sides) of a shape.

Perpendicular bisector: a line perpendicular to another that also cuts it in half.

Plan view: the view of an object from directly above.

Plane shape: two-dimensional shape.

Polygon: a closed plane shape with three or more straight sides.

Polyhedron (plural polyhedra): a solid shape with flat faces that are polygons.

Polynomial: an expression made up of many terms with positive powers for the variables.

Population: the name given to a data set.

Position-to-term rule: operations applied to the position number of a term in a sequence in order to generate that term.

Prime factor: a factor that is also a prime number.

Product: the result of multiplying numbers and/or terms together.

Proportion: the number or amount of a group compared to the whole, often expressed as a fraction, percentage or ratio.

Find answers at: cambridge.org/ukschools/gcsemaths-studentbookanswers

Pythagorean triple: three non-zero numbers (a, b, c) for which $a^2 + b^2 = c^2$.

Q

Quadratic: an expression with a variable to the power of 2 but no higher power.

Quadratic equation: an equation that contains a variable squared term, like x^2, but no variable term with a power greater than 2. $x^2 = 4$ and $x^2 + 2x - 6 = 0$ are quadratic equations. $x^3 - 1 = 0$ and $6x + 7 = 35$ are not quadratic equations.

Quadratic expression: an expression in which the highest power of x is x^2.

R

Radius (plural **radii**): distance from the centre to the circumference of a circle. One radius is half of the diameter of the circle.

Random: not predetermined.

Ratio: a comparison of different parts or amounts in a particular order.

Rational number: a number that can be expressed in the form of $\dfrac{a}{b}$ (or as its equivalent as a terminating or repeating decimal).

Real numbers: all the numbers that can be placed on a number line. They include the set of rational and irrational numbers. Numbers that are not real are called imaginary.

Reciprocal: reciprocal is 1. Note that any number can be written as $\dfrac{a}{1}$ For example. 8 can be written as $\dfrac{8}{1}$, and therefore $\dfrac{1}{8}$ is the reciprocal of 8.

Reflection: an exact image of a shape about a line of symmetry.

Regular polygon: a polygon with equal straight sides and equal angles.

Representative sample: a smaller quantity of data that represents the characteristics of a larger population.

Right prism: a prism with sides perpendicular to the end faces (base).

Roots: the individual values of x in a quadratic equation.

Rotational symmetry: symmetry by turning a shape around a fixed point so that it looks the same from different positions.

Round to significant figures: round to a specified level of accuracy from the first significant figure.

Rounding: writing a number with zeros in the place of some digits.

S

Sample: a set of data collected from a population.

Sample space: a list or diagram that shows all possible outcomes from two or more events.

Scalar: a numerical quantity (it has no direction).

Scale factor: a number that scales a quantity up or down.

Second difference: the difference between each term in the first difference.

Semi-circle: half of a circle.

Sequence: a number pattern or list of numbers following a particular order.

Set: a collection. The brackets { } are shorthand for 'the set of'. For example, {2, 4, 6, 8} is the set of the numbers 2, 4, 6, 8, which represents the even numbers between 1 and 9.

Significant figure (s.f.): a position in a number used to decide the level of accuracy. The first significant figure is the first non-zero digit when reading a number from the left.

Simultaneous equations: a pair of equations with two unknowns that can be solved at the same time.

Solution: both possible values of x in a quadratic equation.

Subject: the variable which is expressed in terms of other variables; it is the variable on its own on one side of the equals sign. In the formula $s = \dfrac{d}{t}$, s is the subject.

Substitute: to replace letters with numbers.

Supplementary angles: two angles are supplementary angles if they add up to 180°.

Surd: if $\sqrt[n]{a}$ is an irrational number, then $\sqrt[n]{a}$ is called a surd.

T

Tangent: a line that makes contact with a curve at one point; it does not cut the curve, it just touches it.

Term: a combination of letters and/or numbers. Each number in a sequence is called a term.

Term-to-term rule: operations applied to any number in a sequence to generate the next number in the sequence.

Theorem: a statement that can be demonstrated to be true by accepted mathematical operations.

Transversal: a straight line that crosses a pair of parallel lines.

Trinomial: an expression with three terms.

Truncation: cutting off all digits after a certain point without rounding.

U

Unit fraction: a fraction with numerator 1 and denominator a positive integer.

Unknown: part of an equation which is represented by a letter.

Upper bound: the largest value that a number (given to a specified accuracy) can be.

V

Variable: a letter representing an unknown number.

Vector: a quantity that has both magnitude and direction. For example, displacement (30 m south), velocity (30 m/s forwards) or acceleration due to gravity (9.8 m/s² down).

Vertically opposite angles: angles that are opposite one another at an intersection of two straight lines. Vertical here means of the same vertex or point, not up and down.

X

***x*-intercept:** the point where a line crosses the x-axis when $y = 0$.

Y

***y*-intercept:** the point where a line crosses the y-axis when $x = 0$.

Index

Acknowledgements

Questions from Edexcel past question papers © Pearson Education Ltd.

These questions are indicated by .

Questions from Cambridge IGCSE® Mathematics reproduced with permission of Karen Morrison and Nick Hamshaw.

The authors would like to thank Fran Wilson for her work on GCSE Mathematics Online.

Cover © 2013 FabianOefner www.fabianoefner.com; p1 (top) Henry Gan/Photodisc/Thinkstock; p1 Denis Kuvaev/Shutterstock; p14 (top) Monarx3d/iStock/Thinkstock; p26 kilukilu/Shutterstock; p27 (top) Huang Zheng/Shutterstock; p27 (bottom) Marafona/Shutterstock; p33 © Owen Franken/Corbis; p38 (top) alfimimnill/iStock/Thinkstock; p57 (top) Yuriy S./iStock/Thinkstock; p57 Tyler Olson/Shutterstock; p69 (top) agsandrew/iStock/Thinkstock; p69wavebreakmedia/Shutterstock; p84 (top) SDivin09/iStock/Thinkstock; p84 Chameleons Eye/Shutterstock; p97 (top) Andrey Popov/iStock/Thinkstock; p97 Leah-Anne Thompson/Shutterstock; p99 William West/Staff/Getty Images; p101 © Jumana elHeloueh/Reuters/Corbis; p109 (top) Jeffrey Collingwood/Hemera/Thinkstock; p109 Konstantin Chagin/Shutterstock; p125 (top) Joe McDaniel/iStock/Thinkstock; p125 Dmitry Kalinovsky/Shutterstock; p133 Pixsooz/Shutterstock; p141 (top) Mike Watson Images/moodboard/Thinkstock; p141 Dorling Kindersley/Getty; p148 Taiga/Shutterstock; p165 (top) David Chapman/Design pics/Valueline/Thinkstock; p165 itman_47/Shutterstock; p166 dkART/Shutterstock; p176 iceink/Shutterstock; p183 JLR Photography/Shutterstock; p185 (top) imagean/iStock/Thinkstock; p185 Federico Rostagno/Shutterstock; p191 Stefano Spezi p202 Calvste/Shutterstock; p205 (top) Leigh Prather/iStock/Thinkstock; p205 Dariush M./Shutterstock; p226 (top) LongHa2006/iStock/Thinkstock; p226 Huntstock.com/Shutterstock; p242 (top) AlisonBradfordPhotography/iStock/Thinkstock; p242 Andrey_Popov/Shutterstock; p284 (top) © PhotoAlto/Alamy; p284 © Monty Rakusen/Cultura/Corbis; p287 © Roger Bamber/Alamy; p297 (top) murengstockphoto/Thinkstock; p297 (bottom) Shaiith/Thinkstock; p303 (top) DeyanGeorgiev/iStock/Thinkstock; p303 Leah-Anne Thompson/Shutterstock; p304 Tigger11th/Shutterstock; p314 Laguna Design/Shutterstock; p316 © PCN Photography/Alamy; p319 (top) Phil Ashley/Photodisc/Thinkstock; p319 govicinity/Shutterstock; p320 (top) ArvindBalaraman p320 (bottom) lsantilli/Shutterstock; p325 Dmitry Kalinovsky/Shutterstock; p326 Sergio Bertino/Shutterstock; p328 © Daniel Mogan/Alamy; p330 (left) Courtesy of Newcastle International Airport; p330 (right) © 2ebill/Alamy; p334 (top) Chameleons Eye/Shutterstock; p334 (bottom) kravka/Shutterstock; p335 cpphotoimages/Shutterstock; p336 (top) shutter_m/iStock/Thinkstock; p350 (top) EugenWeide/Hemera/Thinkstock; p350 T. Fabian/Shutterstock; p352 Anteromite/Shutterstock; p354 zentilia/Shutterstock; p355 Adam Gilchrist/Shutterstock; p355 ValentynVolkov/Shutterstock; p362 (top) Chemik11/iStock/Thinktstock p362 racorn/Shutterstock; p364 Galina Mikhalishina/Shutterstock; p378(top) Huskyomega/iStock/Thinkstock; p378 Franz Pfluegl/Shutterstock; p378/380/381 (top) Yulia Glam/Shutterstock; p381 (bottom) Milos Luzanin/Shutterstock; p389 (left) Vector House/Shutterstock; p398 (right) UMB-O/Shutterstock; p393 Gemenacom/Shutterstock; p395 (top) sutichak/iStock/Thinkstock; p395 Michael Winston Rosa/Shutterstock; p398 Herbert Kratky/Shutterstock; p407 (top) KeremYucel/iStock/Thinkstock; p407 Dan Breckwoldt/Shutterstock; p430 (top) shaunnessey/iStock/Thinkstock; p430 © Jenny E. Ross/Corbis; p435 herreid/Thinkstock; p455 (top) Mark_Stillwagon/iStock/Thinkstock; p455 Mikio Oba/Shutterstock; p459 Dmitry Kalinovsky/Shutterstock; p464 Ryan Lewandowski/Shutterstock; p473 (top) sdecoret/iStock/Thinkstock; p473 MarketaJirouskova/Getty Images; p489 (top) maury75/iStock/Thinkstock; p489 angellodeco/Shutterstock; p512 (top)agsandrew/iStock/Thinkstock; p512 Sergey Kamshylin/Shutterstock; p526 (top) Comstock/Stockbyte/Thinkstock; p526 Kletr/Shutterstock; p548 (top) Pietro_Ballardini/iStockEditorial/Thinkstock; p548 Ross Strachan/Shutterstock; p560 (top) © Emma Smales/VIEW/Corbis; p560 © Paul Doyle/Alamy; p572 Bahri Altay/Shutterstock; p573 David Hilcher/Shutterstock; p577 (top) Digital Vision/Photodisc/Thinkstock; p577 GECOUK/Science Photo Library; p581 © Andrew Ammendolia/Alamy; p604 (top)shutter_m/iStock/Thinkstock; p604 Pressmaster/Shutterstock; p607 p615 (top) Karol Kozlowski/iStock/Thinkstock; p615 Michael Jung/Shutterstock; p616 (top) Larik_Malasha/Shutterstock; p616 (bottom)terekhovigor/Shutterstock; p617 ermess/Shutterstock; p618 Maksim Kabakou/Shutterstock; p619 (top) Rtimages/Shutterstock; p619 (bottom) Christian Delbert/Shutterstock; p629 (top) Tabor Gus/Corbis; p629 VadimRatnikov/Shutterstock; p647 (top) shutter_m/iStock/Thinkstock; p647 Chad McDermott/Shutterstock; p650 © Detail Nottingham/Alamy; p664 FilipFuxa/Shutterstock; p676 (top) marekuliasz/iStock/Thinkstock; p676 Brian A. Jackson/Shutterstock; p700 (top) zentilia/iStock/Thinkstock; p700 Zryzner/Shutterstock; p715 (top) ninjacpb/iStock/Thinkstock; p717 Pal Teravagimov/Shutterstock; p739 (top) MarcelC/iStock/Thinkstock; p739 Balefire/Shutterstock; p741 Kristina Postnikova/Shutterstock; p745 Kenny Tong/Shutterstock.

Find answers at: cambridge.org/ukschools/gcsemaths-studentbookanswers